Southern Culture

Southern Culture
An Introduction

Third Edition

John Beck

Wendy Frandsen

Aaron Randall

CAROLINA ACADEMIC PRESS
Durham, North Carolina

Library of Congress Cataloging-in-Publication Data

Beck, John (John J.)
 Southern culture : an introduction / John Beck, Wendy Frandsen and Aaron
Randall.
     p. cm.
 Includes bibliographical references and index.
 ISBN 978-1-61163-104-3 (alk. paper)
 1. Southern States--Civilization. I. Frandsen, Wendy Jean. II. Randall, Aaron
J. III. Title.

 F209.B38 2012
 975--dc23

                              2012021713

                      Carolina Academic Press
                          700 Kent Street
                         Durham, NC 27701
                   Telephone (919) 489-7486
                      Fax (919) 493-5668
                        www.cap-press.com

Printed in the United States of America
2022 Printing

Contents

List of Figures

Introduction

I wish I was in the land of cotton,
Old times there are not forgotten,
Look away! Look away! Look away! Dixie land.
From "Dixie"

The lazy, laughing South
With blood on its mouth;
The sunny-faced South,
Beast-strong,
Idiot-brained;
The child-minded South
Scratching in the dead fire's ashes
For a Negro's bones.
Cotton and the moon,
Warmth, earth, warmth,
The sky, the sun, the stars,
The magnolia-scented South.

From "The South" by Langston Hughes

From the very beginning the South was different. The source and significance of this "differentness" has been argued about, debated, and discussed for two hundred years. Various explanations have been offered to
explain what makes the South uniquely different from the rest of the country:
the presence of slavery and later segregation; the importance of agriculture;
defeat in war (the Civil War); a sort of inborn conservatism; the unique ethnic
origins of inhabitants of the South; and even the weather. It's a popular topic:
a veritable industry—books, lectures, videos, conferences—has arisen in
modern times to not only "explain" the South but also to prophesy its imminent demise or survival as a regional cultural entity. Aside from the inherent
interest in all of this—at least to those who are interested—why bother? Some
differences between people do not much matter—the English drink tea for
breakfast while most Americans prefer coffee—but the differences between the
South and the rest of the nation **have** mattered—the Civil War representing
the most significant example of this. Indeed, from the very beginning, the nation's politics have been shaped by regional differences. Journalist Peter Applebome has made a convincing case in *Dixie Rising* that the contemporary South
has finally put the defeat in the Civil War behind it and is now a "rising" region
that is "putting its fingerprints on almost every aspect of the nation's soul,
from race, to politics, to culture, to values."[1] If this is the case, both Southerners and non-Southerners alike should understand the culture of the South to
better understand what the national culture may be becoming. Certainly if one
is a Southerner, it is well, as the ancient Greeks told us, to "know thyself."

Where Is the South?

While there is some dispute about the precise borders of the South, most
Americans would agree that it is in the southern half of the United States and
perhaps more precisely in the southeastern corner of the US. Then things get
murky. Where does the region stop in the West? No one considers New Mexico
"Southern"; some would argue that Texas is part of the South while others
argue that it is more Western than Southern. Other areas like Miami may be
indisputably part of the region geographically speaking, but today don't seem
particularly "Southern" as that term is popularly understood. Most people who
are interested in the issue of mapping the South start with the eleven states of
the former Confederacy (the band of states stretching from Virginia to Texas
and including Tennessee and Arkansas). Kentucky, Missouri, West Virginia
(once a part of Virginia) and Maryland—slaveholding states and regions be-

---

1. Peter Applebome, *Dixie Rising: How the South is Shaping American Values, Politics,
and Culture* (San Diego, New York, and London, 1997), 22.

fore the Civil War that did not secede from the Union—are also often included as part of the South. As border states, these states always were crossroads of values and customs, and today Missouri seems to have become more "Midwestern" in its values and allegiances than Southern, and parts of Maryland seem to have become part of the "Northeast." Despite the imprecision, this list of states gives us a good working definition of where the South "is," recognizing, of course, that what we are interested in here is not geography but culture. Indeed, it is culture that gives meaning to the term "the South."[2]

Figure I.1   The South and the Nation

What is culture? Culture is the shared values, behaviors (ways of doing things), and material creations (clothing styles, architecture, tools, art, etc.) that define a society and distinguish one society from another. We create culture, and culture creates us. Cultures vary tremendously, as anyone who has traveled knows firsthand. Cultures are normally created by people who live in proximity to each other—hence the connection to geography—and are shaped by a variety of factors—climate, resources, population density, presence or absence of external threats, and even geography itself may be a factor as some scholars have suggested. [3] In all societies of any size, subcultures are to

2. John Shelton Reed has explored this topic at length in several essays. One of the best—"The South: What Is It? Where Is It?" is found in *My Tears Spoiled My Aim and Other Reflections on Southern Culture* (Columbia and London: University of Missouri Press, 1993), 5–28.

3. See Jared M. Diamond, *Guns, Germs, and Steel: The Fates of Human Societies* (New York: W.W. Norton and Co., 1997).

be found. Subcultures are variations of a culture—the values, behaviors, and material creations of some groups differ from those commonly found in the dominant culture. Sociologists once believed that mass society—a term used to describe the kind of society produced by industrialization, urbanization and the growth of mass communication, transportation and universal education—would gradually eliminate subcultures.[4] Certainly strip malls and franchise restaurants and the pervasive influence of the automobile have made one area of the country look more and more like another, but subcultures seem to be persisting.

The South, then, is a subculture of the broader national culture, and, complicated though it may be, subcultures are to be found within the South, too. This is not surprising: the South is a large region consisting of many subregions—coastal plains, mountains, swamps, deltas, and piedmont, with a varied climate ranging from the nearly tropical climate of southern Florida to the decidedly "Northern" climate (short summers and long winters) of northern Virginia, and differing patterns of settlement and development. Thanks to the growing interest in ethnic cuisines, one of the better known subcultures in the South is the Cajun culture of Louisiana. The Cajuns are descendants of a group of French-speaking immigrants expelled from Acadia (now called Nova Scotia) in Canada by the British in the 1700s. Many still speak a unique version of French and their Catholicism, spicy cuisine, and celebratory attitude about life and its pleasures set them apart from most of the rest of the South. Where else in the region do people gather Saturday morning to eat, drink, dance, and listen to music, sometimes well into the night? Mountain folk constitute another well-known subculture, perhaps most noted for birthing the country music industry. The Gullah people—descendants of slaves who speak a unique dialect and live in coastal areas in South Carolina and Georgia—are another. Still another are the "O'cockers"—residents of the Outer Banks' island of Ocracoke (North Carolina) who are noted for their colorful dialect and terms. (For example, they call off island folks "dingbatters.")[5] Along with these variations in Southern culture, there may also be "degrees" of "Southerness." Indeed, sociologist John Reed has studied this issue for years and has even developed a diagram of the region charting how "Southern" different areas of the region are.[6]

---

4. See John Shelton Reed's discussion of this issue in *The Enduring South: Subcultural Persistence in Mass Society* (Chapel Hill, NC: University of North Carolina Press, 1972), 1–2. William Kornhauser's *The Politics of Mass Society* (Glencoe, Ill.: Free Press, 1959) is the most famous exploration of the mass society thesis.

5. Walt Wofram and Natalie Schilling-Estes, *Hoi Toide on the Outer Banks: The Story of the Ocracoke Brogue* (Chapel Hill, NC: University of North Carolina Press, 1997), 41, 45.

6. See Chapter 2, "Southerners: Who, What and Where," in John S. Reed's *The Enduring South: Subcultural Persistence in Mass Society* and Chapter 4, "The Heart of Dixie," in Reed, *One South: An Ethnic Approach to Regional Culture* (Baton Rouge and London: Louisiana State University Press, 1982).

Historian James Cobb would agree; he has argued that the Yazoo-Mississippi Delta is *The Most Southern Place on Earth*.[7] Reed has found a waning of "Southerness" in a number of values and preferences over the years but still believes a number of unique cultural characteristics persist in the region that distinguish it from the rest of the country.

The Creators of Southern Culture

Southern culture (we'll use the term culture in this book rather than subculture) began with four major groups that initially settled the region and contributed distinct cultural influences to the evolving Southern culture. The four groups were Native Americans; West Africans; settlers from the south of England; and settlers from the area of the British Isles bordering the Irish Sea. This last group is usually called "Scotch-Irish" although some now use the term Scots-Irish to be politically correct. (The Scots say Scotch is a drink, not a people.) Many of these settlers were Scots who had initially migrated to Ireland, but as historian David Hackett Fischer has persuasively argued, the group also included English settlers from northern England and Scots from southern Scotland. The major influence on Southern culture would come from the migrants from West Africa and the British Isles who migrated here in the 1600s and 1700s. These migrants brought values and traditions with them that influenced, in subtle and often profound ways, the creation of a new culture in a new land. While the rest of the nation received a steady infusion of new immigrants throughout the 1800s and the 1900s, migration **into** the South largely concluded by the end of the 1700s and would only resume on a significant scale in the 1960s and 1970s. So a fairly stable population was creating this regional culture.

Native Americans (the term American Indian is still in use, too) were the first to settle the region. Native Americans were migrants from Asia and came to the Americas by way of what is today Alaska. They migrated southward and eventually eastward over the course of many centuries. The earliest documented Native American in the South lived in Florida about 12,800 years ago.[8] By about 700 BC, a particular pattern of Native American culture called Woodland had arisen in the South—a region now climatically similar to what it is today—and as historians Theda Purdue and Michael Green note, this tradition would persist "until well after the European invasion that began in the six-

---

7. James Cobb, *The Most Southern Place on Earth: The Mississippi Delta and the Roots of Regional Identity* (New York and Oxford: Oxford University Press, 1992).

8. Theda Perdue and Michael D. Green, *The Columbia Guide to American Indians of the Southeast* (New York: Columbia University Press, 2001), 20–22.

teenth century." [9] Woodland people belonged to tribes, each with a distinct language, and typically lived in small villages. Over time their cultures evolved and became more sedentary and less dependent on hunting and gathering and more dependent on agriculture. Women were the farmers while men hunted and fished. By about 1200 AD, cultivated corn had become, for most people in the South, a major part of the diet. Beans and squash were two other commonly grown staples.

Perdue and Green argue that the Woodland cultures were waning when Europeans were first setting foot in the Americas, and the Mississippian cultures were predominant in much of the region. Mississippian people are sometimes known as "moundbuilders" because of the large earth mounds they constructed in many of their villages. These mounds were topped by buildings used for government and religious purposes. The Mississippian tribes were more involved in trade than neighboring Woodland tribes, and some of their towns were quite large. They engaged in "cleared field" cultivation of corn, they lived in square houses (their neighbors built circular homes), and they crafted more delicate pottery in a wider range of shapes than their neighbors. They had elaborate chiefdoms and fairly complex social hierarchies as compared to the more egalitarian social structures of most Woodland peoples.[10]

Native Americans of the South first encountered Europeans in the early decades of the sixteenth century when Spanish expeditions led by such men as Ponce De Leon and Hernando de Soto began exploring the region. It is difficult today to determine how many Native Americans lived in the South at the time of the initial contact with Europeans, but in excess of one million seems a reasonable beginning point. Over the next two hundred years, disease and war took a tremendous toll, and by the first census the newly created United States conducted in 1790, the native population was a fraction of what it had been. In North and South Carolina east of the Appalachian Mountains, one scholar put the estimate at 600 survivors.[11] In the 1820s and 1830s, President Andrew Jackson attempted to "remove" the small numbers of Native Americans who still remained in the eastern United States to land west of the Mississippi, a policy that led to the "Trail of Tears" and even more deaths. Members of some Southern tribes successfully fought "removal," most notably the Cherokee in the mountains of North and South Carolina and the Seminole in Florida. Other Indian people who were able to remain in the East assimilated into white and black culture, took English and Scottish and Irish names, and lived as their neighbors lived. But interestingly, even though they assimilated, many retained some degree of Native American identity, sometimes creating a new tribal

---

9. *Ibid.*, 25.
10. *Ibid.*, 27–32.
11. *Ibid,* 40–41.

name to identify themselves. Perhaps the most well-known of these groups are the Lumbee of North Carolina. The Lumbee are an amalgam of the descendants of Native American people who lived in the southeastern part of the state. While sharing values and customs and even ancestry with local blacks and whites, the Lumbee still have retained a separate cultural identity and have been and are viewed by their neighbors as a distinct group of people. Groups similar to the Lumbee are to be found throughout the South.

Given the virtual annihilation of the Native American population in the South and the marginalization of the small numbers that remained, Native Americans have had the smallest influence on the region's culture as it developed and spread. Certainly their influence can be seen in many place names and in the region's cuisine, particularly its reliance on corn.

While the Spanish established the first permanent European settlement in the South at St. Augustine in Florida in 1585, migrants from the British Isles, by dint of sheer numbers, would come to dominate the region. English settlers established a short-lived colony on the island of Manteo (on the coast of present-day North Carolina) in the 1580s and later (1607) a settlement that would last on the banks of the James River in the newly established Virginia Colony. This settlement, Jamestown, began to grow after a rocky start, and by the mid-1600s, English settlements had spread throughout the coastal plain of the Virginia colony.

The settlers streaming to Virginia in the 1600s were primarily from the region of England south and west of London, historian David Hackett Fischer tells us in *Albion's Seed*. Fischer has argued persuasively that the regional culture of this area, carried to the New World by the migrants, would profoundly shape the culture of the Chesapeake—a region including coastal Virginia and Maryland—and ultimately the rest of the South. As he notes, "Both regions [the Chesapeake and southern England] were marked by deep and pervasive inequalities, by a staple agriculture and rural settlement patterns, by powerful oligarchies of large landowners with Royalist politics and an Anglican faith."[12] In southern England a small landed gentry owned large estates worked by landless tenants and laborers. Migrants to Virginia would recreate this same system with a small landed elite—derived from the gentry class in England—and a large pool of servants drawn from the landless tenants and laborers of southern England. While the settlers of New England and Pennsylvania brought with them a religion of dissent (Quakerism and Puritanism) and came to America to escape religious prosecution, settlers coming to Virginia belonged to the state-sponsored Church of England (Anglican) and established that faith as the official faith of Virginia. Fischer argues that the unique Southern dialect has its roots in the regional dialects

---

12. David Hackett Fischer, *Albion's Seed: Four British Folkways in America* (New York and Oxford: Oxford University Press, 1989), 246.

of southern England. In both Virginia and in Sussex County, England, for example, many people would have understood what "moonshine," "mess of greens," and "dis" (this) and "dat" (that) meant. Most residents of Hampshire County, England, and Virginia would probably have understood the meaning of such words as "chitlins" (intestines) and "passel" (bunch).[13]

In addition to settling coastal Virginia and Maryland, English colonists settled the coastal plains of the Carolinas and Georgia and later pushed into the Piedmont. Rivers, towns, counties and streets in this region were often named after English people and places. A small stream of English slaveholding planters migrated from the Caribbean to South Carolina and Georgia. Charleston and Savannah are today noted for their unique architecture, which was influenced by Caribbean building styles brought by these migrants.

The migration from what Fischer calls the border region of the British Isles—southern Scotland, northern Ireland, and northern England—came in waves, beginning in the late 1600s. These migrants (we'll call them Scots-Irish in this book) left in search of opportunity, and by the end of the 1700s in excess of 250,000 of them had arrived in America. They tended to be young, they came in family groups, and many came from the middling ranks of society— small landowners, tenant farmers and farm laborers, and small tradesmen— with a smattering from the upper ranks of landowners.[14] The land they left was anything but prosperous. The typical lowland Scot struggled to survive on a stony plot of land, huddled around a peat fire at night, the smoke billowing through a hole cut into the roof of the tiny one-room hut he and his family called home. He ate gruel (oats and water) for breakfast and for supper (the evening meal) fresh mutton and sometimes beef in the summer and salted mutton or beef in the winter. He liked his whiskey when he could get it.[15] Rising rents on the land that most worked as tenants (the so-called rack rent), drought, and the unpopular religious policies of the British government pushed many toward the plentiful, cheap land of North America.[16] The Scots were Presbyterian in their faith; the northern English, while generally Anglican, were often influenced by the New Light movement that was sweeping the British Isles. This movement fostered meetings in fields and pastures for believers (similar to the camp meeting revivals in America) and emphasized an intense, personal religion that ran counter to the ritual and ceremony of the Anglican Church.[17]

---

13. *Ibid.*, 260–261.
14. Fischer, *Albion's Seed*, 613–614.
15. Carlton Jackson, *A Social History of the Scotch Irish* (Lanham, NY and London: 1993), 5; Fischer, *Albion's Seed*, 727–731.
16. James G. Leyburn, *The Scotch-Irish: A Social History* (Chapel Hill: UNC Press, 1962), 158–166.
17. Fischer, *Albion's Seed*, 615–617.

Northern England and southern Scotland were battlegrounds over the centuries as the English fought the Scots for control and Scottish nobles fought each other. Membership in family and clan, the extended family, provided people with a degree of security. Retribution—"an eye for an eye"—was how families and clans protected their own. As one historian noted, "It is the lawlessness and violence of life in Scotland throughout the period from 1400–1600 that made the deepest impression on visitors from more stable countries and that justify one in speaking of the life of Lowland Scotland as barbarous."[18] During the 1600s the English government set out to pacify this "barbarous" region and pacify it it did, but this pacification often involved bloody reprisals that continued the cycle of violence. Ireland was also pacified by the English, and to **permanently** pacify the region, the English began to settle northern Ireland with lowland Scots (from whence we get the term Scots-Irish). Over three hundred years later, many of the descendants of these migrants to Northern Ireland and the native Irish were still at war and still following the principle of an "eye for an eye." The troubled history of the border areas, according to David Hackett Fischer, elevated the warrior over the worker, force over reason, and men over women.[19] This "warrior ethic" stressed a fierce independence, pride, and a sense of equality, but also an equally fierce loyalty to the leadership of one's family and clan.

Most of these migrants would arrive in America at Philadelphia or nearby ports. Many migrated west and settled western Pennsylvania. Others headed south from Lancaster, a small town west of Philadelphia, on the "Great Wagon Road." They settled in the mountain and piedmont areas of Virginia, the Carolinas, and Georgia. As at home, they established small farms and tended a variety of crops including wheat, corn, and oats. They raised sheep but found that hogs were hardier animals requiring less care than the sheep. Increasingly, pork, not mutton, became their meat of choice. Corn meal mush (grits) would replace the oatmeal mush from home. The contentiousness for which they were famous continued. In the mid-1700s, rebellions broke out in Pennsylvania, South Carolina, and North Carolina in areas dominated by settlers from the border regions of Britain. These rebellions, called Regulator movements, were fueled by a variety of grievances against colonial governments on the coast (Philadelphia, Charlestown, and New Bern) that seemed interested in the backcountry only as a source of tax revenue. The ancient animosity between the Scots and the English was also a major factor because the governments were dominated by Englishmen. The largest of the rebellions took place in North Carolina and was fi-

---

18. Leyburn, *The Scotch Irish*, 6; see also Fischer, *Albion's Seed*, 628–629 and Grady McWhiney, *Cracker Culture: Celtic Ways in the Old South* (University, Alabama: University of Alabama Press, 1988), 149–152.

19. Fischer, *Albion's Seed*, 680.

nally crushed when a force commanded by the colonial governor, Lord Tryon, defeated a Regulator army at the battle of Alamance.

The African migration to the South was a forced migration that began in the early 1600s and had largely run its course by the early 1800s. According to one estimate, over five hundred thousand African immigrants would be brought to North America, and most of these people would settle in the South. This is a small fraction of the more than ten million people who were brought in chains to the Caribbean, Brazil, and elsewhere in the Americas as chattel slaves to serve the growing plantations of the New World.[20] The young men and women who made plantation agriculture in the New World feasible and profitable came mostly from long-established agricultural and herding societies of West Africa and to a lesser extent Central Africa. During the sixteenth century, more than a hundred different societies could be found along the West African coast such as the Fon, Yoruba, and Senegambian in the north and the Kongo further south.[21] A variety of political systems could be found in the region from small villages that might form loose alliances with neighboring villages to powerful nations ruled by kings. Between 900 and 1600, three great empires—Ghana, Mali, and Songhai—rose and declined in the western Sudan, a fertile belt of land located just below the Sahara desert which extends well into the interior. Songhai, the last of these empires, was a major mercantile power that thrived on the gold trade. Muhammad Touré was one of its greatest rulers. Touré was a devout Muslim and used his power to spread Islam in his kingdom; Timbuktu, one of the major trading cities in the empire, became a center of Muslim scholarship. Songhai was conquered in the late 1500s by a Moroccan army composed mostly of Spanish mercenaries dispatched south to gain control of the gold trade. The collapse of the empire of Songhai created a political vacuum and a significant increase in the trade in human beings, although some scholars believe the series of droughts that afflicted the region played a more important role in creating the sort of desperate economic and social conditions that would allow the slave trade to flourish. Further south, a number of other states—Benin, Dahomey, Oyo, Kongo to name several of the more prominent ones—flourished at one point or another during the 1500, 1600, and 1700s. The Kingdom of Kongo, for example, ruled an immense region in the Congo River basin in the 1400 and 1500s. This was a kingdom that maintained close ties to Portugal and thrived for a time on the trade with the Portuguese. Nzinga Mbemba, king in the early decades of the 1500s, embraced Portuguese culture and Christianity and tried his best to spread the religion throughout his

20. Herbert S. Klein, *The Atlantic Slave Trade* (Cambridge, United Kingdom: Cambridge University Press, 1999), 210–211.
21. Darlene Clark Hine et al., *The African-American Odyssey* (Upper Saddle River, NJ: Prentice Hall, 2000), 13–16.

kingdom. Ultimately, Kongo devolved into warring factions and became a puppet of Portugal, which greatly expanded the highly profitable trade in slaves.[22]

Prior to the arrival of the Europeans, slavery was a part of the social and economic life of most African societies; the Atlantic slave trade evolved slowly from this indigenous slave trade with Europeans—Portuguese, Spanish and later British, Dutch, and French—partnering with African slave traders and rulers such as the king of Dahomey to feed the growing demand for slave laborers in the plantations of the New World.[23] In Africa, there was a "continuum" between slave and free rather than a sharp division. People in slavery arrived at that status in a variety of ways: some were war captives, others had been kidnapped (possibly as war prizes from a neighboring society or village), some had been purchased, others were born slaves, and still others had "pawned" themselves to pay off a debt. What slavery meant varied according to who the enslaved person was, where he lived, and who his master was. Slaves might be concubines, soldiers, craftsmen, administrators, and, of course, laborers. Slavery could be permanent or temporary; a "pawned" man, for example, might be able to pay off his debt and earn his freedom, and a war captive might be freed when the war ended. In Muslim areas, Islamic law recognized certain rights for slaves. In many households, slaves were treated as members of the family and community, although ones without the same rights and privileges as higher status people.[24] As Olaudah Equiano (an Ibo who had been a slave in both West Africa and the West Indies) observed about West African slaves, "their food, clothing, and lodging were nearly the same as the others except they were not permitted to eat with those who were born free." In amazement he noted "how different was their condition from that of the slaves in the West Indies."[25] It was the West African familiarity with slavery, ironically, that made it possible for African and European traders to begin the trade in human cargoes to distant shores where a harsher form of slavery was instituted.

Sophisticated farming systems, hundreds of years old, formed the base of the economies of West African societies. Agricultural production involved the cultivation of millet on the flat savannas and root crops (especially the yam),

---

22. *Ibid.*, 9–17; Phillip Curtin, "Africa North of the Forest," in Phillip Curtin et al., *African History: From Earliest Times to Independence* (London: Longman, 1995), 168.

23. Klein, *The Atlantic Slave Trade*, 46, 50–72; Phillip Curtin, "The West African Coast in the Era of the Slave Trade," in Curtin, *African History*, 206, 211.

24. John Iliffe, *Honor in African History* (Cambridge: Cambridge University Press, 2005), 120–121; Paul Lovejoy, "Transformation in Slavery," in Robert O. Collins, ed., *Problems in African History* (Princeton, NJ: Markus Wiener Publishers, 2005), 284.

25. Olaudah Equiano, *The Interesting Narrative of the Life of Olaudah Equiano*, edited by Robert J. Allison (1791; Boston : Bedford Books of St. Martin's Press, c1995), 40–41.

fruits, and other vegetables in the tropical forests. Rice was also cultivated in some areas. Trade was often conducted by women in lively West African markets.[26] The local community was the basis of social organization, stability, and order in West African societies. Within communities, people were organized along kinship lines, by age with older free people occupying privileged positions, and by gender. Older males supervised the work of the family, organized hunting parties, and performed religious ceremonies. Councils of elders were often an important part of the local and even national political structure. Monogamy was the usual marriage pattern, but important elders were permitted to take a second, third, or fourth wife if they had the means to provide for them. A code of honor governed relationships with dependent people obligated to more powerful people and younger people to older people. In many societies, such as the Yoruba, honor was accorded to a man on the basis of his rank and reputation in the community; a woman earned honor by protecting her virtue and sacrificing for her children.[27]

Art was an important part of the lives of African peoples. Artisans and craftsmen worked with wood, ivory, gold, glass, terra cotta, iron, and clay and made pots, bowls, baskets, sculptures, furniture, masks, textiles, costumes, fly whisks, and wands. Pots, bowls, and baskets were a very practical part of everyday life; art objects like the masks and costumes served an important role in the religious and social rituals of African societies. Music, an important part of religious and social ceremonies and rituals, was polyrhythmic and was composed of layers of "simple and more complex rhythms." Dance was also ceremonial; it adapted to this polyrhythmic musical structure, and exhibited creativity, improvisation, great precision, and coordination. Musical instruments included flutes, a variety of stringed instruments, and many kinds of drums.[28]

People transported to America as slaves brought a variety of religions with them from Africa. Some captives were very likely Christian, some were Muslims, but most African captives practiced a diverse collection of religions unique to their societies. What most of these religions did share in common was an ethos that the world was an organic unity and that humans were part of a "Oneness that bound together all matter, animate and inanimate, all spirits, visible or not."[29] In the Yoruba culture, for example, àshe was a spiritual force

---

26. Robert W. July, *A History of the African People* (New York: Charles Scribners Sons, 1980), 131–132, 135.

27. Iliffe, *Honor in African History*, 67, 80; Lovejoy, "Transformation," 283–285; John Lamphear and Toyin Falola, "Aspects of Early African History," in Phyllis M. Martin and Patrick O'Meara, eds., *Africa* (Bloomington, IN: Indiana University Press, 1995), 94–95.

28. Patrick R. McNaughton and Diane Pelrine, "African Art" in Martin and O'Meara, *Africa, 223–255;* Ruth Stone, "African Music Performed" in Martin and O'Meara, *Africa,* 257–271; quote p. 264.

29. Lawrence W. Levine, *Black Culture and Black Consciousness: Afro-American Folk Thought from Slavery to Freedom* (Oxford: Oxford University Press, 1978), 1978, 58.

that was given to the world by Yoruba Olorun, the supreme deity, and was invested in both living beings—humans, animals, and plants—and the nonliving parts of the natural world—mountains, rivers, etc. The spiritual ideal for a Yoruba was to "become possessed by the spirit of a Yoruban deity," to imbibe, in effect, àshe and let it flow through "one's body."[30] The role of the priests in Yoruba and other West African societies was to help believers reach this state of openness to the almighty and to perform religious ceremonies; they also served as foretellers of the future and as doctors.

Other migrants who arrived in the South in the late 1600s and early1700s included the French and later the Spanish who settled in Louisiana, Germans who traveled south from Lancaster, Pennsylvania and settled in the piedmont region of Virginia and the Carolinas, and the Irish who settled throughout the region. A smattering of other migrants from Europe settled here and there—in the 1700s Charleston received a small stream of French-speaking people and Sephardic Jews, and in the 1800s, New Orleans became home to a significant population of Irish and German immigrants. Small numbers of Greeks and Jews from Central and Eastern Europe established themselves in the towns and cities of the region. Texas was always home to a large population of Spanish-speaking people, and the border between Mexico and Texas was lengthy and porous with people and customs moving back and forth across it with ease.[31] These "other" migrants who settled in the South would constitute a small fraction of the population that was dwarfed in size and cultural influence by the descendants of the migrants from southern England, the British borderlands, and West Africa who came in the 1600s and 1700s.

Migrant streams mixed; some Scots-Irish migrated to coastal areas while English settlers on the coast moved west. Scots-Irish married English, and African women bore the children of men from both groups. In the years before and after the Revolution, settlers, led by such men as Daniel Boone, crossed over the Appalachians and established settlements in Tennessee and later Kentucky. Later still, in the early and middle decades of the nineteenth century, settlers from Virginia and South Carolina and North Carolina and Georgia pushed into Florida, Mississippi, Alabama, Texas, Louisiana, and Arkansas. Wars were fought to protect and promote this migration: wars with Native

---

30. Robert Farris Thompson, *Flash of the Spirit: African and Afro-American Art and Philosophy* (New York: Vintage Books, 1984), 5–9, quote p. 9.

31. Bennett H. Wall et al, *Louisiana: A History* (Wheeling, Illinois: Harlan Davidson Inc., 2008), 32–35, 67; Randall Miller, "A Church in Cultural Captivity: Some Speculations on Catholic Identity," in Randall Miller and Jon L. Wakelyn, eds., *Catholics in the Old South* (Macon, Georgia: Mercer University Press, 1983), 29; Eli N. Evans, *The Provincials: A Personal History of Jews in the South* (New York: Free Press Paperbacks, 1997), 49; Lee Shai Weisback, "East European Immigrants and the Image of Jews in the Small Town South," in Mark K. Bauman, ed., *Dixie Diaspora: An Anthology of Southern Jewish History* (Tuscaloosa, AL: University of Alabama Press, 2006), 108–110.

American tribes, a war with the Spanish in Florida, and several wars with Mexico in Texas. In the 1850s a guerrilla war broke out between Missouri men who supported slavery ("Bushwackers") and opponents of slavery (including John Brown) in the border state of Kansas. The expansiveness of the South—the desire of its people to settle in new and far off places—is often considered by many historians one of the causes (along with the expansiveness of the North) of the Civil War.

For a hundred years following the Civil War, migration was primarily one way: out of the region. Tens of thousands of blacks left the South for Kansas in the 1880s in the so-called Exoduster migration. The big out-migration of blacks, however, really began around the First World War, picked up momentum during the Depression and finally tapered off in the 1960s. Millions of Southern blacks left the South for the Northeast, Midwest, and far West. Several million whites left the region, too, more often making their way to the Midwest and far West. At the same time, millions of other Southerners, black and white, left the land and moved to the growing cities and towns of the South. By the 1970s many of the rural areas of the South looked like wartime evacuation zones with expanses of crop land gone to weeds and scrub pine, small towns full of boarded up stores, and abandoned, collapsing houses begging to be bulldozed.[32]

Migration into the South began again on a significant scale in the 1950s and early 1960s from two regions: Cuba and the Northeast. The northeastern migration was made up largely of retirees from the cities of the North who were drawn to the east coast of Florida by its sunny weather and beaches. Railroad entrepreneur Samuel Flagler had actually gotten the east coast of Florida off the ground as a tourist mecca in the early years of the twentieth century. Flagler had constructed a railroad line linking the eastern coast of Florida to the cities of the Northeast and had built a string of luxurious hotels up and down the coast. By the 1950s retirees were coming to stay permanently and began packing the highrises going up on Miami Beach and other resort communities on the coast. Migrants brought a piece of northeastern big city life to the formerly sleepy south of Florida. Big name acts—Dean Martin, Frank Sinatra, and others—appeared at Miami Beach hotels, and for a time Jackie Gleason's variety television show broadcast from Miami. Stores and restaurants catered to the tastes and interests of the northeastern migrants. Jewish retirees, for example, could eat real New York-style kosher delicatessen food at Wolfie Cowan's Rascal House restaurant, and gamblers could find racetracks—dog and horse—just like home. In the 1960s this stream of migrants was joined by another; Cuban exiles escaping Fidel Castro's communist revolution poured

---

32. Jack Temple Kirby, *Rural Worlds Lost: The American South, 1920–1960* (Baton Rouge: Louisiana State University Press, 1987), xv.

into Miami and south Florida. The Cubans brought their own distinctive culture with them and began the transformation of Miami into a Latino city.

In the 1960s a new stream of migrants began trickling into the South; by the 1980s this trickle had become a flood. This migration—millions strong by the early 1990s—was made up of people from the Midwest and the Northeast who came south to work in the jobs created by the region's expanding economy. While parts of the Northeast and Midwest were in economic decline (a swath of the region was called the "Rust Belt"), the economies of portions of the South—Houston, Dallas, Atlanta, Charlotte—were growing, even flourishing. Joining this stream of internal migrants into the South was a growing migration from foreign countries. Foreign-born residents of the South increased from 1.8% of the population in 1960 to 5.4% of the population in 1990 and jumped to 9.1% in 2000. Asia was one source of migrants: migrants from India, Pakistan, China, and other parts of Asia settled in the growing metropolitan regions and even the small towns in the region. The largest foreign migration into the region, however, was the growing throng of people coming from the Caribbean, Central America, and South America. As we saw, this began with the Cuban migration to South Florida in the 1960s. For most of the region, Mexico was the largest source of foreign immigrants. There had always been a significant movement of people from Mexico across the border into Texas and other Southwestern states; by the 1970s a sizeable stream of Mexican migrant workers began moving up the east coast of the United States planting and harvesting the crops of farms from Florida to New England. Some began to settle in cities and small rural communities, and these numbers grew even more in the 1990s. Today it is rare to find even the smallest town in the rural South without at least one bodega or tienda that caters to this growing population.[33]

Creating Southern Culture

The English, Scots-Irish, and African migrants to the South who arrived in the 1600 and 1700s established the basic patterns of Southern culture by the late 1700s, and these patterns proved to be remarkably resistant to change well

---

33. Campbell J. Gibson and Emily Lennon, "Historical Census Statistics on the Foreign-born Population of the Unites States: 1850–1990," U.S. Bureau of the Census, Population Division (Washington, D.C.: G PO, February, 1999), http:// www.census.gov/popu lation/www/documentation/twps0029/twps0029.html.; "Current Population Survey: Population in U.S. Regions by Sex and Citizenship Status," U.S. Bureau of the Census, Ethnic and Hispanic Statistics Branch, Population Division (Washington, D.C.: GPO, March 2002), Table 1.14, http://www.census.gov/population/socdemo/foreign/ppl-162/tab01-14.pdf.

into the 20th century. The most important pattern was the predominance of farming and rural living and a set of values supporting this agrarian lifestyle. This agrarian pattern dictated much about how the rest of Southern culture developed, and even today, when very few people farm or live the rural lifestyle any more, agrarian traditions still influence the region's culture in all sorts of ways. The next chapter of this book is devoted to this farming, rural pattern known as agrarianism.

Social class also exerted a tremendous influence on the evolving culture of the South. Attitudes about class shaped in southern England and in the border regions of Britain coupled with the appearance early on of race-based slavery would produce a class system that consigned blacks to the bottom and that paradoxically fostered both the idea of equality for whites and large differences between upper and lower class whites in terms of power, privilege and wealth. On the one hand, less affluent whites were generally anything but deferential to the wealthy, and upper class men sometimes affected the speech patterns of the less affluent (even today an educated, affluent man is not considered odd for using the word "ain't") and enjoyed the same outdoor pastimes—hunting and fishing—as their less well-off neighbors. But looked at another way, the South for much of its history has seemed as oppressively class conscious as an "old" European society. Indeed, before the Civil War, English aristocrats apparently felt some kinship for Southern planters and vice versa. Certainly, classes produced their own unique subcultures. Less affluent Southern whites produced a distinctive religion, music (called "country" today), stories, and spoke dialects that set them off from their neighbors. Affluent white Southerners tended to worship in ways that differed from their less affluent neighbors, often spoke their own unique dialects, and by the twentieth century were inclined to spend time at "the club." Because of the power of race, a separate black class system, with its own unique class-based subcultures, coexisted with the white class system. Culturally, the power and influence of class cannot be denied.

Race—the division of the South into white and black—was another major influence on the culture. Slavery created this division, and segregation would maintain it well into the twentieth century. Race for blacks was destiny: it determined where they could live, whom they could marry and socialize with, and where they could work. Rigid rules and laws created by whites defined what was permissible for blacks to say and do. Violators of these rules and laws were dealt with harshly. For the slave, it might be a whipping; after the Civil War, for the black man or woman who violated one of the rules or laws of segregation, it might be a harsh prison sentence or extralegal violence, which in its most extreme form was lynching. For whites, race established a sense of privilege even for the poorest white person. As a consequence of slavery and segregation, blacks and whites developed two versions of Southern culture that coexisted side by side. However, despite the rigid separation of white and black, whites and blacks and their cultures intermingled and intermixed, each influencing the other and each sharing in the creation of a broader Southern culture. The meaning and impact of race has evolved in contemporary times, but it continues to shape the culture in profound ways.

In modern post-industrial societies, a host of institutions—schools and colleges, families, the mass media, government agencies, churches, groups like the Boy Scouts and the Kiwanis—define and transmit the culture. In the agrarian society that was the South for so long, it was the family that did this with little competition from any other institution save the church. Until the twentieth century, the South was mostly rural with few cities, and many Southerners lived on farms. Each farm was like a small isolated kingdom unto itself, and, particularly on small farms, family members worked, socialized, and played primarily with other family members. Often, only the head of the household had much regular contact with those outside the family. One's values, notions of how to behave, social status and even one's identity came primarily from the family. The prominence of the male head of the household in this traditional family has led many to refer to the family structure as patriarchal (male dominated), and, until recently, the laws and customs of the South promoted and supported this role for the male. For blacks, family and gender roles would play out differently; slavery and segregation would have a tremendous impact on the black family and gender roles. Understanding family and gender and how Southern families and gender roles have changed are keys to understanding the culture of the South.

Politics in the South, as with politics anywhere, reflected the culture, and in turn shaped it. Given the importance of race, not surprisingly Southern politics devoted a considerable amount of attention to it. Indeed, slavery and later segregation were as much political creations as they were social and economic creations. Even today, race is a topic of most Southern political campaigns if only in an unspoken sense as an overwhelmingly white Republican Party contends for power with a multiracial Democratic Party in the region. Class, too, has played an important role in shaping the region's politics and has had a decisive influence on the distinct "styles" of politics, each a creation of a specific era, that have defined the options available to voters on election day. Understanding these styles is a key to understanding contemporary Southern politics and Southern politicians like George W. Bush, Newt Gingrich, and Bill Clinton.

The South is the most overtly Christian region of the country, the most Protestant region of the country, and the most Baptist region of the country. When the Presbyterian churchman James McBride Dabbs wrote his reflection on the South and being a Southerner, he tellingly entitled it *Haunted by God.* (The novelist Flannery O'Conner has also referred to the region as "Christ haunted.") What Dabbs meant by this is that it is a region where religion is pervasive. Understanding the unique brand of Christianity practiced in the South by most people is, therefore, critical to understanding Southern culture.

Finally, certain well-known and not-so-well-known icons, symbols and myths define the South, set it apart from the rest of the nation, and help Southerners make sense of themselves and their history. People understand themselves as different and unique by comparing themselves to others, and these myths and symbols set Southerners apart from the rest of the nation—known collectively in the decades leading up to the Civil War and for over a hundred years later as "the North." The Civil War itself became a myth and a symbol of the South—it was called the "Lost Cause"—and loomed large in the psyches of white Southerners for over one hundred years and played a major role in defining "Southerness." Although it is waning in its influence in the culture as the insularity of the South is eroded by mobility into and out of the region and a rising level of multi-cultural cosmopolitanism, even today, a migrant from the North who offends a native of the region might be denounced as a "damn Yankee," and even today the ceremonial display of the Confederate flag on a government building can draw its passionate defenders. Elvis, moonshine, the cross, the pickup truck, fried chicken, even kudzu, a ubiquitous plant that may grow several feet a day, all represent the region to its inhabitants and outsiders.

Just as important as myths and symbols and institutions in shaping how people understand and define the region's culture are the creative products of Southerners. Building styles, crafts such as pottery-making, cuisine, music—perhaps the South's major creative contribution to the world—story-telling and literature reflect the agrarian heritage of the region as well as the influences of race, class, family, religion, and gender. The cultural products of the South—fried chicken, the Baptist religion, even Elvis—have all, in recent decades, been subject to the same mass production forces that roll over everything in American society for good and ill. These forces, driven by the dollar, seem to be creating a franchised, mass produced, electronically mediated culture that varies only in the consumption patterns of different market segments. So a form of fried chicken joins pizza and hamburgers in the pantheon of American franchise restaurant food, and Elvis is a major interior design element in the franchised nostalgia of rock and roll restaurants found all over the globe. The Baptist faith is still primarily a Southern faith, but PowerPoint, praise songs, and the influences of a national conservative movement seem to be emptying it of "Southerness." But people have been predicting the decline or disappearance of the South as a meaningful entity for a long time, and the South's dogged resistance to change has an equally long history.

Southerners and non-Southerners alike have different perceptions of the region and its culture. For some, it is the last bastion of traditional values—"old times there are not forgotten"—while for others, the progress of the region is what's important and some traditions—slavery and segregation, for example—are best forgotten. Getting at the truth about the region's culture is difficult—the truth is, after all, often elusive—but the "searching for" is as important as the finding and has its own rewards.

Southern Culture

Chapter 1

The Agrarian South

Introduction

For almost three hundred years, agriculture was the major livelihood of most residents of the American South, and the rural lifestyle was the shared experience that tied together a region that rivals most countries in size. The defining institutions of this agrarian tradition were the plantation and the small farm. The first plantations were established around Jamestown in the Virginia Colony in the early 1600s. The labor of choice was indentured servants imported from England, and the crop of choice was tobacco. Later, slaves would replace servants, and still later, in Virginia and across the South, sharecroppers would replace slaves. Rice, sugar, and "King Cotton" would join tobacco as major plantation crops in the region. While plantations eventually could be found from Virginia to Texas, they were numerous only in the areas with the richest, most fertile land, areas like the Tidewater of Virginia, the Low

Country of South Carolina, the Yazoo-Mississippi Delta, and the Black Belt of Alabama. Even so, the plantation would dominate the Southern economy and dictate the course of Southern history until technology, migration, industrial development, and policies implemented by the federal government would finally bring to an end the plantation era in the decades after World War II.

For all of the plantation's economic importance, the great majority of white Southerners before the Civil War were small farmers who owned farms of several hundred acres, worked their land with the help of kin, lived on what they grew and raised on their owns farms, and bartered or sold what was left for the little extras. Small farmers would survive the Civil War and actually grow in number, but, by the late twentieth century, the small farm was on the verge of extinction. In many ways, the plantation and the small farm were in different worlds, but there was also much in common between life and labor on the plantation and on the small farm, enough apparently to unite the farmer and the planter. In this chapter, we will explore the variations of this agrarian tradition, how it evolved over time, and what its influence is today in the contemporary South.

The Birth of the Agrarian Tradition

In 1607 a band of English adventurers who had traveled across the ocean to the New World began building a settlement called Jamestown. The settlement was in a colony established by the Virginia Company as a profit-making venture. The colony (Virginia) and the company were named in honor of Elizabeth, the "Virgin Queen." The earliest settlers, shareholders in the company and their indentured servants, were a rather undisciplined, lazy lot who hoped to find great wealth, ideally lying on the ground somewhere. Virginia was not a place to make a home; the adventurers planned to return to England with their loot. These indolent fellows drove their leader, Captain John Smith, to despair, and the colony very nearly ended in failure.

Back in England, Sir Edwin Sandys, one of the company's shareholders, was elected treasurer and he began to actively promote permanent settlement in the colony as a way of making the colony profitable. Sandys instituted the headright system that gave the settlers moving to Virginia fifty acres for every person ("head") they brought with them. He actively "recruited" poor men and boys to serve as the colony's workforce. Sandys encouraged the production of a variety of agricultural commodities, and one of these commodities was tobacco. Tobacco was a plant native to the New World and was attracting some interest in England and the continent of Europe, although no one was quite certain what to do with the plant initially. It began finding a use in the brothels and taverns of England as a recreational drug, and the demand for it began to grow. Sandys' settlers began establishing plantations to grow the "sotweed." These men were as infused with the profit-making spirit as the earlier treasure hunters had been and were not, for the most part, interested in operating small family farms. The poor migrants from England whom Sandys was recruiting labored in the fields for these planters as indentured servants or tenants. Servants signed contracts (indentures) to labor for the planters for set terms, usually seven years, in return for passage to Virginia, food, clothing, and a place to sleep. Tenants technically were free men who received half of what they earned; in practice, according to historian Edmund Morgan, their rights and privileges were little different from servants. Virginia became a booming plantation colony dedicated to growing and exporting tobacco.[1]

Life on the tobacco plantations was harsh and short. In fact, in an investigation of the colony in the mid-1620s initiated by disgruntled shareholders, it was discovered that the overwhelming majority of immigrants to Virginia since its founding in 1607 had died. Disease, malnutrition, skirmishes with local Native American tribes, and overwork made Virginia a living hell. And it was the indentured servants and tenants who suffered the most.[2] The British government took over Virginia and made it a royal colony. Under the rule of the British government, plantations spread across the land, and thousands of new immigrants, most of them servants, arrived from England. Virginia's appetite for labor and the profit of transporting servants to Virginia led ship captains to scour England looking for people willing to take the voyage. Generally these were marginal people—prison inmates, people hoping to avoid prison time, desperately poor people, and no doubt, a fair number of men who had accepted free drinks from the wrong people. By the 1640s the horrible death rate in Virginia had declined, and some servants even began to live out their terms of servitude and become free men and women.

Rising life spans had an unanticipated consequence: many of the young men—and the servant workforce of Virginia was overwhelmingly male and young—refused to sign up for a second tour of servitude. Few had the funds to return to England or buy much land; many ended up on the frontier where they could squat on unoccupied land, and many others lived by their wits in the more settled areas, squatting, hunting and fishing, and poaching (stealing livestock). Their growing numbers on the frontier led to more conflict with the Indians, and they bombarded a less than sympathetic colonial legislature with demands for troops. The privileged men who served in the legislature came to see these former servants as a threat to order that rivaled even the Indians. In 1670

---

1. Edmund Morgan, *American Slavery, American Freedom* (New York: W.W. Norton and Co., 1975), 44–99. Morgan's brilliant analysis of the evolution of the plantation and slavery in early Virginia is the primary source for this section of the text.

2. *Ibid.*, 100–101.

they decided to deny landless men the vote apparently perceiving them as too irresponsible to be entrusted with the franchise. The legislature also responded with increasingly heavy penalties for the sorts of crimes they were committing. Poaching, for example, could result in a 2000-pound fine, a huge sum.[3]

The situation reached the boiling point, and servants and former servants united under the leadership of a disgruntled planter by the name of Nathaniel Bacon, rose in revolt, marched to Jamestown, and burned it to the ground in 1676. Fortunately for the planters, Bacon became sick and died and the rebellion collapsed, but they still faced a dilemma. The planters needed a growing workforce, but the more servants they imported, the more shiftless, property-less, dangerous young men would be floating around the colony when their terms of servitude were up. The solution was at hand in the growing numbers of African workers being brought in by enterprising merchants to feed the colony's insatiable appetite for workers. Early on, these Africans were technically servants, but they were servants with a difference: they were foreign people from a distant, and to the English strange land, and, unlike the English servants, they had been captured and brought to the colony in chains. The English were certainly aware that the Spanish and the Portuguese were enslaving people like these to work on their New World plantations, and while they had no significant experience with slavery nor laws governing it, their need for a dependable and controllable labor force and their disdain for a strange, heathen people overcame any reticence they may have had about establishing slavery in the colony. By the late 1600s, the legal and practical details of chattel slavery had been worked out: a slave was a slave for life; a slave was property or chattel; and importantly, slavery was only for people of another race. Slavery saved the plantation system in Virginia as slaves became the labor of choice for plantation owners.[4]

But what of the servants? The ranks of the servants dwindled as the importation of African slaves grew. According to historian Edmund Morgan, the planters of Virginia now became very helpful to those whom they had recently exploited. By the early 1700s, freed servants were compensated for their servitude with land, money, and clothing by their masters, and the government provided them each with fifty acres of land. The poll tax, a tax one paid to vote, was significantly reduced. Why had the planters become so generous? According to Morgan, "fear of a servile insurrection" was one important factor.[5] Former servants were needed as allies to keep black slaves under control. But the planters also apparently were coming to believe that since the laboring class now was black, whites, all whites, were members of a "superior race." In short,

---

3. *Ibid.*, 235–249.
4. *Ibid.*, 250–270.
5. *Ibid.*, 344.

a sort of white solidarity resulted from slavery in part because the planters no longer needed to exploit other whites. Land was so plentiful and tobacco prices by the end of the seventeenth century high enough that slaveholding planters could afford to be generous. With a growing population of African slaves to control, they could not afford to be less than generous with their white brethren.

A sizeable class of white yeomanry emerged by the early 1700s in Virginia. A yeoman farmer was one who owned a small farm—often of several hundred acres—used his family for labor and grew food crops and often a bit of tobacco just like his large planter neighbor. A commonality of interests had thus emerged between this new small farmer class and the slaveholding planters, and astute politicians from the planter class would thereafter carefully cultivate that commonality. Importantly, a pattern of plantations **and** small farms was established that was replicated throughout the region as new areas were settled. And this pattern, call it the Southern agrarian pattern, would persist until the Civil War and beyond.

The Spread of the Agrarian Tradition

As new regions of the South were settled—the coastal region of South Carolina, for example, or the piedmont region of North Carolina—the land itself and the accessibility to markets would determine the mix of plantations and farms. Thus, the South Carolina coast in the early decades of the 1700s and the Mississippi Delta during the 1820s and '30s emerged as prime plantation districts with few small farms because these areas were perfectly suited to large-scale cash crop agriculture. The mountain areas of North Carolina and Virginia, on the other hand, became the domain of the small, slaveless farmer because the steep slopes of the Appalachians were no place to grow cotton or rice or tobacco in quantity. The piedmont region of the South, stretching from Virginia into Alabama, a region characterized by rolling hills and rather anemic clay soil, was primarily the domain of the small farmer, but a sizeable minority of slaveholding planters struggled to make a go of it in this region, too. Generally, these planters occupied the best land in the Piedmont, and wherever else they settled, too, while many of the small farmers were more likely to labor away on the less desirable land on the steeper slopes or land bordering swamps.

This was a society that had little need or, it turns out, little use for cities and towns. Small farmers were largely self-sufficient; they produced most of what they and their families ate, wore, and used. They had little need or cash to pay for the products produced or sold in towns and cities. Planters were market-oriented and did need to market their crops and did, of course, have the cash to buy what cities and towns produced. But planters were always small in number and not, therefore, numerous enough to support much of a class of urban artisans or merchants. Furthermore, much of the South was richly endowed with navigable rivers, which served as major thoroughfares upon which to ship cash crops to distant metropolises in the North and Europe, and, of course, to import needed manufactured goods. Had this not been the case, the South would have had more towns and cities than it did. Finally, what we call the South was not completely "settled" until after the Civil War. There was, therefore, always fresh land to clear and settle for a growing population, and this bounteous supply of land certainly kept the agrarian tradition viable. But geographic and economic factors were not the only reason the region was so profoundly rural and devoted to agriculture. Agrarianism had become a deeply embedded set of values in the regional culture, a set of values that might be termed the agrarian ideal.

The Agrarian Ideal

The agrarian ideal was a set of values and attitudes that had become common currency in the South by the 1700s. In this value system farming was not merely a way to survive, it was the best way to live. Thomas Jefferson is no doubt the most famous son of the South to articulate the agrarian ideal. Jefferson was, of course, a planter, a slaveholder, a Virginian, and a prime example, albeit an exceptional example, of the unique world of the eighteenth century. He was the supreme rationalist who argued for human rights and freedoms (for whites, anyway) and who experimented with new crops on his farm, and he was also the supreme romantic who built a plantation atop what can only be described as a small mountain. Monticello had a wonderful view, but building a plantation on a mountain was a foolhardy endeavor that may have contributed to the mountain of debt that he accrued over his long life. The rational and the romantic both influenced the agrarian ideal as articulated by Jefferson and others in the 1700s and 1800s. According to this ideal, farming was a supremely practical endeavor that was also inherently moral, even spiritual. In *Notes on the State of Virginia*, Jefferson observed:

> Those who labor in the earth are the chosen people of God, if ever He had a chosen people, whose breasts He has made His peculiar deposit for substantial and genuine virtue. It is the focus in which he keeps alive the sacred fire, which otherwise might escape from the face of the earth. Corruption of morals in the mass of cultivators is a phenomenon of which no age or nation has furnished an example. It is the mark set on those, who, not looking up to heaven, to their own soil and industry, as does the husbandman, for their subsistence, depend for it on casualties and caprice of customers. Dependence begets

subservience and venality, suffocates the germ of virtue, and prepares fit tools for the designs of ambition.[6]

So for Jefferson and other agrarian-minded Southerners, farming was the only virtuous occupation for men, and the only occupation that truly allowed men to be free. Crafts, industry, and the trades made men dependent on bosses, customers, and suppliers, and created in men greedy, self-serving personalities. Further, for Jefferson, rural living was healthy; city life corrupting. For him, farming and the countryside were necessary preconditions for the growth of democracy. Of cities and government he wrote: "The mobs of great cities add just so much to the support of pure government, as sores do to the strength of the human body."[7] In short, greedy, dependent, ambitious men were not the stuff from which democracies were made. The Republic would only thrive if the nation were an agrarian nation of farmers.

A devotion to, even worship of the land was also an aspect of both the spiritual and practical nature of agrarianism. On the practical side, land was necessary for a farmer, and rich, flat land was better than poor land on a hill or in a swamp. How much was enough? As Ben Robertson, writing in the 1930s, said of his kin in the piedmont region of South Carolina, "there is also a quality within our character that makes us dissatisfied until we have bought all the land that joins our land. We cannot resist buying land."[8] But spending time on a particular piece of land that one's family owned had a more profound influence on the psyche than, say, owning a car or some other piece of property. Robertson noted that "I and all the families of my kinfolks lived for nearly two centuries in two old and fertile valleys at the foot of the Blue Ridge Mountain," and though many of his people had "rambled," and left those valleys as he had done, "Someone is always keeping the homeplace, someone is always there...."[9] This land had become a part of their lives. As he said, "It was disturbing country that rested us and somehow never let us rest."[10]

When Robertson was writing his memoir, a group of young poets and scholars called the Nashville Agrarians (or Southern Agrarians) published a collection of essays entitled *I'll Take My Stand,* which attacked the industrial order in the United States and voiced what was probably the last major defense of agrarianism. Andrew Lytle's essay "The Hind Tit" sounds quite reminiscent of Jefferson. Lytle describes the dominance of an "industrial empire

6. Thomas Jefferson, *Notes on the State of Virginia* in Adrienne Koch and William Peden, eds., *The Life and Selected Writings of Thomas Jefferson* (New York, 1972), 280.
7. *Ibid.*
8. Ben Robertson, *Red Hills and Cotton: An Upcountry Memoir* (Columbia, SC: University of South Carolina Press, 1973), 8–9.
9. *Ibid.,* 5, 20.
10. *Ibid.,* 6.

bent on the conquest of the earth's goods and ports to sell them in." This dominance has set in motion "a war to the death between technology and the ordinary functions of living." For Lytle, industrial capitalism and the cities it spawns have produced "a poison which penetrates to the spirit and rots the soul." The only salvation is "in a return to a society where agriculture is practiced by most of the people. It is in fact impossible for any culture to be sound and healthy without a proper respect and proper regard for the soil, no matter how many urban dwellers think their victuals come from groceries and delicatessens and their milk from tin cans. This ignorance does not release them from a final dependence upon the farm and that most incorrigible of beings, the farmer."[11]

Today, agrarianism as a philosophy or ideology is but a whisper of its former self. How could it be otherwise? Most Southerners troop off to work each day in factories, offices, franchise restaurants, and schools, not the back 40. The region's agriculture is increasingly dominated by large-scale "agribusiness" (Lytle would have been horrified by the term), and the small farmer appears headed for extinction. While the Nashville Agrarians may have shouted the last hurrah for agrarianism as a creed in the 1930s, one can still hear the values of Jefferson and Lytle extolled in countless country music songs (listen, for example, to the lyrics of a tune popular in the 1970s, "Thank God I'm a Country Boy") and in the poetry and prose of Wendell Berry and the few other critics of modern society who still believe a life on the land is the best life.[12] Implicit in this commitment to a life on the land is a commitment to a particular place; one should live one's life, like the Robertson clan, in a particular locale, a place that belongs to you and to which you belong even if you should leave. As James Everett Kibler has noted in his memoir about restoring his family homeplace:

> Indeed, as Carolinians of the last century [he's referring here to the nineteenth century] knew so much better than those of our own day, to live a life of completeness, a mortal must fully concentrate his being upon one finite place on earth and know it both tactilely and spiritually in all the fullness of the seasons, know all the creatures of that place who move there in the night world as well as the day.[13]

---

11. Andrew Lytle, *The Hind Tit*, in Twelve Southerners, *I'll Take My Stand* (Baton Rouge and London: Louisiana State University Press, 1977; first published, 1930), 201–245.

12. See for example, Wendell Berry, "The Regional Motive," in William L. Andrews et al, eds., *The Literature of the American South: A Norton Anthology* (New York and London: W.W. Norton, 1998), 934–937.

13. James Everett Kibler, *Our Fathers' Fields: A Southern Story* (Columbia, SC: University of South Carolina Press, 1998), 396.

The Agrarian Tradition before the Civil War

By the decade before the Civil War, the South was a sprawling fifteen-state region stretching from Maryland on the East Coast over to border states Kentucky and Missouri and finally ending in Texas in the West. If one could have flown over the region in an airplane, it would have appeared as an almost uninterrupted vista of fields, forests, and swamps. With the exception of New Orleans and Charleston, its cities and towns were scattered crossroads settlements, state capitals of a few thousand souls, and small port or river towns of a few hundred or thousand. The plantation, not urban industry, was the engine of the Southern economy. Towns and cities were on the periphery and served primarily as collection points to gather the products of the plantations and send them on to points north and across the ocean.[14] Indeed, the plantation economy was driven by world markets, and changes in world demand for a commodity could create great prosperity or throw planters who specialized in that commodity into a downward spiral. Rice, for example, made the South Carolina Low Country one of the wealthiest areas in the world in the 1700s, but when new sources of rice came into the European market in the early decades of the 1800s, the Low Country went into a serious decline which has only been reversed in recent decades.[15] Towns did serve as centers of local markets where planters and small farmers could market their corn, wheat, swine, and produce, but local trade, while important, as a rule was a limited stimulus to town growth. Planter and small farmer alike strove to be as self-sufficient as possible, and for many, the trip to town was a rare and special occasion.

Plantations produced a variety of staple crops and products—tobacco, sugar, cotton, turpentine, and rice—to sell in markets in the North and across the Atlantic. Plantations were worked by slave labor, and a minimum of twenty slaves were required for a farm to be considered a plantation. Large plantations might have several hundred slaves, and some planters owned several plantations. The planter and his family and perhaps an overseer supervised the slave work force. The plantation system was expanding in the decades before the Civil War. Many of the older plantation regions in the eastern states were in decline, and some planters or their sons set out for the West, a contingent of slaves in tow, to establish new plantations that would save or bolster family fortunes. New plantations were hacked from the wilderness in Alabama, Mississippi, Louisiana, and East Texas. Other eastern planters kept afloat financially

---

14. Ulrich B. Phillips, *Life and Labor in the Old South* (Boston and Toronto: Little, Brown and Co., 1963; reprint of 1929 edition), 140–159.

15. Peter A. Coclanis, *The Shadow of a Dream: Economic Life and Death in the South Carolina Low Country*, 1670–1920 (New York and Oxford: Oxford University Press, 1989), 131–137.

by selling their "extra" slaves, and these men, women, and children often ended up in the newly settled regions of the South.

Plantations were risky investments, and more planters than not carried sizeable debt loads. Many planters strove to be self-sufficient, to produce on the plantation what was needed and to depend on the merchants for as little as possible. James Battle Avirett in his memoir describes in idyllic terms his family's plantation "The Rich Lands." This plantation, located on the New River in North Carolina midway between New Bern and Wilmington was, as Avirett describes it, a self-sufficient enterprise with vegetable gardens, flocks of sheep and herds of cows and hogs, fruit trees, a variety of fowl—chickens, ducks, guinea hens—and fields of black eyed peas, peas, and wheat for home consumption. The plantation had a loom house for the weaving of wool and cotton cloth. Plantation hands dug marl from beds along the New River to enrich the soil. The primary cash crop of the farm was rice.[16] The Rich Lands would not have been unusual; on most plantations, a sizable amount of the acreage was devoted to food crops, particularly corn (for meal for the plantation's residents and for animal feed), and other grains, fruit trees, and vegetables were also cultivated. Slaves were often permitted to tend to their own private gardens. Poultry houses were commonly maintained, and a herd of hogs often roamed a plantation's woodlands and provided meat for the smokehouses. But the cash crop—cotton especially in the decades before the Civil War—was the primary focus of the plantation.[17]

By the 1850s cotton was the king of plantation crops; it was the most profitable cash crop and was grown in a broad belt beginning in North Carolina and stretching to east Texas and up the Mississippi to an area north of Memphis. The Mississippi Delta was becoming the richest cotton-producing area, and, James Cobb has argued convincingly, the heart of the entire South—*The Most Southern Place on Earth*. Most of the cotton crop was produced by slaveholding planters who owned sizeable tracts of farmland. A cotton plantation typically had from several hundred to as many as a thousand or more acres of land suitable for cultivation, not to mention hundreds of acres of woodlands and uncleared acres. Farms of this size required large slave work forces to get the cotton in. The historian Gavin Wright has found that the largest slaveowners in the cotton belt (the top 10%) owned over 60% of the slave workforce.[18] A larger planter often had over a hundred slaves laboring away on his planta-

---

16. James Battle Avirett, *The Old Plantation: How We Lived in Great House and Cabin Before the War* (1901; Chapel Hill: *Documenting the American South*, 1998), 29–32, http://docsouth.unc.edu/avirett/avirett.html.

17. Gavin Wright, *The Political Economy of the Cotton South: Households, Markets, and Wealth in the Nineteenth Century* (New York and London: W.W. Norton & Co., 1978), 55–62. See also Ulrich B. Phillips, *Life and Labor in the Old South* (1929; Boston and Toronto: Little, Brown and Co., 1963), 218–304.

18. Wright, *The Political Economy of the Cotton South*, p. 27.

tion. One authority opined that the ideal plantation in the Delta—one with 1000 acres under cultivation and a slave workforce of 75 field hands—should bring in a crop of a bale per acre and an average of eight bales per hand.[19] Some delta planters did better than that; Wade Hampton II boasted in the fall of 1855 that his Walnut Ridge Plantation was getting two bales to the acre.[20] Figures like this translated into big money in a year when cotton prices were high. But cotton prices often were not high, or the land flooded, or there was a drought, or an epidemic of cholera raged through the slave quarters. Thomas Chaplin, a young planter on St. Helena Island off the coast of South Carolina, struggled to make his plantation profitable growing sea island cotton, a highly prized long fiber cotton grown by island planters. His poor work habits and the loss of a portion of his slave work force—sold to pay his creditors—limited his success. Rarely did he produce more than 10 bales, a modest amount, and his last crop before the outbreak of the war was only 7 bales. He sold his cotton to a "factor" (cotton wholesaler) in Charleston, but he also sold small quantities of the other products of his plantation in local markets. Probably to compensate for his inability to bring in a good cotton crop, he struggled to make his plantation as self-sufficient as possible, but his taste for whiskey, wine, jewelry, and ice—the family used 125 pounds a week in the summer— still kept him in debt.[21]

Plantations were money-making ventures, but they were also something more: they supported a particular lifestyle—the plantation lifestyle—that reflected one version of the agrarian ideal. As noted earlier, the agrarian ideal was built in part on romantic notions of farming and life in the country. The beauty of nature, the joys and bounties offered by the outdoor life, and the slow rhythms of agriculture were part and parcel of this romance for many planters. James Battle Avirett's description of the New River's bounty is nothing less than romantic and that cousin of the romantic, nostalgic:

> One must take into consideration the fact that this beautiful body of salt water constituted the abundant storehouse of nature, from which were taken some of the most valued features of table comfort and luxury. Its waters teemed with the various varieties of fine fish found in this latitude, among which were the mullet, the sea trout, the sheepshead, the flounder, the croaker or pig ash, with others not a few. These fine fish were there in great abundance. In their season were to be had many varieties of water fowl, ducks, wild geese and

19. James C. Cobb, *The Most Southern Place on Earth: The Mississippi Delta and the Roots of Regional Identity* (New York and Oxford: Oxford University Press, 1992), 10.

20. *Ibid.*, 14.

21. Theodore Rosengarten, *Tombee: Portrait of a Cotton Planter with The Plantation Journal of Thomas B. Chaplin (1822–1890)* (New York: William Morrow, 1986), 68–91.

swans. The ducks were very numerous and of the varieties found in that famous storehouse, the Chesapeake Bay. Never in this country has the writer tasted a more delicious breakfast dish than the blue winged teal of these waters, while the blackheads, mallards, and the variety which we call the canvasback were found in large numbers. Rich and abundant as were all these contributions to the planter's comfort, none surpassed the shellfish found so abundantly where this beautiful inland salt lake joined the sea. The oysters were larger and fatter than the celebrated "Blue Points" of the New York market, and in delicacy of flavor quite equaled the "Morris Cove" specimen of the Philadelphia Club House.[22]

Avirett wrote this passage after the Civil War, and his memories of the plantation lifestyle were no doubt colored by nostalgia for his "lost" world. But a reverence for the old seems to have been a common sentiment in the South even before the "Lost Cause" (the Civil War) ended this world. Indeed, as William Faulkner famously observed about the South, "The past is never dead. It's not even past." It was not uncommon for Southerners before the Civil War, for example, to describe the plantation system and the society that supported it as old or ancient and the nicknames for two Southern states— "the Old Dominion" (Virginia) and "the Old North State" (North Carolina)—reflects this habit. John Pendleton Kennedy, in his pre-Civil War novel *Swallow Barn*, describes the plantation of the protagonist of the novel thusly:

Swallow Barn is an aristocratical old edifice, that squats, like a brooding hen, on the southern bank of the James River. It is quietly seated, with its vassal out-buildings, in a kind of shady pocket or nook, formed by a sweep of the stream, on a gentle acclivity thinly sprinkled with oaks, whose magnificent branches afford habitation and defense to an antique colony of owls.[23]

Why the fascination, indeed obsession with oldness in a society that was, relatively speaking, quite new? At bottom, the outlook and attitudes of most Southern planters was conservative despite the prominent role played by some eighteenth-century planters (Jefferson especially) in formulating the basic tenets of American liberalism. Planters wished to maintain or conserve a certain way of life, and the belief that Southern traditions and customs were ancient gave *gravitas* and legitimacy to this way of life. The plantation was thus perceived to be as old as nature itself and just as "natural." To dislodge or dis-

---

22. Avirett, *The Old Plantation: How We Lived in Great House and Cabin Before the War*, 23.

23. John Pendleton Kennedy, excerpt from *Swallow Barn; or A Sojourn in the Old Dominion* (originally published in 1832) in William L. Andrews, general editor, *The Literature of the American South* (New York and London: W.W. Norton & Co., 1998), 60.

rupt it would thus be unnatural; to cherish its memory, mourn its demise or transformation, again, natural.

However important the plantation and powerful the planter, the overwhelming majority of rural white people in the South were not planters and did not own plantations. Rather, they lived and worked on small farms, and small farms numbered in the hundreds of thousands. They could be found throughout the South but were most numerous in the piedmont and mountain areas of the South and less numerous in the rich plantation districts. Most of the small farmers did not own slaves; they used their own families for labor. Those who did own slaves usually owned at best a few, but some might own a dozen or so. Small farmers typically owned farms of 100–500 acres, although some owned 1000 or more acres. Some owned no land and worked the land of others.[24] In Rowan County, North Carolina, a county with many small farms, the average size of the farm of a slaveless farmer was 143 acres and was valued at slightly more than $1000 in 1860. Small farmers with a small slave workforce (less than 10 slaves) owned larger farms that averaged 274 acres with an average value of $2650.[25]

Small farmers ranged from commercially oriented farmers growing a cash crop to purely subsistence farmers growing and raising what they needed to survive. Most small farmers pursued a cautious "safety first" strategy of taking care of their families' needs first and then devoting "extra" time to a cash crop to bring in a little extra money. Most of what they produced they ate or used, so their focus would be on crops like corn and wheat, garden vegetables, hogs for meat, sheep for the wool. A few extra acres might be planted in cotton, tobacco or wheat to sell or barter to buy a few extras. In Rowan County, for example, the typical small farmer produced several hundred extra bushels of corn and small grains which he could sell or barter with neighbors and merchants. On an August day in 1859, Salisbury (Rowan County) merchant McNeely and Young gave cash credit to local farmers for the following items: watermelon, tobacco, whiskey (34 gallons was bartered), and butter. Farmers typically constructed their own homes and outbuildings, and most of what could be found in the typical home—the furniture, beds, possibly even the nails holding things together—was either made on the farm or on a neighbor-

---

24. Frank Lawrence Owsley, *Plain Folk of the Old South* (1949; Baton Rouge and London: Louisiana State University Press, 1982),156, 166, 168–169, 175, 180, 198–200, 204, 206, 207, 208, 221, 223, 225, 227; Steven Hahn, *The Roots of Southern Populism: Yeoman Farmers and the Transformation of the Georgia Upcountry, 1850–1890* (New York and Oxford: Oxford University Press, 1983), 21–28; Paul Escott, *Many Excellent People: Power and Privilege in North Carolina, 1850–1900* (Chapel Hill, NC and London: University of North Carolina Press, 1985), 7–8.

25. John J. Beck, "Development in the Piedmont South: Rowan County, North Carolina, 1850–1900" (Unpublished Ph.D. dissertation, University of North Carolina, Chapel Hill, 1984), Table 1.3, 260.

ing farm. Spinning wheels and looms were quite commonly part of the household goods on a small farm, and many farm women, despite the growing availability of store bought clothes, were probably still spinning thread (generally wool not cotton) on a spinning wheel, weaving cloth on the family loom, and making the family's dresses, shirts, and pants. A limited number of household items and provisions—a clock, perhaps some dinner plates or a rocking chair, tools, coffee—were store bought.[26]

The Transformation of the Agrarian Tradition after the Civil War

The Civil War produced wrenching changes in the nature of agrarianism in the South. The most obvious change was the destruction of slavery. No longer could the plantation system and planters depend on the coerced labor of black slaves. Not that the planters gave up their labor supply easily; while the Thirteenth Amendment to the United States Constitution ended slavery, legislatures in most Southern states attempted to delay if not defeat emancipation by passing a series of laws called the "Black Codes," which were intended to maintain a form of slavery through legal trickery. The ruling Republican majority in Congress would not stand for this and disbanded the state legislatures and re-instituted military rule in the South. And so a new labor system was devised that was part compromise between planters and the people they had once owned and part tragedy that would mire millions of Southerners, black and white, in poverty and hopelessness.

This system was known as tenant farming, or more commonly, sharecropping. It was actually not new; landless whites before the war often farmed as tenants. As it evolved after the war, the tenant system was a simple proposition: plantations were carved up into small farms, and these farms would be worked by families of former slaves. The planter or landlord would provide tenants with land, seed, fertilizer, a mule, and plow; the tenant would provide the labor. The harvested crop—cotton, tobacco, or sugar cane—would be divided between the two, usually on a 50/50 split. If the tenant had his own equipment, he might garner a larger share; those with nothing but their own labor got less.

---

26. Wright, *The Political Economy of the Cotton South*, 62–74; Hahn, *The Roots of Southern Populism*, 29–30; Beck, "Development in the Piedmont South," Table 1.4, 261. On the barter trade at McNeely and Young, see McNeely and Young Daybook, August 1, 1859, 584, North Carolina Division of Archives and History, Raleigh. For evidence on how widespread the ownership of looms and spinning wheels in Rowan County was see "Inventories and Accounts (of Estates)," Rowan County, NC, 1850–1860, North Carolina Division of Archives and History, Raleigh.

Tenant farms were typically small—generally less, much less, than a hundred acres—because the landlord wanted as much land as possible planted in the cash crop on each of his tenant farms to increase what his "share" would bring. Cotton was thus often planted "from the doorstep to the road."[27] In Rowan County, North Carolina, for example, most tenant farmers tended farms with fewer than 50 cultivatable acres, and the average acreage of these small farms that was suitable for planting was less than 27.[28] Tenancy saved the plantation; the Census Bureau, in a study of 325 cotton-producing counties in 1910, found nearly 40,000 plantations worked by five or more tenant families. The average size of a plantation worked by tenants was over 700 acres.[29] Sharecropping grew by leaps and bounds; by 1930, the majority of farmers in the South were engaged in some form of tenant farming.[30] Increasing numbers of whites who had lost their land or never had land to begin with became "croppers."

Figure 1.1   Tenant houses in the Mississippi Delta

27. Three good accounts of the evolution of the sharecropping system after the Civil War are: Roger Ransom and Richard Sutch, *One Kind of Freedom: The Economic Consequences of Emancipation* (Cambridge: Cambridge University Press, 1977), Harold D. Woodman, *King Cotton and his Retainers* (Lexington, KY: University of Kentucky Press, 1968), and Gavin Wright, *Old South, New South: Revolutions in the Southern Economy Since the Civil War*(New York: Basic Books, Inc., 1986), especially 84–115.

28. Beck, "Development in the Piedmont South," Table 2.3, 277.

29. U.S. Bureau of the Census, *Thirteenth Census of the United States Taken in the Year 1910, Vol. V, Agriculture, 1909, 1910* (Washington, D.C.: GPO, 1914), 880–881.

30. George B. Tindall, *The Emergence of the New South, 1913–1945* (Baton Rouge: Louisiana State University Press, 1967), 125.

There was one important additional component of this new "system": the merchant. Prior to the Civil War, stores were few and far between. They were located in towns and, as we saw, the towns were small, widely scattered, and few in number. After the war, agents of the R.G. Dun credit-rating company traveled all over the South building an extensive credit rating system with credit scores on thousands of individuals. Northern supply houses began to extend credit to good risks in the South to open stores and other businesses, and the number of merchants skyrocketed. Stores opened by the hundreds in the growing towns and small cities of the region and began popping up on rural crossroads and country lanes. These stores stocked a dizzying diversity of products from cotton seed to long underwear, and they became a central feature of both the economic and social life of the region. Merchants, in turn, extended credit to their cash-strapped customers to buy corn meal, seed, fertilizer, clothing, coffee, and the host of other items that they stocked. Tenants generally didn't have property of value for collateral on this credit, but they did, assuming things went well, have a share of a crop come harvest time. Merchants would take a lien on this future crop, called a crop lien, and would charge high interest—often exceeding 50%—because of the risk. Merchants joined with landlords to encourage "croppers" to maximize the acreage of cash crops they planted and to tend it well. Sharecroppers thus ended up with two bosses, both of whom they were in debt to.[31] Many have called sharecropping a new form of slavery. Certainly many sharecroppers could never seem to grow enough to get free of their debt to the merchant. Some would slip away at night with their families to start afresh in a neighboring county, but they would get the same "deal" wherever they went.

An unhealthy cycle was thus established: because landlords' and merchants' livelihoods depended on sharecroppers growing a cash crop, when prices declined, the solution was to plant even more to make up the difference. The acreage devoted to cotton, the primary cash crop, skyrocketed after the Civil War from 7½ million acres in 1866 to 25 million acres in 1900 to over 42 million acres in 1930, the peak year of acreage devoted to cotton.[32] With more acreage, time and energy devoted to cash crops, food production in the South plummeted and the region became a net importer of food. By the turn of the century, a large and growing portion of the population of the rural South was terribly poor and even malnourished. Diseases such as pellagra (a nutritional deficiency), hookworm, and malaria were very common. The growing de-

---

31. Ransom and Sutch, *One Kind of Freedom,160–168.*
32. United States Department of Agriculture, *All Cotton: Acreage, Yield, Production, Price, and Value of Production United States: 1866 to Date, Track Records: United States Crop Production.* USDA-National Agricultural Statistics Service, April, 2003, http://ww.usda.gov/nass/pubs/trackrec/track03a.htm.

pendence on a single crop—cotton especially—kept the Southern economy from developing balance and more lucrative occupations. Malnourishment and grinding poverty were a terrible irony in a region of fertile land, bountiful water supplies, and moderate climate.[33]

If sharecropping was becoming the dominant form of farming, this is not to say that the small, landowning farmer disappeared. Small, family-owned farms actually increased in number after the Civil War, and by 1900 there were between 750,000 and 1 million family farms in the South. The number of farms would continue to grow until the 1930s.[34] In North Carolina and South Carolina, the number of farms in the 100 to 500-acre range more than tripled from 1860 to 1900.[35] Like the sharecropper, the small farmer began to focus on the production of cash crops, and the food crop production of small farmers declined. However, many small farmers and even some sharecroppers were able to continue the practices of pre-Civil War small farmers and live largely self-sufficient lives—they ate what they grew.[36] Even today, as one drives down a rural road, it's not uncommon to see fairly sizeable gardens stretched out beside the farmhouses, so a limited degree of self-sufficiency persists even now. President Jimmy Carter recalls his family's farm outside Plains, Georgia (circa 1930s) grew a variety of crops—wheat, oats, and rye—for "food and feed," maintained a garden, and kept milk cows, chickens, and hogs. "Almost all our food was produced in our pasture, fields, garden, and yard," he writes.[37] Self-sufficiency appeared to hang on longest in mountain areas. As late as the 1930s in some mountain counties in North Carolina and Virginia, over half of the farmers were described as self-sufficient by the U.S. Census.[38]

Ultimately however, most small farmers could not resist the lure of the market; the provisions now widely available in the country store often just a few miles away, the chance to make extra money or to buy that extra twenty acres a neighbor was offering for sale all drew farmers to cash crop agriculture. Farmers bought fertilizer, seed, and implements at the merchants; Jimmy Carter remembers that his family bought fish, canned goods, peanut

---

33. Gilbert C. Fite, *Cotton Fields No More: Southern Agriculture, 1865–1980* (Lexington, KY: University Press of Kentucky, 1984), 32–39.

34. *Ibid.*, 32, Table A2, 234.

35. U.S. Bureau of the Census, *Twelfth Census of the United States, 1900, Vol. V, Agriculture, pt.1* (Washington, D.C.: GPO, 1902), 108, 118; U.S. Bureau of the Census, *Eighth Census of the United States, 1860, Vol. 2, Agriculture* (Washington, D.C.: GPO, 1864), 214.

36. On the decline of food production, see Hahn, *The Roots of Southern Populism*, 149–152.

37. Jimmy Carter, *An Hour Before Daylight: Memories of a Rural Boyhood* (New York: Simon and Schuster, 2001), 29–37, 55.

38. U.S. Bureau of the Census, *Fifteenth Census of the United States: 1930, Agriculture, Vol. III, pt. 2—Southern States* (Washington: Government Printing Office, 1932), 109–111, 227–233.

Henderson [NC] Daily Dispatch

Figure 1.2   Plowing with a Mule

butter, rice, and cheese from local merchants and that the white small farmer families in the Plains area mostly wore "store bought" clothing. A successful farmer might have a windmill like his father's—purchased from Sears Roebuck—to pump water and deliver it to "the kitchen and a bathroom with toilet."[39] Merchants extended credit to small farmers and planters and took as collateral for these "loans" liens on the debtors' land to secure the debts. If a debt wasn't paid off, the merchant got the land. Indebtedness was another reason to focus on cash crops, and the "safety first" approach of the pre-war small farmer increasingly gave way to cash crop specialization. Even in the Piedmont, generally not the most suitable land for growing cotton, more and more farmers began growing the white lint. In Rowan County, North Carolina, for example, cotton production jumped from a few hundred bales before the war to over 7000 bales by 1900. By 1880, over half the farmers in the county were growing cotton, compared to less than 10% of the farmers before the war.[40] Tobacco was another cash crop small farmers in South Carolina, North Carolina, Georgia, and Kentucky grew. Small farmers also grew corn, peanuts, wheat, and oats, and frequently would raise a herd of hogs and use part of their corn crop for feed. Jimmy Carter's father primarily grew peanuts (Jimmy would grow them too after completing his tour in the navy) and cotton for his cash crops.[41]

So small farmers were moving in the direction of becoming modern market-oriented farmers who grew a cash crop and little else. The final stage of this transition would have to wait for the advent of machinery, tractors especially. Beginning in the 1930s, tractors began making their appearance in the region on a significant scale, thanks in part to government programs that provided cash subsidies to farmers. The small Farmall was the tractor of choice for many small farmers, and worn out, rusting Farmalls, and a few working ones, can still be seen parked beside barns or sitting in sheds. Mules have now almost vanished. One vestige of the subsistence era would linger: farming folk were slow to accept the market ideal that their neighbors were their competitors, and the practice of neighbor helping neighbor with the work would persist well into the twentieth century. For example, group corn huskings—where neighbors would congregate at each other's farms to husk the harvested corn—were not unheard of as late as the 1930s, and even today rural people are probably more likely than others to help each other out when the weather or the economy turns ugly.

---

39. Carter, *An Hour Before Daylight*, 28, 31, 34.
40. Wright, *Old South, New South*, 110–112; Beck, "Development in the Piedmont South," 93.
41. Carter, *An Hour Before Daylight*, 55.

The Growth of Towns and Industry

We saw earlier that the Nashville Agrarians, writing in the 1930s, warned of the impending destruction of the agrarian way of life by modern industry. The growth of industry in the South actually began on a significant scale fifty years before they wrote. After the Civil War, some Southerners such as Henry Grady, editor of the *Atlanta Constitution*, began urging the region to diversify its economy, quit its dependence on agriculture, and develop industry. Their arguments were purely practical: industry had helped the North win the Civil War, and industry was making the North rich. Grady and others argued that the reliance of the South on the outside world, particularly the North, left it dependent. One of Grady's most famous illustrations of this dependency took the form of a story about a funeral he attended:

> It was a poor "one gallus" fellow, whose breeches struck him under the armpits and hit him at the other end about the knee—he didn't believe in decollete clothes. They buried him in the midst of a marble quarry: they cut through solid marble to make his grave; and yet a little tombstone they put above him was from Vermont. They buried him in the heart of a pine forest, and yet the pine coffin was imported from Cincinnati. They buried him within touch of an iron mine, and yet the nails in his coffin and the iron in the shovel that dug his grave were imported from Pittsburg. They buried him by the side of the best sheep-grazing country on the earth, and yet the wool in the coffin bands and the coffin bands themselves were brought from the North. The South didn't furnish a thing on earth for that funeral but the corpse and the hole in the ground. There they put him away and the clods rattled down on his coffin, and they buried him in a New York coat and a Boston pair of shoes and a pair of breeches from Chicago and a shirt from Cincinnati, leaving him nothing to carry into the next world with him to remind him of the country in which he lived, and for which he fought for four years, but the chill of blood in his veins and the marrow in his bones.[42]

The limits of the cotton economy in the South and of agriculture in general were becoming painfully obvious as the nineteenth century waned. What we need, Grady and others said, is a "New South," a South of not only of agriculture but also industries and cities.[43] Men like Grady were often very circum-

---

42. Joel Chandler Harris, ed., *Life of Henry W. Grady, Including his Writings and Speeches* (Cassell Publishing Company, 1890). The excerpt is from Grady's speech given to the Bay State Club. See 199–207.

43. *Ibid.*, 90–91. The historian Paul Gaston has called this set of beliefs "the New South Creed." Gaston, *The New South Creed: A Study in Southern Mythmaking* (New York: Vintage Books, 1973).

spect in their criticisms of the old regime and agrarianism, but reading between the lines of what they were writing and saying, one could see that they were also calling for a new Southern man who, unlike his agrarian predecessors, was hard driving, competitive, and eager to make a buck. The Old South man—a man who was oriented to the seasons, who spent his waking hours in a tight network of supportive kin folks, who was disdainful of money or at least cavalier about it, who viewed hard work as the province of the slave (this would have been more a planter value than a small farmer value), who was interested more in a pleasant lifestyle and leisure than in business success—this man was a dinosaur.

Even before the growth of industry in the South, an important economic and social change was taking place, and this change would pave the way for industrial development. As we have seen, the expansion of cash crop farming after the Civil War had stimulated the growth of small towns across the South—towns like Macon, Georgia, Laurel, Mississippi, and Darlington, South Carolina—to service and supply the farmers. The number of rural stores skyrocketed to serve the sharecroppers and small farmers of each area, and these stores often became the nucleus of small crossroads settlements. These new and expanding towns became hotbeds of New South boosterism. In short, the merchants and lawyers and warehouse owners and even planters who lived in or near these towns became the sort of New South people that Grady dreamed of. They wanted to make their own towns bigger and better because that would mean their stores would sell more or they would have more clients and the land they owned would be worth more. They worked together to make their towns grow. The most important factor in assuring the continued growth of a town was luring the railroad to build a line (or a second line) to town. Meetings were held, speeches were given, tours for railroad executives were conducted, and money raised in town after town in a frenzied effort to win the favors of a railroad company. The advocates of development also worked to improve town services (roads, sewers, schools), and they established banks and savings and loans and new town organizations such as the chamber of commerce. Much of this activity required political power, and so "progress" became (and still is) a key political issue in towns big and small.[44] The Piedmont was the area of the South where notions of progress took the firmest root and for a simple reason. Given the limits of the anemic clay soil in the Piedmont, agriculture had less allure for men with money to invest than it did in the Mississippi Delta or the Low Country of South Carolina or the other plan-

---

44. David L. Carlton, *Mill and Town in South Carolina, 1880–1920* (Baton Rouge and London: Louisiana State University Press, 1982), 17–39; Beck, Development in the Piedmont South," 98–100, 127–158; Douglas Flamming, *Creating the Modern South: Millhands and Managers in Dalton, Georgia* (Chapel Hill and London: University of North Carolina Press, 1992), 19–24.

tation districts of the South. Too, where the plantation was weakest was also where planter power was less likely to be employed to block development that might attract workers from the countryside to the town or that might cause taxes to go up on land. Planters were famous for protecting their cheap supply of labor and opposing higher taxes.

By the 1880s there was a critical mass of these "New South" men dedicated to making money, and these men were interested in making even more money. While stores had proven to be a good investment, the modern penchant for establishing chains of stores had not yet taken hold. So a successful merchant looking to invest his profit might expand his store, but rarely built other stores in neighboring towns. Here's where the Gradys of the South were important; their non-stop advocacy of industrial investment started to resonate with men with money in their pockets—the merchants, doctors, bankers, and warehousemen—who began to realize that they might be able to make even more money doing something new. The factory of choice in the South was the textile mill, and hundreds would be built in the region. But furniture factories were also established in western North Carolina, tobacco factories were established throughout the region but especially in Durham, North Carolina, Richmond, Virginia and Winston-Salem, North Carolina, and a steel industry arose in Birmingham, Alabama.

Textiles mills were attractive for a number of reasons: for one, the cotton was already there, and many felt it made sense to make a product out of it. Further, it was a common perception that the production of yarn and cloth was relatively simple and did not require a highly skilled workforce, and textile mills had been built here and there in the South even before the war, so there was a degree of familiarity with mills in some areas. And the labor supply was there; hundreds of thousands of families were eking out a bare existence on the land, and it was becoming clearer and clearer to more and more people that life on the land led only to poverty and hopelessness. Also important were the Northern companies that increasingly sent representatives south with enticing "deals" on machinery. Mills were generally built by local people in the towns in which they lived and often, once the first one was built, a number of others followed. In Salisbury, North Carolina, for example, the first mill built after the war was started by three merchants, a banker, and a minister. By 1900, four additional mills had been constructed. The workforce in the mills of Salisbury was overwhelmingly white. In fact, the first mill was promoted in Salisbury not only as a moneymaking venture, but also as the salvation for rural poverty-stricken whites.[45] Textile mills across the South fit the racial pattern found in

---

45. Carlton, *Mill and Town in South Carolina*, 40–81; Beck, "Development in the Piedmont South," 159–196; Paul D. Escott, Many *Excellent People: Power and Privilege in North Carolina, 1850–1900* (Chapel Hill and London: University of North Carolina Press, 1985), 198–219; Flamming, *Creating the Modern South*, 24–27.

Salisbury and would not hire significant numbers of African Americans until the late 1960s and early 1970s.

Figure 1.3   South Henderson mill village

By the early decades of the twentieth century, the South was the number one textile region in the world, and hundreds of thousands would be employed in its mills. While a number of mills would remain locally owned enterprises, some mill men, such as the Cone brothers of Greensboro and James Cannon of Concord, North Carolina, built mill "empires," each with a multitude of mills that were spread across the region. The industrial heartland of the South circa 1900 was concentrated in the hilly Piedmont beginning in Richmond and stretching southward to Birmingham. Unlike the North, where industrialization spawned the growth of large towns and great cities, industrialization in the South was primarily a small town affair. Greensboro, North Carolina, one of the more prominent industrial towns, grew from 500 or so souls in 1870 to around 10,000 in 1900, but would not reach 100,000 until the mid-century mark. Even Atlanta, the most prominent city of the "New South," would only attain major city status in the last three decades of the twentieth century. Most of the mills were built in or near towns much smaller than Greensboro or Atlanta, towns of a few thousand (or less) like Clinton, South Carolina, or Henderson, North Carolina.

If the Old South was rural, this growing New South was rural **and** small town. To an extent, town and country were more a continuum than two separate entities because the interplay between town and country was very strong, and towns had much about them that could be described as agrarian. Many of the residents of the growing towns were recent migrants from the countryside;

over the course of the 1880s, 1890s, and early years of the 1900s, hundreds of thousands of men, women, and children migrated to these towns and mill villages to work in the mills.[46] The ranks of merchants, clerks, lawyers, bankers, and mill superintendents was also fed by rural immigration. Georgia resident L. R. Allen grew up on the farm owned by his parents in the early 1900s. He told his interviewer in 1940:

> All during my boyhood my ambition was to get grown and go to a city and become a merchant. Fame and fortune kept constantly calling me to the bright city lights. When I was 21 years old I launched out for Augusta and got me a job as clerk with a retail grocery store at a salary of $10 a month.
>
> Wanting to be near me, my father and mother moved to Augusta and opened up a boarding house. Thus I was able to continue to live with them.[47]

It was not unusual for town people to own a farm or at least a bit of property in the countryside, nor was it unusual for farmers or planters, at least the more successful ones, to have business interests in town. A planter might sit on the board of the local bank or might be a co-owner of a local store. Merchants often acquired farms when people failed to pay off their loans. The many towns across the South without industry really existed primarily to service agriculture; in these towns farmers' concerns were the concerns of the merchants, bankers, and professionals who served them. Farmers' wagons clogged the streets of these towns on market day. When farmers had good years, the towns prospered; when farmers had bad years, the towns went into a depression. Even in towns with a mill, or two or three, farmers' business was important, and farmers' concerns were taken seriously. Small town life was slow-paced, and restaurants, tall buildings, museums, libraries, and parks were scarce. Vegetable gardens were common in town people's yards, most of the streets were typically packed dirt, and no place in a small town was more than a mile or two from a working farm.

In towns with mills, people lived in two distinct parts of town. Town people lived "in town" while people who worked in the mills typically lived in villages (sometimes called mill towns or mill hills if on a hill) built on the outskirts of a town and outside the town limits. Sometimes, as in the case of Kannapolis,

---

46. Jacquelyn Dowd Hall, James Louloudis, et al., *Like A Family: The Making of a Southern Cotton Mill World* (Chapel Hill and London: University of North Carolina Press, 1987), 34–43.

47. L.R. Allen, "I Wanted to Be a Merchant," Interview by Daisy Thompson, *American Life Histories: Manuscripts from the Federal Writers Project, 1936–1940* (Washington: Library of Congress, Manuscript Division, 1998), http://memory.loc.gov/ammem/wpaintro/wpahome.html.

North Carolina, a complete town—streets, stores, churches, houses, town hall—was built. These mill villages were owned and operated by the factory owners and typically featured simple houses for the workers, more elaborate houses for supervisors, a commissary where workers could buy provisions, and one or more churches. They were self-sufficient worlds, although mill workers would go "to town" to shop for special items or perhaps attend the "picture show." Mill children might attend school in town, too. As we'll see in the next chapter, the division between town and the mill village people was quite distinct, and mill village residents sometimes felt the sting of prejudice when they went to town.

While mill workers in the early decades (1880s–1920s) came for the most part from the countryside, as time went on, a good number of new hires were people who came from nearby towns looking for a better wage, or, increasingly, they were the children of mill workers. Some, unable to accustom themselves to life in the mill, would return to the farm; many others stayed but never fully adapted and longed to return to the countryside. Wesley Renn was one such man. Renn worked in a mill in Durham, North Carolina, and lived in a mill village. He was interviewed in the late 1930s, and the interviewer said of him:

> Wesley Renn lives in the mill village in one of the better houses which has a comfortable stretch of lawn shaded by two or three trees. He likes to sit in his swing on the porch in the springtime and watch day by day as the tree buds grow into leaves and the grass shoots up into a newer, pleasanter green. His first twenty-one years were spent in the country and the sight of growing things still awakens in him an urge to live again on the farm. He says that he will probably die in a mill village but at heart he'll always be a farmer.[48]

Renn moved from mill to mill seeking better pay; at one point he went to barber school to learn a new trade. During World War I, he returned to the country and farmed on shares for a while and did well, but declining prices forced him back to the mill.

For rural people such as Wesley Renn, factory work involved discomfiting adaptations: mill work was tiring, sometimes dangerous work, and the workday was 12 hours. The pace of work was dictated by the machines, and the work was monotonously the same day in and day out. Seasons, the weather, and even day and evening meant nothing; the clock dictated everything. Bosses supervised workers closely, and, as the industry matured, more sophisticated methods of monitoring workers—time-and-motion studies and mechanical devices that recorded the output of machine operators—were implemented. Life on the land had been different: even sharecroppers, comparatively speak-

---

48. The Renns interview, *American Life Histories: Manuscripts from the Federal Writers Project, 1936–1940.* (Washington: Library of Congress, Manuscript Division, 1998), http://memory.loc.gov/ammem/wpaintro/wpahome.html.

ing, had little daily supervision, and small farmers were their own bosses. People from rural areas such as Wesley Renn had to learn the "habits of industry" that would fit them to work in an industrial setting.[49]

However, along with the new, remnants of the old persisted; in the early decades (late 1800s and early 1900s), entire families including young children worked in mills just like on the farm. It was not uncommon for workers, like Wesley Renn, to return to farming at least temporarily. Too, mill families often had a "family farm" somewhere in their extended family so the connection to the countryside was never entirely severed. Mill villages had a rural "air" about them, perhaps even more so than the small towns that they were frequently built near. People often had gardens and chickens, and sometimes even hogs.[50] At Royal Cotton mill village in Wake Forest, North Carolina, a Works Progress Administration interviewer talked to a resident tending his hogs one September day in 1938:

> "Pretty hogs you have there," the woman said.
>
> "Ain't they fine," John said and looked up at the woman.
>
> "Does this land belong to the mill company?" the woman asked.
>
> "Yessum, and this road leads up to the houses. It used to be called Hogpen Lane because then all hogpens had to be built down here. That rule ain't followed now and you'll find plenty up there amongst the houses. I like to have my hogs down here though. They's more space and it's easier to keep clean. Thata way it don't make much of a stink." The woman looked up the avenue of old Spanish oaks green yet with the full ripeness of late summer. There were weeds all along, ragged and disorderly, and there were dilapidated hogpens up as far as the tenth big tree.[51]

Mill workers retained that part of the older agrarian value system that stressed cooperation over the materialism and competitive individualism that were becoming important town values. People helped each other out in times of need, and the village community functioned "like a family" in ways reminiscent of rural communities.[52]

---

49. Jacquelyn Dowd Hall, James Louloudis, et al., *Like a Family*, 44–56, 204–205. See interviews with Grover and Alice Hardin in Allen Tullos, *Habits of Industry: White Culture and the Transformation of the Carolina Piedmont* (Chapel Hill and London: University of North Carolina Press, 1989), 253–276.

50. Kirby, *Rural Worlds Lost*, 298–299.

51. John Pierce interview, *American Life Histories: Manuscripts from the Federal Writers Project, 1936–1940* (Washington: Library of Congress, Manuscript Division, 1998), http://memory.loc.gov/ammem/wpaintro/wpahome.html. See also Jack Temple Kirby, *Rural Worlds Lost: The American South, 1920–1960* (Baton Rouge and London: Louisiana State University Press, 1987), 298–299.

52. Jacquelyn Dowd Hall, James Leloudis, et al., *Like a Family*, 151–152.

Was a new urban, industrial culture replacing agrarian culture? The answer is yes, but slowly and fitfully. As we have seen, much about the culture of these towns remained close to the agrarian roots of many of the towns' residents, and the prosperity of many towns rested on the health of the farming economy. Even in areas with industry, large numbers of people—farmers, tenants, and landlords—continued to till the land. For example, in Vance County, North Carolina, home of several sizable textile mills, farm employment exceeded employment in manufacturing until well into the 1950s. Outside the Piedmont—in the Alabama Black Belt or the Mississippi Delta or the eastern part of North Carolina—agrarianism held undisputed sway. Also, the urban industrial economy was not particularly dynamic. By the 1940s the region's industries were still primarily the ones begun in the late 1800s and early 1900s, and towns were often one-industry towns that grew slowly.

But trends did not auger well for the persistence of the agrarian lifestyle. By the eve of World War II, small towns and cities blanketed much of the South and, particularly in the Piedmont, a growing proportion—although not yet a majority—of the population lived in towns and worked in stores, factories, banks, offices, and small shops. More and more of the children of these folks were born and raised in town and would work in town when they grew up. The locus of economic and political power had, by then, long since shifted from the countryside to the towns and cities, and that was where most of the more affluent people, even many of the larger landowners, resided. Rural areas were, by comparison, poorer and more isolated. Farming people realized their culture was in decline, and this realization fed a persistent discontent in rural areas and a resentment of city and town that was an important factor in Southern politics from the late 19th century well into the 20th and even today to a limited degree.[53]

The Decline of Agrarianism during the Modern Era

Following World War II, massive changes swept the South. Farming as an occupation had reached its numerical peak in 1930; after that, a precipitous decline began during the Great Depression that continued unabated into the new century. For example, in Darlington County, South Carolina, one of the preeminent farming districts in that state, the number of farms declined from

---

53. Raymond Arsenault, *The Wild Ass of the Ozarks: Jeff Davis and the Social Bases of Southern Politics* (Philadelphia: Temple University Press, 1984), 10–13; V.O. Key, Jr., *Southern Politics* (New York: Vintage Books, 1949), 112–118; 510–513.

over 3,000 farms in the 1930s to almost 1,800 in the early 1960s to less than 350 farms by the late 1990s.[54] Today, only a tiny number of Southerners—less than 2%—farm for a living. Even people who live in rural areas are unlikely to be farming; by 2000, only 5% of earnings in rural areas came directly from agriculture.[55] Farming is still very important in the region, but today it is heavily mechanized and capitalized and increasingly the domain of agribusiness. Farmers specialize in at most a few crops such as cotton, tobacco, soybeans, and peanuts, or they raise poultry or hogs in large volume operations. The old subsistence lifestyle has become a thing of the past, and modern farmers purchase what they eat and wear and use in the store just like the rest of us. If the percentage of people farming has drastically declined, so too has the percentage of people living in the rural/small town South; today the percentage of Southerners living in metropolitan areas—75%—is near the national average, and most work in a variety of occupations having nothing to do with agriculture.[56] The transformation of the agrarian lifestyle and economy that began in the decades after the Civil War seems to have been completed in the waning decades of the twentieth century. How and why did all of this happen?

The Great Depression of the 1930s devastated the agricultural regions of the country including the South, and many people lost their land and their homes. Government programs, which were part of President Franklin Roosevelt's New Deal, were established to help struggling farmers, but the rules and policies of the United States Department of Agriculture were designed to create "a rural America of businesslike, mechanized, and efficient farms," and government largess went primarily to the landowners, not the tenants.[57] Farmers were paid to cut back on the acreage they planted, and floor prices were established for many commodities, such as cotton, tobacco, and wheat, that guaranteed farmers at least a minimum price for their harvested crop. Many farmers used this government money to invest in machinery—tractors, harvesters and the like.

---

54. U.S. Bureau of the Census, *Census of Agriculture: 1935, Report of States with Statistics for Counties and a Summary for the United States, Vol. 1* (Washington, D.C.: U.S. Government Printing Office, 1935), 479; U.S. Bureau of the Census, *Census of Agriculture,1964, Volume 1, Statistics for the States and Counties, Pt. 27, South Carolina* (Washington, D.C.: U.S. Government Printing Office, 1967), p. 265; U.S. Department of Agriculture, *1997 Census of Agricultural Profiles, South Carolina State Profiles,* http://www.nass.usda.gov/census/census97/profiles/sc/sc.htm.

55. *The State of the South 2002: Shadows in the Sunbelt Revisited* (Chapel Hill, NC: MDC, Inc., 2002), p. 11; *The State of the South 2010: Chapter 2: Talent and Skill: Antidotes to Uncertainty* (Chapel Hill, NC: MDC, Inc., 2010), 10.

56. *The State of the South 2011: Looking Ahead: Leadership for Hard Times* (Chapel Hill, NC: MDC, Inc., 2011), p. 8; *The State of the South 2002: Shadows in the Sunbelt Revisited,* 16.

57. Pete Daniel, *Lost Revolutions: The South in the 1950s* (Chapel Hill and London: University of North Carolina Press, 2000), 42.

With land kept fallow, many Southern farmers sent some of their sharecroppers packing, and the new tractors enabled them to make do with even fewer "croppers" and laborers. Eventually, cotton picking machines were developed, and these came into widespread use by the 1960s. An early prototype, put to work on the Hopson plantation outside Clarksdale, Mississippi, in the mid-1940s, could do the work of fifty pickers. New herbicides cut down on the amount of hoeing needed to keep a field free of weeds, and better fertilizers and strains of seeds greatly increased yields, allowing farmers to get more and more production out of the land.[58] More and more of the labor needs of farmers could be met by migrant workers who came through at harvest time and then left. By the late 1960s, sharecropping clearly was dying.

Figure 1.4   Tractors replace mules

If the tenant farm was disappearing, the small family farm fared little better. Those who remained in farming had to be highly capitalized to afford the increasingly expensive machinery, and that meant they had to be big farmers; small farmers simply couldn't make it. Tractors now often cost more than $100,000, and a successful family farm today might have well over a million dollars of equipment parked in its sheds and barns. Corporate farms are capitalized at an even higher level and have staffs of professionals to manage the

58. Gilbert Fite's *Cotton Fields No More: Southern Agriculture, 1865–1980* is an excellent treatment of this transformation. See 120–225; Nicholas Lemann, *The Promised Land: The Great Black Migration and How it Changed America* (New York: Vintage Books, 1992), 7. See also: Kirby, *Rural Worlds Lost: The American South, 1920–1960.*

different aspects of the enterprise from the actual planting and harvesting to the marketing of the crop. Wendell Murphy and Frank Perdue and others have mechanized pork and poultry production and have transformed the raising of farm animals for meat into an industrial enterprise. Science and technology rather than tradition guide the modern farmer.

The transformation of agriculture pushed literally millions of people off the land and would reach its peak in the 1950s and 1960s. Migrants streamed into the cities and towns of the South or headed for the cities of the North, West, and Midwest. African Americans were a large part of this migration, particularly the part of it heading north and west.[59] The impact of this "depopulation" of the rural South was devastating, and one can still see the impact of this out migration on the landscape and the built environment of rural areas. Drive east along Highway 158 in North Carolina from Henderson to Roanoke Rapids through one of the major farming regions in the state. In the countryside, you see productive, well-tended farms, but you also see abandoned farmhouses, sometimes fronted by rusted mobile homes perched precariously on cinder blocks, collapsing barns and boarded up country stores, and fields that are weed choked, disused. Substantial tracts of the less fertile farmland are now planted in pine, a new cash crop to be sure, but one offering limited employment opportunities and one that, once harvested by clear cutting, adds to the ruined appearance of the countryside. Once thriving small towns that served area farmers are now more often filled with shuttered, unpainted empty shops, small video rental stores, "antique" shops selling used furniture, and the ubiquitous franchise fast food restaurants.

The massive migration out of the region by African Americans had a profound effect on them and on the region they left behind. Near the turn of the twentieth century, African Americans were overwhelmingly residents of the South. Over the next six decades, they moved out of the region in such numbers that by the 1970s they were evenly split between the South and the rest of the nation. In 1910 they were overwhelmingly rural, farming people; by the 1970s, over 80% of the African-American population lived in urban areas, and black farmers were as rare as hen's teeth. By a cruel twist of fate, Southern African Americans escaped the poverty of the rural South only to settle in an urban America that had begun a downward spiral, losing jobs, middle class taxpayers, and resources to the burgeoning and largely white suburbs.[60] Job-

---

59. Lemann, *The Promised Land*; 3–107; James N. Gregory, *The Southern Diaspora: How the Great Migrations of Black and White Southerners Transformed America* (Chapel Hill: The University of North Carolina Press, 2005), 11–41; Kirby, Rural Worlds Lost, 276–287.

60. Stewart Tolnay, *The Bottom Rung: African American Family Life on Southern Farms* (Urbana and Chicago: University of Illinois, 1999), 23, 171–178.

lessness, high incarceration rates for young black males, and high rates of single parent families were the result. Given the huge out migration of blacks, it is not surprising that the South became whiter. The rural Pee Dee region of South Carolina, for example, was almost evenly divided between whites and blacks in 1950 (53% to 47% respectively). In the 1950s, nearly two times as many blacks as whites left the Pee Dee region; in the 1960s, 380 whites left versus roughly 13,000 blacks and by 1970 the region was almost 61% white to 39% black.[61]

While employment in agriculture steadily declined, employment in city jobs in the South—"public work," rural people called it—skyrocketed. Industry had experienced moderate growth throughout the early decades of the twentieth century, but after World War II, the growth rate took off. Much of the growth was fueled by northeastern and midwestern industries either relocating to the South or building expansion facilities in the region. A trickle of firms relocating to the South in the 1950s turned into a flood of firms by the 1970s. In the 1960s, for example, the small town of Darlington, South Carolina, attracted an electronics manufacturing plant (part of a large multinational corporation) and a gear company from the Chicago area that moved its plant lock, stock, and barrel to the outskirts of town. Some homegrown industries and businesses grew by leaps and bounds, and new ones developed and flourished. In Texas and Louisiana, major oil discoveries led to the development of a petrochemical industry, and in the Research Triangle Park, North Carolina, Atlanta, and Austin, Texas, cutting-edge research industries developed in the 1970s and 1980s with the support of government and area institutions of higher education. A thriving banking industry blossomed in the "Queen City," (Charlotte, North Carolina), and two of the largest banks in the world—Bank of America and Wachovia—were headquartered there, although Wachovia floundered in the rough seas of the banking crisis afflicting the nation in 2008 and was acquired by California-based Wells Fargo in December of that year. Atlanta's greatness is partly built on the success of its most famous corporate citizen, Coke; and discount king Sam Walton and eccentric billionaire H. Ross Perot both began their empires in the South. The region has become one of the leading vacation destinations in the country, and now promoters boast of the massive tourism industry. Resort areas such as Hilton Head, Disney World, Branson, Missouri, and Myrtle Beach are known throughout the nation and, indeed, the world. This industry employs hundreds of thousands in a wide range of occupations including impersonating Mickey Mouse (at Disney World), travel agent, restaurateur, and hotel maid. By the 1970s, the region

---

61. Pee Dee Regional Planning and Development Council, *Population and Economic Study: Pee Dee Region* (SC: Pee Dee Regional Planning and Development Council, 1972), 11, 24.

was touted as a success story and was now often called "the Sunbelt"; per capita income rose in the South an average of 3.7% a year between 1950 and 1980 compared to the national average of 2.6%.[62] The region's growth rate in per capita income slowed in the 1980s and 1990s but still exceeded the national average. Even with this impressive growth, the region's per capita income level still trailed the national average (it was 90% of the national figure).[63] Still, in a region that President Franklin Delano Roosevelt had referred to in 1938 as "the Nation's No. 1 economic problem," the growth was nothing less than amazing.[64] The South had evolved from a dependence on "agriculture and low-skilled manufacturing to a twenty-first century mix of services, and more people were employed in managerial occupations than in blue collar jobs." Between 1990 and 2002, jobs in managerial, financial and professional occupations grew the most in the region.[65]

This growth was not solely the result of the mysterious workings of the market: state governments in the South actively courted Northern industry, extolling the virtues of the region's climate, its large supply of labor, its low taxes, its "competitive" (read low) wage rates, and its "favorable" labor climate, a euphemism that meant that unions were actively discouraged. Industrial recruiters working for towns, counties, and states ranged far and wide searching for companies interested in building plants in the South. Inducements were offered — incentives, they were called — that ranged from road improvements to specialized job training for the company's new employees to reduced taxes.[66] These incentives could be quite substantial; for example, from 2007–2011 the German company ThyssenKrupp was granted over one billion dollars in tax incentives and other forms of aid by the Alabama state government and several local government bodies to build and then expand a steel mill in Mobile County.[67] Southern states, particularly the Carolinas, built scores of new community and technical colleges to train people to work in the new factories. The recruiting campaign, fueled by the incentives program, has been termed "the

---

62. Jim Clinton, Carol Conway et al., *The Mercedes and the Magnolia: Preparing the Southern Workforce for the Next Economy* (Research Triangle Park, NC: Southern Growth Policies Board, 2002), 5.

63. *Ibid.* Alison Greene, Ferrel Guillory, et al, *The State of the South: Fifty Years After Brown v. Board of Education* (Chapel Hill, NC: MDC Inc., 2004), 14.

64. Tindall, *The Emergence of the New South*, 599.

65. Greene, Guillory, et al, *The State of the South*, 14.

66. James C. Cobb, *The Selling of the South: The Southern Crusade for Industrial Development, 1936–1980* (Baton Rouge and London: Louisiana State University Press, 1982). See especially 35–63.

67. Jeff Amy, "Alabama state and local aid to ThyssenKrupp tops $1 billion after vote," *al.com*, 28 April 2011, http://blog.al.com/live/2011/04/alabama_state_and_local_aid_to.html. (accessed 2/17/2012) See also, "Incentives for Nucor could lure recycler too," [Raleigh, N.C.] *The News and Observer*, 30 May 1998.

great buffalo hunt," and its fruits—hundreds and hundreds of new factories and branch offices—would have made Henry Grady's heart proud.

The federal government itself was the source of a substantial number of the new jobs and a significant source of funding for state and local government and private business. During World War II, the federal government had established a number of military bases in the South that provided work not only to armed services personnel, but also to thousands of civilians. The Cold War kept these bases humming with activity. An expanding federal government showered government funds on the South for welfare programs, anti-poverty programs, aid to education, grants for sewer construction, expenditures for military contracts and dozens of other worthy causes. The South received a net inflow of federal tax monies—more money coming in for services than went out of the region in federal taxes—that buoyed the economy. In 1952, for example, the Southeast received 50% more in federal tax dollars for services than its residents and businesses paid in federal taxes.[68] A massive aid program for the South was thus being funded by the rest of the country, although the size of the net inflow would decrease as the South's fortunes rose and the level of opposition in the Northeast and Midwest to this Southern "welfare program" increased. However, even today, the South enjoys an advantage over the other regions in the amount of federal funds coming to the region compared to what goes out in federal taxes.[69] State and local governments began providing countless services, many required by federal legislation or partially funded by federal revenues. These services—welfare, industrial recruiting, parks, mental health centers, a more extensive educational system with expanding universities, new community colleges, and growing public schools—required scores of new, and generally higher paid, employees.

This booming economy fostered the growth of a truly "new" South no longer wedded to the countryside, a metropolitan South where the overwhelming majority of people (as noted earlier, 75%) lived. These metropolises included great cities like Atlanta, Miami, Houston, and Dallas and a number of smaller ones like Little Rock, Raleigh, Columbia, and Richmond. Here was where most of the new jobs were being created—nearly 89% of the new jobs in the period 1987–2007.[70] This metropolitan South is actually more suburban than urban; in many respects, even the larger cities like Atlanta are little more than vast expanses of suburban developments surrounding a relatively small city core and connected to it by a ring of traffic-choked highways. In effect, the South went from rural to suburban and leapfrogged urban. These suburban enclaves, places like Forsyth County, Georgia (outside Atlanta), Cary, North Carolina (outside

---

68. Cobb, *The Selling of the South*, 206–208.

69. "Per Capita Tax Burden and Return of Federal Tax Dollar: 2005," Northeast Midwest Institute (Washington, D.C.), http://www.nemw.org.

70. *The State of the South 2010: Chapter 1: Beyond the Gilded Age* (Chapel Hill, NC: MDC, Inc., 2010), 4.

Figure 1.5   Atlanta

Figure 1.6   Hilton Head

Raleigh), and Plano, Texas (outside Dallas) are composed of a multitude of developments large and small that are carbon copies of developments one could find anywhere in the country. Suburbs, whether in Cary or New Rochelle, New York, are predominantly inhabited by middle class people who reside in single family homes selected from a limited range of housing styles with two-story federal style homes and French inspired "manors" seemingly the most popular of late. The geography of suburbia also follows a national pattern: homes are situated on cul de sacs designed to provide privacy, and traffic is channeled onto a small number of feeder roads which in turn connect to highways. There is generally no functional town core in suburbia, and housing, shopping areas, schools, and places of work are widely dispersed and accessible only (or primarily) by car.

Life in the suburbs is much more regulated than the old agrarian world with a variety of restrictions on individual sovereignty, especially when it comes to property. So in a suburban development, repairing a car propped on cinder blocks—the stereotypical image associated with less affluent rural residents—is simply not done. Of an even more intrusive nature, a suburbanite often must get permission to make changes to the exterior of his home; he may not be permitted to park his car on the street in front of his home, and when he takes the pooch out for a walk—on a leash, of course—he must remove the dog's business from the ground with a plastic baggy. The thought of carrying around a bag of dog excrement would have struck the old-time agrarian as absolutely hilarious.

Attachment to place, so central to the agrarian experience, is clearly not so central to the suburban experience. One suburban community blends into another and then another, and given the dispersed geography of suburbia, suburbanites frequently go far afield to reprovision themselves, find recreation, and get to their jobs and schools and places of worship. Because they spend so much time on the road, the car has become the home away from home for many people, a place to eat, talk on the phone, listen to music, and even watch television (for the passengers). Consumer preferences and lifestyle choices are often more important determinants of where one shops or lives than attachment to a particular community. Suburbanites often see themselves as temporary residents of the places they live, and one of the more popular topics of conversation in the suburbs is the "resale value" of homes. The modern job market for professionals encourages rootlessness: a family may move to another state if the primary breadwinner loses his job or gets a new job, and a promotion may result in a family moving to a more expensive house in another suburb or moving out of state. Retirement also often occasions a move—perhaps to a home in the mountains or to a retirement community in a resort, preferably near water or a golf course or both. Suburbanites establish their place in society primarily through what and how much they make and have—houses, cars, clothing, jewelry, barbecue grills, club memberships—and structure their private lives around particular forms of consumption like golf, dance and soccer for the kids, shopping, membership in a club. The traditional mediums of establishing one's place in society, such as family connections and involvement in community institutions like churches, are less important. Neighbors often are less important, too; one may associate with folks at the club but keep neighbors at arm's length.

The old agrarian South, most of it anyway, was a dichromatic world composed of native born blacks and whites; the new metropolitan South is multiethnic and made up of a large numbers of non-natives. In the 1960s in a small way and in the 1970s in a big way, a massive migration to the South had begun, the first significant migration into the region since the 1700s and most of them ended up in the metropolitan South. By the 1990s, in many booming counties like Wake County, North Carolina (home of Raleigh and Cary), a majority of the residents were out-of-staters, many of them the once-dreaded Yankees, and a significant number of immigrants from other countries, Hispanics especially but a large Asian population too. The cultural homogeneity of the old agrarian South was giving way to the cultural heterogeneity of the metropolitan South, and one could now find temples and mosques and Catholic churches scattered among the Baptist and Methodist churches and a host of ethnic restaurants now joined the barbecue joints and "meat and 3" establishments.

Despite the massive changes that have cleared most of the people out of farming and many out of the countryside, a significant number of people still live "in the country." Indeed, the South has a large share of what is left of the U.S. rural population; 44% of the nation's non-metropolitan population lives in the region.[71] Some of these rural dwellers live in comfortable suburban style houses and commute to work in nearby towns and cities. Here and there one can find a sort of hybrid—a suburban development not on the outskirts of a city or town but plopped down in the middle of the country. Agriculture is still preeminent where the soil is rich and the land is flat, and so in the coastal plain of South Carolina or the Alabama Black Belt, one can find expanses of well-tended fields planted in soybeans, corn, tobacco, and cotton, quiet rural roads where people drive 20 miles an hour and wave at every car they pass, forests, clean air, and old men gossiping at the surviving country stores scattered here and there. Here, it's not unusual to find people who have lived in the same house or at least on the same road all their lives, and who count parents, uncles, aunts, and siblings among their neighbors. Here, place still matters and is part of who you are, and outsiders will always be outsiders. A "newcomer" who had lived most of his adult life in one such town in a rural area was still asked if he was "going home for Christmas" to a place he had not lived in over forty years.

The rural South can provoke nostalgic feelings in both Southerners and non-Southerners; an acquaintance of one of the authors used to refer to largely rural eastern North Carolina as "God's country." But for many of the inhabitants, it's anything but "God's country," and this is true of much of the rest of the rural South. As noted earlier, the changes in farming and the outmigration of millions of farming people has left rural areas depopulated and the small towns that once served the farming population have struggled. Ironically, other developments that most see as good and beneficial—better roads, the expansion of automobile ownership, the growth of national chain stores and franchise operations— have also dealt a serious blow to the economic viability of the small towns that served rural residents. In a good car on good roads, a drive of 20 or more miles to shop for food, cleaning supplies, and so forth is now no big deal. So the eastern North Carolina town of Warsaw, with a population of around 3,000, saw its stores and shops dwindle as local residents increasingly drove to the nearby towns of Clinton, which had a small shopping mall anchored by a Belk's department store, or, thirty-five minutes away, Goldsboro, with an even larger enclosed shopping mall with several department stores. Who can resist lower prices, better selections, and the "pizzazz" of an enhanced shopping experience? Walmart has a special reputation with small town merchants for destroying a variety of stores when it moves into a new area. So metropolitan regions, even the smaller ones, grew and flourished partly at the expense of small towns.[72]

The four poorest regions in the South—the Appalachian Mountains; the delta counties in Mississippi, Louisiana, and Arkansas; the old plantation dis-

71. *The State of the South 2002: Shadows in the Sunbelt Revisited*, 8.
72. *The State of the South 2002,* see"Population and Job Growth by Size of Metro Area, 1980–2000," 33–35.

tricts of Southside Virginia, eastern North Carolina, South Carolina, Georgia, Alabama, and portions of eastern Mississippi; and the Rio Grande Valley—are all predominantly rural. While each of these areas has some economic bright spots—coastal areas that are now thriving tourist destinations and mountain ski resorts, for example—in general, their continuing economic woes have led many to speak of two Souths—a thriving metropolitan South and this "left behind" rural South, the "other South."[73] Because of the high unemployment rates, people of working age leave in large numbers. As one report noted: "Many communities count high school graduates as their biggest export." The population of these areas is thus heavily skewed toward the very young and the very old and is further skewed between a small number of comfortable if not affluent people and a large number of very poor people. Many young people, particularly poor African-American young people, aren't adequately prepared for a productive adulthood in the modern world. They drop out of high school at alarming rates, the girls have children in their teens, and some of the problems associated with poor inner cities—gangs, violence, and the drug trade— are now found in these rural areas. Many of the young people are only qualified to do low-skilled work, but this sort of work that pays any kind of wage is in decline. For example, employment in apparel manufacturing (cut and sew factories), a major employer in rural areas of the South, declined by nearly 200,000 jobs between 1986 and 2000. Whites still tend to own what's worth owning—farms, stores, small businesses—and hold most of the decent paying private sector jobs. So another "shadow" of the agrarian past—of the slavery and segregation eras—is still lingering.[74] The decline of industry in the "other South" has accelerated in the new millennium; in the phenomenon known as globalization, cheap imports from Mexico, China, and other third world countries are leveling what's left of the textile industry. In Cameron County in south Texas, the list of plant closings sounds like a Who's Who of the American textile industry—Fruit of the Loom, Levi, Wrangler, Vanity Fair, Hagger—and nothing has replaced the closed factories. Unemployment has generally been high in the county and underemployment has been a persistent problem; a journalist found an astonishing 40% of those working in 2004 underemployed, many of them engaged in temporary work. Two recessions in

---

73. *Ibid.*, 8–9.
74. See for a good exploration of the economic and social problems of the rural South, Linda Flowers, *Throwed Away: Failures of Progress in Eastern North Carolina* (Knoxville: University of Tennessee Press, 1992), especially 179–205. See also *The State of the South 2002*, 10. Ronald Wimberley and Libby Morris's study, *The Southern Black Belt: a National Perspective* (Lexington, KY: University of Kentucky, 1997) documents the persistent poverty, especially for blacks, in a large swath of the rural South they refer to as the "Black Belt." See also the report, *Dismantling Persistent Poverty in the Southeastern States* (Athens, GA: Carl Vinson Institute of Government, University of Georgia, 2002).

the new millennium, the most severe starting in 2008, have weakened the economy of the "other South" even more. [75]

So with only a tiny fraction of the population farming and many rural areas in a state of decline if not despair, is the agrarian tradition dying in the South? In some places, if it is dying, it is dying a very slow death. Paradoxically, the poverty and isolation of the "other South" has to some degree maintained it as a rural time capsule. Farming is still important here and even if most people no longer farm, many older people once farmed, so a connection to farming, if only in memory, is still quite common. Here you are most likely to find the old style dialects and attitudes about work and life. Here old ways are still respected, and people who have lived on the same road their parents and even grandparents lived on are common. Here attachment to place is still strong and the suspicion of outsiders equally strong. For many, the past isn't even past. In Warsaw, North Carolina, people giving directions for a back road route to Goldsboro commonly included the instruction to "turn left at Mattie Grady's store." This store had been closed for years and while the building was still standing, it took a close inspection of it to make out the faint outline of Mattie Grady's name. To someone born and raised in Warsaw, it would always be Mattie Grady's store, even when the store fell down. But for rural areas like Warsaw, the growing number of people who have never farmed, the big city drug problems, the fleeing young people, and the ubiquitous television culture do not bode well for this time capsule to forever protect its cargo from decay.

What is of more interest and cultural relevance is not where in the South one can still find someone plowing with a mule or sitting around a stove in a country store, but rather, how the agrarian tradition persists with folk who live in the suburbs, commute to their jobs, and work all day in front of a computer terminal. Culture by its nature evolves or dies, and the agrarian culture of the South seems to be both adaptive and persistent. The rural, mostly poor people who migrated to the towns and cities of the South and the North in the 1930s and '40s and '50s did not leave their culture at home; they brought it with them. As historian Pete Daniels notes, "The collision between rural and urban cultures generated creative tidal waves."[76] These waves rolled over the growing modern South of city and suburb and across the rest of the nation. New music, new attitudes about race and class, new recreations and even new modes of speaking and dress have resulted. For example, the polished and stylized rhythm and blues music of the 1960s produced by Detroit's Motown record

---

75. Katherine Boo, "The Churn: Creative Destruction in a Border Town," *The New Yorker*, March 29, 2004: 62, 70; *The State of the South 2010: Chapter 1: Beyond the Gilded Age*, 1–5.

76. Daniels, *Lost Revolutions*, 1.

company and performed today by such entertainers as Mariah Carey had its roots in rural Southern churches and jook joints. The modern country music industry may have gone Hollywood and "pop," but the roots of the music are in the hills and hollows of the Appalachian Mountains. The sport started by rural Southern moonshiners and small town mechanics—stock car racing—now is the banner carrier for corporate America, and the uniforms of racers and their cars are covered with corporate emblems and logos.

Many Americans have some familiarity with Southern cooking via "the Colonel's" chain of fried chicken restaurants (KFC) and Cracker Barrel, a national restaurant chain headquartered in Tennessee that serves country-style food in facilities designed to look like someone's idea of an old country store. In the past this cuisine kept hard-working farming people going; it is high in calories and fat—even vegetables are heavily seasoned with pork fat—and the liberal use of sweeteners (sugar and molasses, especially) on or in staples and treats like "sweet tea" (sweetened iced tea), pies (pecan is a regional favorite), cakes, and biscuits. For many Southerners, the home-cooked version (**and the** restaurant version) of "country cooking" is still a regular part of their diets. However tasty Southern cuisine is, we know today this diet is not particularly healthy, and we know it is not a good diet for people who are sedentary as most Southerners now are. As a result, many Southerners are now, well, fat and are prone to suffer from diseases related to being overweight and eating the wrong foods. Seven of the ten states leading the nation in the percentage of citizens who are overweight are Southern; eight Southern states are among the top ten states in the number of per capita heart disease related deaths.[77]

Also persisting are rural pastimes—hunting, fishing, and gardening—although Southerners aren't hunting or fishing at a rate significantly higher than the rate in other regions of the country (this is probably true of gardening, too).[78] The pickup truck—originally designed for use on the farm—is the vehicle of choice for many in the South, although its popularity has grown elsewhere in the country, too. The music of choice for much of the white population in the South is country music, and this music still celebrates the virtues of rural people and rural living even if some of the performers are no longer from the South (one popular female performer is from Canada) or grew up or lived in the country. More affluent Southerners sometimes live in suburban subdivisions with grand Old South names like Wakefield Plantation. Wakefield is a

---

77. "The Burden of Chronic Diseases and Their Risk Factors: National and State Perspectives, 2002." U.S. Department of Health and Human Services. National Center for Chronic Disease Prevention and Health Promotion, http://www.cdc.gov/nccdphp/burden book2002/02_heart.htm.

78. "2001 National Survey of Fishing and Hunting and Wildlife-Associated Recreation," U.S. Fish and Wildlife Service, 2002, http://www.census.gov/prod/2002pubs/ FHW01.pdf.

real estate development in Raleigh, North Carolina, with a golf course and a clubhouse with huge pillars and an expansive veranda that resembles a gigantic version of the traditional Southern plantation mansion. Wealthy Southerners, like the Charlie Croaker character in the Tom Wolfe novel, *A Man in Full*, will sometimes buy rural retreats.[79] Croaker is a late twentieth century Atlanta real estate developer who is making a lot of money converting a once-rural region into a traffic snarled web of highways, malls, office centers, and suburbs. But Croaker repairs for relaxation and revitalization to a plantation in rural Georgia—Turp'mtine—where he takes visitors on hunts in mule drawn wagons driven by African-American men and amazes his urban visitors with a cage full of rattlesnakes and a peek at his horses breeding.

Some of these examples of agrarian persistence—Turp'mtine, Wakefield, driving a pickup—sound like mere nostalgia on a par with the restaurants crammed with old lanterns and Lucky Strike signs that seem to be so popular. Are deeper values persisting despite the changes in what people do for a living and where they live? Are the agrarian traits of independence and self-sufficiency extolled by Jefferson still imbedded in the characters of Southerners? The South has long been considered a conservative region, and people who call themselves conservatives certainly make much of the values of independence and individualism.[80] Indeed, the white South today is mainly Republican—the party of conservatism—in its politics, and it is white Southerners who seem to be the most conservative members of the Republican Party. Conservative politics often goes hand in hand with conservative religion, which is also a powerful presence in the region. What seems to animate these folks the most is their hatred of government programs and government regulations and the taxes that pay for them. Southern conservatives, particularly those active in churches and religious groups, often see contemporary American society as morally decadent and out of control. One hears again and again references to a time when doors could be left unlocked, when children could roam unsupervised on a summer evening without fear, when a sort of order prevailed that is contrasted with the lack of order and control today. Lurking in the minds of many white Southern conservatives is the idea that things began to go really wrong when segregation died. Many conservatives wish to restore what they believe was the moral system of the past, which was in the South an agrarian past. People should be responsible for themselves and should not be dependent on government handouts. The old family and community values of the countryside and the small town—people married for life, abortion was illegal, men's leadership was unchallenged, and

---

79. Tom Wolfe, *A Man in Full* (New York: Farrar, Straus, Giroux, 1998).

80. Earl Black and Merle Black, *Politics and Society in the South* (Cambridge, Mass. and London: Harvard University Press, 1987), 213–219.

schools reflected community values, not the values of outsiders or "experts"—are idealized by these folks.

This conservatism reflects the persistence of values formed in the agrarian past, but it also reflects the collective uneasiness of a people who once farmed and lived in small communities filled with people they knew who have not yet adjusted to the roar and confusion and pace of the modern economy and modern culture. In short, it's a defensive reaction to change that elevates some agrarian values, but it's important to note that it ignores or discards others. Interestingly, many of the ideas that inform this reaction, both in politics and religion, seem to be shaped by a well-funded **national** conservative movement employing modern technology. If anything, economic and social change seem to be escalating, and with this escalation comes more uneasiness. Globalization cost the region perhaps half a million manufacturing jobs between 1998 and 2001, and two recessions in the new millennium delivered a "one, two punch" to the Southern economy that resulted in higher unemployment, declining wages and family incomes, and soaring poverty rates. People who worked in factories for years, many of them the children of sharecroppers and farmers, have had to troop back to schools and training centers to learn new skills for what they hope are new jobs. Unfortunately, some observers believe the lost manufacturing jobs are being replaced by even lower paying jobs in retail and the service sector.[81] The Southern Agrarians, were they all still alive, would nod glumly and say, "What did you expect"? They saw a restoration of **true** agrarianism as the answer to the economic dislocations and alienation of modern life. Wendell Berry, a native born Kentuckian who splits his time between writing and working a small subsistence farm in Henry County, Kentucky, has noted:

> With the urbanization of the country so nearly complete, it may seem futile to the point of madness to pursue an ethic and way of life based upon devotion to a place and devotion to the land. And yet I do pursue such an ethic and such way of life, for I believe they hold the only possibility, not just for a decent life, but for survival."[82]

It's hard to find many people, including self-professed conservatives, interested in a return to a life of manual labor on the land. Despite their uneasiness, most would probably agree with the older woman who had sharecropped most of her life and said in an interview in the early 1980s:

---

81. Alison Greene, Ferrel Guillory, et al, *The State of the South: Fifty Years After Brown v. Board of Education* calls this the "conventional wisdom" but also argues that economic change is creating "both high- and low-end jobs." See p. 15. See also Amy Martinez, "Workers suffer in global economy," [Raleigh, NC] *The News and Observer*, 30 May 2004.

82. Berry, "The Regional Motive," in Andrews et al, eds., *The Literature of the American South*, 937.

We had a lot of work to do and the children got a thrill out of it. They had so many things that children don't know and don't see today, that we had back then. Still, it's wonderful to know that the times have changed.[83]

---

83. Debbie Heath Best, "Farming is Hard Work," 1980, unpublished interview in the possession of the authors.

Chapter 2

Social Class

Class is a mysterious topic in the United States; the ideals, and for many, the realities of equality and opportunity have rendered it almost irrelevant here as compared to its significance in Europe and many other places. Most Americans, when asked what social class they belong to, reply "middle class." Poor people and rich people alike often respond in this way, from mothers on welfare to the Congressman making over $200,000 a year who told a reporter in 1996 that he was in the "lower middle class." The perception that most Americans are in the middle goes back a long way. In the 1780s J. Hector St. John De Crevecoeur wrote in *Letters from an American Farmer* that "The rich and the poor are not so far removed from each other as they are in Europe," and that Americans lived in housing that possessed a "pleasing uniformity of decent competence."[1] This is not to say that the United States has been and is a "class-

---

1. J. Hector St. John De Crevecoeur, *Letters from an American Farmer*(selections) in Diane Ravitch, ed., *The American Reader* (New York: Harper Perennial, 1991), 33.

less" society or that class has never been an issue. During periods of rapid economic change and depression, the more affluent have often been viewed by many with suspicion, and commentators and politicians who condemned the inequities of the class system have found a receptive audience. But, in general, in America it is more common for less affluent people to aspire to join the favored few (a process known as upward mobility), and the socially acceptable means of doing this has been hard work, the accumulation of wealth through saving and investment, and the proper choice of a spouse. Of course, there's also crime.

The South is a region that has always differed from the American norm and has, not surprisingly, generated an abundance of myths and stereotypes about the poor and the wealthy. So the concept of class is not quite as "mysterious" to Southerners. These myths and stereotypes are clearly in evidence in one of the most popular American films of all time, *Gone with the Wind*. Here was a society of extremes before the war: slaves toiling in the fields, poor whites, and fabulously wealthy planters. Many scholars and writers have argued that there was an element of truth to this picture. The historian Eugene Genovese, for example, grants the pre-Civil War slaveholders tremendous authority and the power to "make" the South be what they wished it to be.[2] But other scholars of the South have maintained that because race was so important, class was relatively unimportant; James Oakes, for example, tellingly entitled his history of the pre-Civil War planters *The Ruling Race*.[3] After the Civil War, one notion that contributed to the romance of the South is that the prewar civilization and the class that made it were swept away—again, think of *Gone With the Wind* and a broken Gerald O'Hara shuffling around Tara. Certainly, for the next 140 years people wrote and spoke of a "New South" rising from the ashes that differed in virtually every respect from the "Old South." However, this "new" South was long in coming. For one thing, the old planter class and the plantation survived the war. Indeed, William Alexander Percy in his memoir, *Lanterns on the Levee: Recollections of a Planter's Son*, was bemoaning the eventual demise of the planter aristocracy as late as the 1930s.[4]

The position taken here is simple: class has been important in the South, although not as important as race. Both class and race are contexts in which one's life is played out; race has been the more powerful of the two, the more difficult to get away from, but class has played and still plays a large role in

---

2. Eugene D. Genovese, *The World the Slaveholders Made: Two Essays in Interpretation* (New York: Vintage Books, 1971).

3. James Oakes, *The Ruling Race: A History of American Slaveholders*(New York: Vintage Books, 1983).

4. William Alexander Percy, *Lanterns on the Levee: Recollections of a Planter's Son* (Baton Rouge: LSU Press, 1973; first published, 1941).

shaping people's destinies. Further, the playing out of class relationships has had a profound effect on the culture of the South and the creation of unique, class-based subcultures. Thus, while people may deny the importance of class in shaping the way they live and the opportunities presented to them, like economist Adam Smith's "invisible hand," it nonetheless has had its way. As if by magic, it compels some to drop out of high school and others to attend college. Contemporary middle and upper class men seem drawn to golf, pastel knit shirts, electronic gizmos and belts embroidered with little alligators or college emblems while lower class men seem just as powerfully drawn to dressing in athletic or hunting garb and driving huge trucks with loud mufflers. Upper class women are often addicted to fitness; lower class women can't afford to join fitness clubs and their jobs and family responsibilities are often so physically challenging, they don't have the time or the energy to do the sort of exercises that counteract the effects of the traditional Southern diet or modern America's diet of processed foods. There are poor women devoted to aerobics and rich women devoted to the comforts of the couch and the products of Frito Lay, and wealthy men who work on their cars and poor men who play golf, but what we're describing here are tendencies, not iron laws.

But, first things first. Class seems to be such a confusing notion in American society that we need to carefully define it.[5] A class is a group of people who share similar amounts of income and wealth, generally have similar occupations, freely interact and intermarry with each other, and share similar values and lifestyles. A three-part separation—upper, middle, lower—has been the most popular way of dividing people into classes although the subtle distinctions between different groups of people have convinced some observers, particularly American sociologists, that layers or strata are a more useful way of thinking about differences, and that there may be a dozen or two dozen or even sixty of these. We think the traditional tripartite separation, with perhaps distinctions made in the middle class for an upper middle and a lower middle and in the lower class for a working class category and a poor category, capture reality more accurately than the plethora of classes (or strata) proposed by sociologists that are generally based on patterns of consumption or lifestyles.

People in a particular class pass on traditions and values from one generation to the next and teach new members of the class—folks from other classes—how to behave. The culture of class prepares children for membership in that class, so one's dialect, interests, skills, tastes (in music, religion,

---

5. Sociological works that have influenced how we approach class in this work are: Herbert J. Gans, *The Urban Villagers: Group and Class in the Life of Italian Americans* (New York: Free Press of Glencoe, 1962); E. Digby Baltzell, *The Protestant Establishment: Aristocracy and Caste in America* (New York: Vintage Books, 1964), 7–8; G. William Domhoff, *Who Rules America?* (Englewood Cliffs, NJ: Prentice Hall, Inc., 1967) 3–4.

and leisure activities) are shaped by class membership. But for the ambitious who wish to move up, where there is a will, there is a way, and new values, attitudes and tastes can be acquired. Class plays a big role in the choice of a mate, friends, a church to attend, and a career. It influences whether one goes to college and even which recreational activities one enjoys—golf vs. coon hunting, for example. In a broad sense, it helps shape individual aspirations, self-concept, and even notions of masculinity and femininity. Because of the overwhelming importance of race, the South has actually had two class systems for much of its history, one white and one black. And so, for example, there was a black middle class and a white middle class, and members of these classes had very little to do with each other socially. Classes, particularly upper classes, may be relatively open (easy to enter) or quite closed (difficult to enter), and the degree of openness can change. Classes stand in a particular relationship to each other not only in terms of money, but also in terms of power and status. In other words, members of higher classes not only have more money than folks in lower classes, but also more political power, and they generally are treated with more respect by the people they encounter. The importance of class can change, too; class may be destiny in one era and merely an advantage or disadvantage in another. As we will see, class *has* become less important in the modern South, as opportunities, primarily middle class job opportunities, have expanded, and poverty has declined.

Social Class in Early Virginia

In early Virginia, the pattern for what would become the South was established, and class was part of that pattern. It was a curious pattern marked by both freedom and servitude as Edmund Morgan has shown in his brilliant book *American Freedom, American Slavery*. The inhabitants of the first permanent English settlement in America (Jamestown) in the decade after its establishment in 1607 were of two classes: shareholders and servants. The shareholders were men who held shares in the Virginia Company and came to the New World to seek their fortunes. They saw themselves as, and indeed, in England were considered, "gentlemen"; that is, they were from the upper reaches of the social order. Had they been men of the landed nobility in line to inherit estates, however, they would not have been in the wilds of Virginia looking for gold. These were men from comfortable backgrounds who were second or third sons of lesser aristocrats or landed commoners. Their older brothers were going to inherit the family estates, or there was no family estate to inherit thanks to a profligate father. They hoped to make money in Virginia, lots of it, and return to England to live the lives of gentlemen. They shared the class prejudices of their brethren back in England: the less affluent were, in the words of one English gentleman, "the vile and brutish part of mankind." They were lazy, dangerous and a threat to social order.[6] Indentured servitude was widely perceived by refined folk to be a good solution to this social problem and was common throughout England. Servants had "masters" with broad powers—including the use of corporal punishment—to make them do as they wished. Thousands of mostly young, mostly male poor English people made the long journey to Virginia to live and work as servants in an alien and often dangerous environment for the terms of their contracts. They got no pay, and they must have known their chances of returning home were slim to none. Why would anyone in England sign up for this kind of life? The answer is simple: it was better than living under a bridge or starving to death. England was in the throes of a major economic transformation, and there simply wasn't enough work. What the gentlemen saw as indolence was actually widespread unemployment, and this fueled the mass migration of English men and women to the New World.

Once the moneymaking potential of tobacco cultivation became clear, plantations spread across the countryside of the Virginia colony, as we saw earlier. More and more servants were brought in, and more and more plantations were established by newly arrived "gentlemen." Life on these plantations was brutal and short. Overwork, disease, warfare with Native American tribes, and malnourishment took their toll, and most of the early settlers died. Planters died too, and one avenue of upward mobility for former servants was marriage to the widow of a planter. But most of the people dying in early Virginia were servants, and the gentlemen-rulers of Virginia were to blame. They weren't feeding the servants enough and were literally working them to death. It was a horrific scandal, and the British government finally disbanded the Virginia Company and made Virginia a royal colony.[7]

Conditions improved in Virginia, but servitude as a labor system was still a powder keg ready to explode. Planters, true to the prejudices of their class, did not worry about the lack of opportunities for servants who served out their terms. Servants could sign another indenture, but many servants did not want to work away their lives as servants in the malarial Tidewater with no hope of ever earning money, getting properly married, or having a stake in society. Unfortunately, with so many servants pouring into the colony, the demand for wage-earning workers was small, and few servants had the funds to buy land. Nonetheless, most servants finishing their terms gambled that as free men something better might turn up. As we saw earlier, many squatted on unoccupied land, mostly on the frontier, or made the best of it in the more settled parts of the colony. Given the moderate climate and the abundance of fish and

---

6. Edmund Morgan, *American Slavery, American Freedom: The Ordeal of Colonial Virginia* (New York: W.W. Norton and Co., 1975), 325.

7. *Ibid.*, 92–101.

game, the life of a scavenger was not the worst life in the world. But it was a worrisome life to the planters. These former servants didn't respect property rights; they squatted on land that wasn't theirs and shot hogs that didn't belong to them, and they fought with the Indians. Planters saw them as a growing threat to social order, and they worried about their loyalty should the Dutch invade, as they threatened to do in the late 1660s.

The planters' fears became a horrible reality when Nathaniel Bacon showed up in the colony. Bacon was a gentleman fresh from England who settled on a plantation on the frontier. He quickly became discontented with his new home: he didn't like being on the frontier, and he resented the colonial notables who were slow to give him the government posts he felt he was due. He was as incensed as his more humble neighbors at the government's unwillingness to provide protection from the Indians, and in short order a sort of frontier movement formed under his leadership. Bacon and his supporters, most of whom were former servants, launched a campaign against local Indian tribes, and Bacon even began threatening the government in Jamestown with his "troops" if his demands were not met. At this point, the rebellion began spiraling out of control as more and more servants and former servants joined and began, apparently, pressing grievances that went well beyond Indian troubles. When Bacon and his men finally did march to Jamestown, they burned a number of plantations along the way and finally Jamestown itself. Irony of ironies, a class snob if ever there was one was leading a revolt that threatened to overturn the colony's class system. Bacon's death ended that possibility, and the growing reliance on slavery, greatly accelerated after the rebellion, slowed the importation of new servants. Former servants received better "severance packages," including land and money, and property qualifications to vote were lowered. By the early 1700s most whites belonged to a comfortable class of small farmers, while the property-less laboring class was now almost entirely made up of African slaves.[8]

Ironically then, by the early 1700s a sort of egalitarian society had appeared in Virginia where, just as Crevecoeur had described, there was no great gulf separating those at the top and at the bottom, as long as you were only looking at free men who were, of course, white. To be sure, there was quite a gulf in the value of property owned by whites at the top and those at the bottom, especially human property. But both groups farmed and lived a rural lifestyle and took pleasure in rural pastimes like hunting. While some planters lived in impressive homes maintained by large staffs of slaves, many others lived in white frame homes little different from those owned by the more successful small farmers. And importantly, planters had no need to employ white labor or control a white workforce. A society that had once been bitterly divided

---

8. *Ibid.*, 250–315.

along class lines was now a society divided more along racial lines. Planters, who largely controlled the colony's and eventually the region's politics, developed astute ways of appealing to their less affluent neighbors for political support. It was a careful cultivation of the commonalties between the big man and the little man and an equally acidulous downplaying of the differences.[9] This downplaying has, some believe, resulted in the "aw shucks, we're just plain folks" style of speech affected by many men of the affluent class in the South one hears even today. As sociologist John Reed has noted, "Authority in the South is often veiled by a style that pays lip service to the useful fiction that all men are created equal...."[10] This even extends to pastimes. Reed notes, for example, that *Southern Living*, a contemporary magazine dedicated to providing a model of genteel life in the South, is the only magazine of its kind to feature a football issue. Elsewhere in the country, football, decorating tips, and the proper pairing of food and wine don't seem to mix.[11]

Social Class before the Civil War

By the midpoint of the nineteenth century, the South had developed a relatively stable class system, although during the decade of the 1850s, some troubling trends were becoming apparent. It was a class system very much like the pattern established in the Virginia colony over a century before. In broad terms, at the top was a slaveholding planter class; in the middle was a class of small farmers, and at the bottom were the slaves. But there was also a small class of urban professionals, merchants, and doctors who mingled freely with the planters, and a small class of rural and urban artisans who made such products as wagons and barrels and clay pots. Perhaps most ominously for social peace, a growing class of poor whites occupied a rung in the class system below the small farmers and artisans. Finally, a class of free blacks, numbering a quarter million people by 1860, occupied the niche above the slave population. Into one of these classes fit the eight million whites of the South (population figures are for 1860) and the more than four million blacks. This class system was kept viable if not thriving by the expansiveness of the South in the decades before the war. Settlers from the less fertile and soil-exhausted regions of the Southeast migrated further and further west, and, by the 1850s, the region's western border had reached Texas in the Southwest and "bleeding Kansas" (where anti-slavery men fought it out with pro-slavery men) further

9. *Ibid.*, 338–387.

10. John Reed, "The Same Old Stand," in *One South* (Baton Rouge and London: Louisiana State University Press, 1982), 180–181.

11. Reed, "Grits and Gravy: The South's New Middle Class," in *One South*, 119–126.

north. Men scratching out a living on worn-out farms, planters interested in expanding their operations, and the youngest sons of planters and small farmers—men who did not stand to inherit much land—moved west where fertile land was plentiful and less expensive.

The Planters

The basic prerequisites to be considered a planter in the antebellum period were the ownership of land and slaves. Around a quarter of the white families of the South owned slaves in 1860, down from almost a third of the families in the 1790s.[12] Only slightly more than forty-six thousand slaveholders owned 20 or more slaves. Twenty slaves was considered the minimum necessary for operating a plantation.[13] The planter class would thus have been quite small—less than 5% of the families in the region would have belonged. There were only a few thousand families in the entire South that owned one hundred or more slaves; these families were the elite of the planter class. Planters and plantations were clustered in the most fertile regions such as the Low Country of South Carolina, the Black Belt of Alabama, and the Mississippi Delta. The Delta was the richest of the plantation districts; its topsoil measured in feet, not inches, and Delta planters were among the wealthiest men in the country, if not the world. Planters across the region formed a wealthy, powerful, and cohesive upper class in the antebellum South. As Albert Bushnell Hart observed in *The Southern South*, "These people were organized into a society of a kind unknown in the North since colonial times. In any one state the well-to-do people, perhaps two to five-thousand in all, knew each other, recognized each other as belonging to a kind of gentry, intermarried, furnished nearly all the college and professional students, and were the dignitaries of their localities."[14] An example of a man of this class was Thomas Chaplin.

In 1845 twenty-two-year-old Thomas B. Chaplin was comfortably settled with his wife and four children on Tombee Plantation on St. Helena Island, an island off the coast of South Carolina near Hilton Head Island. Tombee Plantation was family property, one of several plantations owned by Chaplin's widowed mother, and consisted of nearly four-hundred acres of fields, meadows, and woodlands. In 1845 Chaplin owned between sixty and seventy slaves. With

---

12. Oakes, *The Ruling Race*, 229.
13. U.S. Bureau of the Census, *Eighth Census of the United States, Agriculture of the United States in 1860* (Washington, D.C., Government Printing Office, 1864). 248.
14. Albert Bushnell Hart, *The Southern South* (New York and London: D. Appleton and Co., 1910), 60. See also William K. Scarborough, *Masters of the Big House: Elite Slaveholders of the Mid-Nineteenth-Century South* (Baton Rouge: Louisiana State University Press, 2003), 23–27 and Jane Turner Censer, *North Carolina Planters and Their Children, 1800–1860* (Baton Rouge: Louisiana State University Press, 1984), 7–10, 43, 83.

this workforce, Chaplin grew Sea Island cotton, corn, potatoes and other vegetables, and raised an assortment of livestock. Cotton was the major cash crop, although he seemed to be more interested in and have a knack for his corn crop. As for the home of this young planter, Theodore Rosengarten, author of *Tombee: Portrait of a Cotton Planter*, describes it as follows:

> Tombee was a two-story clapboard house on a high tabby foundation. It was laid out in a modified cruciform, or T, so that all six rooms had windows on three sides, to catch as much breeze as possible. The house had high ceilings, tall sashes, narrow halls, and two exterior chimneys venting four fireplaces, two on each floor. In winter the rooms were difficult to heat, but in summer they stayed cool. A two-story porch, with six square columns on each story, faced Station Creek. On the landside, or back, was a single-story portico.
>
> The house was not luxurious. Its floors were heart pine and the lower portions of the walls were covered in wainscoting, but this was customary even in modest dwellings.[15]

The house still stands, but the outbuildings — sheds, kitchen, barns — and the slave cabins are long gone. While many plantation homes were fairly modest like Chaplin's, some planters lived in substantial and sometimes ornate dwellings popularly associated with the plantation lifestyle.

Chaplin, like many planters, came from a long line of plantation families and had numerous planter relatives scattered throughout the area. Both his first wife and his second wife (his first wife's half-sister) were from planter families. As a young man, his close friends, according to Rosengarten, "included his cousins the three Jenkinses; his three uncles; and Ned Capers, the third son of Charles Gabriel Capers, a wealthy old man who kept close watch over his estate while his sons killed time waiting to inherit plantations of their own."[16] To the north in Rowan County, North Carolina, another young man — John Steele Henderson — also spent his youth and young adulthood in the bosom of the planter aristocracy of his homeplace. Henderson's closest friends were his cousins — Baldy Boyden, son of a planter and attorney, and Stephen Lord, son of a large planter. Henderson's family was interconnected through marriage and blood with a number of prosperous families in the region including the Boydens, Lords, Fishers, and Caldwells, who in turn were connected with other planter families.[17] Fanny Caldwell, for example, married Peter Hairston,

---

15. Theodore Rosengarten, *Tombee: Portrait of a Cotton Planter with The Plantation Journal of Thomas B. Chaplin (1822–1890)*(New York: William Morrow and Co., Inc., 1986), 65.

16. *Ibid.*, 113.

17. John J. Beck, "Development in the Piedmont South: Rowan County, North Carolina, 1850–1900" (Unpublished Ph.D. dissertation, University of North Carolina, Chapel Hill, 1984), 41–50; 265. The John Steele Henderson Papers provide good informa-

master of Cooleemee plantation (one of the largest plantations in North Carolina) and a member of an extended planter family that, a modern day Hairston estimates, owned forty-five plantations in four states and 10,000 slaves.[18]

Figure 2.1   Cooleemee plantation house

The children of planters did not marry each other by happenstance: planter families were very particular about whom their sons and daughters married, and balls, parties, extended visits, and graduations were occasions to pair the right boy with the right girl. Marriage was more than the pairing of people; when two people married, two families merged and kin served not only as a source of friends but also as political and economic allies who could be counted on for help. The Hairstons made doubly certain the right match was made; they often married cousins.[19]

Unfortunately for Thomas Chaplin, his widowed mother had slimmer pickings to choose from than a girl of eighteen did, and she ended up marrying a failed druggist and portrait painter. This turn of events obsessed Chaplin over the next decade in part because of the ignominy of the match and in part because he hated the man. He referred to him in his journal as "so low and vile an insect as that thing that crawls about and calls himself R.L. Baker."[20] His

tion about the planter class in the piedmont region of North Carolina in the 1850s. John Steele Henderson Collection, Southern Historical Collection, University of North Carolina, Chapel Hill.

18. Henry Wiencek, *The Hairstons: An American Family in Black and White* (New York: St. Martin's Press, 1999), 8.

19. *Ibid.* See also Scarborough, *Masters of the Big House*, 22–26.

20. Rosengarten, *Tombee*, "The Journal of Robert B. Chaplin," 342.

main problem with Baker, and the source in all likelihood of his hatred, was money; he feared that his mother's new husband would squander his inheritance. Chaplin's mother had almost guaranteed some level of tension between her sons (Chaplin had a brother) and her new husband by signing a marriage contract prior to the nuptials that had a provision guaranteeing her husband and her the profits from her property but also permitting her to convey property to her sons during her life or at her death. A series of lawsuits and counter suits were filed by Chaplin and his brother and Baker, and the family feud kept the lawyers busy for years.[21] Feud it was, and in more than a legal sense; Chaplin and a friend happened upon Baker's carriage one day, and Baker jumped out and hid behind a tree with his gun. Chaplin did not approach because he had "nothing but a pistol."[22] And this was not the only time guns were brandished and even shots fired. A good marriage made a family stronger; a "bad" marriage did not destroy this family, but it certainly weakened it.

The planter class lived in a social world despite the rural isolation of most plantations. The young Thomas Chaplin, Ted Rosengarten says in *Tombee*, "was busy trying to make himself felt in society. He and his friends, the younger planters of St. Helena, seemed to be in perpetual motion. They gave themselves up to sport and play, to carousing and to conspicuous consumption." He found that "Every day, Chaplin dined somewhere else or had guests at home to dine with him. The Big House at Tombee was the center of a dense social life. Friends, relatives, and slaves, all with strangers in tow, invaded the house by night and day, making privacy impossible."[23] The Hendersons likewise entertained, traveled, bought expensive furniture and silverware (from Charleston and Philadelphia), and sent their two sons to private schools and later college. Not surprisingly, indebtedness was a very common experience for many planters. Chaplin would spend himself into heavy indebtedness at an early age, and a planter of an earlier era, Thomas Jefferson, was over one hundred thousand dollars (a substantial sum in those days) in debt when he died. Archibald Henderson, John Steele Henderson's father, struggled to pay for the lifestyle of his family, and struggle is the appropriate term because the clay soil of Rowan County simply was not productive enough to sustain it or to even keep his hundred plus slaves gainfully employed. His wife frequently complained of indebtedness, on one occasion complaining in her diary about "surplus negroes" the family couldn't support and on another occasion, in a letter to son Leonard, who was off at school at the University of Virginia, that she rarely entered a store any more because she believed the merchants "consume

---

21. *Ibid.*, 98–111.
22. *Ibid.*, "The Journal of Robert B. Chaplin," 380.
23. *Ibid.*, 112. See also, Bertram Wyatt-Brown, *Southern Honor: Ethics and Behavior in the Old South* (Oxford and New York: Oxford University Press, 1983), 327–339; Scarborough, *Masters of the Big House*, 32–44.

our substances to enrich the Yankees and impoverish us."[24] The Hendersons were luckier than they might have been; Archibald Henderson was able to rent a number of his slaves to the North Carolina Railroad for several years for a comfortable sum.[25] Robert Chaplin wasn't so fortunate; he had to sell off a portion of his slave workforce to pay his debts.[26]

The social world of the planter was a world defined by an appreciation of the finer things in life, and a belief that leisure was a better way to spend one's time than work, particularly hard work. While the Puritan work ethic of the North defined work as good and leisure as bad if not evil, the planters saw leisure as the end result and even the goal of accumulating wealth. Dinner parties, balls, card playing, hunting and fishing, and horse racing were also ways to demonstrate social standing. Owning a large house or a fine racehorse, extending hospitality—the fabled Southern hospitality—all showed one was a "big" man. This could become quite competitive; Thomas Chaplin provided dinner for his Agricultural Society meeting one February evening, "five times as much as the men could eat." Ironically, he noted in his journal "There was a resolution passed to fine any member 50 cts. who found [provided] more than six dishes of meat for dinner, which is a very proper thing, it will prevent competition among members in finding dinner."[27] Planters styled themselves aristocrats, but at bottom it was money more than family lineage that provided the wherewithal to lay claim to this status, and the money had to be spent in ways aristocrats spent money. Family honor almost demanded it.

Members of the planter class were obsessed with honor, which at the most obvious level meant having one's family name held in high repute. But honor was more than that and was, in fact, at the very center of the value system of planter and non-planter alike. Originating in England and the borderlands of the British Isles, the code of honor stressed hierarchy, of superiors and inferiors; it established particular behaviors and obligations for men and for women, for planters and common folk, and for family and non-family. Honor demanded caring for family, helping friends, abiding by promises, and treating women, especially upper class women, with respect.[28] Planters had to comport themselves like "gentlemen," which meant adhering to the conventions of man-

---

24. Diary of Mary F. Henderson 22 January 1858; Mrs. Archibald (Mary F.) Henderson to Leonard Henderson, 14 March 1861. John Steele Henderson Collection, Southern Historical Collection, University of North Carolina, Chapel Hill.

25. See for example "Hiring lists," 1858 and 1860. John Steele Henderson Collection, Southern Historical Collection, University of North Carolina, Chapel Hill. In 1860 Henderson earned several thousand dollars, a sizable sum, from hiring out slaves to the North Carolina Railroad.

26. Rosengarten, *Tombee*, "The Journal of Robert B. Chaplin," 346–348.

27. *Ibid.*, 395.

28. Wyatt-Brown, *Southern Honor*, xv–xvi; 34–36; 50–55.

nerly behavior—"thank you sir for your generous hospitality" and so forth—and being "sociable." Gentlemen were also expected to exhibit some of the refining influences of an education, and it was not uncommon for planters' sons to attend at least a few years of college. As the Civil War approached, being a good Christian—upright, sober, church going—was also considered a virtue of gentle folk; Robert E. Lee would come to exemplify this "new" virtue. A planter worked to build respect for his name and worried over slights to it and was constantly seeking the approval of other planters in socially acceptable ways.[29] Performing one's duty to family, friends, and community was the high road to honor, but owning a big house, driving the finest carriage, or hosting the best party also won the respect of others and added to the account of honor. The underside, of course, was to avoid doing something shameful like drinking too much and behaving foolishly, or being dragged into court for bad debts. As James McBride Dabbs observed in *Haunted by God* about his own plantation upbringing decades after the Civil War, "What was really hammered home with us was the avoidance of shame. 'Honey, ain't you shamed?' was the cry of many a nursemaid or other servant. We avoided forbidden things to keep from being shamed, not to keep from feeling guilty."[30] Honor and shame are the flip sides of the same coin, but shame, unlike guilt, is meted out by others when one does something dishonorable.

Because so much rode on others' assessments of one's character and even an ill-thought-out casual remark might prove embarrassing, many Southern gentlemen developed the hair-trigger temper that seems to commonly define the male personality in a shame culture whether of planters in the nineteenth century or African-American ghetto youth in the twentieth. Violence or threatened violence, then, undergirded the honor code. This is not surprising because to lose one's honor was to suffer a social death—that is, to be ignored or ridiculed or lose one's place in the pecking order of the community. Too, one was defending not just one's own name but a family name; an insult to one was an insult to all. For the planter, the proper response to an affront to one's honor depended on the class of the offending party. If it was a man who was not a gentleman, caning was one proper response. Caning literally meant that the offender was beaten over the head with a cane, often without warning. The notion was that an inferior had no right to criticize or insult a superior and deserved whatever he got. Sometimes whether a man qualified as gentlemen or not was in the eye of the beholder. Robert Chaplin went to visit a son of the sister of his stepfather, R. L. Baker, to "demand an apology for some scandalous talk he had taken the presumptuous liberty to make use of toward me."

29. *Ibid.*, 88–97; 99; 102–105; 107.

30. James McBride Dabbs, *Haunted by God* (Richmond, Virginia: John Knox Press, 1972), 107.

In Chaplin's mind, Baker and probably all of his kin were scoundrels, not gentlemen. As he noted in his journal "The fellow hesitated rather long for my patience to endure, so I merely gave him a genteel flogging with a small cane. Made him beg like a Negro...."[31] Caning was not the only way to deal with an uppity inferior. William Alexander Percy describes, in *Lanterns On the Levee*, a post-Civil War encounter in Mississippi which was precipitated when two men refused to stop gossiping about a friend of a third man seated at their table:

> At supper he sat across the table from two strangers who began to disparage General Ferguson. Mr. Merritt said: "Gentlemen, I will ask you not to discuss the General." His manner was quiet, almost diffident, and his appearance belied his stoutness. The strangers looked him over and continued the tenor of their conversation. Mr. Merritt said, still more quietly: "Gentlemen, General Ferguson is my friend." The strangers ignored his warning. Mr. Merritt picked up his coffee cup, a thick old-fashioned weapon weighing about a pound, and hurled it across the table. It hit one of the men squarely between the eyes and laid him low. Before the other could recover from his astonishment, Mr. Merritt was over and across the table and had fallen on him with murderous fists, one on the jaw finally putting him where he belonged. Then Mr. Merritt finished up with the first, who was recovering from his coffee-cup. When it was over, he flicked a crumb from his lapel, strolled forward, sweetly at peace, and watched the moonlight from the bow. The strangers were borne off at the next landing, on stretchers.
>
> I asked Mr. Merritt about it years after when he was well over ninety. He was still diffident and said it was just a little personal matter.[32]

If one was shamed by another gentleman, the proper response was to challenge him to a duel. President Andrew Jackson had been a duelist, and Louis Wigfall, U.S. Senator from Texas in the 1850s and Confederate leader in the 1860s, was a noted duelist. However, on the eve of the Civil War, actual duels were not common in the South because more often than not friends interceded and prevented the duelists from actually going through with the duel. As Ted Rosengarten observed in *Tombee*, "No longer was it necessary to exchange pistol shots. The delivery and acceptance of a challenge was sufficient to give satisfaction. By issuing a challenge, the injured party got to publicize his grievance and show his allegiance to a ritual code. He showed that he belonged. And by accepting the challenge, the offender restored the social balance upset by the original insult." As Rosengarten notes, "At least four times in thirteen years, acquaintances of Chaplin went through the motions of preparing to duel. Signif-

---

31. Rosengarten, *Tombee*, "The Journal of Robert B. Chaplin," 349.
32. Percy, *Lanterns on the Levee*, 72–73.

icantly, none of the duels came off."[33] Likewise, in Rowan County, North Carolina, several challenges were issued during the 1850s, but there is no record of an actual duel being fought. Like much about the South's upper class traditions, dueling was a concept borrowed from the aristocratic traditions of England and the continent which Southern gentlemen carefully and self-consciously copied early and late in the history of the antebellum South and after.

The concept of *noblesse oblige* occupied the moral center of the English and continental aristocratic world. In the South this concept would take the form of paternalism, and it would justify the morality of slavery and the entire Southern social order. At its simplest, paternalism was the notion that superior people must take care of their inferiors like a father would care for his children. It was based on the patriarchal model of the family where the father/husband ruled the wife/mother and the children. As historian Eugene Genovese explains it in *Roll, Jordan, Roll*, it also requires inferiors to loyally serve their superiors, so it was a set of mutual obligations.[34] At bottom, it was rooted in the idea of inequality, that some are born and bred to lead, and others are born and bred to be led. Paternalism most directly informed family relations and the relationship between the planters and their slaves. The paternal relationship between the planters and other whites—small farmers and poor whites—was less obvious for the simple reason that these folks were largely independent of the planter and often quite prideful about their independence; one historian has even described the relationship between planters and less affluent whites as "fraternal." But it's also clear small farmers and poor whites generally deferred to the planters in matters political and military in a tradition rooted in the culture of the colonial era and, before that, southern England and the border regions of Britain. In Rowan County for example, voters—most of them small farmers—generally chose men like Charles Fisher for office. Fisher was one of the wealthiest men in Rowan County and married to the daughter of a wealthy planter. His father had served in the state legislature and in Congress, and he served in the state senate and was one of the leaders of a campaign to build a state-funded railroad line. On the eve of the Civil War, he organized and bankrolled a regiment which he led into battle.[35]

---

33. Rosengarten, *Tombee*, 135.

34. Eugene Genovese, *Roll, Jordan Roll: The World the Slaves Made* (New York: Vintage Books, 1974), 3–7.

35. Rhys Isaac, *The Transformation of Virginia: 1740–1790* (Chapel Hill: University of North Carolina Press, 1982), 131–134; Wyatt-Brown, *Southern Honor*, 62–69; John H. Wheeler, *Reminiscences and Memoirs of North Carolina and Eminent North Carolinians* (1884; Chapel Hill: Documenting the American South, 2001), 403–404, http://docsouth.unc.edu/nc/wheeler/

wheeler.html; John Steele Henderson to Mrs. Archibald Henderson, 21 April 1861, John Steele Henderson Collection, Southern Historical Collection, University of North Carolina at Chapel Hill.

It may seem ironic that paternalism would take root in a region that produced some of the great early proponents of freedom and equality. Ironic, perhaps, but not surprising. Over the long haul, it was simply too difficult and required too many mental gymnastics to both defend slavery and promote
equality. And planters, with their political power, their wealth, their immersion in social relations with other planters, and (for many) their planter lineage, would have been rather exceptional men if they had seen their slaves and
their less affluent neighbors as just like themselves. Indeed, the notion was
even current that they looked different from their more common neighbors.
Slaveholder Daniel Hundley observed in a book published in 1860 (*Social Relations in Our Southern States*) that the typical member of the upper class possessed "that lithe, airy, and graceful carriage, that compactness of muscle"
which distinguished him from his less affluent neighbors whom he did not describe in such complimentary terms. He also argued that "the Southern Gentlemen comes of a good stock. Indeed, to state the matter fairly, he comes usually of aristocratic parentage...."[36] So superior genes made a man superior in
every respect who was ideally suited to rule. And logically, inferior genes produced people suited to follow.

Paternalism, one could argue, had much to commend it, but it could take
strange twists and turns. The Southern philosopher George Fitzhugh, author
of *Sociology for the South or the Failure of Free Society* and *Cannibals All! or
Slaves Without Masters,* used the concept of paternalism to defend slavery
against the attacks of abolitionists. Fitzhugh argued that slavery protected the
weak and less able and was thus a more moral system than the capitalistic free
society of the North that left the poor and members of the working class to
fend for themselves. His logic compelled him to advocate extending the benefits of slavery to laboring whites although he noted that "We need never have
white slaves in the South, because we have black ones."[37] He did believe laborers in Europe (and in the North?) would benefit from being enslaved, although, he argued, "the character of slavery necessary to protect the whites in
Europe should be much milder than negro slavery, for slavery is only needed to
protect the white man whilst it is more necessary for the government of the
negro even than for his protection."[38] While few planters (and probably no
poor whites) were interested in contemplating the concept of white slavery
even in faraway Europe, Fitzhugh's views certainly indicate that a more conser-

---

36. Daniel Hundley, *Social Relations in Our Southern States* (1860; Baton Rouge and
London: Louisiana State University Press, 1979), 84.

37. George Fitzhugh, *Sociology for the South, or the Failure of Free Society* (1854;
Chapel Hill: Documenting the American South, 1998), http://docsouth.unc.edu/fitzhugh
soc/fitzhugh.html.

38. *Ibid.,* 94–95.

vative view of freedom and equality, as opposed to the expansive, liberal view of Jefferson's Declaration of Independence, was taking hold in the South.

Given the planters' aristocratic pretensions, it is not surprising that the planters valued martial skills and experience. Aristocracies began, after all, as warrior classes. In England, the country with the most long-lived aristocracy, titled gentlemen were an important element of the officer corps of the nation's armed services well into the twentieth century. Southern gentlemen likewise made up an important part of the officer corps of the U.S. Army before the Civil War. Manly valor was part and parcel of the code of honor; indeed, war brought esteem to the warrior.[39] Southern planters had quite practical reasons for valuing military skills: much of the South was only recently wrested from the frontier, and fighting Indians and outlaw bands was still a living memory for many. Most importantly, with a large slave population to control, armed watchfulness was a necessity. As a result, the South was virtually an armed camp with a fairly well-developed militia system throughout the region. Units periodically met, much as National Guard units do today, to drill and practice the military arts, and in many areas patrols would make rounds periodically in the evening to ensure that slaves were where they belonged. Militia officers were elected, and planters often ended up with "commissions" as officers. Thomas Chaplin periodically attended militia meetings, led patrols, and at one point served as an orderly sergeant in the St. Helena Mounted Rifles, but he went for long periods when he paid little or no attention to his militia responsibilities. While he apparently did not take his service too seriously, he did enjoy the socializing—militia meetings often concluded with a meal and drinks—and took pride in his shooting skills.[40]

Many planters took the idea of proper military training for their sons seriously; the region supported dozens and dozens of public and private military schools and colleges for young men. While military academies were not uncommon in the North and indeed may have originated in the region, the South seemed to embrace this form of education with more passion than the North in the decades leading up to the Civil War.[41] Two of the military colleges—The Citadel in South Carolina and Virginia Military Institute—still survive today and are the only state-run military colleges in the country. Historian Rod Andrew, Jr., has argued that while sectional tensions leading up to the Civil War were partly responsible for the blossoming of military education, there was

---

39. Wyatt-Brown, *Southern Honor*, 34–42.

40. Rosengarten, *Tombee*, 199–121; "The Journal of Robert B. Chaplin," 335. For more on the role of militia and patrols in "policing" the slave population, see Wyatt-Brown, *Southern Honor: Ethics and Behavior in the Old South*, 402–434.

41. Rod Andrew, Jr., *Long Gray Line: The Southern Military School Tradition, 1839–1915* (Chapel Hill, NC: University of North Carolina Press, 2001), 19.

strong support in the region—especially in the planter class—for the character building element of a military education, particularly its role in promoting "respect for the law, obedience to authority, and stern notions of civic duty and patriotism."[42]

So the planter class was unique and differed in significant ways from the upper class of the North, which was more a class of merchants and increasingly manufacturers. Some historians have disputed this notion, arguing that planters were motivated by profits just like their Northern counterparts and that many of them were not the inheritors of ancient landed estates but men on the make who wrested fortunes from the land. There is no question that most planters liked money and that some planters, particularly those struggling to make a go of it in the Piedmont, were open to innovation and even new kinds of enterprises such as the textile mill. Nor is there is any question that some planters had "common" origins. Recall that in *Gone with the Wind*, Mr. O'Hara (Scarlett's father) was an immigrant from Ireland. The view that planters were merely rural businessmen, however, ignores several key realities. Planters saw wealth as a means to an end: a certain kind of lifestyle of leisure and refinement. This end was to be achieved through the ownership of land and slaves; nothing else would do. The planters' code of honor and commitment to paternalism, however imperfectly acted on by the typical planter, also set them apart from their businessmen counterparts to the north who valued dignity and individual autonomy.[43] Too, wealth and power were more concentrated in a small upper class in the South as compared to the North. This class had old landed families at its core, and the newly rich planters showed an amazing proclivity for emulating the values and lifestyles of the old guard. For example, Virginian Robert Bailey was a gambler, which, while lucrative, was not a high status role in the Old South, but he did his best to be recognized as a gentleman by becoming a militia captain in the "Light Blues" and defending his honor in a duel.[44]

The planter class imparted to antebellum Southern culture its respect for manners and tradition, a disdain for equality as it applied to blacks, and at least a skepticism about the idea of equality in general. Because planters believed in honor and its compatriot, shame, their value system and that of the people they influenced was externally driven compared to the more internally driven guilt value system of the North. Planters were among the freest people

---

42. *Ibid.*, 18.

43. Edward L. Ayers says that the value of dignity, which he defines it as "the conviction that each individual at birth possessed an intrinsic value at least theoretically equal to that of every other person," was "antagonistic" to honor. *Vengeance and Justice: Crime and Punishment in the 19th-Century American South* (New York and Oxford: Oxford University Press, 1984), 19.

44. Wyatt-Brown, *Southern Honor*, 355.

on earth, but, in a peculiar sense, this freedom was profoundly circumscribed by what other people thought. Aside from acquiring more slaves and more land, change and progress for most were at best a minor part of their vocabulary while change and progress were becoming more and more a major part of the vocabulary of the Northern elite. The planters were becoming, in short, conservatives in the truest sense of the term. They were becoming more committed to stability and social order, to the "old" order whether it was in the "Old North State" or the "Old Dominion."

The Small Farmers

Thomas Jefferson saw the small farmer as the heart of the South and indeed the nation. Numerically speaking, small farmers certainly constituted the largest segment of the free, white population. Small farmers ranged from small slaveholding commercial farmers to subsistence farmers. They could be found throughout the South but, as we saw earlier, were most numerous in the piedmont and mountain areas of the South where plantation agriculture was less profitable, and they were less numerous in the rich plantation districts. Most small farmers used their own families for labor, and did not own slaves; those that did own slaves usually owned at best a few, but some might own a dozen or so. Small farmers typically owned farms of 100–500 acres, although some owned 1000 or more acres. Some owned no land and worked the land of others.[45] In piedmont and mountain areas of the region, areas like Rowan County, as much as fifty percent or more of the white male population were small farmers, although this number included individuals who did not own the land they farmed or were farming small parcels of land and producing small crops.[46]

Even those with slaves generally got out in the fields and worked. Families of small farmers lived a life governed by the seasonal patterns of work—planting in the spring, hoeing in the summer and harvesting in the late summer and early fall. The women of the house were governed by daily rituals that revolved around the laborious tasks of preparing cooked meals several times a day, spinning thread and weaving cloth (two activities which were quite commonly performed despite the growing availability of inexpensive store-bought cloth),

---

45. Frank Lawrence Owsley, *Plain Folk of the Old South* (1949;Baton Rouge and London: Louisiana State University Press, 1982), 156, 166, 168–169, 175, 180, 198–200, 204, 206, 207, 208, 221, 223, 225, 227; Steven Hahn, *The Roots of Southern Populism: Yeoman Farmers and the Transformation of the Georgia Upcountry, 1850–1890* (New York and Oxford: Oxford University Press, 1983), 21–28; Paul Escott, *Many Excellent People: Power and Privilege in North Carolina, 1850–1900* (Chapel Hill, NC and London: University of North Carolina Press, 1985), 7–8.

46. Beck, "Development in the Piedmont South," 272.

sewing clothing, making soap, washing clothes, tending the garden, and managing the children. At planting and harvest time, the wife would help her husband and, of course, do all her regular chores. Children were an important source of labor, not an added expense like today; they helped their parents with the tasks that they were capable of doing. When the sun came up, everyone who was able worked; when the sun set, everyone went to bed.[47]

Contrary to popular contemporary notions, it appears small farmers rarely lived in multi-generation households. Occasionally, an aged parent might live with a couple, but usually it was the traditional "nuclear family" that constituted a household, supplemented, perhaps, by a hired hand or young relative who boarded with the family.[48] The ability to work hard was valued in men and women alike. The self-sufficiency of the small farmer bred in him a prickly independence and individualism, or as Hundley said, "a manly independence of character."[49] Independence did not mean isolation, however. While the nuclear family was the primary "world" inhabited by small farmers and their wives and children, extended kin—uncles, aunts, cousins, grandparents—and neighbors were also important. Kin, historian Stephen Hahn found in his study of upcountry Georgia, often lived close to other kin, and this pattern still persists today in some rural areas.[50] Barn raisings, corn shuckings, quilting bees, and other group endeavors where neighbors and kin helped get work done that an individual family would have been hard-pressed to complete were common; individualism and self-reliance were thus diluted by a large helping of communalism and cooperation.[51] The deference shown planters also circumscribed small farmer independence. The small farmer might be king of his domain, but rarely did his kingdom extend beyond the property line of his farm. With the exception of the evangelical churches, the public sphere—the court house, the legislature, the speaker's platform—was generally the domain of the planter.

The simple lifestyle of the small farmers extended to their dwellings, which were typically one-story cottages or more spacious two-story houses. The less affluent small farmers lived in homes of 2 to 4 rooms—little more than cabins really—with the kitchen in an outbuilding. Ben Aycock, a small farmer in Wayne County, North Carolina, lived in a small dwelling consisting of a parlor and dining room heated by a fireplace; three bedrooms, unheated, that opened

---

47. Hahn, *The Roots of Southern Populism*, 30–31; Frank L. Owsley, *Plain Folk of the Old South*, 95.

48. Hahn, *The Roots of Southern Populism*, 30; Sample, U.S. Manuscript Census Returns, 1850, 1860, Rowan County, NC, Population Schedule.

49. Hundley, *Social Relations*, 199.

50. Hahn, *The Roots of Southern Populism*, 53–54.

51. Owsley, *Plain Folk of the Old South*, 104–115.

directly onto the porches, and a fourth room in the unheated attic that served as another bedroom. A variety of structures—a kitchen, slave cabins, and barns—surrounded the main house. One of the most common houses built by small farmers was a two-story clapboarded structure (unpainted or painted white) which consisted of two ground floor rooms and two rooms upstairs. Two chimneys flanked the building, and each room was furnished with a fireplace. Thomas Harper, a county official and small farmer, built an eight-room house in Bentonville, North Carolina, that is a good example of the sort of dwelling a prosperous farmer or even planter would have constructed in the prewar era. Decorations in the homes of small farmers were typically sparse and mostly homemade. For modern tastes, the wooden chairs and benches are far removed from the soft chairs, couches, and recliners modern Americans feel they need for comfort. But, then, comfort or ease was not in the vocabulary of many of these folks.

Recreation for farm families was simple: hunting and fishing for the men, quilting bees (which combined work and play) and conversation after church for the women, and the occasional frolic or party for all. Drinking was an ever-popular diversion for men, and corn or small grains could be fairly easily turned into a supply of drinkable alcohol. However, small farmers were more and more likely to attend Baptist or Methodist churches as the South was transforming into the "Bible Belt," and these denominations (and the Presbyterian) emphasized a strict morality that frowned on such behaviors as gambling, racing, dancing, and especially excessive drinking, and disciplined church members who violated their strict rules of behavior.[52] Planters were affected by this transformation, too—indeed, planters were increasingly members of these churches—but it would still be fair to say that if agrarian values united the planters and small farmers, they were worlds apart in their **professed** moral codes. While the small farmers might defer to the planters in politics and elect planters to lead the militia companies, respectable small farmers looked with disdain at the planters' drinking, partying, and horse racing. Women "were warned against aping the style, dress, and behavior of the idle rich, whose only claim to esteem, according to the Evangelicals, was position based on birth, rather than personal worth."[53]

Small farmers (and poor whites too) did share with the planters one value: honor. As Frederick Law Olmsted noted:

52. Bertram Wyatt-Brown, *The Shaping of Southern Culture: Honor, Grace, and War, 1760s–1880s* (Chapel Hill and London: University of North Carolina Press, 2001), 94–99; Donald G. Matthews, *Religion in the Old South* (Chicago and London: University of Chicago Press, 1979), 44–45, 62–63; Christine Leigh Heyrman, *Southern Cross: The Beginnings of the Bible Belt* (Chapel Hill, NC and London: University of North Carolina Press, 1997), 249–250.

53. Matthews, *Religion in the Old South*, 44; 111.

Every white Southerner is a person of importance; must be treated with deference. Every wish of the Southerner is imperative; every belief undoubted; every hate vengeful; every love, fiery. Hence, for instance, the scandalous fiend-like street fights of the South. If a young man feels offended with another, he does not incline to a ring and a fair stand-up set to like a young Englishman; he will not attempt to overcome his opponent by logic; he will not be content to vituperate, or cast ridicule upon him; he is impelled straightway to strike him down with the readiest deadly weapon at hand, with as little ceremony and pretences of fair combat as the loose organization of the people against violence will allow. He seems crazy for blood. Intensity of personal pride—pride in anything a man has, or which connects itself with him, is more commonly evident.[54]

Honor, as we saw earlier, had both English and Scots-Irish roots. The Scots-Irish influence loomed largest with the small farmers; the "heartland" of the small farmer—the Piedmont and Mountains—was largely settled by Scots-Irish and, as historian David Hackett Fischer has argued, these migrants brought a heritage from Scotland, Ireland, and northern England of bloody family and clan feuds and a prickly sense of independence. Where Scots-Irish settlers predominated in the South, the *lex talionis* (rule of retaliation) prevailed. This rule, like the more aristocratic (and English influenced) honor code of the upper class, required men to defend with murderous violence their family names and reputations.[55] As Olmsted noted, this violence was less stylized than that practiced by the upper class and might involve rough-and-tumble wrestling matches that left participants eyeless or noseless, knife fights, or gunfights. One study of Edgefield County, a county in piedmont South Carolina noted for violence, found a murder rate before the Civil War that makes cities today look positively peaceful by comparison, and the local courts rarely convicted anyone of murder. [56]

Vigilantism, where groups—mobs—took the law into their own hands was another aspect of this code, and David Hackett Fischer has found vigilantism more common in the highlands of the South than in any other region of the South or the rest of the country, a phenomena he attributes to the Scots-

---

54. Frederick Law Olmsted, ed. by Arthur M. Schlesinger Sr., *The Cotton Kingdom: A Traveller's Observations on Cotton and Slavery in the American Slave States* (1861; New York: Modern Library, 1984), 555.

55. David Hackett Fischer, *Albion's Seed*, 765; Ayers, *Vengeance and Justice*, 21–22; Grady McWhiney, *Cracker Culture: Celtic Ways in the Old South* (University, Alabama: University of Alabama Press, 1988), 146–155.

56. Fox Butterfield, *All God's Children: The Bosket Family and the American Tradition of Violence* (New York: Alfred A. Knopf, 1995), 8–9.

Irish origins of much of its white population.[57] Rowan County, with a large Scots-Irish population of small farmers, experienced periodic bouts of vigilantism. It, along with much of the Piedmont of North Carolina, was a hotbed of Regulator activities in the 1760s. The Regulators, folks who were bitterly angry at the royal government over high taxes and poor service, harassed local government officials and finally fought a brief pitched battle with an army led by the royal governor. Vigilantism seemed to escalate in the county immediately before the Civil War. In 1856 a crowd gathered outside the lodgings of a visitor to Salisbury (the county seat) who had achieved some degree of notoriety in the state for criticizing slavery; the crowd hissed and howled and were only quieted "by the appearance of several of our citizens who prevailed upon them to disperse."[58] In 1861 a mob, incensed by the acquittal of a man accused of rape, sledge hammered open the door of the Salisbury jail, took the man out, and hanged him. Several years later, a mob of women, angered by what they believed was wartime price gouging, seized food and provisions from local merchants.[59]

Honor did have an antagonist that would do battle with it. The evangelical Protestantism that flourished in the decades leading up to the Civil War promoted a value system that conflicted with honor in many respects.[60] The movement, as we have already seen, established the overwhelming predominance of two churches in the region—the Baptist and Methodist churches—and these churches struggled mightily to civilize the hard-drinking, hard-fighting males and replace a male subculture rooted in honor with a new code that stressed Christian (and feminine) virtues of modesty, humbleness, and piety.[61] However, honor was deeply entrenched and a wily adversary to boot and was not so easy to vanquish. Most importantly, in such an honor-drenched culture, evangelical ministers had a hard time convincing men that it was "manly" to join a church; then (and now) women were more likely to join. To appeal to men, ministers stressed manliness—that the devil was to be fought in "spiritual warfare," that a Christian man could be, in fact, should be, master of his household, that a minister was courageous in the conventional sense—in an effort to win male support. What would become a stock figure on the revival circuit in later decades (and in religious broadcasting today)—the animated, gesturing, forceful male preacher shouting defiance at Satan, in short behaving not too differently from the prideful Thomas Chaplin—no doubt made its appear-

---

57. Fischer, *Albion's Seed*, 766–767.
58. [Salisbury, NC] *Republican Banner*, 28 October 1856.
59. [Salisbury, NC] *Carolina Watchman*, 6 June 1861, 23 March 1863.
60. Bertram Wyatt Brown, *The Shaping of Southern Culture*, 101–104.
61. Ted Owenby, *Subduing Satan: Religion, Recreation, and Manhood in the Rural South, 1865–1920* (Chapel Hill, NC and London: University of North Carolina Press, 1990), 14–15.

ance at this time. So while Christianity set limits on honor and male freedoms, honor influenced the language of Christianity and the boundaries of church regulation of male behavior.[62]

Poor Whites

Poor whites were people who lived on the margins of the small farmer/plantation economy and society of the South. They were people who owned very little property and generally lived in the countryside. As Hundley observed, "The Poor Whites of the South live altogether in the country, in hilly and mountainous regions generally, in communities by themselves, and far removed from the wealthy and refined settlements."[63] Most poor whites farmed—on their own farms or as tenant farmers for large landowners or as farm laborers; others worked as loggers and miners. In many areas of the South, the poverty that spawned this class was actually increasing before the Civil War. This growing poverty had several sources: soil exhaustion in many of the rural areas of the long settled Southeast coupled with a rapidly expanding population which pushed more and more people into what could best be termed marginal farming on poor land. Migration was an option, and large numbers of residents in the Southeast migrated to the fresh lands of Alabama and Mississippi; unfortunately, then as now, one needed money to start afresh, making migration a daunting prospect for people with no resources. The traditional trades—carriage making, blacksmithing, barrel making and the like—in much of the South actually offered fewer opportunities for employment during the fifties as modern industry arising in the North extended its reach and devastated the old crafts. In Rowan County, North Carolina, for example, a larger percentage of people farmed in 1860 than in 1850 as employment in the traditional trades plummeted. Many of these "new" farmers were eking out a living on tiny plots of land that produced miniscule harvests.[64]

How numerous were these folks? It's hard to say because poor, comfortable, and affluent are subjective terms, and we really don't know an awful lot about less affluent people white or black because they did not leave us much in the way of written records or accounts of themselves. In Rowan County almost 39% of the white males 20 and older owned less than $50 dollars of real and personal property in 1860, an amount which came to little more than personal possessions and perhaps a firearm. These men would be prime candidates for poor white status, although some of them were living and working on the

---

62. Heyrman, *Southern Cross*, pp. 231–252.
63. Daniel Hundley, *Social Relations in Our Southern States,* p. 258.
64. Beck, "Development in the Piedmont South," 68–70; 75–76.

farms of fathers and older brothers. Looking at both the property figures and at the number of farms—about 20%—that produced negligible crops, poor white males were perhaps 20–30% of the male population in Rowan. Historian John Bolton estimates that poor white households constituted between 30–40% of the households in the piedmont North Carolina counties he studied. Bolton found that there were significantly fewer poor whites in the rich cotton lands of Mississippi and that they generally did not establish permanent residency there.[65] So many poor whites who migrated to the Southwest kept moving. In truth, with little property at their disposal, there really wasn't much of a place for poor whites in the antebellum South. As two other historians have noted, "the market for poor white labor would always be varied, fleeting, and unstable."[66]

Accounts of poor whites frequently stressed the meagerness of their homes, farms, and lives. Daniel Hundley said they typically lived in homes of logs and farmed a few acres of land.[67] Many also commonly lived in dogtrot houses. The dogtrot consisted of "two rooms at either end of an open breezeway" and may, in its basic design, have originated in the borderlands of Britain.[68] Frederick Law Olmsted, writing in the 1850s, said of poor whites:

> I have been once or twice told that the poor white people, meaning those, I suppose, who bring nothing to market to exchange for money but their own labour, although they may own a cabin and a little furniture, and cultivate land enough to supply themselves with (maize) bread, are worse off in almost all respects than the slaves.[69]

The meanness of their lifestyle often inspired a moral judgment of their characters: the men were frequently described as lazy and as more inclined to hunt and fish than expend much effort on farming or maintaining their houses or outbuildings. Hundley said of them that they have "a natural stupidity or dullness of intellect that almost surpasses belief...."[70] They are frequently described as having sallow or gray complexions, listless dispositions, and a fondness for strong drink. Terms of derision—"redneck," "white trash," "cracker," "pecker-

---

65. *Ibid.*, p. 262, Table 1.6; Charles C. Bolton, *Poor Whites of the Antebellum South: Tenants and Laborers in Central North Carolina and Northeast Mississippi* (Durham, NC and London: Duke University Press, 1994), 12, 112.

66. Charles S. Bolton and Scott P. Culclasure, eds., *The Confessions of Edward Isham: A Poor White Life of the Old South* (Athens and London: University of Georgia Press, 1998), 31.

67. Hundley, *Social Relations in Our Southern States*, 258.

68. J. Wayne Flynt, *Dixie's Forgotten People: The South's Poor Whites* (Bloomington and London: Indiana University Press, 1979), 16; McWhiney, *Cracker Culture: Celtic Ways in the Old South*, xxii.

69. Frederick Law Olmsted, ed. by Arthur Schlesinger, Sr., *The Cotton Kingdom*, 65.

70. *Ibid.*, 264.

wood"—were commonly applied to poor whites by the more affluent before and after the Civil War. William Faulkner's Wash in the short story by the same name is the perfect fictional representation of the stereotypical poor white. Wash is described as "a gaunt, malaria-ridden man with pale, questioning eyes."[71] He lived in an abandoned fishing cabin, which Thomas Sutpen, a planter, had allowed him to occupy. Even the slaves treated him with contempt, as a figure, in truth, lower in the social order than they. One of the few first-hand accounts we have of the life of a poor white—*The Confessions of Edward Isham*—describes a life of violence, drunkenness, thievery, and murder. Isham was constantly on the move, working here and there, visiting friends and relatives, never stopping too long in one place until the law finally forced him to stop.[72]

While some poor whites were outlaws like Edward Isham or loafers like Wash, most worked hard to eke out an existence. They were generally derived from the same ethnic stock as small farmers—English and Scots-Irish—and most probably shared many of the same values as small farmers even if they didn't always have the means to live by those values. It is not surprising that educated and economically comfortable commentators such as Olmsted—he was the co-designer of Central Park in New York, by the way—would find poor whites strange and their poverty their own fault. The poor often elicit similar reactions today. Poor whites lived hard lives in a society that, thanks to slavery, had little use for them, and hard lives produce hard people.

Slaves and Free Blacks

African Americans had their own class system—free blacks and slaves—which was a product of slavery and the race consciousness of Southern society. Both of these groups will be discussed in greater detail in the next chapter, but we'll sketch out a few details of each of these groups here, too. Slaves were property, pure and simple, and were the foundation of the plantation system and the wealth of the planters. They could be bought and sold "like an ordinary article of merchandise," in Chief Justice Roger Taney's words in the U.S. Supreme Court's famous *Dred Scott* decision (1857). Aside from some restrictions on their treatment—they couldn't be "casually" killed—slaves were little different legally than other forms of property. The Constitution protected the slaveholder, not the slave. As Taney noted in *Dred Scott* "The government of the United States had no right to interfere [with slavery] for any other purpose

---

71. William Faulkner, "Wash" in *Collected Stories* (New York: Vintage Books, 1977), 535–550.
72. Bolton and Culclasure, *The Confessions of Edward Isham*.

but that of protecting the rights of the owner...."[73] Slaves performed the heavy manual labor on the plantations. They planted, tended, and harvested the cotton, tobacco, and sugar that made the region wealthy. They also worked side by side with many of the small farmers on their farms, labored in the lumber industry, and even worked in some of the region's few factories. Some slaves, by virtue of having a white father with a conscience or working especially hard or having a special skill, might take a more comfortable job as a house servant or a craftsman or a driver. Some could actually save enough money to buy their own freedom, but this was rare. So there were a few opportunities for upward mobility. For most slaves, however, slavery and heavy manual labor were all they could expect in life. Their "master" or the master's overseer had the power to make work and life a bit more bearable or a living hell.

Free blacks were a population of people numbering a quarter million by 1860 who were primarily the descendants of slaves who were freed in the late 1700s and early 1800s during a period when this was fairly common. George Washington, for example, had freed his slaves. There was a wide variation in what free blacks did for a living and how well they lived. There were actually a small number of free black slaveholders, which was usually the result of a free man buying his wife who was still a slave. Some free blacks were skilled craftsmen like furniture maker Thomas Day of North Carolina. Other free blacks worked as laborers in cities. Free blacks were neither fish nor fowl in the antebellum South, however, because of the color consciousness of the region and the equation of black with slave. By the 1850s, freeing one's slaves was no longer socially acceptable in white society, although it was still done on occasion. Further, laws were passed by most state legislatures to circumscribe the freedom and rights of free blacks. But free blacks would be the foundation of black leadership that emerged after the war, and small free black communities like Howell Town (later renamed Antioch) outside Oxford, North Carolina, provided postwar freed slaves with models of behavior and places of refuge in an often hostile sea of whiteness.[74]

Honor and shame, so important in white culture, also appeared in the slave quarters. That this was so is not surprising; many of those kidnapped into slavery were from honor/shame cultures, and Southern slaves lived immersed in such a culture every day of their lives. In white eyes, however, honor was a white virtue; when whites looked at slaves, they saw people who lacked (with few exceptions) the capacity to be ashamed or to behave honorably. Indeed, black shamelessness was a source of great amusement and consternation to

---

73. *Dred Scott v. John F. A. Sandford*, 1857, http://www.tourolaw.edu/patch/Scott/.

74. Colin A. Palmer, *Passageways: An Interpretative History of Black America, Volume I: 1619–1863* (Fort Worth: Harcourt Brace College Publishers, 1998), 185–198; Barnetta McGhee White, "History of Antioch Baptist Church, Granville, County, North Carolina," 1990.

whites who would marvel at black guile when it came to stealing food or avoiding work, but would also moan, as Mrs. Archibald Henderson did in a letter to her son, about "the corruption of Negroes."[75] But whites' understanding of black morality was just as limited as their understanding of what slavery did to those enslaved. Whites' ability to control, humiliate, and brutalize slaves did not squeeze shame and honor (or guilt for that matter) out of black consciousness. Rather, the powerlessness and the humiliations, serious and petty, that were the slaves' lot made shame and honor mean something to them that free white men and women could not and would not understand. The slave who spied on other slaves for the master was, for the slaves, shameful; the slave who stole from the master to provide his family with adequate rations was honorable. For whites it was the reverse. Black men apparently did share with white men a common definition of honor in their dealings with each other, when whites were not around, and with the same violent consequences found in the white world.[76]

Both slaves and free blacks were increasingly drawn to the evangelical Christianity that was growing in importance in the white community in the decades before the Civil War. Black Christianity differed in important respects — in theology, ritual, and morality — from white Christianity, and black Christianity, just as with white, struggled to govern the passions of its adherents.

Class after the Civil War

Following the Civil War, a new class system arose and would, in its broad outlines, remain little changed for one hundred years. The demise of slavery played a big role in the appearance of new classes, but so too did the expansion of commercial agriculture, the growth of towns, and industrialization. At the bottom of this new class system were the sharecroppers, and above the sharecroppers in wealth and prestige were industrial workers, men and women who worked in the growing industries of the South, especially the textile industry. In the middle were the small farmers and members of an urban middle class. This urban middle class was quite small and merged almost imperceptibly into the upper class, which now was composed of the planters, the more successful merchants and urban professionals, and the owners of the new industries emerging in the region. The more successful industrialists, like the Duke family, often became part of a broader and

---

75. Mrs. Archibald Henderson to John Steele Henderson, 15 January 1861, John Steele Henderson Collection, Southern Historical Collection, University of North Carolina at Chapel Hill.

76. Brown, *The Shaping of Southern Culture*, 11–27.

fabulously wealthy American upper class that also emerged after the war. Just as before the Civil War, race separated black and white into two class systems.

Sharecroppers and Millhands

The postwar class system was governed by a fact of life in the South that would remain resistant to change for almost a century and that fact was widespread poverty that relegated many to the bottom of the class system. This poverty was common in the rural South and in the towns and villages that popped up all over the region. Poverty had been growing among whites before the war as more and more people pushed into farming a finite amount of arable land. After the war, millions of freed slaves joined them. Most black farmers became sharecroppers and a growing percentage of white farmers worked as "croppers" or tenant farmers (landless farmers who owned their own equipment and got a bigger "share"). By the 1930s over half the farmers in most Southern states farmed on shares, most tending tiny farms as small as 15 or 20 acres. Landlords closely monitored sharecroppers because effort on the part of the "cropper" and his family would mean a larger crop (and larger share for him) in the fall. One white man who sharecropped in the 1950s and early 1960s recalled to one of the authors how his landlord would drive up to the house on a Saturday morning, honk the horn, and discuss business with him through the car window. The close supervision and control that was the slave's lot before the war was now extended to landless white farmers, too.

The landlord also encouraged the "cropper" to plant as much of his land in a cash crop as possible and not waste precious land or labor on crops that could not be sold. Ironically, because of the smallness of the sharecroppers' farms and the pressure exerted by the landlords to grow the cash crop "from the front steps to the road," many sharecropper families came to depend on provisions bought at the country store. The most important of these provisions were the so-called three M's—meat, meal, and molasses. This diet of fatback and cornbread, dressed by molasses, was supplemented by the luxury items of coffee and sugar, and by homegrown vegetables in season, sweet potatoes, and perhaps a chicken dinner on a special occasion. President Jimmy Carter has observed about the diets of black tenants on his father's land in Georgia (circa 1930s):

> During most of the year they ate only two meals a day, usually cornmeal, fatback, molasses, and perhaps sweet potatoes from our common field. The more industrious families also had small gardens that provided some seasonal corn, Irish potatoes, collards, turnips, and cabbage, with a few rows of running peas and beans planted alongside the garden fence. The combination of constant and heavy work, inad-

equate diet, and excessive use of tobacco was devastating to the health of our poorer neighbors. With the exception of a few very old women who could no longer do fieldwork, I don't remember any of the tenant-family members' being the slightest bit overweight.[77]

As we saw in Chapter 1, the provisions the "cropper" bought from the local merchant were often bought on credit at an exorbitant rate of interest; come "settle" time (when the crop was sold and accounts were settled), he often walked away with nothing in his pockets and a continuing debt in the merchant's account book. Because the merchant was interested in having his debt paid, he often took an active interest in his debtors' crops, and the sharecropper acquired a second "boss" as a result. It should be noted that a sharecropper could, unlike the prewar slave, simply walk away from a bad situation, and many did, sometimes in the dead of night, but signing on with a new landlord rarely resulted in an improvement in his life.[78] Some sharecroppers were able to live comfortable, largely self-sufficient lives, and some were even able to use sharecropping as a steppingstone to becoming landowning farmers, but most became mired in debt and lived a life of backbreaking labor and grinding poverty. The poverty and the oppressiveness of the system was probably worse for blacks; at least for white sharecroppers, the landlord might be a relative or friend, there were fewer obstacles in their paths if they wished to buy land, and mill work offered a "way out."[79]

The industrialization of the South after the Civil War resulted in a rapidly expanding class of workers toiling away in factories producing cigarettes, furniture, steel, and textiles. With the exception of the tobacco industry, most factory jobs were reserved for whites; generally only the most menial positions were open to blacks. Southern industries would only begin hiring blacks in significant numbers in the 1960s and 1970s. The primary industry was textiles, and by the 1920s the South was the textile capital of the world with hundreds of thousands of workers laboring in mills scattered across the piedmont region of a five-state area. The textile mills were generally located on the outskirts of small towns, and millowners built villages near their mills to house their workers.[80] The typical village was owned lock, stock, and barrel by the mill and the

---

77. Jimmy Carter, *An Hour Before Daylight: Memories of a Rural Boyhood* (New York: Simon and Schuster, 2001), 53.

78. The U.S. Census found in a study conducted in 1920 that less than half of white tenant families had been on the farms they were working for more than one year. U.S. Census, *Fourteenth Census, 1920, Vol. V: Agriculture* (Washington, D.C.: GPO, 1922), 406.

79. Jacquelyn Dowd Hall, Jim Leloudis, et al., *Like a Family: The Making of a Southern Cotton Mill World* (Chapel Hill and London: University of North Carolina Press, 1987), 12; Steven Hahn, *The Roots of Southern Populism: Yeoman Farmers and the Transformation of the Georgia Upcountry, 1850–1890* (New York: Oxford University Press, 1983), 165.

80. Hall et al, *Like A Family*, 114–116.

homes were rented to the workers. It often featured a mill-owned store where workers could buy food and other items on credit. James Cannon went further than most mill owners and built an entire private town of houses, stores and shops and even controlled the government and police force. He "modestly" named his town Kannapolis. Most mill workers would live in company-owned housing until after World War II when mills began selling off their towns.

Figure 2.2   Furniture Workers in Statesville, North Carolina

A new working class culture arose in the industrializing, urban South, and the heart of this culture was in the mill towns and villages. Initially, this culture was closely connected with farming and the countryside. Most of the workers were recruited from the surrounding countryside, and entire families—father, mother, and children—often worked together in the mills, the younger children doing odd jobs and the older children working more rigorous jobs, just like on the farm. Mill villages had a rural quality to them with gardens behind many of the houses and chickens pecking the dirt around the front stoop. Workers were still, at heart, country people who did not see themselves as a permanent part of an industrial working class and adjusting to industrial life for people accustomed to the rhythms of seasons and sunrise and sunset was difficult. Many returned to farming; others would go to the countryside during planting or harvesting season and then return to millwork. But as time passed, many did come to see themselves as workers, not farmers, and the mill or factory and the town or village defined their lives. Mill towns were tightly knit communities, and village inhabitants were "Like a Family," according to Jacqueline Hall and her collaborators in their fine book on mill town life. If a man became sick, the neighbors would help the family out with food and chores and small monetary contributions. Churches were built by residents, and became an important part of each community. One source of pride for mill town inhabitants was the mill ball team when baseball gained popularity in the early 1900s.[81] A rivalry between the teams of two cross-town mill towns in Henderson, North Carolina, resulted in an annual July 4th ball game in which participants "'played ball for nine innings' then 'fight for two or three hours.'"[82] Milltown culture did not develop in isolation at each mill; millworkers who moved from mill to mill looking for better pay or better conditions spread the culture. One journalist referred to the Piedmont as "one long mill village."[83]

The culture of the mill towns was defined by the unique relationship between workers and those owning and supervising mills and the towns. The mills were pervaded by a form of paternalism that derived from the paternalism of the Old South. At its best, it inspired mill owners to help the workers when they needed help. A good worker who got sick might be kept on the payroll for a while, and workers might get a small Christmas bonus if the company was doing well. But paternalism is always a relationship between people who are not equal, and so the mill owner would talk of doing this or that for "my" people, conjuring up images of the slaveholder saying the same thing about his slaves. Mill owners frequently donated land for churches for millworkers, funds to build the churches, parsonages for the ministers, and sometimes even a yearly contribution to church operating expenses because they believed religion was good for them and, not coincidentally, that church-going people made better employees.[84] One such church in Clinton, South Carolina, had a picture of the mill owner on one side of the vestibule of the church and a picture of Jesus on the other. Indeed, the owner's power and control over the worker was almost god-like—he owned his job, his house, and possibly even his church. As one government study concluded in 1910:

> The president, agent, or superintendent is the mill official usually vested with dictatorial power. His will is supreme in the village; his decisions final, so long as they do not conflict with the laws of the state. He usually controls the community affairs of all in a benevolent and judicious manner.[85]

---

81. *Ibid., pp.* 125–180.

82. Daniel Clark, *Like Night and Day: Unionization in a Southern Mill Town* (Chapel Hill, NC: University of North Carolina Press, 1997), 14.

83. Jacquelyn Dowd Hall, Jim Leloudis, et al., *Like a Family, 144.*

84. *Ibid.,* 124–125. William Hayes Simpson, *Southern Textile Communities* (Charlotte, NC: American Cotton Manufacturers Association, 1948), 71–73; Melton McLaurin, *Paternalism and Protest: Southern Cotton Mill Workers and Organized Labor, 1875–1905* (Westport: Greenwood, 1971), 38–39.

85. *Report on Condition of Women and Child Wage-Earners in the United States, Vol. 1: Cotton Textile Industry* (Washington: Government Printing Office, 1910), 537.

It was, in many ways, all very personal: the mill owner or manager might know the names of each member of a mill family and the fact that the eldest boy played on the ball team, but he also might, as one mill owner did, "chide" women who smoked on their front porches. Workers, for their part, did not necessarily appreciate the meddling and control—"It was almost like slavery" one told an interviewer—but they understood.[86] "Fatherly authority"—paternalism—was, as we saw, deeply embedded in the pre-war culture of the Piedmont within the family (as patriarchy) and between the classes.[87] Thus, wives were expected to obey husbands within the family, an unruly crowd of men could be "dispersed" (usually) by the admonitions of gentlemen, and a gentleman could, during the war, create a regiment led by himself and recruit enough willing local small farmers to fill the ranks. It is not such a leap to understand how desperately poor farmers and tenants after the war could accept the expanded authority exercised by mill owners who offered in exchange jobs and housing.

Paternalism, like all values, would evolve. In the decade before World War I, some owners, inspired by new progressive ideas about management and not coincidentally concerned about workforce turnover and public criticism of dirty mill towns and ill-educated, poorly clothed workers, attempted to beautify the towns, and "provide new social services to their employees." The larger companies began to hire welfare workers who counseled workers, instructed the ladies in proper housekeeping techniques and how to raise their children, and organized wholesome recreational activities.[88] But many owners still dealt with certain problems the old-fashioned way. Wilt Browning notes in *Linthead*, his memoir of growing up in a mill town in the 1940s and 1950s:

> For the most part, though, drinking never became much of a community problem because of a rule that was brilliant in its simplicity: "You get drunk and cause a fuss on Saturday night" Juber [Hairston] said, "and Monday'd be moving day."

> There was no appeal, no trial by jury. No presumption of innocence. Nothing but a summons to the super's [the mill supervisor] office on Monday morning to answer for the binge Saturday night. Final. Effective.[89]

Given the similarities between the Old South's attitudes about slave labor and the New South's attitudes about factory labor, it is not surprising that

86. Jacquelyn Dowd Hall, Jim Leloudis, et al., *Like a Family*, 121–124.

87. Allen Tullos, *Habits of Industry: White Culture and the Transformation of the Carolina Piedmont* (Chapel Hill: University of North Carolina Press, 1989), 77, 82–83.

88. Jacquelyn Dowd Hall, Jim Leloudis, et al., *Like a Family*, 131–140.

89. Wilt Browning, *Linthead: Growing Up in a Carolina Cotton Mill Village* (Ashboro, NC: Down Home Press, 1991), 110. See also Douglas Flamming, *Creating the Modern South: Millhands and Managers in Dalton, Georgia, 1884–1984* (Chapel Hill: University of North Carolina Press, 1992), 134.

unions were bitterly opposed by mill owners and their supporters. The union movement sweeping the industrial regions of the United States in the late 1800s and early decades of the 1900s did not do well in the South, and it would be and remains today the least unionized region of the country. Southern workers, living in small, widely dispersed villages, were difficult to organize. Some historians have argued that Southern workers' values, which emphasized family and personal relationships, made them naturally skeptical of the "new" kind of formal community that unions represented. Workers often did not see themselves as a permanent part of an industrial working class worth fighting for, and, as one historian has noted, "The worker often 'appreciated' his job and deferred to the leadership of the gentry."[90] There was and is an element of truth to all of this. But looming even larger was the mill owners' reaction to union activity.

During the first flurry of union organizing in the South at the turn of the twentieth century, a common response by mill owners was to fire workers associated with union organizing and kick them and their families out of company-owned houses. If there was a strike, sometimes the entire workforce was fired. In Rowan County, North Carolina, for example, three strikes were launched by workers from June 1900 to June 1901. All three ended with the firing of the striking workers and their replacement. One of the strikes involved workers at a textile mill; these strikers were also evicted from company-owned housing. [91] As a government report noted in 1910, "The suddenness and completeness with which the union movement of 1900 was suppressed have prevented any similar movement since that time."[92]

Even after the passage of federal labor laws in the 1930s recognizing the legality of unions, such responses were still not uncommon. For example, in Darlington, South Carolina in the late summer of 1956, workers at the Darlington Manufacturing Company (a textile mill) voted 256 to 248 to organize a chapter of the Textile Workers Union of America. On October 17 the stockholders of the company that owned a majority interest in the plant, Deering Millikin, voted to close the plant. The next day workers were laid off, and over 500 people lost their jobs. A petition was circulated by the laid off workers that begged the company to reconsider. Eighty-three percent of the workers signed the petition. Roger Millikin, the president of Deering Millikin and known for his strong anti-union sentiments, refused to consider reopening the plant saying of the petition, "As long as there are 17% of these hardcore labor people

90. McLaurin, *Paternalism and Protest*, p. 205; Allen Tullos, *Habits of Industry*, xiii; George B. Tindall, *The Emergence of the New South, 1913–1945* (Baton Rouge: Louisiana State University Press, 1967), quote 523.
91. Beck, "Development in the Piedmont South," 245–248.
92. *Report on Condition of Women and Child Wage-Earners in the United States, Vol. I*, 610.

here, I refuse to run the mill."[93] A complaint was filed by the union with the National Labor Relations Board. After almost two decades of appeals, the U.S. Supreme Court finally ruled that the layoff violated labor law and was intended to "chill unionism."[94] Some of the workers who had voted to join the union those many years past couldn't enjoy the belated satisfaction brought by this decision—they had died. When unions were able to establish a foothold in a mill, often it was only a temporary victory.

The Harriet Henderson mills (Henderson, NC) were unionized in the 1940s, but by 1958, the president of the mills, John D. Cooper, Jr., had decided to break the union once and for all. He proposed important changes in the union contract when it came up for renewal, changes he was loath to compromise on. When the workers went out on strike, Cooper brought in strikebreakers—easy to find in a region filled with people desperate for work—and a virtual war broke out between the workers and Cooper and his strikebreakers. The mills were peppered with gunfire, cars were shot at, and homes were dynamited, including the home of mill vice-president Marshall Cooper. The local law enforcement community apparently sympathized with the strikers, so Cooper asked the Governor to send in the highway patrol. At one point a sizable percentage of the state highway patrol was stationed in Henderson; later, the Governor dispatched National Guard troops. Many of the strikers were arrested on a variety of charges (more than 60 strikers and strike sympathizers were convicted), and several key strike leaders were among those convicted of conspiring to bomb the boiler room at the Harriet mill and an electric substation. By 1961 the strike was broken and the union was driven out.[95] Some strikers were ultimately allowed to return to work (most never returned), but according to one resident, they were segregated in one plant and were supervised by a former union official.[96] Cooper understood the value of a living object lesson for his new non-union workforce. A willingness to go to the mat like Cooper did was not exceptional; even as late as the 1970s, an executive of a national textile corporation told one of the authors, "If the unions push us, there will be bloodshed."

Mill work was often an improvement, in terms of living conditions and opportunities, over the life provided by sharecropping. Mill housing was often much better than the one and two room shacks many "croppers" lived in, and the wages paid an entire family could at least keep everyone clothed, fed, and warm in the winter, even if the lifestyle of most mill workers could hardly be called abundant. There were opportunities for upward mobility: one could be-

---

93. Bill Arthur, "The Darlington Mill Case: Or 17 Years Before the Courts," *New South*, Col. 28, No. 3, Summer 1973: 40.

94. *Ibid.*

95. Clark, *Like Night and Day*, 145, 168–198.

96. Interview with James Wheeler, 29 March 2004.

come a mill supervisor or open a small store, restaurant or honky-tonk bar, which catered to friends and neighbors. While many mill workers moved from mill to mill, and others struggled to get out of mill work, by the mid-twentieth century it would not be unusual to find families who had worked in the same mill and lived in the same mill town for several generations. For many, then, mill work and the mill town, limited and limiting though they were, did provide workers with a sense of stability, predictability, and security that is lacking in the modern world of mobility and opportunity. "Lucky is the man who does not secretly believe that every possibility is open to him," Southern novelist Walker Percy once observed.[97]

Figure 2.3   Mr. Bost's Café

People often remember the hardships of the past as something they overcame, and many who worked in mills or sharecropped took pride in how they could work long hours in often unpleasant conditions, make do on little money, and bear up to pain and tragedy without complaint. In living this hard life, both blacks and whites created cultures that were vibrant and alive and would ultimately shape American popular culture. The traditional music of rural whites would become country music, and its themes reflected the lives of hard-working, hard-living people. The blues grew out of the experiences of rural African Americans and was developed by blues artists who took the music to the towns and cities. Both whites and blacks developed rich folklore traditions—stories and tales told again and again—that shaped how people

---

97. Walker Percy, *The Last Gentleman* (New York: Ivy Books, 1966), 1.

understood the world and each other and that still inform the Southern literary tradition. This culture was at its most vibrant on the fringes, the margins. In South Henderson was Moccasin Bottom, a mill neighborhood described in 1927 along with a similar neighborhood in the area as "the haunts of the bootleggers, rum runners, of gamblers, and the roughnecks. Just the same, here is the place you will find the few free men in the village, the scrapers and the well-fed folks. Here you find the people not afraid to talk [the commentator was a union organizer] and not afraid to fight."[98] In the 1950s and 1960s this same neighborhood has been described by two former residents as a tough place, the toughest in the area, where bootleggers sold liquor by the bottle and the shot, and the famous Mrs. Cutts, proprietor of the Loafers' Inn, kept her unruly poolroom clientele in line with a bullwhip and drove to the liquor store to replenish her stock in a big, rumbling, lime green Plymouth Roadrunner. A man could lose his paycheck or his car in a card game, and a bad batch of moonshine could cost him his eyesight or his life. But Moccasin Bottom was also a place where folks "stuck together," where children could roam at night without fear (if they were white and from the area), and a man earned respect by doing what he said, paying his bills, and not backing down. Women from the Salvation Army visited the bootleggers' joints on payday soliciting contributions, and the bootleggers would settle the men down by calling out "There's ladies present." Cock fights could be found on a Saturday night, and, yes, free men still walked the streets, the sort who would inspire country singers like Johnny Cash.[99]

But make no mistake: poverty does grind people down. For one thing, it makes people sick. When public health professionals began surveying the health conditions of the South in the early 1900s, they found pellagra, hookworm, and malaria in epidemic proportions. One study of the diets of mill families in North Carolina and Georgia found that less than half met the standards of the Atlanta prison, which was not, one assumes, a very high standard.[100] In a region rich with natural resources, moderate climate, and fertile land, indeed one of the richest agricultural regions in the world, many people were suffering from diseases resulting from not enough of the right kinds of food and unsanitary living conditions. Pellagra—a niacin deficiency—was "prevalent in rural areas and mill towns" early in the twentieth century until public health educational efforts began to pay off and the incidence of the disease declined.[101] Pellagra sapped the

---

98. Alfred Hoffman, "Henderson or—Hell" (Philadelphia: American Federation of Labor, 1927).

99. Interviews, James Wheeler, 29 March 2004, 1 April 2004; Earl Sorrel, 29 March 2004; 29 April 2004.

100. C. Vann Woodward, *Origins of the New South: 1877–1913* (Baton Rouge: Louisiana State University Press, 1951), 420.

101. Tindall, *The Emergence of the New South, 1913–1945*, 277–279.

energy out of those afflicted with it; their faces were often marked by a distinctive rash shaped like a butterfly. As one affluent Alabama woman recalled:

> You cannot imagine the change pellagra made in children. The poor white children were very pale and thin with stringy hair. The textile mill children always looked thin and pale and had white hair and white eyebrows and eyelashes. The poor black children always looked ashen.[102]

Parasites were also a problem; nearly 40% of the children examined during a campaign launched by the Rockefeller Sanitary Commission for the Eradication of Hookworm Disease had hookworm, a parasite that burrowed into a bare foot, entered the blood stream, and left its victim feeling weak and listless.[103]

Poverty also took its toll psychologically. The children of mill workers and sharecroppers sometimes felt the sting of prejudice from more affluent town children because of their clothes. The adults heard or at least knew the nasty names—"cracker," "redneck," "linthead" for whites, something worse for blacks—and the looks, the blocked opportunities, the constant struggle could make people bitter, filled with resentment and hatred or lost in hopelessness. Journalist James Agee and photographer Walker Evans spent weeks in 1936 visiting several Alabama sharecropper families, and Agee even lived with one family (they're called the Gudgers in the book) for a while. Agee found them decent, generous people despite their terrible poverty. He imagined how one female member of the Gudger family looked at her circumstances:

> How did we get caught? Why is it things always seem to go against us? Why is it there can't ever be any pleasure in living? I'm so tired it don't seem like I ever could get rest enough. I'm as tired when I get up in the morning as I am when I lay down at night. Sometimes it seems like there wouldn't never be no end to it, nor even a let-up. One year it'll look like things was going to be pretty good; but you get a little bit of money saved, something always happens.
>
> I tell you I won't be sorry when I die. I wouldn't be sorry this minute if it wasn't for Louise and Squinchy-here.[104]

Similarly, novelist Reynolds Price found his classmates from the countryside and the mill community (circa 1930s) "steeped in agrarian or proletarian fatalism."[105] If resignation was one response to poverty, drink was and was another; others tried to find solace in the highly personal religion of the region. Anger and

---

102. Hollinger F. Barnard, *Outside the Magic Circle: The Autobiography of Virginia Foster Durr* (University, Alabama: University of Alabama Press, 1985), 31.

103. *Ibid.*, 425–427.

104. James Agee and Walker Evans (with an introduction by John Hersey), *Let Us Now Praise Famous Men* (1941; Boston: Houghton Mifflin Co., 1988), 80.

105. Reynolds Price, *Clear Pictures: First Loves, First Guides* (New York: Atheneum, 1989), 171.

resentment was yet another response. In William Faulkner's short story "Barn Burning," Snopes, a white sharecropper, observes to his son about the large white house of his new landlord: " 'Pretty and white, ain't it?' he said. 'That's sweat. Nigger sweat. Maybe it ain't white enough yet to suit him. Maybe he wants to mix some white sweat with it.' " After a dispute with the landlord, Snopes burns his barn. This was not the first barn he had burned.[106] The angers and resentments of less affluent whites (and other whites, too) could also be directed at a scapegoat: black Southerners. Clever politicians—Georgia's Hoke Smith, Alabama's George Wallace, and North Carolina's Jesse Helms are prime examples—would exploit this knowledge to win elections. Poor blacks had to deal with this and the poverty.

The Middle

Just as before the Civil War, the "middle" of the class system consisted primarily of small farmers; despite the troubles afflicting agriculture, the number of small farmers owning land actually increased in many parts of the South and would really only begin to fall after World War II.[107] Between 750,000 and 1 million of these farmers could be found in the region by 1900. Amazingly, a significant number of African Americans, many of them former slaves, were able to acquire land after the Civil War and become small landowners; by 1900, for example, African Americans owned over one million acres in Georgia.[108] But owning land did not necessarily assure a family of a comfortable livelihood and membership in the middle class; small farmers who owned small parcels of land (less than 100 acres) were often no better off than sharecroppers. President Jimmy Carter recalled of his childhood years in Georgia in the 1930s, "I knew a number of small farmers who owned their own land. Most of them were white, of course, and it was their children who came to our church and were my classmates in school. Many of them were as poor as black day laborers...."[109] Carter's father owned a productive farm of 350 acres, a holding which placed the Carters squarely in the middle or upper middle of the small farmer class in the region. The family mingled freely both with the more affluent families of the area and the less affluent. Carter described his house as "typical of those occupied by middle-income landowners of the time": it had a "broad front porch" and "rooms that were laid out in 'shotgun' style, with a hall that went down the middle of the house dividing

---

106. William Faulkner, "Barn Burning" in *Collected Stories*, 3–26.

107. Gavin Wright, *Old South, New South: Revolutions in the Southern Economy Since the Civil War* (New York: Basic Books, Inc., 1986), 111–112, 245.

108. Gilbert C. Fite, *Cotton Fields No More: Southern Agriculture, 1865–1980* (Lexington, KY: University Press of Kentucky, 1984), 32–39; Wright, *Old South, New South*, 106.

109. Fite, *Cotton Fields No More*, 32–33; Jimmy Carter, *An Hour Before Daylight*, 28.

the living room, dining room, and kitchen on the left side from three bedrooms on the right," and it was surrounded by a white sand yard the family periodically swept. The house was heated by fireplaces, the cooking was done on a wood burning stove, and, until indoor plumbing was installed, the water was drawn from a well in the yard, and the family used a privy in the back yard.[110]

In many ways, the lives of small farmers changed very little in the 70 years following the Civil War. Animal power—the mule—and human muscle did most of the work into the 1930s and beyond; even as late as the 1950s many farmers were still plowing with mules, and the trade in the animal was still big business. It was not uncommon as late as the 1930s (and even later) for small farmers, particularly the ones with larger holdings of land, to grow or raise much of what the family ate. Farmwomen canned vegetables and fruits, and every fall, on many farms, the entire family participated in butchering hogs and putting up the meat in a smokehouse. The primary labor on the small farm was still family members and everyone, from the youngest to the oldest, did some form of work. Some small farmers had a few tenants, but most relied on day labor to supplement family members during planting season or harvest. Jimmy Carter's father had a farm hand to help him, hired day laborers, and also had some tenants.[111]

Small farmers often lived in a tight community of kin. Ben Robertson, in *Red Hills and Cotton*, wrote of his own kin in the piedmont region of South Carolina:

> Most of my kinfolks, when I was growing up, were located on Pea Ridge between Glassy and Six Mile Mountains, on a long rise of fine cotton country between two lonely spurs of pine-grown granite—we lived and some of us still live in the winding open valley of a river called Twelve Mile. The rest of our kinfolks live to the west of us; they have their houses along both banks of the river Keowee.[112]

Robertson also gives us a good insight into the values of white small farmers: "We are farmers, all Democrats and Baptists—a strange people, complicated and simple and proud and religious and family-loving, a divorceless, Bible-reading murderous lot of folks, all of us rich in ancestry and steeped in tradition and emotionally quick on the trigger." He also observed that:

---

110. Fite, *Cotton Fields No More*, 32; Carter, *An Hour Before Daylight*, 29–31, 44; quotes, p. 29.

111. Carter, *An Hour Before Daylight*, 32–44; U.S. Bureau of the Census, *Fifteenth Census of the United States: 1930, Agriculture, Vol. III, pt. 2—Southern States*, (Washington: Government Printing Office, 1932), 109–111, 227–233; Fite, *Cotton Fields No More*, 33–34.

112. Ben Robertson, *Red Hills and Cotton: An Upcountry Memoir* (Columbia, SC: University of South Carolina Press, 1973), 6.

We believe in self-reliance, in self-improvement, in progress as the theory of history, in loyalty, in total abstinence, in total immersion, in faithfulness, righteousness, justice, in honoring our parents, in living without disgrace. We have chosen asceticism because all our lives we have had to fight an inclination to license—we know how narrow the gulf between asceticism and complete indulgence; we have always known much concerning the far outer realms, the extremes. We have tried throughout our lives to keep the Commandments, we have set for ourselves one of the strictest, sternest codes in existence, but our country is Southern and we are Southern, and frequently we fail.[113]

What **was** changing for the small farmer was a growing involvement in the market economy that undercut the independence and self-reliance that Thomas Jefferson and others had celebrated as the most important virtue of the small farmer. Small farmers were increasingly producing cotton and tobacco and other cash crops, and if many tried to maintain the old self-sufficiency, many others were putting more acreage into cotton or tobacco and buying their food and clothing in stores. Bankers, merchants, and warehouse operators became a bigger and bigger part of the lives of small farmers, and the fluctuations of the market became more and more important to them. When prices plummeted and debts weren't paid, a man could lose his land, and many did. The town, not the countryside, was now the focal point of this new market economy; the town and industry prospered while farming and the countryside struggled and seemed to be in a slow but steady decline. The unease of small farmers at this prospect fueled a resentment that has still not run its course. Politically, it first manifested itself in the Populist movement of the 1880s and 1890s when small farmers in the Midwest and South protested the decline of farming and the agrarian lifestyle and worked to establish laws and government programs that would protect the farmer.[114] Rural unrest would bubble up again and again and would continue long after the fortunes of the small farmer were beyond redemption.

The other part of the middle after the Civil War were the grocers, shoe repair shop owners, country storekeepers, owners of service stations (after the advent of the automobile), mill foremen, bank tellers, teachers, preachers, and clerks who worked in the growing small towns, cities, and crossroads settlements of the region. These town folk would grow in numbers and importance as the farming folk declined in numbers and importance, but this transformation would take a long time, and the urban middle class would remain quite small until after World War II. At the upper end of the urban middle class were the successful lawyers, doctors, bank officers and proprietors of large stores;

---

113. *Ibid.*, pp. 9–10.
114. Steven Hahn, *The Roots of Populism*, 137–203.

these individuals and their families really were more a part of the local upper class. At the lower end, many members of this emerging urban middle class lived very modestly, and some were little better off than the mill workers or sharecroppers; it was not uncommon for example, for mill foremen to live in mill towns in houses only slightly bigger than the homes of the people they supervised. Harvie Bost opened a café in the mid-1930s in the furniture manufacturing town of Statesville, North Carolina. Bost's café was tiny and plain — little more than a counter with a half dozen or so stools — but he made enough to afford a small brick house. Bost always wore a white shirt, buttoned at the neck, even when he was fishing at the beach.[115] With such small differences separating most middle class families from those in the working class, propriety, manners, and proper dress were almost an obsession with many middle class families. As sociologist John Dollard noted in his study of a small Southern town the 1930s, "Middle class people must stress sharply the differences between themselves and the lower class whites and Negroes because they are none too sure the differences are very important or permanent."[116] Many middle class families of modest means in Darlington, South Carolina, the boyhood home of one of the authors (1960s), proudly displayed coats of arms in their homes to "document" that they had descended from aristocracy and that there were, in effect, "important and permanent" differences between them and other people.

On the black side, a small but significant group of landowning farmers could be found sprinkled across the region who, with the preachers, teachers, Pullman car porters, funeral home owners, and small storeowners, formed a tiny black middle class. Middle class blacks also worked to differentiate themselves from their less affluent neighbors, perhaps more so than whites, because if the material advantages middle class folk had over poor folk on the white side was small, it was miniscule for blacks given their limited opportunities for advancement. Education, proper speech and dress, and mannerly behavior were thus very important for middle class blacks. The humiliations of segregation had to be avoided as best one could; one interviewee in the PBS series *Take Me to Chicago* remembers that his father, a teacher, went to the segregated movie house only once — to see the Joe Louis/Max Smeling fight. With that exception, he refused to climb the steps to sit in what was called the "buzzard's roost." Only in the bigger towns and cities like Durham, North Carolina, or Atlanta would there have been much of an upper middle class.[117] Here a thriving black business community centered in all-black areas — Hayti in Durham,

---

115. Interview with Wendy Lapish, 20 November 2005.

116. John Dollard, *Caste and Class in a Southern Town* (1937; Garden City, NY: Doubleday Anchor Books, 1949), 77.

117. *Ibid*, 83–92; Wright, *Old South, New South*, 104–106; *The Promised Land: Take Me to Chicago*, video (Bethesda, MD: The Discovery Channel, c. 1995).

Sweet Auburn in Atlanta—was able to make enough from a black clientele to "move up."

Common Values Across Class and Race Lines

When Ben Robertson referred to his kin as "proud and religious and family-loving," and as a "Bible-reading murderous lot of folks" who were "emotionally quick on the trigger," he identified the two touchstones of the prewar moral code which persisted after the war not only with small farmers but also with sharecroppers, millworkers, and town folk. Honor—family name and reputation—continued to loom large in the moral universe of both white and black, and evangelical Christianity actually extended its reach. As we have seen, honor's enforcer was violence, and violence was still a common response to insult, slight, and female infidelity. Jimmy Carter's great grandfather was knifed to death in a dispute with his business partner over, of all things, a merry-go-round, and his grandfather was shot and killed in a dispute over a desk. His great grandfather's assailant fled the state to escape a trial; his grandfather's assailant was tried three times and never convicted. As his uncle Buddy noted, "Taliaferro [the man who murdered his grandfather] had a lot of kinfolks in the county, and some of his drinking buddies were always on the jury."[118] As the twentieth century progressed, this sort of mayhem seems to have diminished among the more "respectable" (i.e. middle class) folk (no latter day Carters apparently have been murdered), but Southern prisons were filled with less affluent blacks and whites who had committed precisely these sorts of crimes, and the South has led the nation in homicides and assaults. As John Reed has pointed out, "The homicides in which the South seems to specialize are those in which someone is being killed by someone he (or often she) knows, for reasons both killer and victim understand."[119]

Vigilantism—mob enforced honor—also persisted in the South well into the twentieth century and for most of that time—nearly a century—was best characterized as white mobs pursuing black victims, although other minority groups, spouse-abusing white husbands, and disreputable white women sometimes experienced the wrath of a mob. Lynchings carried out by mobs reached epidemic proportions in the region in the late 1800s and early 1900s. A lynching was typically precipitated by the commission of, or the **rumor** of the commission of, an "outrage," generally the alleged rape of a white woman by a black man. Lynching was a tool of racial control, but lynching also reflected the old idea that retribution and vengeance were each householder's

---

118. Carter, *An Hour Before Daylight*, 235–240.
119. John Reed, "Below the Smith and Wesson Line," *One South*, 144.

responsibility, and whites and even women were sometimes lynched. Lynchings generally fit a pattern: following an "outrage" or rumor of one, a suspect was identified (often by the "rumor mill"), and a mob gathered and apprehended the suspect, who was generally tortured and finally killed.[120] Lynchings would decline in number as the twentieth century progressed and in the size of the mob doing the deed; by the 1950s they would be furtive affairs carried out by a few men.

Organized vigilantes—white caps, Knights of the Camellia, or the more well-known Ku Klux Klan—served as a shadowy police force enforcing "order." Vigilantism, whether carried out by impromptu mobs or by organized groups like the Klan, claimed participants from all social classes early on. Indeed the first Klan, active in the 1860s and early 1870s "drew from among the best citizens in areas in which it rode." It was strongest in the piedmont and upland South, that region most influenced by the Scots-Irish culture that fostered the *lex talionis*. It served primarily as the terrorist arm of the Democratic Party in its war with the multi-racial Republican Party and declined when the Democratic Party became dominant.[121] A second Ku Klux Klan was officially launched on the night of Thanksgiving, 1915, at Stone Mountain, Georgia. It was the brainchild of an Alabama man working in the new field of marketing. Historian Nancy MacLean's research suggests it was primarily a middle and lower middle class organization, more urban than rural, with little appeal to poor whites or affluent whites. It seemed to have special appeal to small proprietors who had moved up from less promising beginnings.[122] It condemned blacks, Catholics, foreigners, men who drank too much, and illicit lovers, and wrongdoers might experience the late night visit from robed Klansmen who might threaten, whip, or worse. The Klan that resurged in the 1950s and 1960s in response to the Civil Rights movement was even further down the class ladder in its appeal and performed a rearguard defense of segregation that entailed murdering civil rights workers, blowing up homes and churches, and threatening integrationists.

The last **major** incident of vigilantism in the South occurred in 1979 when a caravan of 35 armed Ku Klux Klansman and American Nazis drove to a "Death to the Klan" rally organized by a group of mostly white, mostly college educated members of the Communist Workers Party in a poor, predominately black part of Greensboro, North Carolina. The Communists were expecting trouble; some were armed. A gun battle ensued; seven rally participants were

120. Joel Williamson, *Rage for Order: Black-White Relations in the American South Since Emancipation* (New York and Oxford: Oxford University Press, 1986), 124–126.

121. David M. Chalmers, *Hooded Americanism: The History of the Ku Klux Klan* (Durham, NC: Duke University Press, 1987), 9–10.

122. Nancy MacLean, *Behind the Mask of Chivalry: The Making of the Second Ku Klux Klan* (New York: Oxford University Press, 1994), 4–5, 54–55.

wounded, and five were killed; no Klansmen or Nazis were shot in a massacre that was captured on videotape. Klansmen and Nazis were twice tried and acquitted of criminal charges despite the videotape clearly showing them shooting some of their victims execution-style. Apparently the jury bought the defense's argument that they were only acting in self-defense. Probably, too, the jurors were thinking, "You chant 'death to the Klan,' you deserve what you asked for." In fact, at the beginning of the attack, one of the Klansmen (a paid police informant) shouted, "You asked for the Klan! Now you've got 'em!"[123]

The South truly became the "Bible Belt" after the Civil War as hundreds and hundreds of new evangelical Christian churches—Baptist especially—were established on rural lanes, in mill towns, and in the expanding cities and towns of the region.[124] These churches and the Pentecostal and Holiness churches that began spreading out across the region after the turn of the twentieth century exhorted members even more stridently than before the war to live a Christian lifestyle and to turn their backs on dancing, cursing, gambling, and drinking in any amount. While they continued to support male authority in the family, increasingly they held up the traditional feminine virtues—passivity, humbleness, and faithfulness—as the model for Christian behavior. Churches launched a virtual war on the male subculture that drew men away from this model and established standards of respectability for working class and middle class folk. A flurry of laws (often called blue laws) poured forth from Southern legislatures that were designed to control if not eliminate the most objectionable vices. At the top of the list was drinking. Responding to pressure from churches and church influenced groups like the Anti-Saloon League and the Women's Christian Temperance Union, many Southern state legislatures passed laws that regulated alcohol sales, if not prohibiting them entirely, long before national prohibition was enacted.[125] Even after national prohibition was rescinded, much of the South remained "dry" until the 1970s, and the region was characterized by a crazy quilt of local and state laws that ranged from outright prohibition to limited retail sales (in North Carolina, for example, only the state could sell liquor in its "ABC" stores) and the famous "brown bagging" that permitted drinkers to bring their beverage of choice to a licensed restaurant or private club in a brown bag. This "legal" approach paid off: nightclubs, bars, and "social" drinking occupied a much less prominent part of respectable social life than was the case in the rest of the country. Indeed, in much of the South, proscribed

123. PBS Online, "88 Seconds in Greensboro," *Frontline* broadcast, 24 January 1983, http://www.pbs.org/wgbh/pages/frontline .

124. C. Vann Woodward, *Origins of the New South*, 170; 448–449.

125. *Ibid.*, 171; 389–392; Ted Owenby, *Subduing Satan,*170–177; 203–210; James Sellers, *The Prohibition Movement in Alabama, 1702–1943* (Chapel Hill, NC: University of North Carolina Press, 1943), 86–189; Daniel J. Whitener, *Prohibition in North Carolina, 1715–1945* (Chapel Hill, The University of North Carolina Press, 1945), 116–171.

recreations went "underground" even when laws technically permitted the activity, and gambling, drinking and even music and dancing took place in storerooms behind gas stations, back rooms in country stores, "shot houses," county line juke joints, and private clubs. In these places a morally suspect culture flourished that reputable people might slip away to on occasion. If a drink was offered at a home one was visiting, it might be consumed in the kitchen, standing up—a guilty pleasure; in male company, drinking took place around a campfire, in a workshop or the backyard, quickly, furtively, liquor sipped from the bag, straight, maybe chased with a swig of cola. Moonshine, illegally produced homemade liquor—corn liquor usually—was produced throughout the region. Jimmy Carter recalls both the "furtive" tradition and a more open acceptance of recreational pleasure among the adults he observed during his boyhood. "Everyone knew my daddy liked to have a good time," he notes. His father built a small cabin on his farm equipped with a pool table and a jukebox where he hosted parties for the local "gentry" featuring beer, wine and whiskey, and dancing. These affairs were for the adults. When the local farm couples were invited over, it was a family affair, children included, with sweet tea and chicken and the more wholesome square dancing. The men, however, would sneak outside to sip moonshine.[126] So organized religion's attempts at "taming" Southerners, especially less affluent males, was only partially successful. As Ben Robertson observed, "we have set for ourselves one of the strictest, sternest codes in existence, but our country is Southern and we are Southern, and frequently we fail."

The Upper Class: Planters, Merchants, Urban Professionals, and Mill Owners

After the Civil War, the growth of commercial agriculture, the expansion of the railroad network, and the growth of industry resulted in a boom in small cities, towns and crossroads settlements. The more successful businessmen who presided over these growing towns and cities became a key part of a new "hybrid" upper class that consisted of the wealthy and a relatively small class of comfortable "good" families (what might be termed today an "upper middle class") that merged imperceptibly with the wealthy. Some members of this affluent class belonged to "old" families that had been part of the slaveholding plantation class for generations; others were upwardly mobile people from humbler beginnings. As Clarence Cason has noted:

> Those natives who possess considerable wealth may be known as Bourbons; those next in the scale may compose the middle class....

---

126. Carter, *An Hour Before Daylight*, pp. 224–225.

But their inheritance of a southern way of life is more effective in emphasizing what these groups share in common than the economic difference could possibly be in separating them from each other.[127]

Planters were a key part of this new postwar upper class. Not everyone agrees with this assertion; a whole bevy of historians have championed the idea that affluent townfolk "with little but a nominal connection with the old planter regime" replaced the planters as the leaders of the "New South."[128] There is no question that towns emerged as the new centers of wealth after the war, nor is there any question that the war and the loss of their slaves dealt the planters a serious blow. Thomas Chaplin, master of Tombee plantation, was truly broken by the war. A portion of his land and his house at Tombee plantation had been seized during the war, and he contended with federal officials for over two decades trying to regain this property. He finally succeeded in 1890, 25 years after the war ended. During this period, Chaplin struggled with opium addiction and drifted from one poorly paying job to another; at one point, irony of ironies, he taught in a school for the children of former slaves.[129] But many planters did not end up like Chaplin. In the rich plantation districts such as the Mississippi-Yazoo Delta and the Black Belt of Alabama and elsewhere where the land was flat and the soil was fertile, planters continued to own large landholdings and grow large crops of cotton with the help of sharecroppers, and continued to hold much of the area's wealth and political power well into the twentieth century. Delta planters, for example, remained at "the very top of the region's socioeconomic and political pyramid" seventy years after the end of the war, and even today exercise considerable clout in this region of rich land and poor people.[130] Planters persisted elsewhere, too; Henry Wiencek found Judge Peter Wilson Hairston (the grandson of the Peter Hairston men-

---

127. Clarence E. Cason, "Middle Class and Bourbon," in William T. Couch, ed. *Culture in the South* (Chapel Hill, NC: University of North Carolina Press, 1934), 500. Anthropologist Hortense Powdermaker could find only a "middle class" in the town she studied in the 1930s but what she seemed to actually describe was more an upper class as the term is used here. See *After Freedom: A Cultural Study in the Deep South* (New York: Atheneum, 1939), 15.

128. Woodward, *Origins of the New South*, 20. See for other examples of the middle class thesis David L Carlton, *Mill and Town in South Carolina, 1880–1920* (Baton Rouge and London, Louisiana State University Press, 1982) 13–14, 26–27; Lacy K. Ford, "Rednecks and Merchants: Economic Development and Social Tensions in the South Carolina Upcountry, 1865–1900," *Journal of American History, LXXI* (September 1984): 294–318.

129. Rosengarten, *Tombee*, 287–288; 291–295,"Journal," 713–716.

130. Cobb, *The Most Southern Place*, pp. 184. See for Alabama Jonathan M. Wiener, *Social Origins of the New South: Alabama, 1860–1885* (Baton Rouge: Louisiana State University Press, 1978), 8–14, 26–28. See also V.O. Key, Jr., *Southern Politics in State and Nation* (New York: 1949), 5–6; Jay R. Mandle, *The Roots of Black Poverty: The Southern Plantation Economy After the Civil War* (Durham, NC: Duke University Press, 1978), 15, 23, 50.

tioned earlier) presiding over the Cooleemee plantation manor (in North Carolina) in the mid-1990s, although by then Cooleemee was no longer a functional plantation.[131] In areas where the soil was less fertile and the land hilly, agriculture was less lucrative, and planters abandoned farming as a primary source of income and invested in stores, urban real estate, and factories. John Steele Henderson was never a planter like his father, although he owned substantial landholdings; instead, he practiced law, speculated in real estate, represented the Southern Railroad, and served several terms in Congress.[132]

The planters' most important resources before the war were land and slaves; after the war, they worked vigorously throughout the South to hold onto their land and establish a secure (and cheap) labor supply to replace their slaves. Planters wanted low taxes on land, an objective that sometimes put them at odds with the urban business leaders who saw taxes as a way of paying for the new town services—water, sewers, rail lines, libraries, schools—that spelled "progress" to them and also, not coincidentally, made their town properties more valuable. Planters had enough political clout to work out an understanding with mill owners, merchants and other urban interests: land taxes, and in fact taxes in general, would be kept low and economic development would not "upset" the social order, particularly the relationship between the races. Planters' low wage workforce was thus largely protected from competition with industrial employment in the region; industrial jobs were reserved for whites only so black sharecroppers, who constituted the majority of the sharecropper workforce in plantation areas, could not be lured to the mills and factories for higher wages. The exact terms of this understanding varied from state to state. Where planters and the plantation were strongest, taxes were lowest, government services fewest, opportunities for the less affluent most limited, and segregation the harshest. Where planters were weakest and not coincidentally most likely to have mercantile and industrial interests, taxes were higher, government services like schools and public colleges better developed, economic development more extensive, and segregation a bit less extreme.[133] This deal would hold up at least until the late 1960s, and the consequences would be, for much of the South, underfunded schools, especially for blacks, an absence of

---

131. Wiencek, *The Hairstons*, 283–291.

132. John Beck, "Building the New South: A Revolution from Above in a Piedmont County," *Journal of Southern History*, LIII (August 1987): 441–470. For a similar view on a "transformed" planter class see Michael Wayne, *The Reshaping of Plantation Society: The Natchez District, 1860–1880* (Baton Rouge and London: Louisiana State University Press, 1983), 203–204 and Harold D. Woodman, "Sequel to Slavery: The New History Views the Postbellum South," *Journal of Southern History*, XLIII (November 1977): 523–554.

133. Wiener, *Social Origins of the New South: Alabama, 1860–1885*, 91–93; 222–227; Michael Schwartz, *Radical Protest and Social Structure* (New York: Academic Press, 1976), 283–284; Beck, "Building the New South: A Revolution from Above in a Piedmont County," 467–470.

services governments elsewhere typically provided, and, of course, routine job discrimination against blacks. The effects linger on even today. An extreme example would be Alabama, a state where planters maintained substantial power long after the Civil War. Alabama today is 50th in the country in per capita taxation. Taxes on land are still extremely low, and the Alabama state tax code can only be revised by a constitutional amendment—a provision written into the state constitution over one hundred years ago. The tax system is heavily tilted in favor of large landowners and the rich: the poorest Alabamians pay 10.6% of their income in state and local taxes; the richest Alabamians pay 4.9% of their income in taxes. Not surprisingly, Alabama provides one of the lowest levels of government services in the nation; its prisons are terribly overcrowded, and its public schools are among the most poorly funded in the nation and rank at the bottom in terms of student performance.[134]

The more successful merchants, especially those in the towns, were important members of this new post war upper class. Smaller merchants, especially rural merchants, would have belonged more to the middle class of small farmers. Merchants made much of their income from extending high interest credit secured with liens on crops, land, and even wages, and sharecroppers, small farmers, millworkers, railroad workers, and others had credit accounts in local stores.[135] Because they took liens on the land of the small farmer, many merchants ended up owning sizeable landholdings acquired when small farmers couldn't pay their debts. Now, however, the truly valuable land was not farmland, but land in town. Merchants and lawyers and bankers worked vigorously to promote the towns they lived in and worked especially hard in the late 1800s to bring in the railroad. A railroad line and a growing population meant not only more customers for their businesses, but rising real estate prices. Then as now, real estate speculation was one of the better ways to become rich. In the 1880s and 1890s merchants began to invest in cotton mills and other industries, and often would invest in businesses in other towns when an opportunity seemed especially promising. Henry Belk, the son of a small slaveholding farmer, would become one of the more successful merchants of the region. He began his mercantile career as clerk in a store in Monroe, North Carolina. After 12 years of clerking, he bought his own store and later (1891) brought in

134. Dale Russakoff, "Alabama Tied in Knots by Tax Vote," *The Washington Post*, 17 August 2003, http://www.washingtonpost.com/ac2/wp-dyn/A4130-2003Aug16?language=printer ; Press Release, "Alabama's Taxes Hit Poor and Middle Class Far Harder than the Wealthy," Institute on Taxation and Economic Policy (Washington, D.C.) 7 January 2003, http://www.itepnet.org/wp2000/al%20pr.pdf .

135. Clarence E. Fesperman, transcript of interview by William F. Hennessee, Federal Writers Project, Life Histories Collection, North Carolina (microfilm, Southern Historical Collection, University of North Carolina at Chapel Hill); Richard Ransom and Robert Sutch, *One Kind of Freedom: The Economic Consequences of Emancipation* (Cambridge, Eng., and other cities, 1977), 160–168; Carlton, *Mill and Town in South Carolina*, 20–26.

his brother, a medical doctor, as a partner. The brothers, like many merchants, invested in a local cotton mill, but the Belks were more farsighted than most and began establishing new stores with partners in other towns. By 1915 Henry Belk lived in Charlotte and headed a regional chain of department stores that still plays an important role in the commerce of the South. In that year, the society page of the local newspaper grandly announced his impending marriage (he married late in life) to the daughter of "one of Charlotte's most prominent physicians and leading citizens."[136]

The early industrialists typically began their careers in some other line of work. Many were merchants like the Belks, some were bankers, some owned farms or plantations, and lawyers were well represented, too. David Y. Cooper was a tobacco warehouse owner in Henderson, North Carolina, who was being squeezed out of business by the emerging Duke family tobacco monopoly on one side and farmer discontent with his prices on the other. With the help of his brother, John D., and Henderson investors, he started a textile mill on the outskirts of town, which grew to two mills, each surrounded by its own mill village.[137] Frank Murdoch was the priest of St. Luke's Episcopal Church in Salisbury, North Carolina, who joined with several local merchants and a banker to start the first cotton mill in that town. By the early 1900s he had invested in four mills in Salisbury.[138] These industrialists were risk-takers and often lost money on bad investments. But they also often made money, big money. The successful ones accumulated much more wealth than most merchants could even imagine; they built elaborate homes, drove expensive automobiles, and not only sent their children to colleges but even built colleges like Duke University. Some industrialists, such as textile man James Cannon and tobacco man James "Buck" Duke, were so successful they joined the ranks of the wealthiest men in the United States.

While families like the Duke's had immense wealth, many families in this "hybrid" upper class, particularly the ones in the small towns and rural areas, seemed to be rather unprepossessing in their ownership of "things" and the nature of their occupations, especially to outsiders from more affluent places. The novelist and essayist V.S. Naipaul, for example, expressed surprise in his account of his travels through the South in the mid-1980s at the humbleness of the occupations—druggist and postmaster for example—of some of the upper class folks he met and opined that "class was something in the mind and consciousness of a family, related to an idea of good behavior and seemliness." On another occasion, he observed of Mississippi, "Unlike the Delta where

---

136. Le Gette Blythe, *William Henry Belk: Merchant of the South* (Chapel Hill: University of North Carolina, 1950), 37–39; 44–49; 107–109.

137. Clark, *Like Night and Day*, 9–11.

138. Beck, "Building the New South: A Revolution from Above in a Piedmont County," 468.

there were rich and poor and caste or class distinctions, in the hills there were no social distinctions, except between black and white."[139] No doubt Naipaul is right that class is "in the mind and consciousness," but there is more to it than mere self-definition. He committed a common mistake for the visitor, which is to miss the subtle distinctions in the places he is visiting. As we have seen, the South as a region was very poor for a long time (parts of it are still very poor), and this affected what people did for a living and what they accumulated. Virginia Durr notes of her own upper class childhood in Alabama during the early decades of the twentieth century, "It is difficult for those who didn't experience it to realize how poor the South was then. Despite Daddy's inheritance from Grandmother Foster, my family lived in genteel poverty, trying to keep our best foot forward on very little money. But we were surrounded by abject poverty." Her father owned land (quite a lot) which was worked by tenants, he was a Presbyterian minister for a time, and he sold insurance.[140] In an area where the typical person was a sharecropper or struggling small farmer or mill worker, the small town druggist with his store, comfortable house on Main Street, and two-year-old Buick was well-off. In short, wealth is a relative concept, but that does not make it any less real, and, just as importantly, the druggist, the large landowner, and the mill owner saw themselves as members of an upper class or at least among the "better families" and were perceived by others to be members of this group. But Naipaul is on to something that bears noting, however self-evident it is, and that is that class distinctions were and are less important (not nonexistent) where inequality is less pronounced.

While the planters persisted, their unchallenged domination of the South obviously did not, and this was probably the root of the laments about the passing of a way of life. Certainly Ashley Wilkes, the object of Scarlett's desire, voiced this lament as did William Alexander Percy in *Lanterns on the Levee*. Percy wrote in the 1930s, "As a class I suppose the Southern aristocrat is extinct, but what that class despised as vulgar and treasured as excellent is still despised and treasured by individuals scattered thickly from one end of the South to the other. Those individuals born into a world of tradesfolk are still aristocrats, with an uncanny ability to recognize their kind."[141] So Percy saw a world of "tradesfolk" (urban businessmen) despoiling the honor and tradition-bound world of the planter class, and while the "aristocratic virtues never die completely," for Percy that did not alter the fact that he belonged to "an aristocracy in the act of dying." But it wasn't dying; it was merely being transformed. It had been the dominant element in the upper class before the war, and now the urban industrialist/merchant/professional element, by dint of wealth and numbers, was becoming predominant.

---

139. V.S. Naipaul, *A Turn in the South* (New York: Alfred A. Knopf, 1989), pp. 170; 199.

140. Barnard, *Outside the Magic Circle*, p. 31, 36.

141. William Alexander Percy, *Lanterns on the Levee*, 62.

In truth, the postwar upper class was more profit oriented and competitive than the old planter class had been in business dealings, and, as a general rule, more committed to the ideas of progress and growth. Most were not interested in simply maintaining a way of life, but in creating a new way of life. However, contrary to William Alexander Percy's gloomy assessment, there were strong social and cultural connections with the old prewar planter class, and this had an effect on how progress was understood. There were limits on how far they would go to change things. Anything that would upset the relationship between the races, which by 1900 was defined by segregation and the loss of the vote by black citizens, was forbidden. Equality in general was viewed with suspicion even as it applied to whites. For one thing, the South's grinding poverty seemed impervious to change despite the growth of towns and the rise of new industries. Many probably subscribed to the biblical fatalistic view—"the poor ye will always have with you"—and were skeptical that poverty stricken and poorly educated maids, sharecroppers, and millhands could ever become like themselves. As Virginia Durr recalled:

> I was told by my mother and father and everybody whom I respected and loved that these people [miners in Birmingham] were just that way. They were just poor white trash. If they had pellagra and worms and malaria and if they were thin and hungry and immoral, it was just because that was the way they were. It was in their blood. They were born to be poor white trash. They dipped snuff and drooled tobacco juice. If they smelt bad and were dirty, well, they liked being that way.
>
> I was told the same thing about the black people.[142]

The belief in progress was thus always hedged with doubt. And the psychology of scarcity—that there was a limited amount of money to go around and you had to grab what you could for yourself and your family—gave the civilized gentility of many of the affluent a hard edge. Lillian Smith recalled in *Killers of the Dream* the inspiring religiosity of her businessman father who was so devoted to his faith that one evening he calmly finished a family prayer even though he knew his lumber mill had caught fire and he needed to organize the fire brigade. But his religiosity did not inspire him to pay his poorly paid workers more or to charge a fairer price for the supplies workers bought at the mill's commissary.[143] It was not just the always-present poverty and the competition that dulled the ardor of these businessmen for change and progress, but the amazing persistence of old ways and ideas, a persistence helped along by the blending together of New South businessmen and the old planter class.

---

142. Barnard, *Outside the Magic Circle*, 31.
143. Lillian Smith , *Killers of the Dream* (Garden City, New York: Anchor Books,1963; first published, 1949), 22–23.

As before the Civil War, members of this class were tied together by economic, social and familial connections and a common sense of manners, morality and even how to speak.[144] Many lived in spacious, often ornate homes that were cleaned and maintained by small staffs of black servants. Their wives organized parties and teas for "our kind of people." They socialized in a very limited way with those beneath them in the public sphere. As one of V.S. Naipaul's informants noted: "When I was growing up, we went to high school and grammar school with them. But we did not socialize. Our social lives were entirely different."[145] Indeed, the way the schools worked tended to separate people by class as well as the more obvious racial segregation. In the 1960s at St. John's, the white high school in Darlington, South Carolina, many of the less affluent students dropped out in the 10th or 11th grades—nearly half the students never graduated—to go to work in the factories and farms and shops of the area. Those who remained tended to take "vocational" courses that were typically offered in a shop building behind the school or in the basement. College "prep" courses were typically taught on the top floor, and most (although not all) of the college prep students were from the more affluent families. Girls from the better families joined the Anchor Club and boys joined the Key Club; they ran the school newspaper, worked on the annual staff, and were typically the ones recognized at the end of the year for their achievements. Boys and girls from less affluent families belonged to the Bus Drivers Club or The Future Homemakers of America or the Future Farmers of America.

Affluent families established social clubs and finally country clubs, when golf began gaining popularity, that were their exclusive preserves. John D. Cooper, Jr., general manager of the cotton mills his father had helped start, served as the first president of the newly formed West End Country Club (later renamed Henderson Country Club).[146] When they could manage it, they organized that ritual known as the debutante ball to formally "introduce" their daughters to society and, importantly, the "right sort" of young men. For example, the Men's Dance Club of Darlington, South Carolina, sponsored a "coming out" ball for the "right" young ladies for many years. Weddings and graduations were celebrated by a flurry of parties and dances. These affairs not only celebrated a special event but also threw together eligible young men and

---

144. See for example "Interview: A Perspective on the 1930s," "in Claudia D. Johnson's *To Kill a Mockingbird: A Student Casebook to Issues, Sources, and Historic Documents* (Westport Conn.: Greenwood Press, 1994), 145–154.

145. Naipaul, *Journeys Through the South*, 111. Novelist Reynolds Price, whose family was on fringe of the affluent class in Warrenton, North Carolina, got in a fight as a boy with his affluent friends and was "forced to seek friendship among the bused in farm children" and the "poorly fed, thin-faced children of production line workers...." He says these new friends saw the "prosperous and idle town children" as "stuck-up rich fops." Reynolds Price, *Clear Pictures: First Loves, First Guides* (New York: Atheneum, 1989), 171.

146. Clark, *Like Night and Day*, 15.

women—often from towns across the state and even the region—at a particu-larly propitious time. In the late 1800s and early 1900s the commencement at the University of North Carolina was accompanied by a round of parties and dances (germans, they were called) and provided "the most coveted social op-portunity which a young lady of North Carolina could ask to enjoy." Bessie Henderson, John Steele Henderson's daughter, traveled from Salisbury to Chapel Hill in June of 1892 for the round of parties and wrote her mother that she was attending the Gimghoul german, "the most select thing of all."[147]

Just as before the war, "old" families served as the guardians and gatekeepers of the upper class; for the young people who were trying to "fit in" and the up-wardly mobile who were trying to gain acceptance, these old families had to be placated, complimented and honored. Those who didn't pass muster with them might be shunned or pushed to the periphery of proper society. In Rowan County, for example, the Henderson family along with two other fami-lies prominent before the war—the Boyden and the Shobers—were said to be the "pillars" of local society.[148] They acted as social guardians in hundreds of ways small and big, as a matter of course, and sometimes quite consciously. John Steele Henderson, for example, would write his wife several weeks before Christmas one year "we must have a reception for the young 'tigers' at the close of the holidays."[149] Virginia Durr nicely captures the intricacies of the sorting process in her description of the Birmingham social order:

> Mother divided the world into types of people. The nice people lived on the Southside and were the Presbyterians and Episcopalians [Mr. Durr was a Presbyterian minister]. They lived in nice houses and had ser-vants and automobiles and belonged to the country club. They were the people that you associated with. Beneath the nice people was a group that she strongly resented and which she called "the climbers," the new rich. They had money, and they might get in the country club—finally. Of course, they always did if they were rich enough. It was always said, "Well, nobody knows who they are or where they came from. Nobody has ever heard of them before, and I have never been able to place who they were." Then beneath them came the "good plain people." These were people who might rise eventually into the nice people.[150]

---

147. Hope Summerell Chamberlain, *This Was Home* (Chapel Hill: University of North Carolina Press, 1938), 155; Bessie Henderson to Mamma (Bessie Henderson), 2 June 1892, John Steele Henderson Collection, Southern Historical Collection, University of North Carolina at Chapel Hill.

148. Hart, *The Southern South*, 61; Chamberlain, *This Was Home*, 276; Beck, "Build-ing the New South," 453–457.

149. John Steele Henderson to Bessie Henderson, 18 December 1892, John Steele Henderson Collection, Southern Historical Collection, University of North Carolina at Chapel Hill.

150. Barnard, *Outside the Magic Circle*, 45–46.

Not that the young and the newly rich always followed the lead the old established families. In her memoir, Hope Summerell Chamberlain remembered the younger members of this class in turn-of-the century Salisbury, North Carolina, hosting cocktail parties, which was somewhat scandalous. This young set was known as "the Bathtub Aristocracy" because they were also the first families to install indoor plumbing.[151]

The children of the upper class and of those who aspired to upper class status were carefully educated by parents and others in the behaviors and values of the upper class. Generally, the more affluent the family, the more formal (and expensive) the training. Young women were sometimes sent to finishing schools or, less formally, to spend time in the home of a "sophisticated" lady to be instructed in the finer points of the proper behavior of a lady. Virginia Durr's Aunt Mamie maintained a "salon" of sorts in New York where young Southern women could spend some time under the tutelage of a Southern belle and get a "taste of New York life and some culture and social life."[152] Children, males especially, attended the region's colleges and universities, although some colleges in the North, Ivy League especially, were also popular. Virginia Durr attended an Ivy League women's college (Wellesley); John Steele Henderson's son attended the University of North Carolina and was a member of Gimghoul (a secret society) and "all the class societies."[153] New public and private institutions of higher education, places like The Agricultural and Mechanical College of the State of Mississippi (Mississippi State), North Carolina State College, Presbyterian College and Coker College for Women (both in South Carolina), were established to meet the growing demand for a college education. While there was some effort to keep tuition low at land grant institutions (new colleges such as Clemson that were established with the proceeds of the sale of federal land), broad participation in college education by the children of the less affluent would not begin until after World War II. There was some "refocusing" in higher education; many of the new colleges were "technically" oriented as befitted the emphasis on business and industry in the "New South." However, certain public and private colleges—the University of Virginia, the University of the South (Sewanee), the University of North Carolina, Hampden Sydney, Tulane, Mary Baldwin to name a few—kept their liberal arts emphasis and retained, even to the present, the cachet of special privilege that conveyed more status to those who attended than the more technically oriented and often newer institutions. They also were considered to be bastions of proper values and behaviors. As Bessie Henderson noted to her husband in a

---

151. Chamberlain, *This Was Home*, 200, 276, 278–280.

152. *Ibid.*, 30.

153. John Steele Henderson, Jr. to Bessie Henderson, 24 October 1900, John Steele Henderson Collection, Southern Historical Collection, University of North Carolina at Chapel Hill.

letter written in the spring of 1892, "It simply fills you with pride to go from Chapel Hill to St. Mary's [a woman's college in Raleigh]—to see the refined polished air of everything—and the good manners and accomplishments of the young people."[154] In the late 1960s a woman told the mother of one of the authors of this book, "Your son will leave Presbyterian [College] a gentleman."

Military education, which suffered immediately after the Civil War, rebounded, and by the turn of the century military schools and colleges flourished. Some of the new land grant colleges such as North Carolina State, Clemson, and Texas A&M were both technical colleges and military colleges.[155] Many of the private colleges required military training; Presbyterian College, for example, required freshmen and sophomore males to serve in the corps of cadets of the ROTC as late as the early 1970s (female students were given a bye on this requirement). Private and land grant colleges would all eventually eliminate the military requirement, leaving only the Citadel and VMI as full-fledged military colleges, but most of these colleges continue to host a voluntary ROTC program. At several, Texas A&M in particular, this program is highly visible and has a large enrollment. At the least, ROTC remains popular on many other college campuses in the South.[156]

Did the martial ethic persist? It appears to have carried on most robustly in the decades immediately after the Civil War as an important part of the definition of honor for men who aspired to be gentlemen. Wrapped up in this value was the perception that the men defeated in the Civil War, the "Lost Cause," were superior men worthy of emulation in every respect. Military service seemed to reflect this value; in 1910 an overwhelming percentage of the general officer corps of the U.S. Army had Southern affiliations. However, military service today does not seem any more popular with the privileged in the South than it is anywhere else, although military participation by less affluent Southerners is quite high compared to rates for other regions. General support for the military (in all social classes) seems to remain strong in the South.[157]

What of the code of honor? It also persisted just as it had in the other classes, but, as one would expect, what it meant underwent change. For one

---

154. Bessie Henderson to John Steele Henderson, 12 June 1892, John Steele Henderson Collection, Southern Historical Collection, University of North Carolina at Chapel Hill.

155. Andrew, *Long Gray Lines*, 36–45.

156. *Ibid.*, p. 118. John. H. Napier III, "Military Schools," in Charles R. Reagan and William Ferris, eds., *Encyclopedia of Southern Culture* (Chapel Hill and London: University of North Carolina Press, 1989), 257–259. Georgia Military College is a two-year college that, despite its name, enrolls only a small percentage of its students in the corps of cadets.

157. John. H. Napier III, "Military Schools," in Charles R. Reagan and William Ferris, eds., *Encyclopedia of Southern Culture*, p. 259. A Defense Department study reported that in 2000, 42% of military recruits were from the South. Chuck Crumbo, "Military attracts

thing, the duel disappeared. The last formal duel fought in South Carolina, for example, was fought in Darlington County in 1880.[158] But gunplay and murder by upper class men as an accepted expression of manhood was still in evidence as late as the turn of the twentieth century. J. William Thurmond, the state prosecutor for South Carolina (father of Strom Thurmond, longtime U.S. senator from South Carolina), shot and killed a traveling salesman for calling him a "G-d damn dog and scoundrel." Thurmond claimed the man had boasted that he had "a d—good knife and a Colt's pistol," but neither was found. Thurmond was acquitted by a jury, resumed his post as state prosecutor and later was appointed United States attorney for the state of South Carolina.[159] Whether armed with a knife and pistol or not, apparently a salesman had no business calling Mr. Thurmond a "dog and scoundrel." As the twentieth century progressed, violence as the ultimate response to personal affronts seemed to be replaced among upper class men by litigation, and the court room and the board room seem to have become the new fields of honor on which upper class men demonstrated their manliness.

Vigilantism likewise became less acceptable for the affluent, as we have already seen. With their hold on the levers of state and local power, the affluent could not help but see mob activity as a threat or a least an affront to their authority. A lynch mob that gathered before the Salisbury jail in mid-July 1906, jeered the district's congressman, who was trying to calm the crowd. He became flustered (and probably frightened), and said "Let me out of here. Where is my umbrella?" The crowd responded (probably laughing and cat-calling), "What are you doing there? You ain't got no umbrella." The town mayor, "Baldy" Boyden, was also shouted down. The lynch mob only broke up when several members were admitted into the jail to see for themselves that the accused were no longer there.[160] It was not, however, uncommon for the affluent to turn a blind eye to the activities of lynchers and the Klan. As historian Joel Williamson has noted, newspaper editorialists might condemn lynching in the abstract but often acknowledged the necessity of the deed given the nature of the crime it punished.[161] In the 1920s challenging the Klan might be hurtful to one's political prospects, and in the Deep South in the 1950s and 1960s, Klan murders and church bombings were rarely prosecuted in state courts, despite the fact that it often was common knowledge in the white community who the perpetrators were.

---

blue-collar recruits," [Columbia, SC] *The State*, 25 May 2003, http://www.thestate.com/mld/state/news/columnists/6915404.htm.

158. Colleen Rhodes, "The Last Duel Fought in South Carolina" in Eliza Cowan Ervin and Horace Fraser Rudisill, eds. *Darlingtoniana: A History of People, Places, and Events in Darlington, South Carolina* (Columbia: R.L. Bryan Co., 1964), 356–359.

159. Butterfield, *All God's Children*, 50–51.

160. *Charlotte Daily Observer*, 16 July 1906.

161. Williamson, *Rage for Order*, 126.

Figure 2.4   The Citadel

Evangelical Christianity made inroads into the ranks of the affluent classes. As Virginia Durr noted in an earlier quote, the Episcopal Church was still a stronghold of the more affluent, but well-off people also belonged to the Presbyterian Church (Durr was a Presbyterian and ranked it just below the Episcopal church), and it was not uncommon for affluent planters, mill owners, bankers, lawyers, and merchants to belong to the Methodist and Baptist churches. The larger Baptist and Methodist and Presbyterian churches in the towns—invariably the "first" Methodist or Baptist or Presbyterian church in town—were often where these folks were sitting each Sunday morning. The moral preoccupations of these denominations undoubtedly became more of an influence on the more affluent, at the least by redefining propriety. But it is also true that the moral concerns of the evangelical churches coincided with some of the political concerns of many affluent white Southerners, evangelical or not. At the turn of the twentieth century, affluent whites across the South were convinced that blacks were a threat to order, and that poor white sharecroppers and mill workers would also benefit from more regulation. For example, in North Carolina, Heriot Clarkson, a future state Supreme Court judge, was a leader in the state prohibition campaign and an ardent supporter of the white supremacy movement that established segregation. Clarkson's biographer refers to him as a "social engineer," reflecting his desire to re-engineer society for the better; although he was an Episcopalian, he could also use the language of the evangelical church: he argued in one speech that the prohibition campaign arrayed the forces of good against the "flesh and the devil."[162] For Clarkson and other reformers, drinking and the saloon were a problem for the less affluent, African Americans especially, who needed to be protected from themselves. As one commentator noted, the "advanced" race had a responsibility to blacks, who were still in an "irresponsible stage of development."[163] In any event, the affluent seem to have often built in loopholes for themselves in the law when restricting recreational activities that they saw as disorderly in the lower classes. North Carolina's prohibition law, enacted in 1908, permitted the purchase of alcohol via the mails, a loophole that favored drinkers from the affluent classes who could afford to buy in bulk.[164] Later, when national prohibition was rescinded, laws in many parts of the South permitted beer (considered a "weaker" from of alcoholic beverage) to be bought and consumed in a variety of bars, honky tonks, gas stations, even drive-ins, but the sale of liquor by the drink would not reappear until the 1970s or later. Laws in most states did permit the brown-bag-

---

162. Johnnie V. Anderson, "Heriot Clarkson: A Social Engineer" (Unpublished M.A. thesis, Wake Forest University, 1972), 32–33, 40; "Perseverance: the Duty of Temperance Advocates," 1904; "Fifteen Bills of Indictment against the Saloon," n.d., Heriot Clarkson Collection, Southern Historical Collection, University of North Carolina, Chapel Hill.

163. "The Saloon in the South," *The Outlook*, 14 March 1908: 581–582.

164. Whitener, *Prohibition in North Carolina*, 171.

ging of liquor, and the establishments that were granted brown bagging per-mits—country clubs, restaurants, Shrine clubs, and so forth—tended to cater to the white middle and upper classes. Of course a plethora of **illegal** establish-ments, bootleggers, and moonshiners still catered to the less affluent. Horse racing could take place at high prestige venues for the more affluent like the Kentucky Derby or the Carolina Cup (in Camden, South Carolina) while it van-ished elsewhere, and other forms of contests that could be bet on—cock fight-ing and dog fighting—were driven underground.

By the 1950s the affluent in the South appeared to be reasonably comfortable with a show of real or feigned propriety before the public, and an acceptance, if not always approval of, the traditional upper class lifestyle of recreational pleas-ure—drinking, dancing, card playing, golf—in private. James Conaway grew up on the periphery of the upper class in Memphis during this period and recalls that while the town was ostensibly "dry," liquor could be had at any of the country clubs in town, and these clubs and spacious homes fostered a "private" social life for the town's affluent. As Conaway saw it, the world "of young, privileged white Memphis mirrored its adult counterpart, its compulsions played out in the street, in clubs, and on the lawns of those big houses in Chickasaw Gardens and along the western verge of the MCC [Memphis Country Cub] golf course...."[165] The right young men and women pledged fraternities and sororities in high school, attended fraternity and sorority parties and debutante balls and, the special event of the year, the Cotton Carnival festivities. If fortunate enough and male, they at-tended Memphis University School in preparation for attending Sewanee or Duke or some other prestigious private college.[166] Lurking beneath this sheen of propri-ety was the "other" social world: fast girls from the wrong side of town one would never marry; the new music that was produced by blacks and poor whites like Elvis Presley (a resident of Memphis); and the exciting if dangerous clubs and roadhouses—the Plantation Inn and the Cotton Club were the most famous—that provided respectable people with the chance to hear disreputable music, drink, and consort with disreputable people.[167] This picture was played out in hundreds of other towns and cities across the region in the 1950s and the 1960s.

Despite all the talk about a "new" South and "dying" traditions and virtues, much about this transformed upper class bore the imprimatur of the prewar upper class. The power of the industrialists, merchants, and planters over the labor force, while in no sense as total as the power of the pre-war planters over the lives of the slaves, was still distressingly similar. Certainly the disparity in wealth between those at the top and those at the bottom was huge, while the middle (small farmers and the small urban proprietors) was for many decades

165. James Conaway, *Memphis Afternoons: A Memoir* (Boston and New York: Houghton Mifflin, 1993), 102.
166. *Ibid.*, 84–85; 116–120; 96.
167. *Ibid.*, 94.

quite small. And the political power wielded by the affluent was just as considerable as it had been before the war. The paternalism of the prewar planter certainly persisted. Mills and mill towns were run very much like plantations, and sharecroppers, white and black, were dependent on merchants and planters for their livelihoods and their homes. Paternalism could take a kind and gentle form in the charity work performed by Junior League members (an upper class women's organization) or the actions of a fair-minded lawyer like the fictional Atticus Finch (in the novel *To Kill a Mockingbird*). It could also take a harsh and demeaning form.

Class in the Modern Era

The 1960s was a decade of momentous change in the South. Legal segregation collapsed, the region finally began experiencing significant economic development, and what can only be described as a new class system evolved. As we saw, the mechanization of agriculture and the application of new technologies—better fertilizer, herbicides, and pesticides—revolutionized agriculture and sent millions streaming from the land. By the 1970s, sharecropping and other forms of tenancy had virtually disappeared after forty years of decline. A substantial percentage of the poorest of the poor in the South left the countryside and often the region. African Americans were most likely to leave the region, although several million whites also left for Chicago, Cincinnati, and other northern and western industrial cities. In a sense, then, the South "exported" a significant percentage of its rural poor. There are still pockets of rural farm workers, the heirs of the sharecroppers, scattered throughout the South, especially in the old plantation districts, but a lot of the heavy lifting of farm work is either done by machinery or by temporary migrant workers.

The old class of mill workers changed, too. Industry in the South is much more diversified today, and textile mills no longer dominate the industrial landscape. Competition from foreign textile factories (some of them owned by Southern textile concerns) has taken more and more of the textile market and resulted in the closing of a growing number of Southern mills. While the number of millworkers plummeted, the number of people working in other kinds of blue collar jobs (jobs outside management and the professions) in industry, government, and the service sector, healthcare and retail, especially, has skyrocketed. Recruiting efforts by state and local governments have brought in a number of new industries, and the region's entrepreneurs have developed new enterprises such as the mini steel mills. Some of the new industries provide high-paying jobs, like the Saturn factory in Tennessee or the IBM facility in Research Triangle Park in North Carolina. Others pay poorly, particularly those which are located in the small towns and rural areas of the South to take advantage of the surplus labor pool created by the changes in agriculture. In eastern North Carolina, for example, cut and sew factories, poultry and hog processing facilities, and mobile home manufacturers dominate much of the industrial landscape. New service jobs have also appeared in great numbers, many of them low-paying positions in fast food restaurants, but some—in hospitals, business and government offices, and computer-servicing concerns—offer relatively good wages and pleasant working conditions.

The new working class, then, is more complex than the old working class of sharecroppers and millhands, and a significant part of it is much more affluent. There are certainly more employment opportunities in many parts of the South, particularly in the rapidly growing areas like Atlanta, Raleigh, and Dallas. Many sharecroppers and millhands and their children were thus able to "move up" into better paying jobs. Several of the children of the desperately poor Gudger sharecropper family mentioned earlier, had, by the late 1970s, decent working class jobs and lived in mobile homes.[168] Training for the more lucrative working class jobs is available at the ever expanding community colleges, and this training has been relatively inexpensive, although this is beginning to change.

The mill town is a thing of the past, and with its passing, so too went the plantation atmosphere of industrial work. Workers, especially those in the more prosperous areas of the South, can choose where to work and live, and the intense scrutiny of the boss, at least away from the workplace, has largely disappeared. The Gudgers are not unusual in their choice of homes; many working class Southerners live in mobile homes; indeed at one point in the 1980s, half the new homes sold were mobile homes.[169] But many workers, particularly those in two-income households, own three-bedroom homes in suburban subdivisions or along rural roads, which today are often lined with such dwellings. For many in the working class, their possessions and lifestyles are little different than neighbors who are educators, loan officers, or sales representatives. They have, in fact, become members of the middle class. Perhaps the biggest change in the working class has been the substantial increase in the number of blacks working in non-farm occupations. Until the 1960s, blacks were rarely permitted to take industrial or even retail jobs. As more and more whites moved into middle class jobs, blacks, protected now by civil rights legislation, moved into the factory and retail and government jobs upwardly mobile whites left behind.

Many of the controls on the less affluent—for example laws restricting drinking and, in some states, gambling—have been lifted, and the market-driven shopping extravaganza that is modern America is operating full bore in the South. No matter how meager an income, few have missed the delights of

---

168. Pete Daniel, *Standing at the Crossroads: Southern Life in the Twentieth Century* (New York: Hill and Wang, 1986), 222.
    169. *Ibid.*

fast food, movies, television, and, now, the World Wide Web. Poverty once dictated that the poor walked and the more affluent rode and that less affluent people dressed in distinctive costumes (bib overalls, worn slouch hats, for the men, washed out gingham dresses for women) that set them apart from their more affluent neighbors who also had distinctive costumes (suits for the men, or, for farmers, starched, creased tan work shirts and pants with a tie and a well maintained slouch hat; women wore silk or wool or starched cotton dresses and hose). Now it can be hard to tell from a distance and sometimes close up who is poor, although poor diets and poor medical and dental care still leave their marks. The cultural creations of less affluent Southerners—the blues, country music, rock and roll, stock car racing, cuisine—were once ridiculed and condemned, but now are celebrated, marketed, and franchised.[170] Memphis business leaders, for example, are proud of Graceland (Elvis's home) and Beale Street (a once disreputable street where the blues and jazz were played, which is now a major tourist magnet). People go to Memphis to visit these attractions, not the country clubs or tree-shaded neighborhoods of the wealthy.

The old poverty-ruled South is not dead, however. Much of the rural South is still dreadfully poor. Jobs are scarce, and many people eke out livings working as day laborers for area farmers, doing odd jobs, perhaps collecting a government benefit check or moonlighting in the drug trade, which is surprisingly active in some rural areas. Some of these "left behind" folks move between poorly paying town jobs and farm labor; others work in rural industries—poultry processing plants, cut and sew factories and the like—that rarely pay well. People are ever on the lookout for panaceas. Mississippi has abandoned its Baptist probity with both hands and has become a gambling center rivaled only by Las Vegas and Atlantic City; however, it is still wracked by poverty. Journalist Peter Applebome found in his travels in the Delta in the late 1990s a blighted region that looked "as if an ancient civilization had died out, leaving behind only a desultory colony of black survivors and ramshackle houses and ghost towns baking under the Mississippi sun."[171] The land is still fertile and the plantations still thrive—Tunica County in the heart of the Delta was supposed to have over 30 millionaires when Applebome visited—but like the poor whites of the Old South, the poor blacks of Tunica and the other Delta counties just don't fit in anywhere, weren't needed, were said by the local whites to disdain work, and couldn't do some of the work because their poor educations and limited life experiences did not prepare them for these kinds of jobs.[172] Center cities in many

---

170. *Ibid*, 91–95, 117, 147.

171. Peter Applebome, *Dixie Rising: How the South Is Shaping American Values, Politics, and Culture* (San Diego, New York and London: Harcourt Brace and Co., 1997), 274–286; quote on p. 278.

172. *Ibid*.

of the metropolises are almost as desperate—many employers and jobs have fled to the suburbs, leaving behind two extremes: high wage professional jobs at the banks and corporate headquarters and low wage retail jobs. While opportunities expanded dramatically in the 1970s, 1980s and 1990s, at the turn of the twenty-first century, globalization and two recessions have wreaked havoc on the manufacturing sector, and some of the manufacturing jobs that have disappeared paid relatively decent wages. Many displaced workers simply do not have the educational skills necessary for the new technical jobs and, given their educational deficits, will have a hard time acquiring these skills. Many of the young people entering the job market will also miss these disappearing manufacturing jobs. Many lack the skills required by the technical and managerial positions leaving them with little to choose from but the poorly paying service sector jobs: Ronald McDonald and "Mr. Sam" (legendary founder of Walmart), happy, friendly icons of modern America though they are, represent companies that don't pay a living wage to many of their employees.

Less-affluent families throughout the region often live in tightly packed trailer parks, urban projects, and small, sagging houses on country roads. Their jobs are often dangerous and debilitating, their health benefits meager. They still feel the sting of prejudice. Ironically, while public expressions of racial prejudice are less socially acceptable today, derogatory terms about less-affluent white people still are. For example, the terms "white trash" and "redneck" are still commonly used. Paula Jones, President Bill Clinton's nemesis, was described as "trailer park trash." Sometimes the terms are used humorously; Jeff Foxworthy has made a career out of his "you might be a redneck …" routine, and a white trash cookbook has been published. But prejudice and stereotypes hurt and diminish people; the humor just makes the insults a bit more tolerable.

To the middle class observer, it seems as if many of the less affluent—poor folks and even working class people—reject on some level the values and work behaviors of modern America. Historian Jack Kirby calls them members of the "countercultural South."[173] While most Americans are slaves to schedules, and clocks, and deadlines, the "countercultural South" seems to refuse to be bound by such restraints. Its members refuse to work "on the clock" or indoors in some airless factory or office or for someone they don't like, and they won't move (or even commute) to places where there are jobs. The men can be seen "piddling" around in the sheds behind their houses or trailers at mid-day or hanging around run-down stores where such people congregate and where an ill-thought-out remark can lead to some foolish misfortune. One of the authors recalls stopping at the Darlington race track—it was quiet, no races or time trials—where two scraggly looking white men had set up a crude lean-to

---

173. Jack Temple Kirby, *The Countercultural South* (Athens, GA and London: The University of Georgia Press, 1995).

constructed out of scrap lumber and plastic sheeting. They were selling boiled peanuts out of a drum filled with a murky liquid, $1.00 a bag. Clearly they were doing what they wanted to do, but it sure wasn't for the money. As one of V.S. Naipaul's Mississippi informants said to him:

> I admire them for their independence. But it's not right for society now. No question about it. It was great a long time ago. But not now. You can't get business done in a modern city with that kind of mentality. We got to change that redneck society and black society, or the wealth is going to be just in the few hands that it's always been in.[174]

The women spend their time caring for children—their own and the children of siblings, daughters, mothers, and friends. Often, these women are not married to the fathers of their children; divorce is common and marriage rates for less affluent people have been plummeting, part of a national trend but one that is perhaps most advanced in the "countercultural South."[175]

For the black members of this counterculture, the core of their psychology is a rejection of the society that rejected them; to a lesser extent this is in the heads of the poor whites, too, who often sport Confederate flag paraphernalia and long hair (still a sign of trouble in the South) and have a penchant for weaponry that goes beyond the typical American's affection for guns. Rejecting those who have rejected you was a survival mechanism for outlaws like the mythic Staggerlee in black folklore or the real life inhabitants of Moccasin Bottom. But in modern America, this outlaw life can lead to heavy drug use, prison time, and a short lifespan and has had an especially disastrous impact on young black men.[176] For many who exist on the fringe, white or black, this "choice" is not exactly a choice. Culture "catches" them just as the Gudgers were caught. Their grandparents and parents worked on farms and in mills; the work they did required little formal education and was learned "on the job" from elders and coworkers. The parent coming from this background now faces a dilemma: what to teach the young now that what you have learned is irrelevant and choices multiply daily, and how do you motivate them to be something you are not and to take seriously, **and for 12 years**, something—education—you never had much use for? The old support systems have weakened: the two-parent family is in decline, important institutions—schools, stores, even churches—often are no longer located in the communities they serve, and towns and neighborhoods that once were like extended "families" are hard to find now. Moccasin Bottom

---

174. Naipaul, *A Turn in the South*, 210.
175. Charles Murray, *Coming Apart: The State of White America, 1960–2010* (New York: Crown Forum, 2012), 149–167. National and state-level data on the relationship between poverty and single-parent families can be found at the National Center for Children in Poverty Web site at http://www.nccp.org/index.html.
176. Kirby, *The Countercultural South*, 8–32.

may have once sheltered gamblers and bootleggers, but it was also home to many folks who worked regular shifts in the mill and families who lived there for years if not generations; they're virtually all gone now, and the mill is closed. The new residents include Hispanic folk who appear to be settling in—they've established several bodegas and a church—but many of the houses in the neighborhood have fallen down or burned down, and some of the residents don't appear to work. The area has a reputation as a haven for crack dealers.

The small farmer class is now verging on extinction; its numbers have declined year by year since the 1930s. The future of farming is corporate farms or at least large, heavily capitalized family farms. Such farms are to be found throughout the richer agricultural regions. For the small farmer, tractors costing $100,000, expensive fertilizer, and the farmer's perennial complaint—low prices—have driven more and more small producers out of farming. Expanding employment opportunities have attracted the young away from the land, leaving family farming increasingly to older men, and often no one in a family is interested in continuing the tradition when the time to retire comes. Even in prime agricultural counties, only very small numbers of people are directly involved in farming anymore. The remnants of the small farmer class are hanging on in the countryside by investing heavily and specializing in the growing of a few commodities. They expand their operations when they can by buying or renting more land. Government crop subsidies have also helped the small farmers stay in business, but these subsidies tend to benefit the larger farmers the most. Some innovators such as Frank Perdue and Wendell Murphy have "industrialized" the raising of chickens, hogs, and turkeys (and even catfish) and have created a new kind of farming which seemingly "helps" the small operator—who actually does the raising of these critters—stay in business. But the power and control of these large chicken and pork and turkey processors over their "growers" does not bode well for the continued survival of the independent small farmer of the past. So the small farmer class, once the largest class in the South, now is a tiny minority. Even in a major agricultural county like Darlington County, South Carolina, only a few hundred families belong to this class today.

The "big" story of the last three decades is the rise of a "new" middle class. The "old" urban middle class of professionals, merchants and mill managers was very small in much of the South, and the upper part of it constituted a portion of the upper class rather than existing as a distinct class. By the 1960s, a rising economic tide created scores of better paying professional jobs, jobs such as teacher, accountant, college professor, loan officer, computer programmer, real estate agent, and a plethora of jobs in the ever expanding healthcare field. This new middle class was made up mostly of employees; many in the old middle class owned businesses of one sort or another or were self-employed professionals. Earle and Merle Black have argued in *Politics and Society in the South* that nearly sixty percent of white Southerners and nearly thirty percent of black Southerners belonged to the middle class by 1980. While the Blacks' definition of middle class is more expansive then the one used here—they include clerical and sales workers—there is no question that the number of middle class jobs exploded, and this allowed hundreds of thousands of Southerners, whites especially, to move up into jobs that could be performed in a white shirt and tie and that paid enough to afford a three bedroom house in one of the new suburban developments going up even in many of the smaller towns.[177] As the Blacks have noted, "Judged by labor force characteristics, the South's social structure is now [early 1980s] scarcely distinguishable from the non-South."[178]

People in the middle class in the South have increasingly adopted the values and lifestyles of the broader American middle class. This is not surprising for many reasons. For one, many members of the middle class in the South were not originally from the region but came south in search of jobs or because their companies relocated to Atlanta or Columbia or Austin. One can see the influence of these immigrants' tastes in the subdivisions growing around urban areas like kudzu. Too, the media today has substantially greater influence over tastes and probably values than it did thirty years ago. Whatever the reasons, most middle class Southerners apparently prefer to live in suburban developments and even the smallest towns now often have a "suburb" grafted onto the old town, the development separated from the road by a row of dirt berms with bushes and trees planted atop and entered via an impressive baronial gateway graced with some pretentious English name like Collinsford Downs or Grayson Manor. Their homes are surrounded by nicely tended yards, and they drive well-maintained cars. Middle class men and some women enjoy playing golf, a good recreation in the temperate South, and golf courses have sprouted throughout the region. Like their counterparts elsewhere, middle class people like to eat out at franchise restaurants where they expect mixed drinks, wines, and light and imported beer to be available. Drinking is no longer morally suspect in the middle class, and the collapse of the more significant legal restrictions on alcohol sales in much of the South (1970s and 1980s) coincided with the explosion in the numbers of middle class people. Middle class people are also more tolerant of gambling—Las Vegas is now a family vacation destination—and so many states now have state run lotteries, just like the northern and western states. Profits from the lotteries often go to benefit education, which makes it seem like a good civic venture. Several states, like Mississippi, now permit casino gambling.

---

177. Earl Black and Merle Black, *Politics and Society in the South* (Cambridge, Mass. and London: Harvard University Press, 1987), 52–56.

178. *Ibid*, 57.

Middle class people like to shop in malls filled with national retail outlets, wear brand name clothing and use brand name products. They enroll their children in a variety of enriching activities like dance classes, gymnastics, and music lessons because they want their children to grow up to be "well-rounded" adults. "Well-rounded" is a term that means "knows a little bit about a lot of things," and such a person is thought to be comfortable in a variety of social settings. Middle class people live very social lives, or "other-directed" lives, to use sociologist David Reisman's term.[179] They thus spend a lot of time talking—at work, at home, and at play—and they must have something to talk about with each other. While its members look, often behave, and even often talk like middle class people from anywhere else in the country, the homogenization process is far from complete. Middle class Southerners generally see themselves as Southerners, while people in the rest of the country are more likely to give you a puzzled look if you ask them if they are "northern" or "midwestern." Middle class Southerners also are more likely than their northern counterparts to be active churchgoers, and the Baptist church still draws the bulk of all churchgoers in the region of whatever class.[180] They are also more likely to be Republicans, if they are white and particularly if they are white males, than their northern counterparts.[181]

The tremendous expansion of the job market in the 1960s, 1970s, and 1980s facilitated a great deal of upward mobility in the South, and many people, white males especially, were able to acquire middle class jobs with only a high school diploma. Today, however, as hundreds of thousands of college graduates pour out of the colleges and universities each year, the four-year degree is becoming more of a necessity for middle class status. So education is one of the top priorities in the middle class. Politicians woo middle class votes with promises to improve the schools. Some middle class parents, particularly those living in the more poverty-stricken areas of the South, send their children to private schools to ensure that they get a good education that prepares them for college. College has now become a lifetime passion for many of the middle class (even if they never attended college). They emblazon their cars with school nicknames or the names of school mascots—Ole' Miss, Gamecocks, Carolina—and they indoctrinate their children in the advantages of one college over another. They attend football and

179. David Riesman with Nathan Glazer and Reuell Denney, *The Lonely Crowd: A Study of the Changing American Character* (New Haven: Yale University Press, 1961), 19–25.

180. *Southern Focus Poll*, Fall 1992, Institute for Research in the Social Science, University of North Carolina at Chapel Hill; Reed, "Plastic Wrapped Crackers," *One South*, 135.

181. Exit polls show nearly 70% of Southern whites voting for the Republican candidate for president in 2000. More than 70% of middle and upper income white males voted Republican. Voter News Service Exit Poll, in *SouthNow #1* (June 2001).

Figure 2.5   A North Carolina State University football game

basketball games at the colleges they attended or wished they attended, sometimes paying thousands of dollars for this privilege, and they wear festive school colors on game days. All of this energy, commitment, and activity is important; it actually gives the children of middle class parents an advantage over the children of less affluent parents by socializing them to be ready for the college experience. Choosing to go to college, staying in college, and graduating from college have as much to do with proper socialization as with intelligence or even commitment.

Indeed, even with expanded educational opportunities, educational attainment is still strongly tied to class. The children of the less affluent often do not attend good public schools, often get sidetracked into the less demanding high school courses, often don't have adults around who are interested in their schoolwork, and generally do not participate in the whirl of "enriching" activities. The South still leads the nation in the percentage of high school drop outs; generally, children from less affluent parents are the most likely to drop out and stay "dropped out."[182] For students who finish high school, class again comes into play with the children of the more affluent more likely to complete

182. Jay P. Greene and Greg Foster, *Public High School Graduation and College Readiness Rates in the United States,* Education working Paper, No. 3, September 2003, Center for Civic Innovation at the Manhattan Institute, 9; *Subsequent Educational Attainment of High School Drops, Statistical Analysis Report,* June 1998, U.S. Department of Education, Office of Educational Research and Improvement, iii.

a four-year degree than the children of the less affluent.[183] They are also more likely to attend the more prestigious colleges. For example, the average family income (1995–1996) of a student at the University of North Carolina was $75,000; at the University of Virginia it was $94,000.[184] People from less affluent families are more likely to attend community colleges. While the results of research on what college does for one's earning power (never mind its other benefits) are more complicated than one might imagine, in general people with four-year degrees on average earn a higher income than people with two-year degrees.[185] Higher family income seems to be an especially strong predictor of completion, and students attending a Duke or a University of Virginia nearly all finish, while students attending community colleges earn degrees or diplomas at a much lower rate. And so while education offers the less affluent opportunities to "move up," it's often the exceptional person who can overcome skill and experience deficits and money problems to take advantage of this opportunity at the four-year level. As the expansion of middle class jobs in the region slows, and the number of four-year degree holders rises, people without the four-year degree are finding it more difficult to land a good job than in the past. An acquaintance of one of the authors "moved up" from clerk to manager of a video rental store (part of a national chain) with "some college" under his belt, but to move up to the next level, he was told he'd need a four-year degree.

There is still a wall of separation between black and white, but it is a wall with many gaps. Suburban developments are now frequently racially integrated, but it is still true that whites tend to live in neighborhoods populated primarily by whites, and blacks tend to live in neighborhoods populated primarily by blacks. There is still a significant disparity between the size of the black middle class and the white middle class. Drive through some of the old plantation districts or the poor areas of virtually any Southern city or town, and you will see terrible poverty afflicting many blacks. This disparity is not likely to disappear soon even if racial discrimination stopped tomorrow. The absence of educational capital, the sort of capital middle class parents are able to provide their children, is such a huge obstacle for poor youth to overcome.

183. "Postsecondary Attainment for 1988 8th Graders," *Student Effort and Educational Progress: Postsecondary Persistence and Progress,* National Center for Education Statistics, 2003, http://nces.ed.gov/progrms/coe/2003/section3/indicator22.asp.

184. "UNC, Public College Students Post High Family Income," *Clarion Call,* Vol. 1, no. 44, 2 December 1999. The Pope Center for Higher Education Policy, Raleigh, NC., http://www.popecenter.org.

185. W. Norton Grubb, "Learning and Earning in the Middle: The Economic Benefits of Sub-Baccalaureate Education," Community College Research Center, April 1999, Table 1, p. 64, http://www.tc.columbia.edu/ccrc/PROJECTS/Grubb.htm ; *The State of the South 2004: Fifty Years After Brown v. Board of Education,* (Chapel Hill: MDC Inc., May 2004), 16, 18.

The upper class today in most of the South is decidedly rooted in business and the business values of competition, growth, and materialism. Its wealth comes from banking, investments, successful law firms, real estate, business and corporate ownership, and management. There are really two upper classes: a fabulously wealthy one which is part of the greater American upper class and a local one planted in the small towns and cities of the region. Much as it was at the turn of the 20th century, the local one is still a hybrid class of wealthy people and what today would be called upper middle class people. It is typically composed of people earning a spectrum of incomes ranging from millions to the two hundred thousand dollar income of the lawyer, businessman, or two-income professional couple. Families in this class sometimes have "old" names, which means they have been affluent for several generations. The names, and the manners and traditions that presumably go with them, are vitally important in places like Charleston and New Orleans, but less important in many other places where money, an appropriate occupation, some familiarity with "proper" manners (especially important for women), and a desire to belong will sometimes suffice. Upper class families live in upscale developments or neighborhoods clustered around country clubs, on estates, or in the older part of town like the Battery in Charleston or the Garden District in New Orleans or "inside the beltline" in Raleigh. They own houses at resort areas, and they often vacation in exotic spots all over the world.

Members of the local upper classes generally play a large role in town and county politics, the local charities, and other ceremonial events. They have a major influence on the politics of their states because they provide the bulk of the contributions to candidates for office. They often are familiar with other members of the upper class through business dealings, college connections, membership in private clubs and, of course, politics. They prefer that their children marry children from other upper class families and while the debutante ball, a once important ritual for pairing the right boys and girls, has waned in popularity over the course of the late twentieth century, one still finds it in many towns and cities. In North Carolina, the "right" families are invited by the Terpsichorean society to send their daughters to a big state-wide debutante ball held in Raleigh. But many affluent families are only vaguely familiar with it (if at all); the national and even global mobility of an important element of the affluent has rendered such institutions parochial. Golf continues to be a favorite leisure activity, and upper class men make business deals at "the club," meet new people, and visit other clubs to extend their network of important acquaintances. Golf is also the great equalizer because many middle class men play it, too, and so the gulf between the middle and upper is diminished. Education is also an equalizer; upper class children generally attend the same sorts of colleges as middle class children, although certain colleges and universities are traditional favorites; in North Carolina the University of North Carolina is a popular choice, and in Virginia it's "UVa." Among some, there is a

Figure 2.6   Terpsichorean Society debutante ball

preference for small private colleges such as Mary Baldwin, Hampden Sydney, and the University of the South (Sewanee) and, of course, Ivy League institutions are always popular.

What's left of the planter class seems thoroughly merged today with the urban upper class in the culmination of a process that began long ago. Interestingly, Walker Percy, the nephew of William Alexander Percy, has studied in novelistic form the same issues that so intrigued his uncle: the decline of gentility and the disappearance of the aristocrat. Perhaps his best novel is tellingly entitled *The Last Gentleman*. Materialism (measuring success by the possession of things), a respect for business ("trade" as Percy's uncle would have referred to it), individualism, competition, varying degrees of cosmopolitanism (an appreciation for others' ideas and customs), and a helping of hedonism realized largely through consumption (BMWs, fine wine, and plasma televisions) are values the contemporary upper class shares with the middle class not only of the South but of the nation.

Honor, surprisingly, is still alive and kicking in all social classes although in a much attenuated form. Shame seems to play less of a role as a restraint, and Southerners seem to be as likely to say shameful things in public, wear embarrassing clothing, and submit to invasions of their privacy by bureaucrats and TV personalities as anyone else. But Southerners of all classes still support a retributive view of justice, and so the region has more folks on death row than anywhere else and actually periodically executes some of these folks. Social psychologists Richard Nisbett and Dov Cohen have found the South still leads the nation in homicides and that crimes arising over insult or loss of face are a lead-ing cause of homicides.[186] There is a significant class differentiation in honor's application here; less affluent Southerners, especially less affluent black South-erners, are the ones most likely to be locked up for these offenses while the courts, the institution doing the locking up, are firmly in the hands of the more affluent. In controlled experiments, Nisbett and Cohen found that Southern college students reacted more angrily to perceived slights than students from elsewhere, and that Southern employers were more willing to consider employ-ing someone who had committed an honor-related felony than folks from other regions. They also found Southerners more accepting of violence as a solution to a problem than folks in other regions. Recall that honor and patriarchy (male predominance) go hand in hand, and Nisbett and Cohen find evidence of per-sistence here, too. Laws regulating domestic abuse as late as the early 1990s were much less onerous for the abusive spouse (generally the male) in the South than elsewhere in the nation. Spanking children is still widely approved of, and peo-ple in some areas of the South are still happy to have school personnel whip their children.[187] In a recent news story, a recently appointed assistant principal in a Mississippi middle school apparently did not understand that. As the story notes, "he did not realize he would be expected to paddle as many as 10 to 15 students a day. When he sought to use other methods of disciplining students, such as detention, his colleagues complained that he was shirking his duties." Ultimately he resigned. As he noted, "I decided I did not get my master's degree in education to spend my time paddling students."[188]

Honor's old adversary, evangelical religion, is still a vital institution for all Southerners white and black, rich and poor. Nationally, the more affluent are most heavily concentrated in the Episcopal and Presbyterian denominations with Methodist, Baptists, and Pentecostals denominations having proportion-ately fewer affluent families; this is undoubtedly the case in the South.[189] But if the average income of members of the **First** Baptist and **First** Methodist churches in the region were computed, they would probably rival the averages for the Episcopalians and Presbyterians. A form of upward mobility of several sorts has been going on and for quite some time; old downtown Baptist churches (the First Baptist) have become staid and even "high church" (we'll explain this term in our religion chapter) and attract mostly educated, affluent people as members. Meanwhile, some Baptists and members of other evangel-

186. Richard E. Nisbett and Dov Cohen, *Culture of Honor: The Psychology of Violence in the South* (Boulder, Colorado: Westview Press, 1996), 13–24.
187. *Ibid.*, 25–80.
188. Michel Dobbs, "Spared the rod, lost his job," [Raleigh, NC] *News and Observer*, 22 February 2004, sec. A.
189. Barry A. Kosmin and Seymour P. Lachman, *One Nation Under God: Religion in Contemporary American Society* (New York: Harmony Books, 1993), 260.

ical denominations who are doing well join the Episcopal or Presbyterian churches to signal their arrival among "better folks." With the prosperity in much of the South providing many with new opportunities, some Pentecostalists who have done better in life are signaling their arrival not by leaving their church but by elevating it (materially speaking) and are building the imposing Pentecostal complexes one sees on the outskirts of many Southern towns and cities. While some denominations—particular the Episcopal, Presbyterian, and Methodist—have renounced the code of honor at least in formal pronouncements (for example, by opposing the death penalty), others have not. Many evangelical denominations—most notably the huge Southern Baptist Convention—support capital punishment, and for many in these denominations, spanking is a biblically supported method of disciplining children. For example, one of the colleagues of the Mississippi assistant principal mentioned earlier, a special education teacher and the "co-pastor of a local church," noted about spanking "Are we going to believe man's report or God's report?" One Baptist church in the Piedmont of North Carolina posted the following on a billboard during the second Iraq war: "War Brings Peace." Christ would not be amused, but honor would understand. The patriarchy that is part and parcel of the code of honor is likewise still a vital part of evangelical Christianity. The Southern Baptist Convention forcefully promotes the idea that males should head the families and the churches. To some extent, support for retributive justice and patriarchy not to mention opposition to evolution and abortion and homosexuality are found in churches and denominations where the less affluent predominate; in the churches where the more affluent predominate, the positions are reversed as witnessed by the recent (2003) ordination of a gay Episcopal bishop. But these disputes are so complex and the role of middle class leaders and followers so important on both sides of the issues that they simply cannot be understood as primarily class issues.

This brings us to our conclusion which is that the old class system of the South is dying. It is a slow death to be sure, but it is dying. The growth of the middle class, more than anything else, is breaking the tight grip of class and changing the South in profound ways. No longer is the region as a whole characterized by extremes of poverty and affluence with little between, and no longer are those born in poverty doomed to die in poverty. It's easier now. There are still poor people, to be sure, and pockets of poverty in certain areas, particularly the old plantation districts and mountain regions. Certain areas of eastern North Carolina or the Mississippi Delta look more like Third World nations than parts of the United States, and it is hard to imagine these areas or many of the people changing much. But it is easier now for a lot more people, and that hard edge of the older South—the terrible, smothering poverty, the need to control and manipulate the less fortunate, the racism that pitted, tooth and claw, the poor white against the poor black—seems to be dissipating. Class means less and dictates less in the lives of Southerners.

Janis Evans

Chapter 3

Race

Introduction

Early on in the history of the American South, the institution of slavery established race as one of the dominant influences shaping Southern culture. Chattel slavery, as it was practiced in the American South, was restricted almost exclusively to the enslavement of Africans or those of African descent; those who were white were free, those who were black were slave, or in the case of the small population of so-called free blacks, semi-free. After the Civil War, race continued to play a major role in the South. Blacks and whites lived in two social "worlds" which were defined by an institution, segregation, which persisted until the 1970s. These "worlds" were very different in terms of economic opportunities, political power, civil and legal rights, and status. The South of today is still coming to terms with the heritage of slavery and segregation.

Race in the Western World: A Brief History of a Concept

Ask the randomly selected person on the street what race is and the answer will undoubtedly begin with skin color and perhaps certain other physical characteristics and cultural traits associated with particular colors of people. This was not always so. During the sixteenth and seventeenth centuries, Europeans used the term to describe descendants of a common ancestor, emphasizing kinship linkages rather than physical characteristics such as skin color or hair type.[1] The concept of race as a biological category was formulated by northern Europeans, and most probably had its origins in the events following European voyages of discovery to the New World and beyond. For most of their histories, Europeans had been largely isolated from contact with people who differed from them physically or culturally. Before the development of large sailing ships in the late 1400s, they had limited contact with people from Asia and Africa, and virtually none with the people of the Americas (save the few Viking excursions to North America). During the age of exploration and conquest, Europeans were struck by the fact that the people they encountered were physically and culturally different from them and sought to both explain these differences and justify their treatment of the peoples they came to dominate and exploit.

Francois Bernier, a Frenchman who lived during the 1600s, was one of the first Europeans to sort human beings into distinct categories, based mainly on skin color. Carolus Linnaeus, a Swedish botanist working in the mid decades of the 1700s, embarked upon an ambitious project to categorize all living things, a project which necessarily included humans. Linnaeus was influenced by the medieval concept of the "Great Chain of Being" and arranged his categories in a hierarchical order. When he turned to humans, he organized people by geography—the "'four quarters' of the globe" ascribing to people of each region specific characteristics. The German anatomist Johann Blumenbach (reputedly the founder of modern physical anthropology) eventually had the most influential impact on the Western conceptualization of race. In 1795 Blumenbach introduced his typology of the "races of mankind," a classification containing five racial groups or "human varieties": the Caucasians (Europeans), the Mongolians (Asians), the Ethiopians (Africans), the Americans (Native Americans), and the Malays (Polynesians). It was Blumenbach who coined the term "Caucasian" to refer to Europeans and believed that human beings originated in the Caucasus Mountains of Russia and that the other races were descended from

---

1. Wilton M. Krogman, "The Concept of Race," Ralph Linton ed., *The Science of Man in the World Crisis* (New York: Columbia University Press, 1945) 38–62.

this group. (Twentieth century anthropologists would later establish that the first humans originated in Africa.) While Blumenbach himself disputed the notion that one race was "better" than another, eventually a hierarchy of physically distinct groups came to be popularly accepted. Different racial groups with differing physical traits (e.g. skin color, nose shape, hair texture) were viewed as having more or less mental and reasoning ability and differing levels of capacity for civilization or cultural achievement. White Europeans or their colonial offspring held down the top position, and Africans were ranked at the bottom of the scale, partly because of their color and alleged primitive culture, but perhaps more so because Africans had been introduced to European societies as slaves by the Moors (North African Muslims) during their occupation of the Iberian Peninsula and southern Europe.[2] No racial idea was more universal at this time than that of European superiority over the red, yellow, brown, and black "racial" stocks of distant lands.

Americans played an important role in developing racial thought in the nineteenth century in large measure because of the presence on the continent of two large groups of people not of European origin—Native Americans and Africans. How to explain these people and justify how they were being treated by the dominant white majority? South Carolinian Josiah C. Nott was one of the most prominent racial theorists in the decades before the Civil War.[3] As he observed in an 1849 publication, "The dark races borrow the vices, but never the virtues of the white man, and wherever the later encroaches on the former, in temperate latitudes, colonization is synonymous with extermination."[4]

Nott's views about the superiority of the white race were fairly typical of the times in both the North and the South, and even a man as enlightened as Abraham Lincoln shared them. One undercurrent in nineteenth-century racial thinking was a fear of what was called "amalgamation"—the "mixing" of races through sexual interaction. Given the prevalence of views about white superiority and black (and Native American) inferiority, amalgamation was perceived to be a dire threat to the "purity" of the white race and its superiority. The fear of amalgamation was a major stumbling block in the way of black emancipation because many believed freedom and equality for blacks would

---

2. C. Loring Brace, *"Race" Is a Four-Letter Word: The Genesis of the Concept* (New York: Oxford University Press, 2005), 24–27, 44–47; Thomas F. Gossett, *Race: The History of an Idea in America* (New York: Shocken Books, 1965), 32–33; Winthrop C. Jordan, *White over Black: American Attitudes toward the Negro, 1550–1812* (Baltimore, MD: Penguin, 1969), 217–227; Audrey Smedley, *Race in North America: Origins and Evolution of a Worldview* (Boulder, CO: Westview Press, 1999), 163–164, 321–322.

3. Brace, *"Race" Is a Four Letter Word*, 77, 110–117.

4. Josiah C. Nott, *Two Lectures on the Connection Between the Biblical and Physical History of Man* (1849; New York; Negro Universities Press, 1969), 18.

promote amalgamation.[5] Interestingly, Adolph Hitler had the same obsession with racial purity a century later, and he attempted to purge Germany and areas he had conquered of what he considered inferior races so that they could not "pollute" the "master race."

In the later decades of the nineteenth century, a new formulation of race gained currency in Europe and America called Social Darwinism. Social Darwinism was loosely (very loosely) based on the ideas of biologist Charles Darwin; it accepted the older notion that the races of mankind were organized in a hierarchy of intelligence, abilities, and moral worth and asserted that the races and people of the Earth were engaged in a struggle for survival. It was viewed as only natural that the superior races (Europeans or descendants of Europeans) should dominate and exploit millions of their fellow human beings, and that inequality, poverty, conflict and struggle were the natural, inevitable features of social life. It was the obligation of the "civilized" races to control the inferior races lest they be pulled down by them, and the "uncivilized" could benefit and learn under the tutelage of the "civilized."[6]

Over the course of the twentieth century, Social Darwinism and the older ideas about race would be called into question. The shaky empirical support for both the concept of race and the notion that races exist in some sort of hierarchy collapsed under the scrutiny of new generations of scientists and scholars. The revulsion with which many people regarded Adolph Hitler's efforts to rid the world of what he considered "inferior" races also played a role in the process of rethinking race and racial thinking. The new view among scholars and scientists is that race is not a valid way of categorizing human beings biologically, and this view has been supported by a mountain of research, especially the latest research in genetics. In this new view, people are people; to be sure, different ethnic groups do have genetic propensities to have different skin tones, to be taller or shorter, and to be resistant or susceptible to different diseases and medical conditions, but intelligence, creativity, and morality are all culturally and individually determined.[7] In popular culture in much of the Western world, overt racism—treating people as inferior because of their skin color and physical characteristics—has become less and less acceptable, and systems of racial oppression—colonial rule by European powers in Asia and Africa, apartheid in South Africa, and segregation in the American South—have all collapsed. Higher levels of education, upward economic mobility of people from groups once considered inferior, immigration that has resulted in greater diversity in many Western countries (the United States, especially), and a media that por-

---

5. Jordan, White Over Black, 542–544.
6. George M. Frederickson, *The Black Image in the White Mind: The Debate on Afro-American Character and Destiny, 1817–1914* (New York: W.W. Norton & Co., 1977), 228–255.
7. Smedley, *Race in North America*, 273–318.

trays a wider palette of people all have undercut old racial thinking. Increased interracial marriages and the children resulting from them also directly challenge and erode the boundaries between "races." But race is not so easily vanquished; color is still a common way of categorizing people in most of the Western world and certainly in the United States, and the association of certain cultural traits (ideas, beliefs, values, musical tastes, and athletic skills) with people of particular skin colors, however erroneous, is likewise still quite common. It is also still common for people to regard their skin color as an important part of their identity. Attitudes and customs that existed for centuries are not quickly undone, and whom one worships with or lives near, who is the best "fit" for a vacant job, and who is a proper marriage partner for oneself or one's offspring are still often influenced by older racial ideas and prejudices.[8]

Slavery and Race in the South

> Both thy bondsmen and thy bondsmaids, which thou shalt have, shall be of the heathen that are around about you; of them shall ye buy bondsmen and bondsmaids. And ye shall take them as an inheritance for your children after you, to inherit them for a possession; they shall be your bondsmen forever. (Lev. 25:44)

In the early Virginia colony, race was important, but the racial divide was between Native Americans and Englishmen, not between Africans and Englishmen because Africans would not make up a significant part of the population until the later decades of the seventeenth century. The English were of mixed minds about the people they encountered when they first began settling Virginia. There was current in England the idea that Native Americans came in two varieties—good and bad. On the one hand, "good Indians" would be helpful and generous to the English and would welcome their rule. The romantic story of Pocahontas is an example of this viewpoint. On the other hand, "bad Indians" were heathens (non-Christian), savages, thieves and possibly even cannibals.[9] In real life, these views were childishly simplistic and, as it turns out, irrelevant. However the English settlers viewed Native Americans, a central fact ultimately governed the relationship between the two cultures: Native Americans stood in the way of what the English wanted, and what they wanted was unfettered access to the land of Virginia, all of the land. What was driving the settlement of Virginia was not small farms worked by families, but tobacco plantations employing scores of workers, and the desire to seize Indian

---

8. *Ibid.*, 319–338.
9. Edmund S. Morgan, *American Slavery, American Freedom: The Ordeal of Colonial Virginia* (New York: W.W. Norton & Co., Inc., 1975), 18–24, 44–48, 98–100.

land was ultimately a desire for riches and power. Native Americans did not prove to be a good source of labor for these plantations, and so they became to the English nothing more than a nuisance, a sometimes deadly nuisance to be sure, to be either driven out or killed. Bitter wars ensued, resulting in the virtual annihilation of the Native American people of Virginia and ultimately the entire South.

If the Native Americans presented problems for the builders of the plantation society of early Virginia, so, too, did the English men and women brought to the New World to labor in the fields. They were temporary servants obligated to work only until their indentures expired, and thereafter were free men and women; as free men and women in a new land, many were unwilling to do what was expected of them and labor as servants their natural lives, and many struck out on their own, squatting on land, stealing if that didn't work out, demanding the protection of the colonial government when they settled on the frontier, all of which was inconvenient and profoundly disturbing to the planter lords of Virginia. As we have seen, all of this culminated in Bacon's Rebellion and forced planters to look for a better source of labor to supply Virginia's ever expanding plantation economy. If the plantation system was to survive, what they needed was a stable and controllable workforce.[10]

The solution to this problem had already been worked out by the Portuguese and Spanish; both countries had introduced slavery in their colonies in the 1400s and 1500s. While both had enslaved Native Americans in their early New World settlements, their major source of slaves became captives from Africa. The Portuguese played the most significant role in establishing an African slave trade to feed the growing New World demand for unfree labor. Portugal was a country on the move in the 1400s; it was aggressively seeking new trade routes with Asia and exploring other trade possibilities closer to home. The Portuguese were aware of the potentially lucrative West African slave trade through their contact with the Moors—today's Algerians, Libyans, and Moroccans—of North Africa, who controlled this trade. One of the main goals of Portuguese expansion in the fifteenth century was access to the profitable trade in West African slaves that earlier had been dominated by the Moors. By the 1450s, a small but consistent slave trade between Portugal and West Africa was in place. Initially, the largest market for the African slaves imported by Portugal was the sugar plantations the Portuguese had established on the island of Madeira, off the coast of Northern Africa. After Portugal colonized Brazil, a huge territory with a tropical environment ideal for growing sugar cane, sugar plantations and slavery were established in the Americas. The growing European demand for sugar led to a the steady growth of this planation system in Brazil and the de-

---

10. *Ibid.*, 235–270.

mand for slaves, and Portuguese slave traders ranged up and down the coast of West Africa buying slaves from African intermediaries.[11]

Spain, Portugal's economic and political rival during this period of initial European expansion, introduced sugar production on the Caribbean island of Hispaniola and bought Africans from Portuguese slave traders to work its plantations. As early as the mid-1500s, at least one English ship captain participated in this slave trade. Ultimately, the Dutch, English, and French would establish plantation colonies in the Caribbean, and all would become deeply involved in the slave trade on a large scale. Caribbean sugar and African slavery had become the basis of European colonial expansion and also the basis for the development of what historian Paul Gilroy calls *The Black Atlantic*—the blending and mixing of European and African cultures throughout the Atlantic Basin.[12] What Spain and Portugal, and later England, the Netherlands, and France, would establish in their New World colonies was chattel slavery, a form of slavery in which the human being was considered property (chattel) with few, if any, rights. This was not the only form of slavery; many of the African societies from which most of the slaves would be obtained practiced a form of slavery known as service slavery. In this form of slavery, slaves did have some rights and privileges, and slavery often was a temporary condition rather than a life sentence passed on to succeeding generations.

The Atlantic Basin slave trade initiated perhaps the largest forced human migration in world history and lasted from the fifteenth century until the mid-1800s. Slavers took over ten million people from their loved ones and homes, marched them to coastal forts, loaded them on ships, and sent them to destinations in the Americas. The peak years of the trade were between 1740–1810, and during this period tens of thousands of captives were shipped from Africa each year. Most of the captives were delivered to Dutch, French, and British sugar plantations in the Caribbean, Portuguese Brazil, and Spanish South America. The rest, numbering perhaps 5% of the total, went to territory that would later become the United States.[13] More men than women were enslaved and shipped to the Americas, and the proportion of males enslaved climbed throughout the duration of the slave trade, exceeding seventy percent by the early 1800s. More adults than children were taken, but the percentage of chil-

---

11. David Richardson, "The Rise of the Atlantic Empires," in Anthony Tibbles, ed., *Transatlantic Slavery: Against Human Dignity* (Liverpool: Liverpool University Press, 2005), 17–24.

12. Jordan, *White over Black*, 56–59; Paul Gilroy, *The Black Atlantic: Modernity and Double Consciousness* (Cambridge, Mass.: Harvard University Press, 1993).

13. Herbert S. Klein, *The Atlantic Slave Trade* (Cambridge, United Kingdom: Cambridge University Press, 1999), 210–211.

dren enslaved also climbed over the course of the trade, and nearly half the captives taken in the early 1800s were children.[14]

In the eighteenth century, English sailors christened the middle part of the triangular trade — from Africa to the Caribbean and the North American mainland —"the Middle Passage." Slave captives were collected at African coastal forts and then rowed to waiting ships to begin an Atlantic journey of unspeakable horror. The length of the captives' journey grew shorter with improvements in ship design, but still typically took 6–8 weeks by the 1800s. Aboard ship, the men were chained in pairs, the right ankle of one connected to left ankle of another, and oftentimes their wrists would be restrained as well. They were taken below deck where men were housed in one area, children in another, women in a third. Packed tightly together on shelves where they would spend most of their time on the journey across the ocean, they could not stand up or lie down comfortably but were forced to lie "spoon fashion," often in their own excrement and vomit. One commentator observed that a "corpse in a coffin" had more room. The women were likely to be raped and sexually abused by the crew. Ventilation was poor, and the stench below decks was suffocating. The unsanitary conditions, poor food, and horrific treatment caused many captives to sicken and die during the voyage, and suicide was quite common.[15] One observer described a slave ship as "half bedlam and half brothel."[16] It was commonly estimated that between one in six and one in three captives died on the voyage; recent scholarship shows significant variation depending on the length of the voyage. The longer the voyage, the higher the death toll, and death rates of thirty percent were common for slaves transported greater distances, while the death rate for slaves transported shorter distances was much lower. The death rate also varied by voyage, with some ships reporting mortality rates as high as fifty-five percent on some voyages. The death toll declined over the course of time, and several studies have found death rates of under ten percent by the late 1700s and early 1800s.[17]

The first Africans arrived in the Virginia colony in 1619 when a Dutch warship exchanged 20 Africans for supplies. The exact status of these first African immigrants—17 men and 3 women—was unclear; to be sure, they had been sold to the English settlers by the Dutch, but in Virginia there were no laws defining or regulating slavery, and English laws on the subject were vague.

---

14. *Ibid.*, 161–162.

15. Hugh Thomas, *The Slave Trade: the Story of the Atlantic Slave Trade, 1440–1870* (New York: Simon Shuster, 1997), 418–424; Colin A. Palmer, *Passageways: An Interpretative History of Black America, Volume I: 1619–1863* (Fort Worth, TX: Harcourt Brace College Publishers, 1998), 19–21; Oscar Reiss, *Blacks in Colonial America* (Jefferson, NC: McFarland & Co., Inc., Publishers, 1997), 23–39, quote p. 34.

16. Thomas, *The Slave Trade*, 418.

17. Klein, *The Atlantic Slave Trade*, 140; Phillip D. Curtin, *The Atlantic Slave Trade: A Census* (Madison: The University of Wisconsin Press, 1969), 275–282.

African and African-descended people would dribble into the Virginia colony from 1619 on, but Virginia law did not formally recognize the condition of perpetual slavery or systematically mark out servants of African descent for special treatment until 1661.[18] They were often housed with white indentured servants and given the same work responsibilities; some were able to gain their freedom. One man, Anthony Johnson, even became a slaveowner himself.[19] The lack of clarity about the status of African workers persisted so long in part because of the small numbers of African people in the colony; by 1650 there were no more than 500 or so people of African descent in Virginia. High death rates in Virginia made owning a human being a less than pressing issue—most workers would die in a few years, and so the impetus to lay claim to a person for his or her natural life was not a strong one. But conditions improved, workers lived longer, and the number of African workers grew.[20] The status of these non-English people brought to labor in the tobacco fields of Virginia had to be spelled out.

Their willingness to consign African workers to permanent servitude was not that great a leap for the tobacco lords of Virginia. The English certainly were familiar with slavery in the colonies controlled by Spain and Portugal, and their participation on a modest scale in the slave trade gave them some direct knowledge. The term they used for African slaves—"negro"—was actually a term they borrowed from these two countries. Enslaving African people was advantageous to Virginia planters for a key reason: however poorly white indentured servants had been treated in the New World, and they were treated terribly for much of the seventeenth century, English traditions provided some restraints on their exploitation. No such traditions applied to people of African descent. Too, the English were placing a higher and higher value on liberty as a defining feature of their culture and were becoming quite prideful of the "rights of an Englishman."[21] It was, in short, becoming unseemly to treat English servants—free men and women after all—little better than slaves. Finally, the racial views of the era, as we have seen, consigned Africans to the bottom of the hierarchy of the world's peoples, and the English shared that belief and with that belief a willingness to treat Africans differently from Europeans. While the English had not practiced slavery on any significant scale, like other Europeans, their traditions did permit enslaving war captives from "heathen" nations.[22] Few African people were Christian, and many people ending up as

---

18. Reiss, *Blacks in Colonial America*, 97.

19. Jordan, *White Over Black*, 74; Reiss, *Blacks in Colonial America*, 97–99.

20. Morgan, *American Slavery, American Freedom*, 154, 297–299.

21. Jordan, *White Over Black*, 60–61.

22. George M. Frederickson, *White Supremacy A Comparative Study in American and South African History* (New York: Oxford University Press, 1981), 72; Jordan, *White Over Black*, 91–98.

slaves had initially been captured in war or at least by a raiding party, and so this legal loophole, coupled with English racial views and the need for labor, paved the way for a series of laws establishing de jure (legal) slavery.

In 1661 the Virginia colonial legislature passed a law that in effect recognized permanent servitude for Africans in the colony; it stipulated that an English servant who ran away "in company with any negroes who are incapable of making satisfaction by addition of time" would be penalized with additional time in servitude for himself and his companions.[23] One of the early stipulations for different treatment of Africans was that they were heathens. What if, however, they converted to Christianity, as some of them did? Up until the 1660s, "Negroes and Indians held in slavery who could prove they had been baptized sometimes sued for their freedom and won it."[24] In 1667 the assembly passed legislation that shut this door. Afterwards, if slaves converted to Christianity and were baptized, they were no longer entitled to freedom. If slaves were mere property, could they be treated like any other property? Yes and no. An act passed by the Virginia assembly in 1669 gave slaveholders the power of life and death over their slaves by declaring that the death of a slave during punishment "shall not be accompted felony," although the act did draw the line on the "casual killing of slaves."[25] Another law passed in 1705 gave private citizens the right to kill runaway slaves and authorized owners of incorrigible slaves (those who kept running away) to petition the court to be allowed to dismember the guilty parties. Robert Carter did just that; he asked the court to permit him to cut off the toes of two "incorrigible negroes."[26] To further define who could be a slave, the assembly passed laws in 1670 and again in 1682 that limited slavery to "non-Christian servants"; the 1670 act applied to people brought in by sea; the 1682 act referred to people brought into the colony by land or sea. In effect, both laws applied to people who weren't English or European people.[27] Slavery was a status reserved for those of another race.

But what would the status be of the offspring of a slave woman if the father was a free white man? The Virginia colonial assembly addressed this problem in 1662 by passing legislation stipulating that the status of a child went with its mother. This law was a departure from English common law and tradition; it established that the child of an unmarried slave woman was not filius nullius (child of no one) but rather belonged to her master and that the father bore no responsibility to support his child or do right by the mother. It established permanent servitude as a condition a child inherited from his or her mother and laid the groundwork for a slave system that need not depend on imports of

---

23. Morgan, *American Slavery, American Freedom*, 311.
24. *Ibid.*, 331.
25. *Ibid.*, 312.
26. *Ibid.*, 313.
27. *Ibid.*, 329.

new captives from Africa to grow and thrive. Perhaps to make it clear that the colonial government was not encouraging white men to have sex with black women now that they did not have to worry about assuming responsibility for the children that resulted, this same legislation also established a double penalty on whites who fornicated with blacks. The assembly returned to this issue again in 1691 with an act that outlawed sexual relations between white and black of any sort in or out of wedlock, referring to children produced by interracial liaisons as an "abominable mixture." [28] Slaveowners and other white men were apparently undeterred by the prospect of producing an "abominable mixture" and commonly had sexual relations with female slaves, often by force. However white the offspring might look and however exalted the status and wealth of the father, the product of such a liaison was by definition a slave.

As chattel, the slave was property and could be disposed of at will, but, after 1691, could only be freed if the slaveowner paid for his or her passage out of the colony; later, emancipation of a slave required the permission of the governor. To further distinguish between slaves and free, slaves were prohibited from owning property, and a law proscribed 30 lashes to any slave who "shall presume to lift up his hand in opposition against any christian." A later law specialty prohibited masters from lashing white servants who were naked, a punishment considered at that point suitable only for black slaves, not white servants, no matter how poor their condition.[29] Such regulations, accumulating piecemeal over several decades in the late 1600s and early years of the eighteenth century, established a system of race-based slavery that consigned virtually all blacks to the bottom of the Virginia social order while elevating even the poorest of whites—a group once exploited unmercifully—to a higher position. By the early 1700s, indentured servant immigration had slowed to a halt while the number of African slaves imported increased dramatically. Virginia, Maryland, and eventually the rest of the Southeast were committed to a plantation system based on slavery.

All Southern colonies and later states would eventually create and establish a body of laws called slave codes similar to the laws passed in seventeenth-century Virginia. In prescribing the condition of servitude, the codes were invariably harsh, with a simple basic thrust—the total submission of all slaves to their masters, and by extension to all whites. These codes specified restrictions on slaves' activities and would evolve over time. For example, following rebellions such as the Stono revolt in South Carolina in 1739 or the Nat Turner Rebellion in Virginia in 1831, legislative bodies revised slave codes to restrict blacks even more.[30] Fear of abolitionist-inspired slave uprisings, concern about

---

28. *Ibid.*, 333–335, quote 335.
29. *Ibid.*, 331, 333, 337, quote 331.
30. Reiss, *Blacks in Colonial America*, 198–211.

runaways, and a general sense of being embattled by the foes of slavery made for more restrictive slave laws in the decades leading up to the Civil War. Manumission was made very difficult, and freed slaves often had to leave the state. Slaves could not testify against a white person in a court, a prohibition that sometimes hindered courts when the witnesses to a crime were black. Slaves were required to have passes to travel off the plantation and could be stopped at will by any white. They were not permitted to gather in large concentrations. Slave marriages were not recognized by law, although many enslaved people married nonetheless. Slave couples had no legal rights to their children; children were owned by the slaveowners. Slaves were not permitted to have guns, and it was illegal for slaves to own property or purchase alcohol. Slave patrols (comprised of local white community members) were given wide legal authority to police slaves outside the borders of their own plantations. Slaves caught without a pass or suspected of an infraction could be whipped, with twenty lashes being a typical penalty. The codes did provide some protections to slaves; slaves were, for example, entitled to a trial if accused of a crime. If a white man killed a slave, he could be charged with a misdemeanor if it was in the heat of passion, or a felony if the act was judged to be premeditated and malicious. While it was rare for a white person to be charged with a crime against a black person, slave or free, it did happen on occasion. The protection of the law did not extend, however, to the crime of rape. No law in the codes addressed the rape of a slave woman; in effect, according to the law, a slave woman could not be raped, although a master might punish a slave man for raping a slave woman if he chose.[31]

For the most part, the codes were designed to control a population of people that at bottom slaveowners could never fully trust and were designed, revised, and interpreted by the courts with this end in mind. Truth be told, slaveowners could and often did ignore the codes, and the law for the most part stood back and allowed them to do it. While no colony or state permitted slaveholders to "casually" kill slaves, authorities and courts rarely investigated the death of a slave. Grief Mason, overseer at Cooleemee plantation in North Carolina, broke up a fight in the slave quarters one day and in the process killed two slaves. When the owner of the plantation castigated Mason, he threatened to quit; he did not expect to be criticized for how he controlled the plantation's slaves and in all likelihood never even considered legal repercussions from his action.[32] Slaveholders obviously violated laws against miscegenation, some permitted trusted slaves to hunt with firearms, and some taught their slaves to read and write. The slaveholder was the law on the plan-

---

31. Eugene D. Genovese, *Roll, Jordan, Roll: The World the Slaves Made* (New York: Vintage Books, 1976), 30–32, 37–41, 406, 617–619.

32. Henry Wiencek, *The Hairstons: An American Family in Black and White* (New York: St. Martin's Press, 1999), 81–82.

tation, and the Slave Codes backed up the power of the slaveholder, only occasionally intervening when a slaveholder violated the law. [33]

White Supremacy

While race-based slavery developed in the South for the very practical reason of keeping the plantation system supplied with low cost labor, it could only have developed if white Englishmen were willing to consider other human beings as little more than beasts of burden. They were willing to do so; as we have seen, they had been quite willing to treat their own countrymen in such a way, so it is not surprising that people from another continent who did not look like them or think like them or act like them could also be treated that way. But the willingness to consider Africans as suitable subjects for slavery evolved into a well-developed ideology in the South called white supremacy, which posited black inferiority and white superiority in all avenues of life—intellectual, moral, and physical. This ideology reflected racial views common in the Western world, the North included. However, in the doctrine of white supremacy that developed in the South, ideas on race became more extreme and unequivocal as spokesmen for the South, elected and self-appointed, became more and more strident in their defense of slavery, particularly as the rise of King Cotton in the early decades of the nineteenth century made the plantation and slavery immensely profitable and Northern abolitionists became more and more strident in their attacks on slavery. In the racial views of these spokesmen, blacks were not merely different and inferior; they were on the one hand brutes and on the other hand childlike creatures incapable of taking care of themselves, and this was their "natural" condition as opposed to a consequence of "environmental" conditions that might change in the foreseeable future. With such a primitive and potentially dangerous population—and here was an argument not commonly advanced by other racial thinkers—blacks could live orderly and productive lives only if under the direct control of whites. Slavery was thus a good thing both for the slave and the slavemaster and was the "natural" condition for an inferior race.[34] These views were reflected in Alexander Stephens's famous "Corner-Stone Speech," delivered shortly after his election as vice president of the Confederacy in 1861. As Stephens noted in this speech,

> Many governments have been founded upon the principle of the subordination and serfdom of certain classes of the same race; such were and are in violation of the laws of nature. Our system commits no such violation of nature's laws. With us, all the white race, however

---

33. Eugene D. Genovese, *Roll, Jordan, Roll,* 41, 47–48.
34. Frederickson, *White Supremacy,* 52–54, 58.

high or low, rich or poor, are equal in the eye of the law. Not so with the negro. Subordination is his place. He, by nature, or by the curse against Canaan, is fitted for that condition which he occupies in our system.[35]

Those who criticized slavery on humanitarian grounds or religious grounds—the Methodist church in its early years had been opposed to slavery, for example—were silenced, and white supremacy would become the unchallenged reigning doctrine in the South.

A new political party (Republican Party) arose in the North and Midwest in the 1850s which was committed to controlling the growth of slavery and which seemed to many in the South bent on ultimately destroying slavery. While ending slavery was not a stated purpose of this party, many Republicans were convinced that slavery ultimately had to go because it put in their midst a population of people who were inferior, who could never be assimilated, and who could never truly be part of the American democratic experience. Ironically, their take on white supremacy led them to oppose slavery. When Republican Abraham Lincoln won the presidential election of 1860, the Deep South, that portion of the South where blacks outnumbered whites and the commitment of whites to the doctrine of white supremacy and slavery was strongest, left the Union before Lincoln even took office; other Southern states would later follow. The South would lose the Civil War, but the doctrine of white supremacy would exert a powerful influence on Southern culture for another 100 or more years.[36]

Making Slaves

When captives arrived from Africa, they were typically auctioned off at slave markets and transported to the farms and plantations where they would live and work. A process that had begun the moment they were captured would move into high gear—the education on how to be a slave. This process was sometimes called "seasoning" and involved instruction in the work regimen of the farm or plantation on which a newly arrived African found himself or herself, the rules he or she would be expected to follow, and the necessity of obedience to the slavemaster and, in fact, all whites. It also involved instruction in the new language slaves would be expected to speak and, indirectly at least, the new culture in which they were now immersed.[37] But if seasoning was a form of education, it was a hard-hearted and often brutal education; masters en-

---

35. Henry Cleveland, ed., *Alexander H. Stephens in Public and Private: With Letters and Speeches Before, During and Since the War* (Philadelphia: National Publishing Company, 1866), 722–723.

36. Frederickson, *White Supremacy*, 145–152.

37. Palmer, *Passageway*, 24, 42.

deavored to "break in" newly arrived slaves, and this process necessarily was designed to make these men, women, and children give up hope of returning to their homelands and accept their lots in life.[38] Ideally, it would make them adopt the personae of slaves, obedient, trustworthy, passive, hard-working, unquestioning, and value what the slaveholders set before them however unpleasant the assignment or meager the reward. The slaveholders had no intention of making their captives into likenesses of themselves; if they had, they would not have passed the sorts of laws they did or limited what they taught them. What they wanted were robots with smiles on their faces.

But the men and women who arrived in the South in chains would not become robots, nor would they be, in the words of an early historian of slavery, "coerced into self-obliterating humility."[39] They would resist in small ways and large, including rebellion, although slave uprisings were few. Slaveholders would apply the lash to discipline slaves who resisted their authority or misbehaved; some resorted to it frequently, while others tried their best never to whip their slaves.[40] One former slave recalled that the overseer on his plantation—he called him "the meanest man that ever walked on earth"—whipped his mother "with a long leather whip" because "they said they couldn't teach her no sense" and whipped a man "until he was bloody as a pig cause he went to the mill and stayed too long."[41] On another plantation, one slave recollected, the master "didn't 'low mucher whipping. Driver do whipping, but if he whip too severely, Maussa would sometime tek field hand and mak him driver and put driver in field." [42] Other slaveowners attempted to employ the carrot more than the stick. Frank Gill recalls on his plantation that his master was a kindly man. Once, as a boy, he was threatened with a whipping by his master; he pulled the master's coattails, causing him to fall down, and then ran to the planter's wife to escape punishment. According to Gill, women were never whipped. On this plantation, slaves were permitted to tend their own private cotton patches and keep chickens; the master would sell what the slaves produced and give them the money.[43]

---

38. Peter Kolchin, *American Slavery: 1619–1877* (New York: Hill and Wang, 1997), 57.

39. Ulrich Bonnell Phillips, *Life and Labor in the Old South* (1929; Boston: Little, Brown and Company, 1963), 194.

40. Genovese, *Roll, Jordan, Roll*, 63–67.

41. Hal Hutson interview, *Born in Slavery: Slave Narratives from the Federal Writers' Project, 1936–1938* (Washington: Library of Congress, Manuscript Division, 2001), http://memory.loc.gov/ammem/snhtml/snhome.html.

42. Sam Mitchell, interview by Chlotilde R. Martin, *Born in Slavery: Slave Narratives from the Federal Writers' Project, 1936–1938* (Washington: Library of Congress, Manuscript Division, 2001), http://memory.loc.gov/ammem/snhtml/snhome. html.

43. Frank Gill, interview by Ila B. Prine, *Born in Slavery: Slave Narratives from the Federal Writers' Project, 1936–1938* (Washington: Library of Congress, Manuscript Division, 2001), http://memory.loc.gov/ammem/snhtml/snhome.html.

In the struggle between master and slave over the conditions of slavery, slaves did have something the masters wanted which gave them some bargaining power: their labor. Their raw numbers also gave them some leverage; in the plantation districts where whites were often outnumbered 10 to 1 by slaves, slaves could easily have overpowered slaveholders any time they wished. But a plantation was a workplace, not a prison, and simply could not have functioned if slaves were under armed guard at all times. Masters had to think about this when they applied the lash, made unreasonable work demands on their slaves, sold children from parents or husbands from wives, or denied slaves some measure of private life. Perhaps the greatest resource for slaves was the masters' own values. Most slaveowners were Christians, and slaves could and did gently remind slaveholders of the golden rule, "the meek shall inherit the earth" and other tenants of the faith that stressed kind treatment to the powerless. Slaveholders generally saw themselves as patriarchs of their plantations, and all souls on the plantation—men, women and children, black and white—were under their authority and protection. This bound slaveholder to slave in an often intimate relationship. A good patriarch acted paternalistically, treating slaves as his children, firm but fair. Slaves could and did remind slaveholders of this responsibility. Slaveholders could and often did ignore their duty and the pleas of slaves and sell a child from a mother or whip a young boy for a trivial reason. But many men and women who owned slaves measured themselves as worthwhile human beings in part by how well they lived up to their responsibilities as slaveholders. And so on more than a few plantations, slave men were given passes to leave plantations to visit wives, Christmas celebrations with bountiful food and drink for all were held, slaveholders tried to keep slave families together, and the lash was a last resort.[44] Slaves got not only better treatment in this "bargain" but the breathing room to create some semblance of a life for themselves; slaveholders got a more productive workforce and perhaps a restful night's sleep that comes to those who aren't worried about being killed in their beds.

In their dealings with whites, slaves knew they were expected to be submissive and deferential. Slaves knew well the penalties for being less than respectful. In order to retain some measure of self-worth, integrity, and personal identity in an often demeaning and brutalizing situation, blacks hid their true feelings and mastered the art of deception—of saying one thing and meaning another—when they were around whites. This act of transformation is called "masking" and is the topic of a well-known poem by Paul Laurence Dunbar:

> We wear the mask that grins and lies,
> It hides our cheeks and shades our eyes,
> This debt we pay to human guile;

---

44. Genvoese, *Roll, Jordan, Roll*, 74–86.

With torn and bleeding hearts we smile,
And mouth with myriad subtleties.

Why should the world be otherwise,
In counting all our tears and sighs?
Nay, let them only see us, while
We wear the mask.

We smile, but, O great Christ, our cries
To thee from tortured souls arise,
We sing, but oh the clay is vile
Beneath our feet, and long the mile;
But let the world dream otherwise,
We wear the mask.[45]

The need for deception would have broader cultural implications—the language (including lyrics to songs and spirituals) of people in slavery was often allusive, symbolic, and indirect. In short, slaves might say one thing and mean another or there might be several layers of meaning, each for a different audience, in what they said or sang: a spiritual might be about Moses and the children of Israel, but it was also about another people in slavery (themselves) who would be delivered from bondage one day. The personalities of slaves were affected by the need to deceive, too. Some slaves refused to be submissive to whites and earned the reputation of being dangerous (they were called "bad niggers"). Most field hands did enough to avoid beatings and were generally "sullenly obedient and hostilely submissive" to whites. At the other extreme, some slaves internalized submissiveness to such an extent they became a "Sambo," a person who seemed to live to serve and amuse his owner. Often, these were the house servants who spent much of their time with whites. For most slaves, their true validation as human beings came away from whites in the slave quarters where they could be, if only for a few hours each day, human beings.[46]

Slavery and Work

For slaves, life was work, and for most, work was farming. Slaves were involved in all phases of agricultural production, including clearing land, preparing the soil for planting, planting and cultivating the crop, harvesting,

---

45. Paul Lawrence Dunbar, "We Wear the Mask," Deirdre Mullane, ed., *Crossing the Danger Water: Three Hundred Years of African-American Writing* (New York: Anchor Books, 1993), 350.

46. John Blassingame, *The Slave Community: Plantation Life in the Antebellum South* (New York: Oxford University Press, 1979), 303–322, quote p. 305.

and processing the crop for market. Men and women frequently performed the same sorts of labor and often worked side by side in the fields, particularly at harvest time. Men typically performed the most physically demanding work, such as the clearing of land and the plowing, but women sometimes performed these tasks, too.[47] As one woman observed, "My grandmother was a field hand. She plowed and hoed the crops in the summer and spring, and in the winter she sawed and cut cord wood just like a man. She said it didn't hurt her as she was strong as an ox."[48] Both males and females served as house servants. While the division of labor was less based on gender in the slave community than it was in the white community, some special kinds of work did exhibit this division. Some women had jobs as plantation cooks and what would today be termed child care providers with responsibility for taking care of the young children during the day while their parents were in the field. Men were generally the plantation craftsmen—wheelwrights, blacksmiths, carpenters, and the like. Craftsmen, cooks, servants, and drivers—a slave man with a supervisory role who typically reported to the overseer—occupied the top of the occupational ladder in the world of the slave. Men were more likely to hunt; women generally spun thread, wove cloth, sewed, and, of course, cooked for their families.[49] Before the age of 8, children were generally not expected to do much work, although this was not always the case. Between 8 and 12, they were expected to dig potatoes, feed chickens, take water to the workers, help around the kitchen, chase birds from the fields, and take part in the harvest. By age 12 or 13, they entered the adult world and were expected to work with the men and women.[50]

Half the slaves of the South lived on farms; most of the remainder lived on plantations. The size of the farm or plantation on which a slave worked had important implications for the sort of life he or she would live. Slaves living on the more prosperous and larger plantations were more likely to have decent cabins and adequate rations of food. As a rule, small farming units were less stable than large units. Small slave owning farmers who encountered financial problems might sell a few slaves and often gave slaves as dowries to their daughters. On a farm with few slaves, such practices could separate husbands from wives, parents from children, and friend from friend and leave those remaining lonely and isolated, not to mention overworked. Slaves on small farms often had to travel long distances to find potential partners for courtship and marriage, and women who married were more likely to end up as single

47. Genovese, *Roll, Jordan, Roll*, 319.
48. Mary Frances Webb interview, *Born in Slavery: Slave Narratives from the Federal Writers' Project, 1936–1938* (Washington: Library of Congress, Manuscript Division, 2001), http://memory.loc.gov/ammem/snhtml/snhome.html.
49. Genovese, *Roll, Jordan, Roll*, 319, 388–398, 486–487, 495.
50. *Ibid.*, 502–503.

parents. Large plantations, particularly the more prosperous ones, were less likely to sell off members of their workforce, and two parent families were less likely to be broken up. Slaves on large plantations had more choices of mates. On a large plantation with many slaves, people in slavery spent most of their time with other slaves in the fields and after work and might see very few whites beyond the master and his family and the overseer. Slaves on small farms spent much of their time with whites with whom they often worked side by side. [51]

On large farms and plantations, slaveholders tended to organize their slave labor force by gang or task. Under the gang system, slaves worked in unison, usually in carefully defined groups that were often segregated by age and gender. Gang members were closely supervised by white overseers and black drivers and were expected to keep up with the pace. "Regimentation and discipline" were the defining characteristics of gang labor leaving "little room" for autonomy or initiative on the part of the slaves. By contrast, under the task system, slaves were assigned an amount of work for the day, or perhaps a week, that was measured in output, not hours—so many rows to be sowed, so much wood to be chopped, so many acres to be harvested. Planters could "measure" the work slaves actually completed and did not need to closely supervise the slaves. When their work was finished, slaves were free to use their time as they saw fit. Skilled or industrious slaves could often complete their "tasks" by early afternoon and have the rest of the day off for leisure or to work for themselves—many had gardens, pigs, boats for fishing, and so on. The "self-regulated" nature of labor and the "absence of direct supervision" gave the slave some measure of control over the amount and pace of the work and some degree, however limited, of freedom. While gang labor was generally limited to plantation-size units, tasking went on everywhere—in herding, on plantations and farms, in industries, mines, and workshops. Different crops and commodities, however, usually lent themselves to one or the other form of labor organization. Sugar production in Southern Louisiana was associated with the gang system; rice cultivation in the Low Country if South Carolina was closely linked with the task system.[52]

The production of certain cash crops tended to "root" slaves in a specific location while others tended to promote mobility, and this had profound impact on the quality of life slaves led and the culture they created. So, too, did the requirements of the crop they were tending. Tobacco cultivation wore the soil out very quickly, and planters periodically moved their workforces to fresh

---

51. Genovese, *Roll, Jordan, Roll*, 7–10; Ira Berlin and Phillip D. Morgan, "Labor and the Shaping of Slave Life in the Americas," in Berlin and Morgan eds., *Cultivation and Culture: Labor and the Shaping of Slave Life in the Americas* (Charlottesville, VA: University Press of Virginia, 1993), 8, 21.

52. Ira Berlin and Phillip D. Morgan, "Labor and the Shaping of Slave Life in the Americas," Berlin and Morgan eds., *Cultivation and Culture*, 14–15.

land. Slaves who worked tobacco could not expect to spend a long time in any one place. Tobacco cultivation itself, however, moved at a measured pace and provided slaves with a stable, orderly work regimen. Sugar and rice plantations produced a very different reality for slaves. Sugar and rice did not deplete the soil like tobacco did, and plantations tended to be large, highly capitalized, and employ large slave workforces. Slaves tended to stay put on the same plantation. On sugar plantations, however, the advantage stability brought the slaves may have been outweighed by the killing pace of work required by the cultivation and processing of this crop.[53] As one observer noted, "the cultivation of sugar in Louisiana is carried on at an enormous expense of human life. Planters must buy to keep up their stock. . . ." These plantations were probably the reason slaves elsewhere feared "being sold down the river."[54] Cotton cultivation, too, had its impact on slave life. A growing demand for cotton in the decades following the War of 1812 resulted in a migration of slaveholders, their agents, and "hundreds of thousands of slaves to the piedmont of the Carolinas and Georgia, further westward to the Mississippi valley, and beyond." Many of these slave migrants were younger people because the rigors of hacking plantations out of the wilderness required the strength and endurance of the young. Thousands of young adults and children would, as a consequence, be separated from their families and communities during this westward migration.[55] Once cotton plantations became well established, cotton cultivation followed seasonal patterns of planting, hoeing, and picking that lent to cotton regions a certain order that became the stuff of legends.

Part of the slave population, a small part, lived in Southern towns and cities laboring at a multitude of non-agricultural pursuits. They worked as factory hands, day laborers, washerwomen, house servants, and skilled craftsmen. For many urban slaves, working in a town or city was as good as it got for a slave. They were able to move freely throughout the city and were often able to hire themselves out during their free time to earn extra money. They were able to engage in activities and pastimes—gambling, gathering in bars, attending their own churches in company with free blacks—that were simply not within the realm of the possible for rural slaves.[56]

Free blacks constituted only 6% or so of the population of the South in 1860 (about 250,000 people). They were an intermediate class between slaves and

53. *Ibid.*, 9.
54. Roderick A. McDonald, "Independent Economic Production By Slaves on Antebellum Louisiana Sugar Plantations," Berlin and Morgan eds., *Cultivation and Culture*, 278.
55. Stephen F. Miller, "Plantation Labor Organization and Slave Life on the Cotton Frontier: The Alabama-Mississippi Black Belt, 1815–1840," Berlin and Morgan, eds., *Cultivation and Culture*, 155, 157, quote, 155.
56. Kolchin, *American Slavery*, 1619–1877, 177–178.

whites as we saw in an earlier chapter; they were free men and women but did not have the full range of rights enjoyed by whites. They were an intermediate group in another respect; many free blacks were mulattoes—people of mixed race. Some ignored the white part of their ancestry, while others took pride in it and saw their light complexions as a sign of superiority. It was not uncommon for free blacks who were mulattoes to get help, financial and otherwise, from their white parents, and whites often preferred to deal with light skinned free blacks. Free blacks were farmers, laborers, craftsmen, preachers, and some, such as the Metoyer family of Louisiana, were even planters who owned slaves.[57] But free blacks really didn't fit into the prevailing racial calculus of the South whereby whites were free and blacks were slaves. In the decades leading up to the Civil War, they were a troubling group of people to the rulers of the region, who worried that they might provoke slave uprisings. Free blacks would perform an important social and political role after the Civil War when they would form a significant element of the black leadership of the South.

Black Culture in a White World

The earliest African migrants to the South were mostly men and often ended up on small plantations; it was for them a male world, a largely white world, and no doubt a world of loneliness and despair. Most learned bits of English and enough of the customs and requirements of their masters to survive. As time went by, a process called "creolization" took place in which slaves, particularly those born in the colonies, adapted to their new world and its culture. As the colonies became more settled, the disparity in numbers between men and women slaves lessened, and more and more people in slavery were able to establish families which encouraged creolization. So, too, did the growing influence of Christianity and the growing diversity of occupations slaves might be engaged in. This process was also helped along by the declining numbers of African born people in the slave population; by the later decades of the 1700s, a great majority of the slave population was made up of people who had been born in America. Unlike the slaveholding societies of the Caribbean where blacks greatly outnumbered whites, slaves in the South lived in the midst of a large white population and were generally in the minority in all but the prime plantation districts. Southwide, slaves would constitute slightly less than 1/3 of the population by 1860; even in the Deep South, whites outnumbered slaves by a small margin.[58]

---

57. *Ibid.*, 241; Palmer, *Passageways: An Interpretive History of Black America*, 185–198.

58. Kolchin, *American Slavery*, 44–57, 242.

The declining influence of African cultures and the rising influence of English and later American culture can be seen in a number of developments. African languages disappeared, leaving behind a small number of words and phrases; English became the language of the slaves. Over time, fewer slave children were given African names such as Quash or Cuffee by their parents and more and more were given Christian names such as John or Mary. Slaves were converted to Christianity in growing numbers from the mid 1700s until the eve of the Civil War; one scholar has estimated that by 1835 nearly 30% of the slaves were practicing Christians. Slave women even adapted the nursing practices of whites and abandoned the African practice of nursing children for several years following their births.[59]

But creolization was much more than slaves simply adopting the culture of their masters. Elements of their old cultures did persist. Slave captives had come from many cultures in Africa, and this made keeping native languages and customs difficult, but there were enough commonalities between many of the African cultures to permit bits and pieces of the old cultures to persist. These bits and pieces—foods and recipes, musical styles, farming knowledge such as the techniques of rice cultivation, building styles, words, phrases, and even certain religious values and practices—came together as an important part of an African-American culture that shared much with the prevailing white culture but differed in important respects. In plantation districts with large slave populations, slaves lived in a largely black world which gave them, however much slaveholders might have objected, more cultural autonomy. Here African-American culture diverged quite vividly from white culture.[60] For example, on the Sea Islands off the coast of South Carolina where slaves outnumbered whites 10 to 1, slaves developed their own language (Gullah) that contained elements of African dialects.[61] In areas where the slave population was sparse, less of the old cultures was retained over time, and white and black cultures were more alike. The internal slave trade served to spread common elements of the culture through the South, although regional variations developed, such as the unique culture on the Sea Islands or the culture spawned in French and Spanish influenced Louisiana.

This was a culture that was in continuous dialogue with white culture; white culture influenced black culture, and black culture influenced white culture in ways that we do not yet fully understand. Take corn shucking, for example.

---

59. *Ibid.*, 44–57; Christine Leigh Heyrman, *Southern Cross: The Beginnings of the Bible Belt* (Chapel Hill: University of North Carolina Press, 1997), 265.

60. Kolchin, *American Slavery*, 43–48; Judith A. Carney, *Black Rice: The African Origins of Rice Cultivation in the Americas* (Cambridge, Massachusetts: Harvard University Press, 2001), 104–105, 116–117, 137.

61. Peter Wood, *Black Majority: Negroes in Colonial South Carolina from 1670 through the Stono Rebellion* (New York: W.W. Norton Co., 1975), 170.

Rural whites throughout the South and the rest of America would gather after the harvest of the corn crop at neighbors' farms to engage in a communal enterprise called a corn shucking. It became a festive occasion with contests, storytelling, eating and drinking as well as the work of shucking piles of corn. In plantation districts, slaves participated in these shuckings and created their own traditions. When a plantation owner sent out word that he wished to have a corn shucking, slaves would gather at plantations for miles around on the appointed evening. They would march in large groups to the plantation where the shucking was to be held, their way lighted by pine knot torches. The groups would converge on the plantation from different directions, their arrival heralded by the corn shucking songs they would be singing that would ring out through the still night air:

> You gwine, aint you gwine,
> Ain't you gwine to the shuckin' of the corn?
> Oh yest I gwine to stay to morning
> When Gable blows his horn,
> Am gwine to stay till the coming of the dawn.

Whites would often gather to view the spectacle, and sometimes the master of the plantation would give a speech to those assembled. The shucking began, and the teams of shuckers would try to outdo each other in both the amount of corn shucked and in song. The team that shucked the most corn might seek out the host and carry him around the plantation yard on their shoulders, singing another song, this one often poking fun at him. Then the men would be treated to a big supper cooked by the slave women; toasts were given, and then those assembled would have a dance that lasted until dawn. In large measure this event—the songs, the ceremony, the toasts, the party—was the creation of the slaves. They had taken an event common in the white world and made it their own. The owner of the plantation in return got his corn shucked and was able to show to one and all that he was the generous patriarch he imagined himself to be.[62] Little wonder whites would wax eloquently about slavery after the war with memories such as this in their heads and other sorts of memories conveniently forgotten.

At the center of African-American culture were family, religion, music, language, and folklore. People in slavery sought order and stability for themselves and their children first and foremost through the family and created family traditions, similar to the whites in many respects and different in others. As we will see in more detail in a later chapter, people in slavery did their best to establish two-parent households and valued their extended families. Slaves did

---

62. Roger D. Abrahams, *Singing the Master: The Emergence of African-American Culture in the Plantation South* (New York: Penguin Books, 1992), 6–21, 52–53, quote, p. 7.

what they could to create and sustain strong family relations despite the terrible possibilities that always hovered in the background. Most slaves adopted a surname (last name), generally of their first owners, and passed this name down to their children despite the sometimes active opposition to this practice on the part of slaveowners. This much was similar to the customs of the whites. But while slaveholders practiced first cousin marriage, slaves observed a taboo against it. Slaves often also practiced a form of trial marriage; if things didn't work out, the couple returned to single status. Children were taught to address older adults as "aunt" or "uncle," residential group members as "cousins," and age mates as "brother" or "sister," regardless of blood relationship. These practices are continued today by many African Americans. This tradition of "fictive kinship" helped enslaved Africans humanize the hostile environment of slavery and communicate to each other "we are part of one family." [63]

Slaveholders had initially opposed active efforts to convert slaves to Christianity, but by the mid-1700s, most had decided that Christianity might encourage slaves to be docile and accepting of their lot in life in hopes of a blissful afterlife. While African-American slaves embraced Christianity, they did not simply accept in toto the version of it offered to them by whites. Slaves rejected the idea that Christianity justified their enslavement, grew restive when white preachers emphasized the importance of obedience to their earthly masters, and used their faith to judge slavery morally and critically. They often attended white churches but were able to create their own "secret churches" where they could practice their own version of Christianity with their own preachers, service, music, and theology. In their religious practices and rituals, they safely vented their frustration and took solace in anticipation of divine deliverance from enslavement in the future. The services in black churches were often exuberant celebrations of the glory of God. Black preachers developed the unique "call and response" style of preaching that ultimately affected preaching styles in many of the white churches.[64] The theology of the black churches is best uncovered in the words of the spirituals, the new religious music African Americans developed for their "new" faith. As historian Lawrence Levine has pointed out, the most persistent image in the spirituals was the idea of African Americans as a chosen people, just like the Hebrews of the Old Testament. Spirituals frequently made references to Old Testament figures who were delivered from some dismal fate, such as Jonah, who was rescued from the belly of a whale, or Joshua, who was assisted by God in fighting the battle of Jericho. Infusing

---

63. Herbert G. Gutman, *The Black Family in Slavery and Freedom, 1750–1925* (New York: Vintage Books, 1977), 12, 47–49, 64–67, 88–93, 96–97, 151, 190–200, 217, 270–277.

64. Blassingame, *The Slave Community*, 130–137; Kolchin, *American Slavery*, 143–148.

slaves with a sense of worth, ultimate justice and change, the spirituals reflected more confidence than despair. While increasing numbers of slaves embraced Christianity, many held fast to beliefs rooted in African traditions, most notably in conjuring, and these beliefs would coexist, often uneasily, with Christian beliefs in the slave community. Root or hoodoo doctors would play a prominent role in most black communities and still may be found in many areas of the South. With their spells and herbal potions, these doctors gave slaves some sense of control in a world in which they had little control, and some of their herbs actually did have medicinal properties, not to mention the psychosomatic benefits a visit to the doctor might provide patients. [65]

The spiritual was not the only "new" musical form developed by slaves; for entertainment slaves sang and played the whole gamut of music found in the white world but also devised work songs and field hollers uniquely their own. Many Africans Americans were accomplished players of stringed instruments, and their style of music emphasized improvisation and rhythmic complexity. Polyrhythmic elements would become permanent, distinguishing features of African-American music. In America, African slaves re-created African instruments, the banjo in particular, and mastered the European violin and guitar. They also produced elaborate rhythmic patterns by "patting juba" (clapping their hands, slapping their thighs, knees and other body parts).[66]

African Americans developed distinctive speech patterns and dialects that differed in important respects from those of whites. Whites were generally dismissive of the way slaves talked; to them, slaves spoke poorly or incorrectly out of ignorance, although they enjoyed some of the more vivid expressions. We now know that these dialects followed rules of grammar and usage and served a variety of functions for people in slavery, not the least of which was as a language that they created themselves and best understood. This language defined them as a distinct people, an important function all languages serve as well as the more obvious function of communicating information. The dialects fell along a range; at one end was Gullah with its large number of African or African-inspired word and language patterns that was often almost indecipherable to whites. One scholar found over 4,000 African words in use in the Gullah language as late as the 1940s. At the other extreme were the dialects spoken by blacks in predominantly white regions of the South, which were often little different from those spoken by whites. A few examples common to many of the black dialects in slavery were the dropping of certain verbs, as in "He tired" ("He is tired"), the dropping of the possessive, as in "Sam coat" (Sam's coat),

---

65. Kolchin, *American Slavery*, 137–146; Lawrence W. Levine, *Black Culture and Black Consciousness: Afro-American Folk Thought From Slavery to Freedom* (Oxford: Oxford University Press, 1977), 26–29, 31–40.

66. Blassingame, *The Slave Community*, 115–116.

and finally using "him" or "he" to refer to both males and females. The influence of black dialects on white Southern dialects is much debated, but the prominence of the drawl in the Deep South, where the black population was largest, suggests a strong influence was likely. Certainly West African terms such as tote, goober, okay, okra, yam, gumbo, and hoodoo became a part of the Southern white vocabulary.[67]

African-American folklore both entertained and instructed; it gave slaves a creative outlet and helped them relieve the frustrations and hostilities a life in bondage produced in human beings. Folklore helped people in slavery reject dehumanizing, stereotypical images, taught them survival techniques, and emphasized the importance of loyalty to friends, kin, and community. Many were "trickster" tales that featured a hero who overcomes a more powerful foe through cunning and trickery. The "Brer Rabbit" tales, for example, demonstrated how a disadvantaged but resourceful individual could outwit a powerful adversary. But the Brer Rabbit tales also taught the foolhardiness of "acting rashly and striking out blindly" as when Brer Rabbit got entangled with the tar baby. The tales often featured animals and amusing dialogue and stories, but the underlying themes of many of the tales went well beyond light entertainment. Many were profoundly critical of slavery. Nonetheless, they were actually popular with whites and became a part of white culture in the South. The criticisms of slavery and whites were on a symbolic level that most whites probably never really "got." Many Americans became familiar with the tales through their retelling by a Southern white man (Joel Chandler Harris) in his Uncle Remus stories and later through Walt Disney's film version of Harris's stories (*Song of the South*).[68]

The End of Slavery and the Rise of Jim Crow

When the Civil War began in 1861, the leadership of the North did not set out to end slavery; its goal was to force the seceding Southern states to return to the Union. President Lincoln and other Northern leaders came to support emancipation only after early heavy losses in the war and the South's bitter resistance transformed the war into an all-out moral crusade to save the union and destroy the institution that most threatened it. The need to impress foreign countries of the rightness of the Union cause, and the need, eventually, for black troops, also convinced the Northern leadership that ending slavery was necessary. The demise of slavery began with Lincoln's Emancipation

---

67. Levine, *Black Culture and Black Consciousness*, 139, 145; Blassingame, *The Slave Community*, 26–30, 99.

68. Levine, *Black Culture and Black Consciousness*, 81–135, quote p. 115.

Proclamation, issued in 1862, which ended slavery in territory controlled by the Confederacy. It was rooted out in its entirety with the passage of the Thirteenth Amendment to the Constitution after the war ended in 1865.[69]

With the end of slavery, race relations in the South took a new turn, although initially the former slaveholders did everything in their power to hold on to their labor source. In 1865 and 1866, the newly reconstituted state legislatures of the South passed a series of laws called "Black Codes" which amounted to little more than an attempt to reestablish a form of "unofficial" slavery through legal trickery. African Americans, many of them traveling by foot throughout the South searching for lost husbands, wives, children and parents, were required to demonstrate that they weren't vagrants (having no home or visible means of support). Of course virtually all of the former slaves of the South were, legally speaking, vagrants and thus subject to arrest. The punishment for this "crime" was often a sentence to work on the same plantation on which they had labored as slaves. The Congress, controlled by the Republican Party, saw through this charade and, a year later, imposed a harsher Reconstruction, which temporarily suspended the operations of Southern state governments and established rule by military governors. Republicans in Congress devised a plan to reintroduce civilian government into the South which would protect Republican power in Congress and limit the power of the prewar slaveholding class. Republicans enfranchised African-American males in the South and endeavored to build a multi-racial Republican Party in the region that would be powerful enough to elect Republicans to Congress. The 14th and 15th Amendments were passed by Congress and ratified by the states. They were designed to ensure, once and for all, that the freed slaves would have full civil and voting rights of American citizens. The multiracial Republican Party dominated the governments of every Southern state in the Second Reconstruction for a brief period of time in the late 1860s and early 1870s and would be a serious contender for office in most Southern states throughout the 1880s and into the 1890s in some states.[70] Arrayed against it was an overwhelmingly white Democratic Party.

The two-party politics of the later decades of the nineteenth century at the least presented the possibility that a new racial accord could be achieved between black and white based on the principle of equality. The educational and economic progress of Southern African Americans also suggested the same possibility. Schools and colleges were started throughout the South by philanthropists, churches, and governments, and hundreds of thousands of former

---

69. Alan Trelease, *Reconstruction: the Great Experiment* (New York: Harper Torchbooks, 1971), 6–9.

70. *Ibid.*, 114–146; Edward L. Ayers, *The Promise of the New South: Life After Reconstruction* (New York: Oxford University Press, 1992), 37–54.

slaves, young and old alike, enrolled. One such student, albeit an exceptional one, was Booker T. Washington. Washington traveled, largely by foot, five hundred miles to attend Hampton Institute in Virginia; later he started his own college in Alabama (Tuskegee), where he built his reputation as the most influential black educator of the era. The development of the sharecropping system, the major form of employment for black families, was, as we saw earlier, ultimately a tragedy, but early on it represented a significant improvement, at least in terms of hope, over slavery. Some sharecropper families were able to wrest from the land (and the landlord) a decent living, and some blacks were able to become landowners. The percentage of black farmers who owned their own farms climbed from 2% in 1870 to 21% in 1890. Some blacks were also able to acquire jobs as skilled and semi-skilled workers, sometimes working side by side with their white counterparts. Nearly 50% of the skilled workforce in Greensboro, North Carolina, was African American during the late 1800s. Blacks and whites often lived on integrated streets in Greensboro. The extent of opportunities for blacks and of residential racial integration in Greensboro may not have been the norm, particularly in the Deep South, but it is illustrative of the "flexibility" of race relations in the decades after the Civil War.[71]

While the years after the Civil War offered greater opportunities for blacks, more rights, and at least the promise of even better things ahead, other developments suggested a very different future. Many conservative Democrats simply did not accept the legitimacy of the Republican Party and were willing to do anything—murder, intimidation, and vote theft—to defeat Republicans. The Ku Klux Klan basically functioned as the terrorist wing of the Democratic Party in the late 1860s and early 1870s and played an important role in the "restoration" of Southern state governments to Democratic control over the course of the 1870s. In the social sphere, blacks and whites were separating themselves from each other in ways that did not bode well for a productive and equitable multiracial society. Some of this was the choice of blacks; for example, in the years after the Civil War, blacks left white churches in droves and formed their own churches. In only a few years, religious worship and religious institutions were overwhelmingly segregated by race.[72] Much of it was the choice of whites who endeavored to replace the rules of slavery with new rules, many of them closely patterned after the old. Blacks were expected to address whites as Mr. or Miss; blacks were called by their first name or "boy," "aunt," or

---

71. Ayers, *The Promise of the New South*, 67–72; Kolchin, *American Slavery*, 216–223; August Meier, *Negro Thought in America, 1880–1915* (Ann Arbor: The University of Michigan Press, 1970), 87–92, 102; William Chafe, *Civilities and Civil Rights: Greensboro, North Carolina and the Black Struggle for Freedom* (Oxford: Oxford University Press, 1981), 14.

72. Eric Foner, *A Short History of Reconstruction, 1863–1877* (New York: Harper and Row, 1990), 184, 160.

"uncle." Blacks did not enter white homes except as servants; whites rarely entered black homes except in the capacity of landlord, sheriff's deputy, or employer. A black person was referred to in newspaper accounts as "a negro"; whites were referred to as "a man" or "a woman." Blacks and whites did not eat together in restaurants, sit together in shows, attend the same schools, or socialize in any capacity. In the public realm of politics, court days, public transportation, and some work situations, there was still a fair amount of interaction.[73] But in many ways, blacks and whites were pulling apart and living in their own worlds.

On the black side, what drove this social separation was the desire to have something (churches, for example) of their own. After centuries of submission to white domination, this is understandable. On the white side, this racial separation of life in some sense was a continuation of the separation of white and black during the slavery era. But it was also much more than that. Whites had suffered terrific losses during the war in blood and wealth. After the war, they struggled to survive, watched in confusion as many of their old leaders were shunted aside, if only temporarily, by the victors, and had to accept the fact that people they had once owned were now, legally speaking, equal to them. With these losses and tribulations went a sense that their world had collapsed and with it the old truths. Planter's son John Steele Henderson reflected this terrible sense of loss and confusion when he confided in his diary in November of 1865 that his life was a "mixture of regret of the past and uneasy forebodings of the future."[74] Southern whites, historian Joel Williamson has convincingly argued, had lost their identity and would have to struggle to rediscover who they were and what their society stood for. This loss of identity was especially pronounced in areas where blacks were most numerous and the possibility of a new multiracial world seemed most likely. It is not surprising that whites would try to restore as much of their old world as possible, nor is it surprising that blacks would resist this. The white solution was to build a wall of separation between black and white and to rebuild their own white world, a world, Williamson has argued, that was defined by a strong commitment to evangelical Christianity and family. Whites refashioned themselves into a people who defined themselves as especially moral and spiritual.[75] As in the past, honor was at the center of this world and the touchstones of honor were now the "Lost Cause" that white Southerners had so nobly fought for and the virtue of white womanhood that had to be protected and defended. The danger to this world was "out there"—the detested Yankee, but more immediate and press-

---

73. Ayers, *The Promise of the New South*, 132–134.

74. John Steele Henderson Diary, 27 November 1865, John Steele Henderson Papers, Southern Historical Collection, University of North Carolina, Chapel Hill.

75. Joel Williamson, *A Rage for Order: Black/White Relations in the American South Since Emancipation* (New York: Oxford University Press, 1986), 36–43.

ing, African Americans and their counter world. Controlling this threatening black world gave white men a mission that rivaled in nobility and purposefulness the mission that had failed—the "Lost Cause." The black world would also serve as a reference point for what whites were—"We are people who are not like them," they might have said loudly and in unison.

The separation of the two worlds, black and white, would become codified into law during the late 1880s, 1890s, and early 1900s and would be given a name and a nickname. The name was segregation and the nickname was Jim Crow, a name derived from a minstrel tune, "Jump Jim Crow." Accompanying the Jim Crow laws were other laws, called disfranchising laws, that took the vote away from all but a handful of African Americans. Why an informal system of separation was replaced by a formal system that consisted of literally thousands of laws and ordinances across the region is hard to say. It is safe to say that the old system left many gray areas and left the principle of white supremacy riddled with qualifications, particularly when it came to black political power. It is also true that there was a strong unease in the white world about the general direction the South was taking. Agriculture and the agrarian culture were struggling; farmers were losing their farms by the score, thousands were reduced to sharecropping, rural areas were in a sad state of decline, and this situation was made worse by a serious depression that hit the country and the region in the early 1890s. The growth of cities and towns and industry was also another source of stress; thousands poured into the region's growing towns and cities to work, and the adjustment to factory work and city life was not an easy one. Some of the men drawn to the cities and towns worked sporadically at best; homeless, jobless young men are, of course, prime candidates to commit petty and serious crimes, and, not surprisingly, crime was a problem and nearly as much of an obsession in the late 1880s and 1890s as it has been in more recent times.[76] As John Steele Henderson, Jr., noted in a letter to his father about his bustling home town of Salisbury, North Carolina, "Prosperity that is accompanied by railroads and contractors brings a fearful train of lawlessness with it."[77] Black men had the hardest time finding employment in the towns and cities; while black women could often find employment as domestic workers, black men were closed out of most forms of employment in towns such as mills or stores. In many towns and cities, young black males often became part of a street corner culture based around pool halls, bars, and gambling joints where petty crime and violent altercations flourished.[78] Whites

---

76. *Ibid.*, 80–82, 145.
77. John Steele Henderson, Jr. to John Steele Henderson, August 7 1906, John Steele Henderson Papers, Southern Historical Collection, University of North Carolina, Chapel Hill.
78. Williamson, *A Rage for Order*, 145.

were appalled; as a Salisbury newspaper opined, the street leading from the business district to the railroad was often crowded with a "worthless sea of humanity"; those who wished to pass down this street often had "to squirm through this filthy crowd of negroes."[79] It would not be too much to say that white concerns about black criminality pushed police to focus their attention on blacks, and blacks could be arrested and jailed for nearly anything. In Atlanta in 1905, almost 60% of those arrested by the police were black. If fear was one motivation to create a better system to separate white from black and solidify white supremacy, envy was another: the gains made by blacks as landowning farmers, craftsmen, businessmen, and politicians were a source of resentment to struggling whites.[80] As we will see, Jim Crow would shut the door on many opportunities for blacks and in the process provide more for whites.

As the white and black worlds grew further and further apart, white attitudes about blacks grew increasingly hostile. The paternalism of old began to fade as the men and women who had been slaveholders were replaced by a new generation that had grown up in a world characterized by racial estrangement. More and more whites believed blacks simply weren't capable of living on an equal footing with whites without dire consequences resulting, violence and crime especially.[81] These views were expressed by growing numbers of newspapers editors, politicians, academics, and writers. Tom Dixon, a successful Baptist minister, authored several popular novels about the Negro "menace." In Dixon's novel, *The Leopard's Spots: A Romance of the White Man's Burden—1865–1900*, Gaston, the leading character, witnesses a brutal lynching of a black man accused of killing a white child and reflects "two such races [black and white], counting millions in number, cannot live together under a Democracy."[82] He speculated that if the "racial fury of the Anglo-Saxon" became aroused, "it would sweep its victims before its wrath like chaff before a whirlwind." He had seen an inkling of this at the lynching, but as horrible as the prospect of a race war was, another prospect was even worse: amalgamation (the mixing of the races), the end result of which would be, he thought (or Dixon thought), the "Africanisation" of the South. "The big nostrils, flat nose, massive jaw, protruding lip and kinky hair will register their animal markers over the proudest intellect and the rarest beauty of any other race."[83]

---

79. *Salisbury Globe* [NC], 26 April 1905.
80. Williamson, *A Rage for Order*, 58–59, 81, 145–146; Edward L Ayers, *Vengeance and Justice: Crime and Punishment in the 19th-Century American South* (New York and Oxford: Oxford University Press, 1984), 235–236, 223, 250–252.
81. Williamson, *A Rage for Order*, 40, 78–79; Ayers, Vengeance and Justice, 241–242.
82. Thomas Dixon, Jr., *The Leopard's Spots: A Romance of the White Man's Burden—1865–1900* (New York: A. Wessels Company, 1906), 386.
83. *Ibid.*

For the new breed of racial theorists like Tom Dixon, the "negro problem" would only get worse: blacks were "retrogressing" into a state of barbarity. Without slavery to guide them, they were becoming savages, and this explained what many believed was the rising incidence of black criminality. The most serious aspect of black criminality was "the new Negro crime," the rape of a white woman, which many commentators of the era seemed to think was of epidemic proportion, although contemporary studies have suggested it may have been more an example of mass hysteria than a significant increase in the crime of rape. There is no question, however, that "the fear of black rape obviously triggered something deep within the psyche of the white South."[84] Rape was the ultimate destination of retrogressing black males and had to be dealt with forcefully and quickly, and lynching became the remedy of choice throughout the South.

Before the 1890s, lynching was most common on the Western frontier, and the victims were generally white. By the 1890s, most of the lynchings in the United States took place in the South, and most of those lynched were black men. Lynching declined by the early years of the century but was still common well into the twentieth century. Over 4,000 lynchings have been documented between 1889 and 1946, but there may have been more. As historian Joel Williamson has argued, lynchings fit a pattern and followed preset if unspoken "rules." A lynching was often preceded by days or weeks of agitation on the part of whites over rumors and gossip of black "uppityness" toward whites and even more outrageous behavior. A crime or a rumor of a crime allegedly committed by a black man, particularly the crime of rape—of violating a white woman—in such a charged environment led to the formation of a mob; the search for the perpetrator; an interrogation of the accused by the mob which was often accompanied by torture; and finally the execution by hanging, shooting, or burning, often by all three. The mob went about its business purposefully and quietly—lynchings were not conducted by crowds of crazed people. The lynching often concluded with the display of the body for a period of time; the body was often dismembered, and fingers, toes, and other body parts were often kept as souvenirs.[85]

A lynching in Salisbury, North Carolina, that occurred in 1906 illustrates all of these points and more. The train of events that led to the lynching began when five black men and one woman were accused of hacking to death with axes a white farm family, the Lyerlys. The six were tenants on the farm, and one had ostensibly threatened the farmer earlier. They had been arrested, and a

---

84. Williamson, *A Rage for Order*, 83–84, 86–106; George M. Fredrickson, *The Black Image in the White Mind: The Debate on African-American Character and Destiny, 1817–1914* (Middleton, Conn.: Wesleyan University Press, 1971), 258–262, 275–282; Ayers, *Vengeance and Justice*, 238–240, quote p. 240.
85. Williamson, *A Rage for Order*, 84–85, 123–126.

mob had tried to take them from the jail soon after the arrests but had been deterred. When the trial commenced, another mob collected one evening and kept growing until perhaps 2,000 people milled around the jail, murmuring and occasionally shouting. The mob ignored local law officers, the local militia, and the pleadings of local notables, most of whom retreated to safety. The mob peppered the jail with gunfire and then broke open the door of the jail. A delegation went inside to find the accused, and the crowd grew still—"all was quiet as death." Three of the men were dragged from jail, run through a gauntlet of flaying hands and feet, and marched to a ball field adjacent to the home of John Steele Henderson. The other two men had been judged innocent by the crowd and had been left in the jail. Apparently the mob was of mixed feelings about the woman; she had been left in the jail, but she had also been beaten. At the ball field, the captives were forced to kneel and pray and were then interrogated; no one confessed. Nooses were prepared and some in the crowd, including a family member of the murder victims, implored the crowd to show mercy to the men, but mercy was not the order of the day. One of the men begged for his life, but the other two stoically awaited their fate. The men were hanged, and their bodies were riddled with bullets. Their corpses were left hanging until the next day and were viewed by thousands, including many women, but that was not all. A "swarm of human vultures cut fingers, toes and ears" from the remains.[86] It's entirely possible that one if not all of the men did not commit the crime, a possibility John Steele Henderson suggested to his wife in a letter.[87] Certainly the behavior of the men—they didn't flee after the crime was committed, for example—seems strange for men who had committed such a heinous crime and would surely have known who would be suspected and what would come next. Too, tantalizing bits of evidence that surfaced during a trial that was cut short by the lynching point in another direction.

It was not unusual for lynch mobs to get the wrong person, and sometimes people were lynched when no crime had been committed, a possibility William Faulkner explored in the short story "Dry September," a fictional but chillingly accurate account of a lynching.[88] Why did whites feel the need to execute blacks outside normal legal channels when they controlled the courts? Lynching, at bottom, very effectively communicated to blacks who was in charge and what the consequences of violent crime against whites would be. They were in-

---

86. *Charlotte Daily Observer* (NC), 15, 17, July, 1906, 7, 8, 10 August 1906; *Carolina Watchman* (Salisbury, NC), 25 July 1906, 8 August 1906; quotes, *Charlotte Daily Observer*, 7 August 1906 and 8 August 1906.

87. John Steele Henderson to Bessie Henderson, 15 July 1906, John Steele Henderson Papers, Southern Historical Collection, University of North Carolina, Chapel Hill.

88. William Faulkner, "Dry September," *Collected Stories of William Faulkner* (New York: Vintage Books, 1977), 169–183.

tended to be as horrific as possible to make this message brutally clear. But lynching served another purpose, too, as Joel Williamson and William Faulkner have suggested. They served as a sort of ritual sacrifice; when white frustration levels were high and the relationship between black and white seemed tense, a lynching was like a thunderstorm that cleared the air, and, in a perverse way, set the world right, right being a dominant white population and a suitably submissive black population. William Faulkner did not haphazardly pick the name "Joe Christmas" for the character in his novel *Light in August* who was lynched for murdering a white woman. Christmas is shot and then castrated, and in his last moment of life, "he looked up at them with peaceful and unfathomable and unbearable eyes," and as the blood gushed from his body "the man seemed to rise soaring into their memories forever and ever."[89]

In the racially charged atmosphere of the 1890s and early 1900s, white racial fears and outrage would sometimes reach such a crescendo that a full scale outbreak of violence—a race riot—would erupt. Race riots in such towns and cities as Atlanta and Wilmington, North Carolina, typically originated with a racial "incident" (or series of "incidents") and ended with a full-scale assault by a white mob on the black areas of town. In Atlanta in 1906, a variety of reformers had launched a concerted campaign against saloons and the "drink evil," which they linked to public disorder and the rising crime rate. Drinking by black men and black bars and dives became a special focus of this mounting campaign. Atlanta had a growing community of marginally employed young black men, and these were portrayed as a special danger to the safety and security of whites, especially white women. Added to the mix was a bitter race for governor in which the candidates (both from Atlanta) tried to outdo each other in advocating tougher and tougher measures to control dangerous blacks. The newspapers of Atlanta competed with each other with lurid stories of black crime, and by late summer the major newspapers announced the city was suffering a rape epidemic characterized by black men raping white women. A journalist who later investigated the rape "epidemic" could only verify two rapes of white women by black men in the six month period leading up to the riot. He found a handful of cases of what may or may not have been assaults by black men of white women and another four cases where the rape charges were simply concocted. Three white men were charged with rape during this same period. As serious as these statistics were, they did not constitute an epidemic, and certainly not a problem best remedied by a race riot, but that is finally what happened.[90]

---

89. Joel Williamson, *The Crucible of Race: Black/White Relations in the American South Since Emancipation* (New York: Oxford University Press, 1984), 309; Joel Williamson, *William Faulkner and Southern History* (New York: Oxford University Press, 1993), 411–412; William Faulkner, *Light in August* (1932; New York: Vintage Books, 1990), 464–465.

90. Williamson, *Rage for Order*, 141–147.

The riot began on a Saturday in mid-September; it was touched off by a newspaper story of an attempted assault, followed by more reports of assaults, several of which were imaginary. Rumors spread of a Negro uprising, and crowds of white men gathered and began attacking black passersby, ransacked black businesses on Auburn Avenue, and finally converged on Brownsville, the home of many prominent black leaders.[91] Walter White, a civil rights leader, lived through the riot and would recall:

> Late in the afternoon friends of my father's came to warn of more trouble that night. They told us that plans had been perfected for a mob to form on Peachtree Street just after nightfall to march down Houston Street to what the white people called "Darktown," three blocks or so below our house, to "clean out the niggers." There had never been a firearm in our house before that day. Father was reluctant even in those circumstances to violate the law, but he at last gave in at Mother's insistence.
>
> We turned out the lights early, as did all our neighbors. No one removed his clothes or thought of sleep. Apprehension was tangible. We could almost touch its cold and clammy surface. Toward midnight the unnatural quiet was broken by a roar that grew steadily in volume. Even today I grow tense in remembering it.
>
> Father told Mother to take my sisters, the youngest of them only six, to the rear of the house, which offered more protection from stones and bullets. My brother George was away, so Father and I, the only males in the house, took our places at the front windows of the parlor. The windows opened on a porch along the front side of the house, which in turn gave onto a narrow lawn that sloped down to the street and a picket fence. There was a crash as Negroes smashed the street lamp at the corner of Houston and Piedmont Avenue down the street. In a very few minutes the vanguard of the mob, some of them bearing torches, appeared. A voice which we recognized as that of the son of the grocer with whom we had traded for many years yelled, "That is where that nigger mail carrier lives! Let's burn it down! It's too nice for a nigger to live in!" In the eerie light Father turned his drawn face toward me. In a voice as quiet as though he were asking me to pass him the sugar at the breakfast table, he said, "Son, don't shoot until the first man puts his foot on the lawn and then—don't you miss!"[92]

---

91. *Ibid.*, 147–148.
92. Walter White, *A Man Called White: The Autobiography of Walter White* (New York: The Viking Press, 1948), 10–11.

Twenty-five blacks died in the riot and one white; perhaps 150 people were seriously injured.[93] Following a riot, many blacks often fled the city or town where the riot occurred, and those who remained kept a low profile and frequently suffered economically. After a riot in Wilmington, for example, the number of black workers in the city (all occupations) dropped by almost a third in the years following the riot, and the number of black businesses declined, particularly in the central business district where businesses catered to both black and white. Black businesses after the riot were more likely located in black parts of town where it was, no doubt, safer and their mostly black clientele would not arouse the jealousies of white businessmen.[94]

Feeding this racist frenzy were politicians like the candidates for governor of Georgia who helped precipitate the Atlanta race riot. Many Democratic politicians bought into the new racial theories but also found "the race card," as it has been more recently called, a vital tool in their drive to defeat their foes. The political contests of the 1890s were not, by any stretch of the imagination, normal contests, but bitterly contested struggles reminiscent of the Reconstruction era. In the 1890s, disgruntled farmers had started their own political party, the Populist Party, and this party and a reviving Republican Party offered the dominant Democratic Party a serious challenge, particularly in states like North Carolina where Populists and Republicans cooperated. Democrats, representing first and foremost the white upper class of the South, saw this challenge as an illegitimate threat to their power and wealth, and they responded with a powerful attack on their enemies. This attack was based on a simple concept: blacks were the source of virtually all that ailed the South, politically, economically, and socially. Democratic politicians loudly asserted that the bitter politics of the era was the fault of a black-dominated Republican Party, which caused division between white men. They also asserted that blacks were taking jobs or might take jobs that rightly belonged to whites and, as we have already seen, that blacks had embarked on an escalating crime spree. As is always the case with scapegoating, a bit of truth was grossly distorted to accomplish a broader goal. Politics was bitter in the 1890s, but then the issues, not the black vote itself, divided people along class lines, racial lines, and rural/urban lines. Jobs were scarce and there was competition for them, which did fuel resentments, racial and otherwise. There was a crime problem. The voters were offered a choice: vote Democratic and support white supremacy or vote for the other parties and choose "negro domination" and chaos. The deepest fears and anxieties of white voters (all males at this time in history) were

---

93. Williamson, *Rage for Order*, 150.
94. LeRae Umfleet, Principal Researcher, *1898 Wilmington Race Riot Report* (Raleigh: Wilmington Race Riot Commission, North Carolina Department of Cultural Resources, Office of Archives and History, May 31, 2006), 228–229, 231–232, http://www.ah.dcr.state.nc.us/1898-wrrc/report/report.htm.

plumbed by skilled agitators versed in the new racial theories: black men not only wanted power, they wanted white women and would do anything to get them. Democratic leaders urged their followers to do whatever was necessary to restore order and protect their womenfolk—steal votes, cheat, and threaten. In some areas the party organized a paramilitary arm to terrorize its opponents into submission. Extraordinary times called for extraordinary measures, and once Democrats were firmly in power, they would fix the problem once and for all. Tom Dixon's hero, Gaston, succinctly expressed this perspective in a resolution he introduced at a political convention: "Resolved, that the hour has now come in our history to eliminate the Negro from our life and reestablish for all time the government of our fathers."[95]

By the early 1900s, in every Southern state, a rigid system of segregation known as "Jim Crow" had been established by the victorious Democrats. Customs of racial separation and discrimination were more rigidly enforced in the workplace and the social sphere, and thousands of laws and ordinances were passed that mandated separate schools, drinking fountains, and bathrooms for white and black. It became virtually illegal for blacks to be in the same room as whites except as servants or customers in stores. Blacks were excluded from most industrial jobs and skilled occupations, and any but the most menial jobs in offices, stores (if white owned) and government agencies were denied them. In Greensboro, North Carolina, for example, 16% of the factory workers were black in 1884; by 1910, none were. The percentage of black men in skilled occupations declined from 30% in 1870 to 8% in 1910.[96] Black public schools were funded at a much lower rate than white schools. Even by mid-century, there was still often a huge disparity; for example, the Clarendon County schools in South Carolina had a budget of nearly $200,000 for 6,500 black students and a budget over three times that much for roughly 2,400 white students. Thirty buses carried white students to schools; not one bus was provided for black students.[97] Blacks did not need much education in the Jim Crow world; they were to be sharecroppers, servants, and custodians, and that was to be it with but few exceptions. Of course, black businessmen could hire black workers, accountants, and secretaries, but then black businesses were generally denied the right to serve white customers or compete with white businesses. Black customers in white stores frequently were denied the right to

---

95. Dixon, *The Leopard's Spots*, 437.

96. C. Vann Woodward, *Origins of the New South, 1877–1913* (1951; Baton Rouge: Louisiana State University Press, 1974), 211–212, 355; George B. Tindall, *The Emergence of the New South, 1913–1945* (Baton Rouge: Louisiana State University Press, 1967) 145–146, 161–165; Williamson, *Rage for Order*, 175–178; Chafe, *Civilities and Civil Rights*, 15–16.

97. Pete Daniel, *Standing at the Crossroads: Southern Life in the Twentieth Century* (New York: Hill and Wang, 1986), 161–162.

try on clothes or shoes, and in some towns were discouraged from shopping on days other than Saturday.[98] Enforcing this brutal inequality was an all-white legal system—sheriffs, police chiefs, judges, prosecutors, and juries were all white—that often denied blacks basic constitutional rights. Local sheriffs and district attorneys often dispensed their own version of "the law" in the black community that could be quite lenient when a crime was black on black, but was swift and harsh if the offense was committed by a black against a white. It was rare for a white man to be convicted of a crime against a black man or woman, and if there was a conviction, the penalty was often trivial. Particularly in areas where blacks outnumbered whites, behind the façade of the law hovered the "unofficial" law: the Klan and the lynch mob.[99]

In such an environment, a multiracial political party was next to impossible. But disfranchisement made it absolutely impossible. A variety of laws were passed in each Southern state mandating that voters must pass a literacy test to vote and pay a special tax, called a poll tax, before they could vote. These laws were a blatant attempt to take the vote away from blacks and were unfairly applied. Many blacks who were quite literate were declared illiterate by Democratic voting registrars, and in most states a "grandfather clause" allowed whites to bypass the literacy test. The black Southern electorate declined to a mere fraction of what it had been, and the Republican Party all but disappeared in most of the region as a viable contender for power; what was left of it became increasingly a white party.[100]

So the possibility of a multiracial South based on the values of equality and respect was brutally smothered. Jim Crow would govern the relationship between black and white until the 1960s and even later in some areas. Whites who suggested an alternative or who condemned segregation and disfranchisement were threatened and often hounded out of the region. For example, John Spencer Bassett, a college professor in North Carolina, wrote an article published in 1903 that condemned those who were "Stirring the Fires of Race Antipathy." Bassett was repeatedly attacked in *Raleigh News and Observer*, a newspaper edited by Josephus Daniels, one of the architects of Jim Crow and disfranchisement in the state. The paper called for Bassett's firing, and his name was often printed bASSett in the headline. Bassett was not fired, but thereafter the scholar was silent on matters racial.[101] If liberal voices were largely stilled, the more extreme viewpoints, like Tom Dixon's, that had so dominated public discourse during the 1890s and early 1900s were less com-

98. Ayers, *The Promise of the New South*, 132.
99. Leon F. Litwack, *Trouble in Mind: Black Southerners in the Age of Jim Crow* (New York: Alfred A. Knopf, 1998), 249–265.
100. Williamson, *The Crucible of Race*, 229–234; Tindall, *The Emergence of the New South*, 167–169.
101. Williamson, *The Crucible of Race*, 261–267, 297.

Figure 3.1   Plantation overseer, Mississippi Delta

monly expressed, although it was not threats or coercion that caused this to happen. Rather, it was as if once the black "menace" had been caged, whites could go on about their business in their secure white world and even say a few kind things about blacks and view them (again) in a paternalistic way as child-like, humorous, easily frightened, sometimes wise people best suited to physical labor.[102] Of course, if a black man did something to rouse the ire of whites—a crime or even not acting "right"—the white fury could return at a moment's notice and a beating might be administered or a man might be lynched.

The new racial solution and black stereotypes were woven into a powerful narrative by Southern whites and those sympathetic to their cause that was told and retold in books, speeches, plays, and films that were distributed through-out the nation. This narrative served to legitimize Jim Crow as part of the nat-ural order of things in the South and became, for those outside the South, the commonly accepted way to understand the region. For example, the notion that the Civil War was a noble defense of a "Lost Cause" was, if not embraced elsewhere in the nation, at least respected. What other country that has gone through a bloody civil war has allowed the losers to build monuments, and im-pressive monuments at that, on the battlefields? Joel Chandler Harris's Uncle

102. *Ibid.*, 460–463.

Remus stories would be quite popular and would, as noted earlier, be made into a successful Disney film in the later 1940s, and Margaret Mitchell's popular novel *Gone with the Wind* was made into an immensely popular film in the late 1930s. Al Jolson, the son of Jewish immigrants, was one of the nation's most popular performers in the 1920s and 1930s and generally performed in black face like the minstrels of old, a white man pretending to be black. The Amos and Andy radio show, popular in the 1940s and early 1950s, also featured white performers pretending to be blacks doing and saying funny and foolish things. Even advertisements employed images and symbols that reflected the Southern racial solution. Who was (and is) not familiar with Aunt Jemima, the epitome of the mammy figure, her beaming face plastered on the front of a pancake mix box? Whites across the nation responded to these images and stories of the South and could thrill to the romance of gallant cavaliers like Ashley Wilkes and laugh or shake their heads at the antics of black characters; they were as receptive as Southern whites because at bottom they harbored many of the same prejudices.[103]

Blacks responded to Jim Crow legislation and disfranchisement in two ways. A group of black intellectuals including, most prominently, W.E.B. Du Bois joined with white liberals and founded the National Association for the Advancement of Colored People (NAACP) in 1909 to fight Jim Crow and disfranchisement. For the next five decades, this organization, headquartered in New York, would use the courts as the battleground and the Constitution as its primary weapon. For the most part, however, the black response to the loss of the vote, civil rights, and job opportunities was accommodation. The leading proponent of accommodation was Booker T. Washington. Washington, in his famous "Atlanta Exposition Address," argued that blacks and whites could be as separate as the fingers of the hand but could work together for mutual progress. What blacks really needed, Washington asserted, was not the right to attend the opera but access to good jobs. However, while Washington pursued a strategy of publicly accepting disfranchisement and segregation, behind the scenes he worked vigorously to protect what little political power blacks still had.[104] For most Southern blacks, accommodation was the only strategy that was practical; confrontation might work for the NAACP, based as it was in the North, but active opposition to Jim Crow in the South was simply too dangerous. Further, support for such an effort was limited; the Supreme Court in its *Plessy v. Ferguson* decision had declared segregation constitutional in 1896 as long as "separate was equal." Too, Social Darwinism was the prevailing viewpoint of most of the educated and powerful people in turn-of-the-century

---

103. *Ibid.*, 464; Grace Elizabeth Hale, *Making Whiteness: The Culture of Segregation in the South, 1890–1940* (New York: Pantheon Books, 1998), 151–168, 281–284.
104. Williamson, *Rage for Order*, 61–64, 66–69; Booker T. Washington, "The Atlanta Exposition Address," Mullane, ed., *Crossing the Danger Water*, 364–367.

America. For people with this mindset, segregation was nothing more than a realistic, even "kindly," system established to separate unequal races and protect the inferior race from the superior race.[105]

Booker T. Washington's accommodationist approach set the pace for countless lesser black leaders who built "islands of certainty" in local communities, churches, schools, and businesses. On these "islands," blacks built a world with limited interaction with the white world, and this world fostered a unique culture. Black leaders often ruled their domains, whether it was a church, a college, an orphanage or a business, with iron hands and jealously guarded their power; they felt they had to because there was little room for error in a dangerous world dominated by whites. They carefully cultivated local white leaders who were reasonable and used this influence to protect members of the black community when they could and get what they could. This sort of behavior in a later era has been called "being an Uncle Tom," but these leaders felt that for the good of their people, they had to flatter and placate whites.[106]

In the countryside the church was the central black institution; churches were social centers and a source of pride for members of the black community, and the preacher was often the most prominent black man in the area. Competing with the church were the less reputable institutions of rural areas—jook joints or party houses where people drank, had fish frys, and listened to music. In every Southern town, there was a black side of town (whites had their own derogatory name for it) where most blacks lived and worshiped. On this side of town, there was generally a black business district of stores, offices, restaurants, jook joints, and poolrooms—in Atlanta it was "sweet Auburn" and in Durham, North Carolina, it was the Hayti area—where blacks could shop, get their shoes repaired or their clothes drycleaned, eat out, and socialize without having to deal with the heavy hand of Jim Crow. In town, businessmen along with the preachers, teachers, and undertakers formed a small black middle class, and from this class came many of the leaders of the black community.[107]

This is not to say that blacks and whites had no interaction with each other during this era. In rural areas, blacks and whites often worked side by side on farms. Black and white children played together until a certain age, and many white children from the middle and upper classes were raised by black maids or "mammies." There were countless acts of friendship and kindness extended

---

105. Fredrickson, *The Black Image in the White Mind*, 228–255.

106. Williamson, *Rage for Order*, 53–56, quote p. 53. See for an account of a local leader, Taylor, *Parting the Waters*, 121–122.

107. Williamson, *Rage for Order*, 53–56; *The Promised Land: Take Me to Chicago*, video (Bethesda, MD: The Discovery Channel, c. 1995); Ayers, *The Promise of the New South*, 68–72, 164; Nicholas Lemann, *The Promised Land: The Great Black Migration and How it Changed America* (New York: Vintage Books, 1992), 36–38.

by blacks to whites and by whites to blacks on a personal level. When it came
to the personal, the worlds often did connect, but when it came to the social,
the worlds were literally "worlds apart."

Figure 3.2   W.E.B. Du Bois

The Worlds Change Orbits: The Civil Rights Movement and the Death of Jim Crow

The black world and the white world were destined to leave their orbits, and the South would again go through another paroxysm of racial conflict and violence. This would happen because, at bottom, the Southern racial solution required time to stand still, which, of course, it doesn't. For starters, many Southern African Americans weren't happy with their world and left it at every opportunity. A massive migration, discussed elsewhere in this text, commenced in the early 1900s, was propelled along by the collapse of the sharecropping system, and would not taper off until the 1960s. Millions would leave the region for the more hospitable North, Midwest, and far West giving blacks a political powerbase in the big cities of these regions and the wherewithal to attack segregation from without. Likewise, after World War II, another migration would bring people and businesses into the region from elsewhere in the country and the world. This migration would take place at an accelerating pace (it's still going on), and it would change the racial calculus. How, for example, would Jim Crow have worked (had it survived) in contemporary Miami with its large population of immigrants from the Caribbean and Central America or at a multinational company in Atlanta with branches all over the world and a workforce of one hundred hues and ethnicities? Importantly, a big change in how people thought about race had taken place by the end of World War II. Nazism had made the blatant prejudices of the prewar era unpopular; talk of inferior people and special laws for certain groups sounded too much like Hitler's vicious racial theories that had led to genocide. The academic community had by now rejected Social Darwinism and was advancing the notion that people were basically the same. Black Southern GIs returning from the war also brought new attitudes with them. They had helped defend the nation and were less willing to accept the insults of Jim Crow than their parents had been. Black migrants to the north periodically returned for visits, and no doubt expressed their incredulity at what their relatives and friends still in the South had to put up with and told them things were different elsewhere. Certainly, whites noticed a difference in the behavior of expatriates who returned home for a visit; police in Clarksdale, Mississippi, referred to it as "The Attitude."[108]

But these developments in and of themselves did not end segregation and disfranchisement; a mass movement composed primarily of Southern blacks, hundreds of thousands of them, with the support, to be sure, of white liberals, would do this. This movement, the Civil Rights Movement, really began in 1909 with the founding of the NAACP. This organization's legal team had

---

108. Lemann, *The Promised Land*, 40.

chipped away case by case at Jim Crow and disfranchisement for decades, backing it into a corner, constitutionally speaking, because clearly it violated and always had the equal protection clause of the 14th amendment, not to mention the 15th amendment. The court decision that broke the legal back of Jim Crow was the Supreme Court decision *Brown v. Board of Education, Topeka, Kansas,* rendered in 1954. The court reversed its stand in *Plessey v. Ferguson* and struck down the constitutionality of segregated public schools and, by implication, segregation in its entirety, although the court did not address segregation outside of education. Some upper South school systems began to integrate shortly thereafter, but in Little Rock, Arkansas, it would take soldiers from the 101st Airborne to quell disturbances when a handful of black students enrolled in previously all white Central High School in 1957.[109] In much of the South, the Deep South especially, segregation continued without pause.

At the time of *Brown v. Board,* the mass movement dedicated to destroying Jim Crow was gathering force; it would challenge segregation not only in courtrooms but in streets, restaurants, hallways, schools, in fact, anywhere it was practiced. The old line civil rights organizations like the NAACP had been fairly small, primarily Northern and confined to intellectuals and members of the middle class, but in the 1940s and continuing in the 1950s, these organizations, the NAACP especially, began recruiting more and more members in the towns and rural areas of the South and reaching further down into the black working class. But whites who opposed equal rights for blacks were organizing, too. In the wake of the Brown decision, the Klan grew in membership and became increasingly committed to violent resistance. A group of ardent segregationists in Mississippi formed the first Citizens' Council to oppose integration and preserve the "Southern way of life." This organization would spread across the South, although its stronghold would be the Deep South. It was sometimes called the "white collar Klan" because many of its members were professionals and businessmen. It supported segregationist candidates for office and used a variety of pressure tactics to discourage civil rights supporters, such as denying them credit in local banks.[110]

Rosa Parks, of Montgomery, Alabama, was one of the NAACP's new recruits. Ms. Parks, a tailor's assistant, served as secretary of the local chapter and had gone to a workshop on organizing at the Highlander Folk School in Tennessee in the summer of 1955. The school, headed by Myles Horton, trained many civil rights activists until forced to close in 1960 and was the source of the movement anthem "We Shall Overcome." Ms. Parks was the

---

109. Taylor Branch, *Parting the Waters: America in the King Years, 1954–1963* (New York: Simon and Schuster, 1989), 222–224.

110. Stephen B. Oates, *Let the Trumpet Sound: The Life of Martin Luther King, Jr.* (New York: New American Library, 1982), 50–51 61; Daniel, *Standing at the Crossroads,* 149, 165–166; Lemann, *The Promised Land,* 310.

woman who, by a single act of defiance, began the Montgomery bus boycott, which launched the modern Civil Rights Movement and the career of the greatest of the civil rights leaders, Dr. Martin Luther King, Jr. Montgomery's segregation ordinance required blacks and whites to sit in separate sections on the bus. One day in December of 1955, Ms. Parks boarded a city bus and sat in the zone that separated white and black seating where either race could sit depending on their relative numbers on the bus. More whites boarded the bus that day and could not find a seat, and the bus driver told black passengers in the area where Ms. Parks was sitting to get up and give their seats to the white passengers. Ms. Parks's act was simple; she refused to give up her seat to a white man, and she was arrested by a city policeman, detained in jail, and finally convicted and sentenced in a court of law. Members of the black community formed the Montgomery Improvement Association and organized a boycott of the city buses. Dr. King, a twenty-six-year-old minister newly arrived in town, was chosen to lead the boycott. The NAACP challenged the constitutionality of her conviction, and ultimately it would be the United States Supreme Court which would end the practice of segregation on the Montgomery bus lines when it upheld a special three judge federal panel that had declared Alabama's laws requiring segregation on buses unconstitutional. But it was the year-long boycott that elevated King to a prominent role in the fledgling civil rights movement. During the boycott, his life had been threatened, he had been arrested, his home had been bombed and shot into, his character had been attacked, and a thousand petty and major obstacles had been thrown up in his path, but he persevered with the steadfast courage that would take him through the next 12 years until that fateful day in Memphis when he would be felled by an assassin's bullet.[111]

King and others formed a new civil rights organization, the Southern Christian Leadership Conference (SCLC), which with older organizations such as the NAACP and new organizations such as the Student Non-Violent Coordinating Committee (SNCC) mobilized hundreds of thousands of Southern blacks in opposition to Jim Crow. A cadre of leaders—John Lewis, Etta Baker, Jesse Jackson, Ralph Abernathy, Andrew Young, Stokeley Carmichael, Medgar Evers, Fannie Lou Hamer, James Forman, and Bob Moses, to name a few of the more prominent ones—emerged to inspire, organize, publicize, and, in the cases of Dr. King and Medgar Evers, to die. The foot soldiers of this movement were everyday people, young and old, male and female, mostly black but some white who might participate in a single protest or be part of dozens. Many did so at great risk to their livelihoods and lives. For example, Hartman

---

111. Branch, *Parting the Waters*, 124–125, 128–130, 143–196; Howell Raines, *My Soul Is Rested: Movement Days in the Deep South Remembered* (New York: Bantam Books, 1978), interview with Myles Horton, 437–443.

Turnbow was a farmer and, by his account, an "ageable man at that time." He was one of the first to attempt to register to vote in his Mississippi Delta community, and, as he said, "I'uz the first one got my house bombed."[112] The movement went into high gear in the early 1960s when boycotts, sit-ins, marches, and voter registration drives would be organized all over the South, guided by a philosophy of civil disobedience and peaceful resistance inspired by Gandhi, Christ, Henry David Thoreau, and the Reverend Martin Luther King, Jr. The Greensboro sit-ins touched off this new phase.

Greensboro was located in a state (North Carolina) often touted as one of the most progressive Southern states on racial issues. And yet the Greensboro public schools were still virtually segregated with a mere handful of black students attending white schools; this was the pattern across the state. The state's "Pupil Assignment Act" gave school boards wide latitude to consider requests to move students to new schools, and school boards routinely denied the requests of black parents to move their children to white schools. In Greensboro, the small number of parents who submitted such a request were often harassed and threatened. The Guilford County Industrial Education Center, part of a state system of industrial training centers for adults, had 2 black students and 1,210 white students. Restaurants, restrooms, waiting rooms and the like were segregated. In a survey conducted in 1958, only 13% of 400 plus Greensboro employers who were surveyed indicated a willingness to hire workers regardless of their color.[113]

Four young men who attended a black college in the city, North Carolina Agricultural and Technical College (generally called A&T), decided to do something to challenge Jim Crow. On February 1, 1960, they walked into the Woolworth's in downtown Greensboro, purchased several items, and then two of them went to the lunch counter—the one reserved for whites—and ordered coffee and doughnuts and were told, "I'm sorry, we don't serve you here." (There was a hot dog stand—no stools—in the basement for blacks.) The other two young men joined their friends at the counter, and they asked the serving staff why they could not, as patrons of the store, be served. A policeman paced up and down behind them, and some whites called them "niggers," although several older white women encouraged them. The manager tried to reason with them, but they remained firm and stayed at the counter until closing time. They returned the next day and the next and were joined by other students and eventually even some sympathetic white students from nearby white colleges. The tactic spread to other cities, and within the next two months, sit-ins were held in 54 cities. A new organization—the Student Non-Violent Coordinating Committee (SNCC)—was founded in Raleigh to coordinate demonstrations in the South. In Greensboro, demonstrations spread to many of the

---

112. Raines, *My Soul Is Rested*, interview with Hartman Turnbow, 288.
113. Chafe, *Civilities and Civil Rights*, 72, 75–76, 107–108.

other restaurants in the city, and at times demonstrators filled the downtown restaurants. Groups of white teenagers and young men heckled the protesters, and customers began staying away from Woolworth's and the other downtown stores. Woolworth's finally closed its lunch counter, and pressure mounted at its national headquarters to find a solution. Negotiations between white merchants and black leaders led by Dr. Hobart Jarrett finally negotiated a deal, and Woolworth's and several other downtown restaurants were desegregated. Protests, however, continued sporadically for the next three years producing more negotiations. The mayor of Greensboro brought together a sort of summit of white businessmen who reached an agreement to desegregate many of the restaurants and provide more jobs to blacks.[114] The bad publicity and lost business resulting from the protests were finally more important than segregation. Greensboro was a city on the move, the "gateway to the New South" as Franklin McCain, one of the four young men who initiated the sit-in, would later note, and segregation and protests simply didn't fit in with the image that the city's white business elite was trying to cultivate.[115] The sit-ins were most effective in the upper South where business leaders were more amenable to negotiations and support for segregation was less profound. Atlanta became known as the "city too busy to hate" after the white Chamber of Commerce negotiated a deal with Atlanta's traditional black civic leaders to end the sit-ins in that city. However, it would take the appearance of Martin Luther King, Jr. to quell dissatisfaction with the pact by young people in the movement who felt it had not gone far enough. A mass meeting was held to discuss the agreement in a black church; King's father, pastor of Ebenezer Baptist Church and one of the leaders who had brokered the deal, was actually booed. King showed up and quieted the crowd; "in a voice close to fury," he told those assembled, "If this contract is broken, it will be a disaster and a disgrace."[116]

The sit-ins had started as spontaneous events; while whites would frequently complain about the role of outside agitators in civil rights demonstrations, local conditions nearly always were the major reason why protests would arise, and local leaders nearly always played the major role. But civil rights organizations were vitally important, too; they provided skilled organizers who would not quit, strategy, and the media attention that proved to be so important. SNCC, for example, excelled at grassroots organizing and reaching young people. Perhaps the most famous SNCC grassroots organizer was Bob Moses, Harlem born and at one point in his life a doctoral student in philosophy at Harvard. Moses had come south to work for Dr. King but realized the SCLC

114. *Ibid.*, 71, 84–85, 94, 97, 112, 115–119,145–149; Raines, *My Soul Is Rested*, interview with Franklin McCain, 73–83.

115. Raines, *My Soul Is Rested*, McCain Interview, 83.

116. Branch, *Parting the Waters*, 397.

was really just a "church office" with a few phones and drifted over to SNCC. He went to Mississippi where he and others planted the seeds of the SNCC voter registration project. It was an uphill battle; Moses was threatened, beaten, shot at, and jailed more than once. Outside the McComb courthouse, he was beaten bloody by the son of the sheriff, a cousin of the sheriff, and the son-in-law of the local state legislator. In Greenwood, he and other protesters attempting to register to vote were repeatedly attacked by police dogs. The threats and beatings were probably not as discouraging as the lack of progress in getting people registered; in a six-month period in Leflore County, 1,500 people took the voter registration test; only fifty were successful. Mississippi whites had much to lose if blacks gained the right to vote because in much of the state, particularly in the Delta, whites were in the minority. In Leflore County, blacks outnumbered whites 3 to 2.[117]

The Congress of Racial Equality (CORE) would briefly hold the spotlight when in 1961 it developed a new tactic to challenge segregation: the freedom rides. The approach as it was first implemented was simple: blacks and whites boarded Trailways and Greyhound buses in Washington, D.C., and rode south to challenge the practice of segregation on interstate buses. All went reasonably well in the upper South, but as one of the buses approached the city of Anniston, Alabama, the tires were shot out, and the bus was surrounded by an angry mob and set on fire. The riders were able to escape the bus and make it to a hospital where they were refused treatment. A mob collected outside the hospital, and they were told to leave. Fortunately, a caravan of cars organized by the Reverend Fred Shuttlesworth pulled up to the hospital to rescue the riders. Shuttlesworth on this day put aside the doctrine of nonviolence; the men in the caravan were armed with shotguns and rifles. They escorted the riders to the cars and whisked them away. Another group of freedom riders that ended up in Birmingham, Alabama, was brutally beaten. The freedom rides continued, by bus and by train, and many of the riders, hundreds actually, were jailed for violating segregation laws.[118]

The SCLC embarked upon a plan in the spring of 1963 to wage a sustained campaign in Birmingham, Alabama. Alabama, along with Mississippi, was the stronghold of segregation; here the white power structure was more willing to ignore if not tacitly support violence to maintain white supremacy—like the beating administered to Bob Moses in McComb by the relatives of local notables. The governor of Alabama, George C. Wallace, was the most famous segregationist politician of the era. He had attained national fame for literally blocking a doorway at the University of Alabama to keep two black students, Vivian Malone and James Hood, from enrolling. Birmingham was presided

---

117. *Ibid.*, 326–331, 494–500, 712–725.
118. Raines, *My Soul Is Rested*, interviews with Hank Thomas, John Lewis, and James Farmer, 119–138.

over by a vicious and corrupt police commissioner, Bull Conner, a man in league with the local Klan and not afraid to break heads to maintain segregation. Birmingham was sometimes called "Bombingham" because of the large number of black churches, businesses, and homes that had been bombed by terrorists intent on keeping blacks in their place; a black neighborhood in Birmingham was nicknamed "Dynamite Hill" for the same reason.[119]

The SCLC's plan, "Project C," would involve civil disobedience on a grand scale—hundreds if not thousands would protest Birmingham and Alabama segregation laws, and many would get sent to jail. The strategy ran into trouble early on; Bull Connor showed a willingness to jail any and all protesters and had gotten an injunction against protest marches; adults with jobs and responsibilities were slow to sign up for events that might result in indeterminate stays in the local jails. King himself spent nine days in solitary confinement in jail where he wrote his famous "Letter from Birmingham City Jail." This letter, more than any other single work, explained the philosophy of the movement with its emphasis on nonviolence and challenging, peacefully, unjust laws and practices. When King got out of jail, other charges still hanging over his head, Project C seemed to be floundering. James Bevel and others urged him to support a young people's march to get back on track. Young people consistently supported civil rights campaigns with enthusiasm throughout the South and were often the shock troops of the movement. King anguished about using children in such a violent city, but finally consented to the plan. The young marchers poured out of the Sixteenth Street Baptist church shortly after 1:00 on May 2 singing the anthem of the movement "We Shall Overcome." The police immediately began arresting marchers, some as young as six, and crammed them into jail cells. Seventy-five were packed into one cell designed to hold eight. When protests resumed the next day, Bull Connor's strategy was to keep the marchers out of the business district; mass arrests were out of the question with jails overflowing. He ordered the fire department to turn powerful fire hoses on the marchers. Black businessman A. G. Gaston was talking on the phone with lawyer David Vann and put the phone aside for a moment to see what was happening in Ingram Park, outside his window. He grabbed the phone and exclaimed to Vann, "They've turned the fire hoses on a little black girl. And they're rolling that girl right down the middle of the street." Some of the marchers threw rocks at the fire hoses and the firemen manning them. Later, police dogs were set on the marchers. But the protesters kept coming day after day; the morale of the police, the jailers, and the firemen began to falter, and white business leaders grew despondent. They had hoped to emulate prosperous Atlanta, "the city too busy to hate"; instead, their city was a war zone, the local economy was in a depression, and images of the battle went around

---

119. *Ibid.*, interview with Ben Allen, 181–185; Branch, *Parting the Waters*, 690–691.

the world at light speed. Sid Smyer, a prominent Birmingham businessman, was called to Washington to meet with President John F. Kennedy. Kennedy told him, in effect, "Either you solve this problem or we will." Smyer convened a meeting of nearly 100 of the elders of the white business community, the so-called "Big Mules" of Birmingham, to consider a modest proposal King had made to end the demonstrations. The businessmen agreed to the basic terms King had put forward—desegregate a variety of businesses and hire more black workers. In return, King agreed to leave the city and allow things to cool off.[120]

President John F. Kennedy's support for civil rights had been guarded; he had won the presidency by a mere 100,000 votes and could not afford to alienate the white South if he wanted another term of office. The Justice Department, headed by his brother Robert, did work behind the scenes to support the movement, although often King and other movement leaders felt the Department was more interested in heading off problems that might embarrass the administration than truly advancing the cause of equal rights for African Americans. But following the Birmingham battles, Kennedy decided to give an address on national television calling for equal rights for African Americans. As he noted in his short address, "the heart of the question is whether all Americans are to be afforded equal rights and equal opportunities, whether we are going to treat our fellow Americans as we want to be treated."[121]

Kennedy's public commitment notwithstanding, opposition to the civil rights cause seemed, if anything, to harden. Murders and beatings continued unabated. The day of Kennedy's speech, Medgar Evers, the Mississippi NAACP leader, was assassinated in his driveway. In Winona, Mississippi, Annell Ponder, a SCLC organizer and Fannie Lou Hamer, one of her literacy school students, were released from jail where they had been imprisoned for four days; in the jail, they had been beaten to a pulp with blackjacks.[122] In the five weeks before and after the speech, nearly 15,000 people had been arrested in demonstrations in 186 cities. Kennedy's civil rights legislation was bogged down in Congress, and some of the other measures he supported also languished because of his civil rights stance.[123] Even those sympathetic to the movement were concerned about the turmoil wrought by the movement. Civil rights leaders, perhaps reflecting on the movement song "We Shall Not Be Moved,"

120. Branch, *Parting the Waters*, 690, 726–781; quote 759; Martin Luther King, Jr., "Letter from Birmingham City Jail," Mullane, ed., *Crossing the Danger Water*, 633–646; Raines, *My Soul Is Rested*, interview with Sid Smyer, 176–181.

121. Branch, *Parting the Waters*, 818–827, quote 824.

122. Branch, *Parting the Waters*, 818–819, 824–825; Raines, *My Soul Is Rested*, interview with Fannie Lou Hamer, 271–280.

123. Branch, *Parting the Waters*, 823, 827–828.

decided to focus the attention of the nation on Washington and laid plans for a large demonstration in the capital itself.

The March on Washington in August 1963 would draw 200,000 people or more from all over the country. The marchers collected on the mall around the reflecting pool in front of the Lincoln memorial to hear speeches by civil rights notables, the most memorable of which was King's "I Have a Dream" speech. King's dream was of a future where color no longer mattered and "little black boys and black girls will be able to join hands with little white boys and white girls and walk together as sisters and brothers." The march gave renewed hope to the hundreds of thousands of civil rights activists and the speeches, especially King's, refocused the attention of the nation on the ideals and aspirations of the movement. But it was the assassination of John F. Kennedy later that year that gave civil rights legislation the push it needed to get through Congress. The new president, Texan Lyndon Baines Johnson, had decided to take up civil rights as his special cause, as a way to set himself apart from the slain Kennedy, whom in life he had resented. Johnson was able to use his contacts in the Senate and the overwhelming public support that flooded over him as the successor of the martyred Kennedy to push the Civil Rights Act of 1964 through Congress. The act unleashed the power of the federal government on Jim Crow; it prohibited segregation in restaurants, stores, and hotels; it gave the Equal Employment Opportunities Commission the power to ferret out discrimination in the hiring, compensation, and promotion practices of businesses; and it unleashed squads of Justice Department attorneys to push school districts to develop comprehensive desegregation plans.[124]

Significant federal support for black voting rights in the South would not come until the following year. Once again, tragedy would push along federal action. Bob Moses and other SNCC leaders had devised a voter registration drive for the summer of 1964, called "Freedom Summer"; the drive would bring hundreds of college students, most of them white, from around the country to Mississippi to help SNCC field workers. Moses and others believed that when the country saw white college students, many of them from influential families, being beaten and jailed, the federal government would be compelled to intervene. The project had barely begun when three SNCC workers, one of them a college student who had just arrived in the state, were arrested by a Neshoba County sheriff's deputy and taken to jail. Thereafter, they vanished; they were found more than a month later buried in an irrigation pond dam. That summer, scores of other SNCC workers were threatened, beaten, and jailed, but by the end of the summer, civil rights workers had registered

---

124. *Ibid.*, 876–887; Adam Fairclough, *Better Days Coming: Blacks and Equality, 1890–2000* (New York: Viking, 2001), 281–282; Martin Luther King, Jr., "I Have A Dream," Mullane, ed., *Crossing the Danger Water*, 649; Earl Black and Merle Black, *Politics and Society in the South* (Cambridge: Harvard University Press, 1987), 110–111, 154–155.

scores of people and had created the Mississippi Freedom Democratic Party (MFDP) to challenge the all-white Democratic Party in the state. The new party sent a slate of delegates to the Democratic National Convention in Atlantic City and argued it should represent Mississippi at the convention, not the delegates selected by the regular party. In hearings organized by party officials to determine which delegation rightfully should be seated, veterans of the voter registration efforts in the state gave graphic testimony, much of it nationally televised, about the perils of trying to register to vote in Mississippi if you were black; Fannie Lou Hamer's was especially moving. But it would take another tragedy before federal action was taken on voting rights. In March of the next year, a protest march of around 600 men, women and children that was scheduled to go from Selma to Montgomery was attacked at the Edmund Pettus Bridge in Selma by Alabama state troopers and Sheriff Jim Clark's deputies and his infamous posse. The lawmen, some riding horses, drove the marchers back with whips, clubs, and tear gas and pursued them down the street indiscriminately beating whoever they could catch; dozens were injured. The attack was captured on film and came to be called "Bloody Sunday."[125] President Johnson, appalled by the violence, announced plans to appear before Congress a week after Bloody Sunday to introduce a tough voting rights bill. Johnson gave a moving speech in his Texas drawl, a white Southerner telling the nation, "Their cause must be our cause too. Because it's not just Negroes, but really it's all of us who must overcome the crippling legacy of bigotry and injustice." He concluded by saying, "and we shall overcome!"[126] Following passage of the act, the percentage of registered black voters surged; by the presidential election of 1968, a majority of blacks was registered to vote in every Southern state, and the huge disparities in voting registration between the Deep South and the Upper South disappeared. The number of black elected officials in the South climbed from 72 in 1965 to 2,601 in 1982.[127]

While many whites were absolutely furious about the marches, demonstrations, and negative publicity and concocted fanciful stories about how the movement was all the work of outside agitators stirring up otherwise contented blacks, white support for segregation did begin to wane in the South. The lonely voices of opposition to the institution in the white community— people like writer Lillian Smith, Presbyterian churchman James McBride Dabbs, Highlander Folklife Center director Myles Horton and newspaper editor Ralph McGill—were joined by a growing throng. Many in the white com-

125. Fairclough, *Better Days Coming*, 284–291; James Cobb, *The Most Southern Place on Earth: The Mississippi Delta and the Roots of Regional Identity* (New York: Oxford University Press, 1992), 234–235; Raines, *My Soul Is Rested*, interviews with Wilson Baker, 214–222, Willie Bolden, 226–228.

126. Oates, *Let the Trumpet Sound*, 354–355, quote p. 355.

127. Black and Black, *Politics and Society in the South*, 136–137, 144.

munity came to the simple realization that fighting to deny people basic rights was a fool's errand. Glenn Evans, an officer on the Birmingham police force, remembers a fellow officer saying, "Evans, ten or fifteen years from now, we will look back on this and we will say, 'How stupid can you be?'" Some came to realize segregation had simply been wrong; Evans himself remembers this belief coming to him as an epiphany one day while riding the bus. A black mother and her little boy got on the bus; while she paid the fare, her son sat in the white section. When she paid, she nervously took him by the hand and told him, "Come on, you can't sit there." As he noted to his interviewer, his eyes filling with tears, "I said to myself, 'Where are we going with this? What's happening here?'"[128] For others, abandoning segregation was simple economic necessity. The old plantation economy was disappearing and with it the need for a large population of low-wage workers, a need segregation had served by limiting the economic and educational opportunities of blacks. Segregation just didn't fit in the new economy that business leaders in places like Atlanta and Greensboro were trying to build. Even in Mississippi, the heartland of white resistance to change, the Mississippi Economic Council had come out with a declaration in the mid-1960s recognizing that the state was not "an island unto itself, but an integral and responsible part of the United States."[129]

However tentative, there was promising movement toward some day achieving King's dream of a colorblind society. In 1965–1966, 6% of the South's black students attended public schools with whites; by the 1976–1977 school year, nearly 4 out of every 5 black students were enrolled in schools with populations at least 10% white.[130] A sea change swept over the culture of Southern public schools. In the 1960s, some white school children were still participating in Confederate Memorial Day ceremonies during the school day (including one of the authors), and most heard nary a word criticizing segregation in their classrooms; by the 1970s, public schools, officially at least, were committed to equality. Lessons promoting the belief that all were equal and that prejudice was a bad thing became an accepted part of most school curriculums, and many schools sponsored at least token programs on black history, white school administrators sitting uneasily on the stage singing "Lift Every Voice and Sing" (a song sometimes called the black national anthem). The sea change affected black children, too. It seemed for many black high school students, integration meant leaving their schools, schools that were often named after notable black leaders like Booker T. Washington and often located in black neighborhoods, and attending what used to be the white schools. Predictably there were clashes —fighting on the school buses between black and white, small scale riots in

128. Raines, *My Soul Is Rested*, interview with Glenn V. Evans, 187–188, quote p. 188.
129. Lemann, *The Promised Land*, 321.
130. Black and Black, *Politics and Society in the South*, 154–155.

some schools, tensions when it came time to picking proms queens or even having a prom. Integration of the universities and colleges moved at a slower pace, although there were some symbolic victories for those who were attempting to build this new colorblind society. For example, at the University of South Carolina, a largely white institution in a state where whites were nearly as obdurate in their commitment to Jim Crow as Mississippi, students selected Harry Walker as student body president in 1971. Walker was the first black student body president at the university and one of the first in the South at a traditionally white college. The Democratic Party, once the party of white supremacy, evolved into a multi-racial party heavily dependent on the black vote, and prominent white Democratic politicians like Georgia's Jimmy Carter emerged who preached the message of racial reconciliation.

The old racial narrative that supported and explained Jim Crow was discredited, even if it still persisted in the hearts and minds of many whites. A new narrative now briefly dominated the public discourse. It featured peaceful, dignified African Americans led by ministers who were simply trying to eat at a lunch counter, register to vote, and carry protest signs; arrayed against them were mobs and police with clubs and dogs and fire hoses and behind them, a shadowy group of terrorists who blew up churches, homes, and businesses and killed, beat, and mutilated scores of people. But this narrative was almost immediately challenged by another narrative dictated more by events elsewhere in the nation than in the South.

In the North and Midwest and West, serious racial problems had long been smoldering. Job discrimination, housing discrimination, segregated schools resulting from segregated housing patterns, and the corralling of large black populations into economically depressed areas of cities known as ghettos created huge disparities in wealth and opportunity between black and white. Race, it turned out, was a national problem, not simply a Southern problem. Civil rights leaders like Dr. King turned their attention to the area of the country outside the South, but the civil rights movement was not nearly as successful in this new phase of the struggle. The goals and enemies were less well-defined, and the old emphasis on building a colorblind society was challenged by a new emphasis on black solidarity and even separatism. A slogan introduced in the South by SNCC's Stokeley Carmichael—black power—replaced the hymns of the Southern movement, and groups like the Black Panthers took the concept to the furthest extent and openly carried guns. The level of organization of the movement in the North, Midwest, and West did not come close to matching that in the South, and without a disciplined movement to direct people's energies, protest often devolved into violent expressions of pent-up rage. In August 1965 a riot broke out in Watts, a predominantly black section of Los Angeles, that was described as "the most destructive race riot in more than two decades." It was the first of nearly three hundred race riots across the country over the next three years, many of them characterized by widespread looting and arson.[131]

Reacting to the disorders of the 1960s and rising crime rates, more and more whites across the nation turned in a conservative direction; "law and order" became their slogan. Conservative whites also saw the expanded welfare programs of the 1960s as primarily benefiting blacks, and affirmative action programs, which pressured private and public employers to actively recruit black employees and institutions of higher education to actively recruit black students, were perceived as giving an "unfair" advantage to minorities and as an example of "reverse discrimination."[132] This new conservatism fostered a new racial narrative: in this narrative blacks were again viewed as a problem reminiscent of the old Jim Crow narrative and efforts to help them had gone too far and were actually holding them back. Ronald Reagan launched his 1980 presidential campaign in Mississippi, where he told a nearly all-white crowd at the Neshoba County fairgrounds, "I believe in states' rights," a term that had been used by segregationists in their battle to turn back federal efforts at ending segregation. Reagan ushered in a conservative political era that would run at least another 25 years; he and most subsequent Republican national leaders attacked welfare programs, affirmative action and court-mandated busing to achieve racial integration in the public schools; enough had been done for blacks seemed to be the subtextual message. White Southerners reflected these national trends and then some; the South became the most reliably Republican region in the country for candidates for national office. Blacks, for their part, were torn between several narratives of their own—the integrationist one envisioned by King and a separatist one that reflected their life experiences in a segregated world, a world in which they had built their own churches, businesses, schools, and traditions. Integration, true integration, would mean an end to this world. And then there was the separatism offered by the black power advocates which urged African Americans to take pride in their culture and deal with the white world from a position of strength.

Race in the Contemporary South

Despite the conservative turn the nation took, in many respects, race matters less today than it ever has in the South. Race is no longer the South's "special problem," and when people discuss racial problems today, they often speak in terms of the nation or perhaps the cities. Laws separating the races are long

---

131. Black and Black, *Politics and Society in the South*, 128–129.
132. *Ibid.*, 166–167.

gone, and open discrimination against non-whites is no longer tolerated. While blacks fled the South by the hundreds of thousands in the first 75 years of the 20th century, over the last 30 years, many have moved into the South from other regions. The South has become the number one destination of blacks relocating from other regions in the United States, with metropolitan areas attracting the most people. Some of these folks are retirees returning to the region they had once fled or their children or grandchildren who are looking for better job prospects and a better quality of life. Many are better educated people with middle class occupations.[133] The number of black families in poverty declined significantly, and the black middle class expanded; by the mid-1990s, over one third of Southern black families were firmly in the middle class in terms of both income and wealth holdings.[134] Colleges and universities in the South are still predominately black or white, although at many institutions there is a slow but steady movement toward a more racially diverse student body.[135] As noted earlier, the Democratic Party in the South has become a truly a multiracial party dependent on the black vote, and thousands of black elected and appointed government officials now serve in various offices throughout the region. Black school superintendents, police chiefs, big city mayors, and congressmen are highly visible public figures. Blacks and whites shop in the same stores and work together. Segregated housing patterns are still common, but integrated neighborhoods and apartment complexes are quite common, too. A black professional couple moving into an upscale development like Preston in Cary, North Carolina, wouldn't raise an eyebrow because the development, like many, is multiracial with representatives from a variety of ethnic groups living there in apparent harmony. While Sunday might still qualify as the most segregated day of the week, the rapidly expanding independent and Pentecostal churches of the region are often racially mixed to a surprising degree. The Assembly of God Tabernacle in Decatur, Georgia, for

---

133. *The State of the South, 2007: Philanthropy as the South's "Passing Gear,"* (Chapel Hill: MDC, Inc., 2007), 9; William H. Frey, "The New Great Migration: Black Americans Return to the South, 1965–2000" (Washington, D.C.: Center on Urban and Metropolitan Policy, The Brookings Institute, May 2004), http://www.frey-demographer.org/reports/Brook04.pdf.

134. *Income and Wealth in the South: A State of the South Interim Report* (Chapel Hill: MDC, Inc., May, 1998), 1–15, http://www.mdcinc.org/docs/income.pdf; *Black and Black, Politics and Society in the South,* 166.

135. See, for example, the data on North Carolina institutions of higher education: *Third Annual Report on University of North Carolina Enrollment Planning,* December 15, 2001, http://www.northcarolina.edu/docs/aa/planning/Rpt_on_Enroll_Plng_2001.pdf; "Racial Composition of Degree Headcount Enrollment in North Carolina colleges and Universities, Fall 2005," http://intranet.northcarolina.edu/docs/assessment/Abstract/2005 –06/section%201/T._1906.pdf.

example, was 55% white and 43% black in 2000; its Web site boasts of having over 50 nationalities in its congregation.[136]

What race means in the South has also changed. Race once was almost exclusively a black and white issue, with Native Americans or Hispanics factored into the equation in some areas. In recent decades, more and more immigrants from South and Central America, the Caribbean, Asia, and Africa have settled in the South, and in 2000 immigrants constituted over 9% of the region's population. Over the course of the first eight years of the new millennium, Hispanics were the fastest growing population in the region, and this held true in every Southern state. Simple black/white distinctions thus are almost archaic. Too, what segregationists once had dreaded is now more common: more interracial couples are taking marriage vows, reflecting a national trend.[137] Interracial couples that the authors have spoken to have talked of getting "looks" and occasional comments, but no one has reported being actively harassed or worse. The issue has been, in effect, put to a vote in two Deep South states in 1999 and 2000. South Carolina and Alabama still had laws on the books that prohibited interracial marriage, and voters in both states, by a significant margin, voted to remove the laws. The votes were largely symbolic because court decisions had rendered the laws unenforceable, but they do indicate that the old taboo no longer generates the passion it once did.[138] There is a movement by interracial couples and their children to end the practice of identifying people on applications and so forth by race. "We are not members of a particular race," say these people. (Tiger Woods, the golfer, would be a well-known example of this group.)

Popular culture now incorporates and even celebrates black culture. In contemporary America and the South, African-American rhythms and patterns of life have had an enormous impact on music, theater, public education, sports, and the arts. Black athletes, such as former basketball star Michael Jordan, are public figures, even idols, for both blacks and whites. Popular music has been shaped by black artists and black music styles such as gospel, blues, and rhythm and blues. Hip hop has displaced rock as the music of choice for many young people, and suburban white youth are just as likely to listen to the music as black youth. Jazz has acquired such status that it is sometimes referred to as "American classical music," and jazz artists such as Duke Ellington, John Coltrane, and Billie Holiday have attained icon status. Modern jazz artists such as Wynton Marsalis

---

136. Kevin Sack, "Shared Prayers, Mixed Blessings," *How Race Is Lived in America* (New York: Times Books, 2001), 3–21; The Tabernacle, http://www.tabernacleag.org/index.php.

137. *The State of the South 2010: Chapter 1: Beyond the Gilded Age* (Chapel Hill, NC: MDC, Inc., 2010), 9; William H. Frey, "Charticle," The Milkin Institute Review, Third Quarter, 2003, http://www.frey-demographer.org/reports/Rainbownation.pdf.

138. "Alabama repeals century-old ban on interracial marriages," *CNN*, 8 November 2000, http://archives.cnn.com/2000/ALLPOLITICS/stories/11/07/alabama.interracial/.

have been successful at expanding the audience for this complex musical form. The works of black painters and sculptors are exhibited in the finest museums and galleries. Black filmmakers such as Spike Lee and John Singleton have reached a broad audience with their provocative films, and black actors like Will Smith or Eddie Murphy are among the highest paid. Toni Morrison, Henry Gates, and Cornel West are not simply good African-American writers and scholars; they are among the very finest writers and scholars in America today. Oprah Winfrey is a major force in television and even has a magazine named after her that features a picture of herself—always dressed in stylish clothing—on the cover each month. Black images are now commonplace in commercial advertisements. The era of the blond, blue-eyed model as the definition of feminine beauty is long over.

But there is another side of the picture in the South. A multitude of ethnic groups may reside in Cary's Preston, but it is, like most of the suburban developments surrounding the cities and towns of the South, predominantly white. Conversely, many Southern cities and even towns are now predominantly black, the result of what has been called "white flight" to the suburbs; Atlanta, for example, was 55% white in 1961, but by 1973 was only 18% white and is less white today, though there is a modest trend of whites returning to the city.[139] So a new form of segregation has emerged; while blacks can generally join the suburban "club" if they choose, there is one admission requirement that keeps many of them out— money. Suburbs are designed to be for middle-class people, and the percentage of black Southerners in the middle class is still around half the percentage of white Southerners in the middle class. The percentage of blacks at the very bottom of the pile in terms of wealth has stayed relatively stable and is still quite large; in 1969, it was 44% and in 1995, it was 42%.[140] The result of these patterns is that suburban whites live in a mostly white world that is defined by a relatively uniform level of affluence. It's a world of 3- to 5-bedroom houses with well-maintained lawns, a thriving job market, thoroughfares lined with strip malls and shopping centers selling every imaginable product, and plenty of soccer fields and dance studios for the kids. Urban blacks live in a very different world that is mostly black and characterized by dilapidated neighborhoods, more expensive consumer goods (the national chains prefer the suburbs), and a paucity of jobs that pay a living wage. For less affluent folks, getting out of the cities and into the suburbs where the jobs are is harder than it sounds; mass transit linking city to suburbs in most of the South is poorly developed, and suburban developers and town governments haven't shown much interest in building low cost housing.

In the rural South, another kind of segregation persists. While hundreds of thousands of blacks fled the rural South over the course of much of the twentieth

---

139. Fairclough, *Better Day Coming*, 328.
140. *Income and Wealth in the South: A State of the South Interim Report* (Chapel Hill: MDC, Inc., May, 1998), 1–15, http://www.mdcinc.org/docs/income.pdf.

century, the old plantation districts such as eastern North Carolina, the Black Belt of Alabama, and the Delta still have large black populations; much of the nation's African-American population still lives in this region, and many of the counties are more black than white.[141] This is an area that is dirt poor; as we saw in earlier chapters, mechanical cotton pickers, tractors and other machines displaced most of the farming people, and rural areas have had a tough time attracting and keeping industry. The industry that is located in rural areas is generally low-paying, and much of it has fled the country in recent years in search of even cheaper labor. Ironically, poverty itself is often the only growth industry in rural areas; federal programs, Medicaid especially, pour millions into poor counties and directly or indirectly create jobs. Over 40% of the 2006 Mississippi state budget, a staggering 5.4 billion dollars, was made up of these federal transfer payments.[142] While many blacks in rural areas have acquired middle class jobs, particularly in the public sector (education, state and local government, and federally funded programs), whites still hold most of the better jobs, and blacks still make up most of the poor.

Recent trends in public schooling offer yet another example of how class and geography now dictate much about what race means. The South's public schools were the most integrated in the nation from the early 1970s until the late 1980s, but in recent years the level of integration has begun to decline, part of a national trend. The resegregation process appears most pronounced in the old plantation region and in many of the cities; here schools are often predominantly black, and the students come from mostly poor families. The Birmingham (Alabama) School System, for example, is only 2.8% white. Rural Halifax County (North Carolina), despite its small population, has three public school systems: two—the Halifax County school system and the Weldon City school system—are overwhelmingly black; the other (in Roanoke Rapids) is predominantly white. Hispanic children are growing in number in the region and are more likely to spend their school days with other Hispanic children and black children and less likely to attend school with white children.[143] Accompanying the growing separation is an even more troubling statistic: many of these rural and urban school systems are classified as low-performing

---

141. Ronald Wimberley and Libby Morris's study, *The Southern Black Belt: a National Perspective* (Lexington, KY: University of Kentucky, 1997) documents the persistent poverty, especially for blacks, in a large swath of the rural South they refer to as the "Black Belt." See also *Dismantling Persistent Poverty in the Southeastern States* (Athens, GA: Carl Vinson Institute of Government, University of Georgia, 2002) and Hayes Mizzell, "Racial Justice and Equity: Challenges for the American South," MDC, 1–2, http://www.mdcinc.org/docs/mizell.pdf.

142. *The Two States of Mississippi* (Jackson, MS: The Mississippi Forum on Children and Families, 2006), http://www.mfcf.org/kc/06_MS_Databook/O6_KC_MS_Databook.pdf.

143. Erica Frankenberg and Chungmei Lee, *Race in American Public Schools: Rapidly Resegregating School Districts* (Cambridge: The Civil Rights Project, Harvard University,

and have high dropout rates. In the Halifax County high schools, for example, less than half of the students pass end-of-course tests, tests which many observers believe adhere to minimal standards at best.[144]

So while white and black are moving closer together on one level, on another level they are moving further apart. Nowhere are these trends more apparent than in politics. As noted earlier, most blacks in the South now vote Democratic, and that once segregated party is now a multi-racial party; Southern whites have increasingly voted Republican, and this party is overwhelmingly white. But these trends mask a high level of complexity and variability. In the Deep South, very few whites vote for the Democratic presidential candidate or candidates for Congress; in the presidential election of 2008, the percentage of whites voting for Barack Obama barely made it into double digits in Mississippi, Alabama, and Louisiana. But in the upper South and Florida, the white portion of the Democratic Party is more robust, and whites, apparently, are not frightened by a black candidate for president from Chicago; Obama took 41% of the white vote in West Virginia, 47% in Maryland, 42% in Florida and in the mid-thirties in Virginia and North Carolina. Obama won in many metropolitan districts with significant white populations such as DeKalb County, Georgia (the Atlanta area) and Wake County, North Carolina (the Raleigh area) while faring poorly in predominantly white rural districts.[145] Race, one might conclude, still means a lot in the politics of the Deep South and the rural South but is less important in Florida, the upper South, and the more cosmopolitan areas of the region.

We are left with a complex picture: race still has a powerful influence on the culture, but its influence is waning, more so in some places than others. Members of the growing black middle class have opportunities, power, and choices, including choices of where to live; for them, race no longer is destiny. Less affluent blacks in rural areas and the inner cities live in a largely segregated world that is, in many ways, as difficult to escape as the Jim Crow world of old and almost as limiting. They are poorly educated and lack job skills. The marginality of their existence has wreaked havoc on the stability of their families, and many of the young men have fallen prey to the lure of illegal drugs and crime. None of this is unique to the South; it describes just as well the urban areas of the North, Midwest and West Coast. No new narrative has yet surfaced that offers a way to bridge this divide.

August, 2002), 1–24, http://www.civilrightsproject.harvard.edu/research/deseg/Race_in_ American_Public_Schools1.pdf.

144. Education First: NC School Report Cards, http://www.ncschoolreportcard.org/ src/.

145. *CNN.com Election Results*, http://www.cnn.com/ELECTION/2004/pages/results/ president/; CNN ElectionCenter 2008, at http://www.cnn.com/ELECTION/2008/results/ president/.

Chapter 4

Family and Gender in the South

Ships at a distance have every man's wish on board. For some they come in with the tide. For others they sail forever on the horizon, never out of sight, never landing until the Watcher turns his eyes away in resignation, his dreams mocked to death by Time. This is the life of men.

Now, women forget all those things they don't want to remember, and remember everything they don't want to forget. The dream is the truth. Then they act and do things accordingly.[1]

Family has always been important in the South, old and new. From the television mountain family the Waltons—three generations living in harmony—to a real life rock and roller named Elvis Presley who loved his momma and

---

1. Zora Neal Hurston, *Their Eyes Were Watching God* (1937; New York: Perennial Library, 1990).

daddy so much that he moved them in with him at Graceland, work, ambition, even love often took a back seat to family. It is still common to find people like Crystal Brantley, a resident of Norlina, North Carolina, who is part of a tightly knit extended family. Ms. Brantley began dating her husband in high school and has been married to him most of her adult life. She has lived within a few miles of her father and mother, her husband's parents, her siblings, and many of her aunts, uncles, and cousins her whole life. Family members tended her children when they were young while she worked as a school teacher; vacations were often spent with uncles, aunts, grandparents, and parents; parties more often than not were family parties; and cousins and siblings were not only cousins and siblings but best friends. Today, fewer and fewer families are like Crystal Brantley's. Two-parent families are still common, but so are families composed of a woman and a child or two, thanks to the higher incidence of divorce and the growing acceptability of single mothers. Blended families—families headed by parents previously married to other partners with the children coming from both marriages—are also more common. It is more and more common for people to have extended families spread all over the country, and to spend little time with uncles, aunts, and cousins.

The way families were organized traditionally followed a certain pattern in the South; it is a pattern familiar to everyone because it is common throughout the world, and it is called patriarchy. In patriarchy, the male heads the family; what this means, however, is surprisingly varied, as we will see. Fundamentally, patriarchy is based on the notion that male and female have different roles in the family and in life. The traditional male role is, at its most basic, to provide the family with food, shelter, and protection. The male's job is also to make the major decisions and to be the family's representative to the world outside the family. The woman's role is to bear and raise children and perform the domestic chores—cooking, cleaning, etc.—and to help the male. In this scheme, most women would be under the care and leadership of a male, generally a parent or husband; the unmarried woman without living parents would often live in the home of a male-headed family of a relative. As should be obvious, today, much about these traditional gender roles no longer applies to many women and men. Many women now live on their own as the average age of marriage creeps upward and divorce sunders many marriages. While almost everyone celebrates the family, many today believe it is a good thing for women to be able to pursue careers and live on their own, perfectly all right for men to raise children and keep house, and only reasonable that married couples make decisions jointly. The "companionate marriage"—a marriage of equals entered into when couples "fall in love" and held together by love, sexual intimacy, and mutual interests—is considered the ideal. While no one celebrates divorce, many people today think no one should have to put up with an abusive or unfaithful spouse and that divorce is sometimes necessary. Conservatives, however, are troubled by these developments. Indeed, there has been a long tradition in the region of opposing the decline of patriarchy and changes in gender roles. Most Southern states opposed the amendment giving women the right to vote that was approved in 1920, and in the 1970s and early 1980s most Southern states opposed the equal rights amendment for women. More recently, the Southern Baptist Convention came out (in 2000) with the following resolution: "A wife is to submit herself graciously to the servant leadership of her husband."[2] And so traditional values, supported by conservative evangelical Christianity, clash with the contemporary values of freedom and individualism, and the clash often takes place in the political arena. This clash is rooted in two different concepts of human nature with many conservatives believing men and women are different in profound ways and that these differences are ordained by God and biology, while "modernists" tend to see gender differences as more culturally determined and think equality of the sexes in most areas of life (with the obvious exception of child bearing) is possible and healthy.

In this chapter, we will explore how family, patriarchy, and gender roles evolved in the South and how there were important differences in what family and gender and patriarchy meant for rich and poor and black and white. We'll explore how they were shaped by the agrarian society that predominated in the region and how they in turn shaped that society, particularly when it came to matters of class and race. The steady decline of agrarianism over the course of the twentieth century would profoundly affect family life and gender roles and touch off the often bitter culture war alluded to earlier.

Family in Early Virginia

Patterns of family, marriage, and gender roles were established by the two groups who predominated in the early settlement phase of the South: English settlers from the South and West of England and Scots Irish settlers. The earliest English settlers, as we have seen, settled on the James River in the settlement of Jamestown and eventually spread throughout the Chesapeake area and later down the coastline of North and South Carolina. These settlers were planters, many of them "gentlemen," and indentured servants. More men than women came to early Chesapeake, and so there was a shortage of women, which necessarily meant that many men, especially indentured servants and the less affluent, never got married. For this and other reasons, attitudes about family, marriage and gender roles that were established in the Chesapeake region not only reflected the culture of southern and western England but also

---

2. "The 2000 Baptist Faith and Message," Southeastern Baptist Seminary, http://www.sebts.edu/prospective_students/what_we_believe/bfm2000.cfm.

had a decidedly upper class cast. Despite the shortage of women and the large numbers of men incapable of supporting a family, both men and women were expected to marry. Marriages were expected to last for as long as both partners lived; one lawyer recollected in 1681 that no one had gotten a divorce in Virginia in the previous sixty years. Marriages were as much between two families as between two individuals, and parents often played a major role in bringing couples together. First cousin marriage was quite common, as we have seen earlier, and further strengthened economic connections within an extended family.[3]

The family was vitally important in Virginia as in England as an economic unit; most work was conducted within the confines of the nuclear family (father, mother, children) supplemented in the case of the planter by indentured servants or slaves and possibly paid workers and relatives who might live in the household. The male head of the family saw himself as the patriarch, and even servants, visitors, and slaves, while in his care, were part of the family. This concept of patriarchy was based on English notions of the father/husband as king of his domain, a notion reflected in the still common saying "a man's home is his castle."[4] The patriarch was expected to make important decisions about the property and rule the family; the wife was expected to follow his lead and be virtuous and modest. But all but the most affluent women were also expected to be good workers at what today would be considered heavy manual labor. Husbands and wives were expected to love each other even if they had not been "in love" when they first married. Naturally, the ideal was not always the reality; wives might bring property to the marriage that husbands had every right to manage, but arguments between husbands and wives over property ensued nonetheless. The Virginia couple Col. John Custis and Frances Parke Custis had bitter, raging arguments over property. After one particularly violent argument, Col. Custis asked his wife to take a drive with him; he drove his carriage into the Chesapeake Bay, and when his wife asked where he was going, he replied, "To Hell, Madam."[5] Another source of contention was the double standard concerning faithfulness; women were expected to be completely faithful to their husbands, while a more lenient attitude toward straying by the husband prevailed. Women were the guardians of the family bloodline; if a woman strayed, she could end up having a child that was not truly a member of the husband's family. If the indiscretion was never found out, the child would bear the family name and might even inherit family property. Men bore

---

3. David Hackett Fischer, *Albion's Seed: Four British Folkways in America* (New York: Oxford University Press, 1989), 274–276, 281–286.

4. *Ibid.*, 274–276, 279; Peter Bardaglio, *Reconstructing the Household: Families, Sex and the Law in the Nineteenth Century South* (Chapel Hill: University of North Carolina Press, 1995), 24–25.

5. Fischer, *Albion's Seed*, 292.

no such responsibility; extramarital promiscuity with a slave or servant woman was winked at, and the child that might result was a bastard with no legal right to paternal property. The culture, in effect, tolerated sexual predators, particularly if the women involved were lower status women. William Byrd, a prominent Virginia planter, may have qualified as a predator; certainly he seemed to regard slave women and Indian women as playthings.[6]

Extended family was important also, and in early Virginia and more broadly the Chesapeake region, cousins, uncles, grandparents, and so forth often settled in the same area. It was even common for members of extended family to be buried together, a practice that was not common in New England. One's personal reputation was influenced by one's family reputation, and awkwardness, or hot-headedness, or dishonesty was often described as a trait of this family or that family.[7] Older males often served as patriarchs of extended families, especially of wealthy families. Even adult sons were expected to show deference to fathers and heed their advice.[8] For upper class families, keeping the wealth in the family was sometimes more important than the happiness or comfort of any single family member. What was important was that the Lee family or Byrd family would be wealthy and powerful one hundred years hence even if individual Byrds or Lees fell by the wayside.[9]

Immigrants from the north of Britain and Ireland, a group we call the Scots-Irish, immigrated to America in family groups in the mid-1700s and brought strong family traditions with them.[10] As we have seen, these were a people who came from a region constantly in violent turmoil. In this troubled region the extended family and the clan—people linked together by a common surname—provided individuals with a degree of security and protection; if one member of a clan was attacked, the other members were obligated by the *lex talionis* to respond in kind to the attacker. Scots-Irish immigrants settled in the back country of colonial America, and it was common for Scots-Irish extended families and even large segments of clans to settle in the same region. In Catawba County, North Carolina, for example, over 300 Alexander families were identified in the first census of the United States in 1790. In the often precarious and dangerous frontier of the back country of the South, extended family and clan functioned in much the same way as they had in the old coun-

---

6. *Ibid.*, 286–306; Louis B. Wright and Marion Tinling, eds., *The Secret Diary of William Byrd of Westover, 1709–1712* (Richmond, VA: The Dietz Press, 1941). See for examples, pp. 337, 423, 425.

7. Fischer, *Albion's Seed*, 274–276, 286.

8. *Ibid.*, 321–323.

9. *Ibid.*, 380–382.

10. *Ibid.*, 610; James G. Leyburn, *The Scotch-Irish: A Social History* (Chapel Hill: UNC Press, 1962), 6; Grady McWhiney, *Cracker Culture: Celtic Ways in the Old South* (University, Alabama: University of Alabama Press, 1988), 149–152.

try, providing family members with support and protection. As in the old country, loyalty to family was paramount; an insult to one member of the clan was an insult to all, and this was the source of sometimes bloody feuds like the famous Hatfield and McCoy feud of a later time.[11] Extended families and clans had patriarchs leading them and matriarchs exerted moral authority over younger folk, but these honored positions only went to the strongest and most able, according to historian David Hackett Fischer. For weaker and less prosperous men and women, old age often brought abandonment and ridicule. One interesting consequence was that Scots-Irish backcountry settlers had something of a youth bias; in a culture that honored successful older people and ignored or cast out the less successful, the general run of men and women wished to appear as young as possible as long as possible.[12]

In many ways, the Scots-Irish immigrants brought with them a frank acceptance of sex; the Scots-Irish women dressed in provocative ways (low cut dresses, for example), and the men dressed in clothing that accentuated the male physique. Suggestive language was more acceptable among the Scots-Irish, and premarital sex—as long as it was followed by marriage—was tolerated and was even a source of humor. Not surprisingly, Scots Irish immigrants married at a younger age than was typical for immigrants from southern England. While men and women often worked together side by side in the fields, this was no culture of gender equality: men were perceived as warriors and family leaders, and women were expected to do the bidding of their husbands "quietly, cheerfully, and without complaint."[13] The notion that women were prizes to be seized persisted in the American colonies, at least symbolically. On the wedding day, for example, it was not uncommon for a bride to be "kidnapped" by her prospective mate and his friends and relatives. The mock kidnapping was accompanied by hard drinking, make-believe gun battles with the bride's relatives and high spirited foolishness that sometimes lasted days.[14]

Family, Marriage, and Gender before the Civil War: Whites

The Scots-Irish and English traditions blended together as the descendants of Scots-Irish and English immigrants intermingled and intermarried, and a new pattern of family and gender roles emerged in the decades before the Civil War based on four key defining features: the nuclear family as the central insti-

---

11. Fischer, *Albion's Seed*, 610, 662–668.
12. *Ibid.*, 691–696.
13. *Ibid.*, 675–677, quote p. 677.
14. *Ibid.*, 669–674.

tution; patriarchy rooted in the honor code; distinct male and female roles in the family and the broader society; and an important role for the extended family. To be sure there were variations: in Louisiana, French and Spanish cultural influences created unique family and gender traditions, one example of which was a more open acceptance of interracial liaisons. In the mountains where Scots-Irish settlers predominated and harsher conditions approximated the border regions of Great Britain, traditions of the Scots-Irish, such as the feud, seemed to persist. The largest variations were dictated by class and race, with significant differences between black and white and rich and poor. The core family and gender role patterns would persist well into the twentieth century and beyond, although evangelical religion and broader cultural changes in how Southern people thought about love and marriage and family and individual freedom would all have an impact in transforming, albeit slowly, the pattern.

The nuclear family was the central institution of both economic and social life of the antebellum South. Most free people lived in households composed of parents and children, a living arrangement often found, as we will see, even in the slave quarters. It was not uncommon, however, for households to include other family members, too. Small farm families might have an aged parent living with them or a nephew boarding with them and helping with the work; planter families often had relatives staying with them for extended periods, and it was common for a niece or the sister of the wife to stay with a family on a permanent basis. On Tombee plantation, the half-sister of Thomas Chaplin's wife stayed with the family and would marry Chaplin when her sister died.[15] By modern standards these households were quite large; families with 10 or 11 children were common and even the more privileged planter women often had 6 or 7 children. One historian estimates that a typical woman had a pregnancy every 2–2½ years from the first year of marriage until she reached menopause. Many women spent thirty years of their lives bearing and raising children. The mortality rate was quite high for children, infants especially, and complications from childbirth took the lives of many women.[16] Thomas Chaplin's wife had four children before her 21st birthday and three more thereafter.

---

15. Steven Hahn, *The Roots of Southern Populism: Yeoman Farmers and the Transformation of the Georgia Upcountry, 1850–1890* (New York: Oxford University Press, 1984), 30; sample, U.S. Manuscript Census Returns, 1850, 1860, Rowan County, NC, Population Schedule; Frank L. Owsley, *Plain Folk of the Old South* (1949; Baton Rouge: Louisiana State University Press, 1982), 18–19; Theodore Rosengarten, Tombee: *Portrait of a Cotton Planter with The Plantation Journal of Thomas B. Chaplin (1822–1890)* (New York: William Morrow and Co., Inc., 1986), 168.

16. Sally McMillen, *Motherhood in the Old South: Pregnancy, Childbirth, and Infant Rearing* (Baton Rouge: Louisiana State University Press, 1990), Table III, 32, Table VII, 167; William Kaufman Scarborough, *Master of the Big House: Elite Slaveholders of the Mid-Twentieth Century* (Baton Rouge: Louisiana State University Press, 2003), 95–98.

Her frequent pregnancies resulted in a debilitating illness that ultimately killed her at age 29. She spent most of the last few years of her life in a darkened bedroom dipping snuff, a habit that apparently provided her with some relief from her pain. Only four of her children reached adulthood.[17]

The nuclear family meant more than family members sleeping under the same roof each night. On the hundreds of thousands of small farms scattered across the countryside of the South, virtually all a family needed to survive was produced by family members on the land around the homestead. Trips to town were special events, and it was often the husband who made that journey. In an era when government, schools, and other institutions were minimally developed and even the church was far from the dominant institution it would become after the Civil War, the nuclear family served as church, hospital, school house, and sheriff's department. Members of farm families, women especially, were likely to spend much of their lives on the farm with family members.[18]

Members of the planter class were more "in the world" than most small farmers. Husbands often traveled to town for court day, to state capitals if they were legislators and even further afield for business reasons. Wives traveled to the homes of neighbors and relatives for short or lengthy (sometimes lasting weeks) visits. Family vacations at resorts, trips to northern cities for shopping and sightseeing, and even overseas trips were not uncommon. The children of planters frequently attended school in nearby towns; many even boarded at schools further away.[19] However, compared to modern folk, even in the planter class, families spent a significant amount of time together.

The nuclear family began with marriage, and marriage was seen as the "natural" state for adult men and women, a state that promoted order and social stability. Its primacy was supported by both law and custom. In an agrarian society, marriage was entered into first and foremost for economic reasons rather than the more modern reasons of sexual attraction and the desire to have a compatible companion. Successful small farms could not easily be managed by solitary individuals, male or female. Work that men and women performed truly was complementary and necessary each in its own way—the

---

17. Rosengarten, Tombee, 168.

18. Stephanie McCurry, *Masters of Small Worlds: Yeoman Households, Gender Relations, and the Political Culture of the Antebellum South Carolina Low Country* (New York: Oxford University Press, 1995), 97, 122, 125.

19. Rosengarten, Tombee 112; Bertram Wyatt-Brown, *Southern Honor: Ethics and Behavior in the Old South* (Oxford and New York: Oxford University Press, 1983), 327–339; Scarborough, *Masters of the Big House*, 32–44, 65–89; Diary of Mary F. Henderson 22 January 1858; Mrs. Archibald (Mary F.) Henderson to Leonard Henderson, 14 March 1861. John Steele Henderson Collection, Southern Historical Collection, University of North Carolina, Chapel Hill.

heavy manual labor that farming required typically could best be performed by a male; whether women were best suited to the spinning, weaving, cooking, darning, gardening and so forth that women did really is irrelevant. What is relevant is that these tasks were just as vital even if viewed as less important "women's work" by men.[20] Any man without a wife certainly knew better. Further, the children borne by the woman became an important part of the farm's workforce, not, as is the case today, an added expense. Even the successful planter needed a wife to manage the household while he managed the field workforce. Unmarried adults were viewed with suspicion, although the greatest onus of singleness rested on unmarried women who were given a variety of less than flattering names such as "old maid" and "spinster."[21] While men might get by on their own as bachelors, there really was no space in society for a respectable single woman on her own, and typically such a woman lived with a family, most commonly with parents or a married brother or sister.[22]

As we saw in an earlier chapter, class played a major role in determining who might be a suitable mate. Planters wanted their daughters to marry young men with land and slaves and their sons to marry young women who would bring property (usually slaves) to the marriage; small farmer parents hoped their children would marry people who would bring property to the new union, but they also valued men and women who were not afraid of hard work. Courtship for members of the planter class and the small farmer class was, by modern standards, quite formal. Peter Hairston, master of Cooleemee plantation, for example, engaged in a lengthy correspondence with Fanny Caldwell, a member of a prominent family in nearby Rowan County (North Carolina) and visited her when he could. In his early letters, he referred to her as "Miss Fanny" and sent her a handwritten copy of the less than romantic "The Charge of the Light Brigade"; later in the courtship, he addressed her as "My Dear Miss Fanny" and later still as "My Dear Darling Fanny."[23] Weddings were ritualized, just as today, and could be quite elaborate affairs when the couple belonged to the affluent planter class, but even folks of more modest means often followed a schedule of dinners, visiting, and partying. At one such wedding in rural Georgia, young women gathered before the ceremony to

---

20. Hahn, *The Roots of Southern Populism*, 29–30; Elizabeth Fox-Genovese, *Within the Plantation Household: Black and White Women of the Old South* (Chapel Hill: University of North Carolina Press, 1988), 165–166.

21. Bertram Wyatt-Brown, *Southern Honor: Ethics & Behavior in the Old South* (Oxford: Oxford University Press, 1983), 228–229.

22. Catherine Clinton, *The Plantation Mistress* (New York: Pantheon Books, 1982), 85; Anne Firor Scott, *The Southern Lady: From Pedestal to Politics 1830–1930* (Chicago: University of Chicago,1970), 36.

23. See, for example, Peter Hairston to Fanny Caldwell, 15 October 1858, 26 January 1859, 12 March 1859, April 1859, Peter W. Hairston Collection, Southern Historical Collection, University of North Carolina at Chapel Hill.

help the bride with wedding preparations. On the wedding day, a party of young men and boys gathered at the groom's house and rode en masse to the house of the bride, approaching the house at a gallop while all the young women rushed to the windows. After the ceremony, a supper followed, and there was much jockeying by the assembled single men to find seats next to the right young ladies. The supper was followed by an impromptu "play" that featured some form of kissing game for the young folk, many of whom spent the rest of the night socializing and courting until the next round of festivities started the following day.[24] A big wedding brought a large number of young people together and provided a good opportunity for courting with less parental supervision.

Marriage was expected to be permanent—literally "until death do us part." As late as the 1830s, many states required the state legislature to approve divorce requests, making divorce nearly impossible.[25] Men did have one way of ending an unhappy marriage—they simply abandoned their spouses and moved away. Women, especially those with children, generally did not have that option. As the Civil War approached, laws were changed in many states to provide women who were being mistreated with legal recourse to ending marriages; even so, the bar was set quite high on what constituted mistreatment. For example, in the early 1860s, North Carolina Chief Justice Richmond Pearson denied the divorce petition of a woman who claimed her husband had horsewhipped her. He noted in his decision: "The law gives the husband power to use the degree of force necessary to make the wife behave and know her place."[26]

On the periphery of white society among poor whites who owned little or no property, marriage was more tenuous and more likely to be forgone. Here flourished a small "subculture of mostly poor people who did not abide by the rules of polite society."[27] Poor whites were generally marginally employed, frequently moved, and had more run-ins with the law than more affluent folks, all of which made marriage less likely or, at the least, a tenuous and fragile relationship. Edward Isham, for example, was a poor man born in Georgia whose father had been a landless miner; his mother and father separated, and his father took up with another woman who served as Isham's stepmother. As an adult, Isham never owned anything that amounted to much and traveled from place to place working at a variety of jobs when he wasn't running from

---

24. Frank L. Owsley, *Plain Folk of the Old South* (1949; Baton Rouge: Louisiana State University Press, 1982), 126–131.

25. Clinton, *The Plantation Mistress*, 79.

26. Victoria Bynum, *Unruly Women: The Politics of Social and Sexual Control in the Old South* (Chapel Hill: University of North Carolina Press, 1992), 61.

27. *Ibid.*, 90.

the law. He married several times and abandoned wives and lovers with equal alacrity. One of his lovers was a free black woman.[28]

The story of Susan Williford of the Tallyho area in rural Granville County, North Carolina, illustrates the elusive nature of marriage for many poor women and the role of the law in enforcing society's marital and racial preferences when women strayed from the norm. Williford was the illegitimate daughter of Elizabeth Williford, a poor woman who never married. Like many illegitimate children, Susan was taken from her mother at the age of six and apprenticed to a man. The man abused her, and it took her mother over a year to convince the court to return her child to her. Like her mother, Williford never married but did have several illegitimate children of own. She had one daughter by John Hobgood, a man in and out of court who finally ended up in the poorhouse. Later, Williford entered into a long-term relationship with Peter Curtis, a man who was part of the area's free black community of small farmers and craftsmen. She had several children by him. She and Curtis were periodically arrested for fornication (they couldn't marry because she was white and he was black), and her children were ultimately taken away from her by the court because they were illegitimate and placed in other households as apprentices just as she had been.[29]

Within most families, patriarchy was still the organizing principal—the male was the head of the family, and his role was to make the decisions, manage the property, provide for the family, and interact with the outside world. His wife was to produce and raise children and manage the household and, as Chief Justice Pearson opined, "know her place." In planter James H. Hammond's words, "Women were meant to breed—Men to do the work of the world."[30] Law supported this male leadership role; in most states upon marriage a husband and wife became in effect a single legal entity with the husband assuming ownership of her personal property (like slaves and cash) and the right and duty to manage her real property (land and buildings).[31] The idea was that whatever assets a woman brought to the marriage would be managed by the husband in return for his protection and support.[32] Legally, the children of the marriage belonged to the husband, although as the Civil War ap-

28. Charles C. Bolton, *Poor Whites of the Antebellum South: Tenants and Laborers in Central North Carolina and Northeast Mississippi* (Durham, NC: Duke University Press, 1994), 1–4, 7–8.

29. Bynum, *Unruly Women*, 88–93.

30. Wyatt-Brown, *Southern Honor*, 199. See also Bardaglio, *Reconstructing the Household*, 31.

31. Bardaglio, *Reconstructing the Household*, 31.

32. Suzanne D. Lebsock, "Radical Reconstruction and the Property Rights of Southern Women," in Catherine Clinton ed., *Half Sisters of History: Southern Women and the American Past* (Durham, NC: Duke University Press, 1994), 113–114.

proached, courts were more inclined to grant respectable women custody of children if their husbands were judged to be unfit.[33] The male prerogative extended, as we saw earlier, even to using physical force to "discipline" a "misbehaving" wife. But there was a check on husbands, and it was not laws and courts as much as it was honor.[34] An honorable man would properly provide for his wife and family and treat all fairly and respectfully; a man who behaved dishonorably—and, despite Justice Pearson's opinion, horsewhipping one's wife would probably have been viewed in such a light by most people—would be shamed by the community. However, given the isolation in which many people lived and the unwillingness to challenge a man's right to do as he wished on his own property, what abuse of women and children that occurred probably often went undetected.

Within the patriarchal system, a woman had specific duties, roles and obligations; she was to protect her virtue, be a good mother, sacrifice herself in quiet forbearance for her husband and family, and be submissive and deferential to her husband. Plantation mistress Ella Gertrude Clanton Thomas referred to her husband in her journal as a suitable "master" and noted "for true to my sex, I delight in looking up and love to feel my woman's weakness protected by man's superior strength. . . ."[35] Upper class antebellum Southern women were also expected to be innocent, delicate, and pure to the point of being almost asexual, in short, a lady who could be put on a pedestal to be worshiped and adored by her husband. These women were the keepers of the family bloodline and, as such, had to be above reproach; manners and propriety—how things looked to others—were of paramount importance, and even married women were expected to have chaperones when they traveled.[36] Ironically, while the delicate, helpless female may have been one set of expectations, Southern ladies were also expected to manage the plantation household workforce and do chores that weren't delegated to the household staff, not to mention instruct the children.[37] The contradictory expectations placed on these women probably are the source of the expression "steel magnolia" as a description of the Southern lady—graceful and beautiful on the outside, but hard as

---

33. Bardaglio, *Reconstructing the Household*, 84–85; Bynum, *Unruly Women*, 99–100.

34. Bardaglio, *Reconstructing the Household*, 5–6.

35. Virginia Ingraham Burr, ed., *The Secret Eye: The Journal of Ella Gertrude Clanton Thomas, 1848–1889* (Chapel Hill: The University of North Carolina Press, 1990), 11 April 1855, 122; Marli F. Weiner, "Mistresses, Morality, and the Dilemmas of Slaveholding: The Ideology and Behavior of Elite Antebellum Women," Patricia Morton, ed., *Discovering the Women in Slavery* (Athens, GA: University of Georgia Press, 1996), 279.

36. Scott, *The Southern Lady*, 4–13; Fox-Genovese, *Within the Plantation Household*, 109, 202, 228; Clinton, *The Plantation Mistress*, 8, 102.

37. Scott, *The Southern Lady*, 30–31; Clinton, *The Plantation Mistress*, 21, 26–27, 90; Fox-Genovese, *Within the Plantation Household*, 118–120.

steel on the inside. The women of the small farmer class did not have the luxury of pretending frailty or delicacy; sturdiness, a strong back, and the absence of vanity were expected of these women.[38]

Naturally, human nature being what it is, the desire for self-fulfillment could not always fit within these constricted standards, and women resorted to subtle and sometimes devious ways of getting what they wanted, the classic response of anyone (male or female) in the subordinate position in a power relationship. However, when a woman was too outspoken trying to get what she wanted, age-old stereotypes could be brought to bear to shame her into submission; women, like men, also lived in a world of shame and honor. Women who berated their husbands were called scolds or were said to be "trying to wear the pants in the family," and males who submitted to this feminine overreaching were called "henpecked."[39] Particularly in the upper class, a form of ultra-femininity associated with the Southern belle of the Scarlet O'Hara sort became a way for at least some women to manage men in the battle of the sexes.

Evangelical Christianity, arising in the mid-1700s and steadily growing in adherents and influence thereafter as Baptist and Methodist churches spread across the landscape, would initially challenge patriarchy by emphasizing a greater degree of equality between the sexes who were, after all, brothers and sisters in Christ. By the early decades of the 1800s, however, evangelical Christianity had made its peace with patriarchy and actively supported the concept of responsible male dominion in all realms of society, including the church. It embraced a view of women common in much of the English speaking world at that time that the "weaker sex" did have a special moral role in the family. Women were believed to be especially spiritual beings who fostered religious values in the family and served as a spiritual counterbalance to males' worldly concerns and predispositions.[40] There was, in this view of reality, an "inborn earnestness in women's nature to teach her to do right" as Ella Gertrude Clanton Thomas noted in her journal. But men, she believed, had a very different nature and simply did not have "control over their passions."[41] The idea was that women should use moral suasion to gently guide men along the right path, although more than a few women discovered that this approach was not always effective. Mary Chaplin had talked to her husband, Thomas, on more than one occasion about his drinking, which disturbed her. On New Year's Eve, 1845, Thomas Chaplin dryly noted in his diary that he "Drank too much

---

38. Bynum, *Unruly Women*, 36, 47–49.
39. Wyatt-Brown, *Southern Honor*, 226–235; Stephanie McCurry, *Masters of Small Worlds: Yeoman Households, Gender Relations, and the Political Culture of the Antebellum South Carolina Low Country* (New York: Oxford University Press, 1995), 215–216.
40. Christine Heyrman, *Southern Cross*, 194–205; Donald Mathews, *Religion in the Old South*, (Chicago and London: The University of Chicago Press, 1977), 112–113.
41. Burr, ed., *The Secret Eye*, 2 January 1859, 167–168.

liquor today. Wife emptied all the brandy out the window. Which closes out the old year, now for the New."[42]

The relationship between Thomas and Mary Chaplin, so neatly summarized by the above quote, suggests for at least some couples patriarchy was limited when it came to the private relationship between husband and wife. If some families were presided over by august patriarchs giving unquestioned orders to wives who dutifully carried them out, in others this was probably more fantasy than reality. At best all we can do is take an educated guess because so little is known about what happened in antebellum families, particularly the families of less affluent folk. We have more information (from letters, journals, and so forth) about upper class families and what emerges in at least some of these marriages are portraits of couples who had more of a companionate relationship (a relationship of equals based on mutual respect and affection) than the more patriarchal model. Planter couples were sometimes more like business partners with different spheres of responsibility, and more than a few women exercised authority in the male realm in special circumstances. For example, Thomas Chaplin's widowed mother tightly held on to her property, neither relinquishing it to her new husband or her sons, and Peter Hairston turned his plantation empire over to his wife (he had married Fanny) when he went off to war, a not uncommon practice. As he wrote her, "I place my entire business under your management until I return. I know that your judgement and your prudence will do all that can be done under the circumstances."[43]

There is no question, however, that the burden of repeated pregnancies (not to mention the health risks this posed), the demands of rearing large numbers of children, and the fact that normally the "world's work" was done by men consigned most women to subordinate roles. Elizabeth and William Wirt, a married couple living in the early decades of the nineteenth century in the upper South, consciously strove to build a companionate marriage, but William's commitment to his career (he was a lawyer) drew him (and his wife) away from this ideal and kept the couple apart for long periods of time. While William was away trying to make his mark in his profession and provide for his family, Elizabeth waited at home, lonely and bitter; her role as dutiful supporter necessarily cast her in the subordinate position and cast the marriage more in the patriarchal model than the companionate. Ironically, when William died, he left the family mired in debt; Elizabeth proved to have an astute business mind and saved the family from financial ruin.[44] One wonders if

---

42. Rosengarten, Tombee, 386.

43. Peter W. Hairston to Fanny Caldwell Hairston, 9 May 1861, Peter W. Hairston Collection, Southern Historical Collection, University of North Carolina, Chapel Hill.

44. Anya Jabour, *Marriage in the Early Republic: Elizabeth and William Wirt and the Companionate Ideal* (Baltimore: Johns Hopkins University Press, 1998), 2–4, 132–133, 163–166.

William had allowed his wife to participate with him in his business dealings, if the family fortunes would have fared better and he could have spent more time at home.

A major source of tension between husbands and wives was the unacknowledged but widespread reality of sexual relationships between white men and slave women. This tension was especially pronounced in the slaveholder class where men had direct control over slave women and thus more sexual opportunities.[45] Relationships between white men and black women ran the gamut of human experience from outright rape on one end to common law marriage at the other. Harriet Jacobs, for example, had the misfortune of being owned by a man who was pathologically obsessed with her; he sexually harassed her and raped her when he could throughout much of her early adulthood.[46] Religious scruples, a commitment to marriage vows, and laws prohibiting miscegenation (sexual relations between blacks and whites) no doubt restrained some men, but, as plantation mistress Ella Gertrude Clanton Thomas bitterly noted in her journal, men "with natures one degree removed from the brute creation" often did not restrain themselves. She despaired over the "standard of morality in our Southern homes" and found it appalling that a man who endeavored to marry his black mistress was condemned by public opinion, but the practice of having mistresses was largely ignored or denied.[47] And it took a blind eye to either ignore it or deny it: Mary Boykin Chestnut happened upon a slave auction one day in Charleston and saw a young woman on the auction block "magnificently gotten up in silks and satins" who clearly was being marketed as a mistress, a not uncommon practice. Chestnut ruefully noted in her diary, "You know what the Bible says about slavery and marriage; poor women! Poor slaves!"[48] Writer Lillian Smith believed white male sexual escapades with the black women in their power before and after the Civil War drove them to idealize white women even more. As she noted, "The more trails the white man made to back yard cabins, the higher he raised his white wife on her pedestal when he returned to the big house. The higher the pedestal, the less he enjoyed her whom he had put there, for statues after all are only nice things to look at."[49]

---

45. Bardaglio, *Reconstructing the Household*, 51–52, 56.

46. Harriet A. Jacobs, *Incidents in the Life of a Slave Girl: Written by Herself*, edited by Lisa Barsky (West Berlin, NJ: Townsend Press, 2004).

47. Burr, *The Secret Eye*, 2 Jan. 1859, 167–169. Historian Nell Irvin Painter believes Thomas suspected that both her husband and her father had children by slave mistresses. See Painter, *Southern History Across the Color Line* (Chapel Hill: University of North Carolina Press, 2002), 87.

48. Mary Boykin Chestnut, *A Diary from Dixie* (1905; Documenting the American South, 1997), 13, http://docsouth.unc.edu/chesnut/maryches.html.

49. Lillian Smith, *Killers of the Dream* (Garden City, NY: Anchor Books, 1963), 103.

Robert Hairston, a member of the wealthy Hairston clan of plantation owners, did try to do right by his slave mistress. Hairston had suffered through a contentious relationship with his wife and had finally left her and his plantation in Virginia and moved to one of his plantations in Mississippi. Here he began a relationship with a slave woman that amounted to a common law marriage. After his death, his will directed much of his property to the daughter, Chrillis, who came from this relationship, an event that made her one of the wealthiest young girls in the United States. Unfortunately for her, Hairstons from several states mobilized to break the will, and both mother and daughter were sold.[50]

That the Hairstons could do such a thing to blood kin is not surprising; generally the children who resulted from liaisons with slave women did not exist as far as white society was concerned, at least not as beings with any connection to the white world. But many black families knew what their true genealogies were. Some of the most prominent families of the South, like the Hairstons and Charleston's Ball family, had a black branch and a white branch.[51] In a region that obsessively tried to separate the races for so long and loudly proclaimed the principal of black inferiority, the close intimacy between black and white, sexual and otherwise, is ironic indeed.

For many Southerners, the extended family and the clan were nearly as important as the nuclear family, continuing a tradition that the early English and Scots-Irish settlers had brought with them. In an area of hills and valleys in upland South Carolina along the Twelve Mile and Keowee rivers, the Robertson clan settled and established large and small farms in the 1700s. Into the early decades of the twentieth century, Robertson and related families were still prominent and numerous in the region, many still farming.[52] The Hairstons were a tightly knit extended family stretched over four states. The first Hairston to come to America was a gentleman nicknamed "Peter the Immigrant" who came in 1715 from Scotland by way of Ireland. Peter Hairston had brought his family with him to America, and they traveled south on the Great Wagon road settling in Virginia where they established a tobacco plantation. Eventually the extended family acquired a series of plantations in Virginia and North Carolina and pushed further south and built plantations as far away as Mississippi; this was a family that was a force to be reckoned with in an immense territory. They kept the wealth together by marrying cousins: three of the most prominent Hairstons in the early 1800s married cousins.[53] Marriage

50. Henry Wiencek, *The Hairstons: An American Family in Black and White* (New York: St. Martin's Press, 1999), 92–97.

51. Edward Ball, *Slaves in the Family* (New York: Ballantine Books, 1999).

52. Ben Robertson, *Red Hills and Cotton: An Upcountry Memory* (1942; Columbia, SC: University of South Carolina Press, 1973), 5–7.

53. Henry Wiencek, *The Hairstons*, 8–9.

to cousins was quite common in the Southern upper class as we saw in an earlier chapter. (It was also common among mountain residents.)[54] Family unity
was strengthened in other ways, too: often a common name would be shared
by several generations of males (like Peter in the Hairston family), and family
surnames were included as either first names or middle names.[55] John Steele
Henderson of Rowan County, North Carolina, for example, had as his middle
name the name of a prominent local family that had married into the Henderson clan.

Property was the glue that held together an extended family; the possibility
of the inheritance of property kept the younger generations connected and deferential to their elders. For a man of modest means like James Davis of Harris
County, Georgia, ownership of property ensured that someone would take
care of him in his old age; as he noted in his will, "Whereas my said daughter
Sarah Jane and her husband James Lysle has agreed to live with and take care of
me during my natural life and also during the lifetime or widowhood of my
beloved wife Judith I therefore give and bequeath unto my daughter Sarah Jane
Lysle . . . for her sole and separate use during her natural life . . . one hundred
and a fourth acres. . . ."[56] In the planter class, property was what made a family
important and powerful, and the family patriarch used his control over property to hold sway over other family members. A capable family patriarch made
decisions that ensured that family wealth and power continued into the future.
A descendent of "Peter the Immigrant" Hairston was master of Saura Town
plantation, one of the largest plantations in the family, and a patriarch of the
clan. "Saura Town Peter," as he was called, was constantly planning and plot-
ting to extend the wealth and power of the clan; one of his most important
tasks was match-making. After Herculean efforts on his part to pair two
cousins, Samuel Hairston and Agnes Hairston, the couple was finally wed in
1818. Saura Town Peter also served as a matchmaker in the pairing of his only
child, Ruth, to one of the larger landholders in the area. When Ruth's husband
died, Saura Town Peter became concerned that a huge holding of family land
and slaves was controlled by two females, Ruth and her young daughter, Agnes,
and that a poorly chosen second husband for Ruth might take the property out
of the family orbit. Again he delved into matchmaking, this time focusing on a
25-year-old nephew, Samuel, whom he urged to marry his cousin Agnes, who
was at this point still an adolescent. As Peter noted in a letter to Samuel, if he
were to marry Agnes, he would have "one of the Best accomplished girls in Virginia as well as a great fortune."[57] The pair finally married four years later, thus

54. Clinton, *The Plantation Mistress*, 233; Bardaglio, *Reconstructing the Household*,
41.
55. Wyatt-Brown, *Southern Honor*, 120–121.
56. Owsley, *Plain Folk*, 19.
57. Wiencek, *The Hairstons*, 76–77; quote 76.

keeping the family's fortunes within the family. As an odd postscript, Ruth married Samuel's brother, further fortifying family finances against outsider intrusions. Mother and daughter were now sisters-in-law and one brother became father-in-law to another and "all became tightly bound to 'Saura Town Peter,' and to each other" by common interests and literally by the complexity of property rights that kept each part of the family entwined financially with other parts.[58] Saura Town Peter's success depended on his being persistent, clever, and unwilling to leave anything to chance.

Samuel Hairston learned these lessons well from the patriarch; he carefully schooled his own son, Peter, in how to be a planter and well that he had: the young man inherited Cooleemee Plantation when he was thirteen from Saura Town Peter, who left him the 2000-acre plantation and 400 slaves.[59] Samuel sent his son to college at the University of North Carolina and to law school at the University of Virginia, and by his twenties Peter was managing more and more of the family businesses. The lessons Samuel taught Peter weren't always pleasant. One time, Peter and Samuel went to talk to the overseer at Cooloomee, Grief Mason, about the death of two slaves. A fight had broken out among some slaves at the plantation, and Mason had killed two of them when he broke up the fight. Peter was appalled by what Mason had done and told him that he should never kill a slave. When Mason said he would quit if the Hairstons didn't like his way of managing slaves, Samuel overruled Peter and told him that if they allowed Mason to leave, the slaves would become ungovernable. The hard lesson Peter learned was that a planter must be willing to use violence to keep what is his and that ultimately slavery rested on a foundation of force, not fairness.[60]

Further south on Tombee plantation on the coast of South Carolina, Thomas Chaplin was making his way in the world without benefit of a patriarch: his father had died, and no older male in his extended family seems to have exercised that role. Not that he did not get the benefits of an extended family; he got numerous loans and gifts of money and livestock and food from his mother and other family members, and, as we saw in an earlier chapter, he spent much of his time with family members, especially his male cousins. But family members failed him at critical points: when he was deeply in debt, an uncle refused to help him forcing him to sell off many of his slaves, and his bitter relationship with his stepfather left him at odds with his mother over the property he thought should properly belong to him. If Samuel Hairston methodically educated his son in the ways of a planter, the less successful Thomas Chaplin was much more haphazard in the education of his three sons. He did

---

58. *Ibid.*, 77.
59. *Ibid.*, 75.
60. *Ibid.*, 81–82; see also Scott, *The Southern Lady*, 14.

send them off to school, a cost that he bitterly complained about given his straitened financial circumstance. One son could barely write at age thirteen, and he considered him "dull"; another son, Daniel, he regarded as spoiled, and the two did not get along when the boy reached maturity. But apparently something of the planter code was passed on; Daniel, in adulthood, married his cousin—the daughter of Thomas Chaplin's brother Saxby—and after the war attempted to maintain the dignified posture of a respected planter, even though his circumstances were less than affluent.[61]

Family, Marriage, and Gender before the Civil War: Blacks

In the early colonial South, the large numbers of captives arriving each year from Africa and the Caribbean as slaves were mostly men. With the resulting imbalance between male and female, many men weren't able to find a mate. By the mid-1700s, the male/female ratio had evened out, and marriage became more common. By the mid-1800s, many slaves, like whites, lived in nuclear families, and two-parent households and permanent marriages were apparently highly valued and common. On the Good Hope plantation in South Carolina, for example, most of the 175 slave residents lived in stable two-parent households; a slave couple on this plantation, Ness and Molly, had lived together over twenty years and had nine children living with them. The commitment of many slave couples to marriage is all the more remarkable because slave marriages were not recognized by law or the church. Slaves were permitted to hold marriage ceremonies of their own, which were sometimes presided over by the masters.[62] James Bolton, a former slave from Georgia, recalled, "Folkses didn' make no big to-do over weddings like they do now. When slaves got married they jus' laid down the broom on the floor and the couple jined hands and jumped backuds over the broomstick. I done seed 'em married that way many times."[63] Finding someone to marry often posed a serious problem. People in slavery were not free to move around, and this constricted their choices of mates; a man or woman living on a small plantation or a family farm might literally have no potential partners to choose from. Slaveholders sometimes allowed men to marry women from other plantations; the couple would live apart during the week,

---

61. Rosengarten, *Tombee*, 172–175.

62. Herbert Gutman, *The Black Family in Slavery and Freedom, 1750–1925* (New York: Vintage Books, 1977), 12, 47–48, 92–93, 96–97, 151, 270–277.

63. James Bolton, interview by Sarah H. Hall, *Born in Slavery: Slave Narratives from the Federal Writers' Project, 1936–1938* (Washington: Library of Congress, Manuscript Division, 2001), http://memory.loc.gov/ammem/snhtml/snhome.html.

and would see each other on the weekend if the husband was granted a pass. One woman recalled that a husband from another plantation was "'lowed to come every Saturday night and stay with you and the chillun 'til Monday mornin.'" He might send food or small household items to his wife during the week by a boy who served as a "runner" between plantations.[64] On this plantation, men who didn't have families lived in a bunk house.

Slave marriages and families existed in an environment that was both supportive and intensely hostile. It was supportive because it was in the slaveholders' interests to have stable families to produce and rear children, and children were like money in the bank. One slaveholder told a slave woman who eventually bore nineteen children that "he didn't care if she never worked if she kept havin' chillun like that for him."[65] Stable black families served slaveholders in another way: then as now, unattached young males are the most volatile of beings, and men with wives and children were less likely to run away or resist authority. But slaveholders also wanted to buy and sell slaves as they wished, and slave couples were often broken up by sale; the deed books of the era are filled with transactions recording the sale of women and their children. The break-up of families was probably most common in the Upper South where agriculture was declining and slaveowners kept themselves afloat financially by selling slaves to the flourishing plantations of the Deep South. Sarah Byrd's family was separated like that; her father was sold to a slaveowner in Tennessee and her mother, herself and her siblings, were sold to a doctor who lived in Georgia. As she observed, "Chile in them days so many families were broke up and some went one way and der others went t'other way; and you nebber seed them no more."[66] One study of a group of slaves in Mississippi found one in six had lost their spouses due to a forced sale.[67] Children were sold away from parents, too. The sale of very young children would not have been common, but the sale of children seven, eight, and nine years of age was quite common and certainly by the time a boy or girl reached puberty, the possibility of being sold away from family and home loomed large. In Granville County, North Carolina, for example, the county deed book has numerous entries documenting the sale of

---

64. "Compilation Richmond County [GA] Ex-Slave Interviews: Work, Play, Food, Clothing, Marriage, etc.," interview by Louise Oliphant, *Born in Slavery: Slave Narratives from the Federal Writers' Project, 1936–1938* (Washington: Library of Congress, Manuscript Division, 2001), http://memory.loc.gov/ammem/snhtml/snhome. html.

65. *Ibid.*

66. For example, see Barnetta McGhee White, ed. "Enslaved Ancestors Abstracted from Granville County, North Carolina Deed Books, A–Z & 1–21, 1746–1864," http://afrigeneas.com/library/ncdeeds (accessed 10/14/06); Sarah Byrd interview, Born in Slavery: Slave Narratives from the Federal Writers' Project, 1936–1938 (Washington: Library of Congress, Manuscript Division, 2001), http://memory.loc.gov/ammem/snhtml/snhome.html.

67. Gutman, *The Black Family in Slavery and Freedom*, 146.

children, such as the nine-year-old boy William Amis sold to his own son-in-law in 1832 or the fourteen-year-old girl named Harriet that Jesse Barnett sold to Willie Smith in 1834.[68] Sometimes it was the parents who were sold away: a young Ike Thomas lost his parents that way. His mistress decided to raise him to be a carriage boy and let him sleep in a trundle bed she kept under her bed. At mealtime, he would sit under the table, and she would feed him table scraps.[69]

Slavery had a profound effect on gender roles. Slave men owned no property and had no control over their livelihoods; economically, they were as dependent as children. Nor could they prevent their families from being broken up by sale, protect their wives from sexual exploitation by white men, or keep their children from being treated like house pets begging for table scraps. Driving home the point of their powerlessness, a young or middle aged man was called "boy" by whites as a term of address and "uncle" when he became old; he was never called a man because he did not have the power to be a man as white society understood the term.[70] As male slaves aged and their ability to perform hard physical labor declined, they became less valuable, and they were sometimes assigned women's duties such as child care or spinning.[71] In short, patriarchy as it existed in the white world could not exist in the world of the slave, and slave husbands and wives had relationships that were more equal than was typically the case with white couples. Women, married or otherwise, were more independent than their white counterparts.[72] Not surprisingly, male and female children were treated more the same, at least until puberty, than was the case in the white world and were often assigned similar duties on the plantation.[73]

The primary duty of slave women, like white women, was producing children, but the children they produced could be claimed by the slaveowner at any time to live in the "big house" as a house boy or girl, sent to another plantation he might own, or sold. While white women were expected to be dedicated to their families and place their own needs and desires second, slave

---

68. White, ed. "Enslaved Ancestors Abstracted from Granville County, North Carolina Deed Books, A–Z & 1–21, 1746–1864."

69. Ike Thomas, interview by Alberta Miner, *Born in Slavery: Slave Narratives from the Federal Writers' Project, 1936–1938* (Washington: Library of Congress, Manuscript Division, 2001), http://memory.loc.gov/ammem/snhtml/snhome.html.

70. Gutman, *The Black Family in Slavery and Freedom*, 306.

71. Deborah Gray White, *Ar'n't I a Woman: Female Slaves in the Plantation South* (New York: W. W. Norton & Company, 1999), 114–115.

72. *Ibid.*, 153, 157; Fox-Genovese, *Within the Plantation Household*, 299; Jacqueline Jones, " 'My Mother Was Much of a Woman': Black Women, Work and the Family Under Slavery," Paul Finkelman, ed., *Women and the Family in a Slave Society* (New York: Garland Publishing, 1989), 218; White, *Ar'n't I a Woman*, 153.

73. White, *Ar'n't I a Woman*, 94, 118; Jones, " 'My Mother Was Much of a Woman,' " 206–207.

women were expected to do the work required by the master, whether that was cooking for his family, cleaning his house, or caring for his children. Their own families came second.[74] Marriage for a white woman defined who she was and where she fit in the social order; for a slave woman, slavery first and foremost defined who she was. Marriage could bring the comfort and support of a mate and a family, but it could not provide slave women with security or an identity in the way it did in the white world.[75] Slave women did the chores commonly performed by white women, but they also often worked in the fields with the men; the notion that women were delicate and fragile apparently did not apply to them.[76] Given the large numbers of women who were separated from husbands periodically (when husbands lived on another plantation) or permanently through sale, it is not surprising that slave women developed particularly strong bonds with other women.[77]

While many aspects of marriage and family were dictated by slavery and the slaveholders, people in slavery did what they could to create and sustain their own family traditions and maintain a network of kin. As one former slave observed, "White folks do as they pleases and the darkies do as they can."[78] Slave couples would frequently live together for a time before deciding to marry; if the couple proved to be incompatible during this trial period, they would end the relationship. Generally, if a trial relationship resulted in a pregnancy, the couple married. Once married, couples were expected to be faithful to each other.[79] While slaveholders frequently married first cousins, slaves had a taboo against first cousin marriage which may have originated in West Africa. Following this taboo was not always easy, particularly on small plantations where the pool of potential marriage partners might be so small that a slave man might have to look for a spouse on another plantation with the permission, grudging or otherwise, of the master.[80] Extended kin were important, and many slaves did what they could to keep a close connection to

---

74. White, *Ar'n't I a Woman*, 69; Fox-Genovese, *Within the Plantation Household*, 138, 173; Jones, "'My Mother Was Much of a Woman,'"203.

75. White, *Ar'n't I a Woman*, 16; Deborah Gray White, "Female Slaves: Sex Roles and Status in the Antebellum Plantation South," Paul Finkelman, ed., *Women and the Family in a Slave Society* (New York: Garland Publishing, 1989), 395; Fox-Genovese, *Within the Plantation Household*, 373.

76. Jones, "'My Mother Was Much of a Woman,'"200, 205; Fox-Genovese, *Within the Plantation Household*, 173.

77. White, "Female Slaves," 394–395; Fox-Genovese, *Within the Plantation Household*, 318.

78. William Gant, interview by Irene Robertson, *Born in Slavery: Slave Narratives from the Federal Writers' Project, 1936–1938* (Washington: Library of Congress, Manuscript Division, 2001), http://memory.loc.gov/ammem/snhtml/snhome.html.

79. Gutman, *The Black Family in Slavery and Freedom*, 64–67.

80. *Ibid.*, 88–91.

kin, even those on other plantations. As one former slave woman noted, "I 'membah how I use t' lie 'wake till all de folks wah sleepn', den creep outen do do' and walk barfoot in de snow, 'bout two mile t' mah ole Auntie's house. I knowed when I git dar she fix hot cawn pone wif slice o' meat an' some milk foah me t' eat."[81]

People in slavery ostensibly had no last name; they were Joe or Mary and were often listed as such in records and legal documents. But early in the history of slavery, many slaves adopted the last names of their first masters, and these names were passed down to later generations unchanged even when people were sold to slaveholders with different names. This was not done to honor slaveholders; many were astonished to learn slaves even had last names. Rather, last names allow us to keep track of who is and isn't in our kin group, and people in slavery, as we have seen, valued and depended on their kin. Generally, the husband's surname became the surname of the children, even if they lived on another plantation, showing that some degree of patriarchy existed in the slave quarters.[82] Children were frequently named for blood kin—fathers (but, interestingly, not often mothers), grandparents, aunts and uncles—which is a practice that people the world over use as a way of showing family solidarity and for slaves may have had roots in West African practices. People in slave communities also created "fictive kin" to communicate to one and all that their circumstances compelled them, for survival's sake, to treat everyone in the slave quarters like kin with responsibilities for each other.[83]

Free blacks lived in a sort of netherworld poised between whites and slaves; they could legally marry, but they were not permitted to marry either slaves or white people. Some free black men and women would skirt this provision by cohabiting with a white person or a slave, but, as we saw earlier, this could incur the wrath of the community if not a jail sentence. It was also not unusual for a free black man to buy a wife and then set her free and marry her or simply cohabit with her because in some states slaves who were recently freed were required to leave the state. Many free black women never wed, and a significant percentage of free black households were headed by women. In Petersburg Virginia, for example, over half the free black households were headed by women who owned a large share of the property of the free black community. They were still quite poor as a group, the poorest group in Petersburg, but in a curious way they were probably the most autonomous women in the town.[84]

---

81. Sarah Gudger, interview by Marjorie Jones, *Born in Slavery: Slave Narratives from the Federal Writers' Project, 1936–1938* (Washington: Library of Congress, Manuscript Division, 2001), http://memory.loc.gov/ammem/snhtml/snhome.html

82. Gutman, *The Black Family in Slavery and Freedom*, 230–252.

83. *Ibid.*, 190–200, 217.

84. Suzanne Lebsock, *The Free Women of Petersburg: Status and Culture in A Southern Town, 1784–1860* (New York: W. W. Norton & Co., 1984), 89, 100, 103–104.

Whites developed stereotypes about the nature of black men and women that proved to be remarkably long-lived after slavery ended. For whites, black men were either lazy, docile, and subservient or sexually aggressive and potentially dangerous. Black women were often viewed as either motherly "mammy" type figures who just loved children, especially white children, cooking, sewing, cleaning house and serving whites, or they were "Jezebel" figures who were sexual, immodest, and dangerous in a way different from their male counterparts. These stereotypes reflected white fears and desires projected onto blacks— white men wanted black women to be sexually available for obvious reasons, and white women could fantasize that black women were uninhibited and incredibly alluring and that is why their men snuck off at night to the slave cabins. The docile, lazy black man (called a "Sambo"), however infuriating such behavior might be to whites, was also a projection of whites' desires because if most black men were truly like this, they posed no threat and clearly validated the idea that slavery helped a "child race." The menacing, sexual young black man —a "Buck" he was called—was almost pure animal in the white imagination and represented for both white men and women their greatest fear.[85]

Family, Marriage, and Gender after the Civil War

The Civil War and its aftermath posed tremendous challenges to Southern families and traditions. A substantial portion of the white male population was away at war; in the absence of fathers and husbands, women ran many of the region's plantations, farms, and businesses, and traditional gender roles and patriarchy were put on hold.[86] Several hundred thousand men in the prime of their lives would never return from the war, and for the next two decades there were more women than men of marriageable age, resulting in an elevated number of women who would never marry. As a result of this disparity and the large number of war widows, female headed households were a larger percentage of households than was the case before the war and the old "rule" of patriarchy that women should live under the authority of males had many more exceptions.[87] In the prominent Petigru family of South Carolina, for example, a number of the male Petigrus never returned from the war, and several

---

85. Catherine Clinton, "Bloody Terrain: Freedwomen, Sexuality, and Violence During Reconstruction," Catherine Clinton, ed., *Half Sisters of History: Southern Women and the American Past* (Durham: Duke University Press, 1994), 145–148; Fox-Genovese, *Within the Plantation Household*, 291; White, *Ar'n't I A Woman*, 29–34, 46–48.

86. Bardaglio, *Reconstructing the Household*, 129; Scott, *The Southern Lady*, 81–82.

87. *Ibid.*, 130–131; Scott, *The Southern Lady*, 92, 106; Bynum, *Unruly Women*, 154–155.

who did were left broken men by their wartime experiences. Louise, the matri-arch of the clan, had 18 great granddaughters of whom at least 10 never mar-ried.[88] Patriarchy was also diminished by the straightened circumstances of many planters and farmers after the war; planter Thomas Chaplin of South Carolina, for example, lost control of most of his property after the war, and he and his wife moved from place to place looking for work and literally had to depend on charity at times. Patriarchy depended on economic mastery and control, and if most planters and small farmers weren't out begging for work like Chaplin, many were at best scraping by, and few controlled the resources and people they had before the war. This turn of affairs diminished their per-sonal authority.

The war and the ending of slavery obviously had a tremendous impact on slaves. Thousands of slave men and women fled the Confederate-controlled territory, scores of others were displaced by the battles, and thousands of men joined the Union Army, some never to return. After the war, hundreds of thousands lived in camps run by the Union Army and later the Freedmen's Bu-reau. In the midst of this confused situation, the former slaves struggled to keep their families together, put scattered families back together again, and begin new lives as free men and women able to legally wed and truly call their children their own. Hundreds of thousands of former slaves filled the roads of the South searching for loved ones lost as the result of sale or the disruptions of war. Former slaves rushed to magistrates by the thousands to obtain marriage licenses to legalize their marriages.[89]

Despite tremendous disruptions in their lives, the former slaves were re-markably successful at building stable family units. In the decades after the war, the majority of people lived in households composed of family members, and most young children were being raised in two parent households. The ex-tended families, so laboriously cultivated before the war, continued to be a powerful part of black family life and were, historian Herb Gutman has ar-gued, an important reason many former slaves opted to stay in the areas where they had lived before the Civil War.[90] Many black married couples moved at least a step or two toward the more patriarchal model of family common with whites as both men and women tried to establish more gender specific duties for themselves. They rejected the old ways that often had men and women la-boring in the fields together and did their best to establish a division of labor that had women working around the house and men working in the fields. Black men also wanted to keep their women at home to protect them from the sexual advances of white men, something that they had been forced to tolerate

88. Jane H. Pease and William Pease, *A Family of Women: The Carolina Petigrus in Peace and War* (Chapel Hill: University of North Carolina Press, 1999), 275–276.

89. Gutman, *The Black Family*, 140–141, 412–417.

90. *Ibid.*, 443, 445, 209, 212–213.

Figure 4.1   Boyd Jones family, Greene County, Georgia

during slavery times. Many women still did fieldwork, but there is no question fewer women were mixed among men working in large gangs under the supervision of white men.[91] Children were an important source of labor, and black rural families were quite large; in 1910, for example, the average rural black family had nine children.[92]

Despite the success of many men and women emerging from slavery at creating stable, two-parent homes, a significant number of children after the war were raised in single-parent homes, the homes of relatives or other adults. This ranged from as many as 34% of black children in 1880 to roughly 20% of rural black children in 1910 and 23% in 1940. These were significantly higher percentages than was the case with white families.[93] Sociologist Charles S. Johnson studied a group of rural black families in a plantation area in Georgia in the 1930s and found a quarter of the families headed by women. Separation and remarriage were quite common, and in a substantial portion of the households headed by two partners, one or both of the partners had been married before.[94] Ruby Lee Daniels (later Haynes) spent her early adulthood on planta-

91. Jones, "'My Mother Was Much of a Woman,'" 214, 219; White, *Ar'n't I A Woman*, 185.

92. Stewart E. Tolnay, *The Bottom Rung: African American Family Life on Southern Farms* (Chicago: University of Illinois Press, 1999), 78.

93. Gutman, *The Black Family*, 445; Tolnay, *The Bottom Rung*, 108, 111.

94. Charles S. Johnson, *Shadow of the Plantation* (Chicago: University of Chicago Press, 1934), 33, 71–72.

tions around Clarksdale, Mississippi. She married several times—only once happily—and told journalist Nicolas Lemann that few people she knew got the "'til death do you part" relationship. At one point she gave up one of her children to a childless couple she was friends with when she moved to Chicago. For her, marriage didn't work out because of the constant struggles of poverty and the general "no-goodness of most men." Her extended family and her close friends, on the other hand, were a frequent source of emotional and financial support.[95]

Some scholars have attributed the higher levels of family instability in the black South to a cultural heritage of slavery, when marriages were easily dissolved, or even the persistence of West African traditions, which stressed the importance of extended family over the nuclear family.[96] Certainly many cultural traits persist over a long period, but poverty and the special problems black men experienced loom largest in explaining the higher incidence of family breakup among black families as compared to white. It wasn't that men were "no good," as Ruby Daniel saw it, but rather that Southern society and culture had no place for them that amounted to much: black men were alternately despised, ridiculed, and feared by white society, treated as children or wild animals, hunted down for real or imagined crimes and murdered, denied even the smallest opportunities for advancement, and limited primarily to sharecropping or some job with "boy" in the title. In towns, jobs for black women were generally more plentiful than jobs for black men. Black women were less tolerant than white women of abusive behavior and more willing to abandon a bad marriage, attitudes that may trace back to the more egalitarian marriages of slavery times but also reflected the limited resources most men brought to a marriage and the lower "cost" to a woman of ending a marriage. As one rural Georgia woman who was living with a man told Charles Johnson, "He's nice all right, but I ain't thinking 'bout marrying. Soon as you marry a man he starts mistreating you, and I'm not going to be mistreated no more."[97] It's not surprising that less resolute men simply gave up on respectable society and walked away from their families or entered into a series of temporary liaisons with women. Male rootlessness worsened during times of economic depression (the 1890s and again during the 1920s and 1930s) when significant numbers of black men were unable to find employment, or at least employ-

---

95. Nicholas Lemann, *The Promised Land: The Great Black Migration and How It Changed America* (New York: Vintage Books, 1992), 32–33, 52, quote p. 33.

96. Sociologist E. Franklin Frazier is the most famous proponent of the notion that slavery had a lasting effect on the black family. See *The Negro Family in the United States* (1939; Chicago: University of Chicago Press, 1968), 15, 17–18.

97. Joel Williamson, A *Rage for Order: Black-White Relations in the American South Since Emancipation* (New York: Oxford University Press, 1986), 57–58, 145; Johnson, *Shadow of the Plantation*, 83.

ment that paid a living wage, and traveled from place to place looking for work. The steady decline of the sharecropping system beginning in the 1930s forced thousands off the land with growing numbers traveling to the Northeast and Midwest in search of work. Family ties in such situations stretched under the strain, and the extended family often picked up the slack. Preston Moseley left the rural community of Townsville, North Carolina, and settled in New Jersey. His wife followed him several months later, but two of his children stayed in Townsville with his brother and his wife until they finished high school.[98]

The marginality of the black male's position in Southern society led to the development of an alternative male subculture outside the family and church-centered culture of most blacks. This culture celebrated the street corner values of the hustler too "smart" to work and too jealous of his freedom to settle down. Pud Bosket, son of sharecropper Aaron Bosket of Saluda, South Carolina, was one of this new breed. Pud worked as a sharecropper but took a new path in life when his landlord tried to whip him (the year was 1910), and he pulled the whip from his hands. He turned his back on sharecropping that day (whites wouldn't hire him anyway) and took to a life of thievery. He was arrested and sent to the chain gang. When he got out, he was greeted by some of the young men in his community as a sort of hero; for them prison time was a badge of honor. He sold moonshine, gambled, and got into numerous scraps. As his brother said of him, "Step on his foot, at a dance or walking by, just brush him, and there'd be a fight." Once a man called him a liar, and he cut him repeatedly across the chest with a knife and almost killed him. Pud lived by the code of honor, but it was an honor code that was purely personal, bereft of the old defense of family and family name; in truth, family didn't mean much to him. The rambling men and "bad" men like Pud Bosket were celebrated in song and lore as heroic figures who "got over" whites and didn't have to work in their fields or live by their rules.[99] The most famous of the "bad" men who emerged in this era was the mythical Staggerlee or Stackolee (and several other variants of the name) who was renowned for his skill as a fighter, gambler, drinker, and lover.[100] Figures like the make-believe Staggerlee and the real life Pud Bosket would serve as role models, albeit unfortunate role models, for disaffected men then and in later generations.

---

98. Williamson, *Rage for Order*, 56–59; "An Interview with Preston Moseley of Townsville," unpublished interview by Thomasina Jefferson, December 8, 1998.

99. Williamson, *A Rage for Order*, 58–59, 145–146; Fox Butterfield, *All God's Children: The Bosket Family and the American Tradition of Violence* (New York: Alfred A. Knopf, 1995), 58–67, quote 63.

100. Lawrence W. Levine, *Black Culture and Black Consciousness: Afro-American Folk Thought From Slavery To Freedom* (Oxford: Oxford University Press, 1978), 413–415.

At the top of the black social structure, a small middle/upper class emerged with its own family and gender traditions. Here stable, formal marriages were the rule, and the more traditional patriarchal family structure was most in evidence with men earning the primary livelihood either as property-owning farmers or professionals in town and the women managing the households and children. Respectability was paramount and sexuality, especially for girls, strictly regulated. Most girls of this class remained chaste until marriage.[101]

The issue of sexual relations between whites and blacks continued to be a powder keg and would remain so well into the twentieth century. By the conclusion of Reconstruction, Southern states had laws against miscegenation (sexual relations between blacks and whites) and interracial marriages, and these laws would be enforced in most Southern states until the 1960s.[102] In effect white men and black women and black men and white women were to keep at arm's length in all social encounters; in practice, however, some white men still had sexual relations with black women, and this was winked at by the law and white society as long as it was discrete. One attractive young woman in Smithville, Georgia, was told by white men she was "just too good-looking for a nigger man"; her family finally sent her away to protect her. Pud Bosket's mother had had a long-term affair with a white man before she married Aaron Bosket, and several children resulted from this liaison. As we saw earlier in this volume, noted South Carolina segregationist politician Strom Thurmond fathered a child by his family's black maid, and Thurmond went to no great lengths to conceal the paternity of the child.[103] The law turned a blind eye to forced sexual relations between white men and black women (otherwise known as rape); according to one historian, no Southern white man was ever convicted of "raping or attempting to rape a black woman" during the hundred-year period following the Civil War.[104]

The biggest concern in the white South—obsession is the better word for it—was sexual contact of any sort between a white woman and a black man, and harsh penalties, legal and outside the law, enforced this "color line." The nightmare for whites was the "violation" of a white woman by a black man, and even the rumor that this crime had been committed often galvanized a lynch mob. Several thousand black men were lynched between 1889 and 1946, the

---

101. Hortense Powdermaker, *After Freedom: A Cultural Study in the Deep South* (1939; New York: Atheneum, 1969), 148–151; Charles S. Johnson, *Growing Up in the Black Belt: Negro Youth in the Rural South* (Washington, D.C.: American Council on Education, 1941), 63, 65, 231; John Dollard, *Caste and Class in a Southern Town* (1937; Garden City, New York: Doubleday Anchor Books, 1951), 85–88.
102. Bardaglio, *Reconstructing the Household*, 177–181.
103. Leon F. Litwack, *Trouble in Mind: Black Southerners in the Age of Jim Crow* (New York: Alfred A. Knopf, 1998), 36–37, quote p. 37; Butterfield, *All God's Children*, 44–45.
104. White, *A'rn't I a Woman*, 188.

peak period of the lynching era, most for allegedly raping white women, but often the transgression ranged from simple discourtesy to being in the wrong place at the wrong time.[105] As late as the Civil Rights era, men were still being lynched for violating the old taboo, although now lynchings were no longer public spectacles but were carried out, often furtively, by a few men. Henry Marrow was beaten and then shot and killed in Oxford, North Carolina, in 1970 by several white men after he directed foul language at the wife of one of them (there is a dispute about what he said and to whom he said it). As one of the men who killed Marrow later noted, "That nigger committed suicide, wanting to come in my store and four-letter-word my daughter-in-law."[106]

Despite the turmoil of the war and its aftermath, pre-war family and gender patterns for whites proved to be remarkably resilient, particularly in the countryside. Certainly there were more female-headed households than before, and laws were passed in many states giving women more control of property and their own children and a way out of abusive marriages.[107] But men and women were still expected to get married, and women were still expected to live in male-headed households. Female-headed households and unmarried women were still viewed as aberrations. By 1910, 87% of the white households in the rural South were composed of married couples, a figure that would be remarkably stable for the next 30 years. Children typically grew up in two-parent households: in 1910 and thirty years later in 1940, over 90% of white children resided in households headed by a father and mother. Women still derived their status from the male heads of those households, and family name still counted for much, particularly in the middle and upper classes. Marriage itself was still firmly tied to economic necessity in the rural South where farming would continue to be powered by muscle, human and animal, into the 1930s and was not much different than farming in the 1830s. Men and women had specific and complementary roles with men leading, a role supported by both custom and law, and women in subordinate positions. Men did the work that required brawn and dealt with the outside world. Women cooked, raised the children, tended the gardens, helped at harvest, and bore children who were still an important source of workers for the farm. Family sizes were still quite large, averaging 7 children in 1910, and, as before the war, bearing and rearing large numbers of children kept women tied to the homestead more so than men and was still a major measure of their worth.[108]

---

105. Joel Williamson, *A Rage for Order*, 84–85.
106. Timothy B. Tyson, *Blood Done Signed My Name: A True Story* (New York: Crown Publishers, 2004), 118–125, 293.
107. Bardaglio, *Reconstructing the Household*, 134–135, 138.
108. Tolnay, *The Bottom Rung*, 32, 54–55, 65, 78, 111; Melissa Walker, *All We Knew Was to Farm: Rural Women in the Upcountry South* (Baltimore and London: The Johns Hopkins University Press, 2000), 21–23, 28.

Men and women were, in many respects, residents of different subcultures. Away from home, men moved in a male subculture of the back room in the general store, the court house, the hunting camp, the church steps after Sunday service, the beer joint, and the stock barn or the "hooch" tent in the midway at the county fair. They enjoyed male pleasures—stories, hunting, fishing, drink more often than not, jokes—often kept secret from women. For most, this "world" shared space with a world of church, family, and domestic life; for some, the allure of gambling and drinking and "loose" women took them permanently away from family and respectability. There was on the fringe of white society, as with black, a dangerous male subculture that at the least skirted the law, and this culture flourished in such places as Moccasin Bottom—a rough neighborhood in the milltown of South Henderson, North Carolina—and in swampy, hilly, or mountainous areas not fit for productive agriculture where poor people congregated. The law wasn't terribly interested in these places, and moonshining was common, illegal liquor or shot houses operated openly, and a cockfight or a woman willing to sell her favors could often be found on a Saturday night. Women in the company of women had their own stories and pastimes, although more often than not their pastimes involved some form of work. Women gathered for quilting bees, which were still common in the countryside, cooking for family reunions, church suppers, weddings, and funerals, showers for women getting married or having babies and, like the men, chit chat after church. At the county fair, they were most likely visiting the household exhibits where prize-winning preserves and pies and quilts were on display, although the new rides like the Ferris wheel that were featured at fairs also had their allure with women.[109]

Evangelical religion, by the turn of the 20th century, worked to control the male world as best it could and make it more like the more domestic female world. Much of this effort turned on pressuring state legislatures to pass laws restricting or prohibiting the more objectionable male pastimes. Evangelicals would work vigorously with other reformers to regulate if not eliminate drinking and would work to "clean up" fairs and even establish controls on hunting. There is no question that this evangelical drive had an effect; the sort of public drunkenness common in the 19th century became much less common, legal public bars dispensing liquor disappeared in most places and would not reappear until the 1970s, and horseracing, cockfighting, and gambling as open community activities all but disappeared.[110] Despite the best efforts of the evangelical community, however, the rougher side of the male subculture persisted, much of it underground and out of sight, which itself may have ap-

109. Ted Owenby, *Subduing Satan: Religion & Manhood in the Rural South, 1865–1920* (Chapel Hill: University of North Carolina, 1990), 21–99.
110. *Ibid.*, 167–193.

pealed to the Southern male personality anyway by making the drink from the bag on the back porch or the cockfight at midnight in some isolated barn even more exciting.

On the Fred Wilkins farm outside of Stem, North Carolina, a photographer spent several days with the Wilkins family in the late 1930s and documented with pictures their daily routine. On one of these days, the family had a corn shucking and members of the Wilkins extended family gathered at their kinsman's home to help along with neighbors both black and white. The men shucked mountains of corn; the women, meanwhile, prepared the food. At mealtime, the men sat down and ate in the dining room while the women served and stood in the background. (A picture of this meal is at the beginning of this chapter.) The pictorial series also shows the Wilkins women feeding the hogs, churning butter, and sorting tobacco. While no photos were taken of the menfolk working in the fields (it was late fall), no doubt a visit in the spring would have found the Wilkins men plowing and planting. Fred Wilkins earned extra income for the family by selling the butter his wife churned door to door in nearby Creedmoor.[111] So it was all there on the Wilkins farm much as it had been before the Civil War—patriarchy, a strong and supportive extended family, and the men's world and the women's world.

But even for farm families like the Wilkins, changes in family and gender roles were slowly making inroads into this tradition. While the Wilkins women of an earlier time would have rarely gone to town, Mrs. Fred Wilkins accompanied her husband to the tobacco market in Durham and spent her free time shopping. Most of the South may have opposed the 19th amendment which gave women the right to vote, but it was ratified anyway, and on Election Day, she could cast her ballot. Her family was smaller than the typical family of the past; rural women were exercising greater control over how many children they would have through contraception, and by 1940 the average rural family had shrunk to 5 children. The number of families with large numbers of children —10 or more—had declined from almost 24% in 1910 to a little over 8% by 1940.[112]

In the growing towns of the South, changes in family and gender roles were even more in evidence. The household was no longer the center of economic activity; "work" took place in offices, factories, and stores. Men were still the primary "breadwinners," and typically left each morning for work, generally leaving the household in the care of wives. However, increasing numbers of

111. "Fred Wilkins," *America from the Great Depression to World War II: Photographs from the FSA-OWI, 1935–1945*, Farm Security Administration-Office of War Information Photograph Collection (Washington: Library of Congress, American Memory, 1998), http://lcweb2.loc.gov/ammem/fsaquery.html.

112. Scott, *The Southern Lady*, 167–169; Tolnay, *The Bottom Rung*, 79. Walker, *All We Knew Was to Farm*, 44.

women worked away from the home, too, as seamstresses, teachers, mill work-ers, and clerks, jobs that allowed them, to some degree, to support themselves and possibly even live on their own. The idea of a woman on her own, at least while she awaited marriage, was no longer an aberration. Divorce was still rare but no longer virtually impossible, and the incidence of divorce was rising and was probably more common with residents of cities and towns. The pressure on married women to produce large numbers of children, particularly in the middle and upper classes, was much diminished because children were no longer an important source of household labor. The typical middle class woman was a homemaker, a role that entailed keeping house, cooking, caring for children, and being a companion to her husband. The sort of work that once took up much of a farm woman's time—spinning, weaving, sewing, tending a large garden, helping with the harvest—was no longer performed. Many middle class women had housekeepers, and children were now spending more and more time at school as the school year lengthened and the number of years children (middle class children, especially) attended school in-creased.[113] Children were now getting more of their preparation for adulthood at school, and parents assumed a smaller role in teaching the young. Increasing numbers of middle and upper class children, male and female, extended their schooling beyond high school to college. In short, the family as the all-encom-passing institution was being redefined as schools, stores, restaurants, and doctors, teachers, social workers, and other professionals increasingly per-formed functions families once performed.

It should not be surprising that as the family began losing many of its func-tions in urban households, more privileged women (those in the upper and middle classes) who did not work outside the home began filling their days with activities like bridge clubs, afternoon luncheons and teas, and the more traditional church meetings. Women's clubs and associations were formed in towns and cities across that region that offered women opportunities for cul-tural enrichment; some also became forums for issues that seemed to be espe-cially relevant to women such as child labor, public health, education, women's suffrage, and social problems like the lynching epidemic. The women did more than talk about these issues; their organizations began to function as political advocacy groups even before suffrage was achieved.[114] The Federation of

113. Jacquelyn Dowd Hall, "Disorderly Women: Gender and Labor Militancy in the Appalachian South," Catherine Clinton ed., *Half Sisters of History: Southern Women and the American Past* (Durham: Duke University Press, 1994), 185–186; Scott, *The Southern Lady*, 118–123, 214; Walker, *All We Knew Was to Farm*, 22, 188; George B. Tindall, *The Emergence of the New South*, 1913–1945 (Baton Rouge: Louisiana State University Press, 1967), 493–496.

114. Scott, *The Southern Lady*, 154–161, 177–179, 188, 195–197; Mary Martha Thomas, "The Ideology of the Alabama Women's Suffrage Movement, 1890–1920," Vir-

Women's Clubs of North Carolina, for example, began holding a yearly state convention in the early 1900s, often meeting in county courthouses. The convention met in the legislative chamber of the North Carolina House in 1909, and the assembled delegates heard a presentation on hookworm, voted to contribute to a scholarship that would pay for a young woman to attend Oxford University in England, and transferred ownership of "traveling libraries" established by the Federation to the North Carolina Library Commission. The ladies posed for a picture in front of the capital building, all of them with enormous hats (the current fashion) perched on their heads. Interestingly, at the next convention, they resolved to stop wearing hats at their meetings because apparently they felt the hats took away from the seriousness of what they were doing.[115] However innocuous as all of this might seem today, the women's clubs and organizations and even the afternoon bridge games undercut the traditional patriarchal family by engaging women in activities outside the home and away from the family and were steps toward a greater role for women in society's affairs, including the formally all male domain of politics. Even the "hat controversy" illustrated a sea change that was taking place, in this case in woman's apparel; the constrictive wear of the past—cumbersome hats and voluminous dresses with yards of fabric gave way very quickly to more modern attire by the 1920s featuring calf and knee length dresses (and even shorter for the youthful roaring 20s "flapper"), pants for the adventuresome, smaller hats and the growing acceptability of "hatlessness" in public.

Jimmy Carter's family story provides a good illustration of the "new" style of family and gender roles that were beginning to emerge in the early decades of the twentieth century. His mother had gotten a job in the post office in Richland, Georgia, as a young, single woman. Tiring of that, she left home to move to Plains, Georgia, to train to be a nurse at Wise Sanitarium. Her family was concerned when she made this decision because they feared she was on her way to being an old maid (she was 22). She was largely on her own in Plains and dated several young men including a fellow in his late twenties named Earl Carter who worked for his older brother at Plains Mercantile and ran a pants pressing business on the side. They would marry and have four children. He would return to farming (he came from a family of farmers), and she would work as a nurse at the hospital, a job that would sometimes take her on trips around the county visiting patients. Her relationship with her husband appeared on the surface to her son as straight ahead patriarchy, but as he observed, "All the time I was growing up, it seemed on the surface that my father

---

ginia Bernhard, et al., *Southern Women: Histories and Identities* (Columbia, Missouri: University of Missouri Press, 1992),116–120, 124.

115. Sallie Southall Cotton, *History of the North Carolina Federation of Women's Clubs, 1901–1925* (Raleigh: Edwards and Broughton Printing Company, 1925), 29–33, 36.

made the final decisions in our house. In front of us children or visitors, Daddy's word was law, and it was not until I was older, perhaps in high school, that I realized how strong-willed my mother was and how much influence she had in our family affairs."[116] So Carter's mother was more like an independent modern woman than the dependent, housebound woman of the past, and the Carter marriage was, in many respects, a companionate marriage.

Family and Gender in the Contemporary Era

Huge changes in the form and function of families and in gender roles would sweep the nation after World War II, and the South would experience this social "revolution," too, but in its own way and at its own pace. Initially, the nation seemed more committed to restoring traditional family and gender roles, as veterans returned to civilian work and many women, who had replaced men in many traditionally male occupations during the war, left the workforce and returned to domestic pursuits. Traditional gender roles were celebrated by women's magazines, politicians, and preachers, and much energy was expended on instructing women on how to be good wives, mothers, and homemakers. But change began to accelerate again in the 1960s; the middle class had expanded dramatically after World War II, and the major growth in new jobs was in offices, hospitals, and government, jobs that either gender could do equally well. Growing numbers of women began to work outside the home. The percentage of women in the workforce jumped from 29% in 1950 to 40% in 1975 and to nearly 60% by 2004. While many of these women worked in traditionally female jobs like secretary and teacher, more and more began taking traditionally male jobs in a process helped along by anti-discrimination legislation passed in the 1960s and 1970s by Congress. Women were making inroads even in high prestige occupations, and by 2004 nearly 30% of both lawyers and medical doctors were women.[117] More and more jobs required a college degree, and both women and men attended college at an increasing rate. In the 1950s and early 1960s, many women still majored in traditional fields like home economics and education, but this, too, began to change, and by the end of the century, more and more women were majoring in traditionally male fields and making up a larger percentage of the classes in professional schools, especially in law, medicine, and business. Women were now more likely than men to attend college, whether it was at a prestigious in-

116. Jimmy Carter, *An Hour Before Daylight: Memories of a Rural Boyhood* (New York Simon and Schuster, 2001), 109–121; quote p. 110.

117. Alice Kessler-Harris, *Out to Work: A History of Wage-Earning Women in the United States* (New York: Oxford University Press, 1982), 301; *Women in the Labor Force: A Databook* (U.S. Department of Labor, U.S. Bureau of Labor Statistics, May 2005).

stitution like the University of North Carolina at Chapel Hill or an "open door" community college.[118] With the emphasis on education and careers for women came delayed marriage, and the average marriage age of men and women edged upwards into the mid to late twenties. Large families, as we have seen, gave way to small families, and today the number of children in a typical American two-parent family is two. Because delayed marriage made "singleness" a respectable choice, and because of the higher incidence of divorce, a growing percentage of both males and females live by themselves.[119]

Changes in gender roles and the family were championed by the feminist movement, a movement which actually began before the Civil War, but one which spoke with a louder and louder voice by the late 1960s and 1970s.[120] Feminism emphasized equality between the sexes in work, politics, and social life, and advocated the same autonomy for women that men enjoyed. Women were not special spiritual beings responsible for the virtue of family and society, nor were they so fragile and weak that they needed to be protected by males and chaperones at every turn. Women were more like men with similar needs—sexual, social, psychological—and similar ambitions. Feminists believed women had been oppressed by traditional gender roles and patriarchy to the detriment of their health and happiness, and men had suffered, too, by being forced to forgo natural human emotions and needs in the interests of fulfilling the traditional masculine gender role. In the new world envisioned by feminists, women could wear work boots and drive trucks or serve in the infantry or run a corporation, and men could cook and clean and take care of children. Marriage was an option, not a requirement.

Many of the changes the movement supported, such as more opportunities for women in the workforce, were already well under way when the movement reached its stride, and many of the core values supported by the movement became mainstream American values, especially in the urban/suburban middle class. These values became part of a new morality which was based on the idea of social equality between the sexes. In this morality, the companionate marriage replaced patriarchy and was, ideally speaking, entered into by couples who were emotionally, intellectually, and

---

118. Deborah Perry Pisione, *The Many Faces of 21st Century Working Women: A Report to the Women's Bureau of the U.S. Department of Labor* (McLean, Va.: Education Consortium Co., 2004).

119. June Carbone, "Autonomy to Choose What Constitutes Family: Oxymoron or Basic Right?", http://www.scu.edu/law/FacWebPage/Carbone/autonomy.pdf (accessed 12/16/06); U.S. Census Bureau, American FactFinder (U.S. Census Bureau, 2004), http://factfinder.census.gov/jsp/saff/SAFFInfo.jsp?_pageId=tp3_gender.

120. For a general overview of the feminist movement see, Kathleen C. Berkeley, *The Women's Liberation Movement in America* (Westport, Conn.: Greenwood Press, 1999), 39–79.

sexually compatible. Both partners would now typically work, and marriage would be entered into later in life so that both partners could complete college educations, get work experience, and make a mature decision about marriage.[121]

Sexuality was cut loose from marriage and procreation; sex outside marriage was increasingly viewed as acceptable, and the birth control pill in the 1960s and later the legalization of abortion in the 1970s made sex outside the confines of marriage less risky in terms of an unwanted pregnancy. Women now could be, many felt, truly on an equal footing with men because they could control the one thing that had made them dependent on men—their fertility. The changes in both sexual attitudes and behavior were so pronounced, they were heralded as a so-called sexual revolution. Marriage was no longer necessarily till death do you part; if the couple proved incompatible or "grew apart," there was growing acceptance of divorce as a socially acceptable response, although ideally not before counseling and therapy were tried. The incidence of divorce had steadily risen after the Civil War and now reached a point where pundits commonly claimed that half of all marriages ended in divorce, although it turns out this overstated the actual rate of divorce. Increasing numbers of women even opted to have children outside marriage, and the "unwed mother" as a social pariah became a thing of the past. Accompanying all of these changes was the growing acceptance of homosexuality as a legitimate form of human expression (as opposed to an illness or a sin); by 2000, opinion polls were showing a majority of Americans polled believed sex between consenting adults, homosexual or otherwise, was their own business.[122]

Given the connection between the rise of industry, cities, and the middle class and the decline of patriarchy and the transformation of gender roles, it is not surprising that the South, much of it still agrarian until well into the twentieth century, would serve as a stronghold of traditionalism. In the 1970s and early 1980s, most of the nation supported the Equal Rights Amendment (ERA) which was designed to provide constitutional guarantees of equality for women, but in the South a powerful movement opposed to the amendment arose. In a replay of the region's hostility to women's suffrage earlier in the century, many argued that the ERA was a threat to the family and would undermine the traditional male role of breadwinner and protector and the traditional female role of wife and mother. Ten of the 15 states that failed to ratify the amendment were Southern (the other 5 were Western states).[123]

---

121. Carbone, "Autonomy to Choose What Constitutes Family: Oxymoron or Basic Right?"

122. *Ibid.*

123. Riane Tennenhaus Eisier, *The Equal Rights Handbook* (New York: Avon, 1978), 43.

Today, Southerners are still more likely to marry than people elsewhere in the nation, Southern women are still more likely than women elsewhere to bear children in their teens, and it is still quite common, particularly in rural areas and small towns, to find members of extended families living up and down the same road, attending the same church, spending much of their free time with uncles, aunts, siblings, cousins, and depending on kin for financial assistance, baby-sitting, and jobs.[124] A picture like the one at the beginning of this chapter could still be taken today at countless family reunions or church suppers.

The "manners" of traditional gender roles also seem to have persisted longer in the South than elsewhere; men still opened doors for women and helped them with packages well after it became politically incorrect elsewhere; it was still common for women to feign helplessness with recalcitrant mechanical devices. The image of the ultra-masculine working class white Southern male, a "Bubba" he was called, with his pickup truck equipped with gun rack and a six-pack of Blue Ribbon beer on the seat, emerged as a popular national stereotype in the 1970s. More than a few men in real life approximated this stereotype; they typically had little to say, but were generally hard workers and more than willing to help a stranded motorist or a woman in distress. The ultra-feminine Southern woman skilled in the ability to manipulate men still seemed to be common, as Florence King humorously documented in her book *Southern Ladies and Gentlemen*. Door opening and other mannerly behavior seems to have waned in recent years, and even grown men now seem to think that it is just fine to eat dinner in a restaurant with a baseball hat on. While "Bubbas" are still common, the Southern belle seems to have survived primarily in the numerous beauty contests found in the region for women and girls ages two to forty plus and in the debutante balls.

Conservative Protestant religion has supported patriarchy and traditional gender roles, even as the region changed. Sometimes this has involved an unsettling disconnect between beliefs and practices; Ruby Haynes, for example, was never able to have a traditional marriage for any length of time but supported the concept. As journalist Nicolas Lemann noted, "she believes, that as a matter of principle, God made man to have dominion over everything, to rule his home and family—but in her own life she has never been able to stand it when a no-good man tried to tell her what to do."[125] An organized Protestant fundamentalist movement began to gain strength in the middle decades of the

---

124. "Percent of Men 15 and Over Who Were Never Married: 2005" and "Percent of Women 15 and Over Who Were Never Married: 2005," U.S. Census Bureau, American FactFinder (U.S. Census Bureau, 2005), http://factfinder.census.gov; "Teen Motherhood at Record Low in the United States, Figure 4" (2003), Annie E. Casey Foundation, Kids Count, http://www.aecf.org/kidscount/.

125. Lemann, *The Promised Land*, 338.

1900s; this movement was opposed to "modernism" within the church and in society and forcefully promoted traditional gender roles and patriarchy, arguing that both were biblically based.[126] This movement would eventually fold into a broader movement of conservative Christians that emerged in the 1970s called the Christian Right that was particularly influential in the Baptist and Pentecostal denominations. This was a national movement, but one with its center of gravity in the South, and it would oppose the new sexual morality, especially abortion, and assert male preeminence as leaders in family, church, and society.

The South is less tolerant of homosexuality than the rest of the nation. While the level of toleration has grown in the South in recent years, as it has in the rest of the nation, the region has become a center of opposition to public acceptance of openly gay people, and this issue now rivals abortion as the major concern of conservative Christians. The national Southern Baptist Convention passed a resolution in 1980 that sums up that denomination's stance on homosexuality: "That our Convention deplore the proliferation of all homosexual practices, unnatural relations of any character, and sexual perversion whenever found in our society." Recent Southern Baptist Conventions in several states have passed resolutions promising expulsion to any member congregation that accepts openly gay members. The issue of same-sex marriage has become a major political issue, and polls show people in the South more opposed to it than folks from any other region. Not surprisingly, conservative Christians are most opposed, and many are willing to support a constitutional amendment prohibiting gay marriage.[127]

While tradition still exerts a powerful pull in the South, in many respects the South reflects changes in the rest of the nation fairly closely. This should not be too surprising given how much the region has been transformed over the last thirty years by the flood of immigrants from elsewhere pouring in, dizzying economic change, growing cities and suburbs, and a rapidly expanding middle class. Today, only 50% of the households of the South, for example, are headed by a married couple, the same percentage as the nation as a whole.[128] The companionate marriage appears to have, for many, supplanted

---

126. Shain Gerami, *Women and Fundamentalism: Islam and Christianity* (New York: Garland Publishing, Inc., 1996), 49–52.

127. James T. Sears, *Growing Up Gay in the South* (New York: Harrington Park Press, 1991), 10, 44; "Resolution on Homosexuality," SBC Resolutions, June 1980, SBC Net, Southern Baptist Convention, 1999–2007, http://www.sbc.net/resolutions; "Most Oppose Gay Marriage; Fewer Back an Amendment," June 2006, ABC News Polling Unit, *ABC News*, http://abcnews.go.com/US/Politics.

128. "The Types of Households in the South in 2005," and "The Types of Households in United States in 2005," U.S. Census Bureau, American FactFinder (U.S. Census Bureau, 2005 American Community Survey), http://factfinder.census.gov.

patriarchy as the ideal, even if women still end up with more of the household duties than is their fair share.[129] Mobile Southern suburbanites generally do not live in the bosom of an extended family, nor do many wish to. In the novel *Raney*, Clyde Edgerton humorously explored the clash of the old and new with Raney, small town born and raised, representing the old and her Atlanta born husband Charles representing the new. They live in Raney's hometown where Charles is a librarian in the local community college, and Raney works for her parents. Charles struggles with Raney's ever-present extended family and their disregard for the couple's privacy, something his suburban upbringing did not prepare him for.[130] While Southerners are a bit more likely than the nation as a whole to marry (males especially), they no longer believe (if recent opinion polls are to be believed) that people must be married to be happy and are actually more likely than folks in the nation as a whole to get a divorce. In 2004, 7 of the 10 states with the highest reported divorce rate were in the South. The region also leads the nation in the incidence of female headed households and the percentage of children living in households headed by grandparents.[131]

Family breakup and the decline in the number of stable two-parent households, particularly when coupled with poverty, have been linked to a host of social problems—dropping out of high school, youth crime, drugs, and teenage pregnancy—and the South has more than its share of these. The region has the highest incarceration rate in the United States and the highest incidence of children living in poverty; single parent households are especially likely to live in poverty. Kentuckian Della Mae Justice grew up poor in the Appalachian mountains of Kentucky; her father left the family, and her brother sometimes had to help feed the family by hunting squirrels. Her mother remarried, but eventually this relationship "imploded in violence," and Della ended up in a foster home for nine months. She was fortunate; her cousin, a lawyer, felt the pull of kin ties and took her in, and she ended up going to college and becoming a lawyer herself.[132] Most are not that lucky.

---

129. See, for example, some of the responses to questions about marriage in the *Southern Focus Poll, Spring 2001* (Chapel Hill: UNC Center for the Study of the American South, 2001).

130. Clyde Edgerton, *Raney* (New York: Ballantine Books, 1986).

131. "Percent of Men 15 and Over Who Were Never Married: 2005" and "Percent of Women 15 and Over Who Were Never Married: 2005," U.S. Census Bureau, American FactFinder, http://factfinder.census.gov ; *Southern Focus Poll, Spring 2001*; "Divorce rates by State: 1990, 1995, and 1999–2004," Division of Vital Statistics, National Center for Health statistics, Centers for Disease Control and Prevention, http://www. cdc.gov; "Children in Single Parent Families, 2004," "Grandchildren in the Care of Grandparents, 2004," Annie E. Casey Foundation, Kids Count, http://www.aecf.org/kidscount/.

132. "Prison and Jail Inmates at Midyear 2002," Bureau of Justice Statistics Bulletin, (U.S. Department of Justice, 2003), http://www.ojp.usdoj.gov/bjs/ pub/pdf/pjim02.pdf ; David T. Courtwright, "The Drug War's Perverse Toll," Issues in Science and Technology Online, University of Texas at Dallas, 2006, http://www/issues.org/ 13.2/courtw.htm;

The changes in family structure have been the most dramatic in the black community where there has been a tremendous increase in the percentage of children being raised by single mothers, relatives, and folks who aren't kin. Nationally, 66.3% of black children are raised in such homes compared to 25.9% of non-Hispanic white children. The South mirrors these rates: for example, in old plantation district counties such as Conecuh County, Alabama, and Vance County, North Carolina, between 60–70% of black children do not reside in a household with two parents. In metropolitan Atlanta, the figure is an astonishing 81%. All three areas report a high incidence of black children living in poverty: in Atlanta, it is 47% (compared to 7.4% of white children), in Conecuh, nearly 47% of black children live in poverty (compared to 22.2% of white children), and in Vance County, 37% of black children live in poverty (compared to 15.9% of white children).[133] The street corner subculture exemplified by Pud Bosket that appeared at the turn of the twentieth century is now less at the fringe and more at the center of black life in the South and across the nation, and even rural areas and small towns have a drug trade and youth gangs.[134] Pud's great grandson, Willie, is a lifer in the New York prison system, and his crimes—many committed before he was out of his teens—make his great grandfather's depredations pale by comparison and have earned him the reputation of being the most dangerous man in the system.[135] Nationally, over 10% of black males between the ages of 20–34 were in prison in 2002; by their thirties, 6 out of 10 black males who dropped out of high school will end up in prison.[136] The South has long led the nation in its incarceration rate, which increased dramatically during the 1990s, and most of those incarcerated in the region have been young black males.[137]

It now appears that the new morality has worked best for middle class people; middle class women are more likely to avoid pregnancy prior to marriage, and middle class men and women are more likely to earn college degrees and delay marriage until they are financially stable. They are also more likely to have two-income families; in the mid-1990s, for example, more than two

---

"Children in Poverty, 2005," "Single Parent Families in Poverty, 2005," Annie E. Casey Foundation, Kids Count, http://www.aecf.org/kidscount/; Tamar Lewin, "Up from the Holler: Living in two Worlds, at Home in Neither," *New York Times*, 19 May 2005. Http://www.nytimes.com (accessed 19 May 2005).

133. Regional, county, and metropolitan data on poverty and race from Annie E. Casey Foundation, Kids Count, http://www.aecf.org/kidscount/.

134. Lemann, *The Promised Land*, 336–337.

135. Butterfield, *All God's Children*.

136. Erik Eckholm, "Plight Deepens for Black Men, Studies Warn," *New York Times*, 20 March 2006, http://www.nytimes.com/2006/ (accessed 12/16/06); "Prison and Jail Inmates at Midyear 2002."

137. *State of the South, 1998* (Chapel Hill: MDC, Inc., 1998), 30, 35; "Prison and Jail Inmates at Midyear 2002."

thirds of the top 20% of income earners in the South were two-income families; nearly half of the lowest 20% were female-headed families.[138] Less affluent people often can't take advantage of the extra income two earners generate; daycare costs would eat up the extra income earned by a woman working at Walmart or as a secretary or bank teller. Middle class people have another advantage: they're more likely to get married and their marriages are more stable. National studies have found that divorce in the middle class is trending down, while the rate for less affluent folk is little changed. Declining marriage rates common among less affluent blacks have now become a characteristic of less affluent whites too. These national trends likely hold true for the South.[139] Even when middle class family breakups occur, their families are better able economically to weather the disruption. Less affluent people simply don't have the incomes to support two separate households if a divorce occurs, and so it's not uncommon for one of the partners (generally the male) to abandon the family or for there to be a struggle over child support payments. Court dockets are kept full by child support disputes.

And so we are back to the continuing influence of race and class. Middle class folks who are mainly white and generally live in the suburbs have embraced changes in family and gender roles and have benefited in many ways; women now play a larger role in the social, political, and economic life of the nation, and both men and women have more choices of how to live. They attend college at growing rates, and they prepare their children for college so that they can get middle class jobs when they grow up. Both men and women have benefited economically from having two earners in a family. The downside is a frantic lifestyle, some degree of male resentment of women's gains, and a higher incidence of marital breakup than in the distant past.

Less affluent people living primarily in urban areas and rural areas and small towns have seen far fewer of the benefits and more of the costs of the new style family and gender roles. Family breakups and children borne out of wedlock have left women, especially black women, bearing more of the burden and expense of child rearing. This is not simply the result of the "no goodness of most men"; the radical transformation of the job market has destroyed millions of the kinds of jobs working class men once did, and many men have not been able to adjust to a new world that requires less brawn, more education, and the sorts of social skills traditionally associated with women. Many men, particularly black men, have become marginalized and drift in and out of jobs,

138. Carbone, "Autonomy to Choose What Constitutes Family: Oxymoron or Basic Right?"; *State of the South, 1998*, 41.
139. Steven P. Martin, "Growing Evidence for a 'Divorce Divide'?: Education and Marital Dissolution Rates in the U.S. since the 1970s ," Russell Sage Foundation, http://www/russellsage.org/publications; Charles Murray, *Coming Apart: The State of White America, 1960–2010* (New York: Crown Forum, 2012), 149–167.

relationships, and prison. Drug use has taken a tremendous toll. A growing number of men have simply opted out of the workforce; workforce participation levels of men, particularly those without a high school diploma, continue to decline while the prison population surges.[140]

But economics is not the only explanation; culture plays a big role in explaining these changes. In the agrarian world that characterized much of the South well into the twentieth century, the family was an all-encompassing institution that provided people with work, leisure, friends, job training, rules to live by, an identity, and a sense of stability. Each member of the family served an important and necessary function in the family, even the children. Men led, women followed, and honor, shame, and religion enforced the rules. Today, other institutions perform many of the functions families once performed. Marriage is a choice, not a necessity, and can be entered into or gotten out of relatively easily. Women can live fruitful lives without the guidance and care of men. The heavy labor that once characterized "men's work" is now generally done by machines; the work most of us do can be performed by either sex equally well. Women can be leaders now and men can be followers. Today's world is more individualistic than the more communal world of the agrarian era; people choose what they want rather than relying on tradition to guide them. To be successful, people need to be open to change, and this might mean moving 1000 miles away to take a better job or going back to school to learn a new skill. People who are flexible, autonomous, rational, and self-controlled seem to do best in this new world.

The agrarian culture did not prepare people, particularly less affluent people, to be flexible, autonomous, and rational, and it relied on shame and sometimes physical force to "make people do right" rather than self-control. Clearly, many people today are still products of the agrarian culture, and they struggle because this culture no longer works. Children still drop out of school, just like they used to do when there were plenty of jobs in farming. Loyalty to family keeps many people in areas (like the old plantation districts) that are desperately poor, decisions that often doom them and their children to a life of poverty. Shame can no longer be depended upon as an enforcement mechanism; the media driven consumer society in which we all live elevates shamelessness to new heights. And the media is at the center of an alternative culture that can be found even in the most isolated area; it challenges both the middle class culture of self-control and rationality and the remnants of the old agrarian culture and takes some of the young, particularly the least advantaged, down a path that leads nowhere. Novelist Randall Kenan discovered this when he returned to his hometown in rural Eastern North Carolina:

---

140. *State of the South, 1998*, 30–36.

More to the point, those things that I had taken so for granted about being black, which had come from my mama and my grandfather and Uncle Roma and Aunt Lillian and Aunt Mildred in third grade, and Reverend Raynor and Miss Ruth, were now dictated by the Martin Lawrence Show and Snoop Doggy Dogg and Dr. Dre and Russell Simmons and Vibe magazine and, yes, Paramount. Chinquapin was becoming more like the rest of America. It was being absorbed by the vast cultural soup of consumeristic we-think.[141]

---

141. Randall Kenan, *Walking on Water: Black American Lives at the Turn of the Twenty-First Century* (New York: Alfred A. Knopf, 1999), 612–613.

Chapter 5

Religion

Introduction

The South has been called "the Bible Belt" and for a simple reason: its people are arguably some of the most religious folks in the country if not the world, and the religion most of them profess and often practice is Christianity, primarily the Protestant version of Christianity. This wasn't always true, as we will see, but it has been true for at least the last one hundred years. And this is not all: in the South most of the church-going population are evangelical Protestants, such as Baptist, Methodist, or Pentecostal, but especially Baptist. In a majority of Southern counties, there are more Baptists than there are members of any other denomination, making the region, without qualification, the most Baptist place on earth. It is not, therefore, surprising that the largest Baptist denomination in America is called Southern Baptist.

Baptists and other evangelical Protestants believe it is the Christian obligation to "save" other individuals and convert them to Christianity. This obligation, called the "great commission," has driven evangelicals to continually seek out converts, and this tremendous energy directed at conversion has helped account for the success of evangelical denominations in the region and has left a deep imprint on the culture. Evangelism became as common a part of everyday experience in the South as eating and sleeping; Bibles were routinely passed out at graduations, prayers routinely delivered at public events, neighbors "witnessed" with neighbors, and telephone answering machines urged callers to "have a blessed day." This evangelical Christian culture has proven to be fertile soil for what could best be described as a religious entrepreneurialism of a very democratic sort; hundreds of variations on the evangelical Protestant theme have sprung up as churches and denominations in the region, and new variations appear each year. On any given day, someone, somewhere feels "called" to start a new church, and one doesn't have to look long in most places to find a storefront or former welding shop on a rural road graced with a sign proclaiming "Sister Mary's House of Prayer" or "God's Love Bible Church." Sometimes these "start-ups" evolve into large congregations housed in imposing facilities located on the bypass outside of town and surrounded by acres of parking lots.

Despite the proliferation of denominations and independent churches, most evangelical Protestant churches have followed to a greater or lesser degree a common pattern, what we will call the "shared religion" of the South. The worship service in most Southern churches adhering to this pattern has been informal with few, if any, rituals, the focus of the service is on a sermon that is "preached," often in a way that elicits strong emotional reactions from those in attendance, and believers are urged to repent and to establish a personal relationship with God. Evangelicals of whatever denomination or church have traditionally subscribed to a strict moral code. Until relatively recently, for example, most Southerners considered drinking morally suspect if not sinful. Some people drank anyway, of course, and often on the sly, and the region undoubtedly led the world in the number of alcoholic beverages consumed out of brown paper bags (generally by men) in tool sheds, backyards, and parking lots. Flannery O'Conner once described the South as "Christ haunted"; certainly we can say evangelical Protestantism has permeated all aspects of Southern culture, and the unique drinking customs of the region are but one example. But the South has been washed over by a tidal wave of economic and social change over the last four decades and has been reintegrated into the culture and life of the nation in small ways and big, and this has, as we will see, affected religion and the role of religion in the culture of the South.

Religion in the Early South

The early settlements in the South offered virtually no indication that the region would someday become known as the "Bible Belt." Few of the early colonists coming to Virginia came for religious reasons. Undoubtedly, they were acquainted with Christianity, and most probably professed to be believers, but, unlike their Puritan brethren to the north, they had not come to the New World to create a religious utopia or to escape religious persecution. They came to make money or escape a debtor's prison or to make a new start. In England, most men and women belonged to the Church of England (also called the Anglican Church), and the leaders of the Virginia Company expected their new colony to be no different. Aboard one of the three small ships that brought the first English settlers to Virginia was Robert Hunt, an Anglican minister.[1]

The Church of England was a product of the Protestant Reformation that swept through much of Europe in the 1500s. Recall that the initial goal of Reformation leaders like Martin Luther had been to reform the Catholic Church; the 95 theses that Luther nailed on the church door in Wittenberg were a list of reforms that, he believed, would bring the church back to a biblically based, truer Christianity. Ultimately, Luther's followers started a new church (called the Lutheran Church) when it became apparent that the reforms they supported were not going to happen within the Catholic Church, and Luther's protectors, the north German princes, found it politically advantageous to permit a breakaway Christian church to form in their domains. Reformers in England also agitated for change in the church, and King Henry VIII, the king famous for his succession of wives, came to support the critics of the church. He created a new church headed, then and now, by the sitting monarch of England (himself), got the divorce he wanted and seized the church lands he had his eye on.

The Church of England had much in common with the Catholic Church. Like the church it replaced, it was the "official" church in England, and people were expected to participate. Dissenters (people who wished to practice another version of Christianity like the Puritans) were not treated kindly. An official church functions as one of the ordering institutions in a society much like the government itself; indeed, headed as it was by the king, it was an arm of the government, and taxes actually helped support it. The church, and later its American offspring, the Episcopal Church, were and are liturgical churches just like the Catholic Church. The church service is built around a set of rituals

---

1. Martin E. Marty, *Pilgrims in Their Own Land: 300 Years of Religion in America* (New York: Penguin Books, 1987), 54.

(the liturgy), particularly the sacrament of communion, and the sermon is typically a short, thoughtful reflection punctuating the rituals of the rest of the service rather than serving as the focal point of the service. Early church leaders developed the *Book of Common Prayer* to guide worshippers, and this book would become a central part of the Anglican experience. Anglican priests represented the church members before God and had the special and sacred responsibility of performing the necessary rituals. Churches built by Anglicans typically were and are ornate structures featuring elaborate altars and elevated pulpits. For them, the church sanctuary truly is "God's house" and should reflect this fact. With its emphasis on ritual and formality, this church was a relatively small step away from Catholicism, but the differences between the two in belief and practice were still significant. Anglican Church services were conducted in English, not Latin, priests could marry, and the highest ordained official in the church was the Archbishop of Canterbury, whose powers were more limited than those of the Pope. In an era of growing English nationalism, the Church of England became very much an **English** church in contrast to the more universal emphasis of Catholicism.

This church was established by colonial authorities as the official church in Virginia, the Carolinas, Georgia, and even Maryland, which had been founded by Lord Baltimore as a haven for English Catholics. The church was to perform in the colonies the same function it performed at home: "to establish the rule of religion," a rule that integrated the sacred and the secular by tying the individual to the community, strengthening the bonds between communities, and bolstering the authority of the government. Colonists were expected to be members and were expected to participate. In Virginia, for example, people were required by law to attend church services.[2] To hold other beliefs or to refuse to participate was viewed "not as a mere difference of opinion, but as a challenge to authority and therefore a disruption of community."[3] In short, religious freedom was at best tolerated by the early leaders in the South.

Part and parcel of the church's role of binding individuals together into a community was lending support to the class system. Within the church sanctuary, the social order of the world outside was replicated; the more affluent gentlemen and their families sat in pews at the front of the church nearest to the pulpit and altar while the small farmers sat on benches at the rear. At Christ Church in Lancaster County, Virginia, an edifice constructed in the new "Greek-cross" style in the 1730s, it was the custom of the local gentry to talk outside until the service began, "when they enter[ed] as a body" and to "leave

---

2. *Ibid.*, 82–86; Donald G. Mathews, *Religion in the Old South* (Chicago and London: The University of Chicago Press, 1977), 1–5; quote p. 1.
    3. *Ibid.*, 5.

in the same manner" when services were over.[4] This was their church, they were saying, and this was not only communicated in symbolic gestures and seating arrangements; they also controlled the vestry and thus all church business. In a sense, even the service itself was theirs. Worship services would have largely consisted of recitations from the *Book of Common Prayer*, recitations that may have left many of the illiterate and less-literate folks (a sizable portion of the small farmer population) sitting mutely. The language of the recitations may have also been problematic for many; the *Book of Common Prayer* reflected the education and sophistication of the "English Christian gentry" that produced it.[5] This is not to say that the small farmers of the early South necessarily sat in church steaming in sullen anger at a religion designed for their betters. Recall that the colonists brought with them a society based on class distinctions that all, high and low, accepted to a greater or lesser degree as natural. The seating arrangements may have struck most as perfectly normal, the recitations of the *Book of Common Prayer* heard often enough could be memorized, and the nod from the big planter on his way out of the church one Sunday might have provided a gratification to the recipient of the nod that more egalitarian-minded modern folk might not be able to imagine.[6]

In practice, the Anglican Church's ability to connect individuals to a community and knit communities together into a society dutifully following the laws, customs, and preferences of a political authority based in England was less than ideal. The Church of England in America had become the responsibility of the Bishop of London and the Society for the Propagation of the Gospel in Foreign Parts, an arm of the church that was established to carry Anglicanism to the far corners of England's emerging empire. Clearly, neither the Bishop nor the Society was up to the task of adequately serving the widely dispersed small settlements and isolated farmsteads of the colonial South. The church required an educated clergy, and, until the College of William and Mary was created, ministers had to be dispatched from England. Generally only the most settled areas were adequately served by Anglican clergy. Virginia and Maryland, the two oldest colonies were thus best served; the church wasn't even established in Georgia until 1758, and North Carolina was considered the

---

4. Rhys Isaac, *The Transformation of Virginia, 1740–1790* (Chapel Hill: The University of North Carolina Press, 1982), 59–61. Quote, p. 61.

5. *Ibid.*, 64.

6. *Ibid.*, 65. See also Hunter Dickinson Farish, ed., *Journals and Letters of Philip Vickers Fithian, 1773–1774: A Plantation Tutor of the Old Dominion* (Charlottesville, VA: Dominion Books, 1968). Philip Fithian a tutor for the children of Robert Carter, a big planter, found that the planters at the Anglican Church he attended socialized on the lawn outside the church after services and would conduct business with each other and extend dinner invitations. He noted that on Easter Sunday "all the Parish seem'd to meet together High, Low, black, white all come out" suggesting that while class and race may have separated church-goers, all still were members of the same church community. See p. 89.

least well-served.[7] For many colonists in the frontier regions of the South, attending a church service was at best an infrequent occurrence. Colonel William Byrd, the leader of a team of surveyors who, in 1728, laid out the boundary between Virginia and North Carolina, wrote of the North Carolinians he encountered: "they are not troubled with any Religious Fumes, and have the least Superstition of any People living. They do not know Sunday from any other day...."[8] Several decades later "Religious Fumes," at least of the Anglican variety, were still not "troubling" most of the people of North Carolina; only six Anglican priests were assigned to serve the entire colony at a time when over 100,000 colonists were settled in an expanse of territory extending hundreds of miles from the coast to the mountains.[9] Nor did the church services that were held always conform to the ordered ideal envisioned by early colonial leaders. One priest, for example, reported that at a service he conducted, "according to Custom, one half of them got drunk before they went home."[10]

In the long-settled regions, the influence of the Anglican clergy and church hierarchy was often circumscribed by local planters. As at Christ Church, the planters typically dominated the vestry boards of churches, and the planters, ever protective of their powers and prerogatives, worked to undercut the influence of the church leadership over local priests and replace it with their own.[11] In Virginia, in particular, disputes in the mid-1700s between several big planters and clergymen they wished to remove devolved into vicious name-calling that blackened the reputation of the ministers and established in the public mind the idea that the Anglican clergy offered a haven to drunks, philanderers, and layabouts.[12]

The Southern colonists were an ostensibly Christian people served by a church that seemed to lack either the will or the ability to marshal the resources necessary to meet their religious needs. They lived lives filled with danger and uncertainly; death and misfortune came easily and quickly, and they needed institutions like the church to provide them with some semblance of order and stability. In retrospect, the Anglican Church may have been good at

---

7. Patricia Bonomi makes a case that colonial churches before the Great Awakening of the 1730s and 1740s were better established than most historians have been willing to admit, but she undercuts her case, at least as it applies to the Southern colonies, in her description of weak church establishments in several Southern colonies and the bitter conflicts that embroiled the Anglican churches in Maryland and Virginia. Patricia U. Bonomi, *Under the Cope of Heaven: Religion, Society, and Politics in Colonial America* (New York: Oxford University Press, 2003), xvii–xx; 41–50.

8. William Byrd, *Histories of the Dividing Line Betwixt Virginia and North Carolina* (New York: Dover Publications, 1967), 72.

9. Mathews, *Religion in the Old South*, 5–6.

10. *Ibid.*, 7.

11. *Ibid.*, 6; Rhys Isaac, *The Transformation of Virginia*, 143–145.

12. Bonomi, *Under the Cope of Heaven*, 44–45.

maintaining order at home, but clearly it was not good at **creating** order on the frontier of a distant land.

Change was in the wind, or more precisely in the holds of ships bringing new immigrants from Scotland and Ireland and Germany. In the early decades of the 1700s, more and more settlers from these countries began to settle in the South and with them came the religions they practiced at home, especially the Presbyterian and Lutheran faiths. Quakers had also made their appearance in the South, and in North Carolina, a group of German colonists called Moravians established communities based on the teachings of their church in a settlement they named Wachovia. The colonial governments of the South permitted colonists to practice these dissenting religions but imposed strict regulations on the churches. Dissenter ministers, for example, were licensed to preach only at specific locations, and all weddings were to be performed by Anglican priests. Nonetheless, dissenters were quite numerous in some areas, particularly in the backcountry, and the Anglican Church was not effective in fending off this new challenge to its position in society.[13]

The Great Awakening and the Introduction of Evangelical Protestantism to the South

The early dissenters posed a challenge to the predominance of Anglicanism largely because the Anglican Church was so inert and passive. However, not one of these denominations blanketed the region with churches; evangelicalism, a passion for converting the unconverted, was not the central organizing principle of any of them, although several, the Presbyterian in particular, would develop an evangelical wing. Thus, for example, the Lutheranism brought by German immigrants took root primarily where German immigrants settled in the Piedmont and few other places, and the Presbyterian Church, even with its evangelical wing out seeking converts, would at best provide the region with a "sprinkling" of churches as opposed to a blanket.

However, a movement was building within western Christianity in the 1700s, particularly in the individualistic Christian societies of northwestern Europe, which fed the American colonies with immigrants and ideas, that would be, among its other qualities, profoundly evangelical. The movement was a reaction to the formality, aloofness, and increasingly rationalistic emphasis of the established Protestant churches, whose leadership was becoming comfortable with ideas generated by the Enlightenment. While the Enlightenment elevated man and celebrated his capacity to reason, members of this

---

13. Mathews, *Religion in the Old South*, 7–8.

movement believed humans were depraved sinners who could not "reason" their way to salvation; only repentance and God's grace could do that. The emphasis on human depravity and the necessity of God's grace clearly reflected the teachings of John Calvin, who had profoundly influenced Presbyterianism and the religious beliefs of the Puritans, but much about the movement's key tenets would have made Calvin's head spin. Most importantly, movement members believed believers must experience God directly and in their hearts, not only in their heads, and, in this sense, the movement espoused a Christianity that was inherently emotional, a religion of the heart. God was active in the world and involved with his creation and would enter into the human heart if that heart was open to Him. Later day converts would refer to this as establishing a "personal relationship with Christ (or God)." This new style of Christianity would be promoted by its adherents with an unusual zeal because they believed that, like the original disciples, the primary role for a good Christian was converting non-believers and bringing those who have strayed back to the faith. God had high expectations for his creations (another Calvinist notion), thus making this new version of Christianity a demanding choice for the convert.[14] The movement would, in effect, pare away another layer of ritual, priestly control of faith, and complex theology in a process that had begun during the Reformation. It would also establish the notion that religion was an individual choice, not a community custom or legal requirement, and in that sense, ironically, it reflected one of the key ideas that surfaced during the Enlightenment—religious freedom.[15] It would find its truest and deepest expression in the American colonies and especially the colonies of the South. It would forever change the religious landscape of the South.

The Great Awakening was the movement that introduced this evangelical, personal, highly charged Christianity to the American colonies and the South, and it would bring thousands of sinners to their knees if not laying them prostrate on their faces. It began in New England and the Middle Colonies in the early decades of the eighteenth century and spread south in a wave of revivals in the 1740s. One of its earliest leaders was Jonathan Edwards, a minister of the Congregational Church (the Puritan's church) in New England who began in the 1720s to preach a new style of intense, highly emotional sermon—his most famous was "Sinners in the Hands of an Angry God"—that stressed the terrible fate that awaited the unrepentant sinner. Its most prominent leader was George Whitefield, the Billy Graham of eighteenth-century colonial America. Whitefield was a British Anglican who had become dissatisfied with the lack of emotion and piety in his church and the focus of its theology on the rational. He preached in both England and the American colonies and would die

---

14. *Ibid.*, 11–13. Patricia Bonomi, *Under the Cope of Heaven*, 131–132.
15. Martin E. Marty, *Pilgrims in Their Own Land*, 108.

in the colonies on his last visit there. For him Christianity was the word of God, not the rituals of the church, and it was the word that saved people. He was not afraid to castigate traditional religious leaders for their wrong-headed theology and lack of piety, and this willingness to challenge established religious (and secular) leaders became a hallmark of this movement.[16] Like Edwards, Whitefield gave highly emotional sermons that focused on the contrast between salvation in heaven and damnation in hell, and this too became another defining characteristic of the evangelical movement. What he hoped to do is break through the normal reserve and worldly concerns of his listeners and bring about a radical change in both belief and behavior. In Charleston, South Carolina, for example, he addressed a crowd that was "very polite" as the members stood listening to him in their "affected finery," an entirely inappropriate response in his mind for folks "who have had such Divine judgment sent amongst them." The next day he addressed another crowd and was pleased when "many were melted into tears" especially "one of the town, most remarkably gay, [who] was observed to weep."[17] Whitefield was in the business of saving sinners and would become the model for evangelical ministers who would be called preachers in recognition of their primary function as exhorters.

Whitefield began a preaching tour in America in 1739 that would take him the length of the colonies. He was only 25 years old, and in a society that valued age in its leaders, religious and otherwise, Whitefield must have struck many as presumptuous. His appearance—he was cross-eyed—may not have helped. But he had a certainty about him and an integrity that impressed a man as perceptive as Benjamin Franklin, who counted Whitefield one of his friends. Franklin, Enlightenment rationalist that he was, was somewhat perplexed by Whitefield's broad appeal; in his *Autobiography* he noted that Whitefield was "admir'd and respected" by the people who flocked to hear him, "notwithstanding his common abuse of them, by assuring them that they were naturally half beasts and half devils." If Franklin was puzzled by Whitefield's message, he seemed to approve of its effect, noting, "It was wonderful to see the change soon made in the manners of our inhabitants. From being thoughtless or indifferent about religion, it seem'd as if all the world were growing religious...." Whitefield's secret weapon was a powerful voice; Franklin conducted an impromptu study at one of his appearances and estimated that he could be heard by a crowd of 30,000.[18] Whitefield drew crowds in Franklin's words,

16. Mathews, *Religion in the Old South*, 13; Marty, *Pilgrims in Their Own Land*, 118–121.

17. George Whitefield, *George Whitefield's Journals to which is Prefixed his "Short Account" (1746) and "Further Account" (1747)* (Gainesville, FL: Scholars Fassimiles [sic] and Reprints, 1969), 382.

18. Benjamin Franklin, *Benjamin Franklin's Autobiography*, ed. by J.A. Leo LeMay (New York and London: W.W. Norton & Co., 1986), 87–89.

"from all sects and denominations"; sometimes he was welcome in local churches and sometimes, because he was critical of established church leaders, he was not. If he could not find a place to meet or the crowd he expected to draw was bigger than available meeting places could accommodate, he would often preach in a field or from the front steps of a court house, a practice that would be the basis for the later day outdoor or tent revival service. Whitefield probably drew larger crowds in the North where the population was more concentrated, but his influence was still profound in the South. Whitefield noted in his journal in 1739, "I could not but think, that God intended, in His own time, to work a good work in these southern parts of America. At present they seem more dead to God, but far less prejudiced than in northern parts."[19]

Followers of this new style of worship were sometimes called "New Lights" or "New Sides" and initially organized reform factions within established churches such as the Presbyterian Church; later, new denominations would be formed. This process began literally at the grass roots. In Hanover County, Virginia, for example, in 1743, Samuel Morris, a bricklayer, led a small group that began holding meetings apart from Anglican services to read and discuss religious tracts by Whitefield and other ministers. As time went on, more people joined them, and they began to think of themselves as a church and even constructed a meetinghouse. They weren't sure what to call themselves until a Presbyterian New Side missionary came to speak to them; after that, they decided they were Presbyterians. The new church was served by traveling evangelical ministers who preached the new style gospel and weren't afraid, apparently, to criticize the Anglican clergymen for their "degeneracy." The crowds that came to hear these ministers and the attacks on the established clergy worried the local Anglican rector, the Reverend Patrick Henry, Sr., and led him to request help from the government. One of the visiting preachers was indicted by a grand jury, and several laymen were "fined for unlawful assembly."[20]

Into this tense situation came Samuel Davies. Davies was a graduate of one of the new "log colleges" started by evangelical Presbyterians to properly train new ministers and came to Hanover County to serve as the permanent minister of the new church. He worked hard to get along with local Anglican ministers and political authorities; although relations were sometimes less than amicable, Davies was successful in gaining some measure of acceptance. However politic Davies may have been with local leaders, he still followed in the path blazed by Whitefield and the other New Lights in his sermons and ministry and largely rejected much of the world he found in Hanover County, including

---

19. Whitefield, *George Whitefield's Journals To Which is Prefixed His"Short Account" (1746) and "Further Account" (1747)*, 369.
20. Rhys Isaac, *The Transformation of Virginia*, 148–149. See also Donald Mathews, *Religion in the Old South*, 15–17.

the theology and morality of the Anglican Church and the social system that placed the planters above all others. Davies' sermons were intense and highly personal: hell awaits us; only those who repent may be saved by the grace of God. Converts should live simply, in prayerful reflection, should avoid many of the pleasures enjoyed by "worldlings" such as drinking, dancing, and gambling and should separate themselves as much as possible from "worldlings."[21]

The Presbyterians "New Sides" were the cutting edge of the evangelical movement until the appearance of the Baptists, but it would be the Baptist faith in its myriad variations (it eventually split into more than a dozen denominations, not to mention large numbers of independent churches) that would eventually dominate the religious life of the South. This was a new church established in the Northern colonies and was initially called the Separate Baptist to distinguish it from a small non-evangelical sect of traditional or "Regular" Baptists. The Separates were people who had been deeply affected by the message of Whitefield and other new-style preachers. They combined the highly personal and emotional Christianity of the New Lights with some of the practices of traditional Baptists. It was a faith that adhered to a simple theology based on the Bible, and it was evangelical with a capital "E." Shubal Stearns, a New Englander, is credited with bringing this new faith to the South.[22] He arrived in North Carolina in 1754 and established the first Separate Baptist church in North Carolina at Sandy Creek. Stearns was a powerful speaker, and, like Whitefield, his sermons drew people to this new religion, sometimes in spite of themselves. A doubter, Elnathan Edwards, attended one of Stearns's services intent on amusing himself, a common occurrence because many came to gawk at the emotional outbursts of believers at the meetings of evangelicals. When people started weeping and trembling, Edwards tried to walk away but found "the enchantment of Stearns' voice drew him to the crowd...." As he stood and listened, "the trembling seized him" and finally caused him along with many others to fall to the ground. "When he came to himself, he found nothing in him but dread and anxiety, bordering on horror. He continued in this situation some days, and then found relief by faith in Christ."[23] Central to the Baptist faith was this conversion experience (today, often called a born-again experience). Although the conversion experience need not be this dramatic, many were and often followed the same pattern: conviction (a change of heart), followed by a period of deep despair, and then redemption. Baptists disavowed baptizing infants or young children because they believed only the converted should be baptized, and infants and young children were too young to have had the experience. Baptism must be by immersion, a belief that dis-

---

21. Mathews, *Religion in the Old South*, 17–22.
22. *Ibid.*, 23.
23. Elder John Sparks, *The Roots of Appalachian Christianity: The Life and Legacy of Elder Shubal Stearns* (Lexington, KY: University Press of Kentucky, 2001), 66.

tinguished Baptists from most other evangelical groups. The Baptist faithful were expected to live by the rigid moral code that was the hallmark of the evangelical movement, and the church community itself served as a social support network and sanctioning body to keep believers on the straight and narrow path of righteous living.[24] Fancy clothing, prideful speech, or a bit too much to drink might bring one before a church committee for disciplinary action. Thus, while reflecting a more individualistic notion of religion that put the believer in a direct relationship with God, it also established a community of believers in an often intense relationship with each other. In fact, believers frequently would touch, hug, and kiss each other to show their love for their fellow Christians and would share their most personal feelings with other believers at church meetings sometimes called love feasts; delivering these confessions came to be called testifying, and the practice became a key part of revival services and was institutionalized in the typical service of most Baptist churches.[25]

The ministerial style Whitefield had introduced also became institutionalized in the Baptist Church. The Baptist minister was not an intermediary between man and God like the Anglican priest but an exhorter: his job was to exhort sinners to repent. The speaking style was highly emotional, and at its most extreme was sometimes termed the "holy whine" which mixed "soothing tones" with "loud and harsh" tones.[26] All the tools a speaker could bring to bear on his audience should be used by the preacher, and, like the good actor, eliciting emotion was for the preacher a sure sign that the audience was responding. While emotional outbursts in church offended and appalled the typical Anglican, for the Baptist these were also signs that God was at work. The church service in effect became a continuous campaign to convert the sinner. It made no difference if the sinner was an elderly woman who regularly attended church and seemed the epitome of piety or a drunken, foul-mouthed loafer who never attended; the regular church goer was still a sinner and needed spiritual renewal, and the unrepentant loafer needed a conversion experience. Both needed to be told and told again how a good Christian should live. Given the depraved nature of people, moral and spiritual decline for the individual and the broader community was an ever-present possibility. So Baptists and later Methodists believed that regular church services needed to be supplemented periodically by extraordinary efforts to fend off individual and collective spiritual decline and reach the unrepentant. Thus was born the revival, a special service modeled after Whitefield's preaching in fields and city streets that would be sponsored by individual churches, entire communities, or self-

---

24. Mathews, *Religion in the Old South*, 23–24.
25. *Ibid.*, 24–26; Isaac, *The Transformation of Virginia*, 164–165.
26. Mathews, *Religion in the Old South*, 24; Sparks, *The Roots of Appalachian Christianity*, 67–68.

appointed revival preachers. Revivals might last days or weeks, and might feature teams of preachers; they were held in fields, campgrounds, churches, tents, and, much later, auditoriums, sports arenas, and convention centers. They featured particularly intense preaching and emotional calls by the preacher to come forward and be saved.

It's hard to know precisely who joined these new churches, but it appears that its early appeal was to the so-called "common" folk—the small farmer, the blacksmith, the small trader—and to folks in the less settled regions. Certainly the Baptist Church (and later Methodism) was more accessible to ordinary people than Anglicanism or even Presbyterianism because it was based on a personal experience of faith rather than knowledge of church theology, tradition, and liturgy, and it did not recognize, in ways the Anglican Church did, social distinctions. The small farmers were not relegated to benches in the back of the church, nor were front row seats reserved for the gentry. Its leadership, in fact, could and often did come from "common" sources because any man could become a preacher if he had the conversion experience and he felt "called" (chosen by God); seminary training and even literacy were not required.[27] In a society with fairly rigid class distinctions, then and later, the Baptist faith and later other evangelical faiths were quite egalitarian. We know that opposition to Baptist organizing was strong in the planter class, and sometimes this opposition was less than genteel. A Brother Waller, for example, was preaching in Tidewater Virginia in 1771 and was interrupted by a party of gentlemen including the local Anglican parson and the sheriff. While Waller was trying to sing, the parson "would Keep Running the End of his Horsewhip in [Waller's] Mouth"; not content with merely disrupting Waller's meeting, the group then pulled him from the stage and "Beat his head against the ground" and finished with the sheriff giving him "Twenty lashes with his Horse Whip...."[28] Efforts to suppress the Baptists in Virginia and elsewhere were to no avail. Seven Separate Baptist churches could be found in Virginia in 1769; five years later, fifty-four had been established.[29]

The Baptist Church represented a radical departure from the ordered, top-down emphasis of the Anglican Church, and the theology was a loosely drawn statement of basic principles. Churches could pick their own ministers, and the ordination of a minister was a relatively simple procedure governed by few rules or requirements. There would never be a shortage of ministers as there had been with the Anglican Church. Churches governed themselves and answered to a higher church authority at their own choosing. Baptist churches

27. Bonomi, *Under the Cope of Heaven, 184;* Isaac, *The Transformation of Virginia,* 164–166; Mathews, *Religion in the Old South,* 27–28.
28. Isaac, *The Transformation of Virginia,* 162.
29. *Ibid.,* 173.

themselves could be cheaply and quickly built (they were simple structures with few adornments), and this simplicity was elevated to an ideal because it reflected the Baptist commitment to humility. This was a denomination designed for expansion and a mass audience, particularly a mass audience with no great loyalties to an established church.

Methodism would mount a strong challenge to this Baptist surge in organizing. Methodism was a movement within the Anglican Church and was headed in England by John Wesley who was ably assisted by his brother Charles, the author of many superb hymns. The Wesleys led their movement from within the Church of England, but their followers in the colonies would split off after the Revolution and form a separate denomination. Like the Baptists, Methodists were committed to spreading the word and to preaching a personal form of Christianity that stressed the relationship between each believer and God. While most Baptists were Calvinistic (like the Puritans and Presbyterians) in their belief that God had selected a few to be saved (the elect), the Methodist doctrine posited a God who extended grace more freely, excluded fewer sinners, and gave imperfect humans more chances at redemption. While it was still up to God to extend his grace and thus make a choice of whom to save, what people seemed to hear was that sinners could choose to accept God and were thus responsible for their own salvation (with God's help of course).[30] So while Methodists were just as likely to emphasize the frightening prospects of an eternity in hell for the unconverted, they also introduced a kinder, gentler God and the idea that the sinner was capable of taking his own fate in his hands. But Methodists were just as demanding of those who repented as the Baptists, and expected converts to follow strict moral precepts.

Methodists did follow the Anglican lead and established a fairly elaborate church hierarchy headed by bishops, and the most famous of the early bishops was Francis Asbury. Bishop Asbury and other church leaders took the traveling preacher concept of the evangelical movement and systematized it; Methodist ministers were famous for riding extensive "circuits." On the circuit of each minister were a number of churches that he would visit. The churches would be responsible for supporting the visiting minister so the costs of maintaining a cleric were spread out. Traveling ministers were typically highly motivated unmarried young men who were willing to travel great distances, sleep in haylofts, and endure the vagaries of the weather and bad food. Asbury himself traveled thousands of miles and never married and seemed to resent losing any of his traveling ministers to marriage. Methodism had started as lay movement within the Church of England, and it continued to rely heavily upon its lay leaders who kept churches active in the absence of the traveling ministers.[31]

---

30. Mathews, *Religion in the Old South*, 31.
31. *Ibid.*, 30; Marty, *Pilgrims in Their Own Land*, 170–173.

By its very nature, evangelical Protestantism, particularly of the sort introduced by the Baptists and Methodists, was radical. It urged its adherents to live humbly and eschew the worldly pleasures and passions that drove most people; for men, competition with other men and defense of manly honor were replaced by brotherhood with fellow believers and turning the other cheek when insulted or affronted. Brother Waller responded to the humiliating treatment he received from the Virginia gentlemen as a good Christian, not as a man who followed the code of honor. Women were to dress modestly and drive all but pious thoughts from their heads. The converted were to keep apart from "worldlings" as much as possible and reject their moral leadership no matter how elevated in status, no matter how wealthy, no matter how educated, no matter how accomplished in politics they were. Theologically, evangelicalism rejected the Anglican understanding of man and God which stressed a benevolent God who granted humans reason to discover, in a calm and measured manner, spiritual truth and encouraged them to do good in the world. God for the evangelical was beyond understanding and could only be feared, loved, and worshiped; salvation came not from study, thought, and good deeds but from the death of the old self during the conversion experience and the birth of a new self. Anything less was false piety, and this attitude explains evangelicals' often bitter criticisms of the Anglican faith. Evangelical religion also threatened to undercut patriarchy, that set of values that established male leadership in the family and over women and that gave older, accomplished males dominion over younger males. Young people and women were especially drawn to the New Light message, and sometimes they attended over the objections of parents or husbands. Men and women often sat in separate areas in the church rather than in family groups, so people worshiped in church as individuals, not as members of a family. Women were permitted to testify and sometimes even to "exhort" (a form of preaching). As we have seen, it was often young men who served as preachers and who were thus in the position of instructing church members, older men included, on how to live and behave. Even the authority of the church to discipline its members in a sense competed with the authority of fathers and husbands to control their families.[32] As followers of a radical version of Christianity, many took seriously Christ's admonition to follow him regardless of the costs, and one would assume more than a few preachers would point to the passage in Matthew where Christ says, "For I have come to set a man against his father, and a daughter against her mother, and a daughter-in-law against her mother-in-law; and one's foes will be members of one's own household."[33] Evangelicals made the conversion of slaves a priority,

---

32. Christine Leigh Heyrman, *Southern Cross: The Beginnings of the Bible Belt* (Chapel Hill, NC and London: University of North Carolina Press, 1997), 116; 128–134; 142–143; 167–168; Mathews, *Religion in the Old South*, 102–105.

33. Heyrman, *Southern Cross*, 134. Quote in Matthew 10:34–10:42.

and some Baptist and Methodist preachers urged believers to give up their slaves, arguing that slavery was inconsistent with the gospel; at one point the Methodist Church threatened to excommunicate slaveholding members who did not free their slaves within two years.[34]

It is not surprising that evangelicals ran into opposition, sometimes violent opposition, from planters, nor is it surprising that while winning many converts, evangelical religion would find critics in other quarters too who found its moral code extreme and the raw emotionalism of its services and revivals frightening and contrary to the quiet reserve that normally counted for much among respectable folk. The strict ways of the evangelicals drew folk away from the popular amusements and community gathering places and by establishing categories of "saved" and "worldling" sometimes split communities and families. The challenge to patriarchy was just as troubling to the man who owned a small farm as it was to the big planter. Evangelical ministers were sometimes accused of breaking wives away from husbands and children away from parents, and this sometimes led to violent confrontations between a preacher and a disgruntled husband or parent.[35] Ordinary folk might feel more at home in a church that spoke their language and that did not put them in the back rows, but ordinary folk generally also wanted to get along with the gentry, and following the evangelicals often meant they had to turn up their noses at the character, lifestyle, and hospitality of the local planters.[36] Evangelicals' criticism of slavery was naturally enough unpopular with the planters, but it often fell on less than receptive ears in the small farmer class, too; it was not uncommon for a small farmer to own a slave or two or to aspire to own slaves. Further, slavery had a deeper significance for the small farmers than dreams of "getting ahead"; as we saw in an earlier chapter, it was the establishment of slavery that pushed whites out of the plantation workforce and made possible the more democratic society (for whites anyway) that existed by the early 1700s.[37] Attacks on slavery threatened to upset all of this.

By the beginning of the American Revolution, by one estimate no more than 10% of the adult whites in the South belonged to evangelical churches, and only a small number of blacks belonged. This does not include the sizeable number of people who attended church on occasion but never joined. Slaves, for obvious reasons, were probably especially likely to attend a church but not to formally join. Still, the great majority of Southerners were outside the evangelical fold, and while more folk were attending evangelical churches than the

---

34. Mathews, *Religion in the Old South*, 68–69; Heyrman, *Southern Cross*, 17.
35. Mathews, *Religion in the Old South*, 103–105. Heyrman, *Southern Cross*, 184–190.
36. Heyrman, *Southern Cross*, 17–26.
37. Edmund Morgan, *American Slavery, American Freedom: The Ordeal of Colonial Virginia* (New York: W.W. Norton and Co., 1975).

Anglican Church, Anglicanism was down but not out; it was still quite strong in the more settled areas where evangelical inroads were more limited.[38]

The Triumph of Evangelical Protestantism

It would take perhaps one hundred years for evangelical Protestantism to completely dominate the religious life of the South and to emerge as one of the defining institutions in the culture of the South. During this period, lasting roughly from the late 1700s to the late 1800s, it would splinter into hundreds of variations; certain core beliefs would persist relatively unchanged, while other beliefs and practices would be discarded or would evolve. The onset of the Revolutionary War set the stage for the rise of evangelicalism by effectively taking the Church of England out of the picture as a serious rival. When the war began, many Anglican clergy returned to England, leaving many churches in the hands of lay leaders. The state legislatures in the newly created nation struck another blow at the church when they disestablished it as the official state church. Weakening the church even more was the stigma that naturally was attached to attending a church called the Church of England during the war with England. It wasn't until 1789 that the Anglican Church in America was reborn as a new denomination—the Protestant Episcopal Church; by then the church had lost too much ground to evangelicalism, ground that it would never recoup.[39]

A massive revival, sometimes called the Second Great Awakening, started in Kentucky in the early 1800s and swept the frontier South and the piedmont South, introducing a new generation to evangelical religion and bringing many others back into the fold. The revival was preceded by years of laments throughout the South that spiritual decline was everywhere in evidence; preachers and laymen pointed to declining church memberships, abandoned churches, and widespread abuse of liquor.[40] Despite these gloomy assessments, many felt that God would intervene; He was everywhere and always involved in His creation; if humans repented, He would bring them back into the fold.[41] The spark that set off the region-wide revival was a local revival organized by several Presbyterian congregations in southern Kentucky. Four or five hundred gathered in June of 1800 at the Red River meeting house to hear preaching

38. Heyrman, *Southern Cross*, 13. John B. Boles, *The Great Revival, 1787–1805: The Origins of the Southern Evangelical Mind* (Lexington, Kentucky: The University Press of Kentucky, 1972), 8–10.

39. Heyrman, *Southern Cross*, 22.

40. Boles, *The Great Revival, 1787–1805*, 12–24.

41. *Ibid.*, 26–33.

from their own ministers and two visiting preachers, one a Presbyterian and one a Methodist. Expectation was in the air; for several years members of the three congregations had been looking for a sign of God's presence. An intense round of preaching by several of the ministers finally resulted in a woman rising up "shouting and singing" which led to an outbreak of crying. Then, John McGee, one of the ministers, began to preach. As he related later, "losing sight of the fear of man, I went through the house shouting, and exhorting with all possible ecstasy and energy, and the floor was soon covered with the slain [worshippers who had fallen to the floor]." And it didn't end with this service. Crowds of people, some from many miles away, began collecting at a camp at nearby Gasper River hoping for a similar religious awakening. Preaching lasted for days and many came forward to be saved; ministers worked night and day in the crowds to console and encourage those who had had the conversion experience. Many of the converts were children, and this was seen as a special sign of God's providence.[42]

The next summer the mammoth Cane Ridge camp meeting was held. Cane Ridge, located in the center of Kentucky where most the state's population lived, attracted as many as 25,000 men, women, and children who camped out for days and listened to virtually round the clock preaching by teams of ministers. The level of emotionalism among the converted was exceptionally high; many fell to the ground crying and shrieking, and some exhibited what became known as "exercises"—singing, dancing, rolling on the ground, and even barking.[43] The fame of Cane Ridge spread, and similar, although much smaller, revivals spread through Kentucky and Tennessee and back to the more settled areas of the coastal South. Many evangelicals came to believe that society was on the doorstep of the millennium, a 1000-year reign of the godly that Christ Himself would usher in or, in another version, a 1000-year reign of the godly that would **precede** the appearance of Christ on earth. These two versions of millennial thinking became embedded in evangelical thought for the next 200 years, waxing and waning in influence and locked in a struggle for the hearts of the converted.[44]

The Great Revival extended the reach of evangelical Christianity in the South, but the region was **still** not the Bible Belt. By one estimate, evangelical denominations still had memberships of less than 17% of the white population and 8% of the black population by the early decades of the 1800s. Even by a less demanding measure, "adherence" (attending but not necessarily joining), only a little over 40% of the white population and 20% of the black population were adherents by 1813.[45] Christine Heyrman has made the persuasive and

---

42. *Ibid.*, 53–57; quote, p. 54.
43. *Ibid.*, 64–68.
44. *Ibid.*, 102–104.
45. Heyrman, *Southern Cross*, 23, 265.

quite commonsensical case that what held evangelical Protestantism back was its very radicalness, which necessarily put it outside the realm of the conventional and respectable. The arbiters of this realm ultimately were not the people who attended the churches in such numbers—young people, women, and slaves—but property-owning white males. As long as evangelical religion threatened what they held dear—male dominion over women and families; age over youth; and white over black—it would not dominate the social and religious life of the South. Evangelical religion would, over the course of the decades leading up to the Civil War, make accommodations to these values. In the process, it would become primarily a conservative religion rather than a radical one. By 1835, it would succeed in drawing in a majority of the white population as adherents and a significant minority of the black population.[46]

Opposition to slavery was the first radical practice of evangelical Christianity to be jettisoned. Even before 1800, evangelicals were becoming less and less strident in their attacks on slavery and less likely to suggest to slaveholding converts that they ought to free their slaves.[47] By the second decade of the nineteenth century, churchmen in the Methodist and Presbyterian churches were still questioning the morality of slavery but acknowledged that there was little that could be done about it. Even the willingness to question slavery would disappear as abolitionism gained momentum in the North and Southern defensiveness over the issue of mounted. Ironically, the Nat Turner slave revolt in Virginia in the early 1830s pushed white evangelical Christianity into an even firmer embrace of slavery. White evangelicals responded to this horrifying uprising that took the lives of sixty whites by working that much harder at converting slaves and bringing them into the churches. Historian Charles Irons has persuasively argued that the success of this effort—slaves joined white churches in droves—convinced whites that "slavery was central to God's plan for their region." Tiring of Northern criticism of slavery and buoyed by the success of this outreach effort with slaves, Southern Baptists and Methodists eventually split from their Northern brethren; Southern Methodists formed the Methodist Episcopal Church, South, and Baptists formed the Southern Baptist Convention. Presbyterians would also split into sectional branches. Southern evangelicals created a "slaveholding ethic" for their members and for Southern society at large. The foundation of this "ethic" was the quite conservative notion we have encountered earlier that humans are, far from being equal, inherently unequal and are ranked in a hierarchy of abilities, intelligence, and character. Evangelicals would come to accept the popular notion (among whites) that people of African descent were for genetic or cultural reasons (there was disagreement on this point) inferior and therefore at the bottom. Slavery

---

46. *Ibid.*, 265.
47. *Ibid.*, 155.

merely recognized this fact and provided a means by which the superior folk (whites) could guide, teach, and control the inferior folk.[48] In the words of historian Donald Mathews, "Slaveholding was seen as not merely a permissible act, but as a positive, Christian, responsibility."[49] Thus, within a few decades, evangelical churches had abandoned criticisms of slavery and had become supportive of the institution; ministers preached sermons urging slaves to "obey your masters" and masters to rule their slaves as good Christians should. After the Civil War, white evangelical churches fended off efforts by Northerners to reunite denominations that had split along sectional lines before the Civil War; Southern Methodists, for example, would not reunite with their Northern brothers and sisters until 1939.[50] Support for slavery would morph into support for segregation, and prominent church leaders would defend this institution well into the twentieth century.

As the two primary evangelical churches (Baptist and Methodist) matured, so, too, did the leadership of those churches. There was a strong push to provide worshipers with a better educated, professional clergy, and seminaries were established throughout the region. These colleges taught more than theology; they also tended to promote the idea that "social stability" was of paramount importance to the church. In short, the church's job was to support the social order, not attack it.[51] Too, ministers who earned an education were more "respectable" in a society where education generally was a badge of upper class status, and thus were more likely to be treated as equals by the planter class. Further, men who completed an education were, naturally enough, more likely to be men with a little age on them. As churches matured and raised more funds to support their ministers, men with families could now support themselves as ministers; upon the death of Bishop Asbury, who was a strong proponent of the unmarried itinerant minister, the Methodist General Conference began to actively encourage a married clergy by raising salaries for itinerant ministers and increasing the supplement paid to the wives of ministers. The youthful, unmarried radicals of the early days of the evangelical movement were being replaced by older family men.[52]

Evangelical churches also abandoned or muted practices that threatened patriarchy and kept many men outside the church doors warily eying what went on inside. Evangelical preachers were, after all, men and were not "content

48. Mathews, *Religion in the Old South*, 75, 160–173; Charles Irons, *The Origins of Proslavery Christianity: White and Black Evangelicals in Colonial and Antebellum Virginia* (Chapel Hill: University of North Carolina Press, 2008), 169, quote on page 209.

49. Mathews, *Religion in the Old South*, 174.

50. Daniel W. Stowell, *Rebuilding Zion: The Religious Reconstruction of the South, 1863–1877* (New York: Oxford University Press, 1998), 172–175.

51. Mathews, *Religion in the Old South*, 88–95.

52. Heyrman, *Southern Cross*, 115.

with a religion that was the faith of women, children, and slaves."[53] Evangelical
religion was reshaped to make it more appealing to men and to limit the role in
the church of women and slaves. Preaching for women obviously was out—
there had been some support for the practice in the Methodist Church—and
outspokenness or less than demure behavior in church was also out. Women
were increasingly perceived and portrayed by preachers and others as especially
pious and spiritual beings who served as a bulwark against the evil influences
of the world and "worldlings," but home and family was where women should
be exercising their religious influence. In the home, the wife and mother's duty
was "nurturing the family in Christian love."[54] While men had to deal with the
world, they could retreat to the home for spiritual rejuvenation. African Americans also receded into the background, at least in white churches. Early on,
black men had been permitted to serve as "preachers, deacons, and exhorters,"
although their authority was limited and they could not discipline white members. African-American believers were often portrayed by early evangelical
leaders as especially gifted spiritually.[55] By the mid-1800s, white church leaders
increasingly portrayed African Americans as not truly up to the task of delivering God's word and noteworthy primarily for their humble deference to
whites.[56] In fear of slave uprisings, many state legislatures in the South passed
laws restricting preaching by free blacks and slaves.[57]

While the role and behavior of women and slaves in churches were being
carefully circumscribed, the church's authority within the family was also
being restricted. Church interference in domestic relations became less common; the treatment of wives and children, the proper marriage partner for a
child, the treatment of slaves (also part of any slaveholder's household), were
more and more matters left to the male head of household. Only in the public
realm did the church take an interest in male behavior: public drunkenness,
fighting, cursing, and gambling were still vigorously condemned by preachers
and church disciplinary committees.[58] While evangelical preachers were celebrating the special spirituality of women, they also told them it was their
Christian duty to be submissive and obedient to their husbands.[59]

To appeal more to men, the images of the church and the minister were recast to appear more manly. While the meek man of God like Brother Waller
who was willing to turn his cheek to an affront might still be found, the new-
style preacher in the decades leading up to the Civil War tried to fashion him-

---

53. *Ibid.*, 193.
54. *Ibid.*, 194–205. Mathews, *Religion in the Old South*, 112–113. Quote on page 112.
55. Heyrman, *Southern Cross*, 217–219.
56. *Ibid.*, 223–225.
57. Genovese, *Roll, Jordan, Roll*, 257.
58. Heyrman, *Southern Cross*, 249–250.
59. Mathews, *Religion in the Old South*, 119.

self in the traditional mold of the Southern man, a man of honor willing to defend himself, what he believed, and those in his care. This was not an easy task; ministers were still expected not to fight or duel, and traditional male pursuits (drinking, gambling, and competition in business and recreation) were also forbidden. Sometimes preachers tried to establish that they had been men of honor before receiving the call; this was accomplished by the continuous telling of stories in sermons and memoirs of an earlier life when the horse race and the whiskey bottle were not unknown and when disputes were settled by flying fists. Increasingly, preaching the gospel was portrayed as a form of warfare, and the minister a spiritual warrior. Preaching, in short, was not for sissies.[60] Lillian Smith said of the revival preachers who visited her home in the early years of the twentieth century, "These were potent men—anyone is wrong to think otherwise—who used their potency in their ardent battle for souls."[61] And one thinks of the image of the modern televangelist, sweating, strutting, holding a Bible aloft and challenging the devil to combat, as a current example of this style. At camp meetings, young men were recruited and organized into military style companies to patrol the grounds and insure order, thus providing them with a special role in revival services. The day often started at camp meetings with the blowing of a bugle. Many evangelicals defended secession and supported the Confederate cause when war broke out in1861. The Presbyterian minister James Henley Thornwell, for example, argued that slavery was a "natural" institution that had arisen from the "operation of moral causes" and was recognized by the Constitution; it was the North that was abandoning the Constitution in its revolutionary zeal to end slavery and had to be resisted with force of arms if necessary.[62] As Christine Heyrman notes, all of this was designed to create for evangelical religion a better fit with the code of honor and the "male warrior culture" of the South.[63]

This is not to say that women receded into the church woodwork as efforts to attract more males accelerated. Despite these efforts, women seemed to fairly consistently outnumber men in most churches (and still do), and, by dint of sheer numbers, they would always be an important part of any church.[64] Too, they would find a variety of ways—church committees, prayer meetings, outreach to the poor and simply being the dependable mainstays of

---

60. Heyrman, *Southern Cross*, 233–234.

61. Lillian Smith, *Killers of a Dream* (Garden City, NY: Anchor Books, 1963; originally published, 1963), 87.

62. Heyrman, *Southern Cross* 242–243, 249. James Henley Thornwell, *The State of the Country: An Article Republished from The Southern Presbyterian Review* (1861; Chapel Hill: Documenting the American South, University of North Carolina, Chapel Hill, 1999), http://docsouth.unc.edu/imls/thornwell/thornwel.html.

63. Heyrman, *Southern Cross*, 242.

64. Mathews, *Religion in the Old South*, 102. On female predominance in contemporary religious groups and denominations in the U.S. see Barry A. Kosmin, Egon Mayer,

many a church—to exert an influence on the affairs of churches and denominations.[65] Nor did the evangelical churches abandon the strict code of behavior, a code that, truth be told, aimed to control unruly behavior more common to males than females. This behavior often caused a world of trouble for
wives and their children, and the church's role in curbing it surely was in the
best interests of women. Despite the concessions made to honor and patriarchy, evangelical religion was still, at bottom, antagonistic to the male world
of honor, competition, and the pursuit of pleasure, particularly drinking and
sex. Evangelical ministers urged churchgoers to be humble, passive, cooperative, and loving, and these characteristics were most associated with women
and children. In a sense, evangelical religion would pit the female world
against the male world.[66]

While pushing males to become more humble, meek, and sober—ambitious goals, to be sure—in most other respects evangelical churches had become vigorous defenders of the status quo in Southern society.[67] This conservatism would be a powerful force in the evangelical community for the next
hundred and fifty years, serving as a sea anchor holding back those who would
try to recover the social radicalism of the early churches. As evangelicalism became more conservative, its practices became, in turn, more "orderly," especially in white churches. The "warm, pathetic style" of preaching would never
go out of fashion, but the emotional displays of believers so common in the
early years of evangelicalism became less common by the 1830s.[68] Churches
that were well established and attended by prominent and affluent people
seemed to be the least emotional, and by the twentieth century, in the typical
first Baptist church or first Methodist church in most towns, college educated
ministers delivered thoughtful sermons in measured tones with only an occasional stirring in the congregation; only during revival might the emotionalism
of old resurface. Mainstream Presbyterianism seemed to move the furthest
away from its radical past and toward a staid respectability that dimmed its
evangelical fervor and the emotional level of its services and led it to largely
abandon the revival. While evangelical religion had made itself acceptable to
the leaders of the South, they and their families still were drawn in great numbers to the Episcopal Church, both before and after the Civil War.[69] For exam-

Ariela Keysar, *American Religious Identification Survey, 2001* (New York: The Graduate
Center of the City University of New York, 2001), 32.

65. Mathews, *Religion in the Old South*, 110–111.

66. Ted Owenby, *Subduing Satan: Religion, Recreation, and Manhood in the Rural
South, 1865–1920* (Chapel Hill, NC: University of North Carolina Press, 1990), 14–15.

67. Mathews, *Religion in the Old South*, 93.

68. *Ibid.,*124.

69. William Kauffman Scarborough, *Masters of the Big House: Elite Slaveholders of the
Mid-Nineteenth-Century South* (Baton Rouge: Louisiana State University Press, 2003), 53;
Edward Ayers, *The Promise of the New South: Life After Reconstruction* (New York and Ox-

ple, South Carolinian Thomas Chaplin, master of Tombee plantation, was a member of the Episcopal Church, although he sometimes attended a Baptist Church, and North Carolinian John Steele Henderson was an active member of the Episcopal Church for decades.[70] Class played an important role in influencing a believer's choice of denominations and congregations to join.

As evangelical religion matured, dissenters unhappy with a particular church or denomination arose, and another characteristic of Southern religion—sectarianism—became a permanent feature of the religious life of the South. Sectarianism is the splintering of religion into a variety of sects and independent churches. Tennessee, Western North Carolina, and frontier areas in the west were especially productive of new sects. People left churches when the preaching became too dry, the service too formal, or there was a difference of opinion in the congregation about a theological point or the proper approach to seeking converts. Baptists were especially prone to spinning off new churches and sects because Baptist churches were largely independent entities, and the theology (what people believed) was only generally sketched out, leading to frequent disputes about specific beliefs. New churches, new denominations, and independent churches too numerous to count were formed by people convinced that the "true" religion had been tampered with, abandoned, or seriously altered and had to be recovered. The Primitive Baptists and the Landmark Baptists were two such sects started before the war by folks who decried new-fangled beliefs, creeds, or practices that took folks away from the "pure" or true church of the apostles and the unadorned Bible. The founders of the Primitive Baptist Church believed that mainstream Baptists had moved away from the traditional Calvinist notion that God selects those who will be saved and toward the idea that salvation was a choice (an exercise in free will); Primitive Baptists believed that God selected the saved, and some eventually argued that God determined **everything** that happened down to a wrong turn taken on a country road; these folks became known as "absoluters." They also opposed the growing emphasis in the Baptist Church on missionary activity and on education for ministers and argued that the denomination was being taken over by ambitious men who were trying to usurp the autonomy of local churches. The Landmark Baptists organized a separate sect that maintained

---

ford: Oxford University Press, 1992), 167; Hollinger F. Barnard, *Outside the Magic Circle: The Autobiography of Virginia Foster Durr* (University, Alabama: University of Alabama Press, 1985), 45–46.

70. Theodore Rosengarten, *Tombee: Portrait of a Cotton Planter* with "The Plantation Journal of Thomas B. Chaplin (1822–1890)"(New York: William Morrow and Co., Inc., 1986), 145–146. On Henderson's religious life see, for example, Bessie Henderson to Mrs. S. J. Cain, 11 April 1876; Jas. H. Enniss to John Steele Henderson, 16 May 1876, John Steele Henderson Collection, Southern Historical Collection, University of North Carolina, Chapel Hill.

that the Baptist Church was the only true church, one that traced its origins in a direct line to John the Baptist, and that churches that did not baptize via immersion were not truly Christian churches.[71] The most significant creation of new churches before the Civil War took place in the slave quarters across the region, where African-American believers fashioned their own version of Christianity.

African-American Christianity

Slaveholders initially opposed the conversion of slaves to Christianity, fearing that Christianity would "spoil" the slaves by encouraging ideas of equality. It's not surprising that the Anglican Church, dominated as it was by slaveholding planters, did not aggressively seek converts in the slave quarters. What most slaves initially practiced was undoubtedly the religions or remnants of the religions they brought from West Africa.[72] The Great Awakening and the slow but steady rise of evangelical religion changed all this. Evangelicals' deep commitment to bringing all, slaves included, to Christ brought growing numbers of slaves into the new evangelical churches. By 1835 nearly 30% of the slave population, according to one estimate, was attending the churches; more than likely, the number of believers was greater than that.[73] Before the Civil War, the Christianity practiced by slave converts took place both in the formal setting of the churches and in a variety of other informal settings—brush arbors, barns, fields and the like—where preaching and instruction and prayer took place away from the watchful eyes of whites.

The churches that Christian slaves attended were usually white churches presided over by white ministers, although sometimes black members outnumbered white members. Blacks sat in balconies or in the back rows of these churches, and their roles in church affairs were limited, particularly as evangelical Christianity became more conservative. By the early decades of the 1800s, a number of black congregations across the region had established churches, generally in towns or cities, presided over by black ministers, some slave, some free. Most of these churches adhered to the Baptist faith, which granted individual churches great autonomy and was thus more tolerant of slave congregations.[74] In Savannah, Georgia, for example, the First African Church of Savan-

---

71. *Ibid.*, 126–128; 132–134. See also Richard T. Hughes, "Restorationist Christianity," Charles Reagan Wilson and William Ferris, eds., *Encyclopedia of Southern Culture* (Chapel Hill, NC: University of North Carolina Press, 1989), 1303–1306.

72. Eugene D. Genovese, *Roll, Jordan, Roll*, 185.

73. Christine Heyrman, *Southern Cross*, 265.

74. Albert J. Raboteau, *Slave Religion: The "Invisible Institution" in the Antebellum South* (Oxford: Oxford University Press, 1980), 137–138.

nah was organized in 1788 by Andrew Bryan, a slave. Bryan had begun preaching in the early 1780s after his conversion, and he and his followers began gathering on the outskirts of Savannah to worship. Local whites, concerned, apparently, about the growing incidence of slave runaways, had Bryan and some of his followers arrested on several occasions and at one point "about fifty were severely whipped." Bryan persevered and was finally permitted to hold services (perhaps because his tormenters were shamed by their treatment of him). Bryan's master gave the congregation the use of a barn, and a white Baptist minister who visited the congregation licensed Bryan to preach. After his master's death, Bryan became a free man and ultimately became a slave-owner himself. The church he started grew and by 1830 reported a membership of over 2400; it spawned several offshoot churches.[75] Churches such as the First African Church of Savannah were at best tolerated by whites; there was always the fear that unchaperoned slaves and free blacks might stir up a slave rebellion or encourage runaways, and this fear grew after the Nat Turner rebellion in the early 1830s. Various restrictions were applied to black churches: as we saw earlier, laws restricted preaching by free blacks and slaves, and denominational bodies attempted to establish white rule over black congregations. The First African Church of Savannah sat on land that was by law administered in perpetuity by white trustees, and ministers who served the church had to be approved by at least two white Baptist ministers. At one point the local Baptist Association attempted to, in effect, disestablish the church and place its congregation under the authority of a local white church.

Important as the black churches were, they were relatively small in number, and, as mentioned, primarily in towns. Of greater significance to rural slaves was the "secret" religion practiced in the informal settings of field, slave quarters, brush arbor, and barn. Here, slaves who attended white churches and those who did not could worship freely. These meetings were often held in secret because of white fears that any gathering of slaves might breed a rash of runaways or even a revolt. The meetings consisted of prayer, song, and preaching. As one former slave noted after the Civil War, "Meetings back there meant more than they do now. Then everybody's heart was in tune, and when they called on God they made heaven ring."[76]

In the black churches and in the brush arbors and barns where slaves met to worship, black Christianity coalesced.[77] In many ways it mirrored the Christianity of whites; after all, many blacks had been converted by white preachers, many worshiped with whites, and the churches that blacks established before and after the war were overwhelmingly evangelical (especially Baptist) just like

---

75. *Ibid.*, 141–142; 189–194.
76. *Ibid.*, 217.
77. Raboteau, *Slave Religion*, 212.

the whites'. Like white evangelical Christianity, black evangelical Christianity preached a strict moral code, followed informal worship practices, and stressed the importance of the conversion experience. True to the evangelical tradition, theirs was a religion of the heart, and church services and prayer meetings were often fraught with emotion. But much about black Christianity was different; while it coexisted with and overlapped white Christianity, it reflected the special needs of a people whose lives were very different than whites, and it drew on cultural traditions rooted in the lost homelands of West Africa. Although people in slavery were not free to move about, their unique form of Christianity spread throughout the South, nonetheless; for example, "Hark From the Tomb," a spiritual sung at slave funerals, could be heard in several variations throughout the region.[78]

People in slavery did not accept the morality of slavery and came to identify themselves with the Old Testament children of Israel—enslaved, oppressed, but ultimately to be set free, in this world or the other, by the hand of God. They were the chosen people; whites, on the other hand, would do well to tremble on judgment day given their sins.[79] The sense of the sinful nature of humans and the guilt that went with this sinfulness pervaded white evangelical Christianity; this sense was not as evident in black Christianity. For example, the dominant themes in the spirituals, the religious music of black Christianity, were "change, transcendence, ultimate justice, and personal worth"; these themes uplifted a downtrodden people who did not need reminding that life was harsh and people often perverse.[80] Nor did black Christianity completely embrace the dichotomy in white Christianity of a corrupt material world and a perfect heaven; black Christianity also drew on the West African traditional worldview which had God, nature, and humans tied together in a seamless whole.[81] Black Christianity was influenced by other West African cultural traditions; the spirituals drew on West African musical forms, and African-American preachers developed a unique style of preaching—the call and response—that had its roots in West Africa. This style established a dialogue between minister and congregation; the preacher would deliver a few sentences or an extended thought and solicit a response for the congregation ("Can I hear an Amen"?), and the congregation would respond. If the response was weak or hesitant, the minister might go back over the point he wished to make. Ministers schooled in this style became highly skilled preachers and orators, and whites would frequently flock to hear certain black ministers.[82] Some of the

78. Genovese, *Roll, Jordan, Roll,* 199.

79. Lawrence W. Levine, *Black Culture and Black Consciousness: Afro-American Folk thought From Slavery to Freedom* (Oxford: Oxford University Press, 1977), 33–35, 50–51.

80. *Ibid.,* 39. See also Eugene Genovese, *Roll, Jordan, Roll,* 246–247.

81. Levine, *Black Culture and Black Consciousness,* 32.

82. Raboteau, *Slave Religion,* 73–74, 243–265; Genovese, *Roll, Jordan, Roll,* 271.

great modern orators—Martin Luther King, Jr., for example—were schooled in this oratorical tradition, which continued to flourish after the end of slavery. Hymns were often "lined" out, another style derived from traditional West African cultures. In lining, a line would be sung by a lead singer, and the congregation would repeat the same line.[83] The "ring shout" was a common form of worship that persisted into the twentieth century. Worshipers gathered in a circle and walked slowly around, swaying, chanting, clapping, and singing in a rising level of excitement.[84] As former slave Silvia King told an interviewer in the 1930s,

> De black folks gits off down in de bottom and shouts and sings and prays. Dey gits in de ring dance. It am jes' a kind of shuffle, den it git faster and faster and dey gits warmed up and moans and shouts and claps and dances. Some gits 'xhausted and drops out and de ring gits closer. Sometimes dey sings and shouts all night, but come break of day, de nigger got to git to he cabin. Old Marse got to tell dem de tasks of de day.[85]

Certain burial customs—placing personal objects of the deceased on the grave and burying the body along an east/west axis—were other examples of the persistence of West African traditions.[86] The spiritual (from which would evolve gospel music), the call and response preaching style, and possibly even the joyful exuberance of black worshipers, which many observers, black and white, felt was more pronounced than that exhibited by white worshipers, would all exert an influence on white churches and white Christians. Black Christianity and white were different, but they were on the same street, and that street went both ways.

While Christianity made deeper and deeper inroads in both the black and white communities in the South, beliefs in magic, conjuring (the working of spells), and healing with herbs and roots also were quite common.[87] For blacks, these beliefs were rooted in the religions and folk traditions of West Africa and were called hoodoo, voodoo, or root working. In this belief system, illness, unhappiness, and misfortune were all ascribed to an imbalance in one's relationship with the rest of creation or to the effects of a spell or hex. The sufferer went to a root (or voodoo or hoodoo) doctor for a cure. Root doctors often treated "natural" ailments with remedies made from such plants as mint,

---

83. Levine, *Black Culture and Black Consciousness*, 33.

84. *Ibid.*, 37–38, 165–166.

85. Silvia King interview, *Born in Slavery: Slave Narratives from the Federal Writers' Project, 1936–1938* (Washington: Library of Congress, Manuscript Division, 2001), http://memory.loc.gov/ammem/snhtml/snhome.html.

86. Genovese, *Roll, Jordan, Roll*, 198–200; Robert Farris Thompson, *Flash of the Spirit: Afro-American Art & Philosophy* (New York: Vintage Books, 1984), 132–142.

87. Levine, *Black Culture and Black Consciousness*, 59–60.

jimson weed, or milkweed root, while other ills were treated with rituals involving incantations and concoctions made from powdered roots, lizards and so forth. A believer might also go to the root doctor for a spell to attract a love interest, get something he wanted, or hurt an enemy.[88] Some of the herbs used by root doctors did have medicinal properties; many of the others did not, but given the psychosomatic origins of many illnesses, the soothing tea or protective mojo (an amulet often worn around the neck to ward off spells) prescribed by the doctor probably was just as effective in relieving the anxieties of some believers as any modern nostrum proscribed by an M.D. Hoodoo in the American South was not anti-Christian or even distinct from Christianity. In fact, those who claimed to have the power to work spells were sometimes referred to as "Reverend," "Brother," or "Sister," and Christian symbols and prayers were sometimes incorporated into the spells. Hoodoo was most well developed in Louisiana and the Gulf South where it approached, as it did in Haiti, the status of a religion, but it was practiced all over the South, and root doctors and their clients may still be found throughout the region.[89]

After the Civil War, African Americans in the South left the white churches en masse and formed thousands of new churches. Most of these churches were either Baptist or Methodist, but there was also a sprinkling of Presbyterian churches. New national denominations such as the African Methodist Episcopal Church and the National Baptist Convention were also established. White church leaders were, by turns, surprised by this, devastated and angered; all the effort they had expended before the war at creating biracial Christian communities now seemed so pointless and unappreciated as blacks rejected white religious guidance and authority and charted their own course. Whites would chart their own course in the realm of organized religion too, and it would not include blacks. By the early years of the twentieth century, African-American church membership stood at 3.6 million, nearly all of whom were members of evangelical churches, primarily Baptist.[90] While membership numbers for churches are nearly always inflated, it would not be an exaggeration to say that evangelical religion had established dominance in the black community as total and complete as its dominance in the white community.

---

88. *Ibid.*, 61–67; Raboteau, *Slave Religion, 275–288;* Silvia King interview, *Born in Slavery;* Marion Johnson, interview by Carol Graham, *Born in Slavery: Slave Narratives from the Federal Writers' Project, 1936–1938* (Washington: Library of Congress, Manuscript Division, 2001), http://memory.loc.gov/ammem/snhtml/snhome.html.

89. Harvey, *Freedom's Coming,* 120–123; Holly Matthews, "Doctors and Root Doctors: Patients Who Use Both," in James Kirkland, Holly Matthews, C.W. Sullivan III, and Karen Baldwin, eds., *Herbal and Magical Medicine: Traditional Healing Today* (Durham, NC: Duke University Press, 1992), 68–98.

90. Paul Harvey, *Freedom's Coming: Religious Culture and the Shaping of the South from the Civil War through the Civil Rights Era* (Chapel Hill, NC: The University of North Carolina Press, 2005), 8; Irons, *The Origins of Proslavery Christianity,* 258–259.

Antioch Missionary Baptist Church was one such church formed after the Civil War. It began, according to oral tradition, as a gathering of worshipers meeting in a brush arbor not far from the current location of the church in an area known originally as Howell Town and later called Antioch on the outskirts of Oxford, North Carolina. Howell Town was a small rural community of free blacks before the Civil War that got its name from a free black family that owned land in the area. Following the war, other black families acquired land in the community, and to this day Antioch is a predominately black community. No one knows for sure when the gathering of worshippers became a formal church. What is known is that in 1876 a parcel of land was acquired, and a wood frame building was erected to house the church. The church had a bell tower "which would ring to call the worshippers to service, and was used to ring out the old year and ring in the New Year." Baptisms were performed in a "tributary of Fishing Creek," a small stream that flowed near the church.[91]

Churches like Antioch became the centers of black communities across the South and offered worshipers a haven in an often dangerous and capricious world dominated by whites. The conservatism of Southern evangelical religion and its focus on individual salvation was tempered in the black churches by a strong commitment to social justice largely absent in the white churches. Once segregation was established and blacks lost their political leaders, the ministers (with local businessmen and landowners) became, in effect, the political representatives of the black community. The black minister served a special role as mediator between his flock and the white world, a role that required the skills of a diplomat. When a church member was in trouble with the law, the minister might intercede; when white officials wished to communicate something to the local black community, they went to the ministers. To perform this role, ministers had to keep on good terms with whites, and for this reason many were initially wary of getting directly involved with the Civil Rights movement after World War II.

The black church created after emancipation was built on the religious foundation laid down before the Civil War. Praise-filled worship services, the call and response preaching style, the unique musical heritage rooted in West African traditions, all of these and more persisted. But the participatory style of worship practiced in the brush arbor inevitably gave way to a more formal style of worship in many churches, and what was once practiced secretly now was often observed by whites and compared by both black and white to white religious practices. Notions of propriety, influenced by white perceptions and the desire of black leaders to "uplift" the race, pushed black churches in a less emotional direction. As historian Jerma Jackson has noted, for many ministers

---

91. Barnetta McGhee White, "History of Antioch Baptist Church, Granville, County, North Carolina," 1990.

Jack Delano

Figure 5.1   Singing in church, Greene County, Georgia

and laymen committed to the "uplift" mission, "'emotional religion' amounted to nothing more than ignorance."[92] The ring shout, for example, was strongly discouraged by some ministers; as one minister told a group of worshipers, "it was a heathenish way to worship and disgraceful to themselves, the race, and the Christian name."[93] Baptist church leaders pushed churches to organize church choirs, use hymnbooks, and abandon the older spontaneous and participatory musical styles of the slavery era. While the Fisk Jubilee Singers sang spirituals and celebrated them as a unique and special art form, the group sang "Europeanized" versions of the songs, and this style became quite popular in many black churches.[94] Some of these spirituals eventually were included in hymnals used in white churches, another indication of the constant interaction between white and black religious practices.

The move to root emotional and participatory displays out of black Christianity was especially pronounced in churches that catered to more affluent and influential congregations. Ralph Abernathy told a young Martin Luther King, Jr., in the mid-1950s that at his church (First Baptist Church of Montgomery, Alabama), "the preacher preaches and the congregation listens" with few if any comments coming from the congregation; Abernathy jokingly told King that at

92. Jerma Jackson, *Singing in my Soul: Black Gospel Music in a Secular Age* (Chapel Hill and London: University of North Carolina Press, 2004), 12.

93. Levine, *Black Culture and Black Consciousness*, 165.

94. *Ibid.*, 166–167; Jackson, *Singing in My Soul*, 12–15.

the even more aristocratically inclined Dexter Avenue Baptist Church where King was headed, "if you just have to mention Jesus, they would like you to do it just as quietly and briefly as possible."[95] But while some black Baptist and Methodist churches were becoming more formal and less emotional, others catering to rural and less affluent congregations traveled only a short way down that path, and independent churches and the sanctified church, which emerged around the turn of the twentieth century, offered African-American believers other options for spirit-filled, emotional religion and song.

The Sanctified Church

Pentecostal and Holiness denominations, sometimes referred to as the "sanctified church," were the last major component of the shared religion of the South to develop. The sanctified church was the product of a two successive movements; the first, the Holiness movement, arose within the Methodist Church in the North before the Civil War and swept into the South in the decades after the war. The Holiness movement harked back to the Great Awakening; Holiness preachers preached sermons that brought tears to the eyes of worshipers and brought many to their knees and criticized established churches for the dry formality of their services. Holiness believers expected conversion to be followed by the infusion of the Holy Spirit into the body and soul of the new convert; this infusion was called the "second blessing" or "sanctification." Believers were cleansed of sin and were ready to follow a Christian life. The Holiness movement appealed to less affluent whites and blacks and found many followers in established churches, particularly the Methodist and Baptist churches. Leaders of these denominations were often critical of the movement, resulting in bitter divisions within some churches and ultimately the formation of new sects by Holiness believers such as the Fire-Baptized Holiness Church.[96]

Pentecostalism emerged in the early twentieth century as a sort of expanded version of the Holiness movement; it would ultimately absorb much of the movement and today we often speak of the two as Pentecostal/Holiness or, as noted earlier, the sanctified church. Like the Holiness movement from which it flowed, Pentecostalism emphasized a church service full of emotional fervor, but, as with the Holiness Church, it was more than simple emotion that worshipers were expressing. The Holy Spirit was moving amongst them and joining with them. The Rev. R. W. Stallings, a Church of God minister, recalled his conversion when he was 16:

---

95. Taylor Branch, *Parting the Waters: America in the King Years, 1954–1963* (New York: Touchstone Book, 1988), 107.
96. Harvey, *Freedom's Coming*, 126–128.

Durin' the next few days and weeks I talked to many of those in the church. They were happy for me and encouraged me in my new-found happiness. Though I was just a young boy of sixteen they treated me as a brother and made me appreciate the joys that were to be had in Christian fellowship. Every night I attended the services, en-joyin' more and more the new-found life. But, as I listened to the older ones speak of a further blessin', that of the Holy Ghost, of sanc-tification, I was interested in receiving that, too. Others not satisfied with mere conversion were nightly spendin' hours on their knees prayin' for sanctification, and I began, too, to ask the Lord for the fur-ther blessin'. I prayed and praised Him for days and nights, trustin' and listenin' for His voice, and at last it came. What it was? I don't know how to tell, except that—well, I just gave my whole self away to the Lord and was submissive to His every impulse and let Him have His way.[97]

Speaking in tongues was recognized as a sign of spirit possession and played an important role in the Pentecostal service. It became known as the "third bless-ing." Like Christ's disciples at the Pentecost, believers filled with the spirit would begin speaking "unknown" languages which were often words or sounds that were not recognizably the English language or any known language but were considered to be a language inspired by God.

Pentecostalism emerged as a full-fledged movement in 1906 at a revival in, of all places, Los Angeles at the Azusa Street Mission. William J. Seymour, an African American from Louisiana, conducted the services and was assisted by Sister Lucy Farrow, a charismatic woman who played the piano and spoke in tongues. The audience was a mixed one with whites, blacks, Mexicans, and Asians, although early on, blacks apparently predominated. This interracialism was fairly typical of the early years of both the Holiness and Pentecostal move-ments. The revival continued week after week, and word of it spread in the Holiness community across the country. Several white Holiness ministers from the South traveled west to take part in the revival; one of them, North Carolin-ian Gaston B. Cashwell, attended a service and noted later, "before I knew it, I began to speak in tongues and praise God." Cashwell returned home and or-ganized revival services in a rented tobacco warehouse in Dunn where believers were, Cashwell later related, "speaking in tongues, singing in tongues, writing in tongues, leaping, dancing, and praising God."[98] The Dunn revival served as an incubator for the growth of Pentecostalism in North Carolina and elsewhere

97. "Shouting from Heaven," an interview with the Rev. W. M. Stallings by Robert V. Williams, *American Life Histories: Manuscripts from the Federal Writers' Project, 1936–1940*(Washington: Library of Congress, Manuscript Division, 1998), http://mem-ory.loc.gov/ammem/wpaintro/wpahome.html.

98. Harvey, *Freedom's Coming*, 135.

in the Southeast, and the movement grew rapidly in the early decades of the twentieth century in rural areas and made great inroads in the mill towns of the region in the 1920s.[99] In South Henderson, a mill community built around the Harriet mill on the outskirts of Henderson, North Carolina, the South Henderson Pentecostal Holiness Church was established in June of 1923 following a five-month long tent revival. The church first met in an old house, and then members built a small sanctuary near the mill.[100]

While the Pentecostal Holiness movement would always be marked by a degree of interracial cooperation, particularly in revivals and tent meetings, by the early years of the 1900s, the growing number of churches and the new denominations that were established were segregated along racial lines. Whites formed the Pentecostal Holiness Church, the Assemblies of God, the Church of God, and the Church of God of Prophecy, a church formed when the Church of God was split by charges that its founder had mismanaged church funds. A plethora of smaller sects, many often arising over a dispute within an established denomination like the one that gave rise to the Church of God of Prophecy, also sprang up. Blacks organized the Church of God in Christ and a number of smaller sects.[101]

The sanctified church had arisen during a particularly troubled and stressful time in the South. Sharecropping and rural poverty were growing at an alarming rate; hundreds of thousands of rural people fled the poverty of the countryside and poured into the textile mills and mill towns popping up all over the piedmont South; and bitter political and racial strife characterized much of this period. The message of Pentecostalism and the Holiness movement was that the world was a corrupt and sinful place, and true believers needed to accept this reality and at the same time to keep as far away from the world's corruption as possible. For less affluent whites and blacks struggling to survive as sharecroppers, small farmers, and millworkers, this message was comforting, and the church offered believers a refuge where all were accepted. The Reverend Stallings's family had attended a Baptist church, but when they moved to Gastonia (a milltown in North Carolina), they felt ill at ease in the town Baptist church "with everybody dressed up in store-bought clothes" and began to attend the Church of God following a tent revival sponsored by that church.[102] Ironically, Pentecostal/Holiness believers were quite practical in using what the world could offer for religious purposes; they were quite open to using modern technology to promote their religion — newspapers, and later radio and televi-

---

99. Hall et al., *Like a Family*, 179, 287.
100. See the South Henderson Pentecostal Holiness Church website at http://www.sh phc.org/AboutUs.htm#History (accessed 4/20/06).
101. Harvey, *Freedom's Coming*, 136–147.
102. Shouting from Heaven," an interview with the Rev. W. M. Stallings by Robert V. Williams, *American Life Histories*.

sion—and embraced popular music (when accompanied by the proper religious messages, of course) played on a variety of musical instruments for their church services. One denomination even chose a popular country gospel song, "Great Speckled Bird," as its anthem, and the gospel music that was created in the Church of God in Christ had much in common with the Blues. Bluesman T-Bone Walker claimed to have "first heard boogie-woogie piano playing in the sanctified church in his Texas hometown."[103] But while making use of what the world offered to save souls, Pentecostal/Holiness believers had a decidedly "otherworldly" orientation. Indeed, they expected the imminent end of this corrupt world; the millennium would be ushered in by Christ who would return and save his flock (this became known as "the rapture"). The world would pass through a period of tribulation after which a massive battle between good and evil—Armageddon—would cleanse the earth of evil. When this would occur was and still is debated, and believers constantly looked for signs that the "end-times" were about to occur.[104] One contemporary Web site even maintains a "Rapture Index," which describes itself as the "prophetic speedometer of end-time activity."[105] Given the presence here and now of the Holy Spirit and the expectation that the end of the world was about to occur, believers needed to live impeccable lives to be ready when called by Christ. Pentecostal and Holiness churches developed a strict code of morals that prohibited drinking, dancing, and wearing improper clothing, not to mention dwelling on the mundane concerns of non-believers. Even today, in some churches, women are prohibited from wearing make-up, pants, or shorts.

The sanctified church accepts the Bible as literally true and rejects the notion that it must be "interpreted." For the true believer guided by the Holy Spirit, the meaning is self-evident. Ministers, therefore, are people invested with the Spirit and called to preach and do not require much training; even today, a relatively brief stint at a Bible college is all many have in the way of formal preparation for the ministry. Paul's pronouncements about the proper role of men and women in the church are taken very seriously, and generally men are church leaders and ministers, although there are exceptions to this "rule." In the African American Pentecostal community, women actually created several small sects, and today sometimes serve as ministers of churches in these sects or of independent churches.[106] Because church members understand the Bible literally, they believe that what happened in biblical times is still happening. Thus modern Christians can speak in "foreign" tongues and heal the sick just like the apostles did. An extreme application of this belief is the practice of snake-handling.

---

103. Jackson, *Singing in My Soul*, 23.
104. Harvey, *Freedom's Coming*, 138–139, 142.
105. See the "Rapture Ready" Web site at http://www.raptureready.com/rap2.html.
106. Harvey, *Freedom's Coming*, 147.

Snake handling began around 1910 in the Grasshopper Valley in East Tennessee, and eventually spread to other areas in the Southern Appalachian Mountains in Virginia, West Virginia, North Carolina, and Georgia and to some urban areas where people from the mountains later settled. George Went Hensley is often credited with starting the practice. Hensley began as a Baptist but switched to the Pentecostal Holiness Church. He became a preacher even though he was illiterate; he would have his wife read Bible passages during church services. He spoke in tongues, healed the sick, and drove demons out of the possessed. One day he climbed White Oak Mountain to pray, saw a timber rattler, asked God to "anoint" him with "the power," and on that day he picked up his first poisonous snake.[107] Snake handling is generally practiced in white independent Pentecostal Holiness churches, but it is a practice that few Pentecostal Holiness churches advocate or permit. It is based on biblical texts describing God's followers taking up poisonous serpents and swallowing poison. Snake handlers pray for an "anointing" of the Holy Ghost and believe if they are in the spirit, they will not be harmed. Ministers and some church members at the church services pick up poisonous snakes like Hensley did on White Oak Mountain (usually rattlesnakes or copperheads), sometimes draping the snakes around their necks. Some believers drink strychnine during services or run their hands through fire. Snake handlers **are** bitten; Hensley was said to have been bitten over 400 times during his career. Fatal bites are rare but do periodically occur, and Hensley himself died "vomiting blood" following a bite.[108] Snake handling at church services continues in the southern Appalachians and here and there, although it is illegal.

Snake handling strikes many as bizarre and frightening and far removed from what most Americans consider a religious activity. But in many respects it reflects, at the extreme edge to be sure, evangelical religion's emphasis on the personal encounter with the Almighty. This encounter, by its nature, is a moving beyond the everyday; the ecstasy experienced by some believers is often taken as a sign that God has touched them. Contemporary journalist Dennis Covington describes one service he attended at a small mountain church that illustrates the ecstatic orientation of this sect; the service began with preaching, followed by music and then more preaching and more music; finally a member began to dance, "stomping his feet and tossing his head," and a woman came forward, dancing, opened the box containing the snakes, "took out a two-and-a-half-foot-long canebrake rattlesnake and held it up with both hands. Then she turned a slow circle with the snake outstretched, her face transfigured by something like pain or remorse." Covington notes that for the person in a state

---

107. Steven Michael Kane, "Snake Handlers of Southern Appalachia" (Unpublished Ph.D. dissertation, Princeton University, 1979), 31–35.

108. Dennis Covington, *Salvation on Sand Mountain: Snake Handling and Redemption in Southern Appalachia* (Reading, PA: Addison-Wesley Publishing Co., 1995), 148.

of religious ecstasy, "the first thing that goes is self" as the internal dialogue that constantly goes on in our heads stops, and all of one's being focuses on something outside the self. Snake handlers achieve this state by ignoring the self's most important drive—self-preservation—and literally put their very lives in the hands of their God.[109]

The "Shared" Religion of the South

The beliefs and practices of evangelical Protestantism—Baptist, Methodist, Pentecostal Holiness, and, to a degree, Presbyterian churches—provided the framework for the shared religion of the South. In most of the South for over a century, the great majority of folks attended or at least subscribed to the beliefs of an evangelical Protestant church, particularly the Baptist Church; even today, Baptists are the major religious group in the overwhelming majority of Southern counties. While differences amongst the sects, denominations, and independent churches abounded, important differences separated black and white Christians, and the churches themselves were racially segregated until relatively recently, certain core beliefs and practices have been shared by all.[110] It is not, therefore, surprising that religion and evangelical Protestantism have been virtually synonymous in the minds of most Southerners, nor is it surprising that the shared beliefs of these churches have had such a profound influence on Southern culture in general. This is what sets the South apart from most of the rest of the nation. Certainly evangelical Christianity has been influential outside the region; Methodism, for example, truly is a national church with a large number of congregations scattered across the entire country. But nowhere else, with the exception of parts of the Midwest, has evangelical Protestant Christianity been so dominant as it has been in the South.

Not **every** Southerner has adhered to these beliefs and practices; most towns in the southeast had at least one Episcopal Church, and larger towns and cities and even a few small towns had a Catholic church and a Jewish synagogue. Lutheran congregations could be found here and there; a sprinkling of churches of newer denominations were established such as the Church of Jesus Christ of Latter Day Saints and Jehovah Witnesses. The Catholic Church has

109. *Ibid.*, 99.
110. Much of this section is based on Sam Hill's excellent *Southern Churches in Crisis Revisited* (Tuscaloosa, AL and London: University of Alabama Press, 1999). See especially pp. 21–23; 36; 76–90; 103; "Religious Congregations and Membership in the United States, 2000," Glenmary Research Center, http://www.valpo.edu/geomet/pics/geo200/religion/church_bodies.gif; Charles Reagan Wilson, *Judgment and Grace in Dixie: Southern Faiths from Faulkner to Elvis* (Athens and London: University of Georgia Press, 1995), 7–13.

been locally prominent in portions of Texas, Florida, Maryland, Kentucky and especially Louisiana. In Louisiana, Catholicism played a major role in the religious life of New Orleans and much of the southern part of the state from the founding of the colony by the French into the present. As one history of the state notes of the colonial era, even though many of the settlers weren't regular church-goers, Catholicism infused the colony; for example, church holy days were widely observed as well as the festival before Lent known as Mardi Gras. An influx of Catholic settlers from Canada in the mid 1700s—the Acadians—settled throughout southern Louisiana and spread the reach of the church even further. Protestant settlers poured into the region, especially northern Louisiana, after the colony was acquired by the United States in the Louisiana Purchase. These settlers looked askance at the Catholic sensibilities of New Orleans but were not able to impose the more austere values of evangelical Protestantism on the city or much of southern Louisiana.[111] But for most Catholics and other religious minorities in the South, especially in the rural areas, their churches floated like driftwood in an evangelical Protestant sea, their presence barely registering in the public consciousness, their beliefs little understood. As one Alabama Catholic noted, "we were a group apart." [112]

Of the shared beliefs and practices of the Southern evangelical Protestantism that was so dominant in the region, first and foremost is the heavy focus on individual salvation. The old Calvinist notion of God selecting those He will save, a common belief during the early phase of evangelicalism, has been replaced for most evangelicals by the notion that God extends His grace to all, and it is up to the individual to "accept" salvation. Individuals must be "born again"—an event that can take place in early adolescence or at any time thereafter in a person's life. At this time the individual admits to sin, makes a leap of faith in believing that Jesus Christ can remove his/her sins, and makes a conscious dedication (or rededication) of his/her life to God. Only the individual him/herself can make the decision to be born again, and the only qualification is faith. The conversion experience could be a quiet coming to terms with God or quite dramatic, like the conversions during the revivals of the Awakenings discussed earlier. Some believers have described the experience as the "death" of the old self. As one recalled,

111. Bennett H. Wall, et al., *Louisiana: A History* (Wheeling, Illinois: Harlan Davidson, Inc., 2008), 32–35, 65, 89, 166, 168; Randall M. Miller, "A Church in Cultural Captivity: Some Speculations on Catholic Identity," in Randall M. Miller and Jon L. Wakelyn, *Catholics in the Old South* (Macon, Georgia: Mercer University Press, 1983), 29–33, 44, 52.

112. Miller, "A Church in Cultural Captivity: Some Speculations on Catholic Identity," 45, 52; Andrew S. Moore, *The South's Tolerable Alien: Roman Catholics in Alabama and Georgia, 1945–1970* (Baton Rouge, Louisiana: Louisiana State University Press, 2007), quotes, 38.

When God struck me dead with His power, I was living on 14th Avenue. It was the year of the Centennial. I was in my house alone and I declare unto you when His power struck me I died. I fell on the floor flat on my back. I could neither speak nor move for my tongue stuck to the roof of my mouth. My jaws were locked and my limbs were stiff.[113]

This focus on the individual salvation has resulted in a religion that could be profoundly liberating for the "saved" person, but it also has exerted a profoundly conservative influence on evangelical churches as social institutions which, in turn, has had a powerful influence on the culture. The terrible poverty of the South, the treatment of slaves, sharecroppers or millworkers, the relationship between white and black and rich and poor were, for many evangelicals, not issues the churches should address except on an individual basis. If there was racial strife or the working conditions of the mill workers were a cause of shame, bringing more souls to Christ was the solution. Even churches that catered to the less affluent did not challenge the ways of the world except in matters of personal morality. Mill churches, for example, were often bankrolled by mill managers up until the middle of the twentieth century, and, according to one historian writing in the early 1940s about a milltown near Charlotte, North Carolina, "churches and ministers have adapted themselves to the situation and serve as an arm of the employers in control of the mill villages."[114]

A second major tenet of this mainstream Southern religion is the literal or near-literal interpretation of the Bible and the belief that the Bible is the basis for all Christian thought and action. Most Southern churches use the Bible exclusively and have eschewed prayer books, creeds, and doctrines; sermons are based directly on biblical texts. Southerners today often support their political and legal viewpoints on issues such as abortion, gay rights, and women's rights by citing biblical passages. There is still controversy surrounding the issue of teaching evolution in schools because it contradicts the literal interpretation of the accounts of creation found in Genesis. This strict interpretation goes hand in hand with strict morality. A good Christian is one who does not drink, take the Lord's name in vain, gamble, dance, associate with people who don't fear the Lord, or engage in sexual activity outside of marriage. Sexuality itself is viewed with some degree of suspicion (undoubtedly a holdover of old Victorian ideas), and even today in some Southern states, laws still exist that ban specific sexual practices in any relationship. A good Christian attends church at least once a week, dresses and behaves in gender-appropriate ways, is loyal to his/her family, is a good neighbor, and presents a model of Christian living to others.

---

113. Clifton H. Johnson, ed., *God Struck Me Dead: Religious Conversion Experiences and Autobiographies of Ex-Slaves* (Philadelphia, PA: Pilgrim Press, 1969), 20.

114. Liston Pope, *Millhands and Preachers: A Study of Gastonia* (New Haven and London: Yale University Press, 1942), 161.

The religious practices of the typical Southern church are informal and non-liturgical (there are few rituals that are repeated at every service). The service centers on a long sermon—anywhere from 20 minutes to three hours—bracketed by extemporaneous prayers by the preacher and hymns sung by the congregation and/or the choir (more contemporary music is now favored in some churches). Communion generally occurs once a month or once a quarter. The communion "wine" in the typical church is usually grape juice served in plastic or glass cups, and it and the bread are usually passed among worshipers in their pews. The practice is "in memory" of the Last Supper rather than a sacred ritual performed by a priest as in the Episcopal, Catholic and other liturgical churches where communion is typically observed more frequently, if not every week. Evangelical ministers generally have not worn vestments (robes, clerical collars, etc.), although again, in the larger, older churches, ministers often will wear robes. Services often include or end with "altar call," a time when sinners are invited to come forward to repent and be saved or to re-commit themselves to Christ. It is believed that each individual has equal access to God, so the minister, better known as the preacher because of his primary role, does not listen to confession or serve in any way as an intermediary (go-between) between members of the congregation and God. Depending on the church, the preacher may or may not be required to have attended seminary. Presbyterian and Methodist churches, like the liturgical churches, typically require formal education for their clergy, as do the larger Baptist churches, particularly those in the cities and towns. There are a number of distinguished Presbyterian, Baptist, and Methodist colleges in the South, many of them with seminaries; however, education for preachers tends to depend on the social class of the church with churches catering to middle and upper class congregations (often the *first* Baptist or Methodist church in town) generally favoring ministers with college and seminary degrees. Whether he has a degree or not, for the minister the most important qualifications in leading a church are visible faith and a commitment to his "call." And it's important to note that although preachers may not possess a traditional college and seminary education, and have no powers greater than the members of the congregation, they are still revered in the Southern community. The church buildings, like the services, are typically informal and unadorned, although large congregations in cities and towns, particularly those catering to a more affluent membership, have built imposing edifices with stained glass windows and ornate appointments inside. Even these churches, however, stop short of what one finds in a typical Catholic or Episcopal Church.

The belief that a good Christian should be evangelical and the predominance of the shared religion combine to make religion a public affair. Testifying, or sharing one's religious experience with others, can be a quiet and private practice, but is also practiced very publicly by some. It is a basic part of evangelism. Testifying is most popular at revivals, and involves emotional accounts of a person's life before and after he/she was "saved." Some feel called upon to testify outside of the church, to tell their story to any stranger whom they perceive as lacking God in his/her life. At its most extreme, testifying is expressed by people carrying signs, shouting and preaching in the streets, exhorting sinners to be saved, or in one case, making a public journey down U.S. Highway 1 dragging a large wooden cross. A more common way to share religion is to welcome a newcomer to the area by inviting that person to one's church; religious tracts are issued by many churches, and these may be handed out individually or placed in strategic locations—such as in restrooms in schools or bus stations. Ceremonial occasions—holiday luncheons at work, ball games, graduations and virtually any other public gathering—generally have started with a prayer that often moved well beyond the giving of thanks and into the territory of evangelism. And the prayer is a Baptist or Methodist prayer unlike the kinds of prayers one hears in a Catholic or Episcopal church or certainly a Jewish synagogue. Few have minded because, again, most folks identified with an evangelical church (even if they rarely or ever attended).

Revivalism has been a defining feature of the shared religion of the South, and many Baptist and Methodist and Pentecostal churches routinely scheduled revivals each year, often in the late summer. Traveling independent revivalists organized their own revivals or appeared at the invitation of a church or several churches. In times of stress and rapid change in the region, revival activity has often been at a heightened level; a revival that might normally attract several hundred might attract several thousand, and the number of revivals might go up dramatically. The first and second Great Awakenings are examples of "eras" of revivalism, and the decades bracketing the turn of the twentieth century were another major era of revivalism. During this turn-of-the-century revival era, preachers traversed the region and the nation stressing the theme of repentance, and several of these ministers became regionally and nationally famous. Sam Jones, a prominent Southern Methodist evangelist, saved thousands of souls with his witty, ungrammatical, "plain-folks" sermons. In a crusade he launched in Atlanta in 1896, an estimated 150,000 people came to hear sermons in which he denounced "jackasses" in the state legislature and high-living "dudes" and "dudines." In Jones's famous "for men only" sermon, which he first delivered at a revival service in Memphis, he warned men to steer clear of drinking, profanity, Sabbath breaking, and licentiousness.[115] Billy Graham is the most well-known contemporary evangelist and emerged as a major regional and national religious figure during a revival era that began after World War II.

---

115. Edward L. Ayers, *The Promise of the New South: life After Reconstruction* (New York and Oxford: Oxford University Press, 1992), 173–178. Jones's "for men only" sermon can be found at the Biblebelievers.com Web site at: http://www.biblebelievers.com/jones_sam/.

This "shared religion" described the "norm" or expected and accepted religion in the South for much of the late 19th and the 20th centuries, and it and the broader culture of the South were as interconnected as a jigsaw puzzle. For all intents and purposes, the "shared religion" was an official state religion, and, well into the 20th century, its major denominations were rooted in the region with limited support elsewhere. At least on the white side, these denominations were self-consciously Southern with a particular view of history, of the Civil War especially, that often put them at odds with their Northern counterparts.[116] Indeed, the shared religion validated or at least accepted much of Southern culture, most notably the dominion of men over women, rich over poor, white over black. Whether a person shared this religion or not, he/she was expected to behave by its standards. The life of "personal holiness" urged on believers by evangelical churches was what remained of the radicalism of early evangelicalism because this holiness required, obviously, tremendous self-discipline and a continual struggle for most believers, particularly of the male persuasion.[117] Social critic Wilber J. Cash believed that what resulted of this struggle was a split "psyche" for the Southerner: part of his mind craved pleasure and good times, and part feared the Lord and struggled to deny these urges.[118] Many in the upper class did not buy into this program, as we have seen, and continued to enjoy their pleasures as they always had. The rest of Southern society did, and so the split in the psyche of the individual Southerner was mirrored by a duality in Southern society itself. The churches struggled to control the passions of believers, especially male believers, and this became the accepted value system, but arising in opposition to this world of uprightness was an often secret realm of backyard cockfights, bars in the back of country stores and later gas stations, hunting camps where off-color jokes were told and liquor or moonshine passed around, and, the ultimate transgression for the white male, a late night visit to the slave quarters or later "colored town" in search of female companionship. By the mid-twentieth century, local county fairs across the region featured tents offering displays of local peach preserves, dinners cooked by local churches, and, astonishingly, "hooch" shows featuring women "dancers" who revealed all and often were willing to be "touched" during the show for a sum of paper money. These spectacles were attended by both men and older boys and were presided over by the sheriff's department. For this week and this week only, the normal rules governing male public propriety were suspended, at least in the hooch show tent. Then, the fair would leave town, and the world of church socials and Wednesday night prayer meetings would again reign supreme.

---

116. Stowell, *Rebuilding Zion*, 162–178.
117. Mathews, *Religion in the Old South*, 59–63.
118. Wilber J. Cash, *The Mind of the South* (1941; New York: Vintage Books, 1969), 60.

This may strike many as the height of hypocrisy, but, actually, it was not. In part, it reflected a fatalism that viewed humans as flawed creatures who can never meet the standards set for them; for this very reason, strict standards were necessary, but the expectation that these standards might not be met or might on "special occasions" be winked at was also part and parcel of this pessimistic view of humanity. Ben Robertson believed Southerners found this demanding moral code appealing because the opposite, a life of sensual pleasure, was so close at hand (at least for men). As he noted in his memoir:

> We have chosen asceticism because all of our lives we have had to fight an inclination to license—we know how narrow and shallow is the gulf between asceticism and complete indulgence; we have always known much concerning the far realms, the extremes. We had tried throughout our lives to keep the Commandments; we have set for ourselves one of the strictest, sternest codes in existence, but our country is Southern and we are Southern and frequently we fail. In the end we stake our immortal souls on the ultimate deathbed repentance."[119]

People fall short, but they are given an infinite number of chances at redemption, the last chance being, as Robertson notes, on the deathbed. Thus a prominent contemporary televangelist caught in a compromising situation with a prostitute (who proceeded to tell all) could beg his television audience for forgiveness. They forgave him, or many of them did, because he's still on television. Even a prominent minister is, after all, human.

The duality in Southern culture was also, at bottom, a conflict between honor and patriarchy on the one hand and evangelical religion on the other. As we have seen, evangelical religion never vanquished honor or patriarchy; honor glorifies the competitive male who is able to win—women, wealth, fame, and respect—and patriarchy (unquestioned male supremacy) gives males wide latitude to play this "game." So for example, a leading segregationist politician and Baptist churchman—U.S. Senator Strom Thurmond of South Carolina—could father a child by his family's black maid and rise to a position of prominence despite the fact that more than a few people (his office staff in Washington, for example) knew of his indiscretion. The key, of course, is that neither his daughter nor her mother ever "told" on him during his lifetime (unlike Monica Lewinsky and another famous Southern politician).[120] In a cul-

---

119. Ben Robertson, *Red Hills and Cotton: An Upcountry Memory* (1942; Columbia, SC: University of South Carolina Press, 1973), 9–10.

120. Thurmond retired from the U.S. Senate in 2002 and died in 2003. The daughter he fathered with the Thurmond family's teenaged housekeeper went public with news that Thurmond was her father shortly thereafter. An attorney for the Thurmond family almost immediately confirmed that the story was true. See "Strom Thurmond's family confirms paternity claim," *CNN*, 16 December 2003, http://www.cnn.com/2003/US/12/15/thurmond.paternity/.

ture tending more to shame than guilt, a shameful secret was only shameful if it became public.

While the churches may have made concessions to honor and patriarchy, they never gave up trying to regulate the behavior flowing from these values, and this meant controlling, in some fashion, male behavior. By the late 1800s, the practice of disciplining errant church members had actually declined in many evangelical churches, but this development was paralleled by a rising interest in enforcing the morality of the evangelical churches via law. Evangelicals pushed to outlaw or restrict a variety of behaviors and entertainments they found objectionable: saloons, swearing, gambling, the sale of alcohol, the county fair "shows" mentioned earlier, and later the new motion picture shows.[121] They would form alliances with other reformers, sometimes unlikely alliances; in the early 1900s, progressive reformers intent on "uplifting" the poor joined with them to ban the sale of alcohol, and, in the 1920s, the new Ku Klux Klan got the support (and often the membership dues) of many evangelical laypeople and ministers who supported the organization's drive to enforce, with violence if necessary, moral purity.[122] This moral crusade would wax and wane over the decades, and new issues would replace old. For over a century, liquor was the number one bane of the evangelicals, and state after state restricted or eliminated its sale in the years leading up to the passage of the 18th amendment establishing national prohibition in 1919. Even after the repeal of national prohibition in 1933, alcohol sales were restricted by state law in most of the South, and many Southern counties were completely "dry." Gambling was also targeted. By the later decades of the twentieth century, however, restrictions on the sale of liquor and gambling appeared to be a losing cause as state after state legalized the sale of mixed drinks, state-supported lotteries, and, in a few states, privately operated casinos. In a concession to evangelical sensibilities, in some states liquor by the drink was only authorized in restaurants, a restriction that limited the growth of the still hated "saloon," and lottery profits were generally earmarked for education. The Mississippi state legislature licensed casinos to boost the economy of this desperately poor state, but casinos could only be operated on boats, barges, or ships, and thus weren't technically "permanent" fixtures in the state.[123] The focus of many contemporary evangelical reformers has shifted to rendering abortion illegal and maintaining restrictions on homosexual behavior; fighting the teaching of evo-

121. Owenby, *Subduing Satan*, 208–211.
122. Harvey, *Freedom's Coming*, 227–229.
123. Hurricane Katrina destroyed or damaged all of the floating casinos on the Gulf Coast in 2005. The Mississippi state legislature authorized the rebuilding of these casinos on firm ground following the hurricane. *Lexington Herald-Leader*, 18 October 2005, http://www.kentucky.com/mld/kentucky/business/12929621.htm.

lution and restoring prayer and Christian symbols (like the Ten Commandments) in the schools and other public places are also important issues.[124]

Modernism versus "The Old Time Religion"

The rough, emotional edges of evangelical religion were continually being sanded and buffed by notions of middle class respectability, orderliness, and restraint, but an equally robust process was creating new, vibrant, enthusiastic denominations and independent churches that catered, at least in the beginning, to the less affluent and reflected the cultures of less affluent black and white people. Evangelical religion was not, therefore, static, and the ease with which new churches or even sects could be started kept it vital and meaningfully involved in the lives of most Southerners. While it continued to evolve, and the number of variations seemed to expand on a daily basis as each new storefront church—often emblazoned with a name no one had heard of before—joined the roster of active churches, most of the South's churches from Sister Mary's House of Prayer to the stately First Baptist Church downtown stayed true to the shared beliefs. The advent of "modernism," however, would begin to unravel the consensus upon which the shared religion depended and would ultimately sunder the interconnectedness of the shared religion and the culture.

Modernism was a new way of thinking that developed in the late 1800s in most developed Western countries and began to challenge the Victorian way of thinking that had been dominant in much of the Western world. Modernism would have a small influence in the turn-of-the-century South, but its influence would grow in the region as the twentieth century progressed. While the older Victorian outlook tended to see things—good and bad, right and wrong—in absolute terms and valued tradition and propriety, Modernism questioned established truths and traditions and relied on empirical data collected by the sciences to fashion new ways of understanding humans and the world. It asserted that humans were motivated as much by irrational drives as by reason and that society's rules and traditions were often arbitrary. Sigmund Freud and other Modernists dealt in paradoxes rather than certainties like the Victorians; for Freud, for example, the repression of basic drives, the sex drive especially, was responsible for the development of civilization but also for the prevalence of a variety of major and minor mental illnesses. But Modernism took, in a sense, a mechanistic view of the human personality and society in its belief that both could be understood and "managed." Psychological problems could be treated using the new therapies being devised by Freud and others,

---

124. Hill, *Southern Churches in Crisis*, xxxv–xxxvi.

and social problems such as poverty, violence, crime, even war could also be "fixed" or at least ameliorated through the efforts of organizations staffed by professionals. The increasingly influential and growing institutions of higher education here and abroad became important generators of Modernist thought. Historian William McLoughlin has argued that this new way of thinking was so influential and ultimately pervasive that its introduction and dissemination amounted to a "Third Great Awakening."[125]

Modernism's influence on religion was significant, particularly in the major Protestant churches (sometimes called the mainline Protestant churches) of the North. Aspiring ministers were increasingly being schooled in new ways of understanding the Bible based on a rigorous study of both the ancient texts and the growing body of historical research. The culture of the people that produced the Bible had to be understood in order to properly understand the meaning of the sacred text. For many, much in the Bible was best understand symbolically rather than literally; what was important was not whether the earth really had been created in six days or the Red Sea really had been parted, but the message. Accompanying the new way of understanding the Bible was a new attitude about the obligations of the church; saving souls was still important, but, some Modernists argued, addressing society's ills should also be a major part of the church's mission. This new emphasis was called the Social Gospel and was justified biblically by referring to Christ's interest in "the least of us."[126] While the influence of the Social Gospel movement would wane after World War I, its stress on helping the poor and oppressed became an integral part of the mission of the mainline churches.

Modernism would creep into the South during the early decades of the twentieth century and would, not surprisingly, first find its way into the universities. The University of North Carolina, for example, was becoming, by the 1920s, a center for Modernist thought, and, irony of ironies for such an "establishment" institution, it became the target thereafter of conservative critics for harboring "radicals" and radical ideas.[127] After World War II, Modernism would become the accepted way of understanding reality by much of the educated middle and upper classes.[128] Modernism would exert a growing influence in the seminaries of the more liberal denominations in the South, but even in Baptist seminaries, if conservative critics are to be believed, the new historical

---

125. William G. McLoughlin, *Revivals, Awakenings, and Reform: A Essay on Religion and Social Change in America, 1607–1977* (Chicago and London: The University of Chicago Press, 1978), 141–178.

126. Marty, *Pilgrims in Their Own Land*, 348–355.

127. Daniel Joseph Singal, *The War Within: From Victorian to Modernist Thought in the South, 1919–1945* (Chapel Hill, NC: The University of North Carolina Press, 1982), 265–268, 302–303.

128. *Ibid.*, 373–375.

scholarship would be taught in a growing number of classrooms.[129] The Social Gospel, like the Modernist movement of which it was part, exerted a relatively small influence in the region in the early decades of the 1900s, but what those who subscribed to the Social Gospel lacked in numbers, they made up for in activism. Women, in particular, often played an important role in founding church-related organizations to fight child labor, the lynching "epidemic," and illiteracy. In the decades following World War II, the more liberal denominations were increasingly committed to a mild form of the Social Gospel.

Fundamentalism as a movement surfaced at the turn of the 20th century to do battle with the growing Modernist movement in American society and in the church. The Fundamentalist movement originated in the North where Modernist thought and influence was strongest. It started in "seminaries, Bible institutes, summer camp meetings, and interdenominational schools," and its key precepts were outlined in a series of pamphlets published from 1910–1915 that were financed by a California oil millionaire. Fundamentalists supported the literal interpretation of the Bible; for them, Moses actually did part the Red Sea. They rejected the scientific explanations of the creation of the world, found the theory of evolution abhorrent, and saw the church's role as saving souls, not solving poverty. Many Fundamentalists were committed to the same sort of millennial thinking common in the Pentecostal movement; many believed Christ would return, sooner rather than later, and usher in a new age for true believers, but not before a terrible time of tribulation scourged the earth. The movement rejected much about the modern world and urged its followers to distance themselves as much as possible from its corruption.[130] Initially, Fundamentalism was not well-received in the South; Modernism seemed more of a Northern "problem" in the late 1800s and early 1900s, biblical literalism dominated the region's religious culture already, and the millennial views of the Fundamentalists were not popular with many people outside the Pentecostal fold.[131] Interestingly, Fundamentalism first became widely known as a result of a trial held in the Southern state of Tennessee in 1925. In this trial, the so-called Scopes Monkey Trial, a high school biology teacher accused of violating Tennessee's law against teaching evolution was prosecuted by a state attorney who was assisted by the orator and conservative Christian, William Jennings Bryan. Defending the teacher was perhaps the most famous lawyer in America, Clarence Darrow. Darrow and his client lost, but Darrow made

---

129. David Roach and Jeff Robinson, "Conservative Resurgence about 'Theology,' not 'Politics,' *Florida Baptist Witness,* 3 November 2005, http://www.floridabaptistwitness.com/2478.article.

130. Harvey, *Freedom's Coming,* 222; William R. Glass, *Strangers in Zion: Fundamentalists in the South, 1900–1950* (Macon, Georgia: Mercer University Press, 2001), xiv–xv, 2, 7, 16–17.

131. Harvey, *Freedom's Coming,* 224.

Bryan, and by extension Fundamentalism, look foolish. The trial and declining Fundamentalist influence in several Northern-based denominations set the movement back on its heels.[132]

Rather than concede defeat to the Modernists, Fundamentalist movement members focused on organizing independent churches, interdenominational associations, Bible conferences, and publishing houses.[133] This grass roots organizing began to pay dividends, especially in the South. Several Fundamentalist colleges were established in the region, the most well-known of which was Bob Jones College (later renamed Bob Jones University) in Greenville, South Carolina, and the Fundamentalist perspective began to attract more and more supporters in evangelical denominations in the South, particularly the Baptist and Presbyterian.[134] While Fundamentalism and the shared religion of the South had much in common, there was an important difference: the shared religion was inherently suspicious of creeds or specific "tests" of faith other than an acceptance of Christ as savior. It emphasized the heart over the head, as we have seen. Fundamentalism was very doctrinaire in its insistence on the unquestioned legitimacy of certain ideas and beliefs; with its concern about ideas, it clearly was much more intellectually oriented than traditional evangelical religion in the South.[135] As Modernism became more influential in the seminaries, church-supported colleges, denominational bureaucracies and urban churches, conservative churchmen clung more tightly to their conservative beliefs and become more vocal and assertive about defending them and defining them as the only proper beliefs for true Christians. Not surprisingly, growing numbers of white Southerners with conservative views were drawn to the Fundamentalist cause. Modernism and Fundamentalism thus developed side by side, at war with each other. Of the two, Fundamentalism had an advantage, given the inherently conservative nature of the shared religion of the South. Because support for Modernism seemed strongest amongst elite groups (such as denominational leaders, seminary professors and ministers and laymen in the affluent and influential urban churches), and Fundamentalism seemed to have more of a "just folks" constituency, this conflict would have undertones of the class conflicts that periodically swept Southern religious culture. In retrospect, the battle lines would also be denominational; the Methodist, Episcopal, and Presbyterian churches tended to be more supportive of the Modernist position, while the Pentecostal, Independent, and Baptist churches tended to be more supportive of some or many of the Fundamentalist positions. The Baptist faith was so big and diverse, however, that it also harbored a growing con-

132. Marty, *Pilgrims In Their Own Land*, 379–382.
133. Glass, *Strangers in Zion*, 35.
134. *Ibid.*, 85, 224.
135. Hill, *Southern Churches in Crisis*, xxxviii–xxxix.

tingent of Modernist folks, especially in the larger urban and suburban churches.

The Black Church and the Quest for Social Justice

The black church in most respects was as committed to the shared religion as the white church and thus just as conservative but with one important difference—its commitment to social justice. After World War II, this commitment would take an increasingly militant turn. While whites were fighting battles over Modernism and Fundamentalism, black churches and ministers played a vital role in the fight to end Jim Crow. Activist ministers like Vernon Johns (King's predecessor at Dexter Avenue Baptist Church in Montgomery, Alabama) could be found sprinkled throughout the region, although many ministers were initially wary of getting directly involved with the Civil Rights movement for fear of jeopardizing their own careers and the painstaking work required over the decades to build their churches.[136] When members of the black community in Montgomery, Alabama, gathered in a church in 1955 to discuss boycotting the city bus after the arrest of Rosa Parks, E.D. Nixon recalled standing up in the balcony of the church and angrily denouncing the ministers for refusing to take a stand. "I said, 'You guys have went around here and lived off these poor wash-women all your lives and ain't never done nothing for 'em. And now you got a chance to do something for 'em, you talkin' about you don't want the white folks to know it.'" He then accused them of being "a bunch of scared boys," at which point Martin Luther King, Jr., "hollered that he wasn't no coward, that nobody called him a coward."[137] King would lead the bus boycott, and later he would join with other ministers (one of them was Ralph Abernathy) to form the Southern Christian Leadership Conference, one of the most prominent civil rights organizations in the struggle to end Jim Crow. Across the South, churches served as recruiting grounds for the Civil Rights Movement and the meeting places of choice for activists. In response, hundreds of black churches were vandalized, blown up, or burned down by those willing to use violence to maintain the subjugation of African Americans in the South. Birmingham, Alabama, lived up to its nickname of "Bombingham" when it came to dynamited churches; three black churches were bombed on a single day in January, 1963. Later that year on a Sunday

---

136. See Branch, *Parting the Waters: America in the King Years, 1954–1963*, 7–26 for details about Johns' career.

137. Interview, "E.D. Nixon," Howell Raines, *My Soul Is Rested: Movement Days in the Deep South Remembered* (New York: Bantam Books, 1978), 41.

morning, a bomb exploded at the Sixteenth Street Baptist Church, sending church members streaming from the building, many with their clothes bloodied and tattered from the blast. The bodies of four young girls, each dressed in white "from head to toe," were found in the rubble, murdered in their blameless innocence.[138]

The black church was more to the Civil Rights Movement than just a place to hold civil rights meetings and a source for recruits; the Movement was infused with the Christian spirituality and the deep belief in justice that was the essence of the black church. The philosophy of nonviolent civil disobedience embraced by King and many of the other leaders and foot soldiers of the Movement had many sources, including Henry David Thoreau and Mahatma Gandhi, but it would not be too much to say that it was Christian to the core and was embraced by so many Southern blacks because it reflected the teachings of Christ. Civil Rights protesters marched off to jail by the score singing spirituals and hymns, and prayed when they were beaten and abused. Evangelical religion in the South had always focused on saving souls from sin and damnation; the Movement said, in effect, to white Christians, "join us and save your souls." In his "Letter from a Birmingham Jail," King addressed a group of white Birmingham ministers who wrote a letter published in a Birmingham newspaper criticizing the demonstrations King was leading and as much as made this point, telling the ministers the "judgement of God is upon the church as never before."[139] And, of course, when he wrote "church," he meant the white church. Would white Christians admit that black Christians truly were their brothers and sisters in Christ?

The leaderships of the major white denominations in the South **did** support civil rights for blacks, as did a growing number of moderate and liberal white ministers and laymen, especially in urban areas. Although many of these supporters were, at best, lukewarm in their support, some, such as James McBride Dabbs, a prominent Presbyterian layman from Maysville, South Carolina, courageously stepped forward and forcefully urged white Southerners to do their Christian duty. But many white conservative evangelical ministers and laypersons actively opposed equal rights for African Americans.[140] Charley Daniel, for example, the pastor of the First Baptist Church of West Dallas, Texas, wrote and distributed a pamphlet entitled "God the Original Segregationist."[141] W.A. Criswell, pastor of the First Baptist Church of Dallas, Texas,

---

138. The four girls were Denise McNair, Addie Mae Collins, Cynthia Wesley, and Carole Robertson. Branch, *Parting the Waters*, 570, 889–890.

139. Martin Luther King, Jr., "Letter from a Birmingham Jail," 16 April 1963, *Historical Text Archive* at http://www.historicaltextarchive.com/sections.php?op=viewarticle&artid=40.

140. Harvey, *Freedom's Coming*, 229–236.

141. *Ibid.*, 233.

reputedly the largest Protestant church in America, spoke before the South Carolina state legislature in 1955 and said of the *Brown v. Board* decision, "Let them integrate. Let them stay up there in their dirty shirts and make all their fine speeches. But they are all a bunch of infidels, dying from the neck up."[142] For many conservative white Christians, "integrationism, modernism, and Communism," were all tied together in some sort of ungodly mix.[143] One of the labels applied to Martin Luther King, Jr., by those opposed to integration was "Communist," and it was a common opinion among whites that the Civil Rights Movement was the work of Communists (sometimes referred to as "Godless" Communists) and outside agitators who were stirring up otherwise contented African-American Southerners. In such an atmosphere, it is not surprising that denominational leaders who called for an end to segregation were often bitterly condemned and resented for joining these outside agitators in trying to force unnatural changes on the region, and white ministers who preached racial toleration were sometimes run out of pulpits.[144]

Segregation died nonetheless, and the moral defense of segregation by white preachers and evangelical laymen collapsed; even Criswell admitted he had been wrong about segregation. The Southern Baptist Convention began to actively (and successfully) recruit black churches to join the denomination and came out in the mid-1990s with an apology for slavery and segregation.[145] But if many conservative whites had given up publicly defending segregation, many privately did not, and many believed the end of segregation had brought social upheaval of the worst sort, including disordered and failing schools, rising levels of crime, and expanding welfare rolls.[146] These feelings led to the formation of private (read, white) schools across the region, many of them Christian academies, a mass white exodus from the Democratic Party (the party most associated with ending segregation), and white flight from the cities of the South to the largely white suburbs. Many still harbored the belief that whites and blacks should remain apart in that most intimate of senses; as late as 2000, Bob

---

142. *Ibid.*, 245.
143. *Ibid.*, 230.
144. *Ibid.*, 236–245. See for an account of the battles of one white minister who spoke up for social justice for blacks, Timothy B. Tyson, *Blood Done Sign My Name* (New York: Three Rivers Press, 2004).
145. Harvey, *Freedom's Coming*, 246.
146. Nancy Tatum Ammerman found that moderate Southern Baptists who were surveyed favored the "Civil Rights Revolution" by an overwhelming majority while only a minority of conservative Southern Baptists viewed it positively. *Baptist Battles: Social Change and Religious Conflict in the Southern Baptist Convention* (New Brunswick and London: Rutgers University Press, 1990), 104; Andrew M. Manis, "The Civil Religions of the South," Charles Reagan Wilson and Mark Silk, eds., *Religion and Public Life in the South: In the Evangelical Mode* (Walnut Creek, CA: Rowman & Littlefield Publishers, Inc., 2005), 177.

Jones University still prohibited interracial dating and interracial marriages within its student population (it dropped this prohibition in 2000).[147]

Modernism versus Conservatism: The Culture Wars

The Civil Rights Movement made plain for all to see that the shared religion of the South was split by the chasm of race; while the black church and the more liberal white ministers and laymen believed standing up for social justice for African Americans was a Christian duty, many other white ministers and laymen did not, and others only belatedly came to a grudging acceptance of what was essentially a *fait accompli* imposed by the might of the federal government. Civil Rights also reignited the conflict between Modernists, now generally called liberals or moderates, and Fundamentalists and other conservative Christians by bringing into sharp relief the very different value systems undergirding these two positions. Many prominent conservative leaders, such as Mr. Criswell, were deeply troubled by the changes sweeping Southern and American society and institutional religion. Women were pushing for greater equality, abortion was legalized by a Supreme Court decision, laws regulating pornography were virtually eliminated (also the result of Supreme Court decisions), there was an explosion in premarital sex called the "sexual revolution," the divorce rate increased and with it the number of children being raised by a single parent, and court-imposed restrictions on prayer in the schools and elsewhere seemed to be driving the shared religion of the South out of the public sphere.[148] Religion itself seemed to be coming unglued; religious experimentation flourished with scores across the nation joining a variety of eastern religious sects, self-help groups that functioned like religions, and newly invented religions. Established Christian churches and denominations explored new styles of worship, and some even introduced rock and folk music into the service to reach those turned off by the "stuffy" old-style religion. A "charismatic" movement adhering to some Pentecostal-style worship practices (ecstatic worship, for one) swept through the Catholic Church and some of the more staid Protestant denominations; a number of independent charismatic churches and even a denomination, the Vineyard Church, came out of the movement. In the mid-1990s, a new phenomenon, originating in a charismatic church in Toronto and called the

---

147. "Dr. Bob Jones III Discusses the Controversy Swirling Around Bob Jones University," *Larry King Live*, 3 March 2000, transcript at CNN.COM, http://transcripts.cnn.com/TRANSCRIPTS/0003/03/lkl.00.html.

148. Ammerman, *Baptist Battles*, 100–104; Andrew Manis, "Protestants: From Denominational Controversialists to Culture Warriors," in William Lindsey and Mark Silk, *Southern Crossroads: Showdown States* (Walnut Creek, CA: Altamira Press, 2005), 64–65.

"Toronto blessing," swept the charismatic movement and introduced "holy laughter" and later animal sounds as legitimate manifestations of the possession of believers by the Holy Spirit during church services. The religious change and experimentalism was at such a heightened level that historian William McLaughlin has called this era the "Fourth Great Awakening."[149] It's important to note that this "awakening" was a national phenomenon; the South was no longer the isolated region it had once been, thanks to its burgeoning economy, the growing influence of the media, a more activist federal government and court system, and the substantial migration of "outsiders" into the region.

If conservatives were horrified by many of these changes, the "mainline" denominations (Episcopal, Presbyterian, Lutheran, and Methodist) active in the South often embraced "liberal" changes such as promoting women in the ministry and supporting a greater acceptance of divorce. The United Methodist Church, for example, elected its first female bishop in 1980; by 2005 over 20% of its bishops were female, and nearly 20% of the denomination's ordained ministers were women.[150] The Episcopal Church ordained an openly gay bishop in 2003. Even the more conservative denominations seemed to be moving in the same direction, but at a much slower pace. In the Southern Baptist Convention, for example, the number of ordained women ministers jumped from 8 in 1974 to perhaps 200 by the early 1980s.[151] Religiously inspired cultural restraints and traditions were being demolished all over the South in the 1960s and 1970s, and churches seemed, to many conservatives, to be helping with the demolition. To them, Southern culture was being overtaken by a decadent, permissive and irreligious national culture that was corrupting religion and luring people away from Christ; the old accord between evangelical religion and the culture of the South was crumbling. Conservatives had given ground on racial equality, but they refused to give ground on the issue of the equality of the sexes and a host of other "liberal" issues that they viewed as wrong-headed if not immoral and un-Christian.[152] When W.A. Criswell was asked what he thought about a woman who was "called" by God to preach, he responded "she is mistaken; God never called her."[153]

---

149. William McLaughlin, *Revivals, Awakenings, and Reform*, 179–216; "Vineyard Churches," The Religious Movements Page, University of Virginia, http://religiousmovements.lib.virginia.edu/nrms/Vineyard.html.

150. "United Methodist Statistics on Women Clergy," The United Methodist Church, http://archives.umc.org/interior.asp?ptid=1&mid=2620.

151. Barry Hankins, *Uneasy in Babylon: Southern Baptist Conservatives and American Culture* (Tuscaloosa and London: University of Alabama Press, 2002), 204.

152. Charles Reagan Wilson, *Judgment and Grace in Dixie*, 16. Charles Reagan Wilson, "Preachin', Prayin', and Singin' on the Public Square," 21–22.

153. Hankins, *Uneasy in Babylon*, 231.

A movement of white conservative evangelicals began to form; this was a national movement, but many of its most important leaders were from the South, and the core of its strength appeared to be in the South. Conservative members of the older evangelical denominations, Baptist especially, were joined by members of Pentecostal churches and independent churches in a campaign to restore conservative values and traditions and turn back the liberal tide. In the political realm, the movement became known as the Christian Right and would come to play a significant role in the politics of the region and the nation. It would become a major part of the Republican coalition to the point that to be a conservative Christian was virtually synonymous with voting Republican. The minister of one church in North Carolina even expelled church members who refused to support his Republican views.[154] The battles with liberals in churches, denominational bodies, the media, and politics became known as the "culture wars."[155] Conservatives stood on much of the original Fundamentalist platform, most notably that the Bible was literally true and that evolution was blasphemy. A strong current of millennial thinking ran through the movement, with many conservatives subscribing to Fundamentalist and Pentecostal beliefs about the "end-times" discussed earlier. A series of novels about the "end times" by conservative Baptist minister Tim LaHaye (LaHaye had attended Bob Jones University and was one of the co-founders of the Moral Majority) and Jerry Jenkins sold millions of copies.[156] Social issues were especially important to conservatives: they vigorously condemned abortion as murder, generally criticized the movement toward equality for women within and outside the church, favored corporal punishment of children, hotly contested efforts to recognize the legitimacy of homosexuality, and loudly proclaimed themselves the defenders of family values. They believed they were a beleaguered minority, oppressed by an increasingly secular society and alternately attacked and parodied by an anti-Christian media. In a curious way, they adopted the tactics, rhetoric, and moral tone of the Civil Rights Movement.

While defending tradition, this was a movement that was not afraid to take advantage of new technology and the techniques of interest group organizing to mobilize its followers and recruit new members. Three Southern conserva-

---

154. Kristin Collins, "Church boots 9 over politics," *Raleigh News and Observer*, 7 May 2005.

155. Andrew Manis, "Protestants: From Denominational Controversialists to Culture Warriors," 67–76. Andrew Manis, "The Civil Religions of the South," in Charles Reagan Wilson and Mark Silk, eds., *Religion and Public Life in the South: in the Evangelical Mode* (Walnut Creek, CA: Altamira Press, 2005), 170–171.

156. Robert Dreyfus, "Reverend Doomsday," *Rolling Stone*, 28 January 2004, http://www.rollingstone.com/politics/story/_/id/5939999?rnd=1130860097171&hasplayer=true&version=6.0.12.1040.

tive "televangelists" emerged as major regional and national figures. Billy Graham was the first to emerge and is the best known of the three. Graham first began preaching in the 1940s and by the mid-1950s was organizing huge televised crusades around the country. He did more than any single individual in exporting conservative evangelical Christianity outside the South and presenting it in a form palatable to non-Southern audiences. While Graham accepted much of the conservative message including its millennial views, his was a moderate voice, and his interest was more in saving souls and working cooperatively with a broad spectrum of religious denominations than in building a movement.[157] Jerry Falwell and Pat Robertson were more influential in creating a conservative movement. Falwell started a small Baptist church in Lynchburg, Virginia, in 1956 with 35 or so men, women and children. Falwell, described in his church's online history as "a particularly aggressive young man," set about building his small congregation. Within the year he had found a new home for the congregation and started a radio program which then became a television program. By 2007, his Thomas Road Baptist Church had over 20,000 members, and his *Old Time Gospel Hour* had been a nationally broadcast religious program for several decades. Falwell founded a school and a university to provide young people with a conservative religious education, and in the late 1970s he launched the Moral Majority, a national interest group dedicated to promoting the conservative evangelical position in American society and politics.[158] The *Old Time Gospel Hour* evolved into a mixture of "old time" religion and modern "hardball" politics; in the mid-1990s, for example, Falwell often hawked a videotape (*The Clinton Chronicles*) on the air that purported to prove that President Bill Clinton, a particularly detested figure in conservative circles, had arranged to have several people murdered.[159] Pat Robertson was also an ordained Baptist minister, but had moved more toward Pentecostalism in his beliefs; he began broadcasting a television program (the *700 Club*) out of Virginia Beach in the early 1960s, founded a college there, and established, in the late 1980s, a national organization (the Christian Coalition) to promote the conservative evangelical cause. Like a number of other televangelists who became prominent, Robertson was not afraid to experiment with format and style on his show. His program had some of the glitz of a secular network show, and was a mix of entertainment, news, and talk show-style chat.[160]

---

157. See Billy Graham's autobiography, *Just as I am: The Autobiography of Billy Graham* (San Francisco: HarperCollins, 1997). Interestingly, Graham attended Bob Jones College for a year or so but left because he didn't like being told "what to think." See p. 30.

158. "Our History," Thomas Road Baptist Church website, http://home.trbc.org/index.cfm?PID=9059.

159. Murray Waas, "The Falwell Connection," *Salon Newsreal*, 11 March 1998, http://www.salon.com/news/1998/03/cov_11news.html.

160. "Pat Robertson," *The Museum of Broadcast Communications* website, http://www.museum.tv/archives/etv/R/htmlR/robertsonpa/robersonpa.htm.

By the late 1970s, the so-called "electronic church" had become a powerful medium to promote conservative views and values and one that spoke with a decided Southern accent. Jimmy Swaggert, Jim Bakker, Oral Roberts and a host of less prominent "televangelists" joined Falwell and Robertson in spreading the conservative evangelical message regionally and nationally on the new medium of cable television. These shows raised big money and proved to be an excellent platform to sell a host of other media like books, videos, and audiotapes, and the techniques of the mass mailing industry were expertly applied to keep the money flowing in. For the most part, mainline Christian denominations were skeptical of on-air fundraising and the "electronic church" as a reputable mission; in effect, they refused to compete. Their on-air presence actually declined after the Federal Communications Commission changed broadcast regulations to permit broadcasters to charge for airing "public service" programs. Many of the programs mainline churches and denominations had sponsored disappeared from the airways. While financial and sex scandals would rock the televangelist community and cut into its viewership in the late 1980s, the electronic church is still a powerful voice for the conservative evangelical position.[161]

In the 1970s, two Southern Baptists from Texas, Paige Patterson, a protégé of W.A. Criswell, and Judge Paul Pressler, set out to establish conservative control of the Southern Baptist Convention (SBC), the largest evangelical denomination. Patterson would later observe, "The controversy began in 1979 when some of us just felt that our denomination was slipping over to the left just as most mainline denominations had done." He hoped to bring Baptists back to the "faith of their fathers."[162] A bitter struggle ensued between conservatives and moderates, a struggle that Patterson and his supporters ultimately won. By the mid-1980s, conservatives succeeded in winning control of the Southern Baptist Convention and set about gaining control of the denomination's bureaucracy and seminaries. Inerrancy—the literal interpretation of the Bible—was the test they would apply to staff and faculty members.[163] At Southeastern Baptist Seminary in Wake Forest, North Carolina, for example, moderate Randall Lolley, the seminary president, and eventually most of the faculty were forced out by a new conservative board and replaced. The seminary's daycare, a popular facility in the community, was closed, and the building that housed it was ultimately bulldozed. (Operating a daycare sent the wrong message to

161. Jeffrey K. Hadden, "The Rise and Fall of American Televangelism," at the Religious Broadcasting Web site, University of Virginia, http://religiousbroadcasting.lib.virginia.edu/pubs/risefall.html.; Wesley E. Miller, "A Sociological Analysis of the New Christian Right" (Unpublished Ph.D. dissertation Loyola University of Chicago, 1984), 95–96.

162. Interview with Paige Patterson," Founders Journal (Fall 2000), http://www.founders.org?FJ42/article2.html.

163. Hawkins, Uneasy in Babylon, 4.

working moms who, conservatives believed, should stay home with their children.) Paige Patterson himself would become the seminary's president. Convention policies and publications, not surprisingly, moved in a conservative direction. For example, the *2000 Baptist Faith and Message* passed by the Convention asserted that "the office of pastor is limited to men as qualified by Scripture" and that "A wife is to submit herself graciously to the servant leadership of her husband."[164] Conservatives eventually gained control of all but one of the state conventions in the South, and moderates eventually ceased struggling with conservatives for control of the national convention.[165] Groups of moderates formed a variety of associations representing their position, the largest of which is probably the Cooperative Baptist Fellowship, an organization that is struggling to offer moderate churches the sorts of services provided by the SBC, including a system of moderate seminaries to school aspiring ministers.[166] Many moderate Baptist churches continue to belong to the SBC, and many churches have both moderate and conservative members, but given the bitterness of the debate, what may happen in the long run is a "splitting off" of one or more denominations from the SBC.

The conservative evangelical's message struck a responsive chord: white conservative churches and denominations grew in the South (and elsewhere in the nation), sometimes explosively, while the more liberal mainline denominations and churches were often shrinking.[167] Further, the **relative** size of mainline denominations in the South shrank dramatically; one study estimated that white mainline Protestants declined from 28% of the population in the 1960s to 15% of the population in the 1990s.[168] Conservative evangelical Protestantism offered stability and clarity to people buffeted by waves of social and economic change generated by the transformation of the agrarian economy and society of the South.[169] In many ways, the movement reflected a nostalgia for the rapidly disappearing agrarian South where people married for life, families (not the government) took care of their own, men were the true heads of the households and the providers, women took care of the children and their husbands, children said "yes ma'am" and "no sir," a pregnancy was a time of

---

164. "The 2000 Baptist Faith and Message," Southeastern Baptist Seminary, http://www.sebts.edu/prospective_students/what_we_believe/bfm2000.cfm.

165. Andrew Manis, "Protestants: From Denominational Controversialists to Culture Warriors," 67, 74.

166. Cooperative Baptist Fellowship website at http://www.thefellowship.info/.

167. "Religious Membership Maps and Reports, Individual States, 1990–2000," America Religious Data Archive, http://www.thearda.com/test_main.asp? Show=RCMS2000.

168. John C. Green et al., "The Soul of the South: Religion and Southern Politics at the Millennium in New Politics of the Old South," Charles S. Bullock III and Mark J. Rozell, eds., *The New Politics of the Old South: An Introduction to Southern Politics* (Boulder, NY: Rowman and Littlefield Publishers, Inc., 2003), 287.

169. Wilson, *Judgment and Grace in Dixie*, 14–16.

celebration, doors could be left unlocked, and children could wander on a summer's evening unsupervised. People with agrarian roots were especially likely to belong to conservative churches, as were less affluent and less educated folks, and these were precisely the kinds of people most buffeted by the social and economic changes sweeping the South and the nation.[170] Conservative denominations and churches also appeared to have attracted a substantial helping of folks in the middle class. Given the tremendous expansion of the middle class in the South, many of these were upwardly mobile people. While the upwardly mobile may have "made it," mobility has it own burden of stress; the upwardly mobile often have left something important behind—old lifestyles, friends, neighborhoods—and have come to their new lives without all of the advantages of the more privileged folk already in the middle class. In one survey conducted in 2001, for example, close to a third of the Pentecostals surveyed reported a family income of $60,000 or more, but only 13% reported having graduated from college. In contrast, 40% of mainline Protestants surveyed reported having earned a college degree and over 42% reported a family income of $60,000 or more.[171] Not surprisingly, the expanding suburbs, filling with rural migrants seeking opportunities and people fleeing the troubled cities, were a major growth area for conservative churches, and new Baptist, Independent, and Pentecostal sanctuaries, no-frills warehouse-type structures that could accommodate hundreds, sometimes thousands, of worshipers, now dot the bypasses circling Southern cities and the major suburban arteries.[172]

While conservative churches condemned much that was modern, they were quite willing to accommodate modern sensibilities, and this helped them attract new members. Many conservative churches have moved toward even more informal worship, which is certainly consistent with the evangelical heritage but also reflects the modern penchant for the "laid back." They are also not afraid to introduce technological innovations and lessons learned from the entertainment industry into their services. At a medium-sized conservative Southern Baptist church located in a small town north of Charlotte, North Carolina, for example, worshipers entering the church on Sunday are greeted by a PowerPoint display announcing a variety of meetings and activities; hymns have largely been replaced by praise songs—songs with simple verses that are typically repeated over and over accompanied by "pop" music—the organ has been replaced by what amounts to a small rock band, and some wor-

---

170. *Southern Focus Poll, Spring, 2001*, Odum Institute for Research in Social Science, University of North Carolina, Chapel Hill; Ammerman, *Baptist Battles*, 129, 146, 148; Christine Smith and Robert Faris, "Socioeconomic Inequality in the American Religious System: An Update and Assessment," *Journal for the Scientific Study of Religion* 44, no. 1 (March 2005), 95–104.

171. *Southern Focus Poll, Spring, 2001*.

172. Ammerman, *Baptist Battles*, 148–149.

Figure 5.2   Germantown Baptist Church, Memphis, Tennessee

shipers raise their hands in the air and sway to the music. A choir director with a hand mike leads the singing, and this musical "master of ceremonies" concept has been observed in other evangelical churches. Neither the recitation of the Lord's Prayer nor the reading of Bible texts appear to be common practices, and the sermons, delivered by a preacher who hails from Ohio, are often seminars on the conservative lifestyle, supported by biblical citations and accompanied by the ever present PowerPoint. The church service concludes with the traditional "altar call." Other than the altar call, much about the service diverges from the Baptist tradition as it was practiced for much of the twentieth century. As one older church member said, "They're trying to appeal to the young people."

Conservative churches often offer a range of activities and services, such as recreational sports teams, prayer groups, elementary and high schools, alternative Halloween festivals, coffee houses, "lock-ins" for teenagers, covered dish dinners, counseling, and special ministries for men and women. For members who wish it, the church can become a sort of exclusive community where they spend most of their free time; this was precisely the sort of closed community apart from "worldlings" that the early evangelicals had hoped but failed to establish. One church has even named its "center" the "Baby Ark," a place where members presumably may escape the deluge engulfing a corrupt society. Mainline churches have tried to keep pace, and many offer a similar whirl of activities and experiment with novel variations on the traditional service, but mainline churches and their members are not as driven to move in this direction and for a simple reason: they simply aren't as critical of modern society as their conservative brethren.

The conservative movement that swept through many white churches in the South has had a limited impact in black churches. Many black churches are every bit as conservative as conservative white churches on such issues as abortion, homosexuality, and corporal punishment of children, and black ministers and laymen will sometimes lend their support to conservative political issues. The minister and some members of the Upper Room Church of God in Christ in Raleigh, for example, have been active in a variety of Christian Right causes including an anti-gay rights campaign and an annual Christmas campaign to compel retailers to greet customers with "Merry Christmas" rather than the more secular "Happy Holidays." The church is part of a local political pressure group ("Called 2 Action") made up of conservative churches and religious organizations.[173] But a linking of white and black conservatives on a significant scale does not appear to be in the cards any time soon; white conservative support for Jim Crow in the 1960s and the continuing support the Religious Right gives to opponents of Civil Rights protections have not gone unnoticed in the black community. Further, the social justice tradition of the black church continues to temper the conservatism of the black churches. This commitment to social justice for black Americans continues to keep many black churches engaged in the liberal side of politics, although overt political activism in the churches has declined since the peak period of the Civil Rights Movement during the 1960s and 1970s. Southern African Americans continue to be a highly religious people, and their participation levels are probably higher than whites, particularly in urban areas.[174] The traditional Baptist, Methodist and Pentecostal churches continue to draw the majority of black Christians.[175] Independent churches following a variety of traditions and mixing elements from different traditions have always been a major feature of Southern black religious culture, and one still finds in the typical medium-sized town a score or more of storefront churches, sometimes presided over by a female preacher. But upward mobility has affected blacks as well as whites, and the upwardly mobile or those who aspire to upward mobility seem to be feeding the growth of a new breed of non-denominational churches.

Many churches now often eschew denominational affiliations to appeal to people "turned off" by denominational bickering, and these churches sometimes have even abandoned the word "church" in their name and have names like Christian Life Center or New Life Ministries. Their sanctuaries now often look anything but "church-like." Virginia Beach's Wave Church recently completed a new sanctuary, a facility described on its web site as a "convention center." As a local reporter observed, "With its sweeping lines and glass-and-metal

---

173. Yonat Shimron, "Group launch holy war against 'Happy Holiday,'" Raleigh *News and Observer*, 3 December 2005, at http://www.newsobserver.com/102/story/373941.html.

174. William E. Montgomery, "Semi-Involuntary: African-American Religion" in Wilson and Silk, eds., *Religion and Public Life in the South*, 87.

175. *Ibid.*, 88.

facade, the modernist building at 1000 N. Great Neck Road invites guesses about what it is." What it didn't have, he noted, "inside or out, are any of the symbols—steeple, bell tower, stained glass, even a cross—that traditionally say 'church' to the public."[176] Non-denominational churches are generally located in the larger towns, cities and suburbs and, if their Web sites are any indication, try to appeal to younger, middle class folks. Many of these churches are more racially diverse than the older denominations (this is true of some Pentecostal churches, too), but it appears that many are either predominantly white or predominantly black, and the clue to which is generally the race of the lead minister. Some are "mega-churches" like The World Changers Church International outside Atlanta, which claims a congregation of more than 20,000. This church features a hard-charging minister by the name of Creflo Dollar who is prominently assisted by his attractive wife, Taffi. Dollar makes appearances at convention centers around the country and has a nationally broadcast television show. Supporting this ambitious endeavor is an elaborate Internet site offering streaming video, a multitude of services, and a full catalog of DVDs, CDs, and books available for purchase.[177] In the ever-expanding world of non-denominational churches, a television show, the bigger the better, seems to be the aspiration of every up-and-coming minister, and many of the churches, even the smaller ones, have "gone electronic." The Wave Church, for example, has a locally broadcast weekly television show and offers visitors to its Web site a menu of audio "podcasts." Non-denominational churches are rarely regional in any sense of the term; they are part of the national religious culture sometimes claiming "international" allegiances. While eschewing denominational affiliations, they are often linked to other churches through networks established by prominent televangelists.

Non-denominational churches adhere to a range of beliefs; some are solidly in the conservative camp, but many others profess a mix of liberal and conservative beliefs that generally have derived from the charismatic movement. Some have female ministers, and husband and wife ministerial "teams" are common. Services are usually very informal and often feature multi-media productions, plays, and praise songs, often accompanied by soft rock music. The focus is on positive messages delivered by the minister in an upbeat style; the fire and brimstone side of the traditional evangelical Southern church seems to be absent in many of these churches. A therapeutic approach to spirituality drawing heavily on the self-help genre of pop psychology is quite popular, and "empowering" people to be successful seems to hold broad appeal. The

---

176. Wave Church Web site at http://www.wavechurch.com (accessed 4/13/09); Steven G. Vegh, "Congregation builds church with new shapes," *The Virginian Pilot*, 3 December 2008, http://hamptonroads.com/2008/12/congregation-builds-church-new-shapes (accessed 4/13/09).
177. See Creflo Dollar's Web site at http://www.creflodollarministries.org/.

Wave Church's Web site proclaimed in 2006, "Our theme for this year is 'Doing Life Well,' and we're committed through all of our conferences, resources, and our preaching and teaching in our services to empower people to do so."[178] A loosely organized national sect called the Word-Faith or Word of Faith movement claims the allegiance of some of these churches and is promoted by several prominent televangelists, including Creflo Dollar and Kenneth Copeland. What unifies believers in this movement is the old idea that faith can move mountains and expressions of faith matter more than doctrine. Faith can heal and faith can bring prosperity; preachers, not surprisingly, are often faith healers, preach a message of "debt-free living and success" and are not reticent about living comfortably, even luxuriously.[179] Some churches belong to a loosely organized national association like the Vineyard churches, while still others are sponsored by a non-denominational church elsewhere. For example, Evergreen Community Church in Raleigh, North Carolina, was started by Grace Community Church in Indiana.[180] The non-denominational movement may very well be the "cutting edge" of religion in the South and the nation, reflecting a turn to an even more individualistic style of worship focused on lifestyle issues and tethered only loosely to any religious tradition.

Conclusion

Evangelical Protestant Christianity is still tremendously important and influential in the region; nowhere else in the country or the world is it so predominant. Nowhere else are there so many Baptists. That said, it is also true that the shared religion of evangelical Protestantism does not dominate the culture like it once did. It comes closest to retaining its old dominance in the rural areas and small towns of the region. Here, evangelical Protestant prayers are routinely recited at ball games and graduation ceremonies with no thought of offending anyone or violating Supreme Court decisions. People want to know what church you attend, wish you a "blessed day," and do not expect neighbors to mow their lawns on Sunday morning. The shared religion reigns supreme, or almost. In the larger towns, cities and suburbs, however, it is a different story; here religion is more a private affair practiced in the church

---

178. Wave Church Web site at http://www.wavechurch.com (accessed 4/12/06).

179. See Kenneth Copeland Ministries' Web site at http://www.kcm.org/ and Creflo Dollar's Web site at http://www.creflodollarministries.org/. The debate about this movement borders on the vicious; one of the "calmer" discussions of its beliefs and leading personalities is "Word of Faith," Wikipedia, http://en. wikipedia.org/wiki/Word_of_faith although in its latest iteration (4/13/09), the tenor of the article has become decidedly more critical.

180. See the Evergreen Church Web site at http://www.evergreench.org. (accessed 4/13/09).

and in the home. It is a choice as opposed to an obligation. Golf, soccer league for the kids, and shopping vie with church on Sunday, and there is no onus attached to choosing golf or soccer over attending church. While few would admit to being atheists or agnostics, many "just don't have time" to attend church or "can't find one I like." For those who wish to attend church, the choices cover a broad spectrum of denominations, sects, independent churches, and non-denominational churches that adhere to a wide variety of beliefs, practices, and traditions. Even within a denomination, the differences can be huge; a Southern Baptist Church following the moderate tradition might perform a marriage ceremony for a gay couple (several have done this and have ultimately been expelled from the SBC) while across the street at another Baptist church, church members might be circulating a petition calling for a constitutional amendment outlawing gay marriage. A more pluralistic range of values and lifestyles now prevails; if there is a unifying ethos in the culture of the South, it is derived from the consumer values of the marketplace, not religion. Materialism has shouldered aside the shared religion's suspicions of sensual pleasure, and 24-hour-a-day, seven-days-a-week shopping, electronic gadgets and games, cable television, chain restaurants dispensing mixed drinks and packaged good times, state sponsored gambling, spectator sports, action films and the Internet have replaced the restricted pleasures of the past. Some churches have even surrendered to the modern penchant for continuous stimulation and have packaged themselves as an alternative form of entertainment, featuring plush theatre-style seating in the sanctuary, plays and coffee house style "chat" in place of sermons, workout rooms, and a message of prosperity for the believers who follow the rules and contribute the money.

The shared religion ultimately reflected first and foremost the values and beliefs of white Protestants born and raised in the South, a group that constituted a large majority of Southerners, not to mention their other advantages. This is no longer the case. We have already seen that white mainline church members are a much smaller percentage of the population of the South, but white conservative evangelical church members are also a smaller percentage of the population, too, down from 45% of the population in the 1960s to 39% of the population in the 1990s according to one study. Together, white Protestants of all stripes were, by the 1990s, a little more than 50% of the population of the South compared to 73% in the 1960s. White Protestants are thus heading for minority status with the number of Catholics (13% of the population and growing) and "secular" folks likely to continue to grow at their expense. Black Protestants have also grown as a percentage of the population (18% of the population), growth fueled by the return of many blacks to the South.[181] The South,

---

181. John C. Green et al., "The Soul of the South," 287. The most recent religious affiliation survey found people in the South who eschewed any religious label roughly doubled as a percentage of the population between 1990 and 2008. See Barry A. Kosmin and

awash in immigrants from elsewhere in the U.S. and the world, is now more of a melting pot of religions with a large helping of secular folks. As one scholar has noted of white Protestants, these are folks who feel they have lost control of their "own country"; numerically, that is exactly what is happening. [182]

Whatever the clout of the Christian Right in current politics and the obvious success of the impressive "mega" churches looming over the bypasses, conservative evangelical Protestantism appears to be fighting a rearguard action. It has been more successful than the more liberal white denominations in attracting and/or keeping members, but it is fishing in an ever smaller pond. It is a movement that is very white in its leadership in a region (and a nation) that is becoming more non-white. It is a movement that stresses male over female in a region and nation where females continue to make up a larger and larger part of the workforce, including the prestigious and higher paying professions, a larger share of the college-attending population, and a larger part of the political power structure. But if conservative Protestantism is a rearguard action, it will not go quietly into the night. While white conservative evangelicals are a smaller part of the population, the percentage of "highly committed" evangelical Protestants grew from 18% (1960s) of the population of the South to 25% (1990s), and most of these folks are conservatives.[183] A quarter of the population speaking as one is a powerful voice. Ultimately, however, that voice is not powerful enough to re-impose the shared religion on the South, nor would that be possible even if conservatives were successful, given the integration of the South into the broader national culture. To dominate the culture, the shared religion would have to go national, and that is exactly how many conservatives see it. Today, the bitterest battles of the cultures wars are often fought on the national stage. Ironically, as the shared religion declines in the South, its adherents work to make it the nation's shared religion.

Ariela Keysar, "American Religious Identification Survey: Summary Report, March 2009," http://b27.cc.trincoll.edu/weblogs/AmericanReligionSurvey-ARIS/reports/ARIS_Report_2008.pdf.

182. Manis, "The Civil Religions of the South," 177.
183. John C. Green et al., "The Soul of the South," 287.

Chapter 6

Politics

Introduction

For most of its history, the politics of the South has been American politics. No one played a larger role in designing the political system of the United States than Virginians Thomas Jefferson and James Madison, and the first and perhaps greatest President was a Southerner. More recently, Southern politicians, such as Bill Clinton, Al Gore, Newt Gingrich and George W. Bush, played a major role in defining the terms of contemporary political discourse in the nation. But the South has had its own unique political traditions, and these traditions have put the region in conflict, sometimes bloody conflict, with the rest of the nation at critical junctures in history. States' rights, nullification, interposition, and secession were all political positions championed by Southern politicians and widely supported in the region at various points in time over the last 180 years; all reflected a fear or distrust of the power of the national government and by implication a wariness of the political objectives of rest of the nation. Nor are these positions ancient history: in April 2009 the governor of Texas, addressing an Austin, Texas, rally organized to protest the taxation and spending policies of the Obama administration, proclaimed that Washington was "overturning our rights, one after another" and chanted "States' rights, states' rights, states' rights." People in the crowd shouted "secede" during the speech.[1] The "pull" of region has affected politics in the South in another important way. John C. Calhoun, the antebellum Southern nationalist from South Carolina, urged Southerners to stand united in politics, and a degree of political unity was forged in the crucible of the Civil War era. For most of the hundred-year period after Reconstruction, the South was the "Solid South," a region so solidly Democratic in its politics that the Republican Party didn't even bother to field candidates for many of the political offices in the region. In the 1960s, whites began shifting to the once-despised Republican Party, and the region seemed to be on its way to becoming as solidly Republican as it had once been Democratic. This shift has led both political parties to pursue a "Southern strategy" in the quest to win control of the presidency and has had a huge impact on the nation's political discourse over the last three decades.

Politics in contemporary America is a much maligned but little understood part of the human experience. Many say the word "politics" with a sneer, and the complaint "why can't they take politics out of it" is on many lips. Unfortunately, politics can't be taken out of anything we as humans do, nor can we dispense with politicians. The reason politics can't be done away with is that it is all about the distribution of things that people want—a paved street, a national healthcare plan, lower taxes, and so on. In fact, one of the more popular definitions of politics is that it is a process of deciding "who gets what."[2] People don't always agree, so we have different groups wanting different things. Some want mass transit, for example, while others want to expand the highway system. Unfair though it may be, people with power "get," while people without power tend to go home empty handed and may even end up paying more in taxes than those who "get." The genius of democracy is that the people, at least those defined as citizens, are guaranteed at least some power, if they choose to exercise it. In other words, they get a shot at getting something they think is valuable for themselves or their community or the nation whether that something is a new road, a ban on abortion, or tax cuts. In a democracy, power starts with the vote; people are free to accumulate **more** power (and have a bigger say about what happens) by getting involved in interest groups and political

---

1. "Governor Perry: Austin Tea Party," You Tube, http://www.youtube.com/watch?v=dbWz1RYGE3Q (accessed 5/24/2009).

2. Walter E. Volkomer, *American Government* (Upper Saddle River, NJ: Prentice Hall, 2001), 3–4.

parties, contributing money, and running for office. Even in a democracy, though, small numbers of people end up with a lot of power and generally "drive" politics, which is to say they determine the issues that are important or at least shape how those issues are understood and make the decisions that determine "who gets what." F. Scott Fitzgerald is said to have observed about the very rich, "They are different from you and me." The same could also be said of powerful people.

The issues and the "doing" of politics, such as running for office, representing voters, championing some issues and opposing others, often fit a pattern that persists over time and will be called here a "**tradition**" of politics. While a crisis, such as a depression or a war, for example, might launch a new tradition, ultimately political traditions are shaped by a set of values, ideas about good and bad and right and wrong that influence the way politicians address issues. **Issues** are the specifics of politics. Issues such as taxes and who pays them, and the kinds of services government provides and to whom, generally reflect the needs of specific groups in society. The other major component of a political tradition is **style**— how politicians talk to the voters, deal with their opponents, and comport themselves. Style is also about how politicians connect (or not) with voters on an emotional level, and this emotional connection can sometimes surpass in importance the so-called "bread and butter" issues. Politics generally takes place in institutions such as political parties, legislatures, and campaigns, and these institutions are like the playing field and rules in a sporting event. Unlike a sporting event, however, rules may be changed by the "team" with the most power while the game is still being played. Groups that are kept out of political institutions, by fair means or foul, will sometimes form social movements to force the leaders of established institutions to take their issues seriously. The Civil Rights Movement in the 1960s was one such movement. Movement members form their own institutions, and these institutions challenge existing institutions for power.

Politics in the South has been defined by a series of crises, and each crisis has established new political traditions or altered old ones. In each crisis, a social movement played an important role in reconfiguring politics. The two most important crises occurred in the 1850s and '60s and, one hundred years later, in the 1950s and '60s. In each crisis, the divergence between the Southern political tradition and the national tradition led to a lengthy conflict. In the 1850s political discord over slavery became so virulent that eleven Southern states left the United States, and over six hundred thousand Americans died in the war that followed. Bitter, often violent, political warfare continued in the South for decades after the Civil War as African Americans and rural whites both fought for a voice in the region's politics. One hundred years later, the South was again on the losing end of a sectional political disagreement. This time the issue was segregation, and some areas of the region, particularly in the Deep South, were virtually occupied by federal troops and agents sent there to ensure civil and voting rights for black citizens. These two eras, when regional values gave way to national values only when troops showed up, demonstrate that the differences between the South's political culture and the rest of the nation's have at times approached the differences one expects between sovereign nations and also illuminate the South's ancient obsession: race. Race is still is at the center of Southern politics, joined in varying degrees of importance by class issues, economic development issues, a debate about the proper role, scope, and size of government, and concerns about cultural values. These issues and how politicians respond to them are shaping Southern politics and the politics of the nation.

Politics in Early Virginia

The first political crisis in the history of the South occurred in colonial Virginia in the mid-1600s. Landowning planters ruled Virginia, while the large majority of the population, indentured servants and former servants, had little or no say in the politics of the colony. As we have seen in earlier chapters, increasing numbers of servants were finishing their terms of servitude and becoming free, and the planters of Virginia and the colonial government that they controlled made no provisions for this growing throng of freed men and women. Many of them were left to scavenge for livelihoods in the settled areas of the colony or take their chances on the frontier, often squatting on land they did not own and fending off Indian attacks, their pleas for military assistance falling on deaf ears in Jamestown. Their discontent flared up as a rebellion in the 1670s that left Jamestown a smoldering ruin and might have overturned the plantation system had the rebellion's leader not suddenly died. The planters' long-term response to this crisis was to end the colony's dependence on "dangerous" indentured servants by replacing them with slaves of a different race. Former servants were now given land, voting privileges, and some degree of respect. The political agenda of the slaveholding planters in Virginia (and later across the South) henceforth would turn on two priorities: protecting and controlling their slave property and keeping on good terms with the expanding class of small farmers.[3]

The Patrician Tradition of Politics

The political tradition developed by the Virginia planters has been called the patrician tradition, and it has a long history extending well into the twentieth

---

3. Edmund S. Morgan, *American Slavery, American Freedom: The Ordeal of Colonial Virginia* (New York: W.W. Norton, 1975), 338–387.

century, although today, in its purest form, it has all but died out.[4] The term patrician was once used as the name of the upper class in ancient Rome, and a patrician tradition is one where, first and foremost, the political leadership comes primarily from the upper reaches of society. The patrician tradition had its roots in both southern England and the border areas of the British Isles, as historian David Hackett Fischer has persuasively argued. Wealthy landowners dominated the politics of southern England, and propertied clan leaders led the unruly Scots and Irish in the border regions.[5] The pattern that had evolved in colonial Virginia, had, by the eve of the Civil War, spread throughout the South. Southern politicians were generally drawn from the more affluent segment of society and were often slaveholding planters or closely connected through marriage and business dealings with planters. In piedmont Rowan County, North Carolina, for example, the Caldwell, Fisher, and Henderson families supplied many of the leading politicians of the county for decades. They were wealthy slaveholding families, they were intermarried, and they were connected by marriage to other wealthy and politically important families in the county and region.[6]

As political historian Paul Conklin has observed, patrician politicians preferred to emphasize universal issues that cut across class lines.[7] One sees the influence of this emphasis in the writings of the "founding fathers" of the nation, James Madison especially, who abhorred the idea of factional bickering and contention. For the patricians, good politics was consensual politics that benefited all. They favored free trade, a position that appealed to planters who produced commodities for sale in the world market and benefited from the free exchange of goods. For the small, subsistence-oriented farmer, free trade really did not matter much one way or the other except, perhaps, as a principle. Patrician politicians also favored low taxes and limited government that, again, often had universal appeal and certainly reflected the basic liberal principles

---

4. We're indebted to Paul Conklin's excellent description of the patrician and the Populist traditions in his article "Lyndon Johnson and the Outer South," in Charles Eagles, *Is There a Southern Political Tradition?* (Jackson: University Press of Mississippi, 1996), 145–166.

5. David Hackett Fischer, *Albion's Seed: Four British Folkways in America* (New York and Oxford: Oxford University Press, 1989), 241, 613, 642–650.

6. James Oakes, *The Ruling Race: A History of American Slaveholders* (New York, Vintage Books, 1983), 143–144; Gail Williams O'Brien, *The Legal Fraternity and the Making of a New South Community, 1848–1882* (Athens and London: The University of Georgia Press, 1986), 63; John J. Beck, "Development in the Piedmont South: Rowan County, North Carolina, 1850–1900" (Unpublished Ph.D. dissertation, University of North Carolina, Chapel Hill, 1984), 29–79.

7. Paul Conklin, "Lyndon Johnson and the Outer South," in Charles Eagles, ed., *Is There a Southern Political Tradition?* (Jackson, MS: University Press of Mississippi, 1996), 152.

that guided both small farmers and planters in the colonial era and in the new nation. But while a patrician politician like Thomas Jefferson could wax eloquently about the virtues of the small farmer, many of his peers had less romantic notions about where power and virtue lay. Few probably would have disagreed with Southern philosopher George Fitzhugh's observation that "some are formed for higher, others for lower stations—the few to command, the many to obey."[8] In this organic conception of politics and society, which was at heart a conservatism at odds with the liberal ideas of freedom and equality found in the Declaration of Independence (which Jefferson largely wrote), each portion of society had its own duties, and what benefited the head of the body politic (the planter class) also benefited the rest of the body (small farmers and tradesmen), too. Patrician politicians, as members or aspiring members of the upper class, saw themselves as the fathers of society who were kindly, just, and responsible, and took care of their inferiors, both free and slave.[9] The responsible politician did not inflame the passions of the voters, but rather met with other responsible politicians to work out agreements and then informed the electorate of their decisions. That was the ideal.

In reality, of course, passions **were** often inflamed, and patrician often contended with patrician for votes and influence. Patricians' interests often diverged because the planter class was not monolithic: coastal planters and upcountry planters often had very different views about the government's role in promoting economic development, for example. Upcountry planters often favored government railroad subsidies because they needed a faster, more dependable way of getting their cotton and tobacco to market; coastal planters had navigable rivers that worked just fine. The South, like the rest of the nation, developed a two-party system almost immediately after the Constitution was ratified, and in the decades before the Civil War, partisan conflict between the Democratic Party and the Whig party (the other dominant party of the era) was often quite bitter. The idea that government policies would benefit all also did not stand up to close scrutiny: the tax codes of most Southern states gave planters a healthy tax break on their most valuable property—slaves— and the few services governments did provide, higher education for example, often primarily benefited the upper class. Patricians sometimes favored positions that many of the common folk did not: secession was more popular among the slaveholding planters and patrician politicians than it was among the small farmers. Nor did patricians always respond to challenges to their power in ways that could be termed "fatherly."

---

8. George Fitzhugh, *Cannibals All! Or Slaves Without Masters* (Richmond, VA: A. Morris, Publisher, 1857), 102.

9. Joel Williamson, *The Crucible of Race: Black/White Relations in the American South Since Emancipation* (New York: Oxford University Press, 1984), 24–25.

Patrician Politics in Crisis

The sectional dispute over slavery in the mid-decades of the nineteenth century dominated the politics of the era and precipitated the most serious crisis in the political history of the South, a crisis that would result in secession, a bloody civil war, and thirty-five years of political upheaval and violence after the war. In the decades leading up to the Civil War, more and more Northerners began to accept the abolitionist argument that slavery was wrong and immoral, but this was still a viewpoint held by a minority. Abolitionist political influence skyrocketed when leading abolitionists began to argue that an evil "slave power," by which they meant a slaveholder dominated South, was intent on spreading slavery to every corner of the nation. Northern workers and small farmers, fearful that their "free labor" might have to compete with slave labor, were especially receptive to this new appeal, and eventually a new political party, the Republican Party, was established which capitalized on this rising anti-slavery, anti-South sentiment.[10] In the South, John C. Calhoun (and others) led a spirited campaign to promote Southern political unity in the face of what he believed was a concerted campaign by Northerners to destroy slavery.[11] Calhoun had mixed success during his lifetime (he died in 1850), but there is no question that criticizing slavery in the South became quite dangerous and "fire eaters"—proponents of secession—grew more influential in the region year by year, especially in the Deep South. Further, the Whig party, unable to stand the stresses of the sectional dispute, collapsed, leaving the South with one functional political party, the Democratic Party. Many planters saw the new Republican Party as a threat, and though the party was publicly committed to **containing** the growth of slavery, they suspected it would destroy slavery if it came to power, a fear that fed the secessionist movement in the South.[12] Fear also pushed the planter class in a more conservative direction as planters attempted to maintain control in the face of this "foreign" danger; in Georgia, for example, the state constitution was rewritten to reduce popular influence in the state senate and on the judiciary.[13]

With the election of the first Republican president (Abraham Lincoln) in 1860, South Carolina immediately left the union and the other Deep South states soon followed, but the Upper South did not rush to join them because

---

10. James Brewer Stewart, *Holy Warriors: The Abolitionists and American Slavery* (New York: Hill and Wang, 1976), 111–112; 166–177.

11. Lacy K. Ford, Jr., "Prophet with Posthumous Honor: John C. Calhoun and the Southern Political Tradition," in Eagles, ed., *Is there a Southern Political Tradition?* 3–25.

12. Stewart, *Holy Warriors: The Abolitionists and American Slavery*, 166–177.

13. Michael P. Johnson, *Toward a Patriarchal Republic: the Secession of Georgia* (Baton Rouge: Louisiana State University Press, 1977), 105–106, 143, 178.

opponents of secession in those states were quite numerous and vocal. Maryland, Kentucky, and Missouri never did secede, and when Virginia finally seceded, western Virginia actually seceded from Virginia. During the war, Union supporters in the seceding states continued to oppose the war, especially in the Upper South and in more mountainous regions where plantations, slaves, and planters were few and far between; over fifty thousand Southern men served in the Union army.[14] Unionist hotbed Eastern Tennessee probably furnished as many troops to the U.S. Army as it did to the Confederate army. So even during the war, the unity Calhoun had worked to build was still elusive, at least in parts of the South.

The South lost the war, and this loss burrowed deeply into the Southern psyche and touched off nearly four decades of often violent conflict between black and white, rich and poor, and urban and rural people. Initially, the victorious North, led now by Lincoln's successor, Andrew Johnson, pursued a conciliatory approach toward the South and for a year or so allowed each state to reconstitute state and local government. Secession leaders and high ranking Confederate officials were prominently involved in politics and even were elected to high state offices, and Southern state legislatures passed a series of laws called the "black codes" that were designed to relegate the former slaves to second class status and keep them tied to the plantations in a sort of shadow version of slavery. Republicans in Congress were furious; they had won the war, hadn't they? Led by the Radical wing of the party, they re-imposed military rule on the South. The state legislatures were disbanded, the governors sent home, and the courts shut down. Thus commenced what has been called the second or congressional Reconstruction. Former slaves were given the vote, and Southern states were ordered to draw up new state constitutions recognizing equality and universal manhood suffrage. The Republican Party, which was heretofore nonexistent in most of the South because of its opposition to slavery, was established in the region by Northern Republicans as a way of "checking" the power of the old planter class. The Southern branch of the Republican Party drew for its support on the newly enfranchised former slaves, but, contrary to legend, it also had a significant white membership. Whites living in the non-plantation areas, the mountains especially, where support for slavery and secession had been weak, and less affluent whites throughout the region were most likely to join the party.[15]

An important part of the drive to organize the Republican Party in the South was sponsored by the Union League. The League had been established in

---

14. Carl N. Degler, *The Other South: Southern Dissenters in the Nineteenth Century* (New York: Harper and Row, 1974), 130–175.

15. Eric Foner, *A Short History of Reconstruction, 1863–1877* (New York: Harper and Row, 1990), 130–132.

the North during the war to support the war effort; after the war some of its members traveled south to organize chapters. Some southern whites joined, particularly in the mountains, but in many areas, especially in the plantation districts, it was the freed slaves who flocked to the organization. The Union League played a major role in transforming a people who had once been slaves into real citizens with the vote. Local League chapters brought in speakers, held meetings, sponsored parades, and often organized members into paramilitary units that conducted military style drills. For the former slaves, the military training was accepted as one of the civic duties of free men, but it also had a political purpose. In York County, South Carolina, for example, the local League chapter organized drills on Election Day as a way of mobilizing black voters. League meetings in many areas were held in secret, and were sometimes protected by armed guards because of white hostility.[16] And the political activism of the former slaves did solicit a great deal of hostility from the white population. For many whites, their minds shaped by the slavery era, the secret meetings, drills, and processions of the Union League were at turns frightening, baffling, aggravating, and ridiculous.

Members of the Republican Party controlled the constitutional conventions organized in each state and won most of the offices in the state and congressional elections that followed. The party of Lincoln, non-existent in the South in 1865, now ruled the region and in only three years! While white Republicans won most of the elective offices, a significant minority of black Republicans were elected. Blacks served in Congress in both the House and the Senate, in the state legislatures, and as lieutenant governors in three states. One historian of Reconstruction in North Carolina has found that Republican officeholders generally were less affluent than their opponents and has argued that the party "seemed inspired by a mission: to open up North Carolina's aristocratic politics and social system." [17] In power, North Carolina Republicans, like Republicans in other Southern states, democratized government by making more offices elective rather than appointive and ending property qualifications to serve in office, and expanded services benefiting the common folk—schools especially.[18]

Not surprisingly, members of the old planter elite took a dim view of Republican success, based as it was on black votes and the support of federal troops, and saw it as, in fact, an "unnatural" development in which roles were reversed and the "proper" leaders of the South were replaced by whites of less

---

16. Steven Hahn, *A Nation Under Our Feet: Back Political Struggles in the Rural South From Slavery to the Great Migration* (Cambridge, Mass.: The Belknap Press of Harvard University, 2003), 177–190; Jerry Lee West, *The Reconstruction Ku Klux Klan in York County, South Carolina, 1865–1877* (Jefferson, NC: McFarland and Co., 2002), 43.

17. Paul D. Escott: *Many Excellent People: Power and Privilege in North Carolina* (Chapel Hill: University of North Carolina Press, 1985), 145.

18. *Ibid.* 144–145.

than reputable character and blacks suited by nature to follow not lead. A common saying of the era captured this sentiment: "The bottom rail's on the top." And it wasn't only political power the planters were worried about; they needed the labor of the former slaves and the talk of "40 acres and a mule," a plan to give former slaves small farms, threatened their labor supply and potentially even their hold on the land. They saw the new Republican governments as corrupt and filled with ignorant, venal officeholders incapable of doing their duty, and they complained about high taxes and rising state indebtedness. They called themselves "conservatives" and came up with a variety of insulting names for white Republicans, "carpetbagger" and "scalawag" being the two most well-known. Conservatives eventually gravitated to the newly reconstituted Democratic Party, and the party became the mouthpiece for the planter class. Many of the civilian and military leaders of the Confederacy were politically prominent after the war, and all but a handful were Democrats.[19]

The multi-racial Republican Party contended with the predominantly white Democratic Party for control of the South throughout the remainder of the Reconstruction era (1867–1876) in a bare-knuckles, no holds barred battle that constituted a second phase of the political crisis that had led to secession and war. Southern Democrats were committed to white supremacy pure and simple, and to ending Northern occupation of the South and Northern meddling in Southern politics. Defeated in war, the old planter elite was not going to lose the peace. The Ku Klux Klan, formed in 1867 by a group of Tennesseans including Confederate general Nathan Bedford Forrest, was an important part of the Democratic Party's campaign to wrest political and social control of the region away from the Republicans. In the words of one historian, "In effect, the Klan was a military force serving the interests of the Democratic Party, the planter class, and all those who desired the restoration of white supremacy." Klan leaders were often drawn from the upper class; in Rowan County, North Carolina, for example, the local chapter of the Klan was said to have been organized by prominent attorney Kerr Craige, Archibald Boyden (John Steele Henderson's cousin), and several others in the Salisbury law office of Craige and Craige.[20]

The Klan and other paramilitary white groups attempted to intimidate Republicans, especially black Republicans, through threats, beatings, murder, and arson. They often wore masks and operated under the cloak of darkness. In Alamance County, North Carolina, for example, Alonzo Corliss, a white

---

19. William B. Hesseltine, *Confederate Leaders in the New South* (Baton Rouge: Louisiana State University Press, 1950), 18–24.

20. Quote, Foner, *A Short History of Reconstruction*, 184; David M. Chalmers, *Hooded Americanism: The History of the Ku Klux Klan* (Durham, NC: Duke University Press, 1987), 9–10; James S. Brawley, *The Rowan Story, 1753–1953* (Salisbury, NC: Rowan Printing Co., 1953), 207.

school teacher from New Jersey who taught in a Freedman's school, was whipped; half his head was shaved and painted black. Sheriff Wyatt Outlaw, a prominent black Republican, was hanged from a tree near the courthouse in Graham.[21] Secrecy was important because federal troops still occupied parts of the South, and Klan leaders did not want to give Republicans in Washington reason to prolong if not extend military occupation. But make no mistake, a virtual war, indeed, the second phase of the Civil War, raged. Klansmen and other white militia groups sometimes fought pitched battles with Republican militia groups. At the so-called Colfax riot in Louisiana, for example, white and black militia units fired on each other in an unequal conflict that left three whites and over one hundred blacks dead.[22] In a small village outside Charleston, South Carolina, a white band tried to silence a Republican speaker at a political gathering; the band confronted a much larger black crowd that included several black militia units. The resulting gun battle left five whites dead and perhaps fifty wounded.[23] The Klan tended to be most active in areas where whites were in the majority or the population was evenly divided between blacks and whites. The piedmont regions of South and North Carolina were Klan hotbeds; in York County, South Carolina, a substantial part of the white population belonged to the Klan.[24] In North Carolina, Klan depredations in a swath of piedmont counties became so bad in 1870 that W.W. Holden, the Republican governor of the state, declared martial law and sent in a small army of militia to round up Klan insurrectionists.[25] Holden's efforts were to no avail. North Carolina Democrats, through legitimate politicking and terror, won most of the state legislative elections in 1870 handily, took control of the state legislature, and impeached Holden.

In South Carolina, two factions sought to lead the Democratic Party back to power in 1876: one headed by Martin Gary advocated a violent confrontation with Republicans; the other, headed by the former Confederate general Wade Hampton, believed a show of armed force would be enough to cow Republicans. Democrats organized rifle and saber clubs, members of which were often called Red Shirts for their distinctive garb. Hampton and his supporters prevailed, Hampton constantly urging his followers to "keep the peace," and the election was marked by "relatively" few deaths—21 blacks and 9 whites.[26]

---

21. Escott: *Many Excellent People: Power and Privilege in North Carolina,* 153–154.

22. Richard Rubin, "The Colfax Riot," *The Atlantic,* July /August 2003, http://www.atlantic.com/issues/2003/07/rubin.htm; James Hogue "The 1873 Battle of Colfax, Paramilitarism and Counterrevolution in Louisiana," unpublished paper, 2006, http://www.libertychapelcemetery.org/files/hogue-colfax.pdf.

23. Hahn, *A Nation Under Our Feet,* 307–308.

24. Foner, *A Short History of Reconstruction,* 186.

25. Escott: *Many Excellent People: Power and Privilege in North Carolina,* 153–154.

26. Jarrell, *Wade Hampton,* 58, 59, 61–62.

The Hampton "non-violent" approach was simple: armed bands of Red Shirts rode to polling places across the state to "discourage" blacks from voting. Red Shirt William Watts Ball claimed that in the election in Laurens, his home county, "Thousands of negroes did not vote—and the Red Shirt riders were the reason."[27]

The terrorist tactics, ballot box stuffing, and, yes, old fashioned political organizing, paid off across the South; by the end of Reconstruction (1877), Democrats dominated the politics of every Southern state. This victory was sometimes called "Redemption," the conservative leaders of Redemption were called "Redeemers," and the old dream of John C. Calhoun of a unified white South seemed closer to realization. White supremacy had replaced slavery as the primary unifying agent, joined with hatred and suspicion of the Yankee, and the glorification of secession and the war as the "Lost Cause." The Democratic Party embraced these themes and vigorously promoted the idea that it was the only legitimate party for "true" Southerners, and the only party that honored the sacrifices of the Confederate heroes. The lost dream of the Southern nation, snatched away by Yankee invaders who left the region in a shambles, would be mourned by party leaders for the next one hundred years. The party also became the sole exemplar of patrician politics because the Redeemers were squarely in that tradition. This tradition would persist well into the twentieth century, particularly in plantation districts such as the Delta and the Low Country of South Carolina.

But the "Redemption" was not as complete as the Redeemers would have liked; Republicans could still win elections and were still capable in most states of mounting a serious challenge to Democratic control, and white small farmers and tenants, while receptive to the emotional appeal of white supremacy and the "Lost Cause," were also beginning to look to politics for answers to more immediate, down-to-earth problems, first and foremost of which was the growing poverty of the rural South.

The Populist Challenge

No challenge to the patrician politics practiced by the Democratic Party was greater than that mounted by the Populists, and the resolution of this "crisis" by the leaders of the Democratic Party in each Southern state would shape the politics of the region for decades to come. Populism was a political and social movement that swept the rural South (and the Midwest, too) in the 1880s and

---

27. William Watts Ball, *The State That Forgot: South Carolina's Surrender to Democracy* (Indianapolis: Bobbs-Merrill, 1932), 164.

1890s. It was a movement spawned by the steady decline of agricultural prices during the decades following the Civil War, the rise of tenancy and sharecropping, and the growing poverty of the rural regions of the country. Then a depression swept the entire country in the early 1890s, making things even worse for farmers. The primary institutions of this movement in the South were the Southern Farmers' Alliance, which grew to hundreds of thousands of members by the late 1880s, the Colored Farmers' Alliance, organized by black farmers, and later the People's Party (sometimes called the Populist Party). The Alliance began in the late 1870s in the Hill Country of Texas and experienced explosive growth throughout the South in the 1880s, especially among small farmers and tenants. It offered despondent farmers a supportive organization of like-minded members, a coherent analysis of why farming was in such trouble, and finally, a plan to address those problems. While the older farm organizations advocated improved farming techniques, the Alliance blamed agrarian woes on the exorbitant rates charged by railroads, the high prices charged by merchants and warehousemen, and a system of credit that discriminated against borrowers. It called for the government to inflate the currency ("free coinage of silver" or "free silver," for short, was the slogan) to ease the debt burden of farmers, the nationalization of railroads to insure fair rail rates, and a government program (called the "subtreasury") that would subsidize crop prices.[28]

Populism also represented what one historian has described as "a politics of cultural resistance."[29] Across the nation, industry and cities were becoming the driving force in the economy, and the countryside and farming were being left behind, growing poorer as the cities grew richer, ignored, even ridiculed. Even in the largely rural South, the small towns and cities were the centers of prosperity. In the past, wealthy men were planters; now, they were more often merchants and mill owners and lawyers. Politics always follows the money, and now politicians were more often town dwellers who made their money in town.[30] The old connection between patrician politicians and the small farmer, first forged by Virginia planters 200 years before, was unraveling. Populism was as much a movement of people angry about being ignored and pushed aside by "progress" as it was about specific reforms. The typical Populist, in his heart of hearts, hoped to restore farming and the agrarian lifestyle to the economic and cultural preeminence of the past.

28. Robert C. McMath, Jr., *Populist Vanguard: A History of the Southern Farmers' Alliance* (New York: W.W. Norton Co., 1977), 3–5, 33–54, 90–131.

29. Raymond Arsenault, *The Wild Ass of the Ozarks: Jeff Davis and the Social Bases of Southern Politics* (Philadelphia: Temple University Press, 1984), 10.

30. *Ibid.*, 11–13; Albert D. Kirwin, *Revolt of the Rednecks: Mississippi Politics: 1876–1925* (Lexington: University of Kentucky Press, 1951), 43–44; Joseph F. Steelman, "The Progressive Era in North Carolina, 1884–1917" (Unpublished Ph.D. dissertation, University of North Carolina at Chapel, 1955), 38.

Alliance members in the South turned to politics with a vengeance in 1890, determined to take over the Democratic Party and bend it to Alliance goals. Only politicians who measured up to the Alliance "yardstick" and were willing to "'stand up and be measured'" were worthy of support.[31] This assertiveness by small farmers was something rarely seen before and flew in the face of the old patrician tradition of politics in which upper class men made the political decisions and less affluent men stood on the sidelines. Alliance members actually expected elected representatives to carry out their wishes and began to publicly denounce, and loudly, those who were evasive. Congressman John Steele Henderson of North Carolina tried to mollify farmers in his district by emphasizing his agrarian roots (his father had been a planter before the war), but Henderson himself was a railroad lawyer, a real estate speculator, and lived in town, and this did not escape notice. He promised to support free silver but waffled on the issue of the subtreasury.[32] When he was attacked for his stand on the issues and his ties to railroads, he was positively bewildered and wrote his wife that there seemed to be a "secret conspiracy" against him.[33] But it wasn't secret, and it wasn't a conspiracy; Henderson simply did not serve the interests of the small farmers and tenants in his district. Loyalty to the Democratic Party ran deep, and he was re-elected anyway, but it would be his last term in office.

Henderson's equivocation wasn't unique; Democratic politicians were mostly talk with little action, especially on the issue of the subtreasury. When it became clear that the existing parties weren't going to enact the Alliance program into law, Alliancemen formed a new party, the People's Party. Alliance members in John Steele Henderson's home county held back from organizing a local chapter of the new party and tried to continue to work within the Democratic Party. The ugly side of patrician politics reared its head when Henderson's cousin and lifelong friend, Archibald Boyden, used trickery and his position as chair of the Rowan County Democratic Executive Committee to outmaneuver Alliance members and keep them from gaining control of the Democratic Party county convention, despite their numerical advantage.[34] Chastened by their naïveté, Alliancemen organized the Rowan County People's Party shortly after the rigged Democratic county convention. In Alabama, Reuben Kolb failed to get the Democratic nomination for governor in 1890 in

---

31. *Ibid.*, 96; C Vann Woodward, *Tom Watson: Agrarian Rebel* (London: Oxford University Press; 1975; first published, 1938), 146.

32. "An Open Letter from the Hon. John Steele Henderson to J. B. Holman Esq., President of the Iredell County Farmers' Alliance," [1890], John Steele Henderson Collection, Southern Historical Collection, University of North Carolina, Chapel Hill.

33. John Steele Henderson to Bessie Henderson, 29 June 1890, John Steele Henderson Collection, Southern Historical Collection, University of North Carolina Chapel Hill.

34. [Salisbury, NC] *Carolina Watchman*, 12, 19 May 1892.

large measure because the Democratic Executive Committee "rigged" the state convention so that some of his delegates failed to be seated. Kolb left the party in 1892 and ran as an independent Democrat with the backing of Populists.[35] Democratic political chicanery repeated again and again across the South, coupled with the actionless lip service offered to the angry farmers by Democratic politicians, accounted for the mass exodus of Alliance members from the Democratic Party to the People's Party.

The People's Party offered candidates who claimed to represent the little man in a battle against the big man or the "masses against the classes" as it was sometimes phrased at the time. Their candidates for office were more like rural voters in terms of where they lived, what they did for a living, and what they were worth than was the case with their opponents. So they rejected the patrician appeal of "vote for me because I am the superior man and will make wise decisions" (what political scientists refer to as the "trustee" theory of representation). Instead, their approach was, "Who better to represent you in this struggle than someone like yourself?" While white Populists shared the racial prejudices of the time (one Populist leader edited a newspaper called *The Caucasian*), some were willing to seek the votes of blacks. The Louisiana People's Party platform made overtures to black voters, telling them that if they stayed with the Republican Party, they would continue to be "hewers of wood and drawers of water."[36] In some Southern states, Populists formed a coalition with the Republican Party to have a better chance at unseating their rivals in the Democratic Party. In these states, Populists and Republicans divided up the elective offices and agreed to support each other's candidates.

The new notions of who should be elected, the new issues, and the new tactics were a repudiation of the patrician political tradition and struck many Democrats as an assault on order rivaled only by the entrance of former slaves into politics twenty-five years before. Populists sometimes acknowledged the magnitude of what they were trying to accomplish; the platform of the Louisiana People's Party warned, "None can yet tell whether this revolution shall be accomplished by peaceable means...."[37] The *New Orleans Times Picayune*, a Democratic paper, headlined a story about the new party "It may be Ridiculous, but it is a Revolution."[38] The radical rhetoric, the rejection of upper class leadership, the willingness to make overtures to black voters and to

---

35. Sheldon Hackney, *Populism to Progressivism in Alabama* (Princeton, NJ: University Press of Princeton, 1969), 14.

36. William Ivy Hair, *Bourbonism and Agrarian Protest: Louisiana Politics, 1877–1900* (Baton Rouge: Louisiana State University Press, 1969), 218.

37. *Ibid.*

38. *Ibid.*, 219.

cooperate with the Republican Party both frightened and infuriated Democrats. Whether Populism was truly "revolutionary" is, in a sense, beside the point; the traditional leaders of the South saw it as such. And it introduced a new political tradition, the Populist tradition, which would influence Southern politics long after the Populist movement and the People's Party disappeared. This was a tradition that stressed the idea that leaders should resemble followers—a small farmer is the best representative of other small farmers. For the Populist, more affluent people simply couldn't understand the needs of "common folk," nor would they support issues that benefited them. Populists also believed government should actually do something to help the "common folk," and, most importantly, to right wrongs and protect the weak from the strong. This might involve, as we saw, establishing a government owned railroad system or government supported crop subsidies for struggling farmers. Ultimately, Populism was a movement that pitted the small farmer and the countryside against town and city interests in the South and Midwest and the growing industrial, banking, and transportation enterprises that were coming to dominate the national economy.

The People's Party was most successful in North Carolina, where a Populist/Republican "fusion" controlled the state legislature for four years, won the governorship, both U.S. Senate seats, and most of the congressional seats (including John Steele Henderson's). In the rest of the Southern states, however, the People's Party was less successful in part because Democrats abandoned patrician niceties and manners and used every tactic at their disposal to defeat their opponents. In Alabama, for example, Populist Reuben Kolb twice was defeated in bids for governor in elections marked by widespread Democratic election fraud, a commonplace occurrence in Alabama elections.[39] William C. Oates, who beat Kolb in his second race for governor, noted in comments to delegates assembled at the Alabama constitutional convention in 1901, "I told them to go it, boys, count them out [steal the vote]. We had to do it. Unfortunately, I say it was a necessity. We could not help ourselves. We had to do it or do worse. White men have gotten to cheating each other until we don't have any honest elections."[40] Across the South, ballot box stuffing, vote stealing, intimidation and assorted other tactics honed to perfection during Reconstruction prevented Populists and Republicans from taking offices they had rightfully won.

---

39. Hackney, *Populism to Progressivism in Alabama*, 22; William Warren Rogers, Jr. *The One-Gallused Rebellion: Agrarianism in Alabama, 1865–1896* (Tuscaloosa and London, Univ. of Alabama Press, 1970), 222, 280–285.

40. *Official Proceedings of the Constitutional Convention of the State of Alabama, May 21st, 1901 to September 3rd, 1901* (Wetumpka Printing Co., 1941), Vol. III, 2788–2789.

The Democrats Destroy the Populists and Break the Republican Party

Ultimately, Democrats developed a one-two punch to put Populism out for good and Republicanism out of power for the next seventy years. First, many Democrats tried to be more like the Populists. They appropriated a few Populist issues ("free silver" was the main one), and some Democrats began to speak and act like Populists. The refined Southern gentleman was "out" and the "salt of the earth" man was "in." At the national level, Democrats nominated in 1896 a man nicknamed "the Great Commoner" (William Jennings Bryan) for president, and his speech at the convention was full of religious and Populist imagery (it has been called the "Cross of Gold" speech) that captured the imaginations of many rural Americans. The Great Commoner supported free silver, and he attracted the votes of many Populists who thought quite pragmatically that supporting a candidate who championed a few of your issues and might actually win made more sense than supporting a man who championed most of your issues but would definitely lose.

In the South, the man who truly pioneered this new style of Democratic politicking was a South Carolinian named Ben Tillman. Tillman was a member of a prominent upcountry South Carolina family that had owned thousands of acres of land and nearly 100 slaves before the war, and he had been actively involved in the "Redemption" of the state from Republican rule in the 1870s.[41] By the 1880s he had acquired the nickname "Pitchfork" suggesting he was "just folks" despite his privileged background, and he spoke like a man on fire. What set him ablaze was his respect for the farmer and his hatred of their enemies—bankers, merchants, and the despised "money power" of eastern financiers and stock market investors.[42] "Pitchfork Ben" became a major force in South Carolina politics for decades. Many politicians following the patrician tradition, particularly those from Charleston and the Low Country, absolutely despised Tillman. He seemed to be turning his back on his own class, and he called one of their most cherished institutions, the Citadel, a "dude factory."[43] But on most issues, he really wasn't that different than the men he railed against. Aside from supporting free silver and establishing an agricultural college (Clemson), it's hard to see what else of substance he stood for that would have helped the small farmer in South Carolina.[44] However ineffectual he may

---

41. Kant, *Tillman*, 10.
42. *Ibid.*, 114.
43. Francis Butler Simkins, *The Tillman Movement in South Carolina* (Durham, NC: Duke University Publications, 1926), 144.
44. *Ibid.*, 18; Kant, *Tillman*, 150.

have been at actually helping the small farmers, he was standing up for them and loudly singing their praises and giving the people they hated hell.

Ben Tillman owed much of his success to his exploitation of the race issue, and this was the knockout punch other Democrats learned to use against their opponents and the one still used by some politicians today (more on this later). The majority of South Carolinians were black, and Tillman saw this as a permanent threat to white supremacy, particularly if whites split their votes between two (or more) parties, and blacks did not. Tillman, and those who emulated him, rewrote the book of rules for racial politics. Opposing candidates for office who were white were bitterly denounced as traitors to the white race. As he said in his inaugural address after he won the governor's office in 1890, his victory represented a "triumph of democracy and white supremacy over mongrelism and anarchy...."[45] Pitchfork Ben taught Democrats the recipe for winning: a steady stream of "heartfelt" tributes to farming folk, virulent racism, and the championing of a few Populist issues that never seemed to end up as laws or policies. Tillman's new style of politics became a model for other Democratic politicians to emulate and would set the tone for Southern politics for decades to come.

Tillman and Democrats across the South, whether they followed Tillman's new style of politics or the older patrician tradition, had one thing in common: they wanted to solve the "race problem" once and for all, and they believed only electoral "reform" offered a permanent solution to the political and social turmoil of the past three decades. They wished to establish a political system firmly **and permanently** in the hands of "respectable" white Democrats by taking the vote away from blacks. As John B. Knox noted at the constitutional convention called in Alabama to "reform" the electorate: "And what is it that we want to do? Why, it is, within the limits imposed by the Federal Constitution, to establish white supremacy in this State." [46] This approach was first taken in Mississippi in 1890 and was known thereafter as the Mississippi Plan. The plan involved disfranchising most blacks through a combination of literacy requirements to vote and a poll tax that one had to pay to be eligible to vote. In Mississippi, the tax was $2 a year ($4 if one failed to pay 2 or more years) that made voting nearly impossible financially for poor black sharecroppers who might never see $2 in cash in a year. (Recall that most of their purchases were made on credit.) The literacy test, as it was **actually** implemented in Mississippi and elsewhere in the South, disqualified virtually **all** black voters, often even the most literate; loopholes in the laws permitted illiterate whites to

---

45. Walter Edgar, *South Carolina: A History* (Columbia, SC: University of South Carolina, 1998), 438.

46. Address by John B. Knox, president of the Alabama Constitutional Convention, *Journal of the Proceedings of the Constitutional Convention of the State of Alabama* (Montgomery, AL: Brown Printing Co., 1901), 9.

vote. In Mississippi, the electorate declined by nearly half within two years of enactment of these measures. Most blacks lost the vote, but thousands of less affluent whites also disappeared from voter registration lists because the $2 poll tax affected them, too.[47]

Efforts by Democrats to regain power and permanently "fix" the political system took the most violent turn in North Carolina, a state where, as we have seen, Populists and Republicans were most successful. Here, Furnifold M. Simmons (a future U.S. senator), newspaper publisher Josephus Daniels (publisher of the Raleigh *News and Observer*), Charles B. Aycock (a future governor), and others launched the so-called White Supremacy Campaign in 1898 to restore the state to the Democratic fold. Democrats were selling an idea, and that idea was that Populist and Republican rule had brought chaos, disorder, and "negro domination," a term used again and again. In speeches and newspapers articles, Democrats offered white voters a stark choice: vote Democratic and support the supremacy of the white race or vote Republican or Populist and support "negro domination." White supremacy clubs were organized and large rallies were held, especially in the eastern part of the state where blacks made up a large portion of the population and white interest in driving blacks from the electorate was the strongest. In speeches and newspapers articles, Democrats described "outrages" committed by blacks ranging from the alleged corruption of black officeholders to a rising tide of petty and serious crimes committed by blacks. Democrats hammered away at the idea that black men posed a mortal threat to the safety and virtue of white women. Democrat George Rountree went to speak at a meeting of a white supremacy club "to inflame the white men's sentiment, and discovered that they were already willing to kill all of the office holders and all the negroes, and so I immediately reacted and became a pacifist." Others were not so circumspect. Taking their cue from their neighbors to the south, North Carolina Democrats organized Red Shirt clubs to constitute the terrorist wing of the party (the Klan had lapsed into inactivity), and Red Shirts rode out at night to threaten, harass, and beat leaders and members of the opposition. In Wilmington, for example, crowds of armed Red Shirts "milled around" polling places on Election Day; they even threatened the Republican governor of the state who had come to Wilmington to vote at his home precinct and literally had to run for his life. The formula worked; Democrats swept back into control of the state legislature.[48]

---

47. Kirwin, *Revolt of the Rednecks*, 73.

48. Quote from George Rountree, "Memorandum of My Personal Recollection of the Election of 1898," Henry G. Connors Collection, Southern Historical Collection, University of North Carolina at Chapel Hill; Escott, *Many Excellent People*, 253–260; H. Leon Prather, Sr. *We Have Taken a City: Wilmington Racial Massacre and Coup of 1898* (Wilmington, NC: NU World Enterprises, Inc., 1998; first published, 1984), 52–54, 83–85, 92–93, 102–103.

It was also in Wilmington that Democrats started (and finished) a race riot following the election. Democrats had won at the polls, but Republicans and Populists still controlled the city government, and municipal elections weren't for another year. A small group of wealthy leading citizens of the city, called "the secret nine," had been working on a plot to take over the city and force the Republican and Populist elected and appointed local officials out of office. The violent tenor of the White Supremacy campaign and an ill-advised editorial by a local black newspaper editor set the stage for the plotters and others of a similar bent of mind to launch their takeover. Following the election, a small army equipped with rifles and even a machine gun ordered specially for the occasion went on a rampage in a sort of paramilitary riot that left a dozen or more blacks dead and drove hundreds out of town in fear of losing their lives. The Republican mayor and the Republican-dominated board of alderman were forced by the mob to resign and were replaced by Democrats. The new mayor was Colonel Alfred M. Wadell, perhaps the most active of the instigators and leaders of the riot. In the aftermath of the riot, black men prominent in politics and the business community were driven out of the city.[49]

The Democrats destroyed the competitive party system in the South. The Republican Party, shorn of the black vote, its leaders almost literally beaten into submission, its white members demoralized by charges of disloyalty to the white race, would not be a viable contender for power in most of the region until the 1970s; only in the predominantly white mountain and upland areas of the South could Republicans routinely win elections. The People's Party died. These parties were not the only casualties of the Democratic "revolution." Thanks to the election "reforms" passed by Democratic controlled state legislatures, voting turnouts declined in many areas of the South and rarely reached fifty percent of the eligible electorate. Often rates were much lower than that (10% turnouts were not uncommon) and averaged such laughably small percentages in some states (Virginia seems to have won the prize) that it's hard to say that some areas of the South even had a democratic system of government in a meaningful sense for the first half of the twentieth century. And this wasn't only because the black vote had all but disappeared; the poll tax and other measures seriously cut into white turnout.[50] This was not exactly a surprise; some of the "reformers" had hoped to eliminate poor whites from the electorate because they distrusted them nearly as much as the black voters. William Oates, for example, was very open about this at the Alabama constitutional convention that rewrote the election laws of that state, telling the assembled

---

49. Prather, *We Have Taken a City*, 49–52, 117–150.
50. J. Morgan Kousser, *The Shaping of Southern Politics: Suffrage Restriction and the Establishment of the One-Party South, 1880–1910* (New Haven: Yale University Press, 1974), 226–227, 236–237; V.O. Key, Jr., *Southern Politics in State and Nation* (New York: Vintage Books, 1949), 20, 533–618.

delegates he wanted to disfranchise not only "densely ignorant and corrupt" blacks but also "the whites of this class...." As he noted, "The privilege of voting is not a natural right."[51]

Other "reforms" also limited democracy. In South Carolina, for example, the constitutional convention that convened in1895 at Ben Tillman's urging passed the usual measures that took away voting rights, but the convention also established a system that severely circumscribed democratic government at the local level by giving each county's legislative delegation, headed by the county's state senator, control over the county's local budget and virtual control over appointments to local offices. Senators, particularly the more powerful ones, would rule their home counties as small bore dictators making decisions that in most other parts of the country were made by elected county commissioners and boards of education. South Carolina would keep this system into the 1970s when a "home rule" amendment and legislation established locally elected county government and local control over taxation and funding decisions. The dramatic changes to the state's system of government in 1895 weren't even sent to the voters for their approval.[52]

The Patrician Tradition in Populist Clothes

Looking back, the triumph of the Democratic Party at the turn of the century seemed to represent the triumph of the upper class and the patrician tradition: low taxes, limited government, limited popular participation in politics and a rural black workforce no more than a step or two beyond slavery would be the rule for the next sixty years. A particular part of the upper class, the planters in the plantation districts, had pushed the hardest for disfranchisement and assumed a sort of veto power in each state when it came to racial matters and, by extension, many other issues because race and labor and taxes were all interconnected. As V.O. Key, Jr., has argued, despite the declining role played in the Southern economy by planters and plantations, the planters had succeeded in imposing their will on the South so that it "presented a solid regional front in national politics on the race issue."[53] But if patrician issues were victorious, the patrician himself and his **style** faced new challenges. Ben Tillman had pioneered the marrying of patrician issues to a Populist style of poli-

51. *Official Proceedings of the Constitutional Convention of the State of Alabama, May 21st, 1901 to September 3rd, 1901*, Vol. III, 2793.

52. Edgar, *South Carolina*, 443–446, 551; Flora Carmichael Hopkins, "A Power Structure Study of a Selected County in South Carolina" (Unpublished Ph.D. dissertation in Education, University of South Carolina, 1978), 31–33.

53. Key, Jr., *Southern Politics*, 9–11.

ticking, and politicians practicing this marriage became so common that the South earned notoriety for the colorful demagogues its politics seemed to produce in such profusion. These politicians spoke the language of the average man—no five dollar words came out of their mouths—and they loudly championed "the farmer" or "the working people" and boasted that they were not afraid to stand up to the "big shots" or the politicians, or the bankers, or whatever privileged target resonated with the public at the time. An affluent background, a refined manner, a college education became handicaps in the political arena, not virtues. Candidates with "common" origins had the advantage, and a rural birthplace counted for much. So, for example, it was commonly understood in Mississippi that hill country small farmers would not vote for a delta planter running for a statewide office.[54] Even today in North Carolina, a home address in Charlotte (Charlotte's the state's largest city) is considered the kiss of death for most politicians aspiring to state office; being born and raised in the rural eastern part of the state is a strong plus.

Lee "Pass the Biscuits, Pappy" O'Daniel, flour salesman, radio personality, governor of Texas and later U.S. senator, was a classic practitioner of this style. Pappy was accompanied by his studio band, the Hillbilly Boys, when he campaigned for governor of Texas in 1938. The band was as likely to play a hymn as a popular tune at appearances that resembled revival meetings more than political meetings. He told voters his platform was the Ten Commandments, boasted that he would throw out the "the professional politicians," and promised that he would establish a pension plan for older Texans. In office, however, he seemed more interested in representing the oil and gas industry and other corporate interests than the common folk he so ardently embraced on his radio show and the campaign trail. But piety and tributes to family and farm apparently counted for a lot with his supporters, and "Pappy" was re-elected governor and later elected to the U.S. Senate.[55]

Were "Pass the Biscuits, Pappy," Pitchfork Ben, and other Populist-style politicians merely scoundrels who pretended to be the common man's friends while secretly representing the interests of the affluent? In some cases they were, and in other cases they were merely inept and confused. Here and there a few Democrats followed both the style and the substance of the Populist tradition. Huey "the Kingfish" Long is often mentioned as a leading exemplar of this tradition. Long came from one of the poorest counties in Louisiana, one with a tradition of Populist dissent. While his own family was affluent by local standards, his biographer has argued that he realized that he would be viewed

---

54. J. Todd Moye, *Let the People Decide: Black Freedom and White Resistance Movements in Sunflower County, Mississippi, 1945–1986* (Chapel Hill: University of North Carolina Press, 2004), prologue.

55. On Pappy O'Daniel see Robert A. Caro, *The Years of Lyndon Johnson: The Path to Power* (New York: Alfred A. Knopf, 1982), 695–703.

as a "hick" by the upper class men of New Orleans or the plantation districts, and this realization helped him identify with the small farmers of Louisiana.[56] Long campaigned for governor of Louisiana in 1928 with a promise that he would represent the people, not big oil companies, planters, and entrenched political interests. He won election by taking the parishes in Louisiana where small farmers were most numerous. As governor, he pushed for tax reforms that pushed more of the tax burden onto the corporations (particularly in the oil industry), increased funding for hospitals and schools, and provided free textbooks to school children. While his accomplishments were relatively modest, he was immensely popular with less affluent Louisianans without resorting to the virulent racism so characteristic of many of his peers. Long's Populism was accompanied by an unquenchable thirst for power that had many worried that he was an American version of Hitler.[57] He began campaigning for the presidency in 1935 with a promise to create a "share the wealth" program if elected, but his campaign ended when he was assassinated. Long would be joined in the pantheon of Democrats whose Populism moved beyond style to substance by Ralph Yarborough, Lyndon Johnson (both of Texas) and Albert Gore (Vice President Al Gore's father) of Tennessee to name a few.[58] None were his equal in terms of charisma.

Ultimately, what most Populist-style Democrats ran into was the hard reality that turning around the declining fortunes of the small farmer and restoring the agrarian lifestyle to its former glory would have required radical reforms that would have led to a resumption of the pitched battles of the Populist era. At heart, the typical Populist-style Democrat wasn't a radical with a serious alternative to offer; he shared (or appeared to share) his constituents' prejudices, hatreds, and romantic illusions, but he had no earthly idea how to save the small farmer from extinction or give "common folks" more power. Nor was he truly willing to challenge the way politics was done. He wanted a piece of the system; he didn't want to change the system. Aside from throwing some rascals out of government (replaced, in short order, by new rascals), most Populist-style Democrats, like many of their small farmer supporters, "had limited faith in government as a problem-solving institution and remained wedded to the ideals of low taxes and small government."[59] Ironically, the very culture that was being threatened—the agrarian culture—fostered a value system that discouraged a sustained movement with realistic political objectives that may have been able to help rural people. People who might be in-

---

56. T. Harry Williams, *Huey Long* (1969; New York: Vintage Books, 1981), 24.

57. Alan Brinkley, *Voices of Protest: Huey Long, Father Coughlin, and the Great Depression* (New York: Vintage Books, 1983), 28–34; 273.

58. Raymond Arsenault, "The Folklore of Southern Demagoguery," in Eagles, ed., *Is There a Southern Political Tradition?*, 122.

59. *Ibid.*, 116.

clined to hear and act upon a realistic Populist message were pulled in the other direction by "traditionalist" values that stressed self-reliance, family as the primary support network and source of assistance, obedience and deference to authority, and the right of businessmen to make money as they saw fit. This traditionalist value system proved to be remarkably resilient and outlived the agrarian culture that gave rise to it.[60]

In any event, we cannot discount the psychological gratifications these Populist-style politicians provided to people. As one historian has noted, "They were legitimate folk heroes, yet (with the exception of Huey Long), their heroics were largely illusory. They were agrarian radicals, yet for the most part they practiced a politics of catharsis and symbolic action...."[61] In short, they made the struggling small farmers and white sharecroppers and the burgeoning class of white mill workers feel better about themselves by telling them they were important, affirming their values, and attacking and ridiculing people by whom they felt threatened. They gave them excitement, drama, emotion, clear-cut villains to hate and heroes to cheer, and an outlet for their despair and anger. The planter or the millowner might shake his head and bemoan the disappearance of honorable men from politics, but ultimately government still did his bidding.

Unfortunately, the one indispensable villain in the drama of Southern politics was the African American. George Wallace learned this lesson the hard way. In the 1950s he emerged as a champion of the "little man" in Alabama under the tutelage of "Big Jim" Folsom, the hard-drinking governor of Alabama who actually was as close to being a "real" Populist as the Democratic Party in the South ever produced. Folsom was a racial moderate, and Wallace adopted this position in his first race for governor. His opponent forcefully defended segregation, and Wallace did not. Wallace was defeated and vowed afterwards, "John Patterson [his opponent] out-nigguhed me. And boys, I'm not goin' to be out-nigguhed again."[62] His focus soon fastened on race and the "enemy" became blacks, their Northern liberal allies, and the federal government, which, Wallace argued, was trying to impose foreign ways on the good people of Alabama. Wallace won in his next race for governor and became famous for literally standing in the doorway of a University of Alabama building to prevent the entrance of two black students there to enroll. One of Wallace's early biographers gives him credit for supporting some Populistic measures, such as the creation of the Alabama community college system and an ex-

---

60. Merle Black and Earl Black, *Politics and Society in the South* (Cambridge: Harvard University Press, 1987), chap. 2; Paul Luebke, *Tar Heel Politics 2000* (Chapel Hill and London: University of North Carolina Press, 1998), 20–22.

61. Arsenault, *Wild Ass of the Ozarks*, 7. See also Arsenault, "The Folklore of Southern Demagoguery" in Charles Eagles, ed. *Is There A Southern Political Tradition?*, 114–115.

62. Marshall Frady, *Wallace* (New York and Cleveland: Meridian Books, 1970), 127.

panded system of roads.[63] However, even though Wallace served four terms as governor (his wife was actually elected governor for a term, too), it's hard to find much evidence that the common folk of Alabama were much better off having had him at the center of their politics for so many years. Today, Alabama has one of the most regressive tax systems in the country (a regressive system taxes the poor at a higher rate than the rich), and one recent governor, a conservative Republican, observed in exasperation, "I'm tired of Alabama being first in things that are bad and last in things that are good."[64] But, as we will see later, Wallace **had** updated the formula for political success first pioneered by Ben Tillman, and this formula would be utilized to great effect by the Republican Party in its rise to power in the region.

Populism Today

It should be clear by now that the slow decline of agrarianism in the South, beginning in the waning years of the nineteenth century and continuing into the contemporary era, has had a profound effect on Southern politics. Rural people and city people with rural roots have responded again and again to politicians who spoke the language of the agrarian South. However, the brutal crushing of the Populist movement, the clever use of the race issue, and a one-party political system that discouraged political competition and popular participation rendered this a language that was long on symbol and short on practical issues. It takes institutions to develop issues and pressure politicians, and struggling farmers and sharecroppers and rural folks streaming to the cities and towns to work in the textile mills didn't have the farm organizations or unions that could do this. Certainly the Democratic Party wasn't the institution to do this; it was primarily a "good old boys" club focused on stability, especially racial stability. Here and there a Populist alternative was offered to the voter in an organized and consistent manner, for example Texas during the New Deal years of the 1930s, but generally the Populist voice was the lone voice that spoke and then was gone.

As farming declined as a major employer and more and more people lived in cities and suburbs and worked in factories and offices, a scattering of activists refashioned the traditional Populist economic message to address the new social and economic realities of the region. This reformulated message at-

---

63. *Ibid.*, 137–138.

64. Dale Russakoff, "Alabama Tied in Knots by Tax Vote," *The Washington Post*, 17 August 2003; "Alabama's Taxes Hit Poor and Middle Class Far Harder than the Wealthy," Institute on Taxation and Economic Policy, 7 January 2003, http://www.itepnet.org/wp 2000/al%20pr.pdf .

tacks the power of the big corporations and their servants, and it proposes some level of the redistribution of wealth, through higher taxes on corporations and the wealthy, to benefit those at the bottom and in the middle. As with the message of the agrarian Populists, it says that an unfettered free market is not always a good thing and so, for example, in recent years, free trade agreements like the North American Free Trade Agreement (NAFTA) have been roundly criticized by latter-day Populists for benefiting investors and hurting people in the working class by driving tens of thousands of factory jobs overseas.[65] This contemporary Populism exerts a relatively weak influence today in the Democratic Party and little if any in the Republican Party. Bill Clinton, for example, first appeared on the political scene in Arkansas as a crusading state attorney general in the Populist mold who was not afraid to take on powerful corporate interests. By the time he had begun his run for president, however, this early Populism was seriously diminished.[66] Among Mr. Clinton's "sins" as president from a Populist perspective was his support for NAFTA. Whatever appeal a Populist message might have to struggling middle and working class voters, it has had little appeal for those running for office; that is, if they want to win. Money is the lifeblood of the contemporary Democratic and Republican parties, and no politician has succeeded for very long by biting the hands that dole out the big campaign contributions. Here and there you'll find men and women like Jim Hightower of Texas. Hightower served as the commissioner of agriculture in Texas and often was at odds with the large corporate farming interests of Texas. He's not an officeholder anymore, but does continue to fight the Populist fight on his radio program and in print.

The modern-day Republican Party has assumed, as we will explore in more detail in a later section, the old Populist role of defender of an embattled culture. Today that culture is not so much agrarianism, which has declined well beyond the embattled state, but the traditional values associated with the agrarian culture of the South. The Republican state supreme court judge in Alabama who dragged a 2½-ton stone inscribed with the Ten Commandments into the foyer of the state supreme court building in the middle of the night (in July, 2001) was making a statement that would have caused "Pass the Biscuits, Pappy" to smile knowingly if he were still around to hear about it.[67] Jesse Helms became a powerful presence in North Carolina politics first as a television commentator in the 1960s and then as a five-term U.S. senator (1973–2003) by loudly and often bitterly denouncing integrationists, welfare recipients, government bureaucrats, radical feminists, homosexuals, and big city liberals.

---

65. Luebke, *Tar Heel Politics 2000*, 25–27.
66. Jimmie Lewis Franklin, "Commentary," in Charles Eagles, ed., *Is There a Southern Political Tradition?* (Jackson: University Press of Mississippi, 1996), 201–203.
67. Joshua Green, "Roy and his Rock," *The Atlantic Monthly* (October 2005), http://www.theatlantic.com/doc/200510/roy-moores-ten-commandments (accessed 3/7/06).

The Progressive Tradition

Another tradition of politics also emerged at the turn of the century and would play a major role in defining Southern politics. This tradition, the progressive tradition, was found elsewhere in the nation but would have a peculiarly Southern cast to it as it was practiced in the South. While patricians resisted change and promoted tradition and were rooted in the soil of the plantation South, and Populists (in their pure form) reflected the views and needs of the less affluent, particularly the rural less affluent, progressives were interested in promoting economic growth and positive social change—in short, progress—and reflected the views and goals of urban middle and upper class people. While patricians sought to keep government services and taxes to a minimum, and Populists sought to use government to get fairer treatment and a bigger share of services and benefits for the less affluent, progressives sought to expand government services and use government as a tool to promote economic development and to correct the ills of society.

The progressive tradition was, just like the Populist tradition, the product of a movement, and this movement swept across the nation in the 1890s and early 1900s. The dramatic changes in American society—the rapid growth of industry, the troubles in agriculture that had led to the Populist movement, the explosion in the size and number of cities, the millions of immigrants pouring into cities and working in the growing numbers of factories—seemed to be transforming American society at breakneck speed. Strikes, violent confrontations between workers and private police hired by factory owners, rising levels of crime, terrible poverty and living conditions in the crowded and ever expanding city slums, and the almost god-like wealth and power of the new class of industrialists and bankers convinced many that the nation might come apart at its seams. Progressives wanted first and foremost to re-establish order in America, and to do this they advocated a wide variety of reforms intended to make things better.[68] They pushed to clean up political corruption, they advocated electoral reforms like the popular election of U.S. senators and the enfranchisement of women, they worked to expand educational opportunities, and they advanced legislation to regulate business, establish rules for child labor, and create safety and sanitary standards for the food industry. They were the first environmentalists. The two most influential politicians of the first two decades of the twentieth century, President Theodore Roosevelt, a Republican, and President Woodrow Wilson, a Democrat, were both considered progressive reformers. Indeed, progressivism was a powerful presence in both political parties.

The roots of progressivism in the South trace back to the 1870s and 1880s when men dedicated to "progress" first made their appearance in the region.

---

68. Robert Wiebe, *The Search for Order* (New York: Hill and Wang, 1967), 11–43.

These were men committed to making their towns grow and prosper, and this meant attracting a rail line to the town, which was a necessity if the town was going to grow, creating or expanding city services like water and sewer service, and building public schools. To accomplish these goals, reformers had to convince voters to raise tax rates and often pitted them against patrician politicians who, as we've seen, were committed to low taxes and limited services. They also often ran into opposition from rural people who were as skeptical of increasing the scope of government and raising taxes as patricians and weren't convinced that "progress" was necessarily a good thing. These folks were often able to cut through all the talk about progress and improvement and see that progressives were really interested in finishing off the very life—the agrarian life—that they wished to rescue. In Rowan County, North Carolina, for example, rural precincts repeatedly voted down railroad bond issues that developers hoped would attract the railroad to the county's major town.[69] By the early 1900s, Southern progressives had moved on to a score of new causes: the regulation of corporations, especially railroads and out-of-state enterprises, prohibition of alcohol and the saloon, the expansion and professionalization of public schools, public heath crusades, and the uplift of blacks and poor whites.[70]

Ultimately, progressivism was rooted in a Victorian mindset common throughout the South (and the rest of America) in the middle and upper classes that saw human history as a battle between civilization and savagery.[71] Educated civilized people, gentlemen and gentlewomen, for that is also how progressives typically saw themselves, needed to uplift the less fortunate, and government was often the best mechanism to do this. Progressives were basically paternalists: "they embraced uplift and progress, yet believed in a hierarchy of race and culture; ... they were fervent advocates of democracy, yet also endorsed measures of coercion and control."[72] In short, they were saying to blacks and poor whites and rural folk, "We know what's best for you." Progressive reformers worked closely with religious groups and denominations in the South which were also involved with uplifting people. Ministers were often leaders in the progressive movement, especially on issues that involved personal morality like prohibition.

While many progressives favored some degree of regulation of business, especially large corporations, this is not to say they had a problem with someone

---

69. Beck, "Development in the Piedmont South," 127–149.
70. Edward L. Ayers, *The Promise of the New South: Life After Reconstruction* (New York and Oxford: Oxford University Press, 1992), 413–422.
71. Daniel Joseph Singal, *The War Within: From Victorian to Modernist Thought in the South, 1919–1945* (Chapel Hill, NC: University of North Carolina Press, 1982), 23–33.
72. William A. Link, *The Paradox of Southern Progressivism, 1880–1930* (Chapel Hill and London: The University of North Carolina Press, 1992), xii. See also Dewey Grantham, *Southern Progressivism: the Reconciliation of Progress and Tradition* (Knoxville: University of Tennessee Press, 1983), 172–177.

making a buck or lots of bucks. As one historian has noted "they were thoroughly committed to the idea of economic growth, industrial expansion, and entrepreneurial opportunity."[73] They themselves were often businessmen or they represented business interests in their private law practices, and certainly they often moved in the same social circles as the more successful business leaders. They did recognize, however, that business, particularly larger businesses, needed some restraint, ideally of the self-imposed sort if businessmen could be convinced that this was in their own self-interest.

North Carolina is generally considered the Southern state harboring the strongest progressive tradition. This is not surprising because it was the state that had experienced the strongest growth of industry, urban development, and had the weakest planter class. Charles B. Aycock, the same Charles B. Aycock who helped lead the White Supremacy Campaign in the late 1890s, is generally considered the state's first progressive governor. Aycock was far from the only Southern progressive to support disfranchisement of black citizens; many Southern progressives had supported it because, they argued, blacks weren't really ready for the vote, and the political turmoil black voting had stirred up threatened social order. Despite Aycock's unsavory role as a white supremacist, he is still remembered and honored in the state today as the father of public education, and there are few counties in the state where one cannot find a public school named after him. He also supported prohibition although he was himself a drinker, but again, the concern of the middle and upper class reformer was generally not his or her own behavior but that of less "civilized" folk in the lower classes.[74] Later progressive governors expanded the state's system of roads and earned for North Carolina the nickname "the good roads state," and after World War II, expanding higher educational opportunities became another plank in the progressive program. The university system grew by leaps and bounds; in the 1960s, Governor Terry Sanford created one of the earliest and most extensive state-funded community college systems in the country. Sanford was noteworthy for steering the state on a moderate course during the Civil Rights era while leaders in other states (George Wallace, for one) opted to vigorously oppose the ending of discriminatory laws and practices.[75] While education and roads may have been the watchwords in the North Carolina progressive tradition, progressives supported a variety of tax incentives and other inducements to attract new industries to the state. The most successful effort to encourage new business and industry was the Research Tri-

---

73. Grantham, *Southern Progressivism*, 158.

74. Oliver H. Orr, Jr., *Charles Brantley Aycock* (Chapel Hill, NC: University of North Carolina Press, 1961), 240.

75. Jack Bass and Walter De Vries, *The Transformation of Southern Politics: Social Change and Political Consequence Since 1945* (New York and Scarborough, Ontario: New American Library, 1977), 230–232.

angle Park. With other government, education, and business leaders, Governor Luther Hodges established the Park in the 1950s, and by the 1980s the project was being touted across the country as a model for government/business cooperation and thoughtful economic development.[76]

Many modern Southern governors fit the progressive mold whether they are Democrats or Republicans. North Carolina's Jim Hunt has been, without a doubt, the most successful governor in the progressive tradition in recent memory. Hunt occupied the governor's mansion for sixteen years in the 1980s and 1990s and, before that, served a four-year term as lieutenant governor. The issues he rode the hardest were education and economic development. An unlikely progressive governor was Republican Bob Riley, who, as member of the U.S. House of Representatives, was a strong proponent of tax cuts and worked vigorously to scale back the size of the federal government, but seemed to have transformed himself into a progressive when he was elected governor of Alabama in 2002 and was faced with a fiscal crisis that left the state over half a billion dollars short of meeting its revenue needs, and this in a state already saddled with grossly overcrowded prisons and poorly funded schools. He forcefully, albeit unsuccessfully, promoted tax reforms that would have made the tax system more equitable and would have expanded funding for the public schools of the state. As he noted, "I believe in a fair tax code. They [his opponents] don't. I believe we have to make investments in education that keep us from being tied for dead last. They don't. They have had special treatment at least for all of my adult life. And even after this modest increase, they'll still be paying less than in any of our surrounding sister states." [77]

While progressives believe in economic progress and the possibility that government reforms and programs can make life better for people, like patricians, they don't like conflict and hope to find policies, better roads for example, that everyone can support. Progressives are insiders; they walk confidently down the corridors of power in government and business, they belong to country clubs and live in nice houses, and they are at home amongst the affluent. In the media-dominated politics of today, much of the money for a successful campaign comes from upper income voters and business interests, and progressive politicians understand this.[78] Not surprisingly, they are nearly as

---

76. Luther M. Hodges, *Businessman in the Statehouse: Six Years as Governor of North Carolina* (Chapel Hill, NC: University of North Carolina Press, 1962), 203–223.

77. Russakoff, "Alabama Tied in Knots by Tax Vote."

78. V.O. Key, Jr. noted the connection between the affluent business leaders and progressives in his classic study *Southern Politics* when he argued that North Carolina, considered then and now one of the most progressive Southern states, was governed by a "progressive plutocracy" (a wealthy elite). Key, *Southern Politics*, 205–228. Paul Luebke, in his more recent study, concludes that nothing has changed. See Luebke, *Tar Heel Politics, 2000*, 48.

wary as patricians of class-based appeals that pit less affluent voters against business and industrial leaders and the rich. They don't want drastic changes in the system; they want to make the system operate better. Their solution to the social fairness issue is to make the pie bigger so that everyone has a bigger piece, but they prefer that the size of the slices not be examined too carefully. Today, for example, public universities, attended primarily by middle and upper class young people, are funded at a much higher level than community colleges, which are more likely to be attended by working class people. State and local governments in the South have long been funded primarily by regressive taxes that hit the less affluent hardest; this is common across the nation but is particularly pronounced in many Southern states. For example, in Georgia, a state with a modest progressive tradition, the poorest 20% of taxpayers pay nearly 12% of their income in state and local taxes; the top 1% pay less than 7% (less than 6% when federal deductions are factored in).[79]

Perhaps the strongest indictment of progressivism is that it looks at the less affluent, the less educated, and minorities as "problems" to be solved. For those viewed as "problems," resentments naturally build up even though the progressive politician is trying to help, and this sometimes surfaces when a seemingly popular progressive politician loses an election in an upset. Too, in the interest of good relationships with powerful economic interests, progressives have sometimes been less than forthcoming about the true costs and benefits of "progress." Progress leaves in its wake winners and losers, and government programs can't always help the people and communities who lose. Communities that lose jobs when factories move overseas often face years if not decades of high unemployment, and laid-off textile workers often can't be retrained for exciting new careers in computers or biotechnology. There is no question, however, that progressive leadership **has** played a vital role in pulling the South out of abject poverty and has defined, in subtle yet profound ways, the political culture of a region most perceive as conservative.

Civil Rights and the Transformation of Contemporary Southern Politics

By the middle of the twentieth century, a new crisis threatened the stable political system crafted by Democratic politicians a half century before. The issue of race, "settled" by Jim Crow laws and black disfranchisement, was again

---

79. Carl Davis, et al., *Who Pays? A Distributional Analysis of the Tax Systems in All 50 States* (Washington, D.C.: Institute on Taxation and Economic Policy, 3rd edition, 2009), 36, http://www.itepnet.org/whopays3.pdf (accessed 3/29/ 2012).

in the forefront of Southern politics. In the 1950s, '60s, and '70s, African Americans and their white supporters would build a powerful movement to wrest political and civil rights for blacks from recalcitrant conservative whites. Southern politics was shaken to its very foundations. The whites-only Southern Democratic Party would become a multiracial party, and the slumbering Republican Party would awaken to become the dominant party in the region with an overwhelmingly white base of support.

The Democratic Party had dominated the nation's politics since the election of Franklin Roosevelt in 1932, and the South, nicknamed the "Solid South" for its unswerving loyalty to the Democratic Party, was an important part of the Democratic power base. But a basic tension existed between the mainstream of the party and its Southern wing. Most importantly, the national Democratic Party depended on the votes of a variety of ethnic minorities, including growing numbers of African Americans who had migrated to the North and Midwest, while the Southern wing of the party, lily-white and dominated in most states by ardent segregationists, was committed to keeping the region's major ethnic minority voteless and out of politics. Too, by the late 1930s, the more conservative Southern Democrats were becoming increasingly disenchanted with the economic reforms coming out of Washington. Governor Eugene Talmadge of Georgia called Roosevelt's reform program "a combination of wet nursin', frenzied finance, downright Communism an' plain damnfoolishness."[80] The national party's growing reliance on the support of unions would not have made these folks happy, either; in the South, as we have seen, unions were bitterly opposed by virtually everyone of consequence.

Southern restiveness with Democratic racial policies increased when Harry Truman became president after the death of Roosevelt and boiled over into a rebellion at the Democratic National Convention in 1948. Hubert Humphrey, a rising star of the Democratic Party from Minnesota, stood up at the convention and spoke forcefully in favor of adding a civil rights plank to the party's platform.[81] The measure passed, and a group of Southern delegates led by Strom Thurmond of South Carolina (a Democrat in those days) walked out of the convention and formed a short-lived third party nicknamed the "Dixiecrat" party. Thurmond ran for President as a Dixiecrat and won the electoral votes of four Deep South states (he also won part of the Tennessee electoral vote), quite an achievement for a third party candidate.[82] Thurmond and most of his supporters returned to the Democratic fold, but ardent supporters of segregation and black disfranchisement in the South, a clear majority of white

---

80. George B. Tindall, *The Emergence of the New South, 1913–1945* (Baton Rouge: Louisiana State University Press, 1967), 617.
81. Pete Daniel, *Standing at the Crossroads: Southern Life in the Twentieth Century* (New York: Hill and Wang, 1986), 157.
82. Key, *Southern Politics*, 329–344.

Democrats in the Deep South, had made an important statement: "We will leave the party if racial equality becomes a political issue." Willingness to consider the Republican alternative increased when the party nominated war hero Dwight D. Eisenhower for president in 1952 and again in 1956; Florida, Tennessee, Virginia and Texas went for Eisenhower both times.[83]

By the early 1960s, the Civil Rights Movement had succeeded in mobilizing hundreds of thousands of Southern black citizens and growing numbers of white supporters from across the country. Movement leaders hoped that Jim Crow could be overwhelmed by the physical and moral pressure of hundreds of sit-ins, protests, boycotts, and marches coupled with political pressure from outside the region. The drive to destroy Jim Crow was met by organized opposition ranging from passive resistance, such as foot dragging on the implementation of the *Brown vs. Board of Education* Supreme Court school desegregation decision, to active, even violent resistance. The opposition was strongest in the Deep South. In Mississippi, for example, the Citizens' Council, an organization opposed to ending segregation and composed primarily of white businessmen, organized chapters across the state. The Council employed a variety of pressure tactics (boycotts and the like) to discourage individuals or businesses from "giving in" to the integrationists.[84] Political leaders from the governor down to the local police chief closed ranks to defend Jim Crow. In some areas of the state, the police functioned almost like an arm of the Ku Klux Klan and dispensed beatings and sometimes death to civil rights workers. When James Meredith arrived at the University of Mississippi in Oxford to become the first black student to enroll, a full scale riot broke out thanks to Governor Ross Barnett's failure to provide adequate security. A contingent of U.S. marshals was dispatched by President John F. Kennedy to protect Meredith, and 160 of them were wounded by the angry mob that roamed the campus and milled around the Lyceum, Ole Miss's administration building where most of the marshals were making a stand. Twenty-eight of the injured marshals had been shot; two civilians had been killed, one apparently by an errant bullet and the other, a reporter for a London newspaper, by a bullet in the back. Kennedy sent 23,000 U.S. soldiers to Oxford to restore order.[85] Political warfare, *literally* warfare, had broken out again, just like the violence of the Reconstruction and Populist eras. This time, however, there were important differences.

President Lyndon Johnson, successor to the slain John F. Kennedy, used his considerable influence and political skill to do something Kennedy could not or would not do: he made a firm commitment for himself, the Democratic

---

83. Bass and De Vries, *The Transformation of Southern Politics*, 26.
84. *Ibid.*, 194–196.
85. Taylor Branch, *Parting the Waters: America in the King Years, 1954–1963* (New York: Simon and Schuster, 1988), 661–670.

Party, and ultimately the nation to civil and voting rights for African American citizens. Johnson shepherded two momentous pieces of legislation—the Civil Rights Act of 1964 and the Voting Rights Act of 1965—through Congress over substantial opposition by Southern Democrats. These laws gave the federal government the power to attack Jim Crow. Johnson knew in charting this course that he might be ultimately dooming his party to defeat by weakening its support among white Southerners, most of whom were still opposed to social and political equality for blacks.[86] Even in North Carolina, a state noted for its moderate racial climate, fewer than 25% of whites surveyed in 1968 favored integrating schools; fewer than 20% favored allowing African Americans to move into white neighborhoods.[87] The full power of the federal government—courts, marshals, troops, lawyers, and agents—enforced the new laws in the region, and legal segregation and disfranchisement died. While Johnson and other Democratic leaders did everything they could to keep the white South in the Democratic fold, including unleashing an avalanche of federal money on the region (the avalanche actually began back in the 1930s during Roosevelt's New Deal), what Johnson had feared began to happen as more and more white Southerners turned to the Republican Party.[88] Ironically, the party of Lincoln, which had been a multi-racial party in the South in the nineteenth century and had been crushed for that very reason, now offered a home to those opposing integration.

The Ascendancy of the Republican Party

The Republican Party was a party in transformation in the early 1960s. Despite its success in electing Eisenhower, it was still the minority party at every level of politics and had been since the early 1930s. It was a party with little hope of becoming the majority party. Nor did the party really offer voters a distinctive alternative to the Democratic Party; many Republicans (the moderate wing) really weren't that different from their Democrats opponents in their views and positions. But on the right, a vocal and increasingly influential group of conservative Republicans began gaining more influence in the party. This group loudly, even bitterly, denounced Democratic policies as socialism. They wanted to adopt a more combative position towards the Soviet Union and weren't afraid to call people who disagreed with this position fools if not traitors. They argued that government was simply too big and that many of the

---

86. Franklin, "Commentary," in *Is There a Southern Political Tradition?*, 204.
87. Luebke, *Tar Heel Politics*, 2000, 191.
88. Conklin, "Lyndon Johnson and the Outer South" in *Is There a Southern Political Tradition?*, 162.

programs Democrats believed had "saved" the country in the 1930s and 40s really hurt the very people they were supposed to help and even served as stepping stones to the sort of government found in the Soviet Union. A member of this wing of the party, Barry Goldwater, was chosen the party's nominee for president in 1964. He represented, his supporters argued, "a choice, not an echo."[89]

Goldwater's attack on the size, power, and scope of the federal government and his promise to shift a variety of responsibilities, including civil rights, back to state governments made the party increasingly attractive to many Southern white voters who opposed the federally imposed changes in racial policies. Goldwater made capturing the white vote in the South a priority; he noted in a speech delivered in Atlanta, "We're not going to get the Negro vote as a bloc in 1964 and 1968, so we ought to go hunting where the ducks are." In the same speech he also made clear his position on integration, declaring it "the responsibility of the states." Goldwater lost the election by a huge margin but won the electoral votes of five Deep South states (the only states other than his home state of Arizona that he won).[90]

Goldwater's success in the Deep South marked the beginning of the rise of the Republican Party in the region and the decline of the Democratic Party. Leading Democratic supporters of segregation and black disfranchisement such as Strom Thurmond and Jesse Helms of North Carolina abandoned the Democratic Party and joined the Republican Party. These leaders were joined by growing numbers of rank and file Democrats who shared their racial views and believed the party and the government it controlled were ruining the South and the nation. As whites poured out of the Democratic Party in the South, newly enfranchised blacks poured in, which in turn accelerated the movement of segregationist whites out of the party. In some parts of the South (Darlington County, South Carolina, for example), Republican Party organizers even made quiet overtures to the Ku Klux Klan.[91]

The Democratic Party faced a challenge from another direction when George Wallace bolted the party in 1968 and ran for president as a third party candidate. Leading up to his run for president, Wallace had repackaged himself; his focus shifted from denying civil and voting rights to African Americans to defending traditional values and customs—the family, belief in God, hard work, local control of schools—and vigorously attacking communism, welfare, high taxes, an elitist federal bureaucracy out of touch with the common man, and "pointy-headed intellectuals" shoving their ideas and social experi-

---

89. Phyllis Schlafly, *A Choice Not an Echo* (Alton, Ill.: Pere Marquette Press, 1964).

90. Bass and De Vries, *The Transformation of Southern Politics*, 27.

91. On Republican organizing in Darlington, South Carolina, Interview, Mildred Beck, 17 November 2004.

ments down common folks' throats. Wallace tapped into the anger or "rage" of working class whites in the South (and elsewhere) who were being buffeted both by economic change as the region abandoned agrarianism and troubling social and cultural changes, including, of course, the most troubling change of all, civil and voting rights for African Americans.[92] Recall that 1968 was a particularly tumultuous year for the region and the nation: racial riots had broken out in a number of cities, the Vietnam War was at its bloodiest, two major political figures were assassinated (Martin Luther King, Jr., and Robert Kennedy), college campuses were rocked by student protests, and the so-called counterculture (the hippie movement), which glorified sex, drugs, unrestricted speech and rock and roll, was mounting a challenge to "straight" society and values. Wallace was saying the sorts of things people were saying to each other at the barber shop or at the VFW hut, and many responded enthusiastically to his message.

Richard Nixon, the Republican candidate for president in 1968, had embraced Barry Goldwater's "Southern Strategy" and now scrambled to siphon off some of the Wallace vote. He used his running mate, Spiro Agnew, as the "heavy" to make some of the same points as Wallace.[93] In the election, Wallace took five Deep South states and received millions of votes in other states, but, ultimately, many of these Wallace supporters ended up in the Republican Party.[94] Republicans had learned an important lesson from Wallace about how to appeal to rural and working class whites that would serve them well in the decades ahead.[95] The party shook off its country club mannerisms and began to fashion an appeal that wedded its traditional support for corporations, small businesses, low taxes, and limited government involvement in the economy with Wallace's largely symbolic support for a variety of traditional values that seemed to be under attack. Where Ben Tillman had denounced Eastern financiers, the new enemy was government bureaucrats and their allies in the universities and the media. Highly charged issues like prayer in the schools, abortion, and homosexuality would, in the hands of skilled politicians like Jesse Helms, be fashioned into an indictment of a government that ignored the values of the people. The "culture wars" had begun, although the term would not gain currency until much later.

While the Republican Party was reforming itself, there was the struggle in each Southern state for the soul of the Democratic Party. While some old-style

---

92. Dan T. Carter, *The Politics of Rage: Wallace, The Origins of the New Conservatism and the Transformation of American Politics* (New York: Simon and Schuster, 1995), 11–12; 345–346; 467.

93. *Ibid.*, 326–331.

94. Black and Black, *Politics and Society in the South*, 263.

95. Wayne Parent and Peter Petrakis, "Populism Left and Right: Politics of the Rural South," in R. Douglas Hunt, *The Rural South Since World War II* (Baton Rouge, LA: Louisiana State University Press, 1998), 167.

segregationist Democrats like Mississippi Senator James Eastland, a delta planter and one of the last of the "old school" patrician politicians, would hang in with the party into the late 1970s and even beyond, the rising stars of the party were new-style Democrats like Jimmy Carter of Georgia, Jim Hunt of North Carolina, and Bill Clinton of Arkansas. These were men who knit together the new black voters with progressive white voters and what remained of the old "yellow dog" Democrats into a new, if fragile, coalition.[96] Their message was moderate progressivism delivered in a folksy, Populist manner; on racial matters, they stressed white/black reconciliation and support for integration. They spoke forcefully for economic development and education and, consistent with the progressive tradition, were able to win the backing of a sizable portion of the business community.

African Americans played a major role in the "new" Southern Democratic Party, and Democratic candidates could only be successful in much of the South if they could get a large black turnout coupled with a respectable showing among whites. Rarely do Democratic candidates for national or state level office get a majority of the white vote in the South. Today, there are thousands of black politicians in the region, and nearly all are Democrats.[97] Black political leaders often combine two styles of politics to reach a black audience that includes a significant number of less affluent people and a white audience that is more middle class. This style is a new hybrid of Populist-style appeals to fairness and equity and progressive promises to expand the pie and create more opportunities and perform government services more efficiently. Examples of politicians who have taken this approach include Douglas Wilder, former governor of Virginia, and Harvey Gantt, former mayor of Charlotte. This style is very difficult to "pull off": less affluent black voters want to be sure that elected officials, white or black, are representing their interests when it comes to such issues as affirmative action and access to quality education. Middle class white voters (and, increasingly, middle class black voters, too) are often more interested in taxation issues, creating a "business friendly" environment, and establishing high standards in education, and are often hostile to affirmative action and social welfare programs.

While the newly reconfigured Democratic Party slowed the hemorrhaging of its white support, it could not stop it. The party wasn't able to make serious inroads in the traditional Republican strongholds in mountain areas, and its racial reconciliation message had a limited appeal in the white community. Race wasn't the Democrats only problem: there was an important cultural dis-

96. "Yellow dog" Democrats were those who, as the saying went, would vote for a yellow dog before they would vote for a Republican. Yellow dog Democrats by the 1970s and 1980s were typically older white voters living in rural areas.

97. David A. Bositis, *Black Elected Officials: A Statistical Summary, 2001* (Washington, D.C.: Joint Center for Political and Economic Studies, 2003).

connect between the transformed Democratic Party and a significant number of white Southerners. Many Southern whites considered themselves conservatives while the party, as it renounced its segregationist past and moved closer to the mainstream of the Democratic Party, became associated more with the liberal policies of the national party. Middle class Southern whites surveyed in the 1970s and early '80s tended to respond positively to authority figures, such as the police and the military, and negatively to individuals and groups, such as women's rights advocates and black militants, that questioned authority and tradition. The Democratic Party's championing of affirmative action for African Americans and women and its emphasis on helping people with such programs as minimum wage and welfare and on protecting individual rights and freedoms really ran counter to the basic values of these conservative Southern whites, especially those living in rural areas and small towns. While the huge infusions of federal funds stretching back to the 1930s had helped lift the South out of poverty and helped propel a major proportion of the white working and small farming class into the middle class, many Southern whites tended to see the benefits they had received as relatively small and most of the benefits paid to "other" people as excessive and wasteful. White opposition to government programs often came back to race given the widespread perception among whites that most federal programs primarily benefited blacks, not whites.[98] As a white restaurant owner in the Mississippi Delta told journalist David Applebome, his town was populated by "two hundred whites and twenty-four hundred welfare recipients."[99] It is ironic that the very programs that Lyndon Johnson and other Democrats had created to lift the South out of poverty contributed to the "loss" of the region by the party.[100]

The economic boom sweeping parts of the South also helped Republican fortunes. The expanding white middle class proved to be a fertile recruiting ground for the party, and its prospects were further fortified by the migrants who began to pour into the region from the North. Many of these new arrivals were middle or upper middle class suburbanites—a prime Republican constituency in the North—and they brought their Republican allegiances with them. The expanding suburbs of the South, where most middle class folks were now choosing to live, were developing their own unique political culture that tilted in a Republican direction. Many of the people moving into the suburbs had "fled" the cities to escape school integration and urban problems in a phenomenon occurring all over the nation called "white flight"; not surprisingly, the suburbs were (and still are) predominantly white. Atlanta, for example, lost 160,000 white residents over the course of the 1960s and 1970s; by the

---

98. Black and Black, *Politics and Society in the South*, 58–64, 214–217.
99. Applebome, *Dixie Rising*, 285.
100. Merle Black and Earl Black, *The Rise of Southern Republicans* (Cambridge: Belknap Press, 2003), 266.

1970s, it was encircled by a ring of growing, overwhelmingly white suburbs while the city was transformed from majority white to majority black. The politics of the expanding suburbs has been described as a "politics of 'suburban secession'" which was driven by a desire to maintain the suburbs as havens apart from the racial discord, higher taxes, poverty and crime of the cities. These concerns, suburban voters believed, were not driven by race or opposition to integration but by fairness and a desire to live in safe neighborhoods, send their kids to good schools, and pay lower taxes. They often believed government programs benefited "other" people, not them, and in this respect they were much like traditional conservatives of the rural South. Court ordered busing, which required suburban and urban children to be bused to different schools to achieve some degree of racial balance, was one issue that mobilized suburban voters who believed it was simply unfair to bus their children to distant schools in the city and worried about their safety and the quality of education they would receive. In Atlanta, MARTA—a mass transit agency organized in the 1960s—became another issue. Many in the suburbs opposed the building of MARTA lines to the ring of suburbs surrounding the city for fear that it would make it easier for inner city people (and in the minds of most suburbanites, this meant black people) and their problems to travel to the suburbs.

Beginning with the presidential campaign of Richard Nixon in 1968, the Republican Party consciously and successfully sought to craft a "suburban" message to appeal to these disaffected voters, part of what Nixon would call the "Silent Majority." This message stressed "law and order," opposition to welfare, support for lower taxes, and fewer federal intrusions—like court-ordered busing—in the lives of law-abiding citizens. The Democratic Party, on the other hand, seemed to many suburbanites to be the agent of cities and government intrusiveness and the champion of people "not like us."[101] Nixon's message had broad appeal to white middle class suburbanites across the country, and in this respect Southern voters were becoming more like voters in the rest of the nation. But it was also true that at this moment in history, the goals of Southern suburbanites and more traditional, mostly rural and small town conservatives merged together, and this gave a tremendous boost to the Republican Party's chances of becoming a truly competitive party in the region. Ronald Reagan, a charismatic figure wildly popular in the South, did more than anyone to bind these two constituencies to the party in a lasting marriage that would persist into the new millennium. The party was able to recruit talented, energetic

---

101. Black and Black, *Politics and Society in the South,* 314; Luebke, *Tar Heel Politics 2000,* 193–194; Kevin Kruse, *White Flight: Atlanta and the Making of Modern Conservatism* (Princeton, New Jersey: Princeton University Press, 2005), 234, 246–249, 251, 253–254; Matthew D. Lassiter, *Suburban Politics in the Sunbelt South* (Princeton, New Jersey: Princeton University Press, 2005), 5, 15, 225, 227, 238.

leaders and provided suburban newcomers—even the once despised "Yankees"—opportunities that the more provincial Democratic Party did not. Many of the new Southern Republican leaders, men such as Representative Newt Gingrich of Georgia and Senator Phil F. Gramm of Texas, were Yankee immigrants.

The last key to Republican success in the region was the emergence of the Christian Right. This was a national movement, but it had its center of gravity in the South, and many of its leaders were from the South. By the 1970s, many white evangelical Christians had come to believe that the United States was in a moral crisis and that traditional values and customs centered in the family, the community, and the church were under attack. They worried about the drug problem, the new racial realities that ran counter to their traditions, the dangerous schools, the growing incidence of abortions, and the sexually explicit movies and song lyrics. The things they hated were so pervasive, how could they keep apart from them? Their own government seemed intent on promoting immorality with laws and court decisions that took kids out of neighborhood schools controlled by local folks, prohibited school-sponsored prayer in the schools, legalized abortion, and loosened restrictions on obscenity in the media. During the Carter administration, all-white Christian academies were threatened with the loss of their tax exempt status if they did not admit black students, another example, for many evangelicals, of a government at odds with the people it represented.[102] To be sure, an important element in the evangelical Christian community, especially in churches following Fundamentalist doctrines, had historically viewed society and all its institutions as totally corrupt, but this viewpoint became much more common among white evangelicals in the South in the 1970s.[103] Important demographic changes also played a role in both radicalizing—this new viewpoint was, by its nature, radical—and mobilizing this group of people. The South was no longer a religious monolith; by the 1990s white Protestants were just a bit over 50% of the population, down considerably from 73% of the population in the 1960s, and evangelical white Protestants were only 39% of the population, down from 45% of the population in the 1960s. Catholics, secular folk (non-religious), and "other" believers (Muslim, Jewish, etc.) constituted nearly 30% of the re-

---

102. Lawrence Kaplan, *Fundamentalism in Comparative Perspective* (Amherst, Mass.: University of Massachusetts Press, 1992), 43–46; Paul Harvey, *Freedom's Coming: Religious Culture and the Shaping of the South from the Civil War through the Civil Rights Era* (Chapel Hill: The University of North Carolina Press, 2005), 229–245; Robert D. Putnam and David E. Campbell, *Amazing Grace: How Religion Divides and Unites Us* (New York: Simon and Schuster, 2010), 114.

103. Sam Hill, "Fundamentalism in Recent Southern Culture: Has it Done What the Civil Rights Movement Couldn't Do?" *Journal of Southern Religion*, 1998, http://jsr.fsu.edu/essay.htm.

gion's population in the 1990s, up from only 13% in the 1960s.[104] So the feeling white evangelicals had of being embattled by a hostile culture was very likely also a feeling of losing control of a culture that they had once dominated by virtue of their numbers and, of course, their race. A significant portion of these evangelicals lived in rural areas, and here the steady decline of the agrarian economy and culture must have also contributed to this sense of being embattled. In earlier times, spiritual crusades to save souls called "awakenings" swept the evangelical community; now evangelicals embarked on a sustained crusade to save the nation. In the political arena, these crusaders came to be referred to as the "Christian Right," and they have been a major force in Southern and national politics for over thirty years.

The movement was led by such individuals as the Reverend Jerry Falwell, the Reverend Pat Robertson, and thousands of ministers and lay leaders in churches large and small. From the pulpit and the television studio, they attacked promiscuity, drug use, abortion, homosexuality, and women's liberation, and decried the disappearance of prayer in the schools and the teaching of the theory of evolution. They painted many established institutions—the federal government, the universities, the media, and even seminaries—as weakening the moral fabric of the nation. This movement took advantage of new technology, especially cable television, which featured a number of popular conservative evangelical preachers who used talk show formats, popular music with Christian themes, and a "show biz" atmosphere to reach home viewers. A group of these evangelicals, led by Falwell, formed an organization called the Moral Majority to promote conservative Christian values in the political system and to support conservative Christian politicians. Later, Pat Robertson formed a similar organization called the Christian Coalition after his unsuccessful run for president in 1988.[105] Given the fact that the Democratic Party was now where most liberals resided and that it championed some of the very issues that the Christian Right despised, it's not hard to understand why this movement would eventually fold into the Republican Party. Despite Ronald Reagan's sketchy church-going track record, he had broad appeal in the Christian Right and played a major role in bringing about this merger. The Christian Right would work to expand the party's base of support in the South, and its strong support among white rural and working class people—once bulwarks of the Democratic Party—helped propel the movement of those voters to the Republican

---

104. John C. Green et al., "The Soul of the South: Religion and Southern Politics at the Millennium," Charles S. Bullock III and Mark Rozell, eds., *The New Politics of the Old South: An Introduction to Southern Politics* (Boulder, N.Y.: Rowman and Littlefield Publishers, Inc., 2003), 287.

105. Mark J. Rozell and Clyde Wilcox, "Virginia: Birthplace of the Christian Right," in John C. Green et al., eds., *The Christian Right in American Politics: Marching to the Millennium* (Washington, D.C.: Georgetown University Press, 2003), 43–45.

camp.[106] One poll estimated that 80% of Southern white evangelical Christians voted for George W. Bush for president in 2004, and in 2008 exit polls show this group supporting John McCain by a similar wide margin, making them one of the most reliably Republican groups in national politics. An astonishing 94% of white evangelical Mississippians voted for McCain.[107]

In the early decades of the twentieth century, only a handful of Republicans represented the South in Congress; by 1970, nearly 25% of the Southern congressional delegation was Republican, and by the mid-1990s it was nearly 60% Republican.[108] The white South became almost as strongly Republican in its voting in presidential elections as it once had been Democratic and played a big role in Republican success at winning the presidency over the last forty-five years. The growing strength of the party in the South helped it take control of the United States Senate in 1994 and, for the first time in decades, the House of Representatives. Southerners Dick Army and Tom DeLay of Texas and Newt Gingrich of Georgia assumed the top House leadership positions, and Trent Lott of Mississippi became majority leader of the Senate a year later. Not surprisingly, the party increasingly reflected the more conservative views of its Southern wing, a trend that was accelerated by the party's declining strength in the Northeast and Midwest where a more moderate Republican tradition had prevailed.[109] The Democratic Party responded to its declining strength in the South with its own version of a "Southern Strategy"; it nominated a number of Southerners for the nation's top office, and both Jimmy Carter and Bill Clinton were able to win the electoral votes of a number of Southern states. This strategy did not work in the election of 2000 when Al Gore failed to take a single Southern state, including his home state of Tennessee, although he did quite well outside the region and actually beat his opponent—another Southerner—in the popular vote.

The Republican Party also made inroads at the state and local level of politics and began fielding competitive candidates for governor, state legislature, and a variety of local offices in every state in the region. Success at the state and local level of politics, however, lagged behind the party's success at fielding

---

106. Black and Black, *The Rise of Southern Republicans*, 227, 265–267.

107. "CNN.com Election Results: U.S. President/Region: South/Exit Poll," *CNN.com*, http://www.cnn.com/ELECTION/2004; ElectionCenter2008 exit polls, *CNN.com*, http://www.cnn.com/ELECTION/2008/results/polls.main/. In the 2000 presidential election one scholar estimates that 84% of Southern white "observant evangelicals" voted for George W. Bush. John C. Green, "Believers for Bush, Godly for Gore: Religion and the 2000 Election in the South," in Robert P. Steed and Lawrence W. Moreland, eds., *The 2000 Presidential Election in the South: Partisanship and Southern Party Systems in the 21st Century* (Westport, Connecticut: Praeger, 2002), 16; Black and Black, *The Rise of Southern Republicans*, 264–267.

108. Bass and De Vries, *The Transformation of Southern Politics*, 36–37.

109. Black and Black, *The Rise of Southern Republicans*, 5–9.

winning candidates for Congress and at putting Southern electoral votes in the Republican column in presidential election years. By 2000, state legislatures across the region were only slightly over 40% Republican.[110]

One advantage the Republican Party has had over its rival is that it has been much more cohesive ideologically; one scholar found that 85% of Republican activists considered themselves conservative, while Democratic activists were spread fairly evenly over the ideological spectrum with, predictably, the larger concentrations of activists describing themselves as liberals or moderates.[111] Republicans have been able to craft a coherent message, which gave them the aura of certitude, while the Democratic message was rarely as coherent because Democrats had to appeal to three often divergent points of view not only among the voters but among their own activists. Democratic candidates who were "too liberal" alienated the conservative activists and voters while moderates sometimes left both liberal and conservatives less than enthralled.

This is not to say the Republican Party has always spoken with one voice; recall that a form of progressivism has been fairly popular among Republican candidates for governor who must appeal to suburban voters who expect good, well-funded schools and decent highways to get them to work. George W. Bush fashioned a message—"compassionate conservatism"—designed to appeal to the suburban middle class voter, the more traditional conservatives, and the Christian Right; this message seemed to incorporate all three political traditions and was well-received in the region. But the dominant message in the Southern branch of the party has been a carefully crafted blend that draws on the old patrician interest in low taxes and limited government services coupled with a cultural Populism that champions traditional values. As we have seen, this cultural Populism has a different list of enemies and friends than the Populism of old; while traditional Populists condemned bankers, merchants, railroads, and other corporate interests and saw government as a tool to right wrongs, the enemies of Republican cultural Populism are big government, feminists, liberal intellectuals, the media and homosexuals. Corporations and small businesses are the "good guys," and wealthy folk are just people who worked hard to get their wealth and deserve to keep as much of it as possible. So, for example, ending the federal inheritance tax was packaged by the Republican Party as a Populist measure that would help small farmers and small businessmen and many other "average Americans" pass their hard-earned

---

110. Harold Stanley, "The South in the 2000 Elections," in Steed and Moreland, *The 2000 Presidential Election in the South*, 222.

111. Diane Blair, "Party Activists: Mirrors and Makers of Change," in Charles D. Hadley and Lewis Bowan, eds., *Party Activists in Southern Politics* (Knoxville, TN: University Press, 1998), 170.

money on to their children, this despite the fact that very few Americans own enough property to be affected by the tax.[112]

While George W. Bush had some success in appealing to Hispanic voters and even black voters, the party has been, for all intents and purposes, a white party, especially in the South. Overt racial appeals are rarely voiced, but opposition to policies that might benefit African Americans or other minorities is common and in the realm of symbolism, the party has fairly consistently sent a message that has repelled rather than attracted nonwhite voters. "Welfare mothers," a term of derision that was a staple of the conservative political lexicon in the 1970s, 80s, and 90s, was a code for "black" welfare mothers, and affirmative action has long been condemned as a new form of discrimination. Opposition to establishing the Martin Luther King, Jr., birthday as a national holiday was led by prominent Republican Southern politicians such as Jesse Helms, and, more recently, Southern Republicans have been in the forefront of the movement to take a "tough" approach with illegal immigrants, a stance that doesn't sit well in the Hispanic community.

Women Become Major Political Players

While the entrance of the black voter has revolutionized politics in the South, the growing role of women in Southern politics has also had a major impact. This has been an uphill struggle for women because opposition to equal rights for women has been stronger in the South than in any other region. Earlier in the twentieth century, most of the Southern states failed to ratify the Nineteenth Amendment to the Constitution, which gave women the right to vote, and more recently, most of the Southern states failed to ratify the Equal Rights Amendment, thus defeating that measure. In recent years the number of female politicians in the region has grown significantly in both parties with increasing numbers of women serving in state legislatures, in the executive branch of state governments, in Congress, and on the courts. However, in general, the region lags behind the rest of the nation in the rate of female office holding. Six of the eleven states with the lowest percentage of female state legislators in 2012 were Southern, and only two states—Georgia and Florida—equaled or exceeded the national average. Southern states were represented by five women in the U.S. Senate in 2012 and nineteen in the House, but this too works out to a rate significantly lower than the national average.[113] Given the strong influence of tradi-

---

112. More than 95% of the population did not own enough property to be subject to the inheritance tax.

113. The data used in this section on women in current Southern politics was derived from "fact sheets" developed by the Center of American Women and Politics, Eagleton Institute of Politics, Rutgers, The State University of New Jersey, http://www.cawp.rutgers.edu.

tion in the region, none of this is especially surprising. One would expect that the Christian Right, with its serious reservations about gender equality, would be a major stumbling block to aspiring female politicians in the Republican Party. Surprisingly, the region was represented by almost equal numbers of female Republicans and Democrats in Congress in 2012. There is, however, a huge difference in the percentage of women serving in Southern state legislatures who are Democrats vs. those who are Republicans, with Democrats holding roughly 60% of the seats held by women.

What of the fabled gender gap in voter preferences? There is one, and like most electoral phenomena, it waxes and wanes from election to election. In the presidential election of 2004, the CNN exit poll found Southern white men voting overwhelmingly for Mr. Bush while Southern white women were less likely to do so, although they still favored him over John Kerry by a large margin. In 2008, most Southern whites again voted for the Republican candidate, and again there was a gender gap in voting preferences with men more likely to vote Republican than women. The gap ranged from 2 to 6% in most states.[114] What gender gap there is seems to turn on differences in attitudes about certain issues. Earl and Merle Black found in a study conducted in the mid-1990s that the majority of Southern white males identified themselves as conservatives, while Southern white women were more likely to identify themselves as moderates and favor at least some positions (like abortion rights) that are traditionally identified with the Democratic Party. In general, they found a fair amount of agreement between the sexes among whites on such issues as lower taxes, less government, and a scaling back of affirmative action, although if women who attend conservative evangelical churches are taken out of the mix, the women remaining were closely split between Democratic and Republican allegiances and tended to lean more toward the moderate/liberal direction on many issues.[115] So with non-evangelical white women, the gender gap was most pronounced, and this still seems to be the case.

Conclusion

The regional solidarity that John C. Calhoun, the antebellum champion of the plantation South, first envisioned over 150 years ago has been reinvented by a Republican Party that now has the allegiance of most white Southerners, just as the Democratic Party once had their allegiance. The fact that for well over a century, the great majority of whites have supported one party, and, by

---

114. "CNN.com Election Results: U.S. President/Region: South/Exit Poll,"*CNN.com*, http://www.cnn.com/ELECTION/2004; ElectionCenter2008 exit polls, *CNN.com*, http://www.cnn.com/ELECTION/2008/results/polls.main/.

115. Black and Black, *The Rise of Southern Republicans*, 252–254.

the same token, the great majority of blacks have supported the other (when they were able to vote) says a lot about the continuing power of race in the region and Calhoun's vision of a "Solid South." The traditional patrician interest in keeping taxes low and government services limited is also still quite strong. The patrician message is now delivered in a down-home way and is coupled with a strong commitment to traditional cultural values. The power of race and the commitment to tradition and the old patrician program are strongest in the Deep South, where conservative evangelical Protestantism is strongest, immigrants from outside the region fewest, racial tensions most bitter, the people the poorest, and where large agricultural interests and traditional business and industry still control much of the economy. Here, taxes are the lowest, government services are the poorest, and resistance to change is the strongest. Alabama, for example, has struggled to provide adequate funding for its schools and its woefully overcrowded prisons for years. To be sure, Alabama has long been one of the poorest states in the union, but the funding crisis was also a consequence of a wildly regressive tax system that taxed the poorest citizens at one of the highest rates in the nation while tax rates for corporations, higher income people, and property holders were among the lowest. In short, the "haves" weren't paying their fair share. The citizens of Alabama were given the chance to rectify this situation in 2003 but voted overwhelmingly against a measure that would have increased taxes on the "haves." The only groups that supported the measure were African Americans, union members, people with graduate or professional degrees, and "outsiders" who had lived in the state for 10–20 years.[116] Since then, the state has continued to struggle to provide adequate funding for its schools, and some school districts have even resorted to taking out bank loans to keep the doors open.[117]

The political continuities with the past are striking, but clearly that is not the whole story. However much conservative rhetoric in the patrician tradition may resonate with Southern white voters, the hand of government and the influence of the progressive tradition are clearly much in evidence in the region, even in the Deep South. The South today is home to major high tech centers, nationally ranked public universities, and state-of-the-art public hospitals all paid for or at least partially subsidized by tax dollars. If some states have heavily regressive tax systems that tax the poor the most, other states, like, surpris-

---

116. Jim Seroka, "Alabama's Tax Reform: What Went Wrong and Why?", *Alabama Municipal Revenue Officers Association*, December 5, 2003, http:// web6.duc.auburn.edu /outreach/cgs/publications/Alabamataxvote2003.pdf; "Alabama's Taxes Hit Poor and Middle Class Far Harder than the Wealthy," Institute on Taxation and Economic Policy, 7 January 2003, http://www.itepnet.org/wp2000/al%20pr.pdf.

117. "Alabama schools turn to bank loans to operate," *CNNMoney*, 31 August 2010, http://money.cnn.com/2010/08/30/news/economy/alabama_schools_bank_loans.fortune/ index. htm (accessed 3/29/2012).

ingly, South Carolina, do not.[118] Extensive systems of highways take Southerners to work, to vacations, and to shopping malls. Young people get subsidies of
various sorts to attend college, and older folks get Social Security checks and
Medicare, and, when they run out of their savings, nursing home care paid for
by Medicaid. Government and politics in much of the region seem to have, on
the whole, a mildly progressive flavor with at least a small helping of the populist urge to help the underdog.

In the early years of the new millennium, it appeared that the "Solid South"
was unraveling, or perhaps fracturing is a better term. The large Republican
gains in the Southern congressional delegation in the 1970s, 1980s and 1990s
plateaued, and Democrats actually gained some seats in the elections of 2006
and 2008. As noted earlier, the Republican Party was never able to match its
success at winning presidential and congressional elections with the same degree of success in state and local elections in many Southern states, and Democrats were able to hold their own. Even in Alabama and Mississippi, two
Deep South states that had consistently gone Republican in presidential elections by wide margins, Democrats still maintained control of the state legislatures as late as 2009. The Democratic Party's candidate for president in 2008,
an African American from Chicago named Barrack Hussein Obama, won four
states in the "fringe" of the South—Maryland, Virginia, North Carolina, and
Florida, and almost won a fifth, Missouri—suggesting that the power of race
in politics was waning, at least in parts of the South. These are all states with
sizable metropolitan areas and more developed economies. Obama performed
well in these states by winning an even larger share of the black vote than Democratic candidates normally received, appealing to other minority groups—a
significant and growing presence—and appealing to a significant minority of
white voters, especially those living in metropolitan areas. White support for
Obama ranged from 35% in North Carolina to a high of 47% in Maryland and
Missouri; at the upper end, these percentages were similar to white support he
garnered in Northern states. Obama easily took heavily suburban Wake
County in North Carolina (where Raleigh is located), Henrico County, a suburb of Richmond, and many of the northern Virginia suburban counties.
While an unpopular war and the economic crisis afflicting the nation in 2008
certainly presented the Democratic candidate with a significant advantage over
his Republican rival, Democratic gains in suburban areas were actually part of
a national trend going back several election cycles and represented a weakening
of the Republican grip on suburbia. In the Deep South, however, old patterns
persisted. There, whites voted Republican by huge margins ranging from 74%
in South Carolina to 90% in Alabama. Obama made some gains in Deep South
metropolitan areas like Charleston and Atlanta, but given the overwhelming

---

118. Davis, et al., *Who Pays?*, 96.

white vote against him, these gains had a marginal impact on election results. The competitiveness of the 2008 election sent voter turnouts in the region soaring: turnouts in six Southern states exceeded the national average, an important break with a past characterized by nearly a century of low voter turnout.[119]

But the Solid South was not dead; within two years old patterns returned, and with vengeance. It all began, oddly enough, on the floor of the Chicago Board of Trade. A month after the inauguration of Barrack Obama, Rick Santelli, CNBC's on-air business reporter and a former stock trader, delivered his famous "rant" from the floor of the Chicago Board of Trade. Santelli passionately denounced a proposal to create a government program to help the millions of people who were in danger of defaulting on their home mortgages, one of the more disturbing consequences of the near collapse of the banking and housing industries during the economic crisis of 2008–2009. He described the proposal as a plan to "subsidize the losers' mortgages" and called for a "Chicago tea party in July" for "all you capitalists" who opposed this measure.[120] His call "went viral," and millions of Americans who said they were fed up with taxes, bailouts, and wasteful government programs and spending began coalescing in hundreds of loosely organized groups across the nation that came to be called the Tea Party. Tea Party activists claimed that the movement was composed of people new to politics and was nonpartisan, but careful studies have since shown that most of its members were conservative Republicans, many of them longtime activists. In effect, it represented a new mobilization of the Republican Party's right wing goaded into action by the electoral victory of a party and a presidential candidate its members absolutely detested. The moderate approach pursued while George W. Bush was president was scorned for supporting bailouts and deficits, and, as the entire party moved further to the right, moderate Republicans became an endangered species. It was movement that was overwhelmingly white, more male than female and most attractive to older people, and it drew significant support from white evangelical conservative Christians. Not surprisingly, it found a receptive audience in the white South, and numerous Tea Party organizations popped up in the region. Over sixty percent of the members of the Tea Party caucus that began meeting in the U.S. House of Representatives represented districts in the region.[121] In the midterm elections of 2010, the reenergized Republican Party

---

119. "2008 Unofficial Voter Turnout," United States Election Project, at http://elections. gmu.edu/preliminary_vote_2008.html.

120. "CNBC's Rick Santelli's Chicago Tea Party," http://www.youtube.com/watch?v=zp-Jw-5Kx8k (accessed 3/22/2012).

121. Theda Skocpol and Vanessa Williamson, *The Tea Party and the Remaking of Republican Conservatism* (New York: Oxford University Press, 2012), chapter 1; David D. Campbell and Robert E. Putnam, "Crashing the Tea Party," *New York Times*, 16 August 2011,

won a solid majority of seats in the U.S. House of Representatives and added to the number of state legislatures and governorships it controlled.

Arguably the biggest Republican gains in the election of 2010 were in the South. Twenty white Southern Democrats running for reelection to Congress were defeated; Congressman Joe Barrow (GA) and Senator Mary Landreiu (LA) became the last white Democrats in Congress representing the Deep South alongside a handful of black congressmen representing "safe" districts with large black populations. The racial polarization of politics that had been waning, at least in the fringe South, seemed to have new life, and analysts predicted more white Southern Democratic congressmen would likely be defeated in the next round of elections. Prior to 2010, Democrats had been able to hold onto significant strength in state legislatures in many states despite decades of Republican inroads, but this strength evaporated on election night in 2010.[122] In North Carolina, Republicans hadn't controlled both houses of the state legislature in over one hundred years but won overwhelming majorities in both houses. In Mississippi and Alabama, Democrats had generally controlled one or both houses of the legislature; this ended and in striking fashion. A number of Democratic legislators in Alabama, Georgia, and elsewhere switched parties. Republican-controlled legislatures and Republican governors responded to the declining tax revenues caused by the 2008 recession by slashing spending, laying off government workers and increasing university tuitions. This was a common approach taken by states across the nation to deal with declining tax revenues resulting from the recession, so it remains to be seen whether this is simply a temporary response to the recession or the beginning of further cuts to state programs and services. In several states, issues dear to the Christian Right were put on the ballot for voters to consider: in North Carolina an amendment to the state constitution outlawing gay marriage was put on the ballot and in Mississippi, voters were given the opportunity to vote on a "personhood" amendment. This amendment would have established fertilized eggs as legal persons but was defeated when the medical community (and others) came out strongly against it. A number of states passed laws that required a government-issued ID to vote, ostensibly to improve "voting security"; critics charged that these laws were designed to suppress the turnout of low income

http://www.nytimes.com/2011/08/17/opinion/crashing-the-tea-party.html?_r=1; "The Tea Party and Religion" The Pugh Forum on Religion & Public Life, 23 February 2011, http://www.pewforum.org/Politics-and-Elections/Tea-Party-and-Religion.aspx (accessed 3/28/2012); "Who Is the Tea Party Caucus in the House?",*CNNPolitics*, http://politicalticker. blogs.cnn.com/2011/07/29/who-is-the-tea-party-caucus-in-the-house/ (accessed 3/30/2012).

122. Ben Evans, "Election nearly wipes out white Southern Democrats," 4 November 2010, *Real Clear Politics*, http://www.realclearpolitics.com/news/ap/politics/2010/Nov/04/election_nearly_wipes_out_white_southern_democrats.html (accessed 3/28/2012).

black voters and young voters, two Democratic constituencies less likely to have such identification.[123] Restrictions on early voting were also passed or considered in a number of states, ostensibly to save money, but again, critics charged that limiting early voting was really aimed at lowering the turnout of low income minorities.

And so the pendulum of politics had swung, but whether this represented a long lasting restoration of an old order Solid South is not a given. The pendulum had swung the other way only a few years earlier, and some pundits then had speculated about the demise of the Republican Party. Clearly, a big part of the explanation of the wild swings in voting is that the worst national economic crisis in recent history, one rivaled only by the Great Depression, had left voters divided and confused. But it does seem likely that Republican electoral success in the South in 2010 also represented the culmination of a trend that began during the Civil Rights era: the exodus of rural and working class conservative whites from the Democratic Party. But other long-term economic and demographic trends are still at work and will again move to the fore, and these trends by their nature will eventually undercut one-party domination and push the region in a more politically competitive direction. For starters, the people most wedded to the old traditions are older whites, and they are an ever-shrinking part of the electorate. The decline of the rural South will also continue apace, as will the rise of the metropolitan South. The suburban voters who predominate in the metropolitan South aren't doctrinaire voters for the most part and often support parts of what both parties have to offer. Clearly, they can't be taken for granted by either party and their votes will be hotly contested. The growing numbers of non-whites in the region, particularly Hispanics, will also make for more competitive elections where these voters are most numerous. Texas, for example, has been a state dominated by conservative white Republicans for two decades, but unless the party becomes more effective at courting Hispanic voters, this domination will eventually end because the Hispanic population is expected to exceed the white population by 2020, and this doesn't even factor in the state's sizable black population.[124] As of this writing, Republicans nationally and in Texas seem disinterested in courting minority groups of any persuasion, but that could change.

---

123. "State Measures to Balance FY 2010—FY 2012 Budgets" and "Voter Identification Requirements," National Council of State Legislatures, http://www.ncsl.org; "Mississippi's 'Personhood Amendment' Fails at Polls," *CBSNEWS*, 8 November 2011, http://www.cbsnews.com/8301-250_162-57321126/mississippis-personhood-amendment-fails-at-polls/.

124. "Texas in Focus: A Statewide View of Opportunities," Window on State Government," http://www.window.state.tx.us/specialrpt/tif/population.html (accessed 3/30/2012).

Marion Post Wolcott

Chapter 7

The Creative South: What People Made with Their Hands

Introduction: Creativity and Culture

In an article published in 1920, H. L. Mencken, a widely read journalist and social critic of that era, referred to the South as the "Sahara of the Bozart." What he meant by this phrase was that the region was "almost as sterile, artistically, intellectually, [and] culturally as the Sahara desert."[1] To add insult to injury, Mencken had deliberately misspelled the French term "beaux arts" (a term meaning fine arts) because he believed Southerners were so cul-

---

1. H. L. Mencken, "The Sahara of the Bozart," in William Andrews, ed., *The Literature of the American South* (New York: W. W. Norton & Co., 1998), 370.

turally ignorant that they wouldn't have a clue how the term was supposed to be spelled or what it meant. Mencken could be quite perceptive in his musings, but in this article he missed the mark. He had, for example, failed to discern the early signs of the golden age of Southern literature that was about to begin, an age that arguably has yet to reach its conclusion. But Mencken's most egregious sin was equating "high" culture (symphonic music, sculpture, poetry, and the like) with culture. If the South had no resident poet of note or a respectable number of symphonic orchestras playing Mozart or Beethoven, for Mencken it was a barren region lacking a creative culture. This, however, is the classic "city boy" putdown of the cultural creations of rural people ("hicks" and "hayseeds" in slang) as some laughably inferior product. This bias is not unique to Mencken; it is a built-in bias of Western culture. Our term "civilization" derives from the Latin *civitas*—"of the city"—and we generally see "civilized" to be preferable to "uncivilized" and, in effect, city culture to be superior to the culture of the countryside. There is a class bias here, too, that reverberates even today; the definers of what is culturally respectable and noteworthy have traditionally been folks from the upper classes or those in their pay, and so the symphony, an entertainment patronized by the more affluent, was deserving of accolades, contributions, and tax funds, while the blues artist might be ignored.

But creativity is creativity whether it is expressed in a blues song played on a battered guitar or a symphony performed by a large orchestra. Only a city can support an orchestra, and only a city can have a talent pool of trained musicians to supply the orchestra with members. The artists who produced the blues had as their palettes lives of poverty and oppression, their songs coming from their experiences and the musical traditions of West Africa, Europe, and the contemporary world they lived in; their training came at the end of a workday in the field. In short, people create with what they have to work with, and the wealth of society, level of urbanization, nature of the class system, what is socially acceptable for women and men to do, and, in the case of the South, race, all shape how people express their creativity. As Lawrence Craig, founder of Craig's Barbecue in Devall's Bluff, Arkansas, has noted: "Folks always talk about how black folks are good cooks. There's a reason for that. Back when I was growing up, there were two kinds of jobs black folks could get without being challenged by white folks: cooking and heavy lifting."[2]

At bottom, the major art forms that were produced in the South reflected a culture that was agrarian for much of its history. People in agrarian societies the world over have expressed their creativity through song and story and the

---

2. Lawrence Craig, "Why I Am a Cook," in John T. Edge, *A Gracious Plenty: Recipes and Recollections from the American South* (New York: HP Books, 1999), 172.

so-called useful arts such as pottery making, homebuilding, furniture making, and cooking. Techniques of producing this art were passed from person to person and generation to generation by seeing and doing and hearing. Southern folk culture was especially rich in aural traditions with a wide variety of musical styles, storytelling, and oratory; indeed, of all the creative arts produced in the South, it has been music that has had the biggest impact on the nation and the world. Country, the blues, gospel, rhythm and blues, and jazz have defined American music and are played and sung and listened to by millions in a host of other countries. As that wild offspring of all of these forms—rock—enters what can only be described as maturity or old age, it now commands the attention if not the approbation of young and old alike, although another offshoot—rap—seems to be a serious challenger to rock's supremacy with the young, and the heir apparent to rock's former position with elders as the "music we most hate." But Southern people created more than good music: potters produced noteworthy pottery, Southern cookery achieved acclaim (some say it is the nation's preeminent regional cuisine), and Southern literature blossomed in the twentieth century and is rivaled by none. Over time, key elements of this created culture—a song like "Dixie" or "Stagger Lee," the white pillared plantation home, the plate of fried chicken or the immortal Elvis Presley—became icons or symbols of the region that helped its citizens understand and define themselves and gave outsiders reference points for understanding the culture.

As the South industrialized and modernized after the Civil War, the arts naturally changed, too. The folk arts became the basis for the more rarefied art forms that a wealthier, urban, educated society could sustain. So, for example, blues evolved into jazz, a musical form now sometimes called American classical music; utilitarian pottery moved from the kitchen to the lighted display case in the living room, and a new "haute" Southern cuisine was pieced together from old recipes and new innovations and is discussed with the same seriousness as the older cuisines of France or Italy. Poets, Mencken would have been happy to learn, became quite common, and novelists became so numerous that they congregated in "colonies," making certain places—Oxford, Mississippi, and Hillsborough, North Carolina, come to mind—seem like small-town Southern versions of the Paris of the 1920s. Southern colleges established programs in some of the traditional Southern art forms (jazz, for example) along with programs that prepared people to perform or practice traditional Western "high" art such as classical performance, ballet, sculpture, and painting. Southern culture reached a wider audience courtesy of such entrepreneurs as Colonel Sanders and Colonel Tom Parker (Elvis's manager). In this and the next chapter, we will examine the more prominent of the traditional art forms, and how these forms gave rise to the arts of the contemporary South and to many of the icons and myths that define the South.

The Cuisine of the South

Southern cuisine is a blending of the culinary traditions and ingredients of three primary groups: Native Americans, immigrants from the British Isles, and West Africans. These influences have resulted in what we will call a "core" cuisine in the South that one can find from Virginia to Texas. Variations in the "core" abound, and one can find particular dishes unique to one area and not found in others. Sometimes these unique dishes are the result of ingredients, seafood for example, only found in certain parts of the South, and sometimes they are simply unique. In certain parts of Virginia, for example, several versions of peanut soup are served; this dish typically can't be found elsewhere in the South. The subcultures of the South often support cuisines that differ, sometimes dramatically, from the "core" cuisine. Cajun and "Tex-Mex" would be two of the most prominent subcultural cuisines, and each, in cooking style and ingredients, varies tremendously from the core cuisine. These cuisines reflect the impact of people—Spanish, French, and Mexican—who weren't found in the rest of the South in significant numbers, nor were many of their recipes and cooking styles much of an influence. It's hard to imagine, for example, crayfish étouffée showing up on the dinner table of a 1930s farm family in South Hill, Virginia, or a burrito making its way to the table of a textile mill worker in Spartanburg, South Carolina, circa 1950.

Today, of course, nearly everyone has had a burrito, and, while crayfish may not be a common food item, many of the millions of Southern tourists who have visited New Orleans have given some version of a "mudbug" dish a try. What people in the South eat today is changing thanks to rising levels of prosperity, mobility, immigration, television advertising of food "products," and the popularity of franchised restaurants. Today, Southerners seem to go out to eat as much as other Americans, and hamburgers, steaks, pizza, and "ethnic" food seem to be at the top of their list of things to eat, judging by the kinds of restaurants found in the typical Southern town or city. These restaurants are, more often than not, national chain restaurants, not local enterprises. Remarkably, when Southerners want Southern cooking, many apparently are quite willing to head off to the Cracker Barrel, a national chain found on many highways in the region, and tuck in to its ersatz Southern cuisine.

Traditional Southern fare was always primarily cooked and consumed at home; this was not, with some notable exceptions, a cuisine fostered by restaurants. Like all cuisines, it had a "common" basis; in other cultures the cooking of the peasantry would have formed this foundation, but in the South it was derived from the cooking of poor African Americans and reasonably comfortable white farm families. At its upper reaches, a "haute" (high) cuisine created in the homes of the planters and the postbellum affluent families by black female cooks would take common dishes and raise them to new levels with better ingredients, greater levels of expertise, and subtle and often complex varia-tions. Folks of more modest means did this, too; the fare they prepared day to day would be raised a notch or more in execution for special events—church picnics, wakes, family reunions, and the like. Southern food traditions are now being taken in new directions, as we will see, by professionally trained chefs often working in restaurants who approach the cuisine with the same reverence as chefs have treated French and other celebrated cooking traditions, but who are intent on exploring its possibilities just as the French chefs have elaborated upon the cooking traditions of their country.

The "Core" Cuisine

When the first English settlers began Jamestown, they brought their own cuisine, a cuisine that depended on: wheat bread; pork, mutton, chicken, and especially beef; vegetables like asparagus, beans, peas, boiled greens such as turnip tops; and a variety of brewed alcoholic beverages. Historian David Hackett Fischer has argued that this was a cuisine common to the south and west of England at that time (the origins of many of the early settlers); here frying, roasting, and grilling were all popular cooking techniques and tastes ran to strongly seasoned food.[3] As historian John Egerton has noted, "They were a meat-and-bread-eating, beer-drinking people."[4] Later, immigrants from England's border regions (the Scots-Irish) would bring their own culinary tra-ditions. Recall that these folks hailed from a troubled region, full of uncer-tainly, poverty, and strife, and it is not surprising that most descriptions of the food they ate are anything but glowing. Many had been herding people, and this lifestyle would influence what they ate and how it was prepared. Their sta-ple foods were clabber (sour milk, curds, and whey), potatoes, a variety of un-leavened breads generally made from oats and cooked on stones, oatmeal mush, and kale cooked in a broth. They ate mutton like their English neigh-bors, although historian Grady McWhiney maintains that their preference was actually for beef and especially pork and that herding sheep (and eating mut-ton) was an English tradition imposed on them. Boiling and frying were their preferred cooking techniques. They also preferred distilled beverages (what we

---

3. David Hackett Fischer, *Albion's Seed: Four British Folkways in America* (New York and Oxford: Oxford University Press, 1989), 350–352.

4. John Egerton, *Southern Food: At Home, on the Road, in History* (Chapel Hill and London: University of North Carolina Press, 1993), 11; C. Anne Wilson, *Food and Drink in Britain: From the Stone Age to Recent Times* (New York: Harper and Row, 1974), 97, 103–104, 199–206.

call today Scotch and Irish whiskey) over the malt beverages imbibed by the folks in England.[5]

But English and Scots-Irish settlers in the South were living amongst a people who had a long history in the region and an established cuisine based on maize (corn), squash, sweet potatoes, pumpkins, wild berries and game, fish, and shellfish. For Native Americans, corn was the "staff of life," and they fixed the corn in a variety of ways: roasted over a fire, ground and baked, and cooked in a porridge. They cooked their meats by roasting and by a slow cook method new to the settlers. As Robert Beverly observed in 1705, "They have two ways of Broyling, viz. one by laying the Meat itself upon the Coals, the other by laying it upon Sticks rais'd upon Forks at some distance above the live Coals, which heats more gently, and drys up the Gravy; this they, and we also from them, call Barbacueing." In short order, the English interlopers and their later arriving Scots-Irish brethren would incorporate the barbecue technique, the various corn preparations and the other Native American food stuffs into their own cuisine.[6]

The first Africans who arrived in Virginia in 1619 and those who would follow brought the culinary traditions of West Africa and to a lesser extent of other parts of Africa and the Caribbean islands where many (including the first arrivals in 1619) had spent time. They brought with them a number of vegetables native to Africa that would become staples of Southern cuisine including okra, described by one food historian as the "continent's culinary totem," black eyed peas, and watermelons.[7] Rice and two ingredients originally brought to Africa from America by the Portuguese—tomatoes and peanuts—were also part of the cuisines of some of the enslaved Africans who ended up in the American South. The yam, an integral part of many African cuisines, gave way in the South to a similar American ingredient, the sweet potato. African cuisines covered a broad range of dishes, but stews were especially popular. Meat was used more as a condiment, and stews consisted primarily of vegetables; greens were boiled down to a soupy consistency, and both the greens and the broth consumed.[8] Steaming, roasting by the fire, baking in the ashes of the

---

5. Fischer, *Albion's Seed*, 728–730; F. Marian McNeil, *The Scots Kitchen: It's Traditions and Lore with Old Time Recipes* (1929; Edinburgh: Mercat Press, 2006), 14–19; Grady McWhiney, *Cracker Culture: Celtic Ways in the Old South* (University, AL: University of Alabama Press, 1988), 83–84.

6. Egerton, *Southern Food*, 13; Robert Beverley, *The History and Present State of Virginia, in Four Parts* (1705; Chapel Hill, NC: Documenting the American South, 2006), Book III, Chapter 3, http://docsouth.unc.edu/southlit/beverley/beverley.html.

7. Jessica B. Harris, *The Africa Cookbook: Tastes of a Continent* (New York: Simon and Schuster, 1998), 10–11, quote 65.

8. *Ibid*, 12; Linda Stanley, "Collard Greens," What's Cooking America: History and Legends of Favorite Foods, http://whatscookingamerica.net/Vegetables/CollardGreens. htm (accessed 1/26/06).

fire, and frying were also popular. Palm oil and sesame oil were two of the more common oils, but as the cultivation of peanuts spread in Africa, peanut oil also came into use. A variety of spices and herbs, many reflecting West Africa's trade with the Arab societies of North Africa and the Middle East and with India, were used to flavor foods, and the use of various peppers, malagueta and cayenne especially, were common.[9]

From these divergent sources and traditions, a cuisine would arise in the South that rested on a foundation of corn and pork.[10] The corn porridge of the Native Americans would become grits and hominy, and their various corn bread concoctions would become the cornbread, cornpone, corn dodgers, hoecake, and hush puppies of the English, Scots-Irish, and African settlers. All cuisines are based on a vegetable or animal fat; the English cuisine relied heavily on butter and secondarily on beef fat and pork fat (lard). In the Southern colonies, pork fat became the fat of choice to fry, sauté, and season, and pork became the meat of choice despite the fact that neither the English settlers nor the West African settlers had come from pork dependent cultures. Indeed, there were suspicions early on by many beef-loving Englishmen that pork was an inferior, even unhealthy meat. William Byrd, planter and surveyor of the dividing line between Virginia and North Carolina in the early 1700s, opined that North Carolina's settlers "live so much upon Swine's flesh, that it don't only encline them to the Yaws, & consequently to the downfall of their Noses, but makes them likewise extremely hoggish in their Temper, & many of them seem to Grunt rather than Speak in their ordinary conversation."[11]

Pork had many advantages over beef for folks living on widely dispersed homesteads in frontier conditions. Hogs were "low maintenance" and could be left to fend for themselves in the woods, fattening on acorns and whatever else they could turn up. Farmers might clip the ears of their hogs to mark ownership and would conduct round-ups when they needed meat or cash or something to barter. Historian Grady McWhiney maintains that pork was

---

9. Harris, *The Africa Cookbook*, 11–13; Robert L. Hall, "Food Crops, Medicinal Plants, and the Atlantic Slave Trade," in Anne L. Bowers, ed., *African American Foodways: Explorations of History & Culture* (Urbana: University of Illinois Press, 2009), 17–44.

10. Joe Gray Taylor, *Eating, Drinking, and Visiting in the South* (Baton Rouge: Louisiana State University Press, 1982), 20–22.

11. William K. Byrd, *William Byrd's Histories of the Dividing Line Betwixt Virginia and North Carolina* (1929; New York: Dover Publications, Inc. 1967), 55. John Lawson, another early chronicler of the Carolinas, also noted the heavy reliance on pork which, he believed was "a gross food" and one that contributed to ill health. See John Lawson, *A New Voyage to Carolina; Containing the Exact Description and Natural History of That Country: Together with the Present State Thereof. And A Journal of a Thousand Miles, Travel'd Thro' Several Nations of Indians. Giving a Particular Account of Their Customs, Manners, &c.* (1709; Chapel Hill: Documenting the American South, 2001), 18, http://docsouth.unc.edu/nc/lawson/lawson.html.

popular for another reason; it allowed the migrants from the border regions of England (he calls them Celts) who migrated to the South in the early decades of the 1700s to continue the herding lifestyle they had practiced in Scotland and Ireland.[12]

Much of the pork that was consumed was cured meat, and the preparation of this meat was an important ritual in the rural South. The fall was the traditional time to slaughter hogs, and on farms and plantations an impromptu factory would be set up to kill the hogs, hang them for bleeding, harvest the organs, carve the carcasses, and process what could be eaten. Novelist Randall Kenan describes a scene that could have taken place any time between the 1700s and the mid-decades of the twentieth century (the period of his story):

> The air would be thick with smoke and the smell of sage and pepper and cooked meats and blood.... [B]eneath the shed, the women would be busy, with knives, with grinders, with spoons and forks; the greasy tables littered with salts and peppers and spices, hunks of meat, bloody and in pans to be made into sausages, pans of cooked liver to be made into liver pudding.[13]

Everything—meat, fat, brains, intestines, kidneys, liver, feet, ears—was used ("everything but the squeal") and would be processed in its own way. Fat would be rendered and intestines would be carefully washed and would become chitterlings ("chitlins") which would be served boiled or fried or used as casings for sausage; the sausage meat was mixed with seasoning, sage especially; ground liver was mixed with pork, onions, seasonings and in some locales rice or cornmeal and made into liver pudding or liver mush; the feet would be cooked and eaten or pickled to be served latter; brains were cooked and served with eggs as a special treat.[14] This was a time of feasting whether on the small farm or the plantation. What would be served at these feasts varied according to status: One former slave remembered:

> But hit wasn't all bad times 'caze us did have planty to eat, 'specially at hog killin' time. Dey would hab days ob hog killin' and de slaves would bake dere bread and come wid pots, pepper, salt. A'ter cleanin'

---

12. Grady McWhiney, *Cracker Culture*, 55.

13. Randall Kenan, *A Visitation of Spirits* (1989; New York: Vintage Books, 2000), 7–8.

14. Liney Henderson, interview by Annie Ruth Davis, *Born in Slavery: Narratives from the Federal Writers' Project, 1936–1938* (Washington: Library of Congress, Manuscript Division, 2001), http://memory.loc.gov/ammem/snhtml/snhome.html; Annie Huff Interview, *Ibid*; Annie Stephenson, interview by T. Pat Matthews, *Ibid*; James Battle Avirett, *The Old Plantation: How We Lived in Great House and Cabin Before the War* (1901; Chapel Hill: Documenting the American South, 1998), 173–174, http://docsouth.unc.edu/avirett/avirett.html; Taylor, *Eating, Drinking, and Visiting in the South*, 23–26.

de hogs, dey would gib us de livers and lights [lungs], and us would cook dem ober a fire out in de open and sho' was good eatin'.[15]

The son of parents who had both been slaves recalled the stories of hog killings his parents had told him and described feasts of "chit'lin's, haslets, pig foots, and sausage, wid good old collard greens, cracklin' bread, and hot coffee."[16] A planter recalled:

> In order that there should be no loss or waste, and that plenty of time should be allowed for consuming the "chines and the chitterlings," the hogs were not all butchered at once, but with an interval of ten days or two weeks between each killing. In this way the sausage, so deliciously seasoned with pot herbs, the juicy tenderloins, the tempting spareribs, the delicious sweetbreads, and perhaps the most delicate of all, the brains of the animals—in fine, everything coming to the old planter's table at this season of the year—made up a breakfast good enough for a king.[17]

The first stages in the preparation of the king of pork products, the ham, would begin on this day. Hams were first produced in early Virginia, and the salted and smoked hams of Smithfield, first produced in the mid-1600s, became famous throughout the South and beyond.[18] Hams could be "dry cured" or "wet cured"; wet cured hams were literally soaked in brine (like corned beef) until the salt penetrated to the bone and were often called "city hams"; dry cured hams, called country hams (Smithfield hams were dry cured) were rubbed with salt and sometimes sugar over a longer period of time and then aged for months. The longer the ham aged, the more flavorful, and thus the "aged" ham acquired a special reputation. Smoking also imparted a special flavor.[19] The curing process, wet or dry, drew out the water from the flesh and prevented spoilage, thus providing families without refrigeration with a steady meat source. Other parts of the pig—the fat on the back, the belly meat and fat, and the joints—would also be cured and the resulting fatback, bacon, and ham hock would be used to season the vegetables and be eaten by themselves

---

15. "Hungry for Pumpkin Pie," Aunt Adeline, interview by Ila B. Prine, *Born in Slavery: Narratives from the Federal Writers' Project, 1936–1938* (Washington: Library of Congress, Manuscript Division, 2001), http://memory.loc.gov/ammem/snhtml/snhome.html.

16. Bill Heard, interview by Grace McCune, *Born in Slavery: Slave Narratives from the Federal Writers' Project, 1936–1938* (Washington: Library of Congress, Manuscript Division, 2001), http://memory.loc.gov/ammem/snhtml/snhome.html.

17. Avirett, *The Old Plantation*, 86.

18. Egerton, *Southern Food*, 256–257.

19. On the tradition of curing hams, see Nancy Newsom Mahaffey, "Kentucky Bacon," interview by Amy Evans, 24 August 2005, Southern Foodways Alliance, http://www.southernfoodways.com/oral_history/bacon/nancy_newsom_mahaffey.shtml (accessed 1/26/06).

when better cuts of meat were not available. These cuts of fat and fatty meat often came from lower on hog; the better cuts (the hams and shoulders) came from higher on the pig, and thus the expression "living high on the hog" means to live bountifully.

This is not to say that the traditional English taste for beef disappeared. Most plantations had a small herd of beef cows and milk cows, and many small farmers kept a few of both, too. Sheep were raised throughout the antebellum period primarily for their wool, although some mutton and spring lamb were eaten. In piedmont Rowan County, North Carolina, for example, slaveless farmers in 1860 averaged five head of cattle and thirteen head of swine, and many maintained small flocks of sheep. Slaveholders in Rowan County maintained even larger herds of cattle. Beef cows and especially young calves were slaughtered for fresh meat, and the flesh could be brined (corned beef), but while fresh beef and veal were popular in the region, corned beef never attained the popularity that salted pork did in the South.[20]

For planters and most small farmers, the kitchen was typically detached from the house to protect the main dwelling from fire and keep it cooler during the hot summers. Less affluent whites and slave families cooked in their cabins; in warm weather they might cook outside, but even the planters enjoyed a good outdoor barbecue. Cooking was largely done in the fireplace or over open fires; cast iron stoves made their appearance in the mid-1800s but really weren't common until after the Civil War. Meats—pork, chicken, beef, game—were roasted on skewers, stewed in big black pots suspended over the fire, or fried in pans with legs on them sometimes called "spiders" which were placed over hot coals on the hearth. Greens and other vegetables were stewed in pots of water nestled in the hot coals on the hearth or suspended over the fire from hooks or cranes. Dutch ovens with rimmed lids that held hot coals even permitted baking in the fire, although the more affluent, planters especially, might have a free-standing oven or a small oven built into the fireplace.[21] Cornbread could be cooked in a Dutch oven or a frying pan placed in the coals although in the most primitive circumstances, corn bread could be cooked on the blade of a hoe (hoe cake) or literally cooked in the ashes of a fire (ash cake). Sweet potatoes (and, later on, Irish potatoes) could also be cooked in the ashes and were an important mainstay of many diets because they could be stored in a cool place and would keep during the winter. Collards would keep on the

---

20. Taylor, *Eating, Drinking, and Visiting in the South,* 26–28; John J. Beck, "Development in the Piedmont South: Rowan County, North Carolina, 1850–1900" (Unpublished Ph.D. dissertation, University of North Carolina, Chapel Hill, 1984), Table 1.15, 270.

21. Fowler, *Classical Southern Cooking,* 11–12; Taylor, *Eating Drinking, and Visiting in the South,* 18–19; Daniel R. Hundley, *Social Relations In Our Southern States* (1860; Chapel Hill: Documenting the American South, 1999), 86, http://docsouth.unc.edu/southlit/hundley/menu.html.

plant for much of the winter in most of the South and were said to be better after a frost. Other vegetables that were commonly planted and might end up on the table were squash, okra, turnips, cabbage, cowpeas, tomatoes, pumpkins, a variety of beans, some of which could be dried and served during the winter, and onions. Herbs, especially sage and spearmint, were also planted and used for seasonings, and apples, peaches, cherries, and a wide variety of other wild and cultivated fruits, nuts, and berries were consumed.[22]

What the families of small farmers ate on a regular basis and how it was prepared varied according to the season and from family to family. One observer opined that:

> In very early Kentucky times, the universal dinner, winter and spring, at every farm-house in the State, was a piece of middling bacon, boiled with cabbage, turnips, greens, collards or sprouts—cabbage-sprouts— according to the season. The pot, if the family was a large one, contained about ten gallons, and was nearly filled with clean pure water: the middling and the greens were put in at the proper time, to give them a sufficient cooking. Almost always the cook would make with water and corn-meal and a little salt, dough-balls, throw them into the pot, and boil them thoroughly with the rest. These were called dodgers, from the motion giving [sic] them by the boiling water in the pot.[23]

Frederick Law Olmstead in his travels through the South in the 1850s recorded meals at several homesteads consisting of corn bread and bacon or salt pork supplemented perhaps by sweet potatoes; he was also served fried eggs with his corn bread and pork, and at one homestead he was given a meal of "barely cooked" food.[24] He describes in almost jubilant terms spending a night with a small farmer family where "The table was abundantly supplied with the most wholesome food—I might almost say the first wholesome food—I have had set before me since I was at the hotel at Natchez; loaf bread for the first time; chicken, stewed instead of fried; two sorts of preserved fruit, and whortleberry and blackberry tarts."[25] In the decades before the Civil War, the typical household in the South consumed more corn and pork and less wheat bread, butter, and milk than their northern counterparts, and apparently vegetables, with the exception of sweet potatoes and perhaps greens, typically played a small role in their daily diets.[26] Whiskey, at least for the males, was the preferred drink over

22. Fowler, *Classical Southern Cooking*, 16; Sarah Belk, *Around the Southern Table* (New York: Simon and Schuster, 1991), 296; Egerton, *Southern Food*, 11–13; Taylor, *Eating Drinking, and Visiting in the Old South*, 37–42.

23. Hundley, *Social Relations in Our Southern States*, 86.

24. Frederick Law Olmsted, *The Cotton Kingdom*, ed. Arthur Schlesinger, Jr., (1861; New York: Modern Library, 1984), 281, 325, 377, 401–402.

25. *Ibid.*, 402.

26. Egerton, *Southern Food*, 21–22; McWhiney, *Cracker Culture*, 81, 82–83, 86, 88.

the English beer or cider, and buttermilk or sour milk (like the clabber of the old country) was preferred over what was called (and still is by some people) "sweet milk."[27] The taste for hard liquor made the South the center of a distilling industry, legal and illegal; not surprisingly, corn was the grain of choice for fermentation, and whiskey was what was produced.[28] Bourbon (produced in Kentucky) and Tennessee whiskey became the standard bearers on the legal side and were distilled from a blend of corn and other grains and aged in barrels; the less-refined "corn liquor" eventually became the specialty of distillers operating outside the law whose product became known as moonshine.

The diets of slaves were based, as those of whites, on corn and pork. On some plantations, the plantation kitchen would fix most of the meals; on most plantations, the slave families cooked most of their meals in the fireplaces of their dwellings.[29] The quantity of food and how it was cooked, predictably enough, varied tremendously. Historian Eugene Genovese estimates that the typical slave got a ration of "a half pound of pork a day" and that most ate as well, calorically speaking, as poor whites.[30] Frederick Law Olmsted visited a rice plantation outside Charleston and found that:

> The provisions furnished them consist mainly of meal, rice and vegetables, with salt and molasses, and occasionally bacon, fish, and coffee. The allowance is a peck of meal, or an equivalent quantity of rice per week, to each working hand, old or young, besides small stores. Mr. X. says that he has lately given a less amount of meat than is now usual on plantations, having observed that the general health of the negroes is not as good as formerly, when no meat at all was customarily given them. The general impression among planters is, that the negroes work much better for being supplied with three or four pounds of bacon a week.[31]

Former slave Allen Parker recalled receiving a weekly ration of 5 lbs. of pork and 4 quarts of cornmeal supplemented by sweet potatoes and occasionally molasses. With these provisions, the typical "bill of fare" for slaves on his plantation was fried salt pork or bacon and baked hoe cake cooked in the fireplaces of the slaves' cabins.[32] Another former slave reported that on his plantation

---

27. McWhiney, *Cracker Culture*, 83, 90, 92.

28. Taylor, *Eating, Drinking, and Visiting in the South*, 45.

29. Eugene Genovese, *Roll, Jordan, Roll: The World the Slaves Made* (New York: Vintage Books, 1976), 544.

30. *Ibid.*, 63.

31. Frederick Law Olmsted, *A Journey in the Seaboard Slave States; With Remarks on Their Economy* (1856; Chapel Hill: Documenting the American South, 2001), 432, http://docsouth.unc.edu/nc/olmsted/olmsted.html.

32. Allen Parker, *Recollections of Slavery Times* (1895; Chapel Hill: Documenting the American South, 2000), 15, 13, http://docsouth.unc.edu/neh/parker/ parker.html.

breakfast consisted of "warm corn bread and buttermilk" served at noon by the plantation cook and dinner (served in the evening) consisted of "corn bread, or potatoes, and the meat which remained of the master's dinner, or one herring apiece."[33] Still another remembered evening meals of corn bread, beans, sweet potatoes, and collard greens, the cornbread wrapped in leaves of elephant ears and cooked in the hot coals of the fireplace of his home.[34] Slave children were sometimes fed sour milk and cornmeal mush or hoecake.[35] The "generosity" of the slave-owner and the freedom he allowed his slaves to grow gardens, hunt, and forage determined how well-fed slaves were and the variety of their diets. Many slave families did maintain small gardens where greens (collards, especially) and other vegetables were grown, and they were sometimes permitted to raise a small flock of chickens, too.[36] Men would often supplement family provisions with fish and game; game would be snared, and some men hunted with the dogs they kept; occasionally, a trusted male slave would be permitted to hunt with a firearm. Because evening was one of the few times a slave could call his own, hunting for nocturnal animals—raccoon and opossum, especially—was popular and the resulting meals savored when prepared properly.[37] As one former slave noted, "The opossum is generally cooked by being roasted in his skin, and when served with roasted sweet potatoes makes a fine dish...."[38] Given the work requirements of slavery, women were hard-pressed to find the time to excel in their cooking, but many must have, for it was in the slave cabins that the culinary traditions of West Africa were kept alive and joined with new traditions and new ingredients to form Southern cuisine. A favorite meal in coastal South Carolina, for example, was "Hoppin' John," which was cow peas (black-eyed peas) seasoned with a piece of bacon and mixed with rice.[39] This dish harked back to Africa, but the seasoning was Southern to the core.

---

33. "Narrative of James Curry," in John Blassingame, ed., *Slave Testimony: Two Centuries of Letters, Speeches, Interviews, and Autobiographies* (Baton Rouge: Louisiana State University Press, 1977), 133.

34. Claude Augusta Wilson, interview by James Johnson, *Born in Slavery: Slave Narratives from the Federal Writers' Project, 1936–1938* (Washington: Library of Congress, Manuscript Division, 2001), http://memory.loc.gov/.

35. Jacob Stroyer, *My Life In the South* (1885; Chapel Hill: Documenting the American South, 2001), 11, http://docsouth.unc.edu/neh/stroyer85/stroyer85.html; Parker, *Recollections of Slavery Times*, 17.

36. Genovese, *Roll, Jordan, Roll*, 535. James Battle Avirett, *The Old Plantation*, 46; Green Willbanks, interview by Sadie B. Hornsby, Born *in Slavery: Slave Narratives from the Federal Writers' Project, 1936–1938* (Washington: Library of Congress, Manuscript - Division, 2001), http://memory.loc.gov/.

37. Genovese, *Roll, Jordan, Roll*, 486–489; Taylor, *Eating, Drinking, and Visiting in the South*, 86.

38. Parker, *Recollections of Slavery Times*, 52.

39. Stroyer, *My Life in the South*, 11.

At the Christmas season, the work demands of the plantation were at their lowest ebb, and slaveowners often allowed the slaves to have time off. Special rations were often provided, and the slaves were permitted to organize parties and feasts. Allen Parker recalled, "One of the slaves would plan for a dance several weeks before the time and word would be sent, not only to the hands on the plantation, but also to the other plantations near by...." and, "Sometimes there would be a supper at the gathering, in which case it would be eaten in the first part of the evening. This supper would consist of hominy, hoe cakes, sweet potatoes, bacon, lamb, coon or 'possum, or any other kind of meat that could be obtained. Sometimes the meat would be given by the masters who might add also flour and molasses."[40] Another recounted Christmas feasts of meats—chickens, turkeys, pigs, even a "wild ox"—roasted in a pit filled with burning coals. Biscuits were served with preserves, and a variety of vegetables, tarts, and pies were laid out. Slaves ate seated at long tables with men sitting on one side and women on the other.[41]

It was in the kitchens of the plantation houses where the diverse culinary traditions of Africa, the Indies, and Europe were married to produce a Southern haute cuisine that became an important element of the legend (and reality) of Southern hospitality. Thomas Jefferson was emblematic of this hospitality; he entertained frequently and lavishly, and his table featured a wide variety of dishes. He was a great proponent of French cuisine, and French dishes came forth in profusion from the kitchens of Monticello and the presidential mansion when he was president of the United States, but Jefferson was also said to be quite fond of such Virginia dishes as sweet potatoes, black eyed peas, turnip greens, and Virginia ham, and it would be dishes like these that would constitute the foundation of Southern haute cuisine.[42] The actual cooking in Jefferson's kitchen and in plantation kitchens across the South was done by black women, and they would use skill and ingenuity to blend the African culinary traditions they learned and practiced at the hearthsides of their small cabins with English and other cooking traditions.[43] These women acquired a certain prominence on the plantation; the cook was, according to Allen Parker, "quite a personage upon the plantation...."[44] The cooks were supervised to a greater

---

40. Parker, *Recollections of Slavery Times*, 64–65.

41. Solomon Northup, *Twelve Years a Slave: Narrative of Solomon Northup, a Citizen of New-York, Kidnapped in Washington City in 1841, and Rescued in 1853* (1853; Chapel Hill: Documenting the American South, 2000), 215, http://docsouth.unc.edu/northup/north up.html#northup208.

42. Marie Kimball, *Thomas Jefferson's Cook Book* (Charlottesville: University Press of Virginia, 1996), 1.

43. Genovese, *Roll, Jordan, Roll*, 540–541; Damon Lee Fowler, *Classical Southern Cooking: A Celebration of the Cuisine of the Old South* (New York: Crown Publishers, Inc., 1995), 3–4.

44. Parker, *Recollections of Slavery Times*, 17.

or lesser degree by plantation mistresses and this interaction, from the earliest times, established an English, or in the case of Louisiana, a French and Spanish, base for the cuisine. "Virginia ladies," opined Mary Randolph in her path breaking cookbook, *The Virginia Housewife*, "who are proverbially good managers" keep a close eye on the glassware and "all the apparatus of the dinner table" and "let all articles intended for the dinner, pass in review before her...."[45]

The cuisine coming out of the plantation kitchen in the decades prior to the Civil War varied from plantation to plantation and by region. Seafood, for example, would form a key part of the diets of coastal residents, and rice dishes would be popular in rice growing areas. French culinary traditions would influence the cuisines of Charleston and especially Louisiana and New Orleans. The affluence and sophistication of the planter family also determined the bounty. As the long suffering Olmsted discovered, particularly on the frontier, some planters made do with the same pork and cornbread fare eaten by small farmers or even slaves. Simple, hardy fare such as chicken and dumplings, ham, biscuits, griddle cakes, sweet potatoes, cornbread, fresh vegetables, especially greens and string beans seasoned with bacon, and perhaps barbecued pork and beef on special occasions was probably what came out of most plantation kitchens. Game was often served because of the prevalence of game animals and the enjoyment many planters took in hunting. South Carolina planter Thomas Chaplin rarely went more than a few days without hunting and would bring home deer and a variety of game birds.[46] Larger game was roasted in the fireplace suspended from hooks. As James Avirett, son of the owner of Rich Lands in eastern North Carolina, reminisced, the hooks "are employed when a wild turkey or a roast of venison are there cooked, basted meantime with vinegar and lard or butter, being constantly turned around so as to present no one side too long to the roaring fire as to burn the meat, while the metal dish underneath catches all the juices as they are distilled by the great heat from the roaring fire."[47] Fish, crabs, oysters, clams, and shrimp were popular in coastal areas. Avirett noted that this bounty from the tidal areas "had become to the planters and their families actual indispensable necessaries." He described an oyster roast where buckets of oyster were set on tables and served with bread and butter and pickled cucumbers.[48] Planked shad—the fish literally nailed to a plank and roasted before a fire—was considered a special

---

45. Mary Randolph, *The Virginia Housewife, or Methodical Cook* (1838; East Lansing, Mich.: Michigan State University Library, 2004), xi, http://digital.lib.msu.edu/projects/cookbooks/html/books/book_10.cfm.

46. Theodore Rosengarten, *Tombee: Portrait of a Cotton Planter; With the Plantation Journal of Thomas B. Chaplin (1822–1890)* (New York: William Morrow & Co., 1986).

47. James Battle Avirett, *The Old Plantation*, 39.

48. *Ibid.*, quote, 24; 137.

treat.[49] It should be noted that there is more to cooking these dishes than meets the eye. As any good cook knows, excellent, simple fare requires great skill to prepare and is as much an art form as is the preparation of more complicated dishes. The famous "beaten biscuits" for example, are light and airy concoctions that are surpassed by none in the world of breads; they are nothing more than flour and lard and perhaps a bit of butter. The "secret" was that the dough to make them was beaten on a large block of wood until it was "perfectly moist and light" by hands that could tell when it was ready for the oven; the final product was flaky, delicate, and delicious.[50]

In an affluent household with an interest in food and graced with a good cook, one could find more elaborate fare during what one writer has called the "golden age" of cooking in the decades before the Civil War. Accompanying the spit roasted pork and beef were yeast breads, fricassees, ragouts, soups, vegetable dishes, fruit cakes, custards, and even ice cream.[51] Mrs. Randolph's cookbook features recipes that reflected English cooking traditions and others that reflected African and Caribbean traditions of the slave women who did all or most of the actual cooking and, of course, a leavening of Native American influences, not to mention the ubiquitous native ingredients. The English influence is clearly reflected in the many recipes for beef and veal, including directions for corning beef, salad preparations dressed in oil and vinegar, and vegetables such as asparagus, cauliflower, and cabbage simply prepared by boiling in salted water. Recipes for curry of catfish, "ochra" (okra) soup, fried chicken, turnips "boiled with bacon in the Virginia style," and "barbecue shote" (a young pig) clearly reflected other influences and document the emerging Southern cuisine. In Kentucky, a "burgou" (sometimes spelled burgoo) became a noted specialty in kitchens of both the rich and not so rich; one recipe reflecting the cookery of the plantation kitchen called for squirrel and birds, barley, tomatoes, corn, oysters, cream, and butter.[52] In rice-growing coastal South Carolina, rice accompanied most meals and even made its way into a variety of breads, muffins, cookies, and griddle cakes.[53] Pilaus were especially popular.

---

49. *Ibid.*, 12; Egerton, *Southern Cooking*, 272.

50. Abby Fisher, *What Mrs. Fisher Knows About Old South Cooking, Soups, Pickles, Preserves, Etc.* (1881; East Lansing, Mich.: Michigan State University Library, 2004), 1, http://digital.lib.msu.edu/projects/cookbooks/html/authors/author_ fisher.html; Avirett, *The Old Plantation*, 39.

51. Fowler, *Classical Southern Cooking*, 6; Taylor, *Eating, Drinking, and Visiting in the South*, 54–59.

52. Minnie C. Fox, *The Blue Grass Cook Book* (1904; East Lansing, Mich.: Michigan State University Library, 2004), 37–38, http://digital.lib.msu.edu/projects/cookbooks/html/books/book_10.cfm.

53. Sarah Rutledge, *The Carolina Housewife* (1847; Columbia, SC: University of South Carolina Press facsimile ed., 1979).

Chicken pilau (also called purloo), for example, was a chicken stew cooked with celery, thyme, red pepper, onion, butter, rice, tomatoes and other ingredients depending on the recipe.[54] A more plebian version of the dish came to be called chicken bog and was generally whole chicken, bones and all, cooked with onion, rice and celery. It became the charity supper par excellence in the twentieth century, and fire departments, churches, and school fund-raising committees cooked up tons of it. Another favorite served in the Lowcountry of South Carolina and Georgia clearly reflected the influences of seafarers familiar with Indian cuisine. This dish, country captain, was a chicken dish cooked with onion, bell pepper, garlic, currents, tomato and curry, and served over rice.[55] The modern cocktail also had antecedents on the plantation; the mint julep was perhaps the most famous of these and was little more than mint, whiskey, water, sugar and ice, but, as with the beaten biscuits, combining these simple ingredients into a decent drink required a special touch. The more elaborate cherry bounce was made, according to one recipe, from a variety of spices including mace, clove, ginger, and nutmeg mixed with cherries, whiskey and sugar, and aged in a barrel for 12 months before bottling. It must have packed quite a kick.[56]

The barbecue was the special event for the plantation and offered planters an opportunity to entertain on a lavish scale. The secret to good barbecue was low heat and long hours; a pit filled with hardwood coals fire would be started the night before the big event, and the meat put on around midnight for a midday meal. The night and morning were spent keeping the fire at the right temperature and basting the meat.[57] Pig, lamb, goat, and beef were all barbecued, although pork would emerge as the favorite meat in most of the South, with beef more popular in the far western part of the region. Generally, the barbecue master was a male slave and was "a person of consequence" on the plantation.[58] The ones with the best reputations would be "loaned out"; whites also barbecued, but, opined Martha McCulloch-Williams, they never attained the same degree of proficiency as blacks, particularly in the mastery of the ideal "'dipney'" sauce.[59] Even today, the masters of barbecue are frequently black men. The barbecue man on McCulloch-Williams's plantation (she called him "Blackdaddy") made a sauce out of lard, black pepper, red peppers, herbs, apple vinegar, and salt. She recalled that cucumbers in vinegar, sliced toma-

54. John Martin Taylor, *Hoppin' John's Lowcountry Cooking: Recipes and Ruminations from Charleston and the Carolina Coastal Plain* (New York: Bantam Books, 1992), 66.

55. *Hoppin' John*, 153–155.

56. Martha McCulloch-Williams, *Dishes and Beverages of the Old South* (1913; Knoxville: University of Tennessee Press, 1988), 72, 77.

57. *Ibid.*, 273.

58. *Ibid.*

59. *Ibid.*

toes, "light bread," and watermelon were served as accompaniments to the bar-becued meat on her plantation.[60]

In Louisiana two unique cuisines, Creole and Cajun developed. The Creoles were the descendent of French and Spanish settlers of New Orleans; the Cajuns were the descendants of French-speaking Acadian settlers expelled from Nova Scotia in the mid-1700s who settled in the rural areas of southwest Louisiana. Historian John Egerton has argued that it's appropriate to consider Creole a close cousin of French haute cuisine and Cajun related to the country cuisine of France and that, given the close proximity of these two groups, where one cuisine began and the other left off is difficult to determine. Creole cooking reached its apogee in the kitchens of wealthy merchants and planters of South Louisiana, especially those with homes in the city of New Orleans. Presiding over these kitchens were black cooks. This city could claim the distinction of being the most cosmopolitan in the South before and after the Civil War, and connections to both France and Spain and a small if consistent stream of im-migrants from Europe enriched its culture and its cooking and informed its tastes. Wine, not bourbon, was the alcohol of choice in Louisiana. As Lafcadio Hearn noted in his famous cookbook published after the Civil War, "The in-herited French taste of the greater portion of the population, and the educa-tion by contact of the American element makes claret the universal table wine." It was "seldom absent from the table of even the most economical."[61] Creole cooking was built on a base of French techniques, sauces, and soups, com-bined with the Spanish appreciation for onion, green peppers, garlic and tomatoes, and enriched by African ingredients (such as okra) and cooking tra-ditions.[62] Louisiana was a world of water—ocean, bayous, lakes, rivers, and streams—and the bounty of this watery world resulted a cuisine rich with dishes containing a variety of local fish and shellfish species, especially the pompano, crayfish, oyster, and shrimp. The foods of the "core cuisine" of the South—cured pork, cornbread, grits, greens—were also integrated into the cooking, but the dishes most emblematic of Creole cooking were the gumbos, bisques, sauces, and broiled and baked meats, fishes, and shellfish. Some of these dishes, gumbo for example, would show up outside Louisiana; most of the others did not. Only in Louisiana would the crayfish end up on the dinner tables of both the wealthy and poor.[63] While the best Southern cuisine was

---

60. *Ibid.*, 274–275.

61. Lafcadio Hearn, *La Cuisine Creole: A Collection of Culinary Recipes from Leading Chefs and Noted Creole Housewives, Who Have Made New Orleans famous for its Cuisine* (1885: East Lansing, MI: Michigan State University Library, 2004), 244, http://digital.lib.msu.edu/projects/cookbooks/index.html.

62. Egerton, *Southern Food*, 110–112; Lafcadio Hearn, *La Cuisine Creole*, Introduc-tion.

63. See Lafcadio Hearn, *La Cuisine Creole* for a sense of the range of dishes in Creole cookery in the 1800s.

largely enjoyed in private homes in most of the region, New Orleans did, before the Civil War, develop a reputation for "superlative dining and hospitality" in its restaurants and hotels.[64] The city was a travel destination for planters across the South; North Carolinian James Avirett, for example, extolled the virtues of "the pompino [sic], that perfection of the Gulf waters, at the old Saint Charles in New Orleans...."[65]

After the Civil War, culinary traditions in the South evolved in two different directions. The terrible poverty of the postbellum South drove more and more people to a diet even more centered on salt pork and cornmeal—the infamous "3 M's" (meat, meal, and molasses). This was the diet of the typical sharecropper and many of the millworkers. It was not simply that people had less money and could only afford this limited fare. The self-sufficiency of the antebellum period had been dealt a blow by the destruction of livestock during the war; after the war, the focus on cash crop agriculture cut into the acreage devoted to food crops and the advent of fencing laws shrank the availability of open land for grazing swine and cattle. More and more of the food consumed by less affluent people, even rural people, came from stores, and diets were constricted. As we saw in an earlier chapter, the incidence of nutritional diseases and malnutrition increased dramatically. Breakfast might be cornbread and molasses; the noon meal might be a sweet potato, cooked in the coals of the fire and accompanied by cold water; fried fatback and corn bread, swimming in molasses, might serve as the evening meal.[66] But some of the less affluent had, predictably, more: the more industrious and fortunate might plant a bigger garden, raise chickens, perhaps a hog or two, hunt, fish, dry berries and fruits, and gather nuts to sell for extra cash. One woman whose family sharecropped remembered that they would cooperate with neighbors and "kill a beef, and each neighbor around would get so much of it, so we would cook it up and use it up cause we didn't have anywhere to store it."[67] Even a poor woman could, on special occasions, assemble the ingredients for a good meal: Sunday dinner might feature chicken and gravy, biscuits, and perhaps some greens, and family reunions, and church dinners "on the grounds" at even the poorest churches often featured a variety of vegetables, meats, cakes, and pies. One woman interviewed in the 1930s spoke of organizing fish fries and oyster suppers to raise

---

64. Egerton, *Southern Food*, 112.

65. Avirett, *The Old Plantation*, 12.

66. Forest McDonald and Grady McWhiney, "The South from Self-Sufficiency to Peonage: An Interpretation," *American Historical Review* 85 (December 1980), 1111–1118; Taylor, *Eating, Drinking, and Visiting in the South*, 139–144; Egerton, *Southern Food*, 26. The sweet potato was a portable luncheon food; for example, Mr. Willie Dunn, of Warsaw, North Carolina, said he often took a sweet potato to school (in the 1930s) for his lunch and put it in the coals of the stove that heated the schoolhouse to cook. Conversation with Willie Dunn, summer, 1985.

67. "Farming is Hard Work," unpublished interview by Debbie Heath Best, 1980.

money for her church and charging a small sum for each plate.[68] Poverty and good food were not mutually exclusive.

As one would expect, the small farmers and the small but growing middle class of town folk ate better than the poor sharecroppers and millhands. Their cuisine closely resembled the cuisine of their counterparts before the war, but it would be fair to say it was more varied. Many of the small farmers still grew and raised some, if not much, of what they ate; it was even common for city folk to have a garden, and to raise chickens and perhaps even a hog or two. But now, more and more people were canning vegetables and even meats, which provided them with a greater variety of foodstuffs year-round, and store-bought food was more readily available to supplement the diet.[69] Georgia-born President Jimmy Carter recalled that his farming family was largely self-sufficient. His father butchered his own hogs, and his specialty at hog killing time was souse meat, a mixture of meats from various parts of the hog. Cured pork and chicken were common meat items in the Carter household with cornbread or grits accompanying most meals; collards were his family's favorite green. The family ate sweet potatoes, butter beans, okra, string beans, peas, and white potatoes, all grown on their farm. But the Carters also consumed store-bought "rice, cheese, peanut butter, macaroni, and canned goods."[70] By the turn of the twentieth century, most people, even the less affluent, had stoves, and the stove made frying and baking so much easier. Commercial baking powder and baking soda and inexpensive flour from the Midwest made biscuits more popular. With cheap flour and stoves, pies, cakes, cobblers and cookies were no longer such an expense or a chore. Eventually, of course, the icebox and later refrigeration would be introduced, permitting the more affluent to keep foods longer and expanding even further the regular availability of a variety of foods.[71] While wives and mothers did much of the cooking in these middle class and small farmer households, it was not unusual for white families of modest means to have black housekeepers who often cooked as well as cleaned; this was common as late as the 1960s and even later in some areas where the persistence of segregation shut blacks out of better paying employment.

The extravagant wealth of the antebellum big planters was replaced by the more straightened circumstances of many of the planters after the war. Affluent

68. Emma Sanders, "Singin' Praises Dat's My Life, Lawd," interview by Caldwell Sims, *American Life Histories: Manuscripts from the Federal Writers' Project, 1936–1938* (Washington: Library of Congress, Manuscript Division, 1998), http://memory.loc.gov/ammem/wpaintro/wpahome.html.

69. Egerton, *Southern Cooking*, 27–29; Taylor, *Eating, Drinking and Visiting in the South*, 108–109.

70. Jimmy Carter, *An Hour Before Daylight: Memories of a Rural Boyhood* (New York: Simon & Schuster, 2001), 33–34.

71. Egerton, *Southern Food*, 27–28.

folk often lived a life of genteel poverty, although the more successful planters, bankers, merchants, and millmen in the new upper class did quite well as we have seen. The cuisine of the upper class was now increasingly documented and influenced by a relative profusion of cookbooks that poured forth from publishers. The *Blue Grass Cook Book,* for example, featured recipes from socially prominent women in Kentucky and Virginia; the cookbook also celebrated the black cooks who did much of the actual cooking and featured pictures of a number of them. Some of the recipes in this cookbook such as saddle of mutton, truffle sauce and hollandaise sauce, and Charlotte Russe (a dessert) were quite sophisticated and reflected the cosmopolitan backgrounds of many of the women. Other recipes were more prosaic, such as the one featuring canned salmon, crackers, and butter. Many of the recipes are very familiar, at least to anyone familiar with contemporary Southern fare, such as the ones for chicken salad, fried green tomatoes, vegetables cooked with bacon, slaw, fruit salad, fried chicken, ham, sweet potato pie, and a variety of preserves.[72]

From kitchens high, middle, and low, and black and white, the "core" cuisine of the prewar period was elaborated upon, expanded, altered. While salt pork in some form continued to be central to the diet of both rich and poor, for the more affluent, it was one of many choices for meat. For them, ham became more of a Sunday dinner or an accompaniment to eggs and grits in the morning, at its best prepared with red-eye gravy. The icebox and later refrigeration and the growing availability of fresh meats and canned (and later frozen) vegetables in stores allowed fresh meat and a wide assortment of vegetables to become a regular part of every meal for comfortable and well-off families. Thanks to the stove, deep-fried foods—chicken, pork chops, seafood, okra, green tomatoes, squash—were probably served more often. (This is probably when Southern cooking got its ill-deserved reputation for frying everything.) As the twentieth century progressed, women, particularly middle class women, began getting recipes from magazines, and the casserole began appearing on dining tables across the region. Green bean casseroles made with canned fried onion rings and canned mushroom soup became a perennial favorite at covered dish suppers. Pecan pie and banana pudding made with store-bought vanilla wafers both emerged as dessert favorites, and a new drink—iced, sweetened tea—became, by the twentieth century, the beverage of choice for the noon and evening meal.[73] Pimento cheese, "Southern caviar" some wags have called it, became the luncheon and party food specialty in much of the South, and women jealously guarded their recipes. If the cookery of the upper class was showcased in cookbooks, middle class people and poor people had their own venues which offered them public opportunities to excel—church

72. Fox, *The Blue Grass Cook Book.*
73. Egerton, *Southern Cooking,* 205.

suppers, wakes, family reunions, Christmas, and other holidays. Here the standard fare, whether everyday cornbread, pecan pie, Brunswick stew, or chicken and dumplings (called chicken pastry some places), was cooked to perfection to show off. Women, rich and poor, white and black, took pride in a table set with a variety of cooked vegetables, meats, fresh sliced tomatoes, cucumbers, congealed salads, and baked goods.

The best of Southern cooking continued to be, for the most part, home cooking well into the twentieth century. This is not to say people didn't eat out; they did when they could, but the poverty and rural quality of the region simply would not support a wide variety of restaurants. Inexpensive "treat" food that people with little money could afford was served in country stores, groceries, and in gas stations (after the turn of the century). The treats are now the stuff of nostalgia—potted meat, Vienna (generally pronounced "vie-ee-na") sausage, sardines, hoop cheese and crackers, a "pack of Nabs" (Nabisco or other brands of peanut butter crackers), eggs preserved in vinegar, boiled peanuts in certain parts of the region (especially South Carolina and Georgia), Moon Pies, and, of course, that special invention of the South, the soft drink, virtually every variety of which originated in the region. In parts of Mississippi, the hot tamale, first introduced, we think, by Mexican laborers around the turn of the twentieth century, could be bought for a few cents at a store or from a vender.[74]

Restaurants, with few exceptions, were no-frills affairs serving inexpensive food and housed in simple structures ranging from meagerly appointed storefronts to cinderblock bunker-like structures. Restaurants often evolved out of a general store or grocery store when the proprietor became more ambitious and began serving sandwiches or hot dogs. Hot dog places still proliferate, and the specialty in much of the South is a hot dog served with chili and onions and topped by slaw, a standard that now is listed on the menus of some restaurants as the "Southern Dog." In Columbia, South Carolina, a number of cafes served the specialty of the town, the pimento cheese burger. This dish was a fried hamburger slathered with pimento cheese; the now defunct Dairy Bar was said to have invented this dish. The hamburger joints in most parts of the South— "Dairy Bar" seems to have been the name for many of them—served a somewhat more prosaic hamburger, often topped with chili and onions; with the explosion in automobile use after World War II, many of these establishments became drive-ins with Atlanta's still thriving Varsity probably the most famous in the region. Most sit-down restaurants typically prepared traditional Southern food served with no fuss—fried chicken, ham, pork chops, fried catfish,

---

74. John T. Edge, *Southern Belly: The Ultimate Food Lover's Companion to the South* (Athens, GA: Hill Street Press, 2000), 138–139.

and fried flounder, oysters, scallops, and shrimp where they were available. A meat and three vegetables became the standard for the noon meal, and the smell of cooked greens and fried meats infused the air of these establishments. Most provided, at best, inexpensive fuel for people of modest and not so modest means, but others excelled. Doe's Eat Place, in Greenville, Mississippi, for example, began life as a grocery operated by the Signa family. In the 1940s the family began selling takeout hot tamales and that trade evolved into an impromptu sit-down business in the Signa kitchen. The specialty of the house was steaks and still is, though the tamales are still served. The restaurant stayed in the old Signa home although a cinder block expansion added seating capacity.[75] The now defunct Lunch Box in Darlington, South Carolina, operated by the Edwards sisters and a staff of elderly black women in the kitchen, served perfectly cooked and seasoned vegetables, ham, chicken, and the best biscuits one could possibly find in a restaurant.

Then there were the barbecue restaurants which popped up all over the region during the course of the twentieth century, housed, generally, in small shed-type buildings or the ever popular cinder block bunker. Pork barbecue prevailed in most of the region, but beef brisket was popular in Texas. Barbecued pork was generally dressed with a sauce: a vinegar-based sauce in eastern North Carolina, and some version of a sweet tomato-based sauce elsewhere. Here and there in South Carolina, most famously at Maurice Bessinger's Piggy Park in Columbia, a mustard-based sauce was used to dress the pork barbecue. Barbecue was no longer cooked in pits but in stoves, the best of which are still wood-fired, but electric and gas cookers are gradually taking over. Certain "sides" typically accompanied pork barbecue with hush puppies (deep-fried cornbread), slaw, and French fries topping the list. Mobile home cookers designed to cook a whole pig that can be towed by a car are now quite common, and charcoal is typically the heat source, although some are propane fired. In eastern North Carolina, an event where a whole hog is cooked in one of these cookers is called a "pig pickin.'"

Memphis acquired a reputation as a sort of barbecue Mecca, serving excellent pork barbecue dressed with a tomato-based sauce. Today, many of the barbecue restaurants of Memphis are modern if tastelessly decorated facilities designed to feed large numbers of people, but some of the best barbecue still comes out of the old-style dump on the side of the road. Payne's, for example, is housed in a converted gas station. It serves a superb barbecue sandwich topped with slaw from a bare bones kitchen that features a wall-mounted grill, a preparation table, and a home-style four-burner stove and refrigerator. Memphis has also become famous for its ribs, and there is a friendly "war" between proponents of wet ribs dressed with a tomato-based sauce and propo-

---

75. *Ibid.*, 144–145.

Figure 7.1   Payne's Bar B Q

nents of a newer-style dry-rub rib introduced, most say, by Charlie Vergos at the Rendezvous restaurant.[76]

Here and there, more ambitious restaurants could be found in the South, but given the rural small town quality of much of the region and the small size of the middle and upper classes, these were few and far between with the single exception of New Orleans. Lusco's, in Greenwood, Mississippi, was one such place, and it is still in operation. The Lusco family began as grocers but branched out from their grocery business after attracting a clientele of cotton men to their backroom to sample Mrs. Lusco's cooking and Mr. Lusco's home-made wine (this was the Prohibition era). Their restaurant began serving steaks and broiled fish (pompano was their specialty), the fish dishes served with sauces inspired by Louisiana recipes. Lucso's was anything but upscale, but its food was well-prepared with quality ingredients, and its waiters—older black men—were exemplary. Its clientele was composed of the delta aristocracy who could come here and relax, eat, and drink, all in an intimate private environment, the privacy enhanced by curtained dining booths.[77] One would think Charleston, the closest rival to the New Orleans culinary tradition, would have fostered a fine dining restaurant tradition, but this was not the

76. Egerton, *Southern Food*, 166.
77. "Lusco's," Karen Pinkston, interviewed by Amy Evans, June 12, 19, 2003, Southern Foodways   Alliance,   http://www.southernfoodways.com/oral_history/delta/green wood/GW06_luscos.shtml (accessed 1/31/06); Edge, *Southern Belly*, 146–148.

case. As late as the 1970s, Charleston arguably supported only one notable restaurant (Perdita's), which was famous for its she crab soup, and another that had seen its better days (Henry's) but could still manage to serve a decent meal and sometimes an excellent meal such as the shad roe wrapped in bacon one of the authors ate there in the late 1970s.

New Orleans's unique restaurant tradition continued after the Civil War. Its most famous restaurant, Antoine's, was established by French immigrant Antoine Alciatore before the war; by the late 1800s the restaurant was thriving under the guidance of son Jules, the creator of Oysters Rockefeller. Antoine's, like Galatoire's and several other restaurants located in or near the French Quarter, specialized in Creole cuisine supplemented with a healthy infusion of classic French cuisine.[78] This cooking was inventive and complex—Oysters Rockefeller, for example, was oysters on the half shell topped with a pureed spinach and cheese mixture that was baked. A popular sauce used on seafood and cold meat appetizers was remoulade, a mixture of parsley, celery, onion, green onion, garlic, finely chopped and combined with seasonings, olive oil, vinegar or lemon juice, and Creole mustard (another specialty of the region). Trout amandine, shrimp Creole, and oysters brochette were three of many seafood specialties originating in New Orleans. The tradition was continually reinvigorated by new entrants, such as the Brennan family, who opened their eponymous restaurant in the late 1940s and began serving their version of Cre-

Figure 7.2   Brennan's

_____

78. Roy F. Guste, Jr., *Antoine's Restaurant Since 1840* Cookbook (New Orleans: Carbery-Guste, 1979), 6–12.

ole cuisine; in the early 1970s, for example, the restaurant served such dishes as redfish Jamie, (redfish topped with crabmeat in a red wine sauce), shrimp Creole (shrimp cooked with green peppers, onions, and tomatoes and served on rice), pompano papillote (fish baked in parchment paper), café brulot (a coffee and liquor drink prepared at the table), and its signature flaming dessert dish, bananas Foster. The family branched out and opened Commander's Palace and a number of other eateries in New Orleans and elsewhere.[79] Italian immigrants to New Orleans imparted their own take on the local cuisine; Mosca's, for example, established in the 1940s and located in a small, white clapboard structure on the side of the Highway 90 West across the river from New Orleans, began serving an oyster casserole that defies description, and Pascal Manale's introduced barbecued shrimp redolent with garlic and swimming in butter. An Italian grocery on Decatur Street, the Central Grocery, began selling a hefty, meat-stuffed sandwich called a muffuletta to workingmen shortly after the turn of the twentieth century. It is truly one of the great sandwiches, and the Central Grocery is still selling them, although it now has many competitors. Its version is described by restaurant critic Michael Stern as "A circular loaf of soft Italian bread … sliced horizontally and piled with salami, ham, and provolone, which are in turn topped with a wickedly spicy mélange of chopped green and black olives fragrant with anchovies and garlic."[80] Notable restaurants owned by African Americans (African Americans were behind the stove in most of the restaurants of New Orleans) offered their own take on local cuisine, leaning more in the direction of the "core cuisine," but with a Creole flair. Dooky Chase and Chez Helene were two of the best. Austin Leslie was the chef at Chez Helene before its lamented closing in the mid-1990s and was famous for his fried chicken served with a Creole twist: chopped garlic and parsley sprinkled on top.[81]

A tidal wave of change in eating and drinking habits swept the South beginning in the 1970s. Certainly one could see these changes much earlier in the larger metropolitan areas of the region, but by the 1970s and certainly the 1980s, they were evident even in the smallest crossroads town. The rising tide of prosperity sweeping the region, the growing throngs of immigrants coming to the South from elsewhere in the nation and the world, the rapid decline of

---

79. Hermann B. Deutsch, *Brennan's New Orleans Cookbook: With the Story of the Fabulous New Orleans Restaurant* (New Orleans: Robert L. Crager & Co., 1964), 3–40. One of the authors worked at Brennan's as a waiter in the early 1970s, and the menu items are based on his recollection.

80. Michael Stern, "Central Grocery-New Orleans, LA," 11/8/2000, Roadfood.Com, http://www.roadfood.com/ReviewsWriteup.aspx?ReviewID=122&RefID=122 (accessed 2/4/06).

81. "Great Chefs of New Orleans: Austin Leslie," 5 November 2005, NOLA Cuisine, http://www.nolacuisine.com/2005/11/05/great-chefs-of-new-orleans-austin-leslie/, (accessed 2/3/06).

the agrarian lifestyle and the rise of urban and suburban lifestyles, and the growing integration of the South into the life of the nation all affected in profound ways what people ate and how they prepared what they ate. The home cook in the South was using more and more of the processed foods available nationwide and cooking dishes like hamburgers and spaghetti that were common throughout the nation. Grocery stores in the region offered a wider variety of foods; a grocery store in Warsaw, North Carolina, that once (late 1970s) offered two kinds of cheese—cheddar and Velveeta—now offered dozens of cheeses; "exotic" meats like lamb were now available in such stores, and more and more "ethnic" foods and ingredients were available. The surging interest in fine dining that had swept the nation's middle class affected the South, too. More and more middle class women and men bought fancy cooking equipment, shopped at higher end food stores like Whole Food, and cooked dishes following recipes culled from *Gourmet* magazine or learned from the latest episode of "Emeril" on the Food Network. Fine wine, not to mention mixed drinks and malt beverages, became a more common feature of the home dining and entertaining experience.[82]

This is not to say Southern cooking has disappeared from the kitchens of the region; some natives, particularly older people, rural and small town folks, and the less affluent, are still cooking Southern style on a regular basis. Some older people cannot fathom why anyone would care to eat a slice of pizza or a taco. Groceries in small towns or on the poorer side of town still feature tubs of lard, fresh pig's feet, fatback, and stacks of glistening collards. Many, particularly in the middle class, continue to cook in the old way for ceremonial occasions (holidays or church suppers), but follow a more "mainstream" American diet for the typical meal. The traditional cuisine will undoubtedly persist, but, for more and more people, it will be an option rather than a mainstay. The decline of home cooking looms large as an important reason for the transformation of the Southern diet.

Southern people are now, like the rest of the nation, eating out more frequently whether at Burger King, the latest "in" table service chain restaurant, or the small Vietnamese restaurant in the strip mall that serves "a really good pho"; Southern young folks have developed the same addiction to "fast food" hamburgers, French fries, pizza, and tacos as their peers elsewhere. In most towns, McDonald's, Wendy's, Pizza Hut, and Taco Bell line the main thoroughfares and scattered amongst them are a variety of more upscale restaurants—many of them national chains—offering such fare as Mexican, Chinese, Italian, and the ever-popular steaks and ribs. The traditional Southern food served in the battered old restaurants has come to seem quaint, not to mention unhealthy, as fat and cholesterol became the new national obsessions. When people go out to

---

82. Taylor, *Eating, Drinking, and Visiting in the South*, 155.

dine at casual restaurants (like Applebee's) or fine dining establishments, they now expect beer, wine, and mixed drinks to be served, and brown bagging and the old restrictions on public drinking have largely disappeared.

Ironically, as the core cuisine of the South has been shouldered aside by a host of other choices, many of them heavily promoted by a steady stream of advertising, a renaissance in Southern cooking began to build steam. Beginning in the 1970s, a few lonely voices began to speak up for the food of the South, telling all who would listen that it wasn't just fried food. Edna Lewis was one of these voices; her cookbook, *The Taste of Country Cooking*, was published in 1976 and was an eloquent testimonial to the "core cuisine" of the South. Lewis was a powerful influence on a number of younger chefs and cooks in the region who were inspired by her dedication to fresh ingredients and traditional, often labor intensive, methods and recipes.[83] In retirement, she collaborated with Atlanta chef Scot Peacock on a new cookbook featuring a dazzling array of inventive new takes on Southern cooking.

By the 1980s, the lonely voices promoting Southern cuisine were lonely no longer. Regional cooking was now trendy, and Southern cuisine benefited. Books poured forth from the publishers, like John Egerton's *Southern Food*, celebrating the riches of the Southern cooking tradition, and popular television personalities emerged like Natalie Dupree and later Paula Deen, who promoted the South's cuisine. Justin Wilson, Paul Prudhomme (inventor of the blackened redfish) and later Emeril LaGasse focused new attention on the cooking of Louisiana and New Orleans with their cookbooks and television shows. The core cuisine of the South, once found primarily in home kitchens and in cinderblock roadside restaurants, now began to appear on the menus of upscale restaurants across the South. This development was more than just a few dishes showing up on a few menus; it was the result of a veritable movement of young Southern chefs and cooks who found their way home to Southern cooking after a detour into other kinds of cooking and began to treat the cuisine of the South with the same seriousness that they had treated the French or Italian or "New American" food that they had been cooking.

Bill Neal was perhaps the most important of this new breed of Southern chef. Neal began cooking while in graduate school in Chapel Hill, North Carolina, and found that he liked cooking better than the graduate work he was doing in English. He eventually opened La Residence (mid-1970s) in an old home in Fearrington, south of Chapel Hill. Neal's cooking was inspired by the cuisine of Provence, and he excelled at it. La Residence would prosper and

---

83. Edna Lewis, *The Taste of Country Cooking* (New York: Knopf, 2006); Gwendolyn Glenn, "Southern Secrets from Edna Lewis-Cuisine," *American Visions*, Feb.–March, 1997, http://www.findarticles.com/p/articles/mi_m1546/is_n1_v12/ai_19257630#continue (accessed 2/3/06).

eventually move to Chapel Hill. Neal was visited by *New York Times* food writer and Mississippi native Craig Claiborne in the early 1980s, and Neal began, at Claiborne's urging, to explore the cuisine of the South. He began to attract a band of like-minded people and in effect started a cooking movement which attempted to do for Southern cuisine what the chefs of France had done for the peasant fare in their country. Neal's signature dish was shrimp and grits, a dish based on the shrimp or fish accompanied by grits that coastal residents sometimes ate for breakfast. In Neal's hands, the grits were prepared more like the polenta of Italy and were full of cheese; the shrimp was redolent of garlic and herbs. A simple dish had become a rich, more complex dish. Neal opened Crook's Corner in a former barbecue joint in nearby Carrboro and began serving this new style Southern cuisine; his approach was driven by ingredients, the freshest and most authentic he could assemble. From Crook's kitchen came several other influential practitioners of this new style of cooking: John Currence, who opened City Grocery (a restaurant) in Oxford, Mississippi; Robert Stehling, who opened Hominy Grill in Charleston, and Bill Smith, who took over at Crook's after the untimely death of Bill Neal.[84] These chefs are part of an expanding list of innovative cooks across the region—people like Ben and Karen Barker (proprietors of the renowned Magnolia Grill in Durham and former chefs at La Residence), Frank Stitt, chef of Highlands Bar and Grill in Birmingham, Louis Osteen, longtime chef in coastal South Carolina, Raleigh's Ashley Christensen and a bevy of other Charleston chefs including Sean Brock and Donald Barickman—who are reinterpreting the "core" cuisine of the South by respecting its traditions (recipes, ingredients, cooking styles) but being open to its possibilities.[85] In the process, they have created a new Southern haute cuisine.

Pottery: From Kitchen Containers to Art

In an age before inexpensive mass-produced plastic, ceramic, tin, aluminum, and glass containers and kitchenware, pottery held the liquids, grains, beans, flour, cooked meals, and odds and ends of the South, just as it had done for millennia before in human societies across the globe. The pottery made in the colonial South came primarily from small producers located in Jamestown,

84. Moreton Neal, *Remembering Bill Neal: Favorite Recipes from a Life in Cooking* (Chapel Hill: University of North Carolina Press, 2004), xiv, 101–103. Neal's path breaking cookbook is *Bill Neal's Southern Cooking* (Chapel Hill: The University of North Carolina Press, 1985).

85. Ben and Karen Barker, *Not Afraid of Flavor: Recipes from Magnolia Grill* (Chapel Hill: The University of North Carolina Press, 2000), ix–xiii, 1; John Edge, "Forward," in Neal, *Remembering Bill Neal*, ix–xiii.

Virginia, Charleston, South Carolina, and later in North Carolina. Most of the early potters were immigrants from England and Germany. These early potters produced earthenware, a pottery that was fired at relatively low temperatures in a kiln and was either unglazed or glazed with a lead solution. Unglazed pottery was porous and could be used as flowerpots or baking dishware; glazed pottery was waterproof and could be used to hold liquids and nearly anything that needed to be kept dry. The Moravians who settled around Salem (present-day Winston-Salem, North Carolina) excelled at producing earthenware pottery that they often decorated with a variety of designs. Earthenware had its limitations; it was fragile and the lead in glazed pottery posed a health risk. By the early decades of the 1800s, most potters had switched to stoneware, although many continued to produce some earthenware for stewpots, candle holders, and flowerpots.[86]

Stoneware was a form of pottery much superior to earthenware; it was made from a higher grade of clay and was fired at a much higher temperature which made it very sturdy—hence its name. Most potters in the South used the groundhog kiln, so called because it was typically built into the side of a hill or under a mound of dirt—to fire their pots. Potters typically dug and processed their own clay, and typically threw their pots standing up at a potter's wheel powered by the potter's foot "pushing a treadle bar out and back into rotary motion."[87] Stoneware would be produced in a variety of locations in the South; one of the earliest stoneware producers in North Carolina, for example, was located in Fayetteville, in the coastal plain. Most of the potters producing stoneware in the early 1800s were located in the piedmont region of North and South Carolina where the yellow clay soil made the ideal raw material for the potter, and a number of potteries producing earthenware had been established in the previous century. There were three areas in the two states that were especially rich with potters: the Edgefield district in South Carolina, the Catawba Valley in western North Carolina, and the area in Moore and Randolph counties in North Carolina that today is known as Seagrove. As migrants became pouring into the Deep South, potters set up shop there, too, and potters would be found as far west as Texas.[88]

Pots until the twentieth century were made for use, not for decoration, and they were produced in volume. Churns, pitchers, and crocks were made by the hundreds by an individual potter and sold for relatively small sums of money. They had to be inexpensive because potters were competing not just with each

---

86. Nancy Sweezy, *Raised in Clay: The Southern Pottery Tradition* (Chapel Hill: The University of North Carolina Press, 1994), 19–22; Charles G. Zug, III, *Turners and Burners: The Folk Potters of North Carolina* (Chapel Hill: University of North Carolina, 1986), 4–5, 23–25.

87. Sweezy, *Raised in Clay*, 34–66. Quote, p. 48.

88. *Ibid.*, 21. Zug, *Turners and Burners*, 27.

other but also with the mass-produced dishware and pots that were being produced in England and the North. Increasing volumes of these goods were making their way to the coastal areas of the South and into the inland regions. Nonetheless, potters took pride in their work and did their best to make good pots with clean, flowing lines and few imperfections, and many worked decorations and conscious artistry into their creations when they could. There were two basic areas in which potters could exercise their creative bent: the form of the pot and the glaze. The form of the pot was influenced by a variety of factors, the most important of which was function: was this pot to be a butter churn or a water pitcher? Pots from a variety of places in the world bear some similar characteristics depending on what the item was intended to do.[89] Potters the world over typically "throw" their clay on a rotating wheel, and this process results in a product with certain characteristics—round surfaces rather than square, generally wider at the bottom where attached to the wheel and narrower at the top, and so forth. The skill at throwing a pot is where the artistry of the pot derives. The pots may be uniform and graceful when thrown by a skilled potter or unsymmetrical, lacking in uniformity, and awkward when thrown by a less skilled one. Tradition also plays a role; whether handles are typically attached to a particular kind of pot, the shape of the spout on a pitcher, the type of glaze all are often influenced by local or regional traditions. Finally the material itself can influence the form of the pot; for example, some clays are more elastic than others, and some clays have more "foreign" materials in them—like bits of quartz—that affect the final product. As contemporary potter Mark Hewitt notes, "One aspect that commands great pride among North Carolina potters is the lightness and balance of the pots they make. This is a function of the excellent making skills fostered here, as well as the plasticity of the local clays."[90] The pot pictured in Figure 7.5 was produced in the Jugtown (NC) pottery in 1988 by Pam Cole and is a good example of a traditional form skillfully executed.

The first glaze employed by Southern potters making stoneware was the salt glaze. Salt was poured in the top of a kiln heated to a high temperature; the salt vaporized and the sodium in the salt bonded with the silica in the clay to form a "sodium silicate glaze in tiny, clear droplets."[91] The pot's color would depend on the amount of iron in the clay, with colors ranging from brown, to gray, to off white (see Fig. 7.3 for examples). Salt-glazed pottery would be produced throughout the region, but the Seagrove area would be noted for its dedication to the salt-glaze technique. Two families—the Cravens and the Coles—an-

---

89. See the comparisons of pottery from Europe, Asia and the South in Mark Hewitt and Nancy Sweezy, *The Potter's Eye: Art and Tradition in North Carolina Pottery* (Chapel Hill: University of North Carolina Press, 2005).

90. *Ibid.*, 14.

91. Sweezy, *Raised in Clay*, 53.

Figure 7.3   Salt-Glazed Pottery
(Pottery from the Tom Hendrickson Collection)

chored a community of potters that have produced pottery from the mid-1700s to the present.[92]

Alkaline glaze was first introduced in Edgefield, South Carolina, in the second decade of the nineteenth century. It spread to western North Carolina (Catawba Valley) and south and as far west as Texas.[93] Dr. Abner Landrum, an Edgefield physician and businessman, was probably the person responsible for introducing the glaze, which was based on Chinese techniques described in the writings of a French missionary in China.[94] The early glazes "were made of ash, clay and sand" ground to a fine mixture. Later potters often added glass, feldspar, and other substances to this mixture. Some potters put large pieces of glass on the handles or mouths of the pots which produced a run of liquid glass down the sides of pots.[95] Alkaline pots are characterized by glossy finishes and typically exhibit streaking. An example of an alkaline glazed pot by the famous slave potter Dave Drake, (of Edgefield County) is in Fig. 7.4. Drake often inscribed poems on his jars as an additional decoration.[96] By the end of the nineteenth century, new glazes had been introduced: most notably clay slip

---

92. *Ibid.*, 52; Zug, *Turners and Burners*, 39–42.
93. Sweezy, *Raised in Clay*, 54.
94. Hewitt and Sweezy, *The Potter's Eye*, 107.
95. Sweezy, *Raised in Clay*, 54–55; quote p. 54.
96. Hewitt and Sweezy, *The Potter's Eye*, 123–127.

glaze, which was made from a highly refined clay, Bristol glaze, which produced vibrant colors, and a variety of materials used in the traditional alkaline glaze. A wide range of commercial oxides were developed by the early 1900s that allowed the potter to produce glazes in virtually any color imaginable.[97]

By the early decades of the twentieth century, mass-produced kitchenware churned out by factories and the slow but inexorable decline of the agrarian South pushed more and more potters out of business. But a surprising number of traditional potters continued to produce the butter churns and pitchers and plates that they always had well into the twentieth century. Jugs for the illegal moonshine business kept some going during prohibition. Others tried to keep up with the times and produce decorative utilitarian items that might allow them stay in business, with earthenware pots for garden and patio leading the way.[98]

The Arts and Crafts movement of the 1920s, a movement that celebrated the so-called folk crafts and hoped to preserve them, focused attention on declining crafts like pottery.[99] In North Carolina, husband and wife Jacques and Juliana Busbee became interested in saving the pottery tradition in Seagrove.

Figure 7.4   Pot by Dave Drake
(Pottery from the Tom Hendrickson Collection)

---

97. Zug, *Turners and Burners*, 393.
98. Sweezy, *Raised in Clay*, 27–28.
99. Hewitt and Sweezy, *The Potter's Eye*, 165.

The Busbees were well-traveled cosmopolitan artists who lived in Raleigh, North Carolina; they visited Seagrove in 1915, surveyed the scene, and began buying the "orange earthenware pottery" that potters had begun making when stoneware sales declined. They sold the pottery in a tearoom in Greenwich Village in New York that Juliana Busbee opened, but they had a broader goal than that. Contemporary potter Ben Owen III has noted that the Busbees "could see that change was necessary if the heritage was to have any future" and they recruited a young potter (Mr. Owen's grandfather, also named Ben) to go to New York with Mr. Busbee on a tour of pottery exhibits in the city's museums. Busbee had in mind a melding of traditional styles and new styles, and this became a hallmark of the Jugtown Pottery he established with Ben Owen at the potter's wheel.[100] Other potters also began to move in the direction of making more decorative pots. Burlon Craig, of the Catawba Valley, continued to make storage jars and churns well into the 1970s, but also began making specialty items such as the face mugs and pots for which he is famous. Georgia's Edwin Meaders made his pottery when he could; in the late 1970s he began to produce pottery on a regular basis thanks to the popularity of the roosters and grape-decorated pitchers he began to make.[101]

Vernon Owens now owns and operates the Jugtown pottery and has been joined at the wheel by his wife, Pam. Pam Owens, New Hampshire born and trained at the High Mowing Pottery School in that state, came to Jugtown to apprentice and stayed when she married Vernon. She says of the influences on her work, "All the stages of Jugtown's evolution influence me today." As she furthers notes "So basically, we're continuing the Jugtown tradition, but we add a few things now and then to follow our own ideas and keep our customers interested."[102] Part of what that entails today is the mastery and application of "a very complex variety of clays, glazes, and kilns that requires careful tracking."[103] Ben Owen III operates his own pottery in the Seagrove area. He is a product of a university ceramics program, has studied pottery making in Japan, and is committed "to make the best we can as carefully as we can."[104] Some potters still turn out fairly sizable quantities of pots, especially mugs and plates, but even these potters are producing pottery that is first and foremost pleasing to the eye.

The Southern folk tradition now is being carried forward by professionally trained potters like Pam Owens and Ben Owen III. They learn from and respect the local traditions, but they range far and wide to study new techniques and other traditions. The best potters today have mastered techniques and

---

100. *Ibid.*, 210.
101. Sweezy, *Raised in Clay*, 89; 103–105.
102. Hewitt and Sweezy, *The Potter's Eye*, 224.
103. *Ibid.*, 224–225.
104. *Ibid.*, 210.

processes that the older potters simply did not have the time for, and their work is featured in art galleries and museums.

Figure 7.5   Pot by Pam Owens

Architecture

What defines Southern architecture is not so much its uniqueness—even the white pillared archetypal Southern plantation mansion may be found in the Northeast—but the prevalence of certain styles, details and building materials, and the locus, until relatively recently, of so much of the architecture in the countryside. Until well after the Civil War, the typical building in the South was a home constructed of wood and located in the country. Architecture, like pottery, was for most people in the South primarily a utilitarian matter. Most buildings were (and still are) constructed to provide shelter, to worship, or conduct business, and artistic concerns were secondary at best. Few of the buildings constructed in the South before the Civil War were designed by architects, and, more often than not, the builders were the people who would be using the building when it was finished. Given the limited resources and skills most builders had to work with, most buildings tended to follow simple designs with limited architectural ornamentation. Simplicity was also dictated by other concerns; people on the frontier needed shelter quickly, and even those in the more settled regions often saw little need to build elaborate and substantial structures given the tendency of so many to pick up and move when the soil was exhausted or opportunities further west beckoned. Cultural traditions that came with the settlers influenced how these simple structures would look: historian Grady McWhiney has argued that "Celts" (folks we call Scots-Irish) came here with a tradition of building simple, unadorned structures that some less charitable observers have labeled crude, and John Michael Vlach has maintained that the single story, one room wide shotgun house was a blending of several traditions that came to the South by way of Haiti with slave immigrants.[105] Evangelical religion would also exert an influence; it urged believers to be humble, so for dedicated evangelicals, homes and places of worship should reflect the modesty expected of the good Christian. Thus, the architecture tradition that was developed by the small farmers and other less affluent folk of the South was a simple, "pared down" style that at its best was characterized by strong, clean lines. This tradition is sometimes referred to as the vernacular architecture.

The other building tradition was developed by the elite of the South and is the one typically featured in books and lodged in the popular imagination. Think of Tara. For those with money and time, conscious artistry in the design and construction of a building, whether a home, a church, a government building, or a place of business, was important. This sort of architecture was strongly influenced by European designs, primarily, as one would expect, designs and trends from England. Before the Civil War, most of the relatively small number of architects responsible for designs used in the South were either British or Northern. Elite architectural styles would also exert an influence on vernacular architecture; small churches, for example, were built throughout the South in the Greek Revival style popular with the elite. Unique architecture subcultures developed in several seaport cities, most notably New Orleans, Savannah, and Charleston, in rural Louisiana where French influences were strong, and in parts of Texas where the Spanish and Mexican influence was prevalent.

The earliest buildings in the South were, of course, structures built by Native Americans. Their building styles had some influence on what English settlers built in the early years of settlement; for example, some of the crude huts the settlers constructed were covered in tree bark, a style they learned from the Native Americans, but many were thatched in a style common in England. When the early settlers set about building more permanent structures, they set timbers upright in holes and these "posts" were either faced with clapboards or caulked with mud and twigs; apparently most of the settlers found the timber-framed construction built on masonry foundations common in England too time-consuming. Later, the log cabin, developed by Swedish settlers in Delaware, would become the most common frontier structure. It could be put up more quickly than the wood frame house and was more durable than the post constructed homes of early Virginia, which tended to rot after a few years.

---

105. Grady McWhiney, *Cracker Culture: Celtic Ways in the Old South* (University, AL: University of Alabama Press, 1988), 236–237; John Michael Vlach, *The Afro-American Tradition in Decorative Arts* (Athens: Brown Thrasher Books, 1990), 125–128.

As settlements became better established, colonists began to build structures patterned after English dwellings with building frames consisting of heavy timbers held together by mortise and tenion joints held in place by pegs. Clapboards covered the frame and small windows flanked by shutters provided interior light. The typical house was two rooms with a loft for the children and was similar in design to small houses common in England. [106]

By the late 1600s, the elite of early Virginia were beginning to invest in more substantial homes, and brick, for those who could afford it, was the preferred building material. The most famous of the early brick dwellings is "Bacon's Castle" which was built in the mid-1660s by a man named Allen but given its current name when Nathaniel Bacon spent time there during the rebellion he led in the 1670s. The "castle" was actually no more than a large house, but it set the pace for subsequent homes for Virginia elite. It followed certain new architectural styles in England with large, impressive chimneys and doorways with pediments (a pediment is a triangular gable).[107] The model for Bacon's Castle was the English manor house of the English rural gentry; the planter elite of Virginia and elsewhere in the Chesapeake copied this model very closely. While building styles would eventually diverge from a slavish copying of British styles, the **idea** of the English manor house would always be the guiding influence for the homes of the planter elite throughout the antebellum South. This was a style that was very formal and cultivated; fences, lanes, gates, lines of trees, and gardens organized plantation space and framed the plantation house, which was situated amongst smaller outbuildings. The visitor often had to march up a long lane and through a gate or even several to reach the planter in his "castle," and the status of the visitor would determine what part of the manor was open to him. The whole effect was to establish the high status of the planter and put visitors, slaves, neighbors, and passersby in their "proper" places.[108]

With the rise of George I to the throne in the early 1700s, the so-called Georgian style swept England, and its influence showed up in construction of homes of the elite, churches and public buildings in the American South and in the other colonies. Sir Christopher Wrenn was one of the early leaders in the development of this new style, and the governor's mansion in Williamsburg and Westover, the home of William Byrd, were good examples of this style.[109]

---

106. Miles Lane, *Architecture of the Old South* (New York: Abbeville Press, 1993), 11–14, 76–81.

107. *Ibid.*, 15–17.

108. John Michael Vlach, *Back of the Big House: The Architecture of Plantation Slavery* (Chapel Hill: University of North Carolina press, 1993), 3–6; Rhys Isaac, *The Transformation of Virginia, 1740–1790* (Chapel Hill, NC: The University of North Carolina Press, 1982), 34–42.

109. Leland M. Roth, *American Architecture: A History* (Boulder, Colorado: Westview Press, 2001), 69–75.

Figure 7.6   Drayton Hall

Georgian style buildings featured large paned windows, flanking halls and low hipped roofs.[110] The style could be scaled back and worked quite well for more modest frame or brick dwellings. By the mid decades of the 1700s, the Georgian style would be influenced by the ideas of an Italian architect of the late 1500s named Andrea Palladio who had himself patterned his designs after "ancient Roman temples." Palladio's writings and drawings were published in England, and his work was promoted by a number of influential English architects, especially James Gibbs and Robert Morris. The architecture was designed to emphasize the size and weight of a building; pediments were larger and buildings featured more decorative detail. For example, Westover, the home of William Byrd II, featured an impressive entrance carved in England and based on a design influenced by the writings of Palladio. Drayton Hall is considered the earliest example of what has been called the Palladian style of architecture in America. The home is situated on the Ashley River outside of Charleston and features porticos supported by columns and the central hall design favored in many Palladian-style homes.[111] Saint Michael's Anglican Church in Charleston is another good example of this style with an imposing steeple that rises 186 feet; it was built in the 1750s and was based on a design in James Gibb's *Book of Architecture*.[112]

---

110. *Ibid.*
111. *Ibid.*, 70, 84, 88. Mills, *Architecture of the Old South*, 36–39.
112. Mills, *Architecture of the Old South,* 43.

The end of the American Revolution ushered in a new era of American architecture for the elite, but European influences, especially English influences, still predominated. This era was called the Federal Era and primarily influenced the architecture of coastal cities, and secondarily some of the homes of the elite that were built in the last years of the eighteenth century and the early decades of the nineteenth.[113] Homes built in this style still reflected the influences of Palladio; Palladium windows, for example, were quite popular. Federal style homes often featured balustrades along the roofline (they resemble railings), more elaborate dentil molding, more delicate columns, colorful paint schemes inside, and unusual room shapes like ovals or octagons.

Charleston was the most populous city of the South in the late 1700s and early 1800s, and a number of Georgian and Federal style homes were constructed in the city for merchants and for planters who moved to the city in the summer to escape the heat and mosquitoes of their plantations further inland. Many of these houses were constructed in a style unique to Charleston called the "single house." This was a two- or three-story house design that was one room wide and was situated sideways on a lot. It had long porches or piazzas shading each floor and faced a garden running the length of the lot, a style that is ideal for a hot climate.[114] It is possible that the concept of the piazza and even the front porch, neither of which were common features in English, Scots Irish, or early colonial architecture, was the result of the influence of West African building traditions brought by the slaves. As one historian has noted, "it is not unreasonable to suppose that millions of African slaves upon whom Europeans depended taught them more about tropical architecture than they cared to remember."[115] Porches, verandas, and piazzas became common features of the homes of the elite by the late 1700s and represented the major modification of English building styles.[116]

If there is one building style that is stuck in the public imagination as uniquely Southern, it is the Greek revival, a style that was in truth quite popular across America in the decades prior to the Civil War and was imported, once again, from England, although Thomas Jefferson designed several buildings in the 1700s that anticipated this style. At its simplest, this was a style that attempted to recreate the temple architecture of ancient Greece and featured columns and impressive pediments.[117] Homes, banks, churches, and government buildings were all constructed in this style, especially in newly settled

---

113. *Ibid.*, 97, 175.
114. *Ibid.*, 135–127, 144–145; Charles W. Moore, "Southerness in Architecture," *Architecture Week* (September 2004), http://www.architectureweek.com/2004/0901/culture_1-1.html (accessed 4 March 2006).
115. Vlach, *The Afro-American Tradition*, 136–138; quote p. 138.
116. *Ibid.*, 136–138.
117. Lane, *Architecture of the Old South*, 177–179.

Figure 7.7   Charleston single house

areas in Mississippi, Louisiana, and Alabama where large fortunes were made by cotton planters in the decades leading up to the Civil War. Oak Alley is one of the most famous examples of this style. It was constructed in the late 1830s in southern Louisiana. Its roof was supported by 28 Doric columns, and deep two-story porches protected the interior from the hot Louisiana sun. In the older settled regions, North Carolina for example, Greek revival was often grafted onto older styles. Somerset Place for example, was built by the Collins family in the 1830s near Lake Phelps and featured the expansive piazzas that now were popular in coastal areas with Greek revival columns supporting the piazzas.[118] Greek revival was especially popular for government buildings, and a number of court houses and state capitals were built in this style.

Vernacular architecture started with the log cabin, as we have seen. On the frontier, log buildings were common for homes, mercantile concerns, and even churches. Homes were often a single room (called a single pen) lighted by small windows with, perhaps, a sleeping loft. For families needing more room, sometimes a second "room" would be added on: if the room was added on next to the fireplace, the house was known as a saddlebag house; if the room was added on the wall opposite to the chimney and a second chimney constructed, the design was known as the double pen.[119] A variation of the double pen sepa-

118. Catherine W. Bishir, *North Carolina Architecture* (Chapel Hill: University of North Carolina press, 1990), 195, 203–204.

119. *Ibid.*, 142–145.

rated the two rooms (or pens) with an open covered walkway. The walkway was called a dogtrot, and this style of house was often known as a "dogtrot." The walkway provided ventilation during the hot months, and one group of contemporary researchers has found that the design was quite effective at providing a good flow of air through the structure.[120] Well into the twentieth century, farmers in many parts of the region continued to use barns made of logs or roughly hewn beams notched together and "chinked" with mud and later cement.

Once areas became more settled, more sophisticated dwellings and buildings were constructed. Wood frame construction was the most popular for homes and churches and followed certain traditional rules on the relative size of rooms, the placement of windows, and the decorations. It was common to raise the structure above the ground to keep out the wildlife, but this also improved ventilation during the hot summer months.[121] Frame houses would be built in the single pen, double pen, and saddlebag styles throughout the South. Two other designs that first appeared in Virginia became popular throughout the South. The "I" house featured two rooms on either side of a narrow entry

Figure 7.8   Oak Alley

120. Aaron Gentry and Sze Min Lam, "Dog Trot: A Vernacular Response," (Mississippi State University School of Architecture: nd), 1–2, http://arch.ced.berkeley.edu/vitalsigns/bld/Casestudies/dogtrot_high2.pdf .

121. Isaac, *The Transformation of Virginia*, 33; McWhiney, *Cracker Culture*, 236.

topped by two more rooms and flanked on either end by chimneys. The roof was steeply pitched, the house was clapboarded, and if the house was painted, it was generally white washed. White is still the most common color for this type of house. The other style was introduced in the Tidewater and was one room deep and two wide and featured a loft and a galley porch in the front and often the back. Portions of the porch were often enclosed and made into shed rooms.[122] The most common "upgrade" was the addition of a "dogtrot" out back connected to a detached kitchen; over time, dogtrots were often enclosed and made into wings extending from the rear of the houses, and one can still find houses all over the Southeast modified in this fashion. Another variation on the "I" house consisted of an added two rooms to each floor; the chimneys generally rose up through the interior of the house and exited through the roof. The dwellings were sometimes expanded further with an extension on the side or back and could end up being quite large. It was common to further customize "I" houses with a single or double porch supported by pillars and other architectural features such as Greek revival flourishes. The more successful farmers and the less affluent (or less ostentatious) planters often lived in modified "I" houses. Thomas Chaplin's house on Tombee plantation in South Carolina, for example, was a two-story clapboarded structure set on a one-story tabby (a form of concrete made of shells) foundation. It had porches serving each floor and a two-story wing jutted out the back, giving the structure a total of six rooms.[123]

Vernacular evangelical churches built in the late 1700s and 1800s were generally frame structures with rows of shuttered windows on each side. Some had steeples but many, if not most, did not. Some were built in the Greek revival style, such as the Baptist church constructed by Warrenton builder Jacob Holt in the 1850s in Wake Forest, North Carolina. Few had stained glass windows, and the interiors were typically of Spartan design as befitted the humble precepts of evangelical churches and the limited wealth of church members.

Louisiana, with its rich French and Spanish heritage, developed its own special architectural tradition. Plantation homes (and even more modest dwellings) were two-story dwellings with high hipped roofs; the main floor was on the second story and was surrounded by wide porches accessed from the interior by French doors.[124] In the major city of New Orleans, a dense concentration of townhouses and business buildings were built in a bend of the Mississippi in an area that came to be called the *Vieux Carre*, or old quarter (now more often called the French Quarter). These houses fronted the street and

---

122. Roth, *American Architecture*, 103–104.
123. *Historic Homes of the South* (New York: Simon and Schuster, 1984), 57.
124. Lane, *Architecture of the Old South*, 83.

Figure 7. 9   Double pen style house with an enclosed dogtrot addition

would be built in two-story and story-and-a-half versions; generally they had a courtyard in back and were often decorated with ironwork filigree. In both the countryside and the city, "American" styles would be introduced after 1800; Greek revival mansions like Oak Alley would be built, and in the city a whole district called the Garden District would be populated by "American" immigrants who built houses that ranged from Greek revival to Victorian styles constructed after the Civil War.[125]

By the mid-1800s the shotgun house was being built in New Orleans in growing numbers for the less affluent. The houses were typically one story and were one room wide and several rooms deep with one room leading into another. The gable end of the house faced the street, and the houses were arranged like row houses, but with spaces between each dwelling. The shotgun design came from Haiti where a basic Yoruban house plan from West Africa was modified with Caribbean Native American and French influences. This is a design that derived from a culture which stressed the communal over the individual and encouraged (or forced) socializing. "A shotgun house is a house without privacy," contemporary residents of these dwellings told one historian.[126] Of course, the single pen houses of early white settlers were also dwellings without privacy, but house designs for the small farmer and the

125. *Ibid.*, 201.
126. Vlach, *The Afro-American Tradition*, 122–129. Quote on p. 123.

**Figure 7.10   Baptist church designed by Jacob Holt
in Wake Forest, North Carolina**

planter would, by the 1800s, move toward providing more privacy for family members. The shotgun would ultimately spread from New Orleans to other cities and towns across the South, and would be common in the countryside, too. It could be quickly and cheaply built, which is a partial explanation of its popularity. While many were little more than crudely built shacks, the design features of a well-constructed shotgun can be quite impressive, and the various influences — Yoruban, French, and Caribbean — can result in a clean, balanced structure that has proven quite popular with restorationists today. Some, built in the Greek revival style, have the appearance of small, well-proportioned Greek temples, while Victorian era shotguns are decorated with the character-istic "gingerbread" detail that many people find appealing.

The pre-war building styles proved to be remarkably durable after the Civil War. The poverty of the South and the slow decline of agriculture created a sort of rural time capsule, and white clapboard churches, "I" houses, shotguns, and one-story houses with porches and dogtrots jutting out the back were common throughout most of the South as the primary types of rural dwellings well into the twentieth century and are still quite common, some still sur-rounded by the traditional swath of dirt yard rather than the more modern grass and shrub landscaping. The old vernacular styles continued to be built into the 1920s both in the countryside and in town. As one scholar noted of North Carolina, "A staunchly rectangular and symmetrical dwelling, one or two stories tall, with a porch and a rear ell or shed containing a kitchen, remained the classic choice."[127] In plantation districts, plantation houses were maintained or not depending on the fortunes of the owners, but the houses themselves or their ruins were a common sight. The upwardly mobile often communicated this fact when they built a Greek revival or Federal style house evocative of the prewar styles.

Figure 7.11   Victorian shotguns, New Orleans

127. Bishir, *North Carolina Architecture*, 288.

Builders began turning to styles popular across the nation in a trend that would eventually spell the decline of the unique regional architecture of the South.[128] Victorian, four square, Queen Anne, bungalow, art deco, colonial revival (generally a mixture of Georgian, Federal, and Greek revival elements), ranch, transitional or contemporary, and mobile home are national design trends that swept the South at different times. Structures were built with mass-produced, standard materials which tended to eliminate some of the idiosyncratic features common in older buildings.[129] A Victorian house built in Charlotte looked just like one built in Pittsburgh. However, the mix of old and new styles of houses, commercial buildings, and churches in a particular town did establish a special identity for that town, and one can see the history of a town in the kinds of houses and buildings that predominate. Asheville, North Carolina, for example, experienced explosive growth in the early decades of the twentieth century; arts and crafts bungalows and art deco public buildings and homes—two popular styles at the time—were built in profusion during this period. The Great Depression killed the building boom and threw the city into an economic tailspin. The population and the local economy grew slowly for the next 40 years, thus preserving many of the bungalows and art deco structures and lending to the city a particular character like no other.[130]

The sort of dense housing common in bigger Northern cities like row houses and high rise apartment buildings were uncommon in the towns and small to middling cities of the South; single family dwellings and duplexes were the most common dwelling types and were often built in suburban developments away from the center of town where business and commerce were located.[131] In the late 1800s and early 1900s, streetcar lines provided transportation from suburban developments to shopping and jobs. Suburban development was not, of course, unique to the South; it was a national trend first for the more affluent and later for the working class and was actively promoted in the early decades of the twentieth century by the "City Beautiful" movement, which advocated landscaped, planned communities served by winding streets that isolated the residents from the hustle and bustle of the city.[132] That this movement would be popular in the South, given its rural tra-

---

128. *Ibid.*, 364; Kenneth T. Jackson, *Crabgrass Frontier: The Suburbanization of the United States* (New York: Oxford university Press, 1985), 240.

129. Bishir, *North Carolina Architecture 275*.

130. "Architecture in Asheville," National Register of Historic Places Travel Itinerary, National Parks Services, http://www.cr.nps.gov/nr/travel/asheville/architecutre.htm (accessed 6 March 2006).

131. David R. Goldfield, "North Carolina's Early Twentieth-Century Suburbs and the Urbanizing South," Catherine W. Bishir and Lawrence Earley, Eds., *Early Twentieth-Century Suburbs in North Carolina* (Raleigh: North Carolina Department of Cultural Resources, 1985), 10–13.

132. *Ibid.*

Figure 7.12   Art Deco city government building,
Asheville, North Carolina

ditions, is not surprising. Suburban developments were generally designed for people in a particular class and race and thus promoted segregation by class and race, which was another reason the "fit" with the South was a good one. Even today, developments cater to people in particular income ranges with the most exclusive (read expensive) keeping out the casual sightseer with guarded gates. The design firm headed by Frederick Law Olmsted (yes, the same Olmsted we've encountered before in this text) promoted the suburban concept and designed upscale developments. His firm designed Druid Hills in Atlanta, one of the more exclusive neighborhoods in the city.[133]

The dramatic transformation of the Southern economy after World War II resulted in the rapid growth of the cities and towns of the region, but a veritable explosion in the growth of suburban areas catering to a predominantly white middle class clientele. Automobile ownership and federal programs that subsidized mortgage loans and built highway systems linking suburbs to cities and towns facilitated this trend in the South and across the nation.[134] While it's often said that California is the national leader in the suburban/highway lifestyle, the South is not far behind. Atlanta, for example, is now a large metropolitan area, but its urban center is relatively small. What makes Atlanta big is the concentric rings of suburban development that surround it and render the urban center almost unnecessary except as a convenient location for corporate headquarters and sports arenas. Developments in the South's suburbs are, with few exceptions, filled with houses designed by national architectural firms that generally follow a particular theme, and the homes could just as well be in Detroit or Poughkeepsie as Suwanee (outside Atlanta) or Cary (outside Raleigh) and have virtually obliterated the last vestiges of the old architecture in many areas.

Air conditioning has also played a role in altering the architecture of the South by rendering porches, dogtrots, and open-aired foundations unnecessary. The mobile home industry's huge success in the region as home provider for the less affluent absolutely depended on this invention. While some have braved a non-air-conditioned mobile home out of economic necessity, few are hardy enough to tolerate the summer heat in what is essentially a metal box, or the noxious odors that are emitted when the plastic, plywood, glue, and synthetic fiber interiors of these boxes begin to cook at 100 plus degree temperatures. Thanks to air conditioning, mobile homes, single wide or the more ambitious double wide, can be found throughout the region. They are called mobile because they are built in factories complete with wheels so they can be towed to their eventual destinations. Many are sited on land bought by the homeowners, but, for financial reasons, many homeowners rent space in developments called parks which are anything but "park-like" because the struc-

---

133. *Ibid.*, 15.
134. Jackson, *Crabgrass Frontier*, 244–248; 265.

tures are often, like shotgun houses in towns, situated lengthwise on the lots with the gables facing the street and only a few feet separating each one. Towns and cities often have building codes that prohibit their erection on lots in town or segregate them to a few parks. Mobile homes are thus most common in the countryside, whether lined up and down rural roads or gathered in parks.

Air conditioning and modern building styles, whether the mobile home or the three bedroom colonial, seem to be driving Southerners indoors and away from the community oriented front porch life many Southerners once lived during the warmer months. The retreat of Southerners from porches and the outdoors was mitigated somewhat by the popularity of the wooden deck added to the rear of the house or mobile home, although, truth be told, these decks seem to be little used as people have retreated more and more to air-conditioned family rooms to watch their daily quotas of television or to "surf the Web," two inventions that seem to be the deadly enemies of the porch and neighborliness.

While the big story of architecture in the contemporary South is the suburban development and, secondarily, the mobile home, the corporations that were now dominating the economic life of the region would require special accommodations found in cities around the world—high rise buildings designed in the modern, international style. Atlanta, in particular, became famous for its glitzy skyscrapers. Interestingly, some of Atlanta's most noteworthy structures were designed by native son John Portman, who became famous for the dramatic hotels that he built all over the United States and the world. His first, completed in 1967, was the Atlanta Hyatt Regency, a 20-plus-story hotel with an immense atrium inside that extended to the top of the building. When the structure was first built and still a novelty, people gasped when they entered, the vista was so breathtaking. On top of the hotel was (and is) a rotating restaurant called the Polaris, made of blue Plexiglas and resembling a flying saucer perched on Portman's creation. Portman may have come from the South, but his primary influences are not native to the region: his designs are in the mainstream of modern international architecture, and he claims the great architect (and non-Southerner) Frank Lloyd Wright as his guiding light. Curiously, his hotels look inward, while Wright did his best to connect his designs to the landscape. Traditional Southern architecture, with its porches and piazzas, also connected with its surroundings, but then traditional Southern architecture was primarily agrarian, not urban.[135] In a sense, however, Portman's design reflects the traditional Southern suspicion of the urban; the Hyatt, futuristic urban architecture though it was widely perceived

---

135. Sandy McLendon, "the beginning of now: john portman's 1967 hyatt regency in atlanta," *jet set modern.com*, http://jetsetmodern.com/hyatt.htm (accessed 3/3/06); "Founder, John Portman," John Portman & Associates. Inc., http://portmanusa.com/ founder.html (Accessed 3/3/06).

to be in the late 1960s, is really, in concept, a suburban shopping mall turned on its end that offers the visitor a haven away from the city. A guest at the Hyatt Regency could literally spend all his time in the Hyatt and the other shopping and dining areas connected to the Hyatt by passageways without ever setting foot on the streets of Atlanta. When the guest does set forth outside the hotel, a common destination is the ever popular Buckhead, which is a suburban area outside of the city proper anchored by—what else?—a huge shopping mall.

Without a significant urban heritage or a regard for the urban, the South tends to have cities with small downtowns that are collections of high rise buildings set amongst parking decks, vacant lots, and older three and four story buildings housing restaurants catering to the lunch trade and marginal businesses. After 5:00, many downtowns are lonely places because so few people live there; home is in the suburbs. Typically, the neighborhoods surrounding Southern downtowns are predominantly poor and black. To be sure, none of this is unique to the South, but it does seem more pronounced in the South. Much time, energy, and money is expended by city promoters trying to come up with ways to get middle class people to live in the city, or at least come downtown and spend a few dollars. This effort has its share of detractors who call it "gentrification" and say it's just another effort to push the less affluent, particularly less affluent blacks, out of the way once again. Defenders respond, "Who benefits from urban decay, high crime, and a declining tax base?" and have supported mixed income development in which a percentage of new or refurbished housing is dedicated to the less affluent. Gentrification has probably impacted Atlanta more than most Southern cities in recent years with a modest influx of middle class people abandoning distant suburbs and hour- and two-hour commutes to relocate in Atlanta proper.[136] Rising gas prices and traffic congestion may do more than anything to establish a significant urban tradition in the region. But for the immediate future, the South will continue to grow more suburban and less agrarian.

Furniture

The story of furniture in the South is much the same story as pottery; the chairs, beds, tables, and cupboards people filled their homes with were primarily designed for utility. In the early decades of settlement, many people didn't really own much in the way of furniture and were described as "squatters or leaners" because to relax or eat, they squatted on the floor or leaned

---

136. Shaila Dewan, "Gentrification Changing Face of New Atlanta," *The New York Times*, 11 March 2006, http://www.nytimes.com/2006/03/11/national/11atlanta.html?th&emc=th (accessed 11 March 2006).

against boxes or chests.[137] Furniture was simply constructed, often of woods such as pine or poplar that were most readily available and easiest to work. Benches, simple tables, and chests for storing clothing were common pieces made early on. Furniture in the typical home of a small farmer on the eve of the Civil War actually would not have been much different than this early inventory supplemented by simple bedsteads strung with rope and supporting corn shuck stuffed mattresses, a cupboard or pie safe, and perhaps a store-bought rocking chair and mantle clock. Historian Grady McWhiney has argued the Scots-Irish and their descendants preferred simple furnishings just as they eschewed ornate homes.[138] Religious values and the fact that subsistence farmers didn't have much cash to spend on furniture also explain these preferences.

As the colonial settlements matured, the more affluent, whether planters, the more successful small farmers, or merchants, purchased fine furniture made by craftsmen in England. This furniture was generally made from fine woods like mahogany and walnut, had complex detailing, and had carefully and laboriously applied finishes that made them gleam. By the early 1700s, colonial craftsmen began making fine furniture. Four main centers of furniture making arose in the Southern colonies: the Chesapeake region, the Lowcountry around Charleston, the northeastern corner of North Carolina and southeastern Virginia, and the backcountry area in the Piedmont. Many of the early craftsmen were from England, Scotland and Ireland, and, early and later, English styles were the dominant influence on the colonial furniture industry.[139] These artisans would make a variety of pieces ranging from simple case furniture (boxes, chests, and cabinets) to more elaborate chairs, tables, and secretaries with carved ornamentation. Some would be made of woods commonly used in the furniture of the small farmers such as pine and poplar; others would be made of hard wood traditionally used for fine furniture, although less expensive soft woods were often used for the support structure.

The Chesapeake was the first area to support a significant fine furniture industry. By the early decades of the 1700s, the houses the elite constructed were larger, and their need for furniture correspondingly greater. English, Scot, and Irish cabinet makers who immigrated to the area began turning out furniture modeled closely on the furniture produced at home to satisfy this rising demand. The affluent continued to buy some of their furniture directly from England, reinforcing preferences for English-style furniture and encouraging colonial craftsmen to keep up with the latest styles in England. In the coastal

---

137. Isaac, *The Transformation of Virginia*, 73.

138. Grady McWhiney, *Cracker Culture*, 243–244.

139. Ronald Hurst, *Southern Furniture, 1680–1830: the Colonial Williamsburg Collection* (Williamsburg, Va.: Colonial Williamsburg Foundation in Association with Harry N. Abrams, 1997), 20.

area of South Carolina, the elite likewise shopped for furniture in England, and locally produced furniture that craftsmen began making there in the mid decades of the 1700s closely followed British design.[140] Norfolk, Virginia emerged as a cabinet-making center, and across the colonial line (the line William Byrd surveyed) a group of cabinet makers with shops in small trading centers on or near the Chowan River began making British style furniture characterized by simple lines and conservative ornamentation such as the "six boarded chests" that were butt joined and nailed together. Craftsman in one of these centers, Edenton, began making more sophisticated furniture in the mid-1700s, much of it made from mahogany. As the prosperity of this region increased, the demand for fine furniture increased, and a number of cabinet makers in the Roanoke River basin, most operating out of shops in the countryside, began turning out fine furniture.[141] A furniture maker known today only as W.H. produced a number of pieces such as the one in Figure 7.13. This piece is of walnut and featured one of W.H.'s trademarks—"a flowing if very stylized, pattern of vines and leafage carved in low relief...."[142]

Back country craftsman in the piedmont settlements of the colonial South were more isolated and more likely to fashion styles that varied from the latest English fashion, but even there, furniture exhibited design characteristics that showed that some craftsman were aware of furniture making trends in England and the coastal cities of the colonies.[143] In some areas of the backcountry, German influences on the furniture can be detected, which is not surprising given the significant German migration down the Great Wagon Road. In Augusta County, Virginia, the German craft tradition influenced the style of clocks made by James Huston, a Philadelphia silversmith and gunsmith who migrated to the area in the late 1750s.[144] In Salem, North Carolina, Moravian craftsmen built simple, utilitarian furniture decorated with wood inlays.

By the early decades of the 1800s, furniture making was becoming an industrial enterprise characterized by mass production techniques, and Northern manufacturers gradually pushed most of the Southern craftsmen out of business.[145] Here and there, a few craftsmen continued to produce furniture until the Civil War. In North Carolina, for example, the largest furniture producing shop in the state was run by craftsman Thomas Day, a free black. He catered to the

---

140. *Ibid.*, 18–20, 25.
141. John Bivens, Jr., *The Furniture of Coastal North Carolina, 1700–1820* (Winston-Salem, N.C.: Museum of Early Southern Decorative Arts, 1988), 108, 132, 140–141, 155, 226–227.
142. *Ibid.*, 293.
143. Hurst, *Southern Furniture, 1680–1830: the Colonial Williamsburg Collection*, 43–44.
144. *Ibid.*, 557.
145. *Ibid.*, 33; Bivens, *The Furniture of Coastal North Carolina*, 112, 230.

Figure 7.13   W.H. secretary (Tom Hendrickson Collection)

planter elite in the state, and his work was highly prized. After the Civil War, the furniture industry, like the textile industry, moved south and located in the Piedmont, especially the Piedmont of North Carolina. Most of the nation's furniture came from these factories until the 1990s when plants began shutting down one after another in the face of competition from overseas manufacturing facilities.[146]

Quilts

A quilt, at its simplest, is a blanket made of two pieces of fabric that are sewn together with some sort of material layered between them to make the quilt warmer. Normally, when people think of a quilt, they think of a blanket with a top made from tiny bits of discarded fabric pieced together in often intricate designs. These are called "pieced quilts." Another kind of quilt is one with in which fabric designs are sewn onto the top piece of quilt fabric. This is called an appliqué quilt. Quilt-making is a craft that was practiced in many parts of the country, typically among frugal rural people, although city and town folk have made quilts, too, and it originated in the British Isles and the European continent.[147] Like the other useful arts, quilts were made for practical purposes, but quilt makers worked in artistry when they could and to the best of their ability. It was and is a craft largely practiced by women and traditionally gave rural women an opportunity to get together and socialize at so-called quilting bees while still getting work done.

Pieced quilts were made all over the South by both blacks and whites. There were differences, however, between the styles of pieced quilts whites made and the style of quilts blacks made. White quilt makers tended to make designs characterized by a "tight and ordered symmetry."[148] The designs were uniform and often intricate; the pieces were often bright colors or pastels, and the colors were coordinated. The famous "double wedding ring" quilt would be an example of this intricate and precise ideal.[149] Black quilt makers often made a ver-

---

146. Robert Lacy, "Economic History: Washstands, Sideboards, and Parlor Suites," Federal Reserve Bank of Richmond, Spring 2005, http://www.richmondfed.org/publications/economic_research/region_focus/spring_2005/economic_history.cfm (accessed 13 March 2006); Robert Lacy, "Whither North Carolina Furniture Manufacturing"? Working paper, Federal Reserve Bank of Richmond, September 2004, http://www.richmondfed.org/publications/economic_research/working_papers/pdfs/wp04-7.pdf (accessed 13 March 2006).

147. Vlach, *The Afro-American Tradition*, 44.

148. *Ibid.*, 67.

149. Susan Roach, "Quilting, Anglo-American," in Charles Reagan Wilson and William Ferris, eds., *Encyclopedia of Southern Culture* (Chapel Hill: University of North Carolina Press, 1989), 518–519.

sion of a pieced quilt called a strip quilt. In this type of quilt, the pieces of fabric were sewn into strips, and then the strips were sewn onto the top piece of the quilt to make a design. African-American women constructed strip lengths that varied in widths, and the patterns and often colors were improvisational and random, like jazz music. White quilters made strip quilts, too; generally, however, they made strips of the same size and pieced them together in an "orderly manner." The classic "log cabin" quilt was made by both blacks and whites; white quilt makers started off with a basic grid pattern (like a checkerboard), while black quilt makers often started with a layout with the focal point of the quilt off center and the design spiraling out from that point. One scholar has traced the African-American style to the techniques employed in African "narrow strip weaving" in which improvisational variations were worked into the design by weavers working at their looms.[150]

There were also often noticeable differences between the appliqué quilts made by blacks and whites. Quilts made by whites were often characterized by a decorative pattern, such as the pattern in the quilt made by Virginian Pocahontas Gay which featured panels of dogs, horses, birds, and statesmen. Quilts made by blacks often told stories and in bold colors and styles that reflected, some scholars believe, the textile-making traditions of West Africa. Harriet Powers's Bible stories quilt, for example, is a narrative of Bible stories starting with Adam and Eve.[151]

Antique quilts are now highly prized and are displayed in museums. Harriet Powers's Bible stories quilt sold for five dollars at one point, but is now displayed in the Smithsonian.[152] Contemporary quilt makers now often make their quilts using sewing machines and use new fabric as well as old. Quilt making was once a folk craft taught by mothers and other female relatives to young women; now it's often learned in a classroom. Traditional patterns are popular, but new, innovative patterns have also appeared.

Basket Making

Today, in Charleston in the old market, along roads leading into the city, and in nearby Mt. Pleasant, African-American women sell sea grass baskets from small stands. These baskets are made from coiled sea grass (also called sweet grass) and palmetto, with pine needles woven in for decoration. The

---

150. Vlach, *The Afro-American Tradition*, 55–75.

151. *Ibid.*, 44–54; Robert Morton, *Southern Antiques and Folk Art* (Birmingham, AL: 1976) 168–169, 171; Maude S. Wahlman, "Quilting, Afro-American," in Wilson and Ferris, eds., *Encyclopedia of Southern Culture*, 517–518.

152. Morton, *Southern Antiques*, 168–169.

Figure 7.14   Charleston sea grass basket

techniques these women employ to make the baskets are centuries old, although today sea grass is hard to come by on the coast of South Carolina, thanks to development. The baskets today are, like the pottery turned out by contemporary craft potters, more art than functional storage items, and they are pleasing to look at and touch. There was a time when baskets were used to store and carry, and looks didn't much matter.

Basket making was common in Europe, West Africa, and among the Native American peoples. Whites in the South would made baskets, generally out of split oak, but the primary basket making tradition in the region was carried on by African-American women. It appears to have first started along the coastal areas and Sea Islands of South Carolina in the late 1600s or early 1700s, and eventually would be found throughout the South.[153] The basket-making tradition of coastal South Carolina was bound together with rice production. Slaves brought to South Carolina were often captured in rice growing areas of Africa, and they brought with them their knowledge of rice cultivation and processing; the baskets and other rice production implements the South Carolina slaves made and used had antecedents in Africa. Slave women wove wide shallow baskets which were used to "winnow the rice after it had been hulled."[154] Baskets with tall sides were used to carry a variety of agricultural products. Both types of baskets were typically made not from the more pliable sea grass, but from

---

153. Vlach, *The Afro-American Tradition*, 8, 16.
154. *Ibid.*, 8–9, quote, p. 8.

the more durable rush with strips of split oak or palmetto inserted to give the basket even more rigidity. Rush baskets, called "rusher" baskets on the South Carolina coast, are still made, although not as often as the sea grass baskets. Generally, the baskets were made without handles because women carried them on their heads; as this practice waned, handles were added, which in turn became an added decorative feature as the baskets became sought after for their beauty rather than their utility.[155]

The need for baskets for agricultural purposes declined as the twentieth century approached, but there still was a market for other kinds of baskets. Women and children had long woven "show" baskets out of the softer sweet grass, and these more refined baskets could be used as sewing baskets and the like. In the 1930s the tourist market for craft items began to take off, and women (it was always a female craft) began producing baskets primarily for the tourist trade. The kinds of baskets and the artfulness of the baskets increased.[156] Today, some women sign their baskets, as well they should.

Painting and Other Visual Arts

The earliest formal works of art to come from the South were the sketches and watercolors of John White, a member of Sir Walter Raleigh's expedition to the coast of North Carolina in the mid-1580s and later governor of the ill-fated lost colony at Roanoke. White drew pictures of the plants and animals of the New World and attempted to capture in his sketches the customs and lifestyles of the Native Americans he encountered. In an era before photography, painting would serve a documentary role as much if not more than a decorative role, and White's sketches gave folks back in England a glimpse of the New World. By the 1700s, a small number of practicing artists worked in the South painting primarily portraits which would be the predominant art form well into the 1800s. Most of the practicing artists of the South were itinerants, often from Europe or the North, who traveled around painting individual or family portraits. These painters also painted coats of arms and occasionally landscapes.[157] In a region with few cities or even towns, there simply wasn't the population to support many artists, and few museums existed in the region until well after the Civil War to display works of art. Most

---

155. *Ibid.*, 9, 13.
156. *Ibid.*, 13, 18–19.
157. Jessie Poesch, *The Art of the Old South: Painting, Sculpture, Architecture and the Products of Craftsmen, 1560–1860* (New York: Alfred A. Knopf, 1983), 28; Estill Curtis Pennington, *Look Away: Reality and Sentiment in Southern Art* (Spartanburg, SC: Saraland Press, 1989), 6.

people in the region did not have the money to commission or buy a painting, so the clientele then as now tended toward the more affluent, a small population to be sure. Most of the paintings and drawings would be displayed in homes, public buildings, and occasionally on the walls of businesses or fraternal organizations or clubs. If an artist did settle in a town, he often did not stay for long.

A small number of nature artists followed in John White's footsteps. Mark Catsby did some nature watercolors in the early 1700s, and John Abbott produced some beautiful watercolors of plants and animals he observed in Burke County, Georgia, where he lived most of his long life (he died in 1840 at the age of 89).[158] The most famous of these nature artists was John James Audubon. Audubon was born in Saint-Domingue (what is today Haiti) and raised in France; he immigrated to the United States as a young man. He engaged in a variety of occupations, but his obsession was to document with drawings and descriptions the birds of the North America. In 1820 he left a business in Kentucky, where he had lived for 11 years, and set out on a famous journey down the Mississippi to sketch the birds of the Deep South. Audubon's primary interest was scientific—he was attempting to document the range of bird species in the United States—but his work is magnificent nonetheless.[159]

The portrait painters of the region varied tremendously in training and skill, resulting in portraits ranging from the awkward and amateurish to the well-crafted. Most of the family or individual portraits they painted had a formal staged look to them, leading some to assume that itinerant painters traveled around with portraits completed except for the heads and faces, which they painted on site. This apparently was not true, but it is true that the painters followed conventions that customers expected, and their skill levels dictated how well these conventions were accomplished. Portraits were expected to convey seriousness and importance; those commissioning them were either well-established affluent folk or the upwardly mobile, and both groups wanted their portraits to convey the high position in society they occupied or aspired to occupy.[160] In the 1700s, a relatively small group of painters traveled around or briefly settled in a city or town and did portraits of the local notables. London born and trained John Wollaston, for example, lived briefly in Annapolis, Philadelphia, and Charleston where he painted the portraits of local notables in the mid-1700s.[161] By the 1800s there were as many as several hundred painters who worked in the South, but most were still traveling. One of the more famous, Thomas Sully, began his career in the Southern cities of

---

158. Estill Curtis Pennington, *Look Away*, 36–37.
159. *Ibid.*, 37–42; Poesch, *The Art of the Old South*, 165.
160. Pennington, *Look Away*, 74–76.
161. Poesch, *The Art of the Old South*, 78.

Charleston, Norfolk, and Richmond, but finally settled in Philadelphia, where demand for his work was greater.[162] Several of the best of the nineteenth century portrait painters were from Kentucky and painted notables in that state and in states to the south. Matthew H. Jouet was one of these Kentuckians; he painted a number of portraits and trained several other artists. His portrait of politician Henry Clay is one of his best and is quite skilled. William Edward West was another accomplished member of this group, and his portrait of Joseph Emory Davis is one of the better portraits done in the prewar era. In it, Davis is posed against a monochromatic background, his black coat in sharp contrast to his brilliantly white shirt. The portrait is spare but conveys a sense of seriousness, purpose, and refinement. West left the South in 1819 to study in Florence, Italy. He returned to the United States several decades later and painted several members of the Lee family, including Robert E. Lee. While painted portraits would never go out of style, photography's rise in the 1850s meant portraiture's decline.[163]

Portraits may have predominated in the pre-war era, but a variety of other kinds of paintings, watercolors, and engravings were done by a small number of artists, both residents and visitors to the region. This was a romantic, sentimental era, and the landscapes, rural scenes, and towns generally portrayed by these artists reflected an idealized vision of the South that suggested the same sense of an "ancient," changeless, natural society that has been discussed before. If there was a Southern style of painting, this was it because it would influence how many painters depicted scenes and people in the region well into the twentieth century. William Frye's "White Bluff," a painting of Demopolis, Alabama, circa 1855 depicts an idyllic river town situated at the top of a high bluff; a steamboat is moored below the bluff, and two men in the foreground are engaged in a leisurely conversation.[164] Thomas Addison Richards, a resident of Penfield, Georgia painted romantic landscapes of the rural South; his "Swamp Scene with Egret" is one of the best landscapes to come out of the period and portrays a mysterious, primeval swamp bathed in the warm shades of sunset; it actually anticipated a style of landscape painting that would emerge in the region after the war.[165] The only images that really suggested that another, more progressive, South even existed were some of the steamboat pictures, featured as lithographs in magazines especially, which showed the vessels in motion chugging down rivers or, if docked, swarming with people boarding or disembarking, loading or unloading bales of cotton, and congregated in groups on the wharf.[166]

---

162. *Ibid.*, 261.
163. Pennington, *Look Away*, 76–82.
164. *Ibid.*, 46.
165. *Ibid.*, 118–123; Poesch *The Art of the South*, 282–285.
166. Pennington, *Look Away*, 54; Poesch, *The Art of the South*, 284.

Depictions of slaves and the lives of slaves ranged from caricatures to rather straightforward documentary type work to a deeper exploration of the moral ambiguities of the institution. Two of the finest are by unknown artists. One, painted in the early 1800s, depicts a man playing the banjo; the other, a watercolor painted around 1800 and set, we think, in the South Carolina coastal rice country, depicts a group of slaves: one is playing a banjo-like instrument made from a gourd, two women are playing the shegureh (a rattle), or possibly dancing with scarves (there is disagreement among historians about this), and a man is dancing with a cane. Both paintings provide visual evidence of the persistence of elements of West African culture.[167] Painter Thomas Satterwhite Noble was a critic of slavery even though he would serve in the Confederate Army during the Civil War. His "The Price of Blood, A Planter Selling his Son," depicts an aged bearded planter seated at table selling the son he had fathered by his slave mistress to a slave trader while his son stands to the side. As one commentator has noted, the father does not show remorse on his face but rather defiance, as if to say, "It is my right to do this," while the son, rather than adopting the pose of a humbled slave, likewise has a defiant and disdainful look on his face. The painting is as much about the shared values of the father and son, despite the difference in their status, as it is about the horror of a man selling his own son.[168] John Antrobus's "The Plantation Burial," completed on the eve of the Civil War, is less clear in its symbolism but suggests Antrobus's mixed feelings about slavery. In the painting, a group of slaves is conducting a burial in the deep woods; the darkness and heaviness of the huge oaks gives the scene a particularly somber and oppressive feeling. A slave preacher is giving a sermon over the casket; in the left foreground, obscured by the shadows, is what appears to be a white overseer, while in the right background the tiny figures of the plantation master and mistress, barely discernible, are viewing the service from a distance.[169] At the least, the artist seems to be saying that in the presence of death, the position and power of whites no longer mattered.

After the war, two types of paintings predominated: romantic, impressionistic landscapes and sentimental odes to the "Lost Cause" of secession and the Confederacy. The most famous of the latter type is Everett B. D. Julio's "The Last Meeting of Lee and Jackson" which depicts the two Confederate generals on horseback discussing battle plans. While intended to touch the emotions, the painting is a good example of realism and is skillfully executed. This painting (and several engraved variations of it) was one of the most familiar images

---

167. Poesch, *The Art of the Old South*, 172–174; Joseph A. Opala, "Rice, Slavery, and the Sierra Leone-American Connection," Gilder Lehrman Center, http://www.yale.edu/glc/gullah/04.htm (accessed, 3/30/09).

168. Pennington, *Look Away*, 18–21.

169. Poesch, *The Art of the Old South*, 293–294; Pennington, *Look Away*, 87.

in the South for decades, at least among whites, and served as an important icon of the "Lost Cause." Less commonly known but still influential was William D. Washington's "The Burial of Lantane" which was actually completed during the war years. It depicts a group of white women and children and several slave men and women burying a Confederate war hero who had been brought to the women's plantation after a battle by the man's brother, also a soldier, who hoped to give him "proper burial." He returns to battle, and the women grieve for this stranger and perform the last rites. The picture is sentimental and celebrates the sacrifices of the Confederate soldier and the idea that duty and honor were the paramount virtues.[170]

Landscapes, not a major form before the Civil War, emerged after the war as a topic for many of a new breed of Southern painters. Artists painting scenes set in Louisiana and later Florida led the way. Some of these artists were natives of those states; others were not, but most shared certain similarities of technique. These painters were especially interested in exploring the effect of light on the subjects of their paintings (the style was called luminism), and in that sense they shared kinship with the more famous New York-based Hudson River school of painting. Like the pre-war artist Thomas Addison Richards, they depicted swamp, bayou, and river scenes filled with light and shadow, oaks dripping with Spanish moss, the scenes illuminated by misty sunrises and red sunsets. If people are depicted in these paintings, they are generally minor figures, perhaps rowing a small boat in the distance.[171] One of the most prolific and most talented of this group of painters was Joseph Meeker, who came south with the Union navy during the Civil War and painted Southern bayous and swamps after the war. George David Coulon lived and worked in New Orleans as both a painter and teacher and was one of group of painters that formed a small artist colony in the French Quarter of the city. Like Meeker, he painted bayous and swamp scenes; perhaps his best work is "Bayou Beauregard, St. Bernard Parish."[172] A similar collection of artists emerged later in Florida, drawn there in part by millionaire Henry Flagler's efforts to entice artists to settle in St. Augustine to provide some culture to the guests at his Florida resort hotels. Their subject was the tropical swamps and rivers of that state, and their work is even more exotic than the paintings of the Louisiana group. Martin Johnson Heade's "The Great Florida Sunset," finished in 1887, was huge and has an almost prehistoric air about it.[173] The best of these paintings are beautiful, and the technical skill exhibited is impressive. It's ironic that while the landscapes were technically quite innovative, they nonetheless reflected the old idea about a timeless, changeless South and have about them a

---

170. Pennington, *Look Away*, 58–63, 22, 24–25.
171. *Ibid.*, 114–116, 120–122.
172. *Ibid.*, 138–139.
173. *Ibid.*, 142–146.

melancholy, nostalgic air—and this at a time when much about the South was changing, however fitfully. Artists continued to paint landscapes and rural scenes in the early decades of the twentieth century. Charleston's Alice Ravenel Huger Smith, for example, painted swamp scenes, such as her "Early Spring," and nostalgic rural scenes of plantation life.[174] When artists like Smith painted city scenes, the paintings often had a dreamy, Old South look about them—again, the draw of the ancient, changeless South still beckoned.

With the huge explosion in the Southern middle class after World War II, the market for decorative art, the real deal rather than prints or posters, expanded astronomically, and professional artists likewise greatly increased in number. Many of the artists catering to this expanded market tended to go with tried and true themes and subject matter and steered clear of the innovative or experimental. Cities like New Orleans, Savannah, St. Petersburg, and Charleston had growing colonies of artists busily turning out quaint city scenes; beach towns became magnets for artists painting seascapes, beach cottages, and children playing on the beach, pastels being the favorite color scheme; and throughout the region, landscapes and rural scenes were big favorites among artists and their customers, with barns, especially tobacco barns, becoming one of the most painted objects. Technology had extended the reach of "real" art even to the less affluent, and airbrush artists, selling their wares at flea markets and the like, painted images of Elvis, Christ, and mothers holding children on various surfaces—black velvet, mirrors, wood planks and so forth. But the region also produced its share of so-called serious artists. These artists tend to fall into three categories: the regionalists, the modernists, and the vernacular artists.

Regionalists struggled to get beyond the nostalgic and romantic to some semblance of truth and would become prominent in the 1930s. They were part of a broader American trend of realism and had much in common with the urban artists of the Northern cities who painted gritty urban scenes (the so-called Ash Can School) in the early decades of the twentieth century and artists like Midwesterner Thomas Hart Benton who painted Depression era rural America. Christopher Clark was one regionalist; his "The Crap Shooters," completed in 1936, depicted five black men shooting craps on a loading dock. Marie Atkinson Hull's "Tenant Farmer" depicts a white tenant farmer seated at his kitchen table, the hardness of his life clearly displayed on his face. John McCrady settled in the French Quarter of New Orleans where he painted and ran an art school that trained a number of artists who emerged in the 1950s and 1960s. One of his more famous works, "The Parade," depicts a parade complete with a huge watermelon float moving slowly down a French Quarter street past a house, its side cut away so that the interior can be viewed; inside

---

174. J. Richard Gruber and David Houston, *The Art of the South, 1890–2003: The Ogden Museum of Southern Art* (London: Scala, 2004), 32.

the house, couples upstairs are dancing and downstairs an artist, McCrady himself, is painting. The scene is confused and lively, much like the vibrant New Orleans itself.[175]

Closely related to the concerns and painting styles of the regionalists are the narrative artists whose pictures tell a story, often in symbolic terms.[176] One of the best was Arkansas native Carrol Cloar, called by one writer "the greatest artist you've never heard of." Cloar painted nearly until his death in 1993 in a variety of styles; some of his paintings are reminiscent of the regionalists like John McCrady or Thomas Hart Benton; others seem more like French impressionist works, but nearly all are compelling and tell a story that the viewer must decipher. In one, a young black girl stands on a dirt road holding flowers while a young white boy in bib overalls picks flowers nearby. Up the road beyond the boy is a sharecropper shack with a black couple working outside, the wife bent over a big pot in the yard, doing her laundry. Cloar did a series of paintings of this girl, who apparently was based on a childhood friend of his. In another painting, a young girl in a bright yellow dress and yellow knee socks with a mischievous look on her face is posed in a graveyard; behind her are impressive statues, gray like ghosts, of men and women and even a man on horseback accompanied by several dogs, as if in a parade frozen in time. The scene is a depiction of an actual graveyard in Mayfield, Kentucky, constructed by a wealthy local eccentric by the name of Henry Wooldridge. The painting, like much of Cloar's work, is beautiful but unsettling because of the way he arranges images in unusual combinations.[177] Contemporary artist Douglas Bourgeois does the same thing with a painting of Elvis ("A New Place to Dwell"): the singer is kneeling holding a glowing guitar and is flanked on one side by his wife, posed in front of a thorn-covered marriage bed, and on the other by his mother, eying his wife suspiciously. Elvis has two choices: his mama or his wife, and we all know whom he will choose. Nostalgia over his lost childhood seemed to have driven Elvis: he moved his parents in with him at Graceland, and his wife began her time with him as a sort of unofficial adopted child, brought into his home when she was in her early teens. Elvis's nostalgia is emblematic of the white South's thirst for nostalgia; as art critic Estill Pennington has noted, "Longing for Elvis is the greatest proof that the central theme of Southern culture at this time is nostalgia."[178]

Some of the best narrative painting was done by Southern black artists, many of them living in the North. South Carolinian W. H. Johnson moved to

---

175. *Ibid.,* 39–48.
176. *Ibid.,* 59.
177. Donald Harrington, "The Witness of Hummingbirds," *The Oxford American 51* (Fall 2005), 70–83; Pennington, *Look Away,* 168–169; Bobbie Ann Mason, "An Ode to a Strange Procession," *The Oxford American 53* (Spring 2006), 40–42.
178. Pennington, *Look Away,* 179; quote p. 176.

New York in the 1920s where he was a participant in the Harlem Renaissance. He painted in the expressionist style but later turned to employing an almost abstract style characterized by bold colors and angular two-dimensional figures in his paintings of everyday life of African Americans. Some of his works, such as "Going to Church," focused on the South of his youth. Charles Alston, born in Charlotte, North Carolina, was also a part of the Harlem Renaissance of the 1920s. He painted and drew works in a variety of styles and was also a respected teacher (one of his discoveries was artist Jacob Lawrence). In the 1930s, he returned to the South and did a series of sketches for his "Family Series."[179] John Biggers was also born in North Carolina, but spent most of his professional life in Houston. He is famous for his murals in which he depicted ordinary African-American rural folk planting, harvesting and engaged in all the other "rituals" of rural life in the South. His aim was to portray "the beauty, dignity, and value of rural black men and women" going about their day-to-day lives. Biggers was also interested in recapturing the African roots of American blacks in his work and visited Africa for inspiration. His "Quilting Party," completed in the early 1980s, depicts women quilting and is an intricate pattern of stylized figures, fantastic shapes, symbols, and subtly blended colors.[180] Benny Andrews was born in rural Georgia in 1930 and moved to New York. Much of his work focused on his experiences in the South and ranged from the highly symbolic "Death of the Crow," which is a statement about the death of Jim Crow, to the more documentary "Revival Meeting" with its worshipers raising their hands in the air. Like an earlier Southern expatriate living in New York, William H. Johnson, Andrews's work combines elements of abstract art with the realistic tradition.[181]

One of the most ambitious works of narrative art was completed by Jacob Lawrence in the early 1940s. Lawrence was born in New Jersey and eventually ended up in Harlem; while not born or raised in the South, his parents were Southern born, and the experience of Southern black migrants to the North captured his imagination. In the early 1940s, he painted a series of paintings on panels entitled "The Migration of the Negro" (sometimes called the "Migration Series") which tells the story of the early phase of the great black migration to the North. The paintings, sixty in all, look at why the migrants left the South, the crucial train trip north, and what happened to them when they reached the North. They are realistic, often brutally so; the colors are bold, the shapes simple and geometric.[182] One panel, for example, features a man and a

---

179. Romare Beardon and Harry Henderson, *A History of African-American Artists from 1792 to the Present* (New York: Pantheon Books, 1993), 185–199, 260–264.
180. *Ibid.*, 430–435; quote, p. 431.
181. Gruber and Houston, *The Art of the South*, 58–59.
182. Beardon and Henderson, *A History of African-American Artists*, 293–303.

woman seated at a table, two bowls set before them. Their heads are bowed in resignation; they are poor and hungry. The room they are in is bare save for the table and a pot hanging on a peg; the blue of the man's shirt and the orange of the woman's housedress punctuate an otherwise bleak, drab scene. Lawrence's series is a masterpiece, its message of suffering and hope neither romanticized nor overdramatized.

Particularly after World War II, many Southern artists turned to styles reflecting national and international trends. Abstract Expressionism—so-called modern art—became the dominant force in the world of high art in the United States and a medium of expression for many Southern artists. Two of the leading lights of modern art—Jasper Johns and Robert Rauschenberg—were from the South. Johns attended college at the University of South Carolina, and in the late 1940s Rauschenberg briefly attended college at Black Mountain in North Carolina, a famous if short-lived experimental school. Art departments in the growing colleges and universities were training grounds for artists interested in creating the new modern art that had its sights firmly on national and international trends that seemed distant from the traditional concerns, topics, and styles of Southern art and Southern culture.[183]

Vernacular art is sometimes called outsider art, primitive art, or folk art, and what should be considered vernacular art is hotly debated in the art world. This is not surprising given the wide range of what now passes for mainstream art in contemporary American culture. At the least, vernacular art is created by people who are not schooled in art techniques or aware of art trends and who are often less affluent working people. Vernacular artists do their art with what's at hand: one artist painted with a mixture of mud and house paint; more than a few construct art objects out of junkyard items, and one even constructed a huge artwork out of tinfoil and items fished from trash cans. The art may be based on folk traditions and generally reflects the particular culture in which the artist is immersed. Black vernacular artists, for example, have drawn on traditions in the African-American community that may trace back to early West African practices. Some find the bold shapes in works of some vernacular black artists rooted in the appliqué art traditions of eighteenth century Dahomey in West Africa. But some of these artists may also draw on the contemporary interest among African Americans in things African, like kente fabrics.[184] Vernacular art is often highly personal, idiosyncratic, and sometimes represents one person's obsession. It often defies categorization.

---

183. Gruber and Houston, *The Art of the South*, 49.
184. Edmund B. Gaither, "Witnessing: Layered Meanings in Vernacular Art," in *Testimony: Vernacular Art of the African-American South* (New York: Harry N. Abrams, Inc., 2001), 73–74.

Religious topics figure prominently in many works of vernacular art. The tin foil covered sculpture mentioned earlier was constructed by South Carolina born James Hampton in a garage in Washington, D.C., and is perhaps the most famous example of vernacular art. The artist was a janitor but saw himself as a prophet—St. James—and believed his project, which he worked on in solitude for years, was his mission from God to "celebrate and forewarn of the Second Coming." It was entitled "The Throne of the Third Heaven of the Nations Millennium General Assembly" and was made by the artist out of cardboard, tin cans, discarded furniture and other items culled from trash cans, which were covered in tin foil. Bible quotes and cryptic notes were inscribed in various places.[185] Despite the common origins of the material from which Hampton's work was made, to view it in person is a moving experience. The Reverend John D. Ruth, a Pentecostal minister, constructed an elaborate "Bible Garden" on a twenty acre plot of land in Woodville, Georgia. The garden was "filled with statues and paintings" illustrating various stories and themes from the Bible. Ruth's garden was dismantled after he died in 1995.[186] W. C. Rice of Prattville, Alabama, specialized in crosses, some large, some small, which he displays on his property, in his home, and even nailed in trees.[187]

Vernacular artists have done works depicting everyday life, abstract paintings and sculpture, and works commenting on contemporary issues. Alabama artist Thornton Dial, Sr. has done paintings portraying President Bill Clinton and the plight of the homeless, and Georgian Leroy Almon has done a piece entitled "Assassinations" on the assassinations of Kennedy, Lincoln, King, and Malcolm X.[188] Some works of vernacular art are whimsical. North Carolinian Vollis Simpson has constructed windmills, some towering forty feet into the air, that are complex and brightly colored machines with turning wheels and moving figures. Ricky Pearce, a backhoe contractor in Henderson, North Carolina, constructed a huge concrete version of Marilyn Monroe's legs with a caption floating above the legs reading "reminiscing." It took him several years to construct and apparently, short of the high heeled shoes he constructed for his sculpture that wouldn't fit, is his only foray into art. Willie Tarver of Watley, Georgia, does sculptures made of cement and metal of a variety of humans and animals. The figures are brightly painted fantasies. Tarver noted to an interviewer, "I got into all this from messin' around with cement, trying to make

185. Jane Livingston and John Beardsley, *Black Folk Art in America, 1930–1980* (Jackson, MS: University of Mississippi, 1982), 93–94.

186. Karekin Goekjian and Robert Peacock, *Light of the Spirit: Portrait of Southern Outsider Artists* (Jackson, MS: University Press of Mississippi, 1998), 96–101, quote p. 98.

187. *Ibid.*, 84–87.

188. *Testimony: Vernacular Art of the African-American South*, 90, 94–95.

a gravestone for my brother years ago. Then I started making the work for my-self. I have always liked statues. I wanted to have a lot of statues around. Now my whole yard is full of statues."[189]

Figure 7.15   Ricky Pearce's Vision

189. Goekjian and Peacock, *Light of the Spirit*, 112–117; quote, p. 112.

Chapter 8

The Creative South: Words, Notes, Myths, and Icons

Introduction

Telling stories and singing songs are an intrinsic part of being human. The people of every culture do these things, some better than others. Some believe that social tension and crisis spawn creativity, and the South certainly has had its share of both, which may account for the excellence of its music and, at least in more recent times, the high caliber of its literature. Some stories become so well-known and important that they enter the realm of myth. These mythic stories, such as that classic American saga of the poor boy who makes good through hard work, help define a culture. Sometimes the images of people and places and even things come to serve as shorthand versions of stories and serve a similar function. We call these images icons, and they can be as

407

mundane as a plate of fried chicken and as controversial as the Confederate battle flag. The language people use to communicate also defines a culture, and is itself the result of an ongoing creative process. People are continuously creating new words, expressions, and pronunciations to suit their needs. Languages and those variations on major languages called dialects also serve as a form of self and group definition. Humorist Roy Wilder, Jr., has written a book on the Southern dialect entitled *You All Spoken Here* that illustrates in its title how the dialect reinforces the group identity of Southerners and distinguishes them from folks who don't say "you all."

Southern Dialect

For many folks, the Southern accent and to a lesser extent the Southern idiom (words and phrases unique to the region) often are the first things to comes to mind when they are asked, "What makes the South different?" Southern visitors or immigrants to the North or Midwest, especially those with "thick" accents, are frequently asked to "talk Southern" by inquisitive if rude locals. The tables are turned on Northern immigrants to the South whose inability to speak the dialect sometimes earns them the epithet "Yankee."

A dialect is generally an important characteristic of a subculture. It develops as a variation of a language when people in a group (usually living in a particular area or region) primarily interact with each other and, in copy-cat fashion, adopt the same speech patterns. Dialects develop when there is a degree of separation between a group and other people speaking the same language. Dialect, like language in general, is constantly changing; speech patterns evolve when group members leave the group and go elsewhere and then return bringing with them new speech patterns, and people from outside the group who enter the group's territory likewise bring new speech patterns. Too, people invent new words, expressions, and pronunciations without outside influences. A dialect serves as a sign of group membership and there can be an element of choice in the speaking of a dialect. The linguist Walt Wolfram has found, for example, that college educated men who left the Outer Banks (off the North Carolina coast) and then returned after many years often had the thickest Outer Banks "brogue." (The brogue's most famous pronunciation is "hoi toide" for the term "high tide.") These men were accentuating their brogue to show that they were truly Outer Bankers, not the off island residents they had temporarily been.[1]

The Southern dialect is actually comprised of many dialects, a not surprising fact given the size of the region. Many of these local and subregional di-

---

1. Walt Wolfram and Natalie Schilling-Estes, *Hoi Toide on the Outer Banks* (Chapel Hill:University of North Carolina Press, 1997), 128.

alects don't vary that much from each, but others, such as the dialect spoken in the Low Country of South Carolina and the almost Brooklyn, New York, style speech heard in parts of New Orleans, are worlds apart. Initially, of course, the earliest English-speaking settlers spoke the dialects of their homeplaces in England, Scotland, and Ireland, and other immigrants, most notably those from West Africa, spoke entirely different languages and generally learned English when they arrived. The English and Scots-Irish also predominated elsewhere in colonial America and so early on there were probably no notable differences between speech patterns in the North and the South. But by the 1800s, a distinct regional dialect had emerged in the South starting roughly at the Mason-Dixon line separating Maryland and Pennsylvania and extending west along the Ohio River and further westward as far as East Texas and parts of Oklahoma. Despite many local variations, the dialect spoken in much of this region had many common features and was the result of a relatively stable population: while the North got continuous infusions of new immigrants, the influx into the South largely stopped by the late 1700s. Further, this population was largely rural and much of it was relatively isolated from the rest of the nation. The result was the persistence of some "obsolete" British English and colonial English terms that disappeared elsewhere and the development of words and pronunciations unique to the region.[2]

One characteristic of this dialect in much of the South was the drawl which was (and is) a "lengthening and gliding of individual vowels."[3] The prominence of the drawl varied from the thick drawl heard in much of the Deep South to the virtually "drawlless" speech of Outer Bankers of North Carolina and much of the mountains. Another characteristic speech pattern common in much of the white South, especially in the Deep South, was the so-called "R-less" speech when R's in most words are not pronounced. (For example, Decatur would be pronounced "Decata.") One scholar believes this pattern was quite common in the Deep South by 1860 among middle and upper class whites, while whites in mountain areas tended to continue to pronounce their R's. He believes the "R-less" speech of the Deep South (it's common in eastern North Carolina and the Tidewater region, too) was the result of African influences because all of these areas had large slave populations. Today, "R-less" speech is disappearing among those born after World War II.[4]

Certain unique words, phrases, and expressions also define the Southern dialect; some are common throughout much of the region while others are com-

---

2. Craig M. Carver, *American Regional Dialects: A Word Geography* (Ann Arbor: University of Michigan Press, 1987), 94.
3. Crawford Feagin, "The African Contribution to Southern States English," Cynthia Bernstein, Thomas Nunnally and Robin Sabino, eds., *Language Variety in the South Revisited* (Tuscaloosa: University of Alabama, 1997), 130.
4. *Ibid.*, 124–130.

mon in particular areas. "Y'all" (for "you all") is nearly universal in the region while "might could" for might and "fixin' to" as in "I'm fixin' to go to the store" were also quite common.[5] In many parts of the South, the trunk of a car has been called the "boot" (also a British usage), the glove compartment the "pocket," children "young'uns," people often greeted one another with the word "hey" rather than "hello," and a person who drove a friend to the store might say "I carried him to the store." In recent decades some of these words and phrases are becoming less common; boot, for example, seems to be leaving the lexicon. The greater mobility and declining isolation of Southerners, the large immigration of outsiders into the South, and the role of the media in introducing the latest words and phrases from the national popular culture into the region all are having an effect on speech patterns. But, as one would expect, there are tremendous variations in how far this process has gone: suburban mall-dwelling middle class young people seem especially prone to speaking a version of "Californese," while young people in rural areas are more likely to speak like their elders.

African-American English is a version of Southern English that may have emerged as early as the 1700s. Slaves recently arrived from Africa were forced to learn English to communicate with slaveholders and with each other and probably first spoke a simplified version of English called Pidgin English. Over time, a more elaborate version of Standard English was developed by African Americans that continues to evolve. The origins of this dialect are the subject of a sometimes bitter debate among language scholars. While both sides of the debate acknowledge that African-American English is based on English, particularly its vocabulary, some scholars maintain that the unique pronunciations, words, and even grammar rules of this dialect derive from the dialects brought by the early English settlers, particularly the poorer sorts like the early indentured servants with whom the early slaves would have had significant contact. Others, however, argue that the language traditions brought by slaves from West Africa played a major role. West African languages don't use the "th" sound, for example, and African-American English typically drops the "th" sound. So "thin" is pronounced "tin," "South" is "Souf," and "them" is "dem." John and Russell Rickford argue that more likely both positions are right and that similar speech patterns from the British Isles and West Africa converged to make Black English. Interestingly, the Rickfords maintain that the Great Migration in the 1900s produced an even wider divergence between black and white speech patterns as greater numbers of blacks settled in largely segregated cities in the North and Midwest. The use of the verb "be," they believe, grew in

---

5. Cynthia Bernstein, "Grammatical Features of Southern Speech: *yall, might could, and fixin to*," Stephen J. Nagle and Sara L. Sanders, eds., *English in the Southern United States* (Cambridge: Cambridge University Press, 2003), 106–118.

the black community ("I be going to the store") while whites adapted new usages not commonly used by blacks.[6]

Southern Music

The Southern musical forms that evolved over the course of the eighteenth, nineteenth, and twentieth centuries had their roots in the cultures of the British Isles and West Africa. Other influences (German and French in particular) were significant but would pale in comparison to these two influences. Because of the role of race in Southern society, two streams of musical traditions would develop, one black and one white. However, while slavery and later segregation separated black from white, the very proximity of the races encouraged an intermingling of traditions and a borrowing back and forth. Both traditions would be profoundly affected and altered by the explosive growth of the commercial music industry after World War I, which would take them from relative obscurity and establish them as major forces in the popular musical culture of the nation and, ultimately, the world. Both traditions had a secular and sacred side. The white secular music would come to be called hillbilly music and later country or country western music; the black secular music would evolve into several distinct forms called ragtime, blues, jazz, rhythm and blues (or later, soul), and finally hip hop. The popular sacred music both produced was called gospel; the antecedent of black gospel was the spirituals of the slavery era. From a fusion of elements of gospel, blues, rhythm and blues, and country would come rock and roll, the giant of modern popular music in America and in much of the world.

Southern Music: The White Tradition

When immigrants from the British Isles arrived in the 1600s and 1700s, they brought with them ballads, instrumental pieces, a variety of dances and dance music, and musical instruments, the fiddle, especially. English, Irish, Welsh, and Scottish ballads told stories of lost loves, military victories, outlaw exploits, travels, good times, and bad times. These ballads became a true part of American "folk music"; the words and music were generally passed on aurally, and variations emerged as different musicians changed words, added a verse, or altered the tune to suit their tastes, and new ballads were written and passed along. In the more isolated areas of the country (the Appalachian

---

6. John Russell Rickford and Russell John Rickford, *Spoken Soul: The Story of Black English* (New York: Wiley, 2000), 145–158.

Mountains, for example), some of these ballads were still a part of the reper-toire of popular music into the early 1900s.[7] Two main forms of dance were brought by the settlers from the British Isles: jigs and country dancing. Jigs were characterized by "solo dance steps," with dancers performing intricate and often energetic steps to tunes also known as jigs.[8] Country dancing was a pop-ular fad in England in the mid-1600s among the upper and middle classes and was popularized by a book, *English Dancing Master*, that drew its inspiration from the dances of rural folk. The text had a number of examples of " 'long-ways' dances in which men and women face each other in two lines" and other dances where dancers formed squares and circles.[9] In France the longways dances were called "contredanses," and these French contredanses were, in the 1700s, exported back to England where they became quite popular. After the Revolution, contredanses were brought to America by French dance instruc-tors; one of the most popular was known as "Sir Roger de Coverley" which be-came the basis for the Virginia reel. The French dance teachers also brought quadrilles to America; quadrilles were often called cotillions in America and were "dances that involved four couples arranged in square formations." Even-tually these became known as square dances. Even today, many French terms are used for various steps in square dances such as promenade and sashay (from the French *chassez*).[10] The fiddle driven music that typically accompa-nied jigs, reels, and cotillions would eventually constitute the lively, high-en-ergy side of country music and served as a counterpoint to the often solemn, mournful ballad tradition.

The sacred music brought by the earliest colonists from the British Isles was Psalm-singing. This was true even in the less formal worship services of the Puritans in New England to the north. In the early and middle decades of the 1700s, a number of songwriters in England began writing a new style of hymn not tied to the Psalms, and these began gradually to replace or at least join the singing of Psalms in church services. Isaac Watt and later John and Charles Wesley were the most prominent of these song writers; perhaps the most fa-mous hymn to come out of this period was "Amazing Grace," which was writ-ten by John Newton, a former slave ship captain.[11] As we have seen, this was an era when religious reformers such as George Whitefield and the Wesleys were leading revivals and promoting a new kind of Christianity that emphasized the

---

7. Bill C. Malone, *Country Music USA: A Fifty Year History* (Austin, Texas: University of Texas Press, 1985), 1–4; Bill C. Malone, *Don't Get Above Your Raisin': Country Music and the South Working Class* (Urbana, Illinois: University of Illinois Press, 2002), vii–viii.

8. Bill C. Malone, *Don't Get Above Your Raisin'*, 154.

9. *Ibid.*, 151.

10. *Ibid.*, 151–152.

11. James R. Goff, Jr., *Close Harmony: A History of Southern Gospel* (Chapel Hill, N.C.: The University of North Carolina Press, 2002), 14–17.

heart as much as the head and the individual conversion experience. Many of the new hymns were clearly designed to touch the emotions and spark a change of heart or a renewal of faith in the listener. As evangelical Protestantism grew in the South after the Great Awakening, the new style of hymn became quite popular in the region, so much so that some of the hymns, "Amazing Grace" in particular, came to be seen by many Southerners and others as Southern hymns.

The British ballads, jigs, and hymns became the foundation for a new musical tradition that would evolve in the folk culture of the rural white South. This tradition would come out of the life experiences and musical tastes and creativity of the white small farmers who largely populated the South. In the decades after the Civil War, the growing population of mill workers, miners, truck drivers and other working people populating the small towns and small cities of the South would also make important contributions. The culture that gave birth to this musical tradition was relatively isolated and conservative in the truest sense of the term; while the rest of the nation urbanized and industrialized and experienced wave after wave of immigration that brought ethnic and religious diversity, industry came to the South much later and at a slower pace, cities later still, and ethnic and religious diversity only in recent years. Musical traditions discarded elsewhere or altered beyond recognition were not so rapidly replaced in the South.[12] But it would be wrong to assume that this music was an unchanging repetition of British originals; it actually was amazingly adaptive and continued to evolve, and this explains both its longevity and later commercial success.

A variety of influences affected the music. Medicine shows, circuses, and minstrel shows all brought outside musical performers to rural areas both before and after the Civil War. Minstrel shows, in particular, were very popular, and featured white professional performers (often from the North) in black face who parodied black life as they imagined it in jokes, songs, and skits. They played banjo and fiddle and some of their songs, such as "Yellow Rose of Texas," "Old Zip Coon," and "Old Dan Tucker," would become part of the folk repertoire of Southern fiddlers and banjo players. Fiddling contests were quite popular in the 1700s and 1800s and gave the fiddle player the opportunity to compare his style and repertoire of songs to those of other fiddlers and pick up new techniques or styles. Rural white Southerners did visit towns and cities, sometimes worked in cities, and traveled outside the region, providing them with other opportunities to hear different forms of music.[13] From black musicians, white musicians got the banjo (an instrument derived from a West African instrument), a fingerpicking style of guitar playing, and later musical

---

12. Malone, *Country Music, U.S.A.*, 1–4.
13. *Ibid.*, 6–9.

styles derived from ragtime, the blues, and jazz. The fiddle and banjo combination used by the minstrels may have been the inspiration for the collection of stringed instruments used by musicians who began playing what would come to be called "hillbilly" or later "country" music, with the guitar gradually joining the other two and eventually supplanting the banjo. Other instruments such as the autoharp, steel guitar, mandolin, and later the dobro were added to the repertoire of instruments played by country artists and would affect the sound of country music immeasurably. The steel guitar, for example, was brought to America by Hawaiian performers in the late 1800s; its "melodious, but crying sound" became an integral feature of many country songs.[14]

Evolving side by side with the popular music of the South was a new form of sacred music. The great revivals touched off by the Cane Ridge revival at the turn of the nineteenth century spurred the development of this new music; to make religious music as accessible as possible, especially to illiterate people, words of hymns were sometimes set to popular music, hymns were often "lined out" by a lead singer and then repeated by the audience, and extended chorus lines were added to hymns. These new songs began to appear in songbooks, and singing schools were started in rural areas throughout the South to promote better singing in church. A new form of musical notation called the "shape note" was taught in these schools; the shape note simplified the learning of musical notation by assigning a particular shape to each note on the scale that could be more easily recognized by the novice. New songbooks employing the shape note were published in the early and middle decades of the 1800s, such as William Walker's *Southern Harmony* and *The Sacred Harp*. With their simple but compelling lyrics and haunting melodies, many of the songs in these songbooks, such as "Wondrous Love," became immensely popular.[15]

What Wondrous Love Is This?

What wondrous love is this,
O my soul, O my soul!
What wondrous love is this, O my soul!
What wondrous love is this
that caused the Lord of bliss
To bear the dreadful curse
for my soul, for my soul,
To bear the dreadful curse for my soul.

When I was sinking down,
sinking down, sinking down,
When I was sinking down, sinking down,
When I was sinking down

---

14. *Ibid.*, 26–27; quote p. 26.
15. *Ibid.*, 11; Goff, *Close Harmony*, 21–24.

beneath God's righteous frown,
Christ laid aside His crown
for my soul, for my soul,
Christ laid aside His crown for my soul.

To God and to the Lamb,
I will sing, I will sing;
To God and to the Lamb I will sing.
To God and to the Lamb
Who is the great "I Am";
While millions join the theme, I will sing, I will sing;
While millions join the theme, I will sing.

And when from death I'm free,
I'll sing on, I'll sing on;
And when from death I'm free, I'll sing on.
And when from death I'm free,
I'll sing and joyful be,
And through eternity
I'll sing on, I'll sing on,
And through eternity I'll sing on.[16]

While singing schools and the shape note songs were not uncommon outside the South, they were heartily embraced in the rural South. A historian of the music argued that "aside from the Holy Bible, the book found oftenest in the homes of rural southern people is without doubt the big oblong volume of song called *The Sacred Harp*," and shape note singing, singing schools, and singing "conventions" could still be found in the rural South well into the twentieth century. [17] The hymns from this tradition together with the Watts and Wesley hymns still constitute an important part of the music many Southerners sing in church on a Sunday morning.

Another revival era produced yet another form of sacred music. In the late 1800s revivals swept the cities of the North and South; one of the more prominent evangelists of this movement, Dwight Lyman Moody, employed Pennsylvania songwriter Ira D. Sankey to produce a new kind of music for his revivals. These songs, called "gospel songs," became quite popular with other evangelists, and a number of songwriters, primarily based in the North, began churning them out. James Rowe penned such songs as "Love Lifted Me," while William Kirkpatrick had a knack for turning out children's songs such as "Jesus Loves Me, This I Know." The most famous gospel composer of this era was New York's Fanny Crosby who wrote over 6000 published songs including "Tell

---

16. William Walker, *The Southern Harmony and Musical Companion* (New York: Hastings House, 1835).
17. Goff, *Close Harmony*, 23.

Me the Story of Jesus," and "He Hideth My Soul." These songs borrowed tunes from popular music of the era, had simple lyrics, and had special appeal to conservative evangelical Christians who would constitute gospel's primary constituency thereafter.[18]

The shape note tradition would play an important role in shaping this new gospel music and establishing it as a Southern musical form. Tennessean James David Vaughan started a new shape note songbook publishing company at the turn of the twentieth century. To promote his publications, he sent out singing school teachers just as shape note songbook publishers had long done, but he came up with a new twist: he put together a touring male quartet to sing his company's songs and promote his songbooks. Thus was born the quartet tradition in the gospel world. Vaughan's quartet established the centrality of four-part male harmony in the new music and touched off a quartet craze. Rival publishers established professional quartets, and all employed professional songwriters to fill the songbooks they published with new material. Albert Edward Brumley was the most influential of the songwriters and wrote both gospel and country tunes in a career that stretched nearly fifty years. Perhaps his most famous gospel tune was "I'll Fly Away," which came out in 1932 and is still a favorite. Ironically, the popularity of the quartets and the songwriters who kept them supplied with new material would eventually supplant the shape note singing schools and conventions as participatory singing gave way to what was essentially professional entertainment provided by hundreds of minor league groups and a much smaller number of star groups like the Chuck Wagon Gang and later the Blackwoods, a group that was popular for decades and was a particular favorite of Elvis's.[19] The shape note would fade into obscurity.

The recording and radio industries were two crucial ingredients of the new entertainment industry that took off after World War I and were essential in both promoting and shaping country and gospel music. Radio first began recruiting country acts to perform in the early 1920s with Atlanta's WSB possibly the first to do so with a performance by Fiddlin' John Carson.[20] John David Vaughan established a station at roughly the same time in Tennessee to broadcast gospel music; he had also begun a small gospel record company.[21] The commercial record industry based in the North turned its attention to regional and ethnic music in the early 1920s when a downturn in the infant industry had cut into profits and sent talent scouts searching the nation high and low for saleable "product." In the South, they hit a gold mine and began recording black and white performers who sang both secular and sacred music. Ralph

---

18. *Ibid.*, 25–32.
19. *Ibid.*, 67–69, 74–76, 89–96, 129–130.
20. Malone, *Country Music, U.S.A.*, 32–34.
21. Goff, *Close Harmony*, 74–75.

Peer was one of these scouts; he had begun with Okeh record label and then switched to the RCA Victor label in the early 1920s. Peer had headed south looking for black performers and quite by chance uncovered Fiddlin' John Carson in 1923 in Atlanta, recorded him, and was amazed at the demand for a record he considered inferior ("pluperfect awful" he called it). It was Peer that may very well have invented the first name for this music when he listed it in a catalog as "hillbilly music," and this was what the music was called for the first few decades of its commercial life. Peer began looking for more Fiddlin' Johns and found Pop Stoneman. Stoneman proved to be a big success and would go on to a long career in country music both as a soloist and as part of a family group called the Stonemans. Peer's greatest success, however, came as result of a series of recording sessions he organized in Bristol, Tennessee, in 1926 that have since become known as the Bristol sessions.[22]

It was at Bristol that the country music industry was born. This was an industry that would thrive on stars, and at the Bristol sessions the first major stars of the business were discovered in Jimmie Rodgers and the Carter Family.[23] Their work would become an almost obligatory part of the repertoire of country performers for the next 80 years in an industry that always paid homage to tradition. While at least one member of the original Carter family singing group would perform into the 1970s, Jimmie Rodgers would die of tuberculosis only a few years after the Bristol sessions. Rodgers and the Carters established a sort of dichotomy in the nascent country tradition that reflected the dichotomy in Southern culture: Rodgers sang songs that often alluded to the rougher side of life, while the Carters were a respectable family whose songs often focused on home, kin, and religion.[24] Rodgers had left home at an early age to join a medicine show and never looked back. He was known as the "singing brakeman," an allusion to his years on the railroad both as an employee and as a hobo. He liked women, according to legend, lots of women, and drink. He was open to various influences including blues and jazz and recorded with black performers. He was famous for his yodel, and his big hit "T for Texas" was also called the "Blue Yodel."[25]

The Carters—A.P., his wife Sarah, and Maybelle, cousin to Sarah and wife of A.P.'s brother—were born and raised in the valleys around Clinch Mountain, Virginia. When they came to be recorded at Peer's makeshift studio in

22. Mark Zwonitzer with Charles Hirshberg, *Will You Miss Me When I'm Gone?: The Carter Family and Their Legacy in American Music* (New York: Simon & Schuster, 2002), 139–141; Malone, *Country Music, U.S.A.*, 81–95.

23. Zwonitzer with Hirshberg, *Will You Miss Me When I'm Gone?*, 142.

24. W. J. Cash, *The Mind of the South* (1941; New York: Vintage Books, 1969), 59–60; Malone, *Don't Get Above Your Raisin'*, 126–130.

25. Pete Daniel, *Standing at the Crossroads: Southern Life in the Twentieth Century* (New York: Hill and Wang, 1986), 100–103; Zwonitzer with Hirshberg, *Will You Miss Me When I'm Gone?*, 139–141; Malone, *Don't Get Above Your Raisin'*, 63, 126–129.

Bristol, they were dressed in their Sunday best—a blue suit for A.P., dresses and silk hose for the ladies. What they recorded was not part of the initial Victor release of the sessions in 1927, but several songs were on a later release, including "Wandering Boy" and "Single Girl, Married Girl." The Carters went to Camden, New Jersey, in the spring of 1928 and recorded 12 songs for Victor including one of the most memorable songs in country music, "Wildwood Flower." Their repertoire then and later consisted of old standards of the British/American ballad tradition, gospel songs, and new songs that often drew on their personal experiences and reflected their evolving musical interests and tastes. Theirs was a simple pared-down style with just guitar and autoharp as instrumentation; the ladies led and A.P.'s bass voice would "drift" in and out. The music they recorded then sounds to the modern ear rough and uncultivated, but it was a musical form in its infancy in a brand new industry. Peer, never one to overestimate the audience for this music, seemed oblivious to mistakes or songs that didn't really work. But listening to Maybelle Carter sing "Wildwood Flower" 45 years later on the Nitty Gritty Dirt Band's country retrospective album *Will the Circle Be Unbroken*, one understands the true potential of this music when performed by highly skilled musicians and a virtuoso with decades of experience. By the early 1930s, Maybelle Carter's guitar work "was the most widely imitated guitar style in music," and she constantly experimented with a variety of styles including "a sort of slide guitar favored by the black blues musicians."[26] Nor was that the only borrowing from other sources: A.P. scavenged far and wide for old songs of any sort that he could use, including songs produced by writers on New York's Tin Pan Alley. Black musician Lesley Riddle was his traveling companion on many of these jaunts and helped him gain entrée with local black performers who would play or sing him songs. Riddle later said some of his own songs ended up as Carter tunes.[27]

Radio stations that had a country format or featured country music shows began, in the 1920s, to proliferate in the South and even in such unlikely places as Chicago. For a time in the late 1930s, XERA broadcasting out of Lacuna, Mexico, was one of the most important country radio outlets. XERA had a signal so powerful it could be heard anywhere in North America; it was located in Mexico to avoid the restrictive broadcasting laws of the United States. The station was owned by Dr. John Romulus Brinkley, a quack doctor who operated a clinic in Del Rio, Texas, that specialized in a bizarre surgical "cure" for men's lack of sexual "pep." The good doctor used his station to promote his clinic and recruited hillbilly performers, most notably the Carter family, to appeal to his largely rural audience.[28] What became the most influential of the radio shows

---

26. Zwonitzer with Hirshberg, *Will You Miss Me When I'm Gone?*, 101–110, 183–184; quotes, pp. 109 and 110.
27. *Ibid.*, 127–132, 183–184.
28. *Ibid.*, 201–216.

was the show broadcast on Nashville's WSM that was originally called the WSM Barn Dance but eventually became known as the Grand Ole Opry. It started on the air in 1925 and, as its popularity surged, it moved to the Ryman auditorium in the early 1940s. Ryman had originally been built as a revival facility by Tom Ryman to honor the man who had converted him, revivalist Sam Jones. Not surprisingly, it was built like a church inside and had pews rather than seats which was a fitting "mother church" for a form of entertainment that liked to see itself primarily as family entertainment. It built up a stable of regular performers like Roy Acuff and Bill Monroe who were joined by a variety of visiting stars and up-and-coming performers. When Monroe joined the show in 1939, he promised to play country music "as she should be sung and played."[29] As Ryman and the Opry emerged as the mother church of country and began attracting flocks of performers to Nashville, Nashville itself emerged as the center of the country music industry with many of the record labels establishing studios in the city.

Motion pictures were another influence on the country music and were partly responsible for the marriage of western and country and the adoption of cowboy attire as the unofficial costume of country music. In the early decades of the twentieth century, the western fringes of the South produced a number of performers who sang straight ahead country music similar to that sung further east, but it also produced "cowboy" singers who sang tunes like "Home on the Range." Western music became part of the commercial music business that emerged in the 1920s, although, in truth, some of the "cowboy" tunes actually came from the music writers of New York's Tin Pan Alley. Jimmie Rodgers may have actually created the "singing cowboy" style after he moved to Texas near the end of his life, but Gene Autry was the man who took the style and rode it to stardom. Autry was a young performer whose early songs were mainstream hillbilly, but in 1934 he went to Hollywood and got a bit part in a cowboy movie which led to a role in a series and then starring roles in feature western films. Autry switched to cowboy music and became the standard bearer for the singing (and acting) cowboy thereafter. His singing style became smoother and the instrumentation for his songs became less "country." Autry's popularity and the immense popularity of cowboy movies into the 1960s, not to mention the appeal of cowboy costumes, helped cement the marriage of country and western music. Performers who had absolutely no connection to the West and sang straight-ahead country songs would dress in ten-gallon hats and flamboyant cowboy outfits with spangles. Some would even change their names; Arkansas native Rubye Blevins changed her name to Patsy Montana and achieved fame for her yodel.[30]

---

29. Malone, *Don't Get Above Your Raisin',* 77–78; quote on p. 82.
30. Malone, *Country Music, U.S.A.,* 141–145.

Honky tonk country music came out of the bars and beer joints that prolif-
erated in the oil boom towns of Texas following the repeal of prohibition in the
1930s. Old songs about mother and the old home place just didn't work in this
new environment; the music had to be louder, the beat stronger, the lyrics
racier. One of the early stars to emerge from the honky-tonk "school" was
Ernest Tubb. Tubb was born in Texas in 1914 and worshiped Jimmie Rodgers.
He performed in honky tonks and anywhere else he could for five years, barely
making ends meet until he landed a deal with Decca records in 1940. He would
stay with Decca and later MCA (MCA bought Decca) for 35 years and became
one of the giants of the business. Tubb was one of the first country stars to use
an amplified guitar, and by 1943 his band was playing several electric instruments on the stage of the staid Grand Ole Opry. Tubb was a star, so he could
afford to be innovative, but not too innovative; several performers went even
further with the electrified, beat-driven style of play, most notably, Bob Wills
and the Texas Playboys. The Playboys band featured horns, reeds, electric gui-
tars, violin, bass fiddle, and sometimes even drums, and combined a variety of
styles including jazz and big band to produce music that became known as
western swing. It blurred the lines between country and other forms of
music.[31]

Country was drifting in a more popular direction (toward "pop" in today's
terms), driven there by the industry's quest for more dollars. What this meant
very simply was that some performers struggled to develop music that appealed to people besides rural and working class white Southerners. Electric instruments, guitar especially, and the virtual abandonment of the banjo and the
fiddle marked this new, more commercial music. Hank Williams appeared on
the music scene in the late 1940s and achieved great success as a "crossover"
artist who could appeal to the traditional Southern audience and a broader
American audience with such hits as "Your Cheating Heart," "Jambalaya," and
especially "Lovesick Blues." He paved the way for the ultimate in crossover
country that would emerge after his death at the age of 29 in 1953.[32]

A year after Williams's death, a wild young artist by the name of Elvis Presley
burst on the music scene with a new sound. No one was quite sure what this
music was or where it fit; it was initially called rockabilly, but it seemed barely
connected to the country music tradition. Elvis's first hit, "That's All Right
Mama," was a blues number originally sung by Arthur "Big Boy" Crudup and
was recorded at Sam Phillips's Sun Records, a studio that specialized in blues
performers. But Elvis was white, and blues performers were black, and the way
he sang the music didn't sound much like the blues. Phillips had been waiting
for someone like Elvis to walk in his door; as he noted later, "They [whites]

---

31. *Ibid.*, 153–158, 170–174, 187.
32. *Ibid.*, 239–245.

liked the music, but they weren't sure whether they ought to like it or not. So I got to thinking how many records you could sell if you could find white performers who could play and sing in this same exciting, alive way."[33] When Elvis's recordings began to sell, he began performing at country music venues including the Opry and the Louisiana Hayride, a radio program broadcast out of Baton Rouge. On the Hayride, the announcer called Elvis's musical style "rhythm and blues" but also exclaimed that it was a "new" kind of music and "they've been looking for something new in the folk music field."[34] "New" was an understatement; Elvis and his band performed it with a driving beat and mixed blues and country guitar styles. Presley was joined by other emerging stars such as Jerry Lee Lewis and Carl Perkins and even a young Johnny Cash.

Rockabilly would eventually leave the country camp, take off on its own as a new form of music—rock and roll—that drew on both the white and black traditions of Southern music. Country would be left to sort out where it should go. Chet Atkins, as both a performer and record industry executive, charted a new course for mainstream country that kept one foot in the traditional camp and one foot in the camp of the "pop" stylists without going the rock route. This "new" sound was called the Nashville sound; it was polished without the harder edges of the old country sound; fiddles and, of course, banjos did not figure in the music, and lush orchestration and smooth background vocals often did. Patsy Cline, Marty Robbins, and Atkins himself were some of the stars of this pop-oriented music that poured out of Nashville in the 1950s and 1960s.[35]

Nashville would continue down this road with many contemporary performers like Dolly Parton, Garth Brooks, and Trish Yearwood singing a soft rock form of the music but with enough of the country kept in—lyrics that respected traditional values, a bit of "twang" in the vocals, western garb for the performers, and at least a nod to old-style country melodies—to keep the music in the country camp. The move of the Opry in the 1970s out of Ryman and into a hotel/theme park complex on the outskirts of Nashville seemed to further exemplify the transformation of country, leading many fans, performers, and industry observers to periodically wonder if country was even country any more. Several performers adopted the pose of "outlaws" in the 1970s to indicate their displeasure with the direction of the industry and industry conformity. Willie Nelson was one of the early outlaws and relocated to Austin, Texas, grew his hair long, and generally thumbed his nose at Nashville propriety. Outlaws often attempted to sing the sort of "pared down" traditional music

33. Peter Guralnick, *Last Train to Memphis: the Rise of Elvis Presley* (Boston, Little, Brown and Co., 1994), 89–96, quote p. 96.

34. A recording of Elvis's first performance on the Louisiana Hayride is in *Elvis Presley Concert Anthology: 1954–1956*, CD (Los Angeles: Master Classics, 2005).

35. Malone, *Country Music, U.S.A.*, 245–267.

without the pop lyrics, rock-style guitar work, and glitzy production values. Nelson, Waylon Jennings, and later George Strait and Ricky Skaggs are several of the more prominent contemporary performers dedicated to playing the "real" country music, although Willie Nelson has also had great success as a crossover artist.[36]

Pop or outlaw were not the only two options, however, for performers or fans. Bill Monroe, Lester Flatt, and Earl Scruggs created a form of music called bluegrass in the late 1940s that, they believe, harked back to the old traditions. This music featured unamplified instruments including fiddle and banjo and performers who attempted to stay true to the "old timey" musical styles, but bluegrass was innovative in what it did with these styles, and the musical virtuosity of some of the performers in itself made the music different than the traditional music it emulated. Traditionalists would draw new recruits to their cause thereafter with Emmy Lou Harris, Iris Dement, Jerry Douglass, and Allison Kraus and her band Union Station among the best of the recent crop of bluegrass artists. Some performers, like Dolly Parton, have gone back and forth between mainstream country and more traditional music. Parton could record a pop song like "9 to 5" and albums of traditional music with Emmy Lou Harris and Linda Ronstadt (*Trio* and *Trio II*) with equal aplomb. Traditional music would have its gospel side, today best exemplified by Ralph Stanley. Stanley's gospel is far removed from the smooth harmony of the quartet tradition and has that simple, heart-felt style one associates with the early days of country and gospel. All of this music achieved a certain national prominence with the success of the film *O Brother, Where Art Thou?*, which came out in 2000. The film was set in the 1930s, and its soundtrack featured a veritable who's who of contemporary traditional performers including Ralph Stanley, Allison Kraus, and Emmy Lou Harris. The *O Brother* soundtrack struck gold despite the fact that most country stations refused to give any of its songs airplay, leading some to wonder if the music industry didn't want people to hear "real" country music.

No conspiracy directs the music industry, although certainly a relatively small number of recording companies and the shrinking play lists on radio stations limit what will get out to a mass audience. The industry is simply in search of dollars and a bigger audience (certainly part of its tradition), and caters to what sells best. Today, country still appeals to working class Southern whites and what's left of the rural white South, but it also appeals to comfortable middle class suburbanites and folks living outside the region who are drawn to it by its "singable tunes and understandable lyrics" and performers who look and dress more like "regular" people.[37] This audience, whether in the

36. *Ibid.*, 398–415; Malone, *Don't Get Above Your Raisin'*, 253–256.
37. Malone, *Don't Get Above Your Raisin'*, 255.

South or outside the South, is plugged into contemporary American culture, and the music must reflect this culture to sell. Hank Williams Junior's pop country song "Are You Ready for Some Football," which introduced "Monday Night Football" for a number of years, is more reflective of this culture than the hauntingly beautiful rendition of "O Death" sung by Ralph Stanley. The more traditional music obviously sells but is more of a niche market; ironically, it seems to be most popular among more affluent college-educated people and is more likely heard on public radio stations rather than on commercial country stations. Folk art has, in a sense, become high art.

Even as mainstream country has moved in a "pop" or "soft rock" direction, it has stayed true to some traditions. The industry still venerates its older stars and songs, and young performers will often perform old standards. It's almost obligatory for a country artist to perform if not record classic tunes from the Carters and Jimmie Rodgers, and the death of June Carter Cash (Maybelle Carter's daughter and wife of Johnny Cash) in 2003 left the industry without the presence of an influential Carter for the first time since the 1920s. In no other form of entertainment has one family played such a prominent role for so long. Explicit references to farming and the rural lifestyle may have nearly disappeared from country lyrics, but traditional values—family, home, religion, hard work, and, a relatively recent addition, patriotism—continue to dominate the lyrics of many songs, while contemporary pop and particularly rap seem fixated on promoting a very different set of values. In a sense, it still can claim "outsider" status as it stands up for old time values against the onslaught of Hollywood, rap, and what many perceive to be declining morals. Not surprisingly, the country demographic matches up closely with the Republican Party demographic, and the music seems to have become part of a conservative white subculture. The female group The Dixie Chicks learned this lesson the hard way when one of the group members criticized President George Walker Bush; in response, many country stations boycotted the group's music. But to watch the Country Music Awards and to listen closely to the music that dominates the airwaves and country record sales is to realize how far removed the music is from the music of those performers who traveled to Bristol so long ago to play a few tunes for Mr. Peer.

Southern Music: The Black Tradition

Architect Benjamin Latrobe visited New Orleans in 1819, and one day he was walking up St. Peter Street approaching an area of the city called Congo Square, when, in his words, "I heard a most extraordinary noise, which I supposed to proceed from some horse Mill, the horse trampling on a wooden floor. I found however on emerging from the houses, onto the common, that it proceeded from a croud [sic] of 5 or 600 persons assembled in an open space or public square."[38] The throngs were slaves participating in a dance the likes of which Latrobe had never seen. Hundreds of dancers were arranged in "circular groupes [sic]"; in the middle of four of these groups was a "ring" of dancers. The largest of these rings consisted of a dozen women who "walked, by way of dancing, round the music in the Center."[39] Musicians in the groups played a variety of instruments including drums and stringed instruments with bodies constructed from large gourds. As historian Ted Gioia has noted, the Congo Square dances, which continued in some form until the 1880s, derived from West African musical and dance traditions. At Congo Square, Latrobe observed an instrument being played that was the predecessor of the banjo, and the patterned dance was likely the forerunner of the ring shout.[40] While Latrobe's observations provide us with evidence of the persistence of West African musical traditions, linking specific West African musical traditions to musical forms developed by people in slavery is not a simple matter. As we have seen, slaveholders did their best to wipe away the cultural traditions of recently arrived African slaves, and some traditions, like drumming, were generally prohibited, although clearly drumming was tolerated in some places like New Orleans. Slaves brought to the South in the 1600s and 1700s came from many different cultures and were generally separated from their countrymen, which made keeping specific traditions alive difficult. But most scholars believe there were enough commonalities in West African cultures to provide slaves from diverse societies who were transported to America with some common reference points, and these reference points would play an important role in the musical culture people in slavery created.

The "core element" of the shared musical tradition many slaves brought to America from Africa was an "extraordinary richness of rhythmic content."[41] The music was polyrhythmic with rhythm layered on rhythm, each rhythm carried along by drumbeat or clap or voice or strummed string instrument. It was a participatory music that generally involved everyone; a singer might sing, but the audience responded back because often music was performed as part of a ritual, and all were participants in the ritual, not mere spectators. The music was often tied to dance, and this made it beat driven, and finally, the musical instruments that were played often emulated the human voice and "talked" to each other. "Talking" instruments and group participation also made the music improvisational; just as a conversation might go in any number of directions

---

38. Edward C. Carter, II, et al, eds., *The Journals of Benjamin Henry Latrobe, 1799–1820: from Philadelphia to New Orleans, Vol..3* (New Haven: Yale University Press, 1980), 203.

39. *Ibid.*, 204.

40. Ted Gioia, *The History of Jazz* (New York: Oxford University Press, 1998), 3–4.

41. *Ibid.*, 9.

and be long or short, so, too, the music might take different directions each time it was played and sung. A variety of vocalization styles including whooping and "voice masking," where the normal sound of one's voice was altered when one put on a mask as part of a ritual dance, were part of the cultural heritage of many newly arrived slaves. Like the British immigrants, most African slaves had come from cultures with ballad traditions; in most West African societies, storytellers called griots would sing stories of the powerful leaders and notable figures of their people.[42]

In America, slaves were exposed to new instruments, the violin especially, and new kinds of secular and sacred music. We know that male slaves sometimes became fiddlers and were sought after by whites for their dances where people danced quadrilles, reels, and cotillions. Richard Mack recalled that before the Civil War, his father, called "Daddy Tony" by the whites, had played the violin at an academy and at parties at the academy and had played such songs as "Cotton Eye Joe."[43] People in slavery listened and danced to the some of the same music enjoyed by whites. One former slave recalled, "About all I remember about the dances was when we danced the cotillion at regular old country break-downs" and that "Turkey in the Straw" was the "oldest dance tune" he could recall. Another recalled dancing to "Old Dan Tucker."[44] Likewise, the British ballads with their stories of conflict, lost love, and outlaws were songs that people in slavery heard and probably enjoyed. This tradition continued after the Civil War when black performers from the South drew on a wide repertoire of traditional British and American folk songs.[45] Religious music, especially during and after the Great Awakening, would play a growing role in the lives of slaves, and the hymns by Isaac Watts and other English composers of the 1700s would have been commonly heard and sung by black believers.

African Americans in slavery took the broader musical influences from their African homelands and melded them with the British and American musical traditions they encountered and created new musical traditions. Slaves might dance, for example, a quadrille, but their version of it was more fluid and improvisational than the stiffer, precise dancing of the whites. They even devised

42. *Ibid.*, 9–11; Robert Palmer, *Deep Blues* (New York: Penguin Books, 1982), 26–33.

43. Lawrence W. Levine, *Black Culture and Black Consciousness: Afro-American Folk Thought From Slavery To Freedom* (Oxford: Oxford University Press, 1977), 15–116; Richard Mack, interview by Martha Pinckney, *Born in Slavery: Slave Narratives from the Federal Writers' Project, 1936–1938* (Washington: Library of Congress, Manuscript Division, 2001), http://memory.loc.gov/ammem/snhtml/snhome.html.

44. John F. Van Hook, interview by Sadie B. Hornsby and Dora Franks, interview by Mrs. Richard Kolb (quote from Van Hook interview), *Born in Slavery: Slave Narratives from the Federal Writers' Project, 1936–1938* (Washington: Library of Congress, Manuscript Division, 2001), http://memory.loc.gov/ammem/snhtml/snhome.html.

45. Levine, *Black Culture and Black Consciousness*, 194–195.

a dance—the cakewalk—that was a pointed satire of the preferred dance of upper class whites, the waltz.[46] Black fiddle players may very well have influenced white fiddle players in playing technique just as later black guitar players influenced white guitarists. But people in slavery also developed new musical forms; one of these forms commonly noted by observers at the time was the work song.

Work songs accompanied chopping wood, picking cotton, and cooking; slaves rowing a boat might time their oar strokes to the rhythm of the song they were singing. Work songs were often dialogues; the song one observer heard rowers singing had a song leader singing a verse and the other rowers responding with a chorus. The songs were as much chants as true songs, and verses would be invented or altered on the spot to acknowledge something new that the workers were discussing or had observed. The subject matter of the songs might be the work itself, gossip, tall tales, or simple nonsense. Frequently, the songs poked fun at the whites, sometimes directly, but often using metaphors or words or phrasings that whites weren't familiar with.[47] While work songs were typically group songs, people in slavery also sang solo songs, and the field holler was the most remarked upon form of solo singing. Field hollers were used to communicate information such as quitting time, vent feelings in song, or simply explore the possibilities of word sounds and rhyming.[48] Blues artist Muddy Waters recalled that as a boy, he sang field hollers to communicate to fellow workers or to express what he was thinking or feeling. "I remember I was always singin', 'I cain't be satisfied, I be all troubled in mind.' Seems like I was always singin' that, because I was always singin' jest the way I felt...."[49] Those phrases would later show up in one of Waters's most famous blues numbers. Hector Smith, a former slave, recalled a holler he sang that went like this:

> Bulldog a barkin'
> Howl! Howl!
> Bulldog a barkin'
> Howl! Howl!
> Bulldog a barkin'
> Howl! Howl!
> Ah-oodle-oodel-ou,
> Ah-oodle-oodel-ou,
> Ah-ou-ah-ou,
> Ah-oodle-ou,

46. Levine, *Black Culture and Black Consciousness,* 16–17.
47. *Ibid.,* 6–15.
48. *Ibid.,* 218–219.
49. *Ibid.,* 203.

Ah-ou-ah-ou,
Ah-oodle-oodel-ou.[50]

The spiritual was the new sacred music people in slavery created in the decades leading up to the Civil War. This was a music that was as likely to be sung in the field as it was in church or brush arbor prayer meeting. The songs were true folk songs learned by hearing, although eventually many would be written down, and today such spirituals as "Swing Low, Sweet Chariot" and "Roll, Jordan, Roll" are in many hymnals. It was a music that had certain themes that we've discussed elsewhere in this text: people in slavery as God's chosen people, the idea of deliverance, like the children of Israel were delivered, and the inevitability of God's judgment on the people keeping slaves in bondage. It was a music designed to uplift the downtrodden, and it promised better times ahead in this world and the next.[51] Spirituals were a blending of old and new; in the words of one historian, they were "forged out of many preexisting bits of old songs mixed together with snatches of new tunes and lyrics and fit into a fairly traditional but never static metrical pattern." So they had much in common with, for example, an Isaac Watts hymn, but unlike a Watts hymn, the typical spiritual constantly evolved with changes in verses, new verses, and even a new tune. Singers would often improvise as they sang, and spirituals might exist in dozens of different versions across the South. Driving the spiritual was a "propulsive" rhythm—clapping, stamping, shouting, carrying the beat—and this rhythm gave spirituals a power that even skeptical white observers remarked upon.[52]

After the Civil War, black Southerners had more freedom, more mobility, and, naturally, more exposure to different kinds of music. Even segregation would not eliminate the "relatively free trade of musical ideas." Whites would hear and be influenced by black musical styles, and blacks would hear and be influenced by white styles. Southern African Americans now had more opportunities as performers; vaudeville, medicine shows, circuses, and minstrel shows toured the South and often featured black performers. To be successful, black performers had to learn different styles of music to suit the tastes of different audiences and had to be willing to perform in a variety of venues ranging from lumber camps to saloons to house parties. Gertrude "Ma" Rainey traveled the South in the early 1900s with a group called the Rabbit Foot Minstrels and sang ballads, minstrel songs, and a variety of songs popular in vaudeville and burlesque.[53] Scott Joplin, setting his sights on becoming a professional pianist,

---

50. Hector Smith, interview by Annie Ruth Davis, *Born in Slavery: Slave Narratives from the Federal Writers' Project, 1936–1938* (Washington: Library of Congress, Manuscript Division, 2001), http://memory.loc.gov/ammem/snhtml/snhome.html.

51. Levine, *Black Culture and Black Consciousness*, 31–40.

52. *Ibid.*, 26–29; quote, p. 29.

53. *Ibid.*, 194–195; quote, p. 194.

left his native Texas and moved to St. Louis in the 1880s where he worked in saloons and night clubs. Joplin would be one of the early innovators of a new musical form called ragtime; Rainey, with W.C. Handy, would be one of the early popularizers of another new musical form called the blues.

Ragtime was created by Joplin and other black pianists sometime in the late 1880s and may have gained broader exposure when black performers played it at the World's Columbian Exposition in Chicago in 1893. It was music primarily for the piano and typically not accompanied by vocals. It featured a two handed playing technique in which the left hand played a steady "four to the bar foundation" while the right hand engaged in "rhythmic acrobatics" that probably gave the music its name for the right hand's "ragged time."[54] Many of the pianists played ragtime quickly and with a great flourish of showmanship. Joplin, unlike some of the other performers, wrote down his compositions and sold them as sheet music. In 1897 he wrote "Maple Leaf Rag," his most famous piece; by 1900 this composition took off in sales and sold more than one million copies. Ragtime became immensely popular for a time; it was a music that, as Irving Berlin noted, captured the "speed and snap" of modern America.[55] As such, the music really reflected the city and the industrializing North and Midwest rather than the still agrarian South, but the Southern roots of Joplin and many of the other ragtime piano players testified to its Southern heritage. In a sense, Joplin and the other rag players were trying to merge European formal music (the left hand) to the more improvisational style of the African-American tradition (the right hand). Ragtime would wane in popularity in the early 1900s, but its influence would be pronounced on another new musical form—jazz—that was developing in New Orleans.[56]

Blues developed in the South in the late 1800s, although its precise origins are unclear and even how to define it is a subject of debate. It was a music with its roots planted firmly in the countryside, although some of its most famous performers left the country behind and traveled from town to town or lived in the city, Chicago especially. The guitar was its chosen instrument, although harmonica, banjo, piano, and even brass instruments might accompany a blues song. Generally blues fit a "twelve bar framework" and featured the so-called "blue notes" which are "the flatted third and seventh notes of the major scale." This produces a music that has a "mournful, lonesome" sound.[57] Blues lyrics often were composed in three line verses, and often one of the lines was repeated and then answered by another line, a pattern illustrated by the first stanza of Charley Patton's "Pony Blues":

54. Gioia, *The History of Jazz*, 20–24, quotes p. 21.
55. *Ibid.*, 25.
56. *Ibid.*, 20–21, 27.
57. Elijah Wood, *Escaping the Delta: Robert Johnson and the Invention of the Blues* (New York: Amistad, 2004), 4–5.

> Hitch up my pony, saddle up my black mare
> Hitch up my pony, saddle up my black mare
> I'm goin' find a rider, baby, in the world somewhere.[58]

Different forms of the blues would emerge in different areas of the South. In Texas and Louisiana, it was often hard driving piano dance music played in the "lumber and turpentine camps"; one of the early stars in the 1920s was Dallas native Blind Lemon Jefferson who played his guitar in the "boogie-woogie rhythm" that characterized this style of blues and whose most popular tune was "That Black Snake Moan." In the Southeastern states, blues songs were more "lilting and melodic" and reflective of the ballad tradition; one of the more famous artists from this region was Blind Boy Fuller. In the Mississippi Delta, what would become the most influential blues of all would flower in the 1920s and 1930s.[59]

Blues was a music that was developing during dark days for African Americans in the South: race riots, Jim Crow laws, and lynching had communicated to black citizens a clear message—stay in your place. Many of the artists and most of the people who listened to the music were poor sharecroppers and laborers and as such were the poorest of the poor. The lyrics of the blues reflected the hard world they lived in. The blues celebrated both the stoic endurance of pain and disappointment and the bit of pleasure that waited at the unexpected moment for those bold enough to seize it. As a music that urged listeners to enjoy the carnal pleasures of drink and sex, it was at odds with the teachings of the church and shunned by good churchgoers as the "devil's music." Many blues artists delighted in cultivating the image of themselves as "bad" men; blues artist Robert Johnson's song, "Me and the Devil Blues" featured lyrics like this:

> Early this morning when you knocked upon my door,
> Early this morning when you knocked upon my door,
> I said "Hello Satan, I believe it's time to go."[60]

If the blues represented a rebellion against the strictures of proper black society, even more it rejected the profound constraints white society tried to impose on blacks. Blues performers lived outlaw-like lives, avoiding the white man's rules and work, traveling far and wide. With the separation of black and white brought about by Jim Crow, the blues turned away from white traditions and embraced African and African-American musical traditions. But while older musical forms from the African-American tradition were largely communal experiences, the blues was generally played by one or two individuals, and the lyrics were intensely personal and individualistic. In that sense it was, as

---

58. Palmer, *Deep Blues*, 63.
59. Palmer, *Deep Blues*, 42–44, 106–107; Wood, *Escaping the Delta*, 34.
60. "Me and the Devil Blues," *Robert Johnson: King of the Delta Blues*, CD (1937; New York: Sony Music Entertainment, Inc., 1998).

Amiri Baraka has argued, "music that developed because of the Negro's adaptation to, and adoption of, America."[61]

Like all of the other musical forms discussed thus far, the blues as it developed was not some "pure" art form unaffected by outside or commercial influences as some fans once thought. In fact, W.C. Handy and Gertrude "Ma" Rainey, the two people generally considered the most responsible for launching the blues as a commercial form of entertainment, were widely traveled professional entertainers. They not only popularized it, they and other professional entertainers from a variety of musical backgrounds (including some white performers) had an important influence on how it sounded and people's expectations of how it should sound.[62] Handy and Rainey both happened upon blues being performed by street performers in the early years of the twentieth century and considered the music on first hearing "strange" and "weird."[63] But both Handy and Rainey adopted the musical style. Handy wrote "Memphis Blues," the first blues "hit," and followed it with several others including "St. Louis Blues." Ma Rainey was one of a number of "blues queens," most of them from the South, most seasoned professionals drawn from vaudeville and minstrel shows, who were commercially successful in the new music industry that emerged in the 1920s. Other queens included Mamie Smith, whose hit "Crazy Blues" encouraged record companies to expand their efforts in the "race" market, Bessie Smith, who could "fix" a man with her stare while she was performing and draw him to the stage, Ida Cox, and Sippie Wallace. Amiri Baraka calls the music these performers produced "classic blues" and argues that they were professionals who took the country blues and polished it up for a wider audience. And polished it was; the blues queens frequently dressed in sequins and silk and fronted jazz orchestras. This classic blues and jazz were kin and there would always be substantial overlap between them. One of the greatest female vocalists of the first half of the twentieth century, Billie Holiday, can justifiably be characterized as both a blues singer and a jazz singer. Classic blues was not just "city music"; even folks living in the Delta considered Rainey and the other queens the big blues stars of the era. Ultimately, the collapse of vaudeville, which had nurtured the female blues singers, and the hard times of the Depression ended the reign of the female stars.[64]

Handy's first encounter with the blues was in Tutwiler, Mississippi, a small town 15 miles from Clarksdale and a bit further from Cleveland, two towns

---

61. Amiri Baraka, *Blues People: Negro Music in America* (1963; New York: Perennial, 2002), 59, 64–67, quote p. 66; William Barlow, *"Looking Up at Down": The Emergence of Blues Culture* (Philadelphia: Temple University Press, 1989), 5.
62. Wood, *Escaping the Delta*, 7–13, 15–21.
63. Palmer, *Deep Blues*, 44.
64. Wood, *Escaping the Delta*, 16–26; Baraka, *Blues People*, 86–87, 99; Francis Davis, *The History of the Blues* (1995; Cambridge, Mass.: Da Capo Press, 2003), 71–85.

that figure prominently in both the history and mythology of the delta blues. Only a few years before Handy's Tutwiler epiphany, Bill Patton, farmer and sometime preacher, had moved his wife and twelve children to the Dockery plantation just outside of Cleveland to work the cotton crop of Will Dockery. Charley, one of Mr. Patton's sons, was by this time in his teens and something of a musician, a pastime not pleasing to his religious father. Apparently at some point he took up with another Dockery resident, Henry Sloan. Sloan played the "rough, rhythmic" music that would come to be called the delta blues, and young Charley learned at his knee. By the time Sloan left Mississippi for Chicago near the end of World War I, Patton was a local celebrity and often played with a sidekick by the name of Willie Brown. Dockery plantation, as well as the neighboring towns of Cleveland, Drew, and Ruleville, had acquired a reputation as the place to go to learn to play the blues, and a number of note-worthy blues artists emerged from this area, most connected in some way to Charley Patton.[65] Tommy Johnson, originally from southern Mississippi, lived at Dockery's for a few years and was one of several blues artists who claimed to have sold his soul to the devil at a midnight meeting at a crossroads in a trade for the ability to play the blues. Aside from the inherent romance of the story, it has its roots in West African tradition: the trickster god Legba often appeared at crossroads and would sometimes bestow special powers on those he encoun-tered. Blues greats Robert Johnson, Son House, and Howlin' Wolf all lived on or near Dockery's at one point. Muddy Waters, with Howlin' Wolf, destined to be among the most commercially successful of the delta bluesmen, was a bit younger than the others. He lived on Stovall plantation outside Clarksdale, 35 miles and some change up Highway 61 from Cleveland, and claimed Robert Johnson as the major influence on his style.[66]

These blues artists and others, most long forgotten, forged a unique style that appealed primarily to black delta residents and a smattering of people else-where. They traded blues songs back and forth, changing them in small ways and large in true folk fashion. "Walkin' Blues," for example, was a standard sung by nearly everyone; Robert Johnson sang a particularly powerful version. They played other sorts of music, too: Patton actually recorded some gospel songs and played the sort of "country" tunes both whites and blacks listened to. It would be a mistake to assume blue artists were isolated country folk; many listened to the popular recording artists of the time, and many of them trav-eled extensively across the country.[67] Many of the best blues songs were polyrhythmic, and blues artists employed a variety of techniques to add den-sity and complexity to their music. Delta blues guitarists often used a bottle-

65. Palmer, *Deep Blues*, 50–62.
66. *Ibid.*, 58–63, 103–104, 111.
67. Davis, *The History of the Blues*, 100–109; Palmer, *Deep Blues*, 103–104, 120–124.

John and Ruby Lomax

Figure 8.1   Blues artist Huddie Ledbetter (Leadbelly) and Martha Ledbetter

neck on the strings to make the instrument "talk," and singer and guitar inter-acted with one another in a unique call and response way. Charley Patton would accent the "first beat in a measure with his guitar and the fourth beat with his voice" and tap on his guitar.[68] Robert Johnson, another bluesmen who allegedly had a fateful meeting with the devil at a crossroads, played a "deliber-ate and driving" rhythm on the guitar in many of his songs but would inter-rupt the rhythm "to hammer and bend a single string" and would alternate "driving bass riffs and high, bottlenecked lead lines."[69] Singing techniques var-ied, but a common technique was the "Delta growl," a low, throaty rumble; Tommy Johnson broke from his normal singing voice and inserted a falsetto yodel into some of his songs, while Muddy Waters employed a variety of voices in his songs ranging from the "purest falsetto to deep, quivering moans, to a grainy, vibrato-heavy rasp."[70]

As rural blacks moved to cities and towns in the 1930s and 1940s, the blues began to take on a "distinctly urban identity," although the blues queens of the 1920s certainly had been city folk, too.[71] Memphis supported a thriving nightlife with Beale Street serving as "the place" for blues and jazz performers, especially pianists. Albert Luandrew, known as Sunnyland Slim, found work as a blues pianist in Memphis and met and played with many blues performers. As

---

68. Davis, *The History of the Blues*, 99; Palmer, *Deep Blues*, 46, 64, 125.
69. Palmer, *Deep Blues*, 125.
70. Davis, *The History of the Blues*, 99, 105; Palmer, *Deep Blues*, 102.
71. Davis, *The History of the Blues*, 164.

Slim noted, "Memphis used to be a barrelhouse town" where a wide variety of joints and dives offered a piano player and card shark like himself opportunities.[72] A young Elvis Presley spent time on Beale in the early 1950s, perhaps drawn there by the lively street scene but certainly by the flamboyant clothing on display at Lansky Brothers clothing store, the early source for his unique street hustler/hipster wardrobe.[73] Beale Street still offers tourists today a time capsule version of the sort of blues folks may have heard in the 1930s, 1940s and early 1950s. Eventually, Sam Phillips would start a small recording company in Memphis—Sun Records—that specialized in the blues. His first "find" was Howlin' Wolf who recorded a song "Moanin' at Midnight" that Phillips leased to Chess records in Chicago.[74] Chicago was the major center of the blues and attracted scores of artists from Memphis and the rural South like Sunnyland Slim,

Marion Post Wolcott

Figure 8.2   Couple jitterbugging in Clarksdale, Mississippi, jook joint

72. Palmer, *Deep Blues*, 152–153, quote p. 152.
73. Peter Guralnick, *Last Train to Memphis: The Rise of Elvis Presley* (Boston: Little, Brown and Co., 1994), 45–46.
74. Davis, *The History of the Blues*, 192.

Howlin' Wolf, who went there to be near his record company, and Muddy Waters. It was in Chicago more than any other place where the new urban-style blues developed. Chicago recording artists like Petie Wheatstraw, Kokomo Arnold, and Big Bill Bronzy were performing and recording in bands that included "bass, drums, and jazz trumpeters and clarinets, in a city style that foreshadowed the rhythm-and-blues of the post-World War II years."[75] Even in the Delta, the blues followed the urban trends. In the early 1940s, a radio program called "King Biscuit Time" (named after a brand of flour that sponsored the show) broadcast out of Helena, Arkansas, just across the river from the Delta. The show featured Robert Longwood, Jr., son of Robert Johnson, who was regularly playing tunes featuring the electric guitar. This instrument would play a major role in driving the blues in a new direction.[76]

Muddy Waters would emerge as the central figure on the Chicago blues scene after World War II. Waters had migrated to Chicago during World War II and struggled to find a place in the music business. After the war, Waters landed a job playing guitar at the Flame Club. The house band at the Flame club was trying to play the more urbane, jazz-influenced "smooth" blues sometimes called jump blues. Muddy wasn't comfortable with this style, but when another delta expatriate—Sunnyland Slim—joined the band, the group began playing a rougher, delta kind of blues with a strong bass and Muddy playing the electric guitar and singing. By the late 1940s, Waters had gotten comfortable with his new style and recorded with Slim and several others his composition "I Can't Be Satisfied" for Aristocrat records. His career began to take off. Waters had something—a willingness to adapt, charisma, and a good rapport with fellow musicians—that attracted some of the best blues artists to work with him. He turned out hit after hit with "I'm Your Hoochie Coochie Man," "Just Make Love to Me," and "I'm Ready" his most successful. The songs Muddy's group put out were employing "stop-time riffs" and a driving drum accompaniment that would play the backbeat (an extra emphasis in the "second and fourth beat").[77] This style and the older styles, too, would play a major role in the creation of rock and roll.

It turns out that the electrified blues Waters and other artists were playing was the end of the road for the blues as a living, evolving art form; the music that would be called rhythm and blues and rock and roll would simply overwhelm it. As Muddy Waters noted, "The rock and roll, this hurt the blues pretty bad.... We still hustled around and made it and kept goin', but we were only playin' for black people when rock and roll came along, and it got so we couldn't play any more slow blues. The people just wanted to 'bug.'"[78] Ultimately, Wa-

---

75. Palmer, *Deep Blues,* 124.
76. *Ibid.,* 178.
77. *Ibid.,* 155–168.; Davis, *The History of Blues,* 188.
78. Palmer, *Deep Blues,* 255.

ters and a number of other blues artists would experience a revival in the 1960s and 1970s when young white rock and roll artists and fans "rediscovered" the early blues artists. They performed on college campuses and at the hangouts of college students and, as time went on, at clubs catering to middle aged white college graduates. A small number of new artists like Taj Mahal produced a kind of studio blues that paid homage to the music and kept blues fans supplied with new material, the music of older, long gone artists was reissued, and rockers like Eric Clapton put out albums that honored their favorite blues artists. Books, television specials, and documentary films on the music and its artists were churned out, and blues fans like record producer Steve LaVere did their best to keep the blues alive in the Mississippi Delta by establishing museums and small blues venues and erecting markers and signs that documented where leading blues artists had lived, played, and died.[79] The blues had become a niche music for a largely white, educated middle class audience.

Blues' urban sibling, jazz, followed a similar trajectory. It seems to have developed in New Orleans where a variety of musical influences bumped into each other in this always culturally rich, always economically poor city that had learned to bear its tragedies and disappointments with celebrations that even a devastating flood (Katrina) has not been able to still. It was music rooted in the classical musical traditions of Europe, in ragtime, and in the blues. It was also influenced by what seems, in retrospect, an unlikely source: brass bands. Brass bands and marching music (think of John Philip Sousa's tunes) were quite popular across the country at the turn of the twentieth century, and New Orleans loved them with a passion; only in New Orleans would a funeral procession be accompanied by a brass band. In popular mythology, jazz was a music that came from Storyville, a district devoted to prostitution and good times bordering the *Vieux Carre*. This story on closer inspection is at best overdrawn, although certainly the profusion of bars, dives, and dance halls in the city provided musicians with places to play for cash. Too, a productive mix of ethnic groups—black and white Creoles (people with some French or Spanish ancestry), Anglo Americans, African Americans, Italian immigrants, each with its own musical traditions, and the New Orleans tolerance for some degree of "mixing" between the races—promoted musical experimentation.[80]

Buddy Bolden is the seminal figure in the genesis of jazz, although undoubtedly there were other key figures now long forgotten. Bolden was born in 1877 in New Orleans, began playing the cornet in the 1890s, and become a member of a band that included several brass instruments, a guitar, bass fid-

---

79. Steve LaVere established a small blues museum and a café featuring live blues music in Greenwood, Mississippi. He also located what he believed is Robert Johnson's grave in a small church graveyard on the Money Road, just outside Greenwood, and marked it with a gravestone.

80. Gioia, *The History of Jazz*, 31–34.

dle, and drums. This band played at parties, and its music evolved from an emphasis on the stringed instruments in the band toward an emphasis on the brass instruments. The music became more bluesy, syncopated, "ragged and raucous" with edgy, suggestive lyrics, and it would lay the foundations for jazz. It appealed largely to a black audience. Bolden's most famous piece was known by a variety of names including "Funky Butt" and "Buddy Bolden's Blues"; one jazz artist recalled that if a band played it and the police were around, the police officers started "whipping heads." Bolden's career was short; he drank too much and had mental problems which landed him in an insane asylum where he spent several decades until his death at age 54.[81]

A second generation of jazz artists followed Bolden and the other pioneers of jazz. These included black Creole players like Jelly Roll Morton, Sidney Bechet, and Freddie Keppard, and black artists like Joe "King" Oliver, and, the most famous of all, Louis Armstrong. There were also white artists like Papa Jack Laine and Nick LaRocca. Jelly Roll Morton was one of the most gifted and influential; he really did learn his trade playing in a whorehouse in Storyville and supported himself from time to time as a pimp and pool shark. Morton was a pianist, composer, and band director, and helped define New Orleans style jazz. This style stressed ensemble work; Morton is said to have taken a pistol out once during a session to "encourage" a trombonist to play exactly the way he told him to. The music was driven by trombone, clarinet, and cornet, each with a specific role; the trombone laid down a bass line, the clarinet filled in with detail, and the cornet provided the lead line. Jazz musicians strove to extract from their instruments a wide range of sounds; in effect they hoped to emulate the range of the human voice, unlike their European counterparts who aspired to produce pure tones. So jazz might wail or cry or whisper. King Oliver's Creole Jazz Band played the ensemble style to perfection and was the most celebrated of the black bands. Louis Armstrong began his career in the big time with King Oliver, but, as it turns out, Armstrong really didn't fit into the ensemble style and paved the way for the more individualistic, spontaneous, improvisational style later associated with jazz.[82]

Jazz would be birthed in New Orleans, but the child would reach maturity quickly and leave home. By the late 1920s, New Orleans jazz artists had left the city by the score, most going to Chicago. Louis Armstrong ended up in New York with the Fletcher Henderson band. The opportunities, particularly in the new recording industry, were simply greater in the thriving cities of the North than New Orleans, always a poor city, could offer. Jazz musicians continued to perform in New Orleans, but the major innovations in the music now took place elsewhere—in Chicago, Kansas City, Los Angeles, San Francisco, and

---

81. *Ibid.*, 34–36, quote p. 36.
82. *Ibid.*, 39–52.

New York, especially. Jazz ceased to be a Southern art form, although the South produced its share of jazz artists, Thelonius Monk and John Coltrane being two of the most noteworthy. Even if most Southern towns and cities didn't have much of a jazz scene (if they had one at all), the recording industry could give young men living in isolated areas exposure to the music.[83] Jazz would, however, continue to be influenced by the blues, which still was deeply rooted in the South, so in that sense there continued to be a Southern connection. Jazz would reach its largest audiences during the 1920s, 1930s, and 1940s with big band jazz (called swing by the 1930s), which was played by bands headed by such well-known figures as Fletcher Henderson, Duke Ellington, and Benny Goodman. These bands and others dominated the record charts and the popular imagination. During the 1940s, the popularity of big bands declined, and jazz began moving in a more experimental direction with bebop leading the way.

Today, jazz appeals primarily to a small audience of well-educated connoisseurs who are drawn to a music that is prized for its complexity and sophistication. What started as a wild, raucous music that might get you a beating if you played it around the law is now, like classical music, set on a pedestal and sponsored by elite institutions. The major figure in modern jazz is trumpeter and composer Wynton Marsalis, who emerged in the early 1980s as a jazz prodigy. Marsalis was born on the outskirts of New Orleans into a musical family; his father is a jazz artist and his brother would also become a jazz performer of note. Marsalis's early stardom drew him into seeing himself not only as a performer but also as the spokesman for jazz. His was a strong voice for mainstream jazz and a sharp critic of experimentalism and as such served as something of a conservator of the music, guarding it like a museum director protects precious artifacts. He has done his best to re-establish his home city as the center of the jazz world and has helped a virtual flood of jazz performers from New Orleans get gigs and recording contracts. As historian Ted Gioia has noted, he has worked hard to promote a jazz rooted in the "sounds of his native New Orleans and the traditional African-American roots of jazz." His own compositions reflect a growing emphasis on the blues, one of the starting points of jazz.[84] His efforts at restoring the New Orleans jazz community to a central role in the music has undoubtedly been dealt a serious blow by Hurricane Katrina.

Yet another musical form developed at the turn of the twentieth century, this one coming out of the sacred music tradition of African-American Southerners. Black churches and sacred music were in transition in the decades after slavery; black leaders pushed and prodded their people to adopt ideas and be-

---

83. *Ibid.*, 55–56, 70, 74–77.
84. *Ibid.*, 387–388, quote, 387.

haviors that would lift them up and to abandon behaviors that might be perceived, by whites especially, as undignified or ignorant. Black church leaders interested in this uplift mission pushed to tone down ecstatic worship services and pushed to replace the free form spiritual and its participatory style with the more controlled music of the hymnal and the church choir. As we have already seen in an earlier chapter, spirituals themselves were recast and formalized by such groups as the Fisk Jubilee Singers, and the formal spiritual became a part of many hymnals.[85] This is not to say older styles disappeared; particularly in rural areas, they persisted. In the largely rural Caswell County, North Carolina, of the 1940s, for example, "jubilee singers" were quite popular. These soloists would travel to different churches and lead the congregation in song; the singer would sing the verse, and the congregation would respond as the chorus. Celester Badgett recalled that "they would talk the verses off, almost like rapping! And they would build it up, until you'd hear those women's feet go 'chit-chat,' 'chit-chat.' "[86]

However, as black church leaders interested in "uplifting" blacks pushed to tame black sacred music, a new kind of sacred music arose that pushed back. This music, gospel, had roots in the spiritual and in the popular hymns of the sort produced by Ira Sankey, and it had a strong, if unacknowledged, kinship with the blues, particularly in its rhythmic quality.[87] Black Pentecostalism was growing in the early decades of the twentieth century, and it would serve as an incubator for gospel and would "nurture many of the singers that helped create and popularize" it.[88] The spirit filled worship service of the Pentecostal church was a good fit with a music that was exuberant, joyful, and "intensely emotional." Pentecostalism appealed to the less affluent, wasn't worried about propriety in the worship service, and did not subscribe to the idea that certain instruments were fit for secular music only; the guitar, the piano, drums, tambourine, and brass instruments were all permitted, and musical styles were borrowed from secular music. The structure of the Pentecostal service itself influenced the direction gospel would take: an individual would sing, testify, and read scripture, and the congregation would respond, spurring on the individual to further reveal his or her "divine gifts."[89] This worship style reflected the older African-American traditions of call and response and unfettered expres-

---

85. Jerma Jackson, *Singing in My Soul: Black Gospel Music in a Secular Age* (Chapel Hill: University of North Carolina Press, 2004), 11–13.

86. Glenn Hinson, Liner Notes, in The Badgett Sisters, *Just a Little While to Stay Here* (cassette) (New York: Global Village Music, 1990).

87. Paul Harvey, *Freedom's Coming: Religious Culture and the Shaping of the South from the Civil War through the Civil Right Era* (Chapel Hill: University of North Carolina Press, 2005), 158.

88. Jackson, *Singing in My Soul*, 16.

89. *Ibid.*, 22–23.

sion of heartfelt emotions, but it also thrust the individual into the limelight and paved the way for solo singing. Women, in particular, occupied a prominent and active role in Pentecostal church services; not surprisingly, when the new recording industry began seeking out gospel performers in the 1920s, women emerged as the first gospel stars.[90]

Sister Rosetta Tharp would become one of these early stars. She was born in 1915 and spent her early years in Cotton Plant, Arkansas. Her mother was a Church of God in Christ missionary, and early in life Tharp accompanied her mother on mission work throughout the South and Midwest and spent time in Chicago. Tharp exhibited an early aptitude for music and would sing and play the guitar accompanying her mother, who played the mandolin. She married a Pentecostal minister who also engaged in mission work, and she traveled extensively with him. Even with a protective mother and a minister husband, Tharp undoubtedly heard and saw a lot leading such a mobile life. She developed a guitar style that probably came from the blues musicians she may have heard on some of the same street corners that she and her mother played on.[91] Certainly, her willingness to take her religious message anywhere prepared her to move into the commercial arena. She sang her music in a wide variety of venues, cut records, and in 1938 appeared at the Cotton Club in Harlem, a well-known jazz nightclub, singing gospel dressed in an evening gown. Gospel had moved unabashedly into the realm of entertainment. Tharp saw this as a new way to do the missionary work she had grown up in; others saw it as debasing sacred music and selling out to make a dollar. To this day, a debate rages over the relationship between gospel and entertainment, and modern gospel stars like Kirk Franklin are often criticized for letting too much of the secular world into their music.[92] Tharp would pave the way for later gospel divas like Mahalia Jackson, Clara Ward, and Aretha Franklin, who would each, in her own way, also have to address the tension between worldly success and the dictates of business and the message of the music they sang.

If Rosetta Tharp was the mother of gospel, Thomas Dorsey was the father. Dorsey was born in 1899; his father was a struggling traveling Baptist preacher who eventually abandoned the ministry, moved the family to Atlanta, and earned a living doing yard work for the white folk. Young Dorsey struggled in Atlanta; he was from the country and subject to the taunts that distinction has always earned rural folk, especially children, in a city environment. To make matters worse, he was also poor and put back a grade in school. Like many unhappy adolescents, he sought acceptance or at least some modicum of happi-

90. *Ibid.*, 22–26.
91. *Ibid.*, 29–33, 40.
92. *Ibid.*, 77, 101–102, 133; Jerma Jackson lecture, 30 March 2006, Vance-Granville Community College, Henderson, NC.

ness in places parents warn their children to stay away from, and began hanging out in the local vaudeville theatres. But in these places he did find a vocation; he decided the life of a musician was a way for him to get ahead, and he eventually ended up in Chicago. He began composing blues numbers and even toured with Ma Rainey at one point under the stage name of Georgia Tom. He achieved minor stardom when a recording he made with Hudson Whitaker called "It's Tight Like That," emerged as the "era's best known party song."[93] But Dorsey also wrote gospel tunes; a life-changing bout with illness caused him to reassess his life, and by the early 1930s, he had dedicated himself to sacred music. What he had learned in the entertainment business as a composer and performer of blues numbers he applied to his new vocation. He composed a number of gospel songs, the most famous of which was "Take My Hand, Precious Lord." Dorsey was a tireless promoter of gospel and his own songs; he hoped to get black churches, the numerous Baptists in particular, to create gospel choirs and, not coincidentally, buy his sheet music. It was tough going; the established black churches in Chicago and many other places were in the firm control of the uplifters who saw the exuberance of the music as too much like the old style worship that they had worked to eliminate. As the Reverend J. C. Austin told his congregation at Pilgrim Baptist Church, an established Chicago church housed in an impressive sanctuary that originally had served as a synagogue, "We are intelligent folk here, and we don't do a lot of hollering and carrying on." But Chicago was receiving on a daily basis hundreds of new migrants from the rural South who were accustomed to a bit of "hollering and carrying on."[94] The Great Depression was in full force, and the restrained and proper hymns they heard in many of Chicago's black churches weren't reaching them, especially in those desperate times. Dorsey had convinced the pastor of a small church to let him start a gospel choir, which became quite popular and began making appearances at other churches. The evident enthusiasm that greeted this choir when it appeared at Pilgrim convinced the Reverend Austin to hire Dorsey to start a gospel choir at his church. The regular choir director resigned; in his opinion, Dorsey's music was "alley junk."[95] Alley junk or not, Dorsey was even more successful with the Pilgrim gospel choir, and success beget more success, in Chicago and around the country. Churches by the score formed gospel choirs. Dorsey established the National Convention of Gospel Choirs and Choruses to promote gospel by holding music conventions in cities across the country; he served as president for 30 years. This organization and the tireless work of Dorsey's right hand, Sallie Martin, of gospel songwriter Lucie Campbell, and of other true believers in the music gradually weakened

---

93. Arthur Kempton, *Boogaloo: The Quintessence of American Popular Music* (New York: Pantheon Books, 2003), 10–13, 24–25, 32–33.

94. *Ibid.*, 37.

95. *Ibid.*, 38–39; quote p. 39.

opposition to gospel as legitimate church music in the Baptist denominations and established Chicago as the headquarters of black gospel. After World War II, gospel would achieve the legitimacy in the black community that Dorsey had always hoped for; middle class uplifters had ceased to actively oppose it, and the music became widely accepted as both "sacred music and an icon of black heritage."[96]

While gospel choirs of the sort led by Thomas Dorsey and female soloists like Sister Rosetta Tharp and later Mahalia Jackson played a major role in black gospel, gospel quartets were also tremendously popular. Just as in the white gospel world, people with the ability to sing formed local quartets across the country that sang for church suppers, family reunions and so forth; a small number of these groups went professional, with the most successful touring the nation and cutting records. A quartet might actually number five or six singers but was still commonly referred to as a quartet; most were all male. There were some female and mixed groups, too; for example, in rural Caswell County, North Carolina, several quartets composed of a father and his daughters performed locally in the 1930s and 1940s.[97] Gospel quartets often sang a capella, their focus firmly set on harmony just like their white counterparts in the gospel world. The "Big Three" of the touring black gospel groups during the heyday of the quartets in the 1940s and 1950s were the Pilgrim Travelers, the Soul Stirrers, and the Five Blind Boys of Mississippi, but there were at least a dozen or so other nationally known groups and hundreds of less well-known groups trying to break into the big-time.[98]

The quartets reflected the grounding of gospel in the sanctified church; the music quartets sang was supposed to be heart-felt, a tool to help listeners get the spirit and not mere entertainment. The top groups were "certified 'house-wreckers'" (a term used in the business) who would deliver performances that would reduce those in attendance, the women especially, into crying, shouting abandon.[99] Singers took pride in their ability to "slay" their audiences and would push themselves and their voices to the limit; Archie Brownlee of the Five Blind Boys of Mississippi dove off stages into the audience and once even checked himself out of a hospital where was being treated for exhaustion and alcoholism so that he could perform. When several groups appeared at the same venue, each would try to outdo the others. While laboring in the service of the Lord, the most popular quartets and singers were, nonetheless, treated

---

96. *Ibid.*, 41–45; Jackson, *Singing in my Soul*, 50–68, quote p. 104; Harvey, *Freedom's Coming*,163–164.

97. Hinson, Liner Notes, in The Badgett Sisters, *Just a Little While to Stay Here.*

98. Peter Guralnick, *Sweet Soul Music: Rhythm and Blues and the Southern Dream of Freedom* (Boston: Little, Brown and Co., 1999), 30.

99. Kempton, *Boogaloo*, 83.

like stars; the pay was meager compared to what secular music stars made, but the other rewards—adulation, applause, and sexual favors—were similar.[100]

The Soul Stirrers, a group established in Texas in the early 1930s, would have, perhaps, the most far reaching influence.[101] The Soul Stirrers' lead singer, R. H. (Rebert) Harris, had grown up singing shape note songs; under his leadership, the group developed a new style with a strong lead singer (himself) parrying lyrics with the second lead. Harris would ad lib and repeat key words in a song, and would sing slightly behind the rest of the group creating "irresistible syncopations." Harris quit the group in 1950, troubled by the classic concern of gospel performers. As he told one writer, "The moral aspects of the thing just fell out of the water." Harris would be replaced by Sam Cooke, a young man (just 20 when he joined the group) originally from Clarksdale, Mississippi, and a member of a young group patterned after the Soul Stirrers called the Highway QCs. Like many in the gospel world, Cooke had come from a background in the sanctified church; his father was a minister who had taken his family to Chicago when Cook was young. Cooke's first recording with the Soul Stirrers was in 1951, and his performance on the song "Jesus Gave Me Water" demonstrated that the young kid was going to be a worthy successor to R. H. Harris. Like Harris, Cooke was no shouter; if anything, he was even smoother than Harris, totally at ease, effortlessly stretching a syllable over several notes; his style was sophisticated, but it suggested to listeners that "an indefinable depth of feeling" lurked beneath his cool demeanor. And he had that appeal to young people. It would be Cooke who would be the first gospel star to take the smooth harmonies of gospel over into the secular music world of rhythm and blues.[102]

Rhythm and blues (R & B) would emerge in the cities of the post-World War II South and North. It would mix straight ahead blues, gospel, and even a bit of jazz and create music with a driving beat and a wide variety of styles. The smooth harmonies of the gospel quartet tradition, the powerful rhythms of the gospel chorus, the gritty, mournful vocalizations of the blues, the jamming jazz combo all would find a place in rhythm and blues. The electrified blues played by artists like Muddy Waters and the smoother sounds coming from artists like Louis Jordan were the earliest forms of R & B and generally featured a strong backbeat. A gospel derived R & B also made its appearance after World War II with male quartets (the groups often actually numbered 5 or 6) like the Ravens, the Orioles, and the Dominoes. These groups took the smooth harmonies of the gospel quartets and "secularized" them, often by simply substituting "baby" or "darling" for "Jesus" in the lyrics of a gospel tune. To

100. *Ibid.*, 81,84, 89, 93.
101. Peter Guralnick, *Sweet Soul Music*, 30.
102. *Ibid.*, 28–36; quotes pp. 30 and 32.

listen to a Soul Stirrers' album of songs from the early 1950s is to hear the source music for the Dominoes or later the Four Tops or Temptations. Ray Charles, a blind young man from Albany, Georgia, came out with a song "I Got a Woman" in 1954 that really launched the gospel/blues blend that would become mainstream R & B. Charles had started his career trying to emulate the smooth sounds of Nat King Cole and claimed to have stumbled on his new sound, but his career suggests it was more than a stumble, and Charles would play a major role in American popular music for nearly fifty years.[103] R & B took off after that, and a host of performers and groups began playing the music; some, like James Brown and the Famous Flames and Solomon Burke, came directly from the gospel world, while others, like Jackie Wilson, front man for the Dominoes, were simply professional entertainers who liked the sound and saw a good thing. Some, like Burke, were from the cities of the North, where, by the late 1940s, a sizable and growing percentage of the nation's black population resided, but R & B would always have a strong Southern contingent of performers, and even the Northern born performers often seemed like Southerners in exile.

R & B's audience was primarily black, in part, because record companies practiced a strict racial division when they marketed music; black artists were marketed to blacks, and white artists to whites (and to blacks if they were interested). However, there was always quite a bit of "crossing over" by the record buying white public if a black artist had a catchy tune. By the 1950s, the youth market was taking off, and a growing percentage of record buyers were white teenagers, especially teenaged girls. Marketing a black male artist to white teenaged girls was a real powderkeg for record companies trying to stay on the right side of segregation, and so if a record company saw that a song by a black artist seemed to be selling well, record companies produced a "cover" version of it by a white artist like Pat Boone. Boone, with his big smile, clean-cut good looks, and white buck shoes was a safe conveyer of Negro music to young white girls and was a popular cover artist. But change was in the wind. The big breakthrough for an R & B song by a black artist was Sam Cooke's "You Send Me" which came out in 1957; it hit number three on the Billboard pop chart and overwhelmed the cover versions by whites which quickly came out.[104] Cooke was the first black artist to garner a large white audience; his sophistication, good looks, and smooth style made him the ideal candidate for a black star in a white world, and he flourished. That he died a violent death in scandalous circumstances did not alter the path-breaking work he had done to break down discriminatory practices in the music business.

At the time Sam Cooke had his big crossover hit, a new form of R & B was being churned out by both white and black performers. When white perform-

---

103. *Ibid.*, 21–27, 63.
104. Kempton, *Boogaloo*, 108.

ers like Elvis Presley were playing it, it was initially called rockabilly to distance it from R & B, but it was still R & B. It would come to be called rock and roll or just rock. Big Joe Turner described it as R & B that had been "pepped … up"; as Elvis and some of the early white rock and rollers played it, it had some country style guitar work and a bit of the country twang, too.[105] Black performers like Little Richard and Chuck Berry also were performing the pepped up version of R & B, and they too got some of the crossover business and helped weaken the racial segregation of the marketing of music. Rock and roll would become the dominant form of popular music in the United States and much of the rest of the world, a position it still holds. Rock would continually be reinvigorated by new transfusions of fresh ideas from the blues, jazz, gospel, and country, the blues especially. Its most explosive period was in the 1960s and 1970s when a number of rockers, the British especially, rediscovered the blues and grounded their guitar-driven take on rock with a heavy dose of delta blues; Eric Clapton, Led Zeppelin, and the Rolling Stones owed a tremendous debt to such blues artists as Robert Johnson and Muddy Waters. Despite the early contributions of Berry, Little Richard, and others, rock was a predominately white offshoot of R & B with few, albeit significant, exceptions (Jimi Hendrix being a giant exception) and more an American (and British) art form than primarily a Southern art form, although a branch of it would come to be called Southern rock.

Southern rock, exemplified by groups like the Allman Brothers and Lynyrd Skynyrd, would emerge in the late 1960s and early 1970s fed by the country tradition, blues, and R & B, especially the R & B coming out of the Fame Studio in Muscle Shoals, Alabama. Skynyrd would produce music heavy on the guitar work; probably their best work was "Free Bird," which featured the electric guitar solo to end all electric guitar solos. The Allman Brothers Band was headed by Duane Allman. Allman had done session work at Fame with R & B star Wilson Pickett where he attracted the attention of Phil Walden, the manager of R & B star Otis Redding. With Walden's support, he formed a band with his brother Gregg, Dickie Betts, and several others.[106] This band played a hard-driving style of bass-oriented music, heavy on the blues, a style best exemplified by the rock classic "Whipping Post." Other examples of bands that played Southern rock include the Texas group ZZ Top and, more recently, the alternative rock bands Southern Culture on the Skids and Drive By Truckers.

While rock and roll would find a receptive audience among Southern white youth in the 1950s and 1960s, a significant number of them would be drawn to

105. Guralnick, *Sweet Soul Music*, 27.
106. *Ibid.*, 376–377.

R & B. Renegade white DJs like Memphis's Dewey Phillips played black artists on their programs and began reaching larger and larger white audiences, and inquisitive white teenagers tuned into black radio stations to hear "the real thing."[107] At Carolina Beach, North Carolina, a hole-in-the-wall dive called the Tijuana Inn had begun playing black R & B music for white, working class patrons after World War II; the beach was a place to go to drink and fight (and do something else, too), a place where home proprieties were temporarily left behind, and this new "negro" music fit the bill for the Inn's clientele and was good to dance to. Eventually, the authorities closed the place down, and its proprietors moved their club down the coast to the vicinity of Myrtle Beach and Ocean Drive in South Carolina. The music became upwardly mobile, and Ocean Drive became known thereafter by young (and later aging) middle class whites across the Carolinas and beyond as the place to go to hear the smooth, upbeat dance-oriented form of R & B that was euphemistically called "beach music" and to learn the latest steps of the curious shuffling, twirling dance called "the shag" that was paired with the music.[108] The Tams, The Drifters, The Dominoes, and The Platters all became popular "beach music" groups.

By the 1960s, legions of young white Southerners were unabashed fans of R & B and watching black performers at clubs and fraternity houses throughout the South. In Memphis, the Plantation Inn in West Memphis achieved fame as the place to go (for whites) to hear black bands; even in the small town of Darlington, South Carolina, circa mid-1960s, there were three clubs—the Coachman, the Po Boy Club, and the Hatchery—operating within a 30-mile radius that catered to young white audiences and featured black R & B acts like The Tams, The Drifters, Jackie Wilson, and more obscure performers like Lee Dorsey and Clifford Curry. These were outlaw places for outlaw music; no one was ever carded at the Po Boy Club when he ordered beer, and the young white couples, girls in Villager dresses, boys in Weejan loafers and V-neck sweaters, back pockets bulging with pint bottles of bourbon, swayed to the music, laughed at the sexual innuendos in the lyrics, and cheered the black performers. For many Southern white young people, black R & B had become their music, a development that undercut segregation's insistence on the superiority of all things white.

While R & B was a musical form rooted in Southern musical traditions, and most of the best of it, the real deal, came from the South, the black migration made it a national music coming out of the cities where these migrants lived, and each city produced, for a time, its own style. In Chicago, there was the

---

107. Peter Guralnick, *Last Train to Memphis*, 4–7, 97–98; Guralnick, *Sweet Soul Music*, 111.

108. Rev. Billy C. Wirtz, "Washed ashore: the long, strange story of beach music," *Independent* (Durham, NC), 5–11 July 2000.

smooth style sung by such artists as Jerry Butler and Lou Rawls; the Philadelphia sound was noted for harmonies; Detroit's Motown produced a bevy of well-dressed, well-coifed, carefully coached acts—The Temptations, The Four Tops, The Supremes—that sang polished, highly produced music that sold well in the white market. Berry Gordy, the head of Motown, was the master of crossover and making a buck and, apparently, of treating his artists like croppers.[109] These Northern centers were fed by a steady stream of singers and groups from the South who trooped north hoping to make it in the big time. James Brown was one of these performers. Brown, reared in Augusta, Georgia, had started with a gospel group, had switched to R & B and had gotten together a band—The Flames—composed of other former gospel performers. His version of R & B was heavily influenced by straight-ahead gospel with his voice leading and The Flames responding, call-and-response style, and his show was like a revival service, Brown working himself to the point of exhaustion (he called himself "the hardest working man in show business"), being led off the stage, and then returning for a high-energy encore that had the crowd screaming for more. But the North and West produced their share of performers such as Solomon Burke, Marvin Gaye (from Washington, D.C.), Tammi Terell, Smokey Robinson, and the daughter of a prominent Detroit minister by the name of Aretha Franklin. The South did have, for a time, several centers of R & B that hosted small record labels that achieved fame for the gritty, bluesy kind of R & B that many still consider the best version of the music. One was at Muscle Shoals, Alabama, where the Fame studio hit it big when Percy Sledge's "When a Man Loves a Woman" was recorded there in 1966 and became famous thereafter for its superb cast of session musicians including Spooner Oldham and Donnie Fritts.[110] But the first center to emerge and the most influential on Southern style R & B was in Memphis, and the record label producing the records was Stax.

Stax was started in Memphis by Jim Stewart and Estelle Axton, a white brother-and-sister team who wanted to get into the music business and make records, of what sort they weren't sure. In 1960 they acquired a run-down theater in a predominantly black part of Memphis that was to serve as their headquarters. Estelle's son Packy and his friends had a group they had started in high school called The Four Spades, and they began hanging around. Estelle Axton also ran a record store at the site, and several kids from the local black high school, Booker T. Washington, also began hanging around. Here would be the nucleus of one of the most famous house bands in R & B, variously known as The Memphis Horns, The Mar-Keys, The Bar-Kays, and Booker T. and the MGs. Literally because it was in a black neighborhood, Stax drifted to

---

109. Kempton, *Boogaloo*, 253–286.
110. Guralnick, *Sweet Soul Music*, 186–219.

recording black artists starting with Rufus Thomas, a Memphis DJ, and then his daughter, Carla Thomas. The company's first real hit was a little tune Carla had written called "Gee Whiz," which she considered childish (she had written it when she was a teenager), but it had nice sound and a good hook, and Stax

Figure 8.3   Stax Museum
(The entrance is a reconstruction of the original Stax building façade.)

was off.[111] Amazingly, in a region that was in the midst of a virtual race war, the talented team that slowly assembled at Stax in the early to mid-1960s was composed of black and white musicians, writers and producers, much of it drawn from the neighborhood and from Packy Axton's high school band mates. (The Fame studio was also integrated.) Isaac Hayes, Steve Cropper, Duck Dunn, David Porter, Al Bell, Al Jackson, Booker T. Jones, Chips Moman and others would play key roles in developing the unique Stax sound which featured a strong horn section, driving rhythms, and a strong blues base. They were all, with the exception of Al Bell and Chips Moman, amateurs who were learning as they went.

Otis Redding would become the catalyst who brought it all together at Stax. Redding was from Macon, Georgia, and had a powerful, expressive voice. Like most beginners, he struggled to make a go of it in the music business and struggled to find his personal style, without which no performer can ever be more than mediocre. Initially, he patterned himself after Little Richard, and Duck Dunn recalled asking, "Who wants another Little Richard?" Redding did a few recording sessions at Stax in 1962 and won converts at the company (Steve Cropper called him "incredible") and by 1963 began to hit his stride. His self-assurance and growing competence drew together the Stax artists and writers who gave him their trust and support. Booker T. Jones said, "He was a leader. He'd just lead with his arms and his body and his fingers."[112] The music mogul Jerry Wexler called him "a natural prince." And so he was. He wrote a number of songs, some in conjunction with Steve Cropper, and did his own take on songs by Sam Cooke and other R & B greats. "Respect," "These Arms of Mine," and "(Sittin' on) the Dock of the Bay" all were written or co-written by Redding.[113] He took the song "Satisfaction" and, backed by Stax's horn section, did a version of it that the English boys who had written it and originally recorded it (The Rolling Stones) could only dream of emulating. Some thought The Stones had gotten the song from him.[114] His version of "Try a Little Tenderness" may very well be the greatest R & B song ever recorded.

Other artists trooped to Memphis to record with Stax, many sent there by Jerry Wexler at Atlantic Records in New York, which had a partnership with Stax. Wilson Pickett arrived one day, and in one session worked out with Steve Cropper the lyrics and tune to the R & B classic "In the Midnight Hour." Sam and Dave, a duo that did an electrifying stage show that even Redding claimed he couldn't keep up with, recorded a series of hits with Stax. The most memorable was "Hold On, I'm Coming," a song written by Isaac Hayes and David

---

111. *Ibid.*, 104
112. *Ibid.*, 131–142, quotes, p. 131.
113. *Ibid.*, 142–151, quote, p. 149.
114. *Ibid.*, 149.

Porter that encapsulated in a few short minutes almost the entire history of black music with its gospel laced blues sound and "call-and-response" vocals.[115] Stax would lose its prince when Otis Redding died in a plane crash just days after recording "(Sittin' on) the Dock of the Bay" in December of 1967; most of the Stax studio group, The Bar-Kays, also died in the crash. Redding's new song, which he had co-written with Steve Cropper, become a major hit on both the R & B and pop charts and would have carried him to new heights had he lived. Stax would have other successes, most notably with Isaac Hayes, who went full time into performing and took the Stax sound in a more pop direction. The productive working relationship between blacks and whites at Stax began to falter after the assassination of Martin Luther King, Jr., in Memphis in 1968, and the riots that followed left Stax brothers eying each other suspiciously. Ultimately, Stax would run afoul of its New York partners and fold, a little fish unable to swim with the big fish of New York.[116]

As the small regional labels disappeared or were bought out, the regional sounds of R & B would fade. The music would grow more polished with performers and groups like Diana Ross (who began with the Supremes), Whitney Houston, Mariah Carey, Prince, and Earth, Wind and Fire taking it to new heights of sophistication, musical virtuosity, and high production values. All of these performers and the more pop-oriented entertainers like Michael Jackson (who began at Motown) were popular with a wide cross section of Americans, and so an element of the music had truly become mainstream American music. But R & B was aging and the record buying public, in a trend that began in the 1950s, was heavily tilted toward young people who now had—thanks to the explosion in service industry jobs employing teenagers—growing amounts of disposable income to spend on recorded music. What many of them began listening to in the early 1980s was a new musical form coming from the cities of the North and the West Coast called rap and later hip hop. The music was a product of young black males for the most part, many of whom affected the pose of ghetto born and raised hoodlums (some were and some weren't) with a penchant for guns, four letter words, and less than pleasant things to say about women. The music would horrify their elders, white and black (just like the blues and rock had done), but would prove and still proves to be immensely popular with young people of both races. Southern versions of it such as "dirty South" and "crunk" developed by the late 1990s, particularly in the major cities of the South (Atlanta and New Orleans, especially). Southern rap artists that achieved some level of prominence include Geto Boys, Petey Pablo, Outkast, Missy Elliott, Bubba Sparxxx, and Ludacris. Hip Hop is derivative of R & B and much of it has been based on electronic "sampling" of pieces of a wide range of

---

115. *Ibid.*, 159–160, 166, quote, p. 159.
116. *Ibid.*, 323–331, 380–394; Kempton, *Boogaloo*, 287–318.

older R & B songs, especially the work of George Clinton, and as such may be the final phase in the evolution of R & B.[117]

Literature

People create literature to explain and to amuse. Great literature does these things in fine fashion; the writing is a thing of beauty, which is satisfying in and of itself, and buried within it are small or large truths that the author has struggled to uncover and share with the reader. What we commonly define as literature—fiction, poetry, essays, memoirs and the like—was not, by most standards, produced in abundance in the South prior to 1900, and great literature even less so; in that respect H. L. Mencken was correct. But there is another way to explain and amuse, and that is storytelling. The region would sustain a strong storytelling tradition well into the twentieth century. Folk tales like the mountain "Jack tales," stories from African-American culture (some set to music) about bad men like Staggerlee and wily animals, and the sort of rich descriptions of people, places, and events that passed for entertainment in an agrarian culture were all part of this tradition. Even today, most small towns support a complement of local "characters" noted for their colorful stories of ill-fated fishing trips and exploding canned goods, complete with sound effects and clever approximations of how local town figures talk and behave. This storytelling tradition, and its inherent rootedness in place and the social and familial connections and relationships that define the meaning of place over time would feed the Southern literary tradition. The strong pull of history—of family, locale, region—would also feed this tradition. History was still relevant in the South long after it had become, in Henry Ford's words, "bunk" in the rest of the country, perhaps because a more stable agrarian culture persisted longer in the South than elsewhere, and perhaps because, as historian C. Vann Woodward has suggested, the South experienced bitter military defeat that forced Southerners to acknowledge and respect history.

The earliest Southern writers were essayists, historians, and social geographers. Captain John Smith wrote a history of early Virginia, and William Byrd wrote a history of the expedition that surveyed the boundary between Virginia and North Carolina. Thomas Jefferson would later write on a variety of subjects, including the history and economy of Virginia and political philosophy. He would author the Declaration of Independence and the Virginia Bill of Rights. As the Civil War approached, essayists, and memoirists turned their at-

---

117. Kempton, *Boogaloo*, 354–447; "Southern Rap," *Wikipedia: The Free Encyclopedia*, http://en.wikipedia.org/wiki/Southern_rap (accessed 6/10/06)

tention to slavery. James Henry Hammond and George Fitzhugh authored works that defended slavery and the Southern way of life. Several works by former slaves, most notably Harriet Jacobs's *Incidents in the Life of a Slave Girl* published in 1861 and Frederick Douglass's *Narrative of the Life of Frederick Douglass* published in 1845 both attacked slavery and questioned the moral character of a society that sustained it.

A small number of writers of fiction and poetry would make their appearance in the region in the years before the Civil War. Most are what we now call local color writers who specialized in describing, often humorously and in great detail, their own locales and the people who lived there, and attempting to approximate local dialect, especially the dialects of poor whites and blacks. A. B. Longstreet introduced readers of his book *Georgia Scenes* to characters like Ransy Sniffle, an odd little man representing poor whites at their worst, and Johnson Jones Hooper introduced his readers to Captain Simon Suggs, a frontier con man. In one story Suggs attends a camp meeting and fakes a conversion experience, telling those assembled that he had originally come to the meeting to "play some trick to turn it all into redecule" but "that brother spoke a word that struck me kleen to the heart, and run all over me like fire in dry grass." Suggs then solicits funds to start his own church and rides off merrily with his loot, comparing his con with the soul saving business; as he says, "They're peart at the same snap game, theyselves."[118]

South Carolinian William Gilmore Simms was, at the time, the most famous of the Southern writers of fiction. Simms was most noted for novels depicting the planter class, of which he was part, and was one of several Southern writers who chronicled the plantation and the stories of its inhabitants. Simms at his best honestly captured the details of the life on the plantation and the class distinctions that separated white Southerners, but for the most part his work glorifies the planter class and romanticizes the plantation lifestyle and slavery. Edgar Allen Poe was the opposite of Simms; he never took much of an interest in the plantation or agrarian culture of the South; while Simms was quite popular and the unofficial poet laureate of the South, Poe was always an outsider who struggled to get published and whose work was dismissed by respectable people. But Simms's work would not stand the test of time and Poe's would. Poe was actually an adopted Southerner who had been born in Boston but grew up in Virginia. His short stories like "The Tell Tale Heart," "The Pit and the Pendulum," and his poems like "The Raven" are well known today as the starting point for the horror genre of fiction in America, although some

---

118. Johnson Jones Hooper, Excerpt, *Some Adventures of Captain Simon Suggs, Late of the Tallapoosa Volunteers*, in William L. Andrews, general editor, *The Literature of the American South* (New York: W.W. Norton & Co., 1998), 161–168; quotes, pp. 165 and 168.

have found in his "The Fall of the House of Usher" an allegory of the corruption afflicting the South that would ultimately bring its downfall.[119]

After the Civil War, the region supported a sizable number of local color writers, many of whom reminisced in essays, memoirs, and fiction about the lost world of the old South. Joel Chandler Harris's *Uncle Remus Tales* and Thomas Nelson Page's *In Ole Virginia* are examples of this style of writing. One of the local color writers, Kate Chopin, was, in retrospect, more than meets the eye and went far beyond the normal boundaries of the genre. Chopin focused on the lives of Louisiana's Creole planters, but she also explored racial issues and, in works such as *The Awakening*, she examined traditional gender roles and the hard choices these roles forced on women.[120] Virginia's Ellen Glasgow also emerged as a significant writer by the turn of the twentieth century as a chronicler of the lives of "ordinary white people and their problems" in such books as *The Voice of the People* and *Barren Ground*.[121] Significant works of fiction by African Americans also began appearing. Charles Chesnutt, originally from Ohio but a long-time resident of North Carolina, wrote challenging novels examining the role of race in the South with a novel on the Wilmington race riot (*The Marrow of Tradition*) and a novel on one of the most controversial topic in the South, the practice of "passing" for white by the light skinned progeny of mixed race relationships (*The House Behind the Cedars*).[122] James Weldon Johnson explored the same topic in *The Autobiography of an Ex-Colored Man*. Johnson was also a poet and the author of "Lift Every Voice and Sing," the unofficial anthem of contemporary black America.[123]

The giant of the postbellum southern writers was Missouri-born Sam Clemens, otherwise known as Mark Twain. Twain would, of course, come to be seen as an American writer, arguably the greatest American writer, but much of his writing clearly derived from his roots in the South and the local color literary tradition of the South, and several of his best novels and short stories are set in the South and have much to say about Southern culture. His masterpiece, *Adventures of Huckleberry Finn*, is a tour de force in the effective use of the techniques of the local color tradition and the use of dialect. But the book is much more; it is an epic adventure on the Mississippi River of the two main characters, Huck Finn, the son of a low-life drunkard, and Jim, a

---

119. Andrews, general editor, *The Literature of the American South*, 69–70, 97–100, 103–116.

120. *Ibid.*, 299–301; Kate Chopin, *The Awakening* (1899; Amherst, NY: Prometheus Books, 1996).

121. Jack Temple Kirby, *The Countercultural South* (Athens: The University of Georgia Press, 1995), 62.

122. Charles Chesnutt, *The House Behind the Cedars* (1900; London: The X Press, 1998); *The Marrow of Tradition* (1901; New York: Penguin Books, 1993).

123. Andrews, general editor, *The Literature of the American South*, 346.

runaway slave, and a biting satire and critique of Southern society and culture. Twain wants us to understand that the value system of Southern society, based as it was on slavery and misguided aristocratic pretensions, was a rather thin soup that did not sustain virtue and character. He sets his two main characters up against the more "respectable" people that they meet to make this case. At one point on their journey, Huck and Jim encounter the Grangerfords and Shephardsons, two families that are "high-toned, and well born, and rich and grand," who nonetheless are engaged in a senseless feud characterized by ambushes and bloody murder.[124] The pair's encounter with two con men called the king and the duke illuminates Twain's suspicion of the privileged and powerful and his democratic sensibilities. It becomes quite clear to Jim that the king and duke are not royalty but rascals, and Huck agrees, but tells Jim it doesn't matter because "all kings is mostly rapscallions, as fur as I can make out." [125] The reader realizes by the end of the book that the true aristocrats in the story by word and deed are Huck Finn and Jim. Slavery is portrayed as the biggest con; the indignities and inequities heaped on one group of people by another are shown time and again as absolutely arbitrary, unfair, and immoral.

By the 1920s, something of a literary revolution was in the works in the South; the region now had cities and towns, expanding industry and a growing middle class of educated professionals, all the ingredients necessary to sustain more writers. The revolution was touched off by a group of poets and essayists at Vanderbilt University in Nashville who began meeting to discuss their work and finally came out with a magazine called *The Fugitive*. They styled themselves literary revolutionaries who would cut loose from the stultifying customs of the tradition-bound South; a few short years later many of the more prominent of them had "done a 360," as they say today, and had published a collection of essays entitled *I'll Take My Stand* in which they vigorously defended the very stultifying customs of the tradition-bound South they had once condemned. Several of the authors would go on to influential careers as poets, literary critics, and novelists, most notably John Crow Ransom and Robert Penn Warren.[126] Ransom would write some fine poetry and help invent the new literary criticism that would dominate the way American literature professors studied literature for decades. Warren would write poetry, short stories and one of the truly great political novels, *All the King's Men*. This novel is the story

---

124. Mark Twain, *Adventures of Huckleberry Finn* (1885; New York: Modern Library Paperback Edition, 2001), 90.

125. *Ibid.*, 129.

126. Andrews, general editor, *The Literature of the American South*, 249; Twelve Southerners, *I'll Take My Stand* (1930; Baton Rouge and London: Louisiana State University Press, 1977).

of a Huey Long type figure's rise and fall and is the classic account of the Southern demagogue politician.[127]

Notable African-American writers also emerged in the decades following the world war, many of them inspired by the intellectual and creative ferment in New York that has come to be called the Harlem Renaissance. Three of the most influential were Jean Toomer, Zora Neale Hurston, and Richard Wright. Toomer was the least productive of the three, but his one notable work—*Cane*—is a wonderful collection of poems and stories that explores black life in the South as Toomer, who was born and raised in Washington, D.C. and lived much of his life in the less rigidly segregated environment of the North, imagined it.[128] Hurston wrote a series of books, some fiction some nonfiction, with *Their Eyes Were Watching God* standing as her enduring masterpiece. Hurston was Florida born and traveled extensively, spending part of her adult life in New York where, like Toomer, she became part of the group of artists and intellectuals that made up the Harlem Renaissance. Hurston was, like many Southern writers, intrigued by the local dialects of the South. *Their Eyes Were Watching God* was largely written in dialect. It is the story of a woman who starts life anew with a much younger man after her overbearing and status-obsessed husband has died. In one sense, it is a classic tale of a woman giving up everything for her man; her new husband is poor and they support themselves as farm workers, a big change from her previous status as the wife of a successful businessman and local political leader. In another sense, it is a feminist tale of a woman ignoring societal conventions to have what she wants. That it ends in misfortune does not, for the heroine, alter the rightness of her choice.[129] Hurston's writing, like Toomer's, is beautifully crafted, and her portrait of black life in the South is both tragic and compelling, a sort of literary version of the blues where her characters are caught by circumstances beyond their control, and yet they forbear and seize, if only for a moment, a bit of happiness.

Richard Wright was the chronicler of Jim Crow, capturing its brutality and tragedy in both fiction and nonfiction, much of it published in the late 1930s and early 1940s. His autobiography, *Black Boy*, is a horrific account of the indignities and dangers facing a black man living in the segregated South. Wright discovered early in life that Jim Crow was something he simply could not adapt to. As a friend told him, "You act around white people as if you didn't know they were white. And they see it."[130] His most notable novel was *Native Son*, a

---

127. Robert Penn Warren, *All the King's Men* (1946; San Diego: A Harvest/HBJ Book, 1974).

128. Andrews, general editor, *The Literature of the American South*, 424–425.

129. Zora Neale Hurston *Their Eyes Were Watching God* (1937; New York: Perennial Library, 1990).

130. Richard Wright, *Black Boy* (1945; New York: Harper and Row, 1966), 203.

dark story of a Mississippi migrant to Chicago, like himself, who accidentally kills a young white girl and, knowing no explanation will ever serve, attempts to cover up her death. The novel generated storms of controversy about the topic and the stereotypes that it seemed to confirm, but at bottom Wright's in-

Carl Van Vechten

Figure 8.4   Zora Neale Hurston

terest was in exploring how segregation, even segregation in the more tolerant North, was a soul-destroying institution.[131] Wright himself would ultimately leave the United States and spend the rest of his life in France.

Other writers also were important in this Southern literary renaissance— Thomas Wolfe, James Agee, and Erskine Caldwell were three of the most noted. Caldwell was the most popular of the three and wrote a series of wildly popular books— *Tobacco Road* is the most famous—exploring in graphic detail the trials, tribulations, and sexual peccadilloes of the poor, a group that Agee wrote about more sympathetically in *Let Us Now Praise Famous Men*. Margaret Mitchell is often not considered a "serious" novelist, but *Gone with the Wind*—both the book and the film—were and still are tremendously popular. Mitchell's book is filled with every stereotype imaginable and plays fast and free with history, but if read as an exploration of the myths of the upper class South, it is very perceptive, and the story of Rhett and Scarlet is quite compelling.[132]

The giant of Southern literature to come out of this period, now residing with Twain at the peak of American literature, is William Faulkner. Faulkner was born in Mississippi in 1897 and spent most of his life in the small town of Oxford, although he traveled extensively and lived for a time in New Orleans (a common destination for many Southern writers), New York, and Paris.[133] He wrote poetry and short stories on a variety of subjects and developed a measured way of letting the narrative take its course in due time, and this at a time when Ernest Hemingway and other modern American writers were paring down their writing to the bare minimum. His greatest writing focused on a fictional piece of real estate in Mississippi that he called Yoknapatawpha County. Faulkner, like many Southern writers before and since, would try to understand "the human condition" by exploring the particulars, the details of the small part of the world he was most familiar with, and in so doing would establish one of the parameters of what "Southern" writing was and is. As Eudora Welty, another great Southern writer, observed, "But in the South, where people don't move about as much, even now, and where they once hardly ever moved away at all, the pattern of life was always right there."[134] For Faulkner, Southerners bore the burdens of a history and culture that created terrible tensions between men and women, rich and poor, and black and white. Violence was often the way this tension could be resolved. In *Light in August* he told the story of Joe Christmas, a mysterious stranger who comes to a small Southern

131. Richard Wright, *Native Son* (1940; New York: Perennial Library, 1989).

132. Margaret Mitchell, *Gone with the Wind* (1936; New York: Warner Books, 1993).

133. Andrews, general editor, *The Literature of the American South*, 435–437.

134. Interview with Eudora Welty by Linda Kuehl (1972), The DNA of Literature: The Complete Paris Review Interviews, http://www.parisreview.com/viewinterview.php/prm MID/4013 (accessed 11 May 2006).

Carl Van Vechten

Figure 8.5   Richard Wright

town. Christmas's history is uncertain; he is not even sure if he is black or white but suspects he is black. Because he is rootless and without history, he is deeply troubled and his presence is troubling to the town. In a cascading series of tragic events, Joe kills a woman who had become his lover and was trying to help him, and is castrated and killed by a lynch mob. For Faulkner, the lynching of Joe Christmas, like lynchings in general, amounted to a ritual sacrifice, an expiation of sins and a righting of the moral order that Christmas's appearance had disturbed.[135] In the short story "Barn Burning," Faulkner explored the tensions inherent in the inequitable class system of the South. The character Snopes is a sharecropper who simply cannot accept the poverty and the petty indignities his status dictates he must accept. His response is textbook passive aggressive behavior: he burns the barns of the people who he feels have disrespected him. Snopes moves his family to a new location after each incident, but his past, his history, always catch up with him, and some slight or disagreement leads to another barn in flames.[136]

Faulkner did not merely chronicle a society caught in its own history; he also explored the social ferment stirred by the decline of the countryside and the rise of the towns. For him, these towns offered common folk from the country opportunities to get ahead if they were cunning and ruthless enough; his fictional representatives of this new class were from the Snopes family, and they possessed the necessary qualities in spades. The old upper class in his stories is impotent to resist these changes. In "A Rose for Emily," Miss Emily Grierson, the daughter of a wealthy antebellum family, supports herself teaching painting in a big old house gone to seed. She's an object of pity and charity in the town, has a short fling with a man who is not her social equal (a Yankee road gang foreman) and is, as it turns out, quite mad.[137] In *The Sound and the Fury*, the aristocratic Compson family is in the process of decline; each member of the family is dysfunctional in his or her own way. The scion of the family, Quentin Compson, brings the decline to an end, for himself anyway, by committing suicide. It's the cunning, hard-driving Snopes who will rule the future, Faulkner was saying. Faulkner's view of the South was conflicted; he saw the tragedy and the damages the heavy hand of tradition had wrought but, like the authors of *I'll Take My Stand*, he also mourned the loss of gentility, the replacement of the personal by the impersonal, and the decline of the more deliberate pace of the agrarian lifestyle.

Following World War II, the South produced a host of writers rivaled in their prominence and productivity only by the Jewish writers coming from the cities of the North. Each in his or her own way explored a different aspect of the South, the writing grounded in the particular, on getting the details right. A bevy of female writers—Carson McCullers, Lillian Smith, Flannery O'Conner, and Eudora Welty—became prominent in the decades following the war,

---

135. Joel Williamson, *William Faulkner and Southern History* (New York: Oxford University Press, 1993), 365–382, 412–413.

136. William Faulkner, "Barn Burning" in *Collected Stories of William Faulkner* (New York: Vintage Books, 1977), 3–25.

137. Faulkner, "A Rose for Emily," in *Collected Stories of William Faulkner*, 119–130.

and Katherine Ann Porter, who emerged in the 1930s as a writer of note, continued to publish. Of this group, Flannery O'Conner is the most respected today. She produced two novels, *Wise Blood* and *The Violent Bear It Away*, and one collection of short stories, *A Good Man is Hard to Find*, during her relatively short life, which she spent almost entirely in Georgia. A second collection of short stories, *Everything That Rises Must Converge*, was published

Carl Van Vechten

Figure 8.6   William Faulkner

138. Andrews, general editor, *The Literature of the American South*, 815–818.

posthumously.[138] Although Catholic herself, many of O'Connor's characters struggle to find their way in the traditional Protestant religious culture of the South, experiencing faith, doubt, sacrifice, salvation, rebirth, and, ultimately, grace. Through ironic and often grotesque events, she exposes how Southerners limit and punish themselves through self-imposed constraints of social class, racial prejudice, gender stereotypes, and religious practices. Her stories highlight Southerners' ignorance, provincialism, and prejudice; however, in true Christian fashion, the characters always receive grace, whether or not it is recognized or accepted.

Ironically, perhaps the most influential female Southern writer of this era wrote only one book, and it was a short one at that, but Harper Lee's novel, *To Kill a Mockingbird*, would have a huge social impact and probably garner more readers than all the works of most other Southern writers combined. It is still widely read, with yearly sales reportedly hitting the million mark. The novel is set in a fictional small Alabama town in the 1930s and is the story of a black man unjustly accused of raping a white woman. It is told through the eyes of a small child, the daughter of the lawyer (Atticus Finch) who is defending the accused man. Despite its brevity, Lee is able to tell a compelling story and explore not only the inequities of the Southern racial tradition and a class system that victimizes the less fortunate, but the positive virtues of the code of honor as exemplified by Atticus Finch. Finch subscribes to the Stoic interpretation of the honor code, which stresses duty as the preeminent virtue; Finch does his duty, and, as we see as the book progresses, so do his children who have learned well from their father. The novel was made into a popular film starring Gregory Peck as Atticus, and both played some small part in preparing the white South for integration by providing Southern whites with a hero on the right side of the race issue with whom they could identify.[139]

An equally impressive group of male writers emerged led by Walker Percy, Tennessee Williams, and Ralph Ellison. Tennessee Williams became one of the nation's great playwrights. Williams was born in Mississippi in 1911, the child of a mother with some claim to upper class heritage and a traveling salesman father who was anything but refined. The family moved to St. Louis when he was a child, and he and his sister never really fit in there. He had had a life-threatening illness as a young child, and his mother became overly protective of him; his father was an alcoholic who ridiculed and abused him. He had a strong relationship with his sister, Rose, who gradually drifted into mental illness and eventually had a lobotomy. Williams himself would suffer a variety of psychological maladies and substance abuse problems throughout his life. His plays explored the tortured dynamics of dysfunctional Southern families, an interest undoubtedly coming from his own upbringing. His most intriguing

---

139. Harper Lee, *To Kill a Mockingbird* (Philadelphia: Lippincott, 1960).

characters were conflicted Southern belles who couldn't manage to live lives on a pedestal but couldn't bear the thought of not being on a pedestal. Williams dealt honestly in his work with sexuality, and this plus his openness about his own homosexuality made him a controversial figure. Two of his most famous plays, *A Streetcar Named Desire* and *Cat on a Hot Tin Roof,* were made into films starring major actors (Marlon Brando and Elizabeth Taylor).[140]

Ralph Ellison was not, strictly speaking, from the South; he was born in Oklahoma City, but both his parents were from the South. Oklahoma did practice segregation and have some degree of kinship with the South, and Ellison would attend college at Tuskegee in Alabama. Ellison was a one-book author (another did come out long after his death), but that book, *Invisible Man,* was a masterpiece. It explored how society marginalized black men and made them, in effect, invisible. As the unnamed lead character notes, "When they approach me they see only my surroundings, themselves, or figments of their imagination—indeed, everything and anything except me."[141] His grandfather tells him on his deathbed that blacks are at war with white society, a revelation he initially rejects in an effort to be the next Booker T. Washington. The speech he gives at his high school graduation wins him recognition, and he is invited to a gathering of local white notables, ostensibly to give his speech. Once he gets there, he discovers that he is also expected to fight other young black men, all against all, for the amusement of those assembled, with the last combatant standing getting a ten dollar prize. Ellison is telling us white society at large worked the same way, keeping blacks weak and divided. His character finally does give his speech, bloodied though he is, and the response is jeers and cat-calls from the drunken crowd. After this second humiliation, he is given a briefcase containing funds to go to college with the admonition to "help shape the destiny of your people." But college (the one he attends resembles Tuskegee) is another disappointment; he finds intrigue and "power struggles" that reveal that both the uplift-oriented president of the college and the powerful white liberal trustee are just as responsible in keeping blacks subservient as the more overt racists he has encountered.[142] Like Wright, Ellison finds that black acquiescence to segregation and racism is as soul-destroying as the more brutal aspects of the institution.

Walker Percy was the cousin and adopted son of William Alexander Percy, the author of *Lanterns on the Levee,* a memoir published in the 1930s that lamented the passing of the old planter aristocracy. Like his kinsman, Walker Percy was concerned about the disappearance of traditional values and virtues. While the elder Percy bemoaned the disappearance of the gentleman and his

140. Andrews, general editor, *The Literature of the American South,* 628–630.
141. Ralph Ellison, *Invisible Man* (1952; New York: Vintage Books, 1995), 3.
142. *Ibid.,* 32; Andrews, general editor, *The Literature of the American South,* 699.

replacement by common tradesmen and the values of the marketplace, Walker Percy's is a more nuanced view. For him the modern society of shopping malls, television, mobility, and suburban living promises more freedom and individuality, but "invisible authority"—science, experts, advertising, and psychotherapy—manipulate, control, and diminish the individual's autonomy.[143] The characters in his novels are typically from "old" Southern families but are cut loose from place, tradition and often family. They are free as birds, but unlike birds, they do not have a clue what to do. Binx Bolling in *The Moviegoer* piddles around as a stockbroker in a small branch office of his uncle's business in Gentilly, a suburb of New Orleans, dating and breaking up with each new office secretary, without a serious career, a family of his own, or a goal. Will Barrett, the lead character in *The Last Gentlemen*, is an anonymous soul living in New York working as a janitor while he tries to figure out what he should do with himself. Will Barrrett's great grandfather had been a man of action and honor and had stood down a Ku Klux Klan leader, but each succeeding generation had gotten further away from that sense of certainty and that grip on what being honorable means. Percy's heroes are suffering from alienation, a condition he believes is part and parcel of modern life. Percy, like Faulkner, is telling us that for all its flaws, the society of the agrarian South did produce certainties and people who believed in them.[144]

Recent decades have seen a tremendous surge in the number of Southern writers emerging, too many to be adequately discussed here, but we'll touch on a few. Many of these writers have come out of college and university writing programs, and many now have teaching positions at institutions of higher education. Some focus on specific Southern themes in their writing; others do not. Maya Angelou, Margaret Walker, and Nikki Giovanni are three black women who emerged as prominent writers in the 1970s. Giovanni is most noted for her poetry; her early writings focused on the national civil rights movement and the black struggle for power. Angelou's work is more grounded in the South; she produced several installments of her autobiography, the most well-known of which is the first, *I Know Why the Caged Birds Sing*, as well as a significant output of poetry. Margaret Walker was a teacher and poet who labored in relative obscurity for decades until her novel *Jubilee* was published in 1966. The novel is based on research she did on her own family history, much like Alex Haley's *Roots,* which came out several years later. Her signature poem

143. Linda Whitney Hobson, "The Study of Consciousness: An Interview with Walker Percy," originally published in *The Georgia Review*, 35 (Spring 1981), 51–60, The Walker Percy Project, http://www/ibiblio.org/wpercy/hobson.html.

144. Veronica Makowsky, "Walker Percy and Southern Literature," The Walker Percy Project, 1996, at http://www.ibiblio.org/wpercy/library.html (accessed 5/14/06); Walker Percy, *The Moviegoer* (New York: Ivy Books, 1961); *The Last Gentleman* (New York: Ivy Books, 1966).

"For My People," published in 1942, is both a celebration of African-American culture and an indictment of the people and institutions that oppress African Americans.[145]

Reynolds Price has written a series of novels exploring the intricacies of family relationships mostly set in eastern North Carolina where he was born and raised. One of his best novels is *Kate Vaiden*. Price has also written collections of poetry and several memoirs. Lee Smith's specialty is Appalachia, and most of her novels are set in that region. *Oral History* is one of the best and is a powerful saga of the Cantrell family, beginning with Almarine Cantrell, and told from multiple perspectives over the generations. In telling this family's story, the novel gives deep insights into mountain culture and where that culture is headed; one current-day descendent of Almarine Cantrell in the story, also named Almarine, is a successful Amway distributor and Junior Toastmaster Club president who is developing the land around the old home place in Hoot Owl Holler into Ghost-land, the "prettiest theme park east of Opryland."[146] The trials and tribulations of his ancestors have become grist for an amusement park. Fred Chappell also focuses on Appalachia in his novels and poems. His most widely known work is *I Am One of You Forever*. Clyde Edgerton is an author whose books explore the clash of cultures produced by a changing South, often in a humorous way. One of his best and funniest is *Raney*, which features two lead characters: Charles, an Atlanta-born, college-educated Episcopalian with modern ideas about race, sex, and family, and, Raney, his wife, who is a small-town Free Will Baptist guided by more traditional ideas and values. The two struggle with each other's beliefs, and at the end of the book, they reach some degree of rapprochement.[147]

Dorothy Allison, Harry Crews, and Tim McLaurin have written books about poor whites, a generally ignored or parodied group that these three authors, all from poor families, write about honestly and sympathetically. For Allison, the crushing weight of an upbringing in poverty often creates people who are psychologically wounded and unable to break free from their pasts. In her *Bastard out of Carolina*, the leading character is a young girl named Bone whose extended family is a hard-drinking, hard-fighting group that gives her reason to be both proud and ashamed. Bone is illegitimate, and the absence of her father's name on her birth certificate obsesses her mother, which only confirms for Bone, again and again, her lowly status. Bone is abused by her stepfather and finally almost killed by him. Nonetheless, at the end of the story, Bone's mother has decided to leave her and go with her husband despite what he has done. Bone wonders if she will be "as hungry for love, as desperate, de-

145. Andrews, general editor, *The Literature of the American South*, 721–724.

146. Lee Smith, *Oral History* (New York: Ballantine, 1983), 291–292.

147. Clyde Edgerton, *Raney* (New York: Ballantine Books, 1985).

148. Dorothy Allison, *Bastard out of Carolina* (New York: A Plume Book, 1993), 309.

termined, and ashamed" as her mother.[148] Allison, along with author Randall Kenan (*A Visitation of Spirits*), has also explored in her writing what it means to be gay in the South, a particularly daunting prospect given the prevalence of traditional attitudes about gender roles.

Two very different writers, both excellent craftsman and both from North Carolina, explore the pull of history on their characters. As one of them, Allan Gurganus, noted in an interview:

> But to have grown up ... we've talked about this before ... to have grown up in a house where four generations could walk through the door at any moment. You literally hear footfalls.... And it also gives you that sense, even if your family, like mine is old fashioned merchant family stock it's not exactly that we are the Cabots or the Lowells. We just owned that patch for a long time and paid our club dues and turned up at church and knew where we were going to be buried. Over enough generations, that really amounts to something. For a story teller it gives you a tremendous kind of fossil fuel, a tremendous sense of material and a tremendous kind of trajectory.... I grew up feeling and knowing ... that history is a daily force. We knew this because we lived with the burned monuments that Sherman had left behind.[149]

Gurganus first achieved prominence when his *Oldest Confederate Widow Tells All* was published in 1989. The novel is the story of Lucy Marsden, a woman born in 1885 who marries a much older man who is a veteran of the Civil War. Her story and that of the people who have touched her life in some way, both living and long dead, takes the reader back and forth through time, an epic story all told in a thicket of details.[150] David Payne has a written series of novels that feature characters in crisis; in *Early from the Dance*, a character returns to his North Carolina home place to confront a childhood tragedy that he had never resolved in his mind; in *Ruin Creek*, the subject is a loveless marriage and the damage it does to all; in *Gravesend Light*, the grown son of the unhappy married couple in *Ruin Creek* is now searching for his own identity.[151]

Probably the most well-known Southern contemporary authors are Alice Walker, Anne Rivers Siddons, Tom Wolfe, and Pat Conroy. Walker, the daughter of a black Georgia sharecropping family, has become one of the region's

149. Robert Birnbaum, "Interview with Allan Gurganus," The Narrative Thread, http://www.identitytheory.com/people/birnbaum29.html (accessed 5/19/06).

150. Allan Gurganus, *Oldest Living Confederate Widow Tells All* (New York: Alfred A. Knopf, 1989).

151. David Payne, *Early from the Dance* (New York: Doubleday, 1989); *Ruin Creek: A Novel* (New York: Plume, 2002); *Gravesend Light: A Novel* (New York: Doubleday, 2000).

and nation's most respected writers. Walker was active in the Civil Rights moment in the 1960s and dedicated herself and her writing to the broader goal of the "survival" of her people.[152] In her first novel, *The Third Life of Grange Copeland*, she explored how segregation and sharecropping had pressed down black men and how they in turn had taken out their frustrations on the women in their lives. In the essay "In Search of Our Mothers' Gardens," written shortly after this, she reflected on the truth in the folklore expression that black women were the "mule of the world." Black women had, she wrote, "been handed the burden that everyone else—everyone else—refused to carry."[153] *The Color Purple*, published in 1982, was her fullest exploration of these insights and is her signature work. It has become one of the most widely read contemporary works of fiction and a popular film and Broadway play. As a story of both racial and gender oppression, the book has earned Walker her share of criticism for its negative portrayal of black men. But *The Color Purple* really comes not so much from Walker's desire to chastise men as her desire to liberate black women. At the end of the novel, Celie, the chief character in the book, is saved from a life of abuse in part by herself and in part with the help of a friend—her husband's lover—who is a strong, independent woman.[154]

Pat Conroy and Anne Rivers Siddons are popular writers with book sales in the millions. Conroy is a master storyteller and a wonderful stylist of words, and this explains his appeal and why most of his books have been made into motion pictures. Conroy was a military brat, the son of a Southern mother and Northern father (the colonel), who spent much of his childhood traveling from base to base. The family finally ended up in Beaufort in the Low Country of South Carolina, and this area became the setting for his books. Conroy writes coming of age stories loosely based on his own history. Conroy is a man of liberal sensibilities, and he finds the strictures of race and class in the South unconscionable. His characters are often in rebellion; in *The Great Santini*, the rebellion is against an overbearing father; in *The Lords of Discipline*, the hero, a cadet at a military academy located in Charleston, rebels against a secret society of well-connected cadets that runs off undesirables at the academy who don't measure up to their standards.[155] The school is patterned after the Citadel, which Conroy attended. In *The Prince of Tides*, perhaps his best book, the lead character has repressed his personal history; in effect he has rebelled against who he is. He must confront this past—an upbringing in a dysfunc-

---

152. Andrews, general editor, *The Literature of the American South*, 1011–1013.

153. Alice Walker, "In Search of Our Mothers' Gardens," Andrews, general editor, *The Literature of the American South*, 1024–1032, quote p. 1028.

154. Alice Walker, *The Color Purple* (New York: Pocket Books, 1985).

155. Pat Conroy, *The Lords of Discipline* (1980; New York: Bantam Books, 2002); *The Great Santini* (1976; New York: Bantam Books, 2002).

tional family capped by a horrific event—to be whole and to help his even more troubled twin sister. While Conroy grew up without a permanent home, his characters are typically rooted in place in true Southern fashion and struggle with what that means. As the hero of *The Prince of Tides* says in the beginning lines of the book, "My wound is geography. It is also my anchorage, my port of call."[156]

Anne Rivers Siddons has more of a reputation as the writer of "page turners" read by women, but in her work she does focus on many of the traditional themes of Southern literature. In her best known work, *Peachtree Road*, she explores the inner secrets of a wealthy family living in a prestigious area of Buckhead, a tony suburb of Atlanta, during the 1960s. Siddons begins her novel with a famous line, "The South killed Lucy Bondurant Chastain Venable on the day she was born," a good line, but as a way of getting across the idea that history can be weighty, it's a bit hyperbolic and the sort of thing that gets Ms. Siddons snickered at. But things calm down a bit after that, and Siddons does a credible job of telling the story of two cousins, Lucy and Shem, who struggle and fail to measure up to upper class standards for men and women. They find temporary solace in an incestuous relationship with each other, and finally Shem flees Atlanta and the South, leaving Lucy behind to find her own escape in madness. All of this is happening against a backdrop of an Atlanta changing from a sleepy regional center into a major city and from a segregated city to an integrated one where blacks are more than maids and butlers.

Richmond-born Tom Wolfe turned to stories with Southern themes or sub themes late in his life as a writer. Wolfe has had a lengthy career beginning with several decades of work as a journalist, writing essays, articles, and books about liberal politics, the art world, modern architecture, the hippie movement of the 1960s, and astronauts. As a journalist, he worked hard to get the details right, and as a practitioner of the so-called new journalism, he didn't mind inserting himself into the pieces he wrote, with often hilarious results because Wolfe can be quite funny. At bottom, he's a conservative along the lines of H. L. Mencken, and he uses his wit and humor to skewer those he thinks are responsible for the decline of good taste, manners, and virtue, and to celebrate (as in *The Right Stuff*) the old virtues. *A Man in Full*, published in 1998, was his first foray into Southern literature and is the story of Charlie Croker, a small town boy who made good in the booming real estate market of modern day Atlanta. For Wolfe, the changes that have swept over Atlanta have left it without a moral and social center, and even the movers and shakers like Croker are rudderless. Croker desperately tries to

---

156. Pat Conroy, *The Prince of Tides* (Boston: Houghton Mifflin Company, 1986), 1.

create an identity for himself in this new society, weaving together the new (a new, much younger wife) and remnants from the old. So Croker has a hunting retreat called Turp'mtine that he's decked out like an old South plantation. When his real estate empire comes crashing down, he finds religion; however, it is not a religion he has roots in nor is it even a part of the South's religious tradition. It is, rather, the musings of another lost soul he has encountered. Wolfe's concern about the loss of civility and order shows up again in *I Am Charlotte Simmons*. Here Wolfe's target is college life and the young, and so the book is not primarily a "Southern" novel, but the book's heroine is from a working class family that lives in western North Carolina and the fictional DuPont University she is attending, while ostensibly in Pennsylvania, seems to be an awful lot like Duke University in Durham, North Carolina. One senses the sympathy he has for Charlotte's working class work ethic and old fashioned ideas about feminine virtue. At college, she's like a character from an English novel of the 1800s, defending her virtue in a school full of privileged, sex mad pagans with high SAT scores. She finally succumbs to one of her three suitors, a fall from grace that leaves her profoundly depressed.[157]

Whether intentional or not, Charlotte Simmons's seduction is a metaphor for the fate of Southern traditional values, and on this point Wolfe and Walker Percy would see eye to eye because neither seems to have much use for what modernism has brought us. More broadly, Simmons's struggle really is at the heart of Southern literature over the last one hundred and fifty years; much of that literature has focused on the clash between traditional values and customs and more modern values and customs. Whether this clash plays out in epic proportions such as in the novel and film *Gone with the Wind* or more modestly in the household of a small town husband and wife in the novel *Raney*, it seems to be the issue upon which many of the best novels (and films) are built. Not surprisingly, some writers like Wolfe and Percy viewed the decline of the traditional culture with sadness and even despair and viewed what is replacing it as, at best, confused, alienating and soulless and, at worst, a return to barbarism; others like Mark Twain or Clyde Edgerton or most African-American writers have seen the transformation in a more positive light or have urged on the change. One gets the sense that Faulkner mourned the decline of the traditional South for personal reasons—it had shaped him and he felt comfortable in it—but that he also believed that it really didn't work well for an awful lot of people. Given the continuing economic and social transformation of the South and the presence of a powerful movement in the region that opposes mod-

---

157. Tom Wolfe, *A Man in Full* (New York: Farrar, Straus, Giroux, 1998); *I Am Charlotte Simmons* (New York: Picador, 2004).

ernism in many of its particulars, the conflict of tradition and modernity will continue to draw the attention of many of the best Southern writers.

Icons, Myths, Symbols

Icons and myths are created in a culture when stories or images of things or people acquire a common meaning to many people. That meaning helps define the culture and helps people, whether cultural insiders or outsiders, understand that culture. For insiders, myths and icons become a part of their personal identity and fill out their sense of self. Icons and myths are not easily created, nor are they easily dispensed with. Part of the reason they can be quite long-lived is that what they mean can change, and so an icon or myth can mean different things in different eras. At bottom, myths are stories, and they may be completely true, partly true, or entirely invented; regardless, they make up what people think of when they say, "This is who we are." Icons are images of people and places and even things and come to serve as shorthand versions of myths and serve a similar function.

One of the earliest myths that developed in the South was that the region's culture and society was ancient. It wasn't ancient at all, but, as we saw in another part of this text, the idea of it being ancient served to justify its institutions, slavery in particular, in the face of challenges from the North, and so that myth was embraced. It's a myth that still resonates, although now it is manifested most often in the pretentious names of suburban subdivisions and resort communities. Apparently, prosperous upper middle class folks can feel more "established" if they live in places with names like Wakefield Plantation. Part and parcel of this myth is the myth of the agrarian ideal, the idea that, as we explored in an earlier chapter, farming, rural living, a pace of life dictated by the seasons, and a life close to nature were what men and women were best suited for and in fact were what God intended for them. By definition, whatever took people away from this lifestyle was bad. And so many Southerners, even in recent times, have a suspicion of cities and the fast paced, impersonal urban lifestyle. The idea of progress, perhaps the most powerful American myth, doesn't carry as much weight in the South because of the continuing if declining influence of the older agrarian myth.

The third in the triumvirate of Old South myths was the myth of the cavalier. This was the notion that white Southerners were derived from the English aristocracy. Certainly, as we have seen, the upper class did its best to emulate early and late the aristocrats of England, but the appeal of this myth led some, against much evidence to the contrary, to imagine that the society of the South was composed only of white planters and black slaves, and even whites of modest means might claim aristocratic ancestry. In the waning decades of the twentieth century, the myth still had enough power to inspire more than a few white middle class Southerners to document their aristocratic heritage by displaying a family coat of arms (easily obtained from a variety of mail order firms) in the foyers of their homes. Historian Frank Owsley, one imagines in exasperation, wrote his *Plain People of the Old South* in the 1930s to make the case that most white Southerners before the Civil War were not actually planter aristocrats. This was a myth that resisted the truth because class mattered so much for so long. For whites to be lower class was to be near, too near, the most despised element of society, and so some struggled to establish some connection to those at the top, if only ancestral. With class less important today, the interest in aristocratic lineage seems to be diminishing, although interest in genealogy is still quite strong.

After the war, the myth of the "Lost Cause" held the imaginations of white Southerners for generations and helped them "retain their identity" despite the "crushing defeat and poverty that the war had brought." The Civil War was not, in this mythic creation, a war over slavery but one over states' rights. Southern idealists fought a hopeless war against a superior foe to uphold this noble commitment but were defeated, and with this defeat an old and honorable way of life died, *Gone with the Wind* in Margaret Mitchell's words. Of all the Civil War leaders, Robert E. Lee emerged as the mythic father who symbolized this idealistic crusade and the ideal of the humble Christian gentlemen dedicated to duty and honor above all else. Lee's image became as familiar as a blood relative's to most white Southerners, and many people had a print of E.B.D. Julio's "Last Meeting of Lee and Jackson" hanging somewhere.[158] A variety of groups arose to keep this myth alive such as the United Daughters of the Confederacy and the Sons of Confederate Veterans. Around the turn of the twentieth century, monuments were erected by the UDC and other groups on courthouse squares, state capital lawns, and battlefields all over the region (and in the North, too, at battlefields such as Gettysburg), thousands of monuments to honor the struggles and sacrifices of those who fought in the war. These monuments became places of pilgrimage each Confederate Memorial Day (observed in May) for countless white school children well into the 1960s in much of the South.[159] "Dixie" was the anthem of the Lost Cause and was sung on ceremonial occasions (college and high school football games, for example) and often ended with a rousing rebel yell.

---

158. Charles Reagan Wilson, *Baptized in Blood: The Religion of the Lost Cause, 1865–1820* (Athens, Georgia: University of Georgia Press, 1980), quotes, p. 139; Estill Curtis Pennington, *Look Away: Reality and Sentiment in Southern Art* (Spartanburg, SC: Saraland Press, 1989), 58–63.

159. Gaines M. Foster, *Ghosts of the Confederacy: Defeat, the Lost Cause, and the Emergence of the New South, 1865–1913* (New York: Oxford University Press, 1988).

Monuments, images of Lee, and the song "Dixie," were all important icons of the Lost Cause myth, but the major icon of the myth has been the Confederate battle flag. While the national flag of the Confederacy has disappeared into obscurity, the battle flag (the stars and bars) is one of the most recognizable images in America. Until relatively recently, many state capital buildings and county and municipal buildings in the South flew the battle flag along with the national and state flags, and even today several Southern states still fly state flags that incorporate the battle flag. The battle flag and the other myths and icons reminded the white South that Southerners were different and, in fact, were morally superior to folks from other regions. Non-Southerners were "Yankees," a group at best good naturedly tolerated and at worst, despised, and these feelings were still quite common in much of the South well into the twentieth century, and even today are still not uncommon, as Yankee immigrants to the region sometimes discover to their chagrin.

The flag has also come to symbolize a variety of other causes besides the Lost Cause. The Ku Klux Klan and other groups long ago appropriated the flag as a symbol of white supremacy, although, to be sure, that was at least an implicit message in the Lost Cause myth. Bikers, rock bands, and other "outsiders," some of whom have never even lived in the South, have also appropriated the flag as a symbol of rebellion and going your own way. Still others have proclaimed that it represents "heritage not hate," in the words of a bumper sticker. Certainly there are enough white Southerners who know their family histories and know that an ancestor fought at Gettysburg or died at Vicksburg, and for many those stories are an important part of the family heritage. But the heritage issue does take some odd twists and turns. Journalist Tony Horwitz found a bitter flag debate going on in a small Kentucky town over the local high school's mascot: "two cartoonish Confederates clutching battles flags and blowing bugles emitting the words, 'Go Rebels, Go!'" The heritage issue was raised by some townspeople who were bitter and angry about a decision by the local school board to retire the mascot.[160] However, as Horwitz noted, Kentucky had never seceded, and the town where the debate was raging had been supportive of the union during the Civil War. In short, its heritage was, if anything, anti-Confederate. And so we are back to race: the one thing most flag proponents have in common is that they are white. The flag seems to have become, in addition to all its other meanings, a sort of generic "white pride" icon for people who feel whites have gotten the short end of the stick in recent times. In the Kentucky town, the mascot supporters even shouted "equal rights for whites!" at a school board meeting, a seemingly strange demand to make in

---

160. Tony Horwitz, *Confederates in the Attic: Dispatches from the Unfinished Civil War* (New York: Vintage Books, 1999), 99.
    161. *Ibid.*, 100–103, quote p. 103.

a country where disparities between black and white in wealth, income, and political power still loom like the Grand Canyon, but not so strange if one realizes that less affluent whites living in declining rural areas don't necessarily enjoy the benefits of this advantage.[161] For many African Americans, the meaning of the flag simply cannot be divorced from slavery and racism, and so a contentious debate periodically bubbles up over the display of the flag.

An alternative myth was spawned after the Civil War, which we can call the myth of the "New South." This myth was part fact, part hope, and part cheerleading and was based on the notion that the South would reinvent itself and become an economic powerhouse through industrial and commercial development.[162] In short, this myth rejected the myths of the Old South, but proponents of the New South myth made concessions to the Lost Cause and the traditions of the Old South when they had to, to head off criticism from folks concerned that the South would cease to be the South or that the baby would be thrown out with the bathwater.[163] Margaret Mitchell actually paid homage to both the New South myth and the myth of the Lost Cause, with Scarlet representing the new hard-driving push to succeed, and Ashley Wilkes representing all of the Old South myths plus the myth of the Lost Cause. Mitchell is telling us, however, that progress will win in the end; even Ashley, after all, has gone along with Scarlet's business plans, however grudgingly. The New South myth has always had a strong dose of hype about it, which has led some wags to speak of a new, New South because the rhetoric always seemed ahead of the actuality. But, after World War II, as we have seen, some areas of the South did grow and prosper and Atlanta, Houston, and Dallas, with their gleaming skyscrapers and ball teams, became iconic representatives of the emergence of the region as, finally, a true economic powerhouse, a truly "new" South. The myth and the reality have certainly captured the imagination of many folks in the less affluent areas who work, often desperately, to accomplish the same transformation. As we have seen, this is easier said than done, often because the older myths still exert a strong influence. It's not uncommon to hear people in poor rural areas say that what's holding back local economic development are the people who want to keep things just like they are.

The Civil Rights struggle has produced new myths and icons. Martin Luther King, Jr.'s brief career as a Civil Rights leader (13 years) and his martyrdom have assumed mythic proportions for many African Americans and white liberals. The image of King is displayed in the homes and offices of many African Americans (and some whites) on a variety of mediums including the ever popular black velvet. The cities where important episodes of the struggle played out—Memphis, Montgomery, and Birmingham—are like Civil War battle-

---

162. Paul Gaston, *The New South Creed* (New York: Knopf Publishing Co., 1970).
163. James C. Cobb, *Redefining Southern Culture: Mind and Identity in the Modern South* (Athens, GA: University of Georgia Press, 1999), 150–156.

Figure 8.7   Confederate memorial, Greenwood, Mississippi, court house

fields with monuments and museums. The museum located at the Lorraine Motel in Memphis, where King was assassinated, is now, fittingly, the best and most moving of the Civil Rights museums. Other figures of the movement such as Rosa Parks and John Lewis have emerged as lesser icons. All represent selfless devotion to freedom, justice, equality, and democracy, and so fit into the greater iconography of America, which values those things above all else, too. But while Movement figures and images have profound and positive meanings for African Americans and white liberals, many other whites are more equivocal if not downright hostile to these icons and myths. This hostility surfaced in the South and elsewhere when the King national holiday was debated in Congress and periodically surfaces when someone proposes to rename a street after King or some other Civil Rights figure. This is not surprising; conservative whites had opposed equal rights for blacks, and it would be amazing indeed if these opponents and the younger people following in their footsteps would wish to accept King as an icon. So, icons and myths can define, but they obviously can divide as well.

Music has provided its share of icons with Elvis at the head of the list, and Elvis's image appears on a wide assortment of pictures, posters, mugs, plates, and black velvet. Artist Clyde Broadway has even done a painting featuring what he considers the three major icons of the South: Robert E. Lee, Elvis, and Christ.[164] In this "trinity," Lee represents duty and honor, Christ represents Southern religiosity, and Elvis represents the wilder side of the male Southern personality. Despite Elvis's suggestive pelvic gyrations when he performed and his reputation, he became acceptable to a wide cross section of white Southerners in part because of his well-known filial devotion to his parents, Mama, especially. Graceland, his home, has become an icon in itself and a place where Elvis pilgrims may walk where he walked, view his possessions, and pay their respects at his grave. For blues fans and some rock fans, several of the early blues greats have become icons. Part of the mystique here is that many of them never enjoyed fame and fortune and died in obscurity, which in a perverse way seems to validate their music for some fans. Robert Johnson is probably the most important of the blues icons; he cut a few dozen songs before his untimely death (some say he was poisoned) in his mid-twenties. His grave (the one outside Greenwood; some claim he is buried elsewhere) is strewn with guitar picks left by fans who have traveled up the Money Road to pay homage. Ryman auditorium is an icon of country music, and while the Opry no longer routinely broadcasts from there, it is still an object of veneration for older fans. Many younger fans don't seem much interested, and so Ryman may fall out of the ranks of icons at some point.

---

164. Broadway's work is entitled "Trinity—Elvis, Jesus and Robert E. Lee." J. Richard Gruber and David Houston, *The Art of the South, 1890–2003: The Ogden Museum of Southern Art* (London: Scala Publishers, 2004), 65.

Figure 8.8   Elvis's grave at Graceland

Religious icons are important as the earlier reference to Clyde Broadway's painting indicates. While Southern evangelical religion is noted for its simplicity and devotion to the word rather than ritual, certain images play an important role in the region. Obviously the cross is one such image, and the widely distributed engraving of Christ (the one in which He has long wavy hair and is looking upward) is another. The cross is, of course, a universal Christian symbol, but crosses are displayed in the South in unique abundance not only on church steeples and in church sanctuaries but in fields, front yards, car bumpers, and even the shoulders of roads to mark where loved ones have died in car wrecks. The white frame church, found throughout the region by the thousands, would certainly constitute another defining icon of the region as would the "Jesus Saves" signs found nailed to trees and fences.

A variety of foods also serve as icons—fried chicken, grits, Vienna sausage, sweet tea, and dozens of others. People from the South delight in seeking out grits (or collards, or sweet tea or any number of food items) when they are outside the region, and outsiders delight in wrinkling their noses at the idea of grits. Both groups are participating in a ritual when they do this: they are acknowledging that Southerners are people who eat grits and people who aren't from the South don't. This, in a nutshell, is what icons and myths do.

As the South became more integrated into the national culture, icons that are popular nationally have become Southern icons. The most notable example of this is the American flag, the display of which has been heartily embraced in the South in recent decades at a time that the display of the Confederate battle

Figure 8.9   Robert Johnson's grave

flag has moved to the fringes of white society. This embrace of old glory reflects the South's emergence—again this is a recent phenomenon dating to the Vietnam war era—as the center of militant patriotism. The corporate logos of Nike, Pizza Hut, et al. are likewise just as prominent in the South as anywhere else on signs, shirts, handbags, shoes, etc., demonstrating the South's incorporation into the consumer culture of America. Some Southern icons have become American icons; the Confederate flag, as we have seen, serves as one to at least some people outside the region, and Elvis and Colonel Saunders—symbol of Kentucky Fried Chicken—serve as well-known national icons. Stone Mountain, the site of a famous monument depicting Generals Robert E. Lee and Stonewall Jackson riding purposefully beside President of the Confederacy Jefferson Davis, is now the site of a theme park. A light show is projected onto the monument in the evening with cartoon figures telling a patriotic story complete with the display of the American flag. So here we have what may be the ultimate transformation of an icon: a monument honoring Confederate war leaders which was also the site of the formation of the second Ku Klux Klan in the early 1900s is now surrounded by a playground and has itself become a screen for the display of consumer and patriotic icons. The park draws a multiracial crowd apparently unaware of or undisturbed by what the site once meant. As one African-American woman visiting the park observed in the summer of 2000, "We don't think about that."

Figure 8.10   Stone Mountain

Conclusion

Will Southern Culture Survive? Three Views.

In *Absolom, Absolom!*, William Faulkner's classic exploration of the Southern psyche, the main character, Quentin Compson, is asked by his Harvard roommate, "Tell about the South. What's it like down there? What do they do there? Why do they live there? Why do they live at all." We have tried to "tell about the South" and undoubtedly have misunderstood and misrepresented some things. We have had only our own experiences in the South and what others have said and written about it over the last three hundred years to go on. There is much we have not seen or experienced and much we have yet to read. I think, however, that there are many truths here and that, I hope, justifies the effort.

Is it still useful to think of the South as a distinct place with a unique culture? My answer to that is a qualified yes. Much, certainly, has changed. During my high school years in Darlington, South Carolina, many of the county's residents still farmed, and many people lived in the country, even if they didn't farm. Newcomers were a curiosity; most of the residents had been born and raised in the area. In much of the county, people could only get two television channels on their sets, so our electronic connection with the outside world was limited by today's standards. Most of the stores we shopped at were locally owned, although there were several stores that were part of regional or national chains such as Belk. If we ate out, it was likely to be at the Southernaire, or the Deluxe Cafe, or the Lunchbox, all locally owned and serving up Southern fare. Darlington would have been typical of much of the South during the mid to late 1960s. Today, very few people in Darlington County or anywhere else in the South farm. The overwhelming majority of Southerners work in IBM plants, medical facilities, schools, Walmarts, government offices, and assorted and sundry other industrial and commercial enterprises unconnected to the land. Even the smallest towns today have residents who have moved there from outside the region and even from other countries. People in the South are as likely to live in a suburban development, shop at Target and eat at McDonalds as people living elsewhere in the country. The Internet and cable television bring the outside world to nearly everyone 24/7, and a media-driven popular culture seems to be just as pervasive in the South as elsewhere. Clearly, the market, more than anything else, has transformed much of the South and has made it more like the rest of the country.

When I started high school, Jim Crow still reigned. My classmates and all my teachers were white; Afro-American young people attended Mayo High School although that began to change my last two years of high school when a handful of black students were admitted to my school. I remember my aunt and uncle, visiting from Pennsylvania, mistakenly attending the state fair in Columbia on the day reserved for African Americans and, when they returned, asking us in perplexity why whites didn't go to the state fair. At the electronics factory where my father worked, the majority of employees were white, but there were a small number of African-American employees too and not just working on the loading dock. As part of a large multi-national corporation, it was less invested in maintaining Jim Crow than the textile mill that had once operated on its site and so it represented, in a way, the first small steps toward a job market that did not discriminate on the basis of race. I also distinctly remember marching to the town square with everyone in my school to the Confederate memorial to observe Confederate Memorial Day. As I recall, the crowds were all white — whites celebrating a white holiday. Today, Jim Crow is long dead; most employers don't routinely discriminate against minorities, and you don't hear much about Confederate Memorial Day any more, although you do hear about Martin Luther King, Jr. Day. This is not to say race is no longer a dominant issue in the region; clearly, we have argued otherwise throughout this book. But the problem of race is now as much a national problem as a regional one.

What hasn't changed? Southern people are still among the most Christian people on the planet, and, of course, among the most Protestant. Wealth, immigration, suburbanization, liquor by the drink, and Sunday morning tee times at the proliferating golf courses in the region may have diluted this religiosity, but it's still a powerful influence, especially in the small towns and rural areas of the region. Churches are still at the center of many Southern communities, and many Southerners still see people, and relationships, and good and bad, and right and wrong through a Protestant (and mainly Baptist) lens. That's why evolution as a concept is not terribly popular in the South, a number of people in the region expect the imminent end of the world, and the progressive view of history—that people of good will can make things better—has never quite attained the popularity in the South that it has elsewhere in the country. There is still in the psyche of many Southerners the biblical belief that humans are flawed creatures who can't change that basic fact no matter how good the schools are that they attend and how wonderful the therapists are that they visit.

The political manifestation of evangelical Protestantism—the Christian Right—is still a potent political force in the region. This movement forcefully advocates traditional values and a return to a traditional lifestyle of two-parent families, male leadership in the church, at home, and presumably elsewhere, quiet Sunday afternoons dedicated to church and repose, and a return of the media to the saner standards of earlier times. Marriage should be between a man and a woman and pregnancies should come to term. For members of this movement, in truth, "old times there are not forgotten." Will these "traditionalists" succeed in halting or reversing the changes that most unsettle them and that also, not coincidentally, erode traditional Southern culture? Probably not. The reason they won't be successful is that while many of them struggle mightily to practice what they preach—they boycott movies with explicit sex scenes, they rail against the "war on Christmas" that they believe is "taking Christ out of Christmas"— most of them avidly embrace the institution that has been the most destructive of tradition: the market economy. And so their efforts to restore a simpler past will probably fail courtesy of Facebook, the iPod, Revlon, the Internet, and such "revolutionaries" as Bill Gates, Ronald MacDonald, and Mark Zuckerberg.

The South still fosters a rich and beautiful musical and literary tradition. It is the heartland of country music, and while the black migration out of the South has spread jazz, gospel, blues, and rhythm and blues across the country, a vital spark for each of these musical forms still comes from this region. In the last decades of the twentieth century and the early years of the new millennium, the nation is experiencing and benefiting from a renaissance in Southern literature. While these writers—Lee Smith, Randall Kenan, Pat Conroy, and Alice Walker, to name a few—are too diverse to create easy generalizations about, most appear to be committed to telling a story and using evocative language to do it. They have, in short, rejected the pared down prose lacking in plot that is so popular in much of the rest of the Western world. Their works often dwell on such Southern themes as family, place, honor, despair, sin, and redemption. To the extent that writers reflect the rest of us, these writers are telling us there is still a unique Southern sensibility.

The continuing persistence of traditional Southern culture is best seen and felt and heard in that "other South," the South left behind by industry, suburbs, and the computer age. In eastern North Carolina, and the Mississippi Delta, and a hundred small towns spread across the region, this other South still has one foot in an older South and is where one can still hear the old-style Southern accents, eat the pork-seasoned traditional food, and spend time with people who don't appear to be rushed. But even here, most people no longer farm although in most cases someone in the family once did. Many of the residents are dreadfully poor, many are marginally literate, jobs are hard to come by, teenage pregnancy rates are high, and there is often a serious drug problem. Dropping out of high school is still common and attending college not common enough. Community leaders desperately seek investments—a new strip mall, a wider highway, a Walmart, a new plant that pays more than minimum wage. None of this—the intractable problems or the solutions—bodes well for this "other South" to continue to serve as a repository of Southern traditions.

John Beck

⌣

Last night I needed a wooden pallet to put under the doghouse. A friend and I drove down a dirt road to a white trailer with a large dirt yard where people can buy corn liquor by the drink for 50¢ (half a shot) or $1.00 (whole shot) or by the pint ($6.00). This is where many of the local field workers come at the end of the day, and there they were, a dozen people sitting on chairs and benches in the yard. They had been pulling tobacco by hand from 6 a.m. to 6 p.m. and had cash wages for the day ($25–$75, depending largely on gender) in their pockets.

One woman came over to my window and said she was tired of working in tobacco; she's getting older and wants a "public job," maybe something at a fast food place. She wanted to know if she could ride into town with me in the mornings if she got a job. I said sure; it was a moot point. She will never really get that job. She has limited writing skills with which to fill out an application, no phone to be contacted by, no clothes that would be acceptable in the "public" world, and no running water to maintain personal hygiene.

My friend asked where we could get a pallet, and a couple of men said their boss had some in his barn. They got in the back of the truck so that people wouldn't say things about black men riding in a car with white women, and we drove to the farm. Their boss was not there, but his father was, an older man whom the workers called by his first name with "Mr." in front of it. He said we could have a pallet, so we drove down to the barn and the men picked it up and put it in the truck. We drove back to the house and they helped us set up the doghouse; then my friend drove them to the general store and bought them a beer as thanks for their help. At the store, she went in alone so that people wouldn't say things about black men going shopping with a white woman.

But things here are about to change. Government regulation of tobacco products and declining cigarette sales will compel the small tobacco farmers to plant sweet potatoes and soybeans instead, crops whose low profits will make small farming an impossibility. Soon, some of the farmers will sell their land to developers and leave their children money instead of land. The state and county are paving the remaining dirt roads. Subdivisions are being built nearby for professionals who work in Raleigh and Durham but prefer the country life. Then someone with a good heart or a critical eye will have many of the field workers' residences—old wooden shacks, tiny cinderblock houses, trailers with no power hook-ups—condemned. The workers will be moved into public housing in the city where they will have plumbing and electricity and welfare. Law enforcement will be obliged to shut down the corn liquor trade. Family graveyards will be moved or paved over. The woods will be cut down and the deer will leave and the local boys will learn another hobby besides hunting. The people who have been living in the area for generations will adapt to newcomers. Already, just in the last few years, general stores have started accepting credit cards. Integration has been in force for thirty years, and attitudes about race are changing.

These are good changes. It is good for racist behavior to be seen as aberrant rather than the norm. It is good for everyone to have plumbing. It is good for America to stop smoking. I would not wish these things to continue as they are. Rural Southerners deserve to benefit from new technology, to profit from new industry, to learn from cultural diversity.

Yet something is sad about the change and, strangely, the people who would seem to benefit from these changes are against them. They have a culture and a community that have been in place for generations. They have the security of knowing that if they follow the community rules that they know so well, they will always have a place and an identity, no matter how flawed that place and identity are. These cornerstones are about to crumble. The oral history, too, will dissipate; the stories of how Granddaddy stood here on the porch and watched the Rebel soldiers walking home along the railroad tracks will not be told on the porch anymore, and the interconnected family histories will be separated. The lifestyle of walking slow and talking slow, pick-up trucks with dogs in the back, snapping beans in a neighbor's kitchen, a job that you got with your daddy's name instead of a resume, credit given for your good name instead of your income—that lifestyle will retire; it is not well-suited to the pace and movement of contemporary America. In every culture there are good and true parts that get lost when it gets overtaken by the next era.

Until recently, a traditional South has still existed, at least in some pockets, complete with all the elements discussed in this text. I'm glad I've had the chance to live in it, but I don't believe it will last much longer. And maybe that's a good thing.

Wendy Frandsen

~

Growing up as an African-American male in the South, at the end of the Segregation Era (1950s and 1960s), I and other African Americans lived at a very heightened level of anxiety, unease, anticipation, and apprehension. Du Bois characterized this mixed and troubling set of emotions as a state of "double consciousness"—the pervasive feeling of being both American and African American, of being both Southern and black. As Americans we loved freedom, of course, but we were the ones who were denied freedom. Like all Americans, we honored justice, but justice was a complete stranger to us (just the mention of the word "justice" would cause us to shriek with hysterical laughter). We admired individualism, individual autonomy and integrity, but we were always stereotyped and treated as though we had no individuality. Like all Americans, we cherished equality, but we were always treated differently, without honor or respect. We lived in two worlds—one was warm, nurturing, full of love and acceptance, usually. The other was often hostile, deadly, and serious.

We lived inside the lion cage with the lion. This required imagination, of course, along with creativity, masking, and improvisation. The lion had to be constantly appeased, amused, soothed, and pacified; otherwise there would be serious consequences, oftentimes lethal ones. Like the grandfather in Ellison's *Invisible Man*, we lived inside the enemy's camp with the enemy, and sought to "undermine 'em with grins," and "agree'em to death and destruction" with meaningless "yessuh bosses." Over time, we mastered the art of masking, of moving without moving, of laughing while crying, of dancing without cross-ing our feet, of saying yes when we really meant no. We learned to take the daily painful and ugly things in life and transform them into amazingly beauti-ful things like spirituals, gospel, blues, and jazz. So it's OK. We managed to forge a culture from the experiences of slavery and segregation with our own distinctly African-American music, religion, literature, folklore, values, ideas, beliefs, and attitudes. And this is what made it possible for us to us to survive both physically and spiritually. The Southern black experience, after all, is that of a people at once American and yet a people apart. Historically, it has been an experience that offers rational grounds for both integrationist and black-nationalist ideologies. There's a part of us that wants to be American, to blend into the social fabric. There's another part that always remembers the pain, the oppression, and the exclusion, and wants to go elsewhere, somewhere, and es-tablish the black nation.

But we are Southerners, too. We still feel like the best place to be on Sunday mornings is in church, praising the Lord. And we still love barbecues, having the family close around, gardening, and going fishing. And what is more beautiful and sublime than the low pitched baying of deer hounds, deep back in the woods, on a clear winter's day?

But unlike white folk, our sense of identity was shaped not so much by a sense of place, but rather by our common, transgenerational experience of racial oppression and subordination. Racial oppression made it impossible for us to practice and fully participate in American culture, Southern or otherwise. We practiced and took refuge and solace in our African-American culture instead, with our own institutions, through which our culture was passed on. This common experience caused us to value, perhaps more so than our white neighbors, freedom, education, hard work, and community. We love the South, but we truly hate what happened to us in this place. Yes, we are Americans, but African Americans; Southern but black; integrationists yet nationalists—the warring souls of our double consciousness.

Things have been changing, some will say, for the better. Since the sixties and the end of legal racial segregation and discrimination, many blacks have achieved the integrationist goal and are happily pursuing the American dream of success. Those with good educations, marketable talents, and professional training and skills are basically free to pursue the American dream. People like Oprah Winfrey, Andrew Young, Alice Walker, and Michael Jordan are all Southerners. The African-American culture still thrives, but it is no longer practiced exclusively by African Americans. Practically the whole of American culture—music, literature, religion, dance, folklore, politics—has been infused, changed, and vitalized by the creativity, wit, and wisdom of the descendants of Southern slaves.

Poor blacks, however, lacking in education and marketable job skills, have fared worse. The Old South and white supremacy may be gone, but the New South is still a nightmare for those who are now held back more by class than race. This portion of the black community faces enormous problems and social ills including high unemployment, unstable families, high rates of teenage pregnancy, problems of drug abuse and high rates of crime and imprisonment. How to address these seemingly intractable problems? At the close of the 20th century, Martin Luther King's message of a colorblind society, of a society of inclusion rather than exclusion seemed to be at best a faintly flickering hope for many in an increasingly conservative society that seemed to feel it had "done enough" to address the "race problem." A new form of separatism began to attract the interest if not the support of many in the black community, and a spokesmen for this position emerged. This new leader was Louis Farrakhan, a minister of the Nation of Islam, and the "million man march on Washington" he helped organize in 1995 made him a national figure. He preached the doctrine of black self-help, of relying on resources that existed within the black community, rather than depending on the federal government to solve our problems. Like Booker T. Washington a century before, Farrakhan seemed convinced that black entrepreneurship and property ownership were the keys to black economic advancement. And so the Black Nationalist separatist addressed the problems of inequality and marginality that afflicted the black community in much the same way that the accommodationist had done one hundred years before.

But now a new black leader has emerged who appeals to whites as well as blacks. Barack Obama, the bi-racial U.S. president, is more or less the living embodiment of racial unity, integration, and the expanding emphasis on cultural diversity and multiculturalism. His surprising, surreal ascendancy to the highest political office in the land—indeed the world—stands as a potent symbol, a representation of what the American nation has become, and ironically, what it always has been—a multiracial, multicultural society. Obama's vision is integrationist and inclusionist, like that of the early W.E.B. Du Bois and more recently Martin Luther King, Jr. Unlike King, however, Obama has his hands on the levers of power and has, at this writing, broad support outside the black community. King, like the Moses of the Old Testament, stood on the mountaintop and saw the promised land but never reached it. It was not, of course, for King a place he saw in the distance but a state of grace—a dream fulfilled where all were brothers and sisters, all belonged to one family that excluded no one, the human family. Is the realization of King's dream closer at hand?

Aaron Randall

Bibliography

Unpublished Sources

Mildred Beck interview, 17 November 2004. Unpublished interview.

Debbie Heath Best, "Farming Is Hard Work," 1980. Unpublished interview.

Henry G. Connors Collection. Southern Historical Collection, University of North Carolina at Chapel Hill.

Heriot Clarkson Collection. Southern Historical Collection, University of North Carolina, Chapel Hill.

Clarence E. Fesperman, transcript of interview by William F. Hennessee. Federal Writers Project, Life Histories Collection, North Carolina, microfilm. Southern Historical Collection, University of North Carolina at Chapel Hill.

John Steele Henderson Collection. Southern Historical Collection, University of North Carolina, Chapel Hill.

Peter W. Hairston Collection. Southern Historical Collection, University of North Carolina at Chapel Hill.

Inventories and Accounts (of Estates), Rowan County, NC, 1850–1860. North Carolina Division of Archives and History, Raleigh.

Jerma Jackson lecture, 30 March 2006. Vance-Granville Community College, Henderson, NC.

Wendy Lapish interview, 20 November 2005. Unpublished interview.

McNeely and Young Daybook. North Carolina Division of Archives and History, Raleigh.

Thomasina Jefferson, Preston Mosley Interview, December 8, 1998. Unpublished interview.

Earl Sorrel interviews, 29 March 2004; 29 April 2004. Unpublished interviews.

U.S. Manuscript Census Returns, 1850, 1860, Rowan County, NC, Population Schedule, microfilm. North Carolina Collection, University of North Carolina at Chapel Hill.

James Wheeler interviews, 29 March 2004, 1 April 2004. Unpublished interviews.

Published Sources

"88 Seconds in Greensboro." *Frontline* PBS broadcast, 24 January 1983, http://www.pbs.org/wgbh/pages/frontline.

"The 2000 Baptist Faith and Message." Southeastern Baptist Seminary, http://www.sebts.edu/prospective_students/what_we_believe/bfm2000.cfm.

"2001 National Survey of Fishing and Hunting and Wildlife-Associated Recreation." U.S. Fish and Wildlife Service, 2002, http://www.census.gov/prod/2002pubs/FHW01.pdf.

"2008 Unofficial Voter Turnout," United States Election Project, at http://elections. gmu.edu/preliminary_vote_2008.html.

Abrahams, Roger D. *Singing the Master: The Emergence of African-American Culture in the Plantation South.* New York: Penguin Books, 1992.

Adeline, Aunt. Interview by Ila B. Prine. *Born in Slavery: Narratives from the Federal Writers' Project, 1936–1938.* Washington: Library of Congress, Manuscript Division, 2001, http://memory.loc.gov/ammem/snhtml/snhome.html.

Agee, James Agee and Walker Evans (with an introduction by John Hersey). *Let Us Now Praise Famous Men.* Boston: Houghton Mifflin Co., 1988; first published 1941.

"Alabama repeals century-old ban on interracial marriages." *CNN*, 8 November 2000, http://archives.cnn.com/2000/ALLPOLITICS/stories/11/07/alabama.interracial/.

"Alabama schools turn to bank loans to operate," *CNNMoney*, 31 August 2010, http://money.cnn.com/2010/08/30/news/economy/alabama_schools_bank_loans.fortune/index.htm (accessed 3/29/2012).

"Alabama's Taxes Hit Poor and Middle Class Far Harder than the Wealthy." Institute on Taxation and Economic Policy (Washington, DC) 7 January 2003, http://www.itepnet.org/wp2000/al%20pr.pdf.

Allen, L.R. "I Wanted to Be a Merchant," interview by Daisy Thompson. *American Life Histories: Manuscripts from the Federal Writers' Project, 1936–1938.* Washington: Library of Congress, Manuscript Division, 1998, http://memory.loc.gov/ammem/wpaintro/wpahome.html.

Allison, Dorothy. *Bastard out of Carolina.* New York: A Plume Book, 1993.

Ammerman, Nancy Tatum. *Baptist Battles: Social Change and Religious Conflict in the Southern Baptist Convention.* New Brunswick and London: Rutgers University Press, 1990.

Amy, Jeff. "Alabama state and local aid to ThyssenKrupp tops $1 billion after vote," *al.com*, 28 April 2011, http://blog.al.com/live/2011/04/alabama_state_and_local_aid_to.html (accessed 2/17/2012).

Anderson, Johnnie V. "Heriot Clarkson: A Social Engineer." Unpublished M.A. thesis, Wake Forest University, 1972.

Andrew, Rod Jr. *Long Gray Line: The Southern Military School Tradition, 1839–1915.* Chapel Hill: University of North Carolina Press, 2001.

Andrews, William L., general ed. *The Literature of the American South.* New York: W.W. Norton & Co., 1998.

Applebome, Peter. *Dixie Rising: How the South is Shaping American Values, Politics, and Culture.* San Diego, New York, and London: Harcourt Brace & Co., 1997.

"Architecture in Asheville." National Register of Historic Places Travel Itinerary, National Parks Services, http://www.cr.nps.gov/nr/travel/asheville/architecutre.htm (accessed 6 March 2006).

Arsenault, Raymond. "The Folklore of Southern Demagoguery." In *Is There a Southern Political Tradition?* Charles Eagles, ed. Jackson: University Press of Mississippi, 1996.

———. *The Wild Ass of the Ozarks: Jeff Davis and the Social Bases of Southern Politics.* Philadelphia: Temple University Press, 1984.

Arthur, Bill. "The Darlington Mill Case: Or 17 Years Before the Courts." *New South*, Col. 28, No. 3, Summer 1973.

Avirett, James Battle. *The Old Plantation: How We Lived in Great House and Cabin Before the War.* Chapel Hill: Documenting the American South, 1998 (first published, 1901), http://docsouth.unc.edu/avirett/avirett.html.

Ayers, Edward L. *The Promise of the New South: Life After Reconstruction.* New York and Oxford: Oxford University Press, 1992.

———. *Vengeance and Justice: Crime and Punishment in the 19thhCentury American South.* New York and Oxford: Oxford University Press, 1984.

Ball, Edward. *Slaves in the Family.* New York: Ballantine Books, 1999.

Ball, William Watts. *The State That Forgot: South Carolina's Surrender to Democracy.* Indianapolis: Bobbs-Merrill, 1932.

Baltzell, E. Digby. *The Protestant Establishment: Aristocracy and Caste in America.* New York: Vintage Books, 1964.

Baraka, Amiri. *Blues People: Negro Music in America.* New York: Perennial, 2002; first published 1963.

Bardaglio, Peter. *Reconstructing the Household: Families, Sex and the Law in the Nineteenth Century South*. Chapel Hill: University of North Carolina Press, 1995.

Barker, Ben and Karen Barker. *Not Afraid of Flavor: Recipes from Magnolia Grill*. Chapel Hill: The University of North Carolina Press, 2000.

Barlow, William. *"Looking Up at Down": The Emergence of Blues Culture*. Philadelphia: Temple University Press, 1989.

Bass, Jack and Walter DeVries. *The Transformation of Southern Politics: Social Change and Political Consequence Since 1945*. New York and Scarborough, Ontario: New American Library, 1977.

Beardon, Romare and Harry Henderson. *A History of African-American Artists from 1792 to the Present*. New York: Pantheon Books, 1993.

Beck, John J. "Development in the Piedmont South: Rowan County, North Carolina, 1850–1900." Unpublished Ph.D. dissertation, University of North Carolina, Chapel Hill, 1984.

———. "Building the New South: A Revolution from Above in a Piedmont County," *Journal of Southern History, LIII* (August 1987): 441–470.

Belk, Sarah. *Around the Southern Table*. New York: Simon and Schuster, 1991.

Berkeley, Kathleen C. *The Women's Liberation Movement in America*. Westport, CT: Greenwood Press, 1999.

Berlin, Ira and Phillip D. Morgan, "Labor and the Shaping of Slave Life in the Americas." In *Cultivation and Culture: Labor and d the Shaping of Slave Life in the Americas*, Ira Berlin and Phillip D. Morgan eds. Charlottesville, VA: University Press of Virginia, 1993.

Bernstein, Cynthia. "Grammatical Features of Southern Speech: *yall, might could, and fixin to*." *English in the Southern United States*, Stephen J. Nagle and Sara L. Sanders, eds. Cambridge: Cambridge University Press, 2003.

Berry, Wendell. "The Regional Motive." In *The Literature of the American South* edited by William L. Andrews. New York and London: W.W. Norton & Co., 1998.

Beverley, Robert. *The History and Present State of Virginia, in Four Parts*. Chapel Hill, NC: Documenting the American South, 2006 (first published 1705), http://docsouth.unc.edu/southlit/beverley/beverley.html.

Birnbaum, Robert. "Interview with Allan Gurganus." The Narrative Thread, http://www.identitytheory.com/people/birnbaum29.html (accessed 5/19/06).

Bishir, Catherine W. *North Carolina Architecture*. Chapel Hill: University of North Carolina press, 1990.

Bivens, Jr., John. *The Furniture of Coastal North Carolina, 1700–1820.* Winston-Salem, NC: Museum of Early Southern Decorative Arts, 1988.

Black, Merle and Earl Black. *Politics and Society in the South.* Cambridge: Harvard University Press, 1987.

————. *The Rise of Southern Republicans.* Cambridge: Belknap Press, 2003.

Blair, Diane. "Party Activists: Mirrors and Makers of Change." In *Party Activists in Southern Politics* Charles D. Hadley and Lewis Bowan, eds. Knoxville, TN: University Press, 1998.

Blassingame, John. *The Slave Community: Plantation Life in the Antebellum South.* New York: Oxford University Press, 1979.

Blythe, Le Gette. *William Henry Belk: Merchant of the South.* Chapel Hill: University of North Carolina, 1950.

Boles, John B. *The Great Revival, 1787–1805: The Origins of the Southern Evangelical Mind.* Lexington, Kentucky: The University Press of Kentucky, 1972.

Bolton, Charles C. *Poor Whites of the Antebellum South: Tenants and Laborers in Central North Carolina and Northeast Mississippi.* Durham: Duke University Press, 1994.

Bolton, Charles S. and Scott P. Culclasure, eds. *The Confessions of Edward Isham: A Poor White Life of the Old South.* Athens and London: University of Georgia Press, 1998.

Bolton, James. Interview by Sarah H. Hall. *Born in Slavery: Slave Narratives from the Federal Writers' Project, 1936–1938.* Washington: Library of Congress, Manuscript Division, 2001, http://memory.loc.gov/ammem/snhtml/snhome.html.

Bonomi, Patricia U. *Under the Cope of Heaven: Religion, Society, and Politics in Colonial America.* New York: Oxford University Press, 2003.

Boo, Katherine. "The Churn: Creative Destruction in a Border Town." *The New Yorker,* March 29, 2004, http://www.newyorker.com/archive/2004/03/29/040329fa_fact (accessed 4/15/2007).

Bositis, David A. *Black Elected Officials: A Statistical Summary, 2001.* Washington, DC: Joint Center for Political and Economic Studies, 2003.

Brace, C. Loring."Race" Is a Four-Letter Word: The Genesis of the Concept.* New York: Oxford University Press, 2005.

Branch, Taylor. *Parting the Waters: America in the King Years, 1954–1963.* New York: Simon and Schuster, 1989.

Brawley, James S. *The Rowan Story, 1753–1953.* Salisbury, NC: Rowan Printing Co., 1953.

Brinkley, Alan. *Voices of Protest: Huey Long, Father Coughlin, and the Great Depression.* New York: Vintage Books, 1983.

Browning, Wilt. *Linthead: Growing Up in a Carolina Cotton Mill Village.* Ashboro, NC: Down Home Press, 1991.

Bryd, William K. *William Byrd's Histories of the Dividing Line Betwixt Virginia and North Carolina.* New York: Dover Publications, Inc. 1967; first published 1929.

"The Burden of Chronic Diseases and Their Risk Factors: National and State Perspectives, 2002." U.S. Department of Health and Human Services, National Center for Chronic Disease Prevention and Health Promotion, http://www.cdc.gov/nccdphp/burdenbook2002/02_heart.htm.

Burr, Virginia Ingraham, ed. *The Secret Eye: The Journal of Ella Gertrude Clanton Thomas, 1848–1889.* Chapel Hill: The University of North Carolina Press, 1990.

Butterfield, Fox. *All God's Children: The Bosket Family and the American Tradition of Violence.* New York: Alfred A. Knopf, 1995.

Bynum, Victoria. *Unruly Women: The Politics of Social and Sexual Control in the Old South.* Chapel Hill: University of North Carolina Press, 1992.

Byrd, Sarah. Interview. *Born in Slavery: Slave Narratives from the Federal Writers' Project, 1936–1938.* Washington: Library of Congress, Manuscript Division, 2001, http://memory.loc.gov/.

Campbell, David D. and Robert E. Putnam, "Crashing the Tea Party," *New York Times,* 16 August 2011, http://www.nytimes.com/2011/08/17/opinion/crashing-the-tea-party.html?_r=1 (accessed 3/26/2012).

Carbone, June. "Autonomy to Choose What Constitutes Family: Oxymoron or Basic Right?" http://www.scu.edu/law/FacWebPage/Carbone/autonomy.pdf (accessed 12/16/06).

Carlton, David L. *Mill and Town in South Carolina, 1880–1920.* Baton Rouge and London, Louisiana State University Press, 1982.

Carney, Judith A. *Black Rice: The African Origins of Rice Cultivation in the Americas.* Cambridge, Massachusetts: Harvard University Press, 2001.

Caro, Robert A. *The Years of Lyndon Johnson: The Path to Power.* New York: Alfred A. Knopf, 1982.

Carolina Watchman (Salisbury, NC).

Carter II, Edward C., et al., eds. *The Journals of Benjamin Henry Latrobe, 1799–1820: from Philadelphia to New Orleans, Vol. 3.* New Haven: Yale University Press, 1980.

Carter, Dan T. *The Politics of Rage: Wallace, The Origins of the New Conservatism and the Transformation of American Politics.* New York: Simon and Schuster, 1995.

Carter, Jimmy. *An Hour Before Daylight: Memories of a Rural Boyhood.* New York: Simon and Schuster, 2001.

Carver, Craig M. *American Regional Dialects: A Word Geography.* Ann Arbor: University of Michigan Press, 1987.

Cash, W. J. *The Mind of the South.* New York: Vintage Books, 1969; first published 1941.

Cason, Clarence E. "Middle Class and Bourbon." In *Culture in the South,* William T. Couch, ed. Chapel Hill: University of North Carolina Press, 1934.

Censer, Jane Turner. *North Carolina Planters and Their Children, 1800–1860.* Baton Rouge: Louisiana State University Press, 1984.

Center of American Women and Politics Web site, Eagleton Institute of Politics, Rutgers, The State University of New Jersey, http://www.cawp.rutgers.edu (accessed March 22, 2012).

Chafe, William. *Civilities and Civil Rights: Greensboro, North Carolina and the Black Struggle for Freedom.* Oxford: Oxford University Press, 1981.

Chalmers, David M. *Hooded Americanism: The History of the Ku Klux Klan.* Durham: Duke University Press, 1987.

Chamberlain, Hope Summerell. *This Was Home.* Chapel Hill: University of North Carolina Press, 1938.

Charlotte Daily Observer (NC).

Chesnutt, Charles. *The House Behind the Cedars.* London: The X Press, 1998; first published 1900.

———. *The Marrow of Tradition.* New York: Penguin Books, 1993; first published 1901.

Chestnut, Mary Boykin. *A Diary from Dixie.* Documenting the American South, 1997 (first published 1905), http://docsouth.unc.edu/chesnut/maryches.html.

Chopin, Kate. *The Awakening.* Amherst, NY: Prometheus Books, 1996; first published 1899.

Clark, Daniel. *Like Night and Day: Unionization in a Southern Mill Town.* Chapel Hill: University of North Carolina Press, 1997.

Cleveland, Henry, ed. *Alexander H. Stephens in Public and Private: With Letters and Speeches Before, During and Since the War.* Philadelphia: National Publishing Company, 1866.

Clinton, Catherine. "Bloody Terrain: Freedwomen, Sexuality, and Violence During Reconstruction." In *Half Sisters of History: Southern Women and the American Past,* Catherine Clinton, ed. Durham: Duke University Press, 1994.

———. *The Plantation Mistress.* New York: Pantheon Books, 1982.

Clinton, Jim, Carol Conway et al. *The Mercedes and the Magnolia: Preparing the Southern Workforce for the Next Economy.* Research Triangle Park, NC: Southern Growth Policies Board, 2002.

"CNBC's Rick Santelli's Chicago Tea Party," http://www.youtube.com/watch?v =zp-Jw-5Kx8k (accessed 3/22/2012).

"CNN.com Election Results: U.S. President/Region: South/Exit Poll," *CNN.com,* http://www. cnn.com/ELECTION/2004.

Cobb, James C. *Redefining Southern Culture: Mind and Identity in the Modern South.* Athens, GA: University of Georgia Press, 1999.

———. *The Selling of the South: The Southern Crusade for Industrial Development, 1936–1980.* Baton Rouge and London: Louisiana State University Press, 1982.

———. *The Most Southern Place on Earth: The Mississippi Delta and the Roots of Regional Identity.* New York: Oxford University Press, 1992.

Coclanis, Peter A. *The Shadow of a Dream: Economic Life and Death in the South Carolina Low Country, 1670–1920.* New York and Oxford: Oxford University Press, 1989.

Collins, Kristin. "Church boots 9 over politics." Raleigh *News and Observer,* 7 May 2005.

"Compilation Richmond County [GA] Ex-Slave Interviews: Work, Play, Food, Clothing, Marriage, etc." Interview by Louise Oliphant. *Born in Slavery: Slave Narratives from the Federal Writers' Project, 1936–1938.* Washington: Library of Congress, Manuscript Division, 2001, http://memory.loc.gov/ammem/snhtml/snhome.html.

Conaway, James. *Memphis Afternoons: A Memoir.* Boston and New York: Houghton Mifflin, 1993.

Conklin, Paul. "Lyndon Johnson and the Outer South." In *Is There a Southern Political Tradition?* Charles Eagles, ed. Jackson: University Press of Mississippi, 1996.

Conroy, Pat. *The Great Santini.* New York: Bantam Books, 2002; first published 1976.

———. *The Lords of Discipline.* New York: Bantam Books, 2002; first published 1980.

———. *The Prince of Tides.* Boston: Houghton Mifflin Company, 1986.

Cooperative Baptist Fellowship Web site, http://www.thefellowship.info/.

Coste, Jay and Sean Trende, "Election Review, Part 2: The South Atlantic," *Real Clear Politics*, January 12, 2009, http://www.realclearpolitics.com/articles/2009/01/election_review_part_ii _the_so.html.

Cotton, Sallie Southall. *History of the North Carolina Federation of Women's Clubs, 1901–1925*. Raleigh: Edwards and Broughton Printing Company, 1925.

Courtwright, David T. "The Drug War's Perverse Toll," Issues in Science and Technology Online, University of Texas at Dallas, 2006, http://www/issues. org/13.2/courtw.htm.

Covington, Dennis. *Salvation on Sand Mountain: Snake Handling and Redemption in Southern Appalachia*. Reading, PA: Addison-Wesley Publishing Co., 1995.

Craig, Lawrence. "Why I Am a Cook." *A Gracious Plenty: Recipes and Recollections from the American South*, John T. Edge. New York: HP Books, 1999.

Creflo Dollar Ministries Web site, http://www.creflodollarministries.org/.

Crumbo, Chuck. "Military attracts blue-collar recruits." [Columbia, SC] *The State*, 25 (May 2003), http://www.thestate.com/mld/state/news/columnists/6915404.htm.

"Current Population Survey: Population in U.S. Regions by Sex and Citizenship Status." U.S. Bureau of the Census, Ethnic and Hispanic Statistics Branch, Population Division, March 2002, http://www.census.gov/population/soc demo/foreign/ppl-162/tab01-14.pdf.

Curtin, Phillip D. *The Atlantic Slave Trade: A Census*. Madison: The University of Wisconsin Press, 1969.

————. "Africa North of the Forest." In *African History: From Earliest Times to Independence*. Ed. by Phillip Curtin et al. London: Longman, 1995.

————. "The West African Coast in the Era of the Slave Trade." In *African History: From Earliest Times to Independence*. Ed. by Phillip Curtin et al. London: Longman, 1995.

Dabbs, James McBride. *Haunted by God*. Richmond, Virginia: John Knox Press, 1972.

Daniel, Pete. *Lost Revolutions: The South in the 1950s*. Chapel Hill and London: University of North Carolina Press, 2000.

————. *Standing at the Crossroads: Southern Life in the Twentieth Century*. New York: Hill and Wang, 1986.

Davis, Carl, et al. *Who Pays? A Distributional Analysis of the Tax Systems in All 50 States.* 3rd edition. Washington, DC: Institute on Taxation and Economic Policy, 2009, http://www.itepnet.org/whopays3.pdf (accessed 3/29/2012).

Davis, Francis. *The History of the Blues.* Cambridge, Mass.: Da Capo Press, 2003; first published 1995.

De Crevecoeur, Hector St. John. *Letters from an American Farmer*(selections). In *The American Reader,* Diane Ravitch, ed. New York: Harper Perennial, 1991.

Degler, Carl N. *The Other South: Southern Dissenters in the Nineteenth Century.* New York: Harper and Row, 1974.

Deutch, Hermann B. *Brennan's New Orleans Cookbook: with the Story of the Fabulous New Orleans Restaurant.* New Orleans: Robert L. Crager & Co., 1964.

Dewan, Shaila. "Gentrification Changing Face of New Atlanta." *The New York Times,* 11 March 2006, http://www.nytimes.com/2006/03/11/national/11atlanta.html?th&emc=th (accessed 11 March 2006).

Diamond, Jared. M. *Guns, Germs, and Steel: The Fates of Human Societies.* New York: W.W. Norton and Co., 1997.

Dismantling Persistent Poverty in the Southeastern States. Athens, GA: Carl Vinson Institute of Government, University of Georgia, 2002.

"Divorce Rates by State: 1990, 1995, and 1999–2004." Division of Vital Statistics, National Center for Health statistics, Centers for Disease Control and Prevention, http://www.cdc.gov.

Dixon, Thomas Jr. *The Leopard's Spots: A Romance of the White Man's Burden—1865–1900.* New York: A. Wessels Company, 1906.

Dobbs, Michel. "Spared the rod, lost his job." [Raleigh, NC] *The News and Observer,* 22 February 2004, sec. A.

Dollard, John. *Caste and Class in a Southern Town.* Garden City, NY: Doubleday Anchor Books, 1949; first published 1937.

Domhoff, G. William. *Who Rules America?* Englewood Cliffs, NJ: Prentice Hall, Inc., 1967.

"Dr. Bob Jones III Discusses the Controversy Swirling Around Bob Jones University." *Larry King Live,* 3 March 2000, transcript at CNN.COM, http://transcripts.cnn.com/TRANSCRIPTS/0003/03/lkl.00.html.

Dred Scott v. John F. A. Sandford, 1857. http://www.tourolaw.edu/patch/Scott/.

Dreyfus, Robert. "Reverend Doomsday." *Rolling Stone,* 28 January 2004, http://www.rollingstone.com/politics/story/_/id/5939999?rnd=1130860097171&has-player=true&version=6.0.12.1040.

Dunbar, Paul Lawrence. "We Wear the Mask." In *Crossing the Danger Water: Three Hundred Years of African-American Writing*, Deirdre Mullane, ed. New York: Anchor Books, 1993.

Durr, Virginia Foster. *Outside the Magic Circle: The Autobiography of Virginia Foster Durr*, edited by Hollinger F. Barnard. University, Alabama: University of Alabama Press, 1985.

Eckholm, Erik. "Plight Deepens for Black Men, Studies Warn." *New York Times*, 20 March 2006, http://www.nytimes.com/2006/(accessed 12/16/06).

Edgar, Walter. *South Carolina: A History*. Columbia, SC: University of South Carolina, 1998.

Edge, John T. *Southern Belly: the Ultimate Food Lover's Companion to the South*. Athens, GA: Hill Street Press, 2000.

Edgerton, Clyde. *Raney*. New York: Ballantine Books, 1986.

Education First: NC School Report Cards, http://www.ncschoolreportcard.org/src/.

Egerton, John. *Southern Food: At Home, on the Road, in History*. Chapel Hill and London: University of North Carolina Press, 1993.

Eisier, Riane Tennenhaus. *The Equal Rights Handbook*. New York: Avon, 1978.

ElectionCenter2008 exit polls, *CNN.com*, http://www.cnn.com/ELECTION/2008/results/polls.main/.

Ellison, Ralph. *Invisible Man*. New York: Vintage Books, 1995; first published 1952.

Elvis Presley Concert Anthology: 1954–1956. (CD) Los Angeles: Master Classics, 2005.

Equiano, Olaudah. *The Interesting Narrative of the Life of Olaudah Equiano* edited by Robert J. Allison. Boston: Bedford Books of St. Martin's Press, c1995; first published 1791.

Escott, Paul D. *Many Excellent People: Power and Privilege in North Carolina, 1850–1900*. Chapel Hill and London: University of North Carolina Press, 1985.

Evans, Ben. "Election nearly wipes out white Southern Democrats," 4 November 2010, *Real Clear Politics*, http://www.realclearpolitics.com/news/ap/politics/2010/Nov/04/election_nearly_wipes_out_white_southern_democrats.html (accessed 3/28/2012).

Evans, Eli N. *The Provincials: A Personal History of Jews in the South*. New York: Free Press Paperbacks, 1997.

Evergreen Community Church (Raleigh, NC) Web site, http://www.evergreench.org.

Fairclough, Adam. *Better Days Coming: Blacks and Equality, 1890–2000.* New York: Viking, 2001.

Farish, Hunter Dickinson, ed. *Journals and Letters of Philip Vickers Fithian, 1773–1774: A Plantation Tutor of the Old Dominion.* Charlottesville, VA: Dominion Books, 1968.

Faulkner, William. "Wash." In *Collected Stories of William Faulkner.* New York: Vintage Books, 1977.

———. "A Rose for Emily." In *Collected Stories of William Faulkner.* New York: Vintage Books, 1977.

———. "Barn Burning." In *Collected Stories of William Faulkner.* New York: Vintage Books, 1977.

———. "Dry September." In *Collected Stories of William Faulkner.* New York: Vintage Books, 1977.

———. *Light in August.* New York: Vintage Books, 1990; first published 1932.

Feagin, Crawford. "The African Contribution to Southern States English." In *Language Variety in the South Revisited,* Cynthia Bernstein, Thomas Nunnally and Robin Sabino eds. Tuscaloosa: University of Alabama, 1997.

Fischer, David Hackett. *Albion's Seed: Four British Folkways in America.* New York and Oxford: Oxford University Press, 1989.

Fisher, Abby. *What Mrs. Fisher Knows About Old South Cooking, Soups, Pickles, Preserves, Etc.* East Lansing, Mich.: Michigan State University Library, 2004 (first published 1881), http://digital.lib.msu.edu/projects/cook books/html/authors/author_fisher.html.

Fite, Gilbert C. *Cotton Fields No More: Southern Agriculture, 1865–1980.* Lexington, KY: University Press of Kentucky, 1984.

Fitzhugh, George. *Cannibals All! Or Slaves Without Masters.* Richmond, VA: A. Morris, Publisher, 1857.

———. *Sociology for the South, or the Failure of Free Society.* Chapel Hill: Documenting the American South, 1998 (first published 1854), http://docsouth.unc.edu/Fitzhughsoc/fitzhugh.html.

Flamming, Douglas. *Creating the Modern South: Millhands and Managers in Dalton, Georgia.* Chapel Hill and London: University of North Carolina Press, 1992.

"Floating casinos." *Lexington Herald-Leader,* 18 October 2005, http://www.kentucky.com/mld/kentucky/business/12929621.htm.

Flowers, Linda. *Throwed Away: Failures of Progress in Eastern North Carolina.* Knoxville: University of Tennessee Press, 1992.

Flynt, J. Wayne. *Dixie's Forgotten People: The South's Poor Whites.* Bloomington and London: Indiana University Press, 1979.

Foner, Eric. *A Short History of Reconstruction, 1863–1877.* New York: Harper and Row, 1990.

Ford, Jr., Lacy K. "Rednecks and Merchants: Economic Development and Social Tensions in the South Carolina Upcountry, 1865–1900." *Journal of American History, LXXI* (September 1984): 294–318.

————. "Prophet with Posthumous Honor: John C. Calhoun and the Southern Political Tradition." In *Is There a Southern Political Tradition?* Charles Eagles, ed. Jackson: University Press of Mississippi, 1996.

Foster, Gaines M. *Ghosts of the Confederacy: Defeat, the Lost Cause, and the Emergence of the New South, 1865–1913.* New York: Oxford University Press,1988.

"Founder, John Portman." John Portman & Associates. Inc., http://portman usa.com/foudner.html (accessed 3/3/06).

Fowler, Damon Lee. *Classical Southern Cooking: A Celebration of the Cuisine of the Old South.* New York: Crown Publishers, Inc., 1995.

Fox, Minnie C. *The Blue Grass Cook Book.* East Lansing, Mich.: Michigan State University Library, 2004 (first published 1904), http://digital.lib.msu.edu/projects/cookbooks/html/books/book_10.cfm.

Fox-Genovese, Elizabeth. *Within the Plantation Household: Black and White Women of the Old South.* Chapel Hill: University of North Carolina Press, 1988.

Frady, Marshall. *Wallace.* New York and Cleveland: Meridian Books, 1970.

Frankenberg, Erica and Chungmei Lee. "Race in American Public Schools: Rapidly Resegregating School Districts." Cambridge: The Civil Rights Project, Harvard University, August, 2002, http://www.civilrightsproject. harvard.edu/research/deseg/Race_in_American_Public_Schools1.pdf.

Franklin, Benjamin. *Benjamin Franklin's Autobiography,* ed. by J.A. Leo LeMay. New York and London: W.W. Norton & Co., 1986.

Franklin, Jimmie Lewis. "Commentary." In *Is There a Southern Political Tradition?* Charles Eagles, ed. Jackson: University Press of Mississippi, 1996.

Franks, Dora. Interview by Mrs. Richard Kolb. *Born in Slavery: Slave Narratives from the Federal Writers' Project, 1936–1938.* Washington: Library of Congress, Manuscript Division, 2001, http://memory.loc.gov/ammem/snhtml/snhome.html.

Frazier, E. Franklin. *The Negro Family in the United States.* Chicago: University of Chicago Press, 1968; first published 1939.

Fredrickson, George M. *The Black Image in the White Mind: The Debate on African-American Character and Destiny, 1817–1914.* Middleton, CT: Wesleyan University Press, 1971.

———. *White Supremacy: A Comparative Study in American and South African History.* New York: Oxford University Press, 1981.

Frey, William H. "Charticle." The Milkin Institute Review, Third Quarter, 2003, http://www.frey-demographer.org/reports/Rainbownation.pdf.

———. "The New Great Migration: Black Americans Return to the South, 1965–2000." Washington, DC: Center on Urban and Metropolitan Policy, The Brookings Institute, May 2004, http://www.frey-demographer.org/-reports/Brook04.pdf.

Gaither, Edmund B. "Witnessing: Layered Meanings in Vernacular Art." In *Testimony: Vernacular Art of the African-American South,* Kinshasha Conwill et al. New York: Harry N. Abrams, Inc., 2001.

Gans, Herbert J. *The Urban Villagers: Group and Class in the Life of Italian Americans.* New York: Free Press of Glencoe, 1962.

Gant, William. Interview by Irene Robertson. *Born in Slavery: Slave Narratives from the Federal Writers' Project, 1936–1938.* Washington: Library of Congress, Manuscript Division, 2001, http://memory.loc.gov/ammem/snhtml/snhome.html.

Gaston, Paul. *The New South Creed: A Study in Southern Mythmaking.* New York: Vintage Books, 1973.

Genovese, Eugene D. *The World the Slaveholders Made: Two Essays in Interpretation.* New York: Vintage Books, 1971.

Genovese, Eugene. *Roll, Jordan Roll: The World the Slaves Made.* New York: Vintage Books, 1974.

Gentry, Aaron and Sze Min Lam. "Dog Trot: A Vernacular Response." Mississippi State University School of Architecture, http://arch.ced.berkeley.edu/vitalsigns/bld/Casestudies/dogtrot_high2.pdf (accessed 3 March 2006).

Gerami, Shain. *Women and Fundamentalism: Islam and Christianity.* New York: Garland Publishing, Inc., 1996.

Gibson, Campbell J. and Emily Lennon. "Historical Census Statistics on the Foreign-born Population of the Unites States: 1850–1990." U.S. Bureau of the Census, Population Division, February, 1999, http://www.census.gov/population/www/documentation/twps0029/twps0029.html.

Gill, Frank. Interview by Ila B. Prine. *Born in Slavery: Slave Narratives from the Federal Writers' Project, 1936–1938.* Washington: Library of Congress,

Manuscript Division, 2001, http://memory.loc.gov/ammem/snhtml/sn home.html.

Gilroy, Paul. *The Black Atlantic: Modernity and Double Consciousness*. Cambridge, Mass.: Harvard University Press, 1993.

Gioia, Ted. *The History of Jazz*. New York: Oxford University Press, 1998.

Glass, William R. *Strangers in Zion: Fundamentalists in the South, 1900–1950*. Macon, Georgia: Mercer University Press, 2001.

Glenn, Gwendolyn. "Southern Secrets from Edna Lewis-Cuisine." *American Visions*, Feb.–March, 1997, http://www.findarticles.com/p/articles/mi_m 1546/is_n1_v12/ai_19257630#continue (accessed 2/3/06).

Goekjian, Karekin and Robert Peacock. *Light of the Spirit: Portrait of Southern Outsider Artists*. Jackson, MS: University Press of Mississippi, 1998.

Goff, Jr., James R. *Close Harmony: A History of Southern Gospel*. Chapel Hill: The University of North Carolina Press, 2002.

Goldfield, David R. "North Carolina's Early Twentieth-Century Suburbs and the Urbanizing South." *Early Twentieth century Suburbs in North Carolina* Catherine W. Bishir and Lawrence Earley, eds. Raleigh: North Carolina Department of Cultural Resources, 1985.

Gossett, Thomas F. *Race: The History of an Idea in America*. New York: Shocken Books, 1965.

"Governor Perry: Austin Tea Party. You Tube, http://www.youtube.com/watch ?v=dbWz1RYGE3Q (accessed 5/24/2009).

Graham, Billy Graham. *Just as I Am: The Autobiography of Billy Graham*. San Francisco: HarperCollins, 1997.

Grantham, Dewey. *Southern Progressivism: the Reconciliation of Progress and Tradition*. Knoxville: University of Tennessee Press, 1983.

"Great Chefs of New Orleans: Austin Leslie." NOLA Cuisine, 5 November 2005, http://www.nolacuisine.com/2005/11/05/great-chefs-of-new-orleans-austin-leslie/(accessed 2/3/06).

Green, John C. "Believers for Bush, Godly for Gore: Religion and the 2000 Election in the South." In *The 2000 Presidential Election in the South: Partisanship and Southern Party Systems in the 21st Century*, Robert P. Steed and Lawrence W. Moreland, eds. Westport, Connecticut: Praeger, 2002.

Green, John C. et al. "The Soul of the South: Religion and Southern Politics at the Millennium." In *The New Politics of the Old South: An Introduction to Southern Politics*, Charles S. Bullock III and Mark Rozell, eds. Boulder, NY: Rowman and Littlefield Publishers, Inc., 2003.

Green, Joshua. "Roy and his Rock," *The Atlantic Monthly* (October 2005), http://www.theatlantic.com/doc/200510/roy-moores-ten-commandments (accessed 3/7/2006).

Greene, Alison, Ferrel Guillory, et al. *The State of the South: Fifty Years After Brown v. Board of Education.* Chapel Hill: MDC Inc., 2004.

Greene, Jay P. and Greg Foster. *Public High School Graduation and College Readiness Rates in the United States,* Education working paper, No. 3, Center for Civic Innovation at the Manhattan Institute, September 2003.

Gregory, James N. *The Southern Diaspora: How the Great Migrations of Black and White Southerners Transformed America.* Chapel Hill: The University of North Carolina Press, 2005.

Grubb, W. Norton. "Learning and Earning in the Middle: The Economic Benefits of Sub-Baccalaureate Education." Community College Research Center (April 1999), http://www.tc.columbia.edu/ccrc/PROJECTS/Grubb.htm.

Gruber, J. Richard and David Houston. *The Art of the South, 1890–2003: The Ogden Museum of Southern Art.* London: Scala, 2004.

Gudger, Sarah. Interview by Marjorie Jones. *Born in Slavery: Slave Narratives from the Federal Writers' Project, 1936–1938.* Washington: Library of Congress, Manuscript Division, 2001, http://memory.loc.gov/ammem/snhtml/snhome.html.

Guralnick, Peter. *Last Train to Memphis: the Rise of Elvis Presley.* Boston, Little, Brown and Co., 1994.

———. *Sweet Soul Music: Rhythm and Blues and the Southern Dream of Freedom.* Boston: Little, Brown and Co., 1999.

Gurganus, Allan. *Oldest Living Confederate Widow Tells All.* New York: Alfred A. Knopf, 1989.

Guste, Jr., Roy F. *Antoine's Restaurant Since 1840 Cookbook.* New Orleans: Carbery-Guste, 1979.

Gutman, Herbert. *The Black Family in Slavery and Freedom, 1750–1925.* New York: Vintage Books, 1977.

Hackney, Sheldon. *Populism to Progressivism in Alabama.* Princeton, NJ: University Press of Princeton, 1969.

Hadden, Jeffrey K. "The Rise and Fall of American Televangelism." Religious Broadcasting Web site, University of Virginia, http://religiousbroadcasting.lib.virginia.edu/pubs/risefall.html.

Hahn, Steven. *A Nation Under Our Feet: Back Political Struggles in the Rural South From Slavery to the Great Migration.* Cambridge, Mass.: The Belknap Press of Harvard University, 2003.

————. *The Roots of Southern Populism: Yeoman Farmers and the Transformation of the Georgia Upcountry, 1850–1890.* New York and Oxford: Oxford University Press, 1984.

Hair, William Ivy. *Bourbonism and Agrarian Protest: Louisiana Politics, 1877–1900.* Baton Rouge: Louisiana State University Press, 1969.

Hale, Grace Elizabeth. *Making Whiteness: The Culture of Segregation in the South, 1890–1940.* New York: Pantheon Books, 1998.

Hall, Jacquelyn Dowd, Jim Leloudis, et al. *Like a Family: The Making of a Southern Cotton Mill World.* Chapel Hill and London: University of North Carolina Press, 1987.

Hall, Jacquelyn Dowd. "Disorderly Women: Gender and Labor Militancy in the Appalachian South." In *Half Sisters of History: Southern Women and the American Past,* Catherine Clinton ed. Durham: Duke University Press, 1994.

Hall, Robert L. "Food Crops, Medicinal Plants, and the Atlantic Slave Trade." In Anne L. Bowers, ed., *African American Foodways: Explorations of History & Culture.* Urbana: University of Illinois Press, 2009.

Hankins, Barry. *Uneasy in Babylon: Southern Baptist Conservatives and American Culture.* Tuscaloosa and London: University of Alabama Press, 2002.

Harington, Donald. "The Witness of Hummingbirds," *The Oxford American* 51. Fall 2005.

Harris, Jessica B. *The Africa Cookbook: Tastes of a Continent.* New York: Simon and Schuster, 1998.

Harris, Joel Chandler, ed. *Life of Henry W. Grady, Including his Writings and Speeches.* New York: Cassell Publishing Company, 1890.

Hart, Albert Bushnell. *The Southern South.* New York and London: D. Appleton and Co., 1910.

Harvey, Paul. *Freedom's Coming: Religious Culture and the Shaping of the South from the Civil War through the Civil Rights Era.* Chapel Hill: The University of North Carolina Press, 2005.

Heard, Bill. Interview by Grace McCune. *Born in Slavery: Slave Narratives from the Federal Writers' Project, 1936–1938.* Washington: Library of Congress, Manuscript Division, 2001, http://memory.loc.gov/ammem/snhtml/snhome.html.

Hearn, Lafcadio. *La Cuisine Creole: A Collection of Culinary Recipes from Leading Chefs and Noted Creole Housewives, Who Have Made New Orleans famous for its Cuisine.* East Lansing, Mich.: Michigan State University

Library, 2004 (first published 1885), http://digital.lib.msu.edu/projects/cookbooks/index.html.

Henderson, Liney. Interview by Annie Ruth Davis. *Born in Slavery: Narratives from the Federal Writers' Project, 1936–1938.* Washington: Library of Congress, Manuscript Division, 2001, http://memory.loc.gov/ammem/snhtml/snhome.html.

Hesseltine, William B. *Confederate Leaders in the New South.* Baton Rouge: Louisiana State University Press, 1950.

Hewitt, Mark and Nancy Sweezy. *The Potter's Eye: Art and Tradition in North Carolina Pottery.* Chapel Hill: University of North Carolina Press, 2005.

Heyrman, Christine Leigh. *Southern Cross: The Beginnings of the Bible Belt.* Chapel Hill, NC: University of North Carolina Press, 1997.

Hill, Sam. "Fundamentalism in Recent Southern Culture: Has it Done What the Civil Rights Movement Couldn't Do?" *Journal of Southern Religion,* 1998, http://jsr.fsu.edu/essay.htm.

Hill, Sam. *Southern Churches in Crisis Revisited.* Tuscaloosa, AL and London: University of Alabama Press, 1999.

Hine, Darlene Clark et al. *The African-American Odyssey.* Upper Saddle River, NJ: Prentice Hall, 2000.

Hinson, Glenn. "Liner Notes." The Badgett Sisters, *Just a Little While to Stay Here.* (CD) New York: Global Village Music, 1990.

Historic Homes of the South. New York: Simon and Schuster, 1984.

Hobson, Linda Whitney. "The Study of Consciousness: An Interview with Walker Percy." The Walker Percy Project, http://www.ibiblio.org/wpercy/hobson. html (originally published in *The Georgia Review, 35,* Spring 1981).

Hodges, Luther M. *Businessman in the Statehouse: Six Years as Governor of North Carolina.* Chapel Hill: University of North Carolina Press, 1962.

Hoffman, Alfred. "Henderson or—Hell." Philadelphia: American Federation of Labor, 1927.

Hogue, James. "The 1873 Battle of Colfax, Paramilitarism and Counterrevolution in Louisiana." Unpublished paper, 2006, http://www.libertychapelcemetery.org/files/hogue-colfax.pdf (accessed 3/21/2012).

Hooper, Johnson Jones. Excerpt, *Some Adventures of Captain Simon Suggs, Late of the Tallapoosa Volunteers.* In *The Literature of the American South,* William L. Andrews, general editor. New York: W.W. Norton & Co., 1998.

Hopkins, Flora Carmichael. "A Power Structure Study of A Selected County in South Carolina." Unpublished Ph.D. dissertation in Education, University of South Carolina, 1978.

Horwitz, Tony. *Confederates in the Attic: Dispatches from the Unfinished Civil War.* New York: Vintage Books, 1999.

Huff, Annie. Interview. *Born in Slavery: Narratives from the Federal Writers' Project, 1936–1938.* Washington: Library of Congress, Manuscript Division, 2001, http://memory.loc.gov/ammem/snhtml/snhome.html.

Hughes, Richard T. "Restorationist Christianity." In *Encyclopedia of Southern Culture,* Charles Reagan Wilson and William Ferris, eds. Chapel Hill: University of North Carolina Press, 1989.

Hundley, Daniel R. *Social Relations In Our Southern States.* Chapel Hill: Documenting the American South, 1999 (first published 1860), http://docsouth.unc.edu/southlit/hundley/menu.html.

Hurst, Ronald. *Southern Furniture, 1680–1830: the Colonial Williamsburg Collection.* Williamsburg, Va.: Colonial Williamsburg Foundation in Association with Harry N. Abrams, 1997.

Hurston, Zora Neal. *Their Eyes Were Watching God.* New York: Perennial Library, 1990; first published 1937.

Hutson, Hal. Interview. *Born in Slavery: Slave Narratives from the Federal Writers' Project, 1936–1938.* Washington: Library of Congress, Manuscript Division, 2001, http://memory.loc.gov/ammem/snhtml/snhome.html.

Iliffe, John. *Honor in African History.* Cambridge: Cambridge University Press, 2005.

"Incentives for Nucor could lure recycler too." [Raleigh, NC] *News and Observer,* 30 May 1998.

Income and Wealth in the South: A State of the South Interim Report. Chapel Hill: MDC, Inc., May, 1998, http://www.mdcinc.org/docs/income.pdf.

"Interview with Paige Patterson." *Founders Journal* (Fall 2000), http://www.funders.org?FJ42/article2.html.

"Interview: A Perspective on the 1930s." In Claudia D. Johnson's *To Kill a Mockingbird: A Student Casebook to Issues, Sources, and Historic Documents* (Westport CT: Greenwood Press, 1994.

Isaac, Rhys. *The Transformation of Virginia, 1740–1790.* Chapel Hill: The University of North Carolina Press, 1982.

Irons, Charles. *The Origins of Proslavery Christianity: White and Black Evangelicals in Colonial and Antebellum Virginia.* Chapel Hill: University of North Carolina Press, 2008.

Jabour, Anya. *Marriage in the Early Republic: Elizabeth and William Wirt and the Companionate Ideal.* Baltimore: John Hopkins University Press, 1998.

Jackson, Carlton. *A Social History of the Scotch Irish.* Lanham, NY and London: 1993.

Jackson, Jerma. *Singing in My Soul: Black Gospel Music in a Secular Age.* Chapel Hill: University of North Carolina Press, 2004.

Jackson, Kenneth T. *Crabgrass Frontier: The Suburbanization of the United States.* New York: Oxford University Press, 1985.

Jacobs, Harriet A. Jacobs. *Incidents In the Life of a Slave Girl: Written by Herself,* edited by Lisa Barsky. West Berlin, NJ: Townsend Press, 2004.

Jefferson, Thomas. *Notes on the State of Virginia* in *The Life and Selected Writings of Thomas Jefferson,* edited by Adrienne Koch and William Peden. New York: Modern Library, 1972.

Johnson, Charles S. *Growing Up in the Black Belt: Negro Youth in the Rural South.* Washington, DC: American Council on Education, 1941.

————. *Shadow of the Plantation.* Chicago: University of Chicago Press, 1934.

Johnson, Clifton H., ed. *God Struck Me Dead: Religious Conversion Experiences and Autobiographies of Ex-Slaves.* Phila., PA: Pilgrim Press, 1969.

Johnson, Marion. Interview by Carol Graham. *Born in Slavery: Slave Narratives from the Federal Writers' Project, 1936–1938.* Washington: Library of Congress, Manuscript Division, 2001, http://memory.loc.gov/ammem/sn html/snhome.html.

Johnson, Michael P. *Toward a Patriarchal Republic: the Secession of Georgia.* Baton Rouge: Louisiana State University Press, 1977.

Jones, Jacqueline. "'My Mother Was Much of a Woman': Black Women, Work and the Family Under Slavery." In *Women and the Family in a Slave Society,* Paul Finkelman, ed. New York: Garland Publishing, 1989.

Jones, Sam. "For Men Only." Biblebelievers.com Web site, http://www.bible believers.com/jones_sam/.

Jordan, Winthrop C. *White over Black: American Attitudes toward the Negro, 1550–1812.* Baltimore, MD: Penguin, 1969.

July, Robert W. *A History of the African People.* New York: Charles Scribners Sons, 1980.

Kane, Steven Michael. "Snake Handlers of Southern Appalachia." Unpublished Ph.D. dissertation, Princeton University, 1979.

Kaplan. Lawrence. *Fundamentalism in Comparative Perspective.* Amherst, Mass.: University of Massachusetts Press, 1992.

Kempton, Arthur. *Boogaloo: The Quintessence of American Popular Music*. New York: Pantheon Books, 2003.

Kenan, Randall. *A Visitation of Spirits*. New York: Vintage books, 2000; first published 1989.

———. *Walking on Water: Black American Lives at the Turn of the Twenty-First Century*. New York: Alfred A. Knopf, 1999.

Kennedy, John Pendleton. Excerpt from *Swallow Barn; or A Sojourn in the Old Dominion* (originally published in 1832). In *The Literature of the American South* edited by William L. Andrews. New York and London: W.W. Norton & Co., 1998.

Kenneth Copeland Ministries Web site, http://www.kcm.org/.

Kessler-Harris, Alice. *Out to Work: A History of Wage-Earning Women in the United States*. New York: Oxford University Press, 1982.

Key, Jr., V.O. *Southern Politics in State and Nation*. New York: Vintage Books, 1949.

Kibler, James Everett. *Our Fathers' Fields: A Southern Story*. Columbia, SC: University of South Carolina Press, 1998.

Kids Count Web site, Annie E. Casey Foundation, http://www.aecf.org/kids count/.

Kimball, Marie. *Thomas Jefferson's Cook Book*. Charlottesville: University Press of Virginia, 1996.

King, Jr., Martin Luther. "Letter from a Birmingham Jail." *Historical Text Archive*, 16 April 1963, http://www.historicaltextarchive.com/sections. php?op=viewarticle&artid=40.

———. "I Have A Dream." In *Crossing the Danger Water: Three Hundred Years of African-American Writing*, Deirdre Mullane, ed. New York: Anchor Books, 1993.

King, Silvia. Interview. *Born in Slavery: Slave Narratives from the Federal Writers' Project, 1936–1938*. Washington: Library of Congress, Manuscript Division, 2001, http://memory.loc.gov/ammem/snhtml/snhome.html.

Kirby, Jack Temple. *Rural Worlds Lost: The American South, 1920–1960*. Baton Rouge: Louisiana State University Press, 1987.

———. *The Countercultural South*. Athens, GA and London: The University of Georgia Press, 1995.

Kirwin, Albert Dennis. *Revolt of the Rednecks: Mississippi Politics: 1876–1925*. Lexington: University of Kentucky Press, 1951.

Klein, Herbert S. *The Atlantic Slave Trade*. Cambridge, United Kingdom: Cambridge University Press, 1999.

Knox, John B. "Address." *Journal of the Proceedings of the Constitutional Convention of the State of Alabama.* Montgomery, AL: Brown Printing Co., 1901.

Kolchin, Peter. *American Slavery: 1619–1877.* New York: Hill and Wang, 1997.

Kosmin, Barry A. and Ariela Keysar. "American Religious Identification Survey: Summary Report, March 2009." http://b27.cc.trincoll.edu/weblogs/AmericanReligionSurvey-ARIS/reports/ARIS_Report_2008.pdf.

Kornhauser, William. *The Politics of Mass Society.* Glencoe, Ill.: Free Press, 1959.

Kosmin, Barry A. and Seymour P. Lachman. *One Nation Under God: Religion in Contemporary American Society.* New York: Harmony Books, 1993.

Kosmin, Barry A., Egon Mayer, and Ariela Keysar. *American Religious Identification Survey, 2001.* New York: The Graduate Center of the City University of New York, 2001.

Kousser, J. Morgan. *The Shaping of Southern Politics: Suffrage Restriction and the Establishment of the One-Party South, 1880–1910.* New Haven: Yale University Press, 1974.

Krogman, Wilton M. "The Concept of Race." *The Science of Man in the World Crisis,* Ralph Linton ed. New York: Columbia University Press, 1945.

Kruse, Kevin. *White Flight: Atlanta and the Making of Modern Conservatism.* Princeton, New Jersey: Princeton University Press, 2005.

Lacy, Robert. "Economic History: Washstands, Sideboards, and Parlor Suites." Federal Reserve Bank of Richmond, Spring 2005, http://www.Richmond fed.org/publications/economic_research/region_focus/spring_2005/economic_history.cfm (accessed 13 March 2006).

———. "Whither North Carolina Furniture Manufacturing?" Working paper, Federal Reserve Bank of Richmond, September 2004, http://www.richmond fed.org/publications/economic_research/working_papers/pdfswp04-7.pdf (accessed 13 March 2006).

Lamphear, John and Toyin Falola. "Aspects of Early African History." In *Africa,* ed. by Phyllis M. Martin and Patrick O'Meara. Bloomington, IN: Indiana University Press, 1995.

Lane, Miles. *Architecture of the Old South.* New York: Abbeville Press, 1993.

Lassiter, Matthew D. *Suburban Politics in the Sunbelt South.* Princeton, New Jersey: Princeton University Press, 2005.

Lawson, John. *A New Voyage to Carolina; Containing the Exact Description and Natural History of That Country: Together with the Present State Thereof.*

And A Journal of a Thousand Miles, Travel'd Thro' Several Nations of Indians. Giving a Particular Account of Their Customs, Manners, &c. Chapel Hill: Documenting the American South, 2001 (first published 1709), http://docsouth.unc.edu/nc/lawson/lawson.html.

Lebsock, Suzanne D. "Radical Reconstruction and the Property Rights of Southern Women." In *Half Sisters of History: Southern Women and the American Past,* Catherine Clinton ed. Durham: Duke University Press, 1994.

————. *The Free Women of Petersburg: Status and Culture in A Southern Town, 1784–1860.* New York: W. W. Norton & Co., 1984.

Lee, Harper. *To Kill a Mockingbird.* Philadelphia: Lippincott, 1960.

Lemann, Nicholas. *The Promised Land: The Great Black Migration and How it Changed America.* New York: Vintage Books, 1992.

Levine, Lawrence W. *Black Culture and Black Consciousness: Afro-American Folk Thought from Slavery to Freedom.* Oxford: Oxford University Press, 1978.

Lewin, Tamar. "Up from the Holler: Living in two Worlds, at Home in Neither." *The New York Times,* 19 May 2005, Http://www.nytimes.com (accessed 19 May 2005).

Lewis, Edna. *The Taste of Country Cooking.* New York: Knopf, 2006.

Leyburn, James G. *The Scotch-Irish: A Social History.* Chapel Hill: UNC Press, 1962.

Link, William A. *The Paradox of Southern Progressivism, 1880–1930.* Chapel Hill and London: The University of North Carolina Press, 1992.

Litwack, Leon F. *Trouble in Mind: Black Southerners in the Age of Jim Crow.* New York: Alfred A. Knopf, 1998.

Livingston, Jane and John Beardsley. *Black Folk Art in America, 1930–1980.* Jackson, MS: University of Mississippi, 1982.

Lovejoy, Paul. "Transformation in Slavery." In *Problems in African History,* ed. by Robert O. Collins. Princeton, NJ: Markus Wiener Publishers, 2005.

Luebke, Paul. *Tar Heel Politics 2000.* Chapel Hill and London: University of North Carolina Press, 1998.

Lytle, Andrew. "The Hind Tit." In *I'll Take My Stand,* Twelve Southerners. Baton Rouge and London: Louisiana State University Press, 1977; first published, 1930.

MacGillis, Alec and Joe Cohen. Democrats Add Suburbs to Their Growing Coalition." *The Washington Post,* November 6, 2008, http://www.washingtonpost.com/wp-dyn/content/article/2008/11/05/AR2008110504824.html.

Mack, Richard. Interview by Martha Pinckney. *Born in Slavery: Slave Narratives from the Federal Writers' Project, 1936–1938.* Washington: Library of Congress, Manuscript Division, 2001, http://memory.loc.gov/ammem/sn html/snhome.html.

MacLean, Nancy. *Behind the Mask of Chivalry: The Making of the Second Ku Klux Klan.* New York: Oxford University Press, 1994.

Mahaffey, Nancy Newsom. "Kentucky Bacon." Interview by Amy Evans, 24 August 2005, Southern Foodways Alliance, http://www.southernfoodways.com/oral_history/bacon/nancy_newsom_mahaffey.shtml (accessed 1/26/06).

Makowsky, Veronica. "Walker Percy and Southern Literature." The Walker Percy Project, 1996, http://www.ibiblio.org/wpercy/library.html (accessed 5/14/06).

Malone, Bill C. *Country Music USA: A Fifty Year History.* Austin, Texas: University of Texas Press, 1985.

———. *Don't Get Above Your Raisin': Country Music and the South Working Class.* Urbana, Illinois: University of Illinois Press, 2002.

Mandle, Jay R. *The Roots of Black Poverty: The Southern Plantation Economy After the Civil War.* Durham: Duke University Press, 1978.

Manis, Andrew M. "Protestants: From Denominational Controversialists to Culture Warriors." In *Religion and Public Life in the Southern Crossroads: Showdown States* William Lindsey and Mark Silk, eds. Walnut Creek, CA: Altamira Press, 2005.

———. "The Civil Religions of the South." In *Religion and Public Life in the South: In the Evangelical Mode,* Charles Reagan Wilson and Mark Silk, eds. Walnut Creek, CA: AltaMira Press, 2005.

Martin, Steven P. "Growing Evidence for a 'Divorce Divide'?: Education and Marital Dissolution Rates in the U.S. since the 1970s." Russell Sage Foundation, http://www/russellsage.org/publications.

Martinez, Amy. "Workers suffer in global economy." [Raleigh, NC] *The News and Observer,* 30 May 2004.

Marty, Martin E. *Pilgrims in Their Own Land: 300 Years of Religion in America.* New York: Penguin Books, 1987.

Mason, Bobbie Ann. "An Ode to a Strange Procession." *The Oxford American* 53. Spring 2006.

Mathews, Donald G. *Religion in the Old South.* Chicago and London: The University of Chicago Press, 1977.

Matthews, Holly. "Doctors and Root Doctors: Patients Who Use Both." In *Herbal and Magical Medicine: Traditional Healing Today,* James Kirkland,

Holly Matthews, C.W. Sullivan III, and Karen Baldwin, eds. Durham: Duke University Press, 1992.

McCulloch-Williams, Martha. *Dishes and Beverages of the Old South.* Knoxville: University of Tennessee Press, 1988; first published 1913.

McCurry, Stephanie. *Masters of Small Worlds: Yeoman Households, Gender Relations, and the Political Culture of the Antebellum South Carolina Low Country.* New York: Oxford University Press, 1995.

McDonald, Forest and Grady McWhiney. *"The South from Self-Sufficiency to Peonage: An Interpretation."* American Historical Review 85 *(December 1980),* 1111–1118.

McDonald, Roderick A. "Independent Economic Production By Slaves on Antebellum Louisiana Sugar Plantations." In *Cultivation and Culture: Labor and d the Shaping of Slave Life in the Americas,* Ira Berlin and Phillip D. Morgan eds. Charlottesville, VA: University Press of Virginia, 1993.

McLaurin, Melton. *Paternalism and Protest: Southern Cotton Mill Workers and Organized Labor, 1875–1905.* Westport: Greenwood, 1971.

McLendon, Sandy. "the beginning of now: john portman's 1967 hyatt regency in atlanta." *jet set modern.com,* http://jetsetmodern.com/hyatt.htm (accessed 3/3/06).

McLoughlin, William G. *Revivals, Awakenings, and Reform: A Essay on Religion and Social Change in America, 1607–1977.* Chicago and London: The University of Chicago Press, 1978.

McMath, Robert C., Jr. *Populist Vanguard: A History of the Southern Farmers' Alliance.* New York: W.W. Norton Co., 1977.

McMillen, Sally. *Motherhood in the Old South: Pregnancy, Childbirth, and Infant Rearing.* Baton Rouge: Louisiana State University Press, 1990.

McNaughton, Patrick R. and Diane Pelrine. "African Art." In *Africa* ed. by Phyllis M. Martin and Patrick O'Meara. Bloomington, IN: Indiana University Press, 1995.

McNeil, F. Marian. *The Scots Kitchen: It's Traditions and Lore with Old Time Recipes.* Edinburgh: Mercat Press, 2006 (originally published in 1929).

McWhiney, Grady. *Cracker Culture: Celtic Ways in the Old South.* University, Alabama: University of Alabama Press, 1988.

Meier, August. *Negro Thought in America, 1880–1915.* Ann Arbor: The University of Michigan Press, 1970.

Mencken, H. L. "The Sahara of the Bozart." In *The Literature of the American South* William Andrews, ed. New York: W. W. Norton & Co., 1998.

Miller, Randall. "A Church in Cultural Captivity: Some Speculations on Catholic Identity." In Randall Miller and Jon L. Wakelyn, eds., *Catholics in the Old South* (Macon, Georgia: Mercer University Press, 1983.

Miller, Stephen F. "Plantation Labor Organization and Slave Life on the Cotton Frontier: The Alabama-Mississippi Black Belt, 1815–1840." In *Cultivation and Culture: Labor and d the Shaping of Slave Life in the Americas*, Ira Berlin and Phillip D. Morgan eds. Charlottesville, VA: University Press of Virginia, 1993.

Miller, Wesley E. "A Sociological Analysis of the New Christian Right." Unpublished Ph.D. dissertation, Loyola University of Chicago,1984.

"Mississippi's 'Personhood Amendment' Fails at Polls." *CBSNEWS*, 8 November 2011, http://www.cbsnews.com/8301-250_162-57321126/mississippis-personhood-amendment-fails-at-polls/(accessed 4/1/2012).

Mitchell, Margaret. *Gone with the Wind*. New York: Warner Books, 1993; first published 1936.

Mitchell, Sam. Interview by Chlotilde R. Martin. *Born in Slavery: Slave Narratives from the Federal Writers' Project, 1936–1938*. Washington: Library of Congress, Manuscript Division, 2001, http://memory.loc.gov/ammem/sn html/snhome.html.

Mizzell, Hayes. "Racial Justice and Equity: Challenges for the American South," draft. MDC, http://www.mdcinc.org/docs/mizell.pdf.

Montgomery, William E. "Semi-Involuntary: African-American Religion." In *Religion and Public Life in the South: in the Evangelical Mode*, Charles Reagan Wilson and Mark Silk, eds. Walnut Creek, CA: Altamira Press, 2005.

Moore, Charles W. "Southerness in Architecture." *Architecture Week* (September 2004), http://www.architectureweek.com/2004/0901/culture_1-1.html (accessed 4 March 2006).

Morgan, Edmund. *American Slavery, American Freedom*. New York: W.W. Norton and Co., 1975.

Morton, Robert. *Southern Antiques and Folk Art*. Birmingham, AL: 1976.

"Most Oppose Gay Marriage; Fewer Back an Amendment." June 2006, ABC News Polling Unit, *ABC News*, http://abcnews.go.com/US/Politics.

Moye, J. Todd. *Let the People Decide: Black Freedom and White Resistance Movements in Sunflower County, Mississippi, 1945–1986*. Chapel Hill: University of North Carolina Press, 2004.

Murray, Charles. *Coming Apart: The State of White America, 1960–2010*. New York: Crown Forum, 2012.

Naipaul, V.S. *A Turn in the South.* New York: Alfred A. Knopf, 1989.

Napier, John. H. III. "Military Schools." In *Encyclopedia of Southern Culture,* Charles R. Reagan and William Ferris, eds. Chapel Hill and London: University of North Carolina Press, 1989.

"Narrative of James Curry." In *Slave Testimony: Two Centuries of Letters, Speeches, Interviews, and Autobiographies,* John Blassingame, ed. Baton Rouge: Louisiana State University Press, 1977.

National Center for Children in Poverty Web site, http://www.nccp.org/index. html. (Accessed 3/6/2012)

Neal, Bill. *Bill Neal's Southern Cooking.* Chapel Hill: The University of North Carolina Press, 1985.

Neal, Moreton. *Remembering Bill Neal: Favorite Recipes from a Life in Cooking.* Chapel Hill: University of North Carolina Press, 2004.

Nisbett, Richard E. and Dov Cohen. *Culture of Honor: The Psychology of Violence in the South.* Boulder, Colorado: Westview Press, 1996.

Northup, Solomon. *Twelve Years a Slave: Narrative of Solomon Northup, a Citizen of New-York, Kidnapped in Washington City in 1841, and Rescued in 1853.* Chapel Hill: Documenting the American South, 2000 (first published 1853), http://docsouth.unc.edu/northup/northup.html#northup208.

Nott, Josiah C. *Two Lectures on the Connection Between the Biblical and Physical History of Man.* New York: Negro Universities Press, 1969; first published 1849.

O'Brien, Gail Williams. *The Legal Fraternity and the Making of a New South Community, 1848–1882.* Athens and London: The University of Georgia Press, 1986.

Oakes, James. *The Ruling Race: A History of American Slaveholders.* New York: Vintage Books, 1983.

Oates, Stephen B. *Let the Trumpet Sound: The Life of Martin Luther King, Jr.* New York: New American Library, 1982.

Official Proceedings of the Constitutional Convention of the State of Alabama, May 21st, 1901 to September 3rd, 1901. Vol. III. Alabama: Wetumpka Printing Co., 1941.

Olmsted, Frederick Law. *A Journey in the Seaboard Slave States; With Remarks on Their Economy.* 1856; Chapel Hill: Documenting the American South, 2001 (first published 1856), http://docsouth.unc.edu/nc/olmsted/olmsted. html.

————. *The Cotton Kingdom: A Travelers Observations on Cotton and Slavery in the American Slave States,* edited by Arthur M. Schlesinger Sr. New York: Modern Library, 1984; first published 1861.

Opala, Joseph. "Rice, Slavery, and the Sierra Leone-American Connection." Gilder Lehrman Center, http://www.yale.edu/glc/gullah/04.htm (accessed, 3/30/09).

Orr, Oliver H., Jr. *Charles Brantley Aycock.* Chapel Hill: University of North Carolina Press, 1961.

"Our History." Thomas Road Baptist Church Web site, http://home.trbc.org/index.cfm?PID=9059.

Owenby, Ted. *Subduing Satan: Religion & Manhood in the Rural South, 1865–1920.* Chapel Hill: University of North Carolina, 1990.

Owsley, Frank L. *Plain Folk of the Old South.* Baton Rouge: Louisiana State University Press, 1982; first published 1949.

Painter, Nell Irvin. *Southern History Across the Color Line.* Chapel Hill: University of North Carolina Press, 2002.

Palmer, Colin A. *Passageways: An Interpretative History of Black America, Volume I: 1619–1863.* Fort Worth, TX: Harcourt Brace College Publishers, 1998.

Palmer, Robert. *Deep Blues.* New York: Penguin Books, 1982.

Parent, Wayne and Peter Petrakis. "Populism Left and Right: Politics of the Rural South." In *The Rural South Since World War II*, R. Douglas Hunt ed. Baton Rouge, LA: Louisiana State University Press, 1998.

Parker, Allen. *Recollections of Slavery Times.* Chapel Hill: Documenting the American South, 2000(first published 1895), http://docsouth.unc.edu/neh/parker/parker.html.

"Pat Robertson." The Museum of Broadcast Communications, http://www.museum.tv/archives/etv/R/htmlR/robertsonpa/robersonpa.htm.

Payne, David. *Early from the Dance.* New York: Doubleday, 1989.

————. *Gravesend Light: A Novel.* New York: Doubleday, 2000.

————. *Ruin Creek: A Novel.* New York: Plume, 2002.

Pease, Jane H. and William Pease. *A Family of Women: The Carolina Petigrus in Peace and War.* Chapel Hill: University of North Carolina Press, 1999.

Pennington, Estill Curtis. *Look Away: Reality and Sentiment in Southern Art.* Spartanburg, SC: Saraland Press, 1989.

"Per Capita Tax Burden and Return of Federal Tax Dollar: 2005." Northeast Midwest Institute (Washington, DC), http://www. nemw.org.

"Percent of Men 15 and Over Who Were Never Married: 2005" and "Percent of Women 15 and Over Who Were Never Married: 2005." U.S. Census Bureau, American FactFinder, http://factfinder.census.gov.

Percy, Walker. *The Last Gentleman.* New York: Ivy Books, 1966.

———. *The Moviegoer.* New York: Ivy Books, 1961.

Percy, William Alexander. *Lanterns on the Levee: Recollections of a Planter's Son.* Baton Rouge: LSU Press, 1973; first published, 1941.

Perdue, Theda and Michael D. Green. *The Columbia Guide to American Indians of the Southeast.* New York: Columbia University Press, 2001.

Phillips, Ulrich B. *Life and Labor in the Old South.* Boston and Toronto: Little, Brown and Co., 1963; first published 1929.

Pierce, John. Interview. *American Life Histories: Manuscripts from the Federal Writers' Project, 1936–1938.* Washington: Library of Congress, Manuscript Division, 1998, http://memory.loc.gov/ammem/wpaintro/wpahome.html.

Pinkston, Karen. "Lusco's," interview by Amy Evans, June 12, 19, 2003. Southern Foodways Alliance, http://www.southernfoodways.com/oral_history/delta/greenwood/GW06_luscos.shtml (accessed 1/31/06).

Pisione, Deborah Perry. *The Many Faces of 21st Century Working Women: A Report to the Women's Bureau of the U.S. Department of Labor.* McLean, Va.: Education Consortium Co., 2004.

Poesch, Jessie. *The Art of the Old South: Painting, Sculpture, Architecture and the Products of Craftsmen, 1560–1860.* New York: Alfred A. Knopf, 1983.

Pope, Liston. *Millhands and Preachers: A Study of Gastonia.* New Haven and London: Yale University Press, 1942.

Population and Economic Study: Pee Dee Region (SC: Pee Dee Regional Planning and Development Council, 1972.

"Postsecondary Attainment for 1988 8th Graders." *Student Effort and Educational Progress: Postsecondary Persistence and Progress,* National Center for Education Statistics (2003), http://nces.ed.gov/progrms/coe/2003/section 3/indicator22.asp.

Powdermaker, Hortense. *After Freedom: A Cultural Study in the Deep South.* New York: Atheneum, 1939.

Prather, H. Leon, Sr. *We Have Taken a City: Wilmington Racial Massacre and Coup of 1898.* Wilmington, NC: NU World Enterprises, Inc., 1998; first published, 1984.

"President Bush, Mobilization Drives Propel Turnout to Post 1968 High; Kerry, Democratic Weakness Shown." Committee for the Study of the American Electorate, circa 2005.

Price, Reynolds. *Clear Pictures: First Loves, First Guides*. New York: Atheneum, 1989.

"Prison and Jail Inmates at Midyear 2002." Bureau of Justice Statistics Bulletin, U.S. Department of Justice, 2003, http://www.ojp.usdoj.gov/bjs/pub/pdf/pjim02.pdf.

Promised Land: Take Me to Chicago. (Video) Bethesda, MD: The Discovery Channel, c. 1995.

Putnam, Robert D. and David E. Campbell, *Amazing Grace: How Religion Divides and Unites Us*. New York: Simon and Schuster, 2010.

Raboteau, Albert J. *Slave Religion: The "Invisible Institution" in the Antebellum South*. Oxford: Oxford University Press, 1980.

"Racial Composition of Degree Headcount Enrollment in North Carolina Colleges and Universities, Fall 2005,"http://intranet.northcarolina.edu/docs/assessment/Abstract/2005-06/section%201/T._1906.pdf.

Raines, Howell. *My Soul Is Rested: Movement Days in the Deep South Remembered*. New York: Bantam Books, 1978.

Randolph, Mary. *The Virginia Housewife, or Methodical Cook*. East Lansing, Mich.: Michigan State University Library, 2004 (first published 1838), http://digital.lib.msu.edu/projects/cookbooks/html/books/book_10.cfm.

Ransom, Roger and Richard Sutch, *One Kind of Freedom: The Economic Consequences of Emancipation*. Cambridge: Cambridge University Press, 1977.

Rapture Ready Web site, http://www.raptureready.com/rap2.html (accessed 3/20/2012).

Reed, John Shelton. *One South: An Ethnic Approach to Regional Culture*. Baton Rouge and London: Louisiana State University Press, 1982.

———. *The Enduring South: Subcultural Persistence in Mass Society*. Chapel Hill: University of North Carolina Press, 1972.

———. *My Tears Spoiled My Aim and Other Reflections on Southern Culture*. Columbia and London: University of Missouri Press, 1993.

Reiss, Oscar. *Blacks in Colonial America*. Jefferson, NC: McFarland & Co., Inc., Publishers, 1997.

"Religious Congregations and Membership in the United States, 2000." Glenmary Research Center, http://www.valpo.edu/geomet/pics/geo200/religion/church_bodies.gif.

"Religious Membership Maps and Reports, Individual States, 1990–2000." America Religious Data Archive, http://www.thearda.com/test_main.asp?Show=RCMS2000.

"The Renns." Interview. *American Life Histories: Manuscripts from the Federal Writers' Project, 1936–1938.* Washington: Library of Congress, Manuscript Division, 1998, http://memory.loc.gov/ammem/wpaintro/wpahome.html.

Report on Condition of Women and Child Wage-Earners in the United States, Vol. 1: Cotton Textile Industry. Washington: U.S. Government Printing Office, 1910.

"Resolution on Homosexuality." SBC Resolutions, June 1980, SBC Net, Southern Baptist Convention, 1999–2007, http://www.sbc.net/ resolutions.

Rhodes, Colleen. "The Last Duel Fought in South Carolina." In *Darlingtoniana: A History of People, Places, and Events in Darlington, South Carolina,* Eliza Cowan Ervin and Horace Fraser Rudisill eds. Columbia: R.L. Bryan Co., 1964.

Richardson, David. "The Rise of the Atlantic Empires." *Transatlantic Slavery: Against Human Dignity,* Anthony Tibbles ed. Liverpool: Liverpool University Press, 2005.

Rickford, John Russell and Russell John Rickford. *Spoken Soul: The Story of Black English.* New York: Wiley, 2000.

Riesman, David with Nathan Glazer and Reuell Denney. *The Lonely Crowd: A Study of the Changing American Character.* New Haven: Yale University Press, 1961.

Roach, David and Jeff Robinson. "Conservative Resurgence about 'Theology,' not 'Politics.'" *Florida Baptist Witness,* 3 November 2005, http://www. floridabaptistwitness.com/2478.article.

Roach, Susan. "Quilting, Anglo-American." In *Encyclopedia of Southern Culture,* Charles Reagan Wilson and William Ferris, eds. Chapel Hill: University of North Carolina Press, 1989.

Robert Johnson: King of the Delta Blues (CD) New York: Sony Music Entertainment, Inc., 1998; first recorded 1937.

Robertson, Ben. *Red Hills and Cotton: An Upcountry Memory.* Columbia, SC: University of South Carolina Press, 1973; first published 1942.

Rogers, William Warren, Jr. *The One-Gallused Rebellion: Agrarianism in Alabama, 1865–1896.* Tuscaloosa and London, Univ. of Alabama Press, 1970.

Rosengarten, Theodore. *Tombee: Portrait of a Cotton Planter with The Plantation Journal of Thomas B. Chaplin (1822–1890).* New York: William Morrow, 1986.

Roth, Leland M. *American Architecture: A History.* Boulder, Colorado: Westview Press, 2001.

Rozell, Mark J. and Clyde Wilcox. "Virginia: Birthplace of the Christian Right." In *The Christian Right in American Politics: Marching to the Millennium,* John C. Green et al. eds. Washington, DC: Georgetown University Press, 2003.

Rubin, Richard. "The Colfax Riot." *The Atlantic,* July/August 2003, http://www.atlantic.com/issues/2003/07/rubin.htm.

Russakoff, Dale. "Alabama Tied in Knots by Tax Vote." *The Washington Post,* 17 August 2003, http://www.washingtonpost.com/ac2/wp-dyn/A4130-2003 Aug16?language=printer.

Rutledge, Sarah. *The Carolina Housewife.* Columbia, SC: University of South Carolina Press facsimile ed., 1979; first published 1847.

Sack, Kevin. "Shared Prayers, Mixed Blessings." *How Race Is Lived in America.* New York: Times Books, 2001.

Salisbury Globe [NC].

"The Saloon in the South," *The Outlook* (14 March 1908): 581–582.

Sanders, Emma."*Singin' Praises Dat's My Life, Lawd,*" interview by Caldwell Sims. *American Life Histories: Manuscripts from the Federal Writers' Project, 1936–1938.* Washington: Library of Congress, Manuscript Division, 1998, http://memory.loc.gov/ammem/wpaintro/wpahome.html.

Scarborough, William K. *Masters of the Big House: Elite Slaveholders of the Mid-Nineteenth-Century South.* Baton Rouge: Louisiana State University Press, 2003.

Schlafly, Phyllis. *A Choice Not an Echo.* Alton, Ill.: Pere Marquette Press, 1964.

Schwartz, Michael. *Radical Protest and Social Structure.* New York: Academic Press, 1976.

Skocpol, Theda and Vanessa Williamson. *The Tea Party and the Remaking of Republican Conservatism.* New York: Oxford University Press, 2012.

Scott, Anne Firor. *The Southern Lady: From Pedestal to Politics 1830–1930.* Chicago: University of Chicago, 1970.

Sears, James T. *Growing Up Gay in the South.* New York: Harrington Park Press, 1991.

Sellers, James Sellers. *The Prohibition Movement in Alabama, 1702–1943.* Chapel Hill: University of North Carolina Press, 1943.

Seroka, Jim. "Alabama's Tax Reform: What Went Wrong and Why?" Alabama Municipal Revenue Officers Association, December 5, 2003, http://web6.duc.auburn.edu/outreach/cgs/publications/Alabamataxvote2003.pdf.

Shimron, Yonat. "Group launch holy war against 'Happy Holiday.'" *Raleigh News and Observer,* 3 December 2005, http://www.newsobserver.com/102/story/373941.html.

Simkins, Francis Butler. *The Tillman Movement in South Carolina*. Durham: Duke University Publications, 1926.

Simpson, William Hayes. *Southern Textile Communities*. Charlotte, NC: American Cotton Manufacturers Association, 1948.

Singal, Daniel Joseph. *The War Within: From Victorian to Modernist Thought in the South, 1919–1945*. Chapel Hill: The University of North Carolina Press, 1982.

Smedley, Audrey. *Race in North America: Origins and Evolution of a Worldview*. Boulder, CO: Westview Press, 1999.

Smith, Christine and Robert Faris. "Socioeconomic Inequality in the American Religious System: An Update and Assessment." *Journal for the Scientific Study of Religion* 44, no. 1, March 2005.

Smith, Hector. Interview by Annie Ruth Davis. *Born in Slavery: Slave Narratives from the Federal Writers' Project, 1936–1938* (Washington: Library of Congress, Manuscript Division, 2001, http://memory. loc.gov/ammem/sn html/snhome.html.

Smith, Lee. *Oral History*. New York: Ballantine, 1983.

Smith, Lillian. *Killers of the Dream*. Garden City, New York: Anchor Books, 1963; first published, 1949.

South Henderson Pentecostal Holiness Church Web site, http://www.shphc. org/AboutUs.htm#History.

Southern Focus Poll, Fall 1992. Institute for Research in the Social Science, University of North Carolina at Chapel Hill, 1992.

Southern Focus Poll, Spring 2001. Chapel Hill: UNC Center for the Study of the American South, 2001.

"Southern Rap." *Wikipedia: The Free Encyclopedia*, http://en.wikipedia.org/wiki/Southern_rap (accessed 6/10/06).

Sparks, Elder John. *The Roots of Appalachian Christianity: The Life and Legacy of Elder Shubal Stearns*. Lexington, KY: University Press of Kentucky, 2001.

Stallings, Rev. W. M. "Shouting from Heaven," interview by Robert V. Williams. *American Life Histories: Manuscripts from the Federal Writers' Project, 1936–1940*. Washington: Library of Congress, Manuscript Division, 1998, http://memory.loc.gov/ammem/wpaintro/wpahome.html.

Stanley, Harold. "The South in the 2000 Elections." In *The 2000 Presidential Election in the South: Partisanship and Southern Party Systems in the 21st Century*, Robert P. Steed and Lawrence W. Moreland, eds. Westport, Connecticut: Praeger, 2002.

Stanley, Linda. "Collard Greens." What's Cooking America: History and Legends of Favorite Foods, http://whatscookingamerica.net/Vegetables/Collard Greens.htm (accessed 1/26/06).

"State Measures to Balance FY 2010—FY 2012 Budgets." National Council of State Legislatures, http://www.ncsl.org/issues-research/budget/state-measures-to-close-budget-gaps.aspx (accessed 4/1/2012).

State of the South, 1998. Chapel Hill, NC: MDC, Inc., 1998.

State of the South 2002: Shadows in the Sunbelt Revisited. Chapel Hill, NC: MDC, Inc., 2002.

State of the South, 2007: Philanthropy as the South's "Passing Gear." Chapel Hill, NC: MDC, Inc., 2007.

The State of the South 2010: Chapter 1: Beyond the Gilded Age. Chapel Hill, NC: MDC, Inc., 2010.

The State of the South 2010: Chapter 2: Talent and Skill: Antidotes to Uncertainty. Chapel Hill, NC: MDC, Inc., 2010.

The State of the South 2011: Looking Ahead: Leadership for Hard Times. Chapel Hill, NC: MDC, Inc., 2011.

Steelman, Joseph F. "The Progressive Era in North Carolina, 1884–1917." Unpublished Ph.D. dissertation, University of North Carolina at Chapel Hill, 1955.

Stephenson, Annie. Interview by T. Pat Matthews. *Born in Slavery: Narratives from the Federal Writers' Project, 1936–1938.* Washington: Library of Congress, Manuscript Division, 2001, http://memory.loc.gov/ammem/snhtml/snhome.html.

Stern, Michael. "Central Grocery-New Orleans, LA." Roadfood.Com, 11/8/2000, http://www.roadfood.com/Reviews/Writeup.aspx?ReviewID=122&RefID=122 (accessed 2/4/06).

Stewart, James Brewer. *Holy Warriors: The Abolitionists and American Slavery.* New York: Hill and Wang, 1976.

Stone, Ruth. "African Music Performed." In *Africa,* ed. by Phyllis M. Martin and Patrick O'Meara. Bloomington, IN: Indiana University Press, 1995.

Stowell, Daniel W. *Rebuilding Zion: The Religious Reconstruction of the South, 1863–1877.* New York: Oxford University Press, 1998.

"Strom Thurmond's family confirms paternity claim." *CNN,* 16 December 2003, http://www.cnn.com/2003/US/12/15/thurmond.paternity/.

Stroyer, Jacob. *My Life In the South.* Chapel Hill: Documenting the American South, 2001(first published 1885), http://docsouth.unc.edu/neh/stroyer85/stroyer85.html.

Sweezy, Nancy. *Raised in Clay: The Southern Pottery Tradition*. Chapel Hill: The University of North Carolina Press, 1994.

The Tabernacle, http://www.tabernacleag.org/index.php.

Taylor, Joe Gray. *Eating, Drinking, and Visiting in the South*. Baton Rouge: Louisiana State University Press, 1982.

Taylor, John Martin. *Hoppin' John's Lowcountry Cooking: Recipes and Ruminations from Charleston and the Carolina Coastal Plain*. New York: Bantam Books, 1992.

"The Tea Party and Religion." The Pugh Forum on Religion & Public Life, 23 February 2011, http://www.pewforum.org/Politics-and-Elections/Tea-Party-and-Religion.aspx (accessed 3/28/2012).

"Teen Motherhood at Record Low in the United States (Figure 4)" (2003). Annie E. Casey Foundation, Kids Count, http://www.aecf.org/kidscount/.

"Texas in Focus: A Statewide View of Opportunities." Window on State Government, http://www.window.state.tx.us/specialrpt/tif/population.html (accessed 3/30/2012).

Third Annual Report on University of North Carolina Enrollment Planning. December 15, 2001, http://www.northcarolina.edu/docs/aa/planning/Rpt_on_Enroll_Plng_2001.pdf.

Thomas, Hugh. *The Slave Trade: the Story of the Atlantic Slave Trade, 1440–1870*. New York: Simon Shuster, 1997.

Thomas, Ike. Interview by Alberta Miner. *Born in Slavery: Slave Narratives from the Federal Writers' Project, 1936–1938*. Washington: Library of Congress, Manuscript Division, 2001, http://memory.loc.gov/ammem/snhtml/snhome.html.

Thomas, Mary Martha, "The Ideology of the Alabama Women's Suffrage Movement, 1890–1920." In *Southern Women: Histories and Identities*, ed. by Virginia Bernhard, et al. Columbia, Missouri: University of Missouri Press, 1992.

Thompson, Robert Farris. *Flash of the Spirit: African and Afro-American Art and Philosophy*. New York: Vintage Books, 1984.

Thornwell, James Henley. *The State of the Country: An Article Republished from The Southern Presbyterian Review*. Chapel Hill: Documenting the American South, University of North Carolina, Chapel Hill, 1999 (originally published 1861), http://docsouth.unc.edu/imls/thornwell/thornwel.html.

Tindall, George B. *The Emergence of the New South, 1913–1945*. Baton Rouge: Louisiana State University Press, 1967.

Tolnay, Stewart E. *The Bottom Rung: African American Family Life on Southern Farms*. Chicago: University of Illinois Press, 1999.

Trelease, Alan. *Reconstruction: the Great Experiment*. New York: Harper Torchbooks, 1971.

Tullos, Allen. *Habits of Industry: White Culture and the Transformation of the Carolina Piedmont*. Chapel Hill: University of North Carolina Press, 1989.

Twain, Mark. *Adventures of Huckleberry Finn*. New York: Modern Library Paperback Edition, 2001; first published 1885.

Two States of Mississippi. Jackson, MS: The Mississippi Forum on Children and Families, 2006, http://www.mfcf.org/kc/06_MS_Databook/O6_KC_MS_ Databook.pdf.

"The Types of Households in the South in 2005." and "The Types of Households in United States in 2005," U.S. Census Bureau, American FactFinder, 2005 American Community Survey, http://factfinder.census.gov.

Tyson, Timothy B. *Blood Done Signed My Name: A True Story*. New York: Crown Publishers, 2004.

Umfleet, LeRae, Principal Researcher. *1898 Wilmington Race Riot Report*. Raleigh: Wilmington Race Riot Commission, North Carolina Department of Cultural Resources, Office of Archives and History, May 31, 2006, http://www.ah.dcr.state.nc.us/1898-wrrc/report/report.htm.

"UNC, Public College Students Post High Family Income." *Clarion Call*, Vol. 1, no. 44, (2 December 1999), http://www.popecenter.org.

"United Methodist Statistics on Women Clergy." The United Methodist Church Web site, http://archives.umc.org/interior.asp?ptid=1&mid =2620.

Unofficial Voter Turnout," *United States Election Project*, at http://elections. gmu.edu/preliminary_vote_2008.html.

U.S. Bureau of the Census. *Eighth Census of the United States, Agriculture of the United States in 1860*. Washington, DC, Government Printing Office, 1864.

―――. *Twelfth Census of the United States, 1900, Vol. V, Agriculture, pt.1* (Washington, DC: U.S. GPO, 1902.

―――. *Thirteenth Census of the United States Taken in the Year 1910, Vol. V, Agriculture, 1909, 1910*. Washington, DC: U.S. GPO, 1914.

―――. *Fourteenth Census, 1920, Vol. V: Agriculture*. Washington, DC: U.S. GPO, 1922.

―――. *Fifteenth Census of the United States: 1930, Agriculture, Vol. III, pt. 2-Southern States*. Washington: US Government Printing Office, 1932.

————. *Census of Agriculture: 1935, Report of States with Statistics for Counties and a Summary for the United States, Vol. 1*. Washington, DC: U.S. Government Printing Office, 1935.

————. *Census of Agriculture,1964, Volume 1,Statistics for the States and Counties, Pt. 27, South Carolina*. Washington, DC:U.S. Government Printing Office, 1967.

U.S. Department of Agriculture. *1997 Census of Agricultural Profiles, South Carolina State Profiles*. Washington, DC: U.S. Government Printing Office, 1997, http://www.nass.usda.gov/census/census97/profiles/sc/sc.htm.

————. *All Cotton: Acreage, Yield, Production, Price, and Value of Production United States: 1866 to Date, Track Records: United States Crop Production*. Washington, DC: USDA—National Agricultural Statistics Service, April, 2003, http://www.usda.gov/nass/pubs/trackrec/track03a.htm.

Van Hook, John F. Interview by Sadie B. Hornsby. *Born in Slavery: Slave Narratives from the Federal Writers' Project, 1936–1938*. Washington: Library of Congress, Manuscript Division, 2001, http://memory.loc.gov/ammem/sn html/snhome.html.

Vegh, Steven G. "Congregation builds church with new shapes." *The Virginian Pilot*, 3 December 2008, http://hamptonroads.com/2008/12/congregation-builds-church-new-shapes (accessed 4/13/09).

"Vineyard Churches." The Religious Movements Page, University of Virginia, http://religiousmovements.lib.virginia.edu/nrms/Vineyard.html.

Vlach, John Michael. *Back of the Big House: The Architecture of Plantation Slavery*. Chapel Hill: University of North Carolina press, 1993.

————. *The Afro-American Tradition in Decorative Arts*. Athens: Brown Thrasher Books, 1990.

Volkomer, Walter. *American Government*. Upper Saddle River, NJ: Prentice Hall, 2001.

"Voter News Service Exit Poll." *SouthNow* # 1 (June 2001), http://www.southnow.org/southnow-publications/southnow-chronicle-1.

Waas, Murray. "The Falwell Connection." *Salon Newsreal*, 11 March 1998, http://www.salon.com/news/1998/03/cov_11news.html.

Wahlman, Maude S. "Quilting, Afro-American." In *Encyclopedia of Southern Culture*, Charles Reagan Wilson and William Ferris, eds. Chapel Hill: University of North Carolina Press, 1989.

Weisback, Lee Shai. "East European Immigrants and the Image of Jews in the Small Town South." In Mark K. Bauman, ed., *Dixie Diaspora: An*

Anthology of Southern Jewish History. Tuscaloosa, AL: University of Alabama Press, 2006.

Walker, Alice. "In Search of Our Mothers' Gardens." *The Literature of the American South,* William L. Andrews, general editor. New York: W.W. Norton & Co., 1998.

———. *The Color Purple.* New York: Pocket Books, 1985.

Walker, Melissa. *All We Knew Was to Farm: Rural Women in the Upcountry South.* Baltimore and London: The Johns Hopkins University Press, 2000.

Walker, William. *The Southern Harmony and Musical Companion.* New York: Hastings House, 1835.

Wall, Bennett H. et al, *Louisiana: A History.* Wheeling, Illinois: Harlan Davidson Inc., 2008.

Warren, Robert Penn. *All the King's Men.* San Diego: A Harvest/HBJ Book, 1974; first published 1946.

Washington, Booker T. "The Atlanta Exposition Address." In *Crossing the Danger Water: Three Hundred Years of African-American Writing,* Deirdre Mullane, ed. New York: Anchor Books, 1993.

Wave Church (Virginia Beach, VA) Web site, http://www.wavechurch.com/.

Wayne, Michael. *The Reshaping of Plantation Society: The Natchez District, 1860–1880.* Baton Rouge and London: Louisiana State University Press, 1983.

Webb, Mary Frances. Interview. *Born in Slavery: Slave Narratives from the Federal Writers' Project, 1936–1938.* Washington: Library of Congress, Manuscript Division, 2001, http://memory.loc.gov/ammem/snhtml/snhome. html.

Weiner, Marli F. "Mistresses, Morality, and the Dilemmas of Slaveholding: The Ideology and Behavior of Elite Antebellum Women." In *Discovering the Women in Slavery.* Athens, Patricia Morton, ed. Athens, GA: University of Georgia Press, 1996.

Welty, Eudora. Interview by Linda Kuehl (1972). The DNA of Literature: The Complete Paris Review Interviews, http://www/parisreview.com/viewinter view.php/prmMID/4013 (accessed 11 May 2006).

West, Jerry Lee. *The Reconstruction Ku Klux Klan in York County, South Carolina, 1865–1877.* Jefferson, NC: McFarland and Co., 2002.

Wheeler, John H. *Reminiscences and Memoirs of North Carolina and Eminent North Carolinians.* Chapel Hill: Documenting the American South, 2001, (first published, 1884), http://docsouth.unc.edu/nc/wheeler/wheeler.html.

White, Barnetta McGhee, ed. "Enslaved Ancestors Abstracted from Granville County, North Carolina Deed Books, A–Z & 1–21, 1746–1864," http://afrigeneas.com/library/ncdeeds (accessed 10/14/06).

———. "History of Antioch Baptist Church, Granville, County, North Carolina," 1990.

White, Deborah Gray. "Female Slaves: Sex Roles and Status in the Antebellum Plantation South." *Women and the Family in a Slave Society,* Paul Finkelman, ed. New York: Garland Publishing,1989.

———. *Ar'n't I a Woman: Female Slaves in the Plantation South.* New York: W. W. Norton & Company, 1999.

White, Walter. *A Man Called White: The Autobiography of Walter White.* New York: The Viking Press, 1948.

Whitefield, George. *George Whitfield's Journals to which is Prefixed his "Short Account" (1746) and "Further Account" (1747).* Gainesville, FL: Scholars Fassimiles [sic] and Reprints, 1969.

Whitener, Daniel J. *Prohibition in North Carolina, 1715–1945.* Chapel Hill, The University of North Carolina Press, 1945.

"Who Is the Tea Party Caucus in the House?" *CNNPolitics,* http://politicalticker.blogs.cnn.com/2011/07/29/who-is-the-tea-party-caucus-in-the-house/(accessed 3/30/2012).

Wiebe, Robert. *The Search for Order.* New York: Hill and Wang, 1967.

Wiencek, Henry. *The Hairstons: An American Family in Black and White.* New York: St. Martin's Press, 1999.

Wiener, Jonathan M. *Social Origins of the New South: Alabama, 1860–1885.* Baton Rouge: Louisiana State University Press, 1978.

Wilkins, Fred. Photographs by Marion Post Wolcott. *America from the Great Depression to World War II: Photographs from the FSA-OWI, 1935–1945.* Washington: Library of Congress, American Memory, 1998, http://lc web2.loc.gov/ammem/fsaquery.html.

Willbanks, Green. Interview by Sadie B. Hornsby. *Born in Slavery: Slave Narratives from the Federal Writers' Project, 1936–1938.* Washington: Library of Congress, Manuscript Division, 2001,http://memory.loc.gov/.

Williams, T. Harry. *Huey Long.* New York: Vintage Books, 1981; first published 1969.

Williamson, Joel. *A Rage for Order: Black-White Relations in the American South Since Emancipation.* New York: Oxford University Press, 1986.

———. *The Crucible of Race: Black/White Relations in the American South Since Emancipation.* New York: Oxford University Press, 1984.

————. *William Faulkner and Southern History.* New York: Oxford University Press, 1993.

Wilson, C. Anne. *Food and Drink in Britain: From the Stone Age to Recent Times.* New York: Harper and Row, 1974.

Wilson, Charles Reagan. *Baptized in Blood: The Religion of the Lost Cause, 1865–1820.* Athens, Georgia: University of Georgia Press, 1980.

————. *Judgment and Grace in Dixie: Southern Faiths from Faulkner to Elvis.* Athens and London: University of Georgia Press, 1995.

Wilson, Claude Augusta. Interview by James Johnson. *Born in Slavery: Slave Narratives from the Federal Writers' Project, 1936–1938.* Washington: Library of Congress, Manuscript Division, 2001, http://memory.loc.gov/.

Wimberley, Ronald and Libby Morris. *The Southern Black Belt: a National Perspective.* Lexington, KY: University of Kentucky, 1997.

Wirtz, Rev. Billy C. "Washed ashore: the long, strange story of beach music." *Independent* (Durham, NC) 5–11 July 2000.

Women in the Labor Force: A Databook. U.S. Department of Labor, U.S. Bureau of Labor Statistics, May 2005.

Wolfe, Tom. *A Man in Full.* New York: Farrar, Straus, Giroux, 1998.

————. *I Am Charlotte Simmons.* New York: Picador, 2004.

Wolfram, Walt and Natalie Schilling-Estes. *Hoi Toide on the Outer Banks: The Story of the Ocracoke Brogue.* Chapel Hill: University of North Carolina Press, 1997.

Wood, Elijah. *Escaping the Delta: Robert Johnson and the Invention of the Blues.* New York: Amistad, 2004.

Wood, Peter. *Black Majority: Negroes in Colonial South Carolina from 1670 through the Stono Rebellion.* New York: W.W. Norton Co., 1975.

Woodman, Harold D. "Sequel to Slavery: The New History Views the Postbellum South." *Journal of Southern History, XLIII* (November 1977): 523–554.

————. *King Cotton and his Retainers.* Lexington, KY: University of Kentucky Press, 1968.

Woodward, C. Vann. *Origins of the New South: 1877–1913.* Baton Rouge: Louisiana State University Press, 1951.

————. *Tom Watson: Agrarian Rebel.* London: Oxford University Press; 1975; first published, 1938.

"Word of Faith." Wikpedia, http://en.wikipedia.org/wiki/Word_of_faith (accessed 6/2/06).

Wright, Gavin. *Old South, New South: Revolutions in the Southern Economy Since the Civil War*. New York: Basic Books, Inc., 1986.

————. *The Political Economy of the Cotton South: Households, Markets, and Wealth in the Nineteenth Century*. New York and London: W.W. Norton & Co., 1978.

Wright, Louis B. and Marion Tinling eds. *The Secret Diary if William Byrd of Westover, 1709–1712*. Richmond, VA: The Dietz Press, 1941.

Wright, Richard. *Black Boy*. New York: Harper and Row, 1966; first published 1945.

————. *Native Son*. New York: Perennial Library, 1989; first published 1940.

Wyatt-Brown, Bertram. *Southern Honor: Ethics and Behavior in the Old South*. Oxford and New York: Oxford University Press, 1983.

————. *The Shaping of Southern Culture: Honor, Grace, and War, 1760s–1880s*. Chapel Hill and London: University of North Carolina Press, 2001.

Zug, III, Charles G. *Turners and Burners: The Folk Potters of North Carolina*. Chapel Hill: University of North Carolina, 1986.

Zwonitzer, Mark with Charles Hirshberg. *Will You Miss me When I'm Gone?: The Carter Family and Their Legacy in American Music*. New York: Simon & Schuster, 2002.

Index